Working with *A Secular Age*

Religion and Its Others

Studies in Religion, Nonreligion, and Secularity

Edited by
Stacey Gutkowski, Lois Lee, and Johannes Quack

Volume 3

Working with
A Secular Age

Interdisciplinary Perspectives
on Charles Taylor's Master Narrative

Edited by
Florian Zemmin, Colin Jager,
and Guido Vanheeswijck

With an afterword by Charles Taylor

DE GRUYTER

ISBN 978-3-11-057315-2
e-ISBN (PDF) 978-3-11-037551-0
e-ISBN (EPUB) 978-3-11-038717-9
ISSN 2330-6262

Library of Congress Cataloging-in-Publication Data
A CIP catalog record for this book has been applied for at the Library of Congress.

Bibliographic information published by the Deutsche Nationalbibliothek
The Deutsche Nationalbibliothek lists this publication in the Deutsche Nationalbibliografie;
detailed bibliographic data are available on the Internet at http://dnb.dnb.de.

© 2017 Walter de Gruyter GmbH, Berlin/Boston
This volume is identical in text and page numbers with the hardcover version published in 2016.
Printing and binding: CPI books GmbH, Leck
♾ Printed on acid-free paper
Printed in Germany

www.degruyter.com

Preface

This book grew out of a conference hosted by the Institute of Advanced Study in the Humanities and the Social Sciences (IASH) at the University of Bern from 5–8 March 2014 and entitled "Working with *A Secular Age* – Interdisciplinary Reflections on Charles Taylor's Conception of the Secular." The conference would not have been possible without the help of Michaela Rossini, who at the time was program coordinator at the IASH, and Michael Frey, who took care of logistical matters. Financial support by various institutions not only made this event possible in the first place, but also helped to create the productive and collegial atmosphere that we were privileged to enjoy over four days. Next to resources of the IASH itself, the conference was generously supported by the Swiss Academy of Humanities and Social Sciences (SAGW), by the University of Bern Intermediate Staff Association (MVUB), by the Mercator Foundation Switzerland, by the Centre for Global Studies (CGS) at the University of Bern, and by the Graduate School TeNOR at the University of Lucerne.

The plan of organizing a conference on *A Secular Age* grew out of a series of smaller workshops around the concept of 'secularity' held at the IASH (which now goes under the name of Walter Benjamin Kolleg). When we considered hosting a larger, and truly interdisciplinary, conference on secularity, however, the very concept itself seemed too broad to provide a common thread or focal point connecting a variety of disciplines and projects. Indeed, if there ever was something close to a consensus about 'secularity,' in hindsight it was a mistaken one. In light of the ongoing deconstruction of 'secularity' and 'secularization,' one wonders whether there ever was any basis to the long-dominant understanding of secularization as the decline of religion, a decline often understood to be an intrinsic element of modernization. It was here that Charles Taylor's *A Secular Age* came into play.

A Secular Age is without any doubt the most prominent contemporary effort of not only deconstructing but also reconstructing secularization and secularity. The success and importance of *A Secular Age* are shown not only in the number of responses to Taylor's work but also in the great variety of disciplines from which these responses have emerged. Thus Taylor's book seemed both rich enough in substance and focused enough in argument to provide that common reference needed for interdisciplinary exchange. In this regard, we planned to *work with* Taylor's book as a tool for promoting dialogue and possible collaboration among research projects on secularity.

The wording of "working with" *A Secular Age* in the conference title also conveyed another intention. After all, Taylor's book had already been extensively worked on. This is not to say that there was (and is) nothing more to say on *A Secular Age*, of course. Still, the major points of criticism had been amply made, be it regarding the role of history in *A Secular Age* or concerning a possible Christian bias in central concepts like "the immanent frame" or "fullness." "Working with" instead of "on" the book was meant, by contrast, to foreground the following questions: What concrete difference does *A Secular Age* actually make for individual research projects? How does *A Secular Age* help in discovering new fields of research or in conceptualizing our own subject matter? Which aspects of our research that otherwise would have gone unnoticed become visible by resorting to *A Secular Age?* In short, what is the potential but also, what are the limits of *A Secular Age* for concrete research projects and for various disciplines? Naturally, as one can only work 'with' what one has worked 'on,' questions of the latter kind were, to various degrees, also tackled in several papers. What is certain is that *A Secular Age* as a tool for interdisciplinary exchange worked even better than we had hoped for, as testified to by the intense and fruitful discussions throughout our conference.

Growing out of this conference, the present volume nevertheless is far from being a mere reproduction of the presentations and discussions held then. At the conference we had the pleasure of listening to three keynote lectures and 25 papers, grouped in seven panels. Out of these contributions, twelve evolved into chapters of this volume, which also includes another four contributions not presented at the conference (the chapters by Koenig, Thomas, Bender, and myself). On behalf of all three editors I want to thank the publisher, especially Alissa Jones Nelson, who accompanied this book project from its first inception to its completion. Thanks are also due to the series editors and the anonymous external reviewer for their substantial and very helpful comments on the original manuscript.

Florian Zemmin   Bern, July 2015

Table of Contents

Florian Zemmin, Colin Jager, Guido Vanheeswijck
Introduction —— 1

I. The Potential of Taylor's Story for Various Disciplines

Matthias Koenig
Beyond the Paradigm of Secularization? —— 23

Günter Thomas
The Temptation of Religious Nostalgia: Protestant Readings of *A Secular Age* —— 49

Jonathan A. Lanman
An Order of Mutual Benefit: *A Secular Age* and the Cognitive Science of Religion —— 71

II. The Story's Normative Implications

Guido Vanheeswijck
The Ambiguity of "Post-Secular" and "Post-Metaphysical" Stories: On the Place of Religion and Deep Commitments in a Secular Society —— 95

Aurélia Bardon
Liberal Pluralism in a Secular Age —— 123

Marian Burchardt
Does Religion need Rehabilitation? Charles Taylor and the Critique of Secularism —— 137

Joyce Dalsheim
Other Sovereignties in Israel/Palestine: The Limited Imaginings of a Secular Age —— 159

Reinhard Schulze
The Quest for the West in an Era of Globalization: Some Remarks on the Hidden Meaning of Charles Taylor's Master Narrative —— 175

III. The Story's Subtler Languages

Colin Jager
Language within Language: Reform and Literature in *A Secular Age* —— 207

Oane Reitsma
Musical Works as 'Higher Times': Concert Culture in a Secular Age —— 229

Thomas A. Carlson
Secular Moods: Exploring Temporality and Affection with *A Secular Age* —— 245

Samuel Shearn
Charles Taylor, Nietzsche and Theology in *A Secular Age* —— 263

Courtney Bender
"Every Meaning Will have its Homecoming Festival:" *A Secular Age* and the Senses of Modern Spirituality —— 283

IV. Islamic Stories

Florian Zemmin
***A Secular Age* and Islamic Modernism —— 307**

Junaid Quadri
Religion as Transcendence in Modern Islam: Tracking "Religious Matters" into a Secular(izing) Age —— 331

Johannes Stephan
Reconsidering Transcendence/Immanence. Modernity's Modes of Narration in Nineteenth-Century Arabic Literary Tradition —— 349

Charles Taylor
Afterword —— 369

Florian Zemmin
An Annotated Bibliography of Responses to *A Secular Age* —— 385

Index —— 421

Florian Zemmin, Colin Jager, Guido Vanheeswijck
Introduction

How long does it take for a book to become a classic? In the case of Charles Taylor's *A Secular Age*, seven years clearly were more than enough. Since its publication in 2007, the Canadian philosopher's book has inspired wide discussion and generated an astonishing number of responses. What is more, the debate has been taking place in a wide range of disciplines: philosophy and sociology, theology and history, political science and literature, anthropology and religious studies, and other fields. In the English language alone there have been far more than 100 direct responses to or reviews of the book since its publication in 2007 (see the annotated bibliography at the end of this volume).

The contributions to the present volume are equally varied. This is a good thing: no contribution in itself can do justice to Taylor's rich work. Rather, the individual responses to *A Secular Age* might better be understood as illuminating its manifold aspects from various angles, and only in their collectivity might they approach something like a 'complete picture.' Part of this picture is that some contributors engage more critically with *A Secular Age* than others, and that Taylor's book can be more fruitfully worked with in some disciplines than in others. With contributions from nine disciplines, this volume illustrates the enormous potential of Taylor's work for interdisciplinary research. It also points to certain limits in this regard.

Stories

The volume is structured around the concept of 'story.' Taylor himself writes that "[i]t is a crucial fact of our present spiritual predicament that it is historical; [....] In other words, our sense of where we are is crucially defined in part by a story of how we got there" (ASA[1]: 29). He offers this in part as a defense of the length of his own book, which audaciously toggles between nuanced intellectual and cultural history, broad empirical observations, philosophical analysis, and normative claims. This generic blend has sometimes been misunderstood by readers, who may wish for something else: more empirical data, perhaps, or less historical texture. But the mixture is crucial to Taylor's own story, which aims among

---

[1] Throughout this volume, reference to *A Secular Age* is made by "ASA," departing from the general style of references, which would demand "Taylor 2007."

other things to get us to feel or sense what it is like to live in a secular age. In this regard, Taylor's "story" demands a kind of interpretive work from its readers, particularly because good stories, or those we deem classics, are always susceptible to multiple interpretations.

In a fundamental sense, *A Secular Age* retells the story of (Western) secularization in order to understand who we are and how we came to be that way. Whilst Taylor does not negate common descriptions of secularity as consisting of social differentiation or the decreasing relevance of religion in the public sphere (which he terms "secularity 1") or as a decline in religious belief and practice ("secularity 2"), his focus is on what he introduces as "secularity 3," namely the background assumptions against which an age or era shows up as "secular." "Why," he asks, "was it virtually impossible not to believe in God in, say, 1500 in our Western society, while in 2000 many of us find this not only easy, but even inescapable?" (ASA: 25).

One answer to that question is what Taylor calls "subtraction stories" (ASA: 22). Subtraction stories offer causal accounts of the spread of secularity: the rise of science and growing urbanization and industrialization brings about an inevitable decline of religion. Taylor opposes this linear description of the gradual decline of religion in human history by describing the vicissitudes and contingencies of religious change as a "zig zag" (ASA: 95). More importantly, he investigates the normative underpinnings of secularity itself, which he understands as something that was built (sometimes deliberately, sometimes haphazardly) rather than simply exposed by the subtraction of religion. This alternative story is what Taylor calls a "Reform Master Narrative." For Taylor, (Western) secularity originates in Christianity, more specifically in a drive for reform that is both theological and behavioral, and which gathered momentum in the early modern period. A summary of this narrative can be found in the first chapter by Matthias Koenig and, with a slightly different focus, in the subsequent contribution by Günter Thomas. It is important to stress that Taylor's "Reform" is not the same as the Protestant Reformation: it is a more encompassing movement, or set of impulses, that picked up speed in the fifteenth century and aimed to bring the details of ordinary human life, in all its contingency and ambivalence, into line with the demands of religious and cultural elites. In a more literary idiom, "Reform" means the imposition of form upon content, with all the gains and losses that attend such an imposition.

The chapters in this volume not only focus on different aspects of Taylor's story but also assess the relevance of the narrative character of *A Secular Age* differently. Taylor's book is most radically treated as a story, as opposed to history, in the contributions by Joyce Dalsheim and Reinhard Schulze, whilst others give it greater historical credibility, for example Jonathan Lanman and Oane Reitsma.

A middle position, if you wish, is taken up by Courtney Bender, who considers Taylor's story as "true insofar as its narrative becomes part of the story that we tell about ourselves." In that line, Florian Zemmin regards Taylor's story as a useful heuristic tool for uncovering other stories of modernity, in this case Islamic ones, while Samuel Shearn takes one kind of story – the genealogy – as a point of contact between Taylor and Nietzsche, and Thomas Carlson assesses the narrative pressure that Augustine's account of time exerts on Taylor's analysis. Whether the book's analysis is treated primarily as story or as history, meanwhile, a critique of *A Secular Age* recurring in all three sociological contributions of this volume (the ones by Koenig, Bender, and Burchardt) is that Taylor neglects the role of institutional power and conflicts around evolving secular convictions.

Social imaginaries

Taylor is concerned throughout the book with the interplay between explicit theories and implicit background understandings. Elite secular ideas make their way to broader populations by way of what he calls "social imaginaries." The origins of this concept, which Taylor elaborates in his book *Modern Social Imaginaries* from 2004, can be traced to an article published two years earlier as part of a special journal issue on *New Imaginaries* (Taylor 2002). The members of the working group behind this special issue employed the idea of social imaginary in quite different ways; in Taylor's case, however, Cornelius Castoriadis's coinage of the concept is still very visible. Castoriadis (1987) had introduced "[t]he idea of a social imaginary as an enabling but not fully explicable symbolic matrix within which a people imagine and act as world-making collective agents" (Gaonkar 2002). Social imaginaries are both fundamental and hard to pin down or delineate; indeed, Castoriadis (1987: 128) likened imaginaries to "what Hegel called 'the spirit of a people'."

Taylor himself defines social imaginaries as incorporating "a sense of the normal expectations that we have of each other; the kind of common understanding which enables us to carry out the collective practices which make up our social life. This incorporates some sense of how we all fit together in carrying out the common practice" (ASA: 172). Taylor, himself a distinguished Hegel scholar, actually locates the concept of social imaginaries in the Kantian tradition, identifying their role with that of Kantian transcendental schemes. When a theory penetrates and transforms the social imaginary, "this process isn't just one-sided; a theory making over a social imaginary. The theory in coming to make sense of the action is 'glossed,' as it were, given a particular shape as the context of these practices. Rather like Kant's notion of an abstract category becoming 'schematized' when it is applied to reality in space and time, the theory is schematized in the dense sphere of common practice" (ASA: 176). However, there remains a central difference between Kant's transcendental schemes and Taylor's social imaginaries. Whereas Kant's transcendental schemes are universal and mainly tailored to the use of scientific concepts, Taylor's social imaginaries are historical and related to the domain of human experiences.

The idea of social imaginaries, as distinguished from explicitly held doctrines or elaborated theories, alerts us to the importance of common implicit understandings lying behind disputes among religious and secular positions. In this regard, the central aim of Taylor's story in *A Secular Age* is to do justice to the specificity of our secular age by articulating these shared implicit understandings, whether we consider ourselves religious or not. Following Heidegger, Taylor defines these implicit understandings as our "pre-ontology" or "background" (ASA: 3, 13, passim). Since social imaginaries are deeply embedded in our pre-ontology, we are in need of stories which make explicit the implicit views lurking in the tacit background and situated in the long historical process of modernity.

The concept of the social imaginary therefore does two distinct kinds of work in *A Secular Age*. First, it aims to illuminate, from the inside as it were, *what it means to live in a secular age*. The shared social imaginary of modern life is what Taylor calls the "immanent frame." While the immanent frame is not necessarily closed to transcendence, its tacit world-picture includes a world defined by natural science and governed by impersonal laws and a social order that is historical in the sense that it has been created by actions that happened in historical time. Thus, when Taylor says that it is a "crucial fact of our present spiritual predicament that it is historical," he is in fact giving voice to a basic part of the immanent frame itself. He aims to give an account of our modern social imaginary *from within that same imaginary*, and that makes his own account, again, an interpretive one. Several of the contributions to this volume, notably those by Carlson, Jager, Shearn, and Reitsma, follow Taylor down this interpretive path, testing his depiction of the immanent frame against alternative possibilities (those found in Heidegger, Schiller, Nietzsche, and classical music, respectively).

Secondly, the concept of the social imaginary also aims to account for the diffusion of elite theories to whole societies – to explain, that is to say, *how we became secular*. Yet from the perspective of social science, the explanatory potential of this concept is debatable. It remains unclear exactly how the interplay of theory and imaginary works (see Bender this volume: 286fn4; Koenig this volume: 41). More fundamentally, the very concept of social imaginaries remains somewhat vague and is problematically identified with abstract cultural entities

(Strauss 2006; Zemmin this volume: 314–315). In this light it is even more interesting that from the perspective of cognitive science, Jonathan Lanman in his contribution to this volume argues that the concept of social imaginary could be fruitfully operated with. At the other end of the spectrum, Reinhard Schulze maintains that "social imaginary" should not be treated as a concept at all, since it is a metaphor which works only within Taylor's particular story. Florian Zemmin argues that the concept can nevertheless be fruitfully applied to other contexts and stories, namely as a "heuristic tool."

Central to the modern social imaginary as depicted by Taylor is the idea of the separation between natural-supernatural or immanent-transcendent. While Oane Reitsma demonstrates how post-romantic classical music absorbs and (he argues) occasionally transcends that same distinction, Junaid Quadri and Johannes Stephan, in their contributions, trace these distinctions in an Islamic context. Meanwhile, the chapters in the second section are concerned with the normative premises and implications of this imaginary and with its limits and contestations.

Taylor's story among the disciplines

From the moment of its publication, *A Secular Age* has inspired disparate responses, and the essays gathered here testify to this diversity. Taken together, the contributors represent nine distinct disciplines, and this variety of approach yields a correspondingly various set of judgements about Taylor's text. It might be helpful, then, to imagine a sliding scale of interdisciplinary engagement. At one extreme, one might extend Taylor's argument more-or-less unmodified into debates in one's own discipline; at the other, one might criticize *A Secular Age* from the perspective of a particular discipline. Though the contributions gathered here necessarily differ in emphasis, all of them move dialectically between these poles. None simply import *A Secular Age* wholesale, nor simply disparage it from a supposedly superior disciplinary standpoint.

With varying degrees of explicitness, one question occurs in each of the essays collected here: is Taylor's account descriptive, interpretive, normative, or explanatory? Put differently, does it aim to *describe* our current condition (the characteristics of being Western and modern at this particular historical juncture)? Does it aim to *interpret* that condition (to dwell on the possibilities and capacities that the secular age opens up and closes down)? Does it *explain* how we got here (giving reasons for the evolution of the immanent frame, or proposing causal accounts of how we moved from a condition of naive to reflexive belief)? Or does it aim at a *normative* account (criticizing the modern condition, offering reasons for thinking of the immanent frame as open or closed, or proposing how we might live under conditions of religious pluralism)? The short answer, of course, is that *A Secular Age* aims to do all of the above – such is the ambition of this ambitious book. But, as always, it is the question of emphasis – both Taylor's emphasis and the emphases of his readers – that will determine how we read Taylor's story.

We have organized the collection into four sections. While most chapters in this volume interweave general reflections on the usability of *A Secular Age* with a specific research project, the contributions assembled in the first section are dedicated more exclusively to evaluating the general potential of Taylor's story for their respective disciplines. The second section treats the normative dimensions of Taylor's alternative story in *A Secular Age*, following Taylor's own lead, if not always his conclusions, by using the various problematics of pluralism to challenge the hegemony of mainstream secularization stories. In a more interpretive vein, the third section uses the concept of "subtler language" to consider alternative accounts of the secular age opened up by Taylor's own descriptive story. And the fourth section explores modern Islamic self-understandings and stories of secularity. The next portions of this introduction contain summaries and analyses of these four sections and their individual chapters.

Beginning the first section, Matthias Koenig explores the potential of *A Secular Age* for sociological theories of secularity and secularization. Summarizing recent assessments of these theories, Koenig formulates three requirements to be fulfilled by any alternative account of secularity: it must explain how secularity became such an important and controversial category (1), it must integrate empirical evidence pointing both to the decline of religion and to religious vitality that varies by region, history, and population (2), and it must explain the diversity of modern religious and political differentiation patterns in cross-national and cross-cultural perspective (3). Closely examining the major premises, concepts, and landmarks of *A Secular Age*, Koenig maintains that Taylor's "culturalist theory of modernity" clearly fulfills the first two requirements, yet fails to deliver on the third. For Koenig, Taylor's story fruitfully brings up historical and sociological questions which cannot be answered by large-scale narratives like Taylor's own.

The Protestant theologian Günter Thomas argues that Taylor's story is fuelled not only by Christian but more specifically by Catholic convictions. Taylor's apologetic approach to history, he writes, results in an unfair treatment of the historical role of Protestantism itself, which for Thomas is a story of "education and freedom, which cannot simply be shelved under Reform." And whilst Taylor allegedly portrays a nostalgic Catholic mysticism as the only remedy for the irreversible result of the process of Reform, "Protestants rely on the many forms of the presence of the resurrected Christ through the Holy Spirit in real, communal and thoroughly plural practices of faith, hope, and love." Despite his rather critical reading of both Taylor's historical narrative and its contemporary diagnosis, however, Thomas points to significant challenges formulated in *A Secular Age* that require an answer by Protestant theologians: a more nuanced relationship to modernity and a Trinitarian theological account of the secular that locates fullness neither exclusively in immanence nor in transcendence but dynamically connects both.

Some readers, including several contributors to this volume, have criticized *A Secular Age* for dwelling too much on broad-based cultural change and not enough on specific institutional configurations and conflicts of interest. By contrast, Jonathan Lanman's contribution, which considers the relevance of Taylor's story for the burgeoning field of cognitive science of religion (CSR), suggests that pieces of a causal explanation do indeed exist in Taylor's account. On first glance, CSR seems methodologically alien to Taylor's story. But Lanman thinks that CSR should aim to complement philosophical and cultural interpretations of religious experiences and actions with explanations of their underlying cognitive dispositions. He suggests that CSR can complement Taylor's account by offering explanations for different levels of belief *within* the North Atlantic world, from the growth of new religious movements to the rise of non-theism. The evidence from cognitive science is that levels of religious belief depend less upon what people say than upon what they do. Thus, the disembodiment of religion brought about by social differentiation (secularity 1) combined with changed conditions of belief (secularity 3) might in turn yield lower levels of belief and participation (secularity 2). Though Lanman remarks that taking social imaginaries as objects of analysis in the study of religious cognition remains a challenge, his proposal has the effect of supporting Taylor's contention that changes in the conditions of belief can causally influence levels of religious participation. In this way, his contribution offers an implicit response to the sociological charge, voiced here by Koenig and Bender, that Taylor is not able to provide a causal account of religious change.

Normative stories in a secular age

The normative discussion about the exact definition of 'religion' and 'secularity' is an old one. But in *A Secular Age* Taylor gives that discussion a new and unexpected twist. *A Secular Age* is explicitly framed as an alternative story to mainstream master narratives of secularization, in part because Taylor believes that the hegemony of such narratives has in fact helped to bring about the present secular age. Taylor's alternative 'Reform Master Narrative,' therefore, is itself a normative account as well as a descriptive one. If Taylor's alternative story about the genesis and evolution of the secular age is accepted as a more convincing genealogical account of modernity, then it implies as well an alternative normative approach to the contemporary relation between secularity and religion.

At the end of *A Secular Age*, Taylor states that in the account he is offering "there is no place for unproblematic breaks with a past which is simply left behind" (ASA: 772). Like Robert Bellah, he believes that with regard to people's past imaginaries and convictions "nothing is ever lost." This emphasis on a narrative of slow change works against a reading of Taylor's initial question ("why was it virtually impossible not to believe in God in, say, 1500 in our Western society, while in 2000 many of us find this not only easy, but even inescapable?") as itself positing a sharp break or abrupt transition. Taylor thinks that simply breaking with a problematic past may give rise to the repetition of its horrors in the modern secular era. He opts instead for a story, through which a fusion of past and present horizons may take place. Especially in the domain of human affairs, where "understanding the other" (Taylor 2011) is at stake, this model of a "fusion of horizons" across both geographic and historical distance is related to the art of telling stories, rather than to the construction of scientific theories.

Taylor proposes that this plea for a "fusion of horizons" – the expression is borrowed from Gadamer – and for normative stories other than those coming from the epistemological tradition is applicable to the contemporary relation between religious and secular stances. Both Gadamer and Taylor challenge any assumption that identities in a secular age are self-enclosed. "Our past is sedimented in our present," as Taylor puts it (ASA: 29), and this demands an equilibrium between acknowledging completely different ways of being human on the one hand and living our own way on the other. It goes without saying that this equilibrium is difficult to achieve (Taylor 2011: 31–38).

From divergent perspectives, the five chapters in the second section all focus upon working with *A Secular Age* in order to approach that balance of understanding. Guido Vanheeswijck in his chapter asks whether the terms 'post-secular' and 'post-metaphysical stories' coined by Jürgen Habermas are humble words or words already surreptitiously transformed into arrogant ones, that is, whether they are successful or not in coping with the predicament of 'understanding the other.' Inspired by Taylor's position in *A Secular Age* and in subsequent essays, Vanheeswijck traces the consequences of divergent interpretations of these two words regarding the role of religious and metaphysical arguments or "deep commitments" in the current debate on the place of religion in the public sphere. He suggests that the controversy around the interpretation of both words is not only due to different epistemological premises, but to divergent political stances as well. Taylor himself has argued that achieving mutual respect and tolerance in this regard is the primary task of democratic societies. Following Taylor, Vanheeswijck proposes that this goal is less amenable to the neutrality of procedural rationality than to the imaginative force of what he calls "subtle words." Therefore, only normative stories that are aware of the subtlety of words can articulate the implicit background understandings that all participants carry with them into discussion.

Coming at the question of neutrality and its limits from a different angle, Aurélia Bardon shows why the liberal pluralism characteristic of our secular age is itself not a neutral story. Taylor's commitment to moral and epistemological pluralisms reveals the fact that the immanent frame, which here stands for modern liberal society, is in fact based on specific normative and epistemological assumptions. Only such assumptions can explain why we expect and accept both moral and epistemological pluralism. Bardon makes it clear that these normative and epistemological assumptions are themselves limited and cannot include certain metaphysical claims. In other words, the liberal commitment to moral and epistemological pluralisms is not and cannot be based on the validity of metaphysical pluralism. This is why in Taylor's view "the language of some public bodies, for instance courts, has to be free from premises drawn from one or another position." If liberal pluralism is taken seriously as a normative story, according to Bardon, the official position has to be no position at all.

The first two contributions in this section mainly elaborate on Taylor's position; the next two are more critical of his general stance when applied to specific situations.

Marian Burchardt explores how *A Secular Age* is related to the normative claims in the fierce debates about secularism in Quebec, and to Taylor's own political interventions in them. He begins by examining Taylor's argument that strong versions of secularization, based on the idea of emancipation from religion, reify secularism as a goal in its own right instead of being subservient to promoting the values of liberty, equality, and solidarity. Next, he evaluates Taylor's claim that the traditional view of religion as playing an ambiguous, if not detrimental, role in the promotion of these values must be reassessed and perhaps even reversed. In the second part of his essay, Burchardt explores how in modern-day Quebec, "this rehabilitation underwrites the project to respect and promote religious diversity." However, it also clashes with notions of secularity as a "lever of national unity and progress."

In her chapter on "other sovereignties in Israel/Palestine," Joyce Dalsheim, too, claims that Taylor's story in *A Secular Age* is not innocent. In particular, she is concerned with those who live in the shadows of the hegemonic secular moral order Taylor describes in *A Secular Age* and who can be produced as enemies of the order itself. Ironically enough, the production of such enemies is especially important in contemporary attempts at peacemaking. This is because attempts at peacemaking take place within the modern social imaginary, an important part of which is the idea of "the sovereign people." As Dalsheim shows, some people in Israel/Palestine have begun thinking and acting in ways that pose challenges to the "sovereignty" component that underlies the modern nation-state. Dalsheim focuses on three examples – each of which poses a different challenge to what is generally thought of popular sovereignty and may therefore be considered "spoilers" of peace. She tells these alternative stories to mark the borders of the moral order of a secular age in which conventional peacemaking is carried out.

In the final contribution to this section, Reinhard Schulze poses the fundamental question of why storytelling has reemerged in the last decade as a "meaning-producing force." Taylor's assertion in *A Secular Age* that "we (modern Westerners) can't understand ourselves except via [...] narratives" (Taylor 2010: 300) becomes for Schulze a method for convincing rather than verifying, whose metaphors and arguments only work within the story itself. The "open secularism" for which Taylor has argued elsewhere is also the endpoint of *A Secular Age*, Schulze proposes, and its goal is that of an affirmative genealogy: reassuring the West of its particularity and excellence in an era of globalization. Noting the Christian roots of the concept 'secular' itself, Schulze proposes not a non-Christian genealogy of secularity but a more Foucauldian genealogy of the modern orders of religion and society, which in almost all great traditions "grew out of a unified normative order which had related the world in its totality to a transcendental truth."

Taylor's story and the subtler languages

The questions of meaning and meaningfulness raised in Schulze's contribution are the explicit topics of this volume's third group of essays. Midway through *A Secular Age*, Taylor writes that "the development of modern poetics, and in general the languages of art, has enabled people to explore [...] meanings with their ontological commitments as it were in suspense" (ASA: 351). Here Taylor proposes that Romantic and post-Romantic aesthetics developed or invented a language that captured the unique phenomenology of the secular age. There were unbelievers before Romanticism, of course, but Taylor claims that, beyond a few elite enclaves, neither their experience nor the experiences of their believing neighbors could have been rendered in the open, tentative fashion that has become familiar to us in the post-Romantic age. Rhetorically, meanwhile, Taylor's claim about modern poetics serves as something of an allegory for his book's own method. The key phrases of the first half of the book – the "buffered self," the "work of reform," the "great disembedding," "discipline," and "social imaginaries" – are terms drawn from or developed out of social and philosophical theories. Taylor's invocation of terms like "commitment" and "suspension" in the second half, then, marks a shift toward the languages of authenticity that will preoccupy him in the remainder of *A Secular Age*, and that have concerned him as well in earlier publications (Taylor 1989; 1992). Thus the appeal to suspension is itself suspended between the two halves of *A Secular Age*, a pause or hesitation before the book pitches fully into its discussion of modernity proper.

Taylor marks this moment with a term borrowed from the English Romantic poet Percy Shelley: the "subtler language." That term signals a new social imaginary: where once artists could assume a common lexicon and a common manner of interpreting both natural and social worlds as structured by a divine hierarchy and benevolent order, that assumption no longer held true by the early years of the nineteenth century. The subtler languages of artistic practice thus come to imagine creativity in a new way, as a space of immanent possibility or what Shelley himself called the "vitally metaphorical" quality of authentic language that "marks the before unapprehended relations of things" ([1821] 2002: 512). Romantic artists, Taylor writes, are "trying to say something for which no adequate terms exist and whose meaning has to be sought in [the] works rather than in a pre-existing lexicon of references" (ASA: 354).

It is important to be clear that this is not a blueprint for unrestrained subjectivity or self-projection – that is a misinterpretation that haunts, Taylor thinks, some aspects of the secular age, which equates authenticity with self-determining freedom. By contrast, the subtler languages do indeed hook onto some aspect of the world; in a philosophic idiom, they have an 'intentional object.' But it remains the case that apprehension of that object may not be widely shared and therefore must be disclosed by the constitutive activity of poetic language itself. Taylor seems to be suggesting that, properly read, the subtler languages hold the key to understanding our secular age itself, to its distinctive feel and mood, its capacities and limitations, its cross-pressures and unquiet frontiers. In this way, the subtler languages are the languages of the immanent frame – the languages of secularity, even if their content may be overtly religious. This helps to explain why Taylor turns increasingly to literary and artistic examples in the second half of the book.

The notion of subtler languages invites a broadly interpretive relationship to Taylor's own text. *A Secular Age* is, after all, a story, and stories demand interpretation. Accordingly, the chapters gathered in the third section consider the interpretive possibilities opened up by Taylor's account.

Colin Jager's contribution, which closely analyzes Taylor's own investment in romanticism, particularly in Shelley and Schiller, suggests a reading of Taylor's story that carries forward the political claims of the book's first section – that secularization-as-Reform was an overt project of elites to separate themselves from popular culture – into the subtler and more aesthetic matters treated in the latter half of *A Secular Age*. In implicit disagreement with Schulze and others for whom Taylor's account is too uncritically celebratory of a certain model of Western modernity, Jager sees Taylor's turn to the aesthetic not as de-politicizing but rather as a means of carrying forward the book's loosely New Left politics within what Jager calls a "fugitive space."

The musicologist Oane Reitsma's contribution adopts Taylor's framework in order to help explain a basic fact about modern art, and music in particular. Whereas music was once embedded in a larger cultural and social matrix – architecture, liturgy, social hierarchy – that contributed to its meaning and significance, music from the late eighteenth century onward had largely to create those contexts for itself. In the abstract, silent, and artificial space of the concert hall, Reitsma argues, music achieves its own "absolute autonomy." He analyzes the identity of post-romantic musical works themselves as markers of the buffered identities of modernity, the secular space of the romantic-era concert hall, with its standardized seating and relative equality of rank, and, finally, the experience of time within modern musical culture. Though largely accepting Taylor's analysis of the secular age, Reitsma shows how close attention to individual works of art reveals that they can "also fulfill a kairotic function in a secular age." Ultimately, this seems a more hopeful description of the secular landscape than that offered by Taylor himself.

Schiller begins his analysis of what he calls "aesthetic education" with the seemingly intractable conflict between will and desire. Friedrich Nietzsche, another of Taylor's philosophical interlocutors, also begins with this conflict. But unlike Schiller, Nietzsche does not think this opposition can be resolved by the free play of aesthetics. Rather, he wants to subvert it altogether. Samuel Shearn nevertheless shows in his contribution that Taylor's account of the secular age remains deeply invested in a Nietzschean critique of humanism and in Nietzsche's genealogical method. Many commentators have noted that Taylor's own theological commitments circulate throughout *A Secular Age*; Shearn's essay, by contrast, offers a deeper reading of Taylor's a-theological sources. Certainly, Taylor in the end proposes that Christianity is superior to Nietzschean anti-humanism because it provides more resources for effecting a transformation that doesn't mutilate our humanity. But, writing from the perspective of Christian theology, Shearn shows how Taylor's theological thinking is enriched by his contact with Nietzsche.

The final two essays in this section are somewhat more skeptical about the adequacy of subtler languages for capturing the nuances of the secular age. Like Shearn, Thomas Carlson turns to a thinker of the counter-enlightenment – Heidegger, in this case – in order to explore the landscape of contemporary spiritual options. But unlike Shearn, Carlson uses this counter-enlightenment tradition to develop an account of love as a "secular mood." Against Taylor's claim that the death of a loved one creates a distinctively modern crisis of meaning, Carlson shows how Heidegger's reading of Augustine enables him to develop an account of love that accepts mortality and does not long for eternity. Taylor, of course, finds Heidegger's well-known critique of instrumental rationality and empty technocratic time very congenial – just as he finds Nietzsche's critique of humanism useful. But Carlson insists that Taylor misses a crucial element of the counter-enlightenment tradition stretching from Nietzsche to Derrida, namely that it is not simply critical of the scientific quest for certainty but also resists the kind of temporal consummation central to Augustinian-Hegelian thinking. To love someone, Carlson argues, is to affirm their mortality and vulnerability. Thus, he concludes, Taylor's reading of the relation between time and meaning, as exemplified for instance in his notion of "fullness," causes him not only to misread Heidegger but to misread the mood of the secular age itself, which is better prepared to deal with death than Taylor is able to acknowledge.

Courtney Bender, likewise, interprets the notion of a subtler language as largely compensatory and dependent upon a notion of lost wholeness. Her ethnographic account of the contemporary North American spiritual landscape, like Carlson's more philosophical version, takes issue with Taylor's language of "fullness," whose nostalgia, she concludes, leads Taylor to miss the possibilities that are actually available within the modern spiritual scene. She notes that in nineteenth-century America, for example, romanticism described less a place of ontic suspension than of interconnection, particularly as the spirits and experiences of the Western frontier began penetrating urban drawing rooms and parlors. In a similar manner, Bender's ethnographic account of contemporary spiritual practitioners in and around Cambridge, Massachusetts, indicates that these subjects too remain porous, open to visitations from worlds beyond the skin and deeply connected to historical traditions. The sensibility of today's subtler languages, then, may be more relational and less buffered than Taylor allows.

Islamic stories

Taylor offers *A Secular Age* as one among several stories of Western secularity. He himself refers to two other accounts: the subtraction narratives that are his running target, and the kind of Intellectual Deviation story developed most prominently by the theologian John Milbank (ASA: 773–776). However, these options are hardly exhaustive. As shown in the contributions of Koenig and Burchardt in this volume, most recent sociological theory-making cannot really be called a "subtraction" story. And neither Taylor nor Milbank's so-called "Radical Orthodoxy," or even a combination of their accounts, will be the last word from the side of Christian thinkers or theologians. Indeed, in the first section of this volume, the Protestant theologian Günter Thomas points to an alternative Protestant account of secularity, criticizing the role Taylor assigns to Protestantism in his own story. There are, moreover, a range of distinctions and issues of 'difference' that are not addressed in Taylor's cultural account of modernity. The issue of gender is entirely absent, as are the problems pertaining to the role of sexuality, class distinctions, immigration, disability, etc. Whilst it is important to keep these other differences in mind, giving them their full due would have made for a totally different work than *A Secular Age*. Aware of the particularity of Taylor's approach and its concommitant omissions, this volume focuses on one 'other' of the secular West which Taylor *explicitly* addresses, namely Islam.

Islam is a crucial 'other' in and to Western self-understandings in general, at once constituent of and set apart from the West. However we conceive of it specifically, the secular is widely regarded as a central characteristic of (Western) modernity, and within this formation Islam marks a crucial boundary. There have thus evolved Western and Islamic visions and stories of modernity, which cling to and perpetuate imagined characteristics and boundaries, quite detached from the historical record of entanglements between Christendom and Islamdom. No other 'other' plays a more significant role in the formation of modern Western self-understanding. The historical evolution of this formation and the power mechanisms at work therein have been aptly discussed in recent scholarship (Hurd 2010; Salama 2011). Taylor's "West," like any other civilization, is not a given but a construction and an imagination. However, this imagined 'Western civilization' has become highly relevant as a marker of identity and of modernity. Even though modern self-understanding only evolved in the "imperial encounter" (van der Veer 2001), it was most closely associated with the European tradition and then with the West, in which it consequently has been developed "most pronouncedly, albeit not without ambiguities" (Wagner 2014: 294). Importantly, many of those identifying themselves as 'non-Westerners' have regarded the West as the epitome of modernity, for better or for worse.

The stories that non-Western Islamic societies tell about secularity and modernity are addressed in the three chapters of this volume's final section, which combine case studies on Islamic contexts with general theoretical, historical, and methodological considerations of the usability of *A Secular Age* beyond the West. Writing from within Islamic Studies as a confessionally neutral discipline, the authors do not develop an Islamic story of modernity themselves. Yet their findings clearly indicate the possibility of such Islamic stories, whether because of convergent developments within Islamic and Western self-understandings or because of Western (colonial and postcolonial) influence on Islamic societies. In their details, these Islamic stories will of course markedly differ from Taylor's story.

Florian Zemmin in his chapter argues that Taylor's story despite its particularity can fruitfully be used for research on modern Islamic self-understandings. *A Secular Age* is for Zemmin a useful heuristic tool precisely because Taylor grasps the profound background understandings of modernity "common not only to believers and non-believers in the West but possibly also to non-Westerners." Islamic societies, too, exhibit all three of Taylor's levels of secularity. Moreover, it is not only modern Westerners who understand their present selves historically. Rather than a different epistemology, it was "the asymmetric power constellations of colonialism [...] that have made it harder for Muslim intellectuals to bring forward their own stories." Zemmin complements his general considerations with a case study on the concept of 'society' in the modernist Islamic journal *al-Manar*.

Complementing Zemmin's focus on 'society,' Junaid Quadri's chapter considers the effect of the transcendent/immanent distinction for modern Islamic 'religion.' While Taylor has been criticized for neglecting non-Western contributions to the evolving modern understanding of religion, Quadri turns the tables on that critique by asking what sort of "conceptual reconfiguring this momentous intellectual shift in the West proceeded to make possible, or indeed necessary, for colonized peoples and knowledge-traditions." How well does the transcendence-immanence distinction travel to the Muslim world? Analyzing legal treatises from the Hanafi school of law, Quadri shows that in pre-modern times religious affairs, for which the sighting of the Ramadan moon is an example, were imbricated as much with immanence as with transcendence. In modernity, then, religion and religious matters came to be exclusively relegated to transcendence, simultaneously making room for an increasingly autonomous worldly sphere.

Johannes Stephan, who is attending to a slightly earlier moment in Arab intellectual history, also discerns the increasing autonomy and importance of the immanent sphere in the writings by two pioneers of the *nahḍa* (Arab Renaissance) he analyzes, the Egyptian Muslim Rifaʿa al-Tahtawi and the Syrian Christian Fransis Marrash. These prominent writers allow Stephan to approach and grasp Arab modernity as reflected in story-telling, and *A Secular Age* becomes a hermeneutic tool to make sense of and contextualize new modes of narration that emerged in modern Arabic literature. In the stories of these Arab intellectuals, "human society can develop independently from transcendent interference." Yet revelation did not disappear but actually regained importance as a marker of the cultural and historical entity that Arab thinkers understood themselves to belong to. Arab or Islamic civilization could thus be conceived as an entity in its own right which was participating in the same universal process as the West, that is, in the common (hi-)story of progress.

Enchantment, unbundling, and narrative

In his Afterword to this volume, Charles Taylor reiterates some of the main themes of *A Secular Age* and responds to several of the matters raised by the volume's contributors. He rejects the charge of nostalgia, raised implicitly or explicitly by several contributors to this volume (Carlson, Bender, Thomas). And he offers several interconnected reasons for the modern sense that both belief and nonbelief are options. Some of these will be familiar to readers of *A Secular Age* itself: disenchantment (both the demise of magic and the transformation of a hierarchically-tiered cosmos) and the consequent development of the immanent frame as our shared background condition. Taylor however here distinguishes between two kinds of enchantment, the first a narrower one, adopted from Weber, having to do with a sense of magical forces operating in the world, and the second a more capacious sense of attunement or kinship with the world beyond the self. This distinction matters when we come to speak of the secular age as one of disenchantment, for the demise of the first kind of enchantment does not necessarily lead to the demise of the second – though for Taylor and others on what he calls the "romantic side of this question," the two seem tightly bound.

Taylor also introduces the concept of "unbundling," and this in two related senses: the unbundling of forms of belonging (family, parish, nation) and the unbundling of spiritual and other activities previously gathered under the church. This seems closely related to social differentiation and therefore part of what Taylor calls "secularity 1" in *A Secular Age*. (As a reminder, secularity 1 for Taylor is the withdrawal of religion from public life, while secularity 2 is the falling-off of belief and practice, and secularity 3, his main concern in *A Secular Age*, involves the background conditions against which the religious and the secular show up as such.) The shift of emphasis that Taylor makes in his Afterword is nevertheless significant; joining unbundling to disenchantment enables Taylor to speak more precisely of the social order, and offers something of a response to those readers, in this volume and elsewhere, who have thought that Taylor concentrates too much on ideas at the expense of socio-political structures. Implicitly, Taylor's point seems to be that spiritual and material factors are mutually dependent, and that secularity 1 and secularity 3 are perhaps more closely bound together than the depiction in *A Secular Age* suggests.

Finally, Taylor reiterates his position on two matters that emerge as key throughout the present volume. The first is the role of narrative, of the stories that societies and cultures tell about themselves and understand themselves to be a part of; the second is Taylor's commitment to the multiple modernities thesis and to the kind of comparative work that it makes possible. Interestingly, the comparative mode that Taylor favors both here and in other publications tends to treat cultures or civilizations as relatively self-enclosed entities, whereas a number of contributors to this volume insist upon a more fractured series of exchanges within as well as among cultures, for instance on the question of the immanent-transcendent distinction and indeed the very development of the idea of 'religion' itself. Thus the question of 'cultures,' and their relative enclosure or openness, remains a key methodological issue in Taylor's work and indeed in the question of secularity itself. On the matter of stories, meanwhile, Taylor writes that narrativity is essential to his project. He reconfirms his sense of what we might call the performative value of stories: that they are true insofar as they become part of a given society's self-understanding. Moreover, he suggests, experience of any kind is itself always embedded in a narrative, replete not with bare data but with a "certain construal of what is to be explained." Perhaps, then, we can read *A Secular Age* in just this fashion: as a narrative, a presentation of experience produced by an immensely gifted and generous writer, a story as true and compelling as he, and we, choose to make it.

Working with *A Secular Age*

This volume is rounded off with an annotated bibliography of previous responses to *A Secular Age*, compiled by Florian Zemmin. Looking both back and ahead, this bibliography gives an overview of the debate sparked by Taylor's book so far and functions as a resource for future contributions. Restricting itself to journal articles, essays, and books written in English, the bibliography still comprises 122 entries.

This flourishing industry of commentary may seem remarkable. After all, the book is very long, often repetitive, and occasionally frustrating in its digressions and swerves. At the same time, this very capaciousness makes it a rich fund of ideas and arguments. Very few writers have Taylor's interdisciplinary reach. Moreover, the book entered a field whose activity and vibrancy made it ripe for a defining statement. Even though a good deal of the response to *A Secular Age* was variously critical, the book has served to invigorate and galvanize broader debates about religion and secularity. These two concepts remain fundamental to the (self-)understandings of modernity, and the relation between religion and society has been hotly debated during recent decades, as the identification of modernization with the decline of religion loses its explanatory force. In this regard, Taylor does much more than argue for the religious genealogy of secularity or the continued salience of religion in modernity. Indeed, he directs our attention to the most fundamental background assumptions of modernity shared by all modern people, believers and non-believers alike. From this it follows that, contrary to one common assumption, controversies between religious and secular positions do *not* necessarily concern fundamental epistemological conflicts but rather play out on a common, if contested, ground. Taylor's "secular age" is not equivalent to an "age of secularism" but is rather a synonym for 'modernity,' in which both religious and secular stances have become an option.

The mutual dependency of religion and secularity also points to a dilemma. What are the other 'others' of religion, and how do we get analytic purchase on them? This is the question addressed in the title of this book series, *Religion and Its Others*. Taylor's implicit answer in *A Secular Age* is that secularity sets the conditions not only for religion but for modern life in all its varieties. By the same token, Taylor's work points the way toward analyses of such 'others' of religion as exclusive humanism, atheism, or religious indifference. In our contemporary societies, where the division between religion and secularity has become dominant, tracing the relation between that divide and others (queer/straight, human/animal, eg.) is work that still largely remains to be done. How might one go about telling such stories? Though the chapters in this volume cannot answer this question, they do jointly illuminate the central categories of modernity, religion, and secularity from which an answer might come. In the meantime, we are confident that *A Secular Age* has been remarkably, even uniquely, fruitful as a tool for interdisciplinary dialogue, and we would be pleased if readers from various disciplines would share in this estimation.

Bibliography

ASA = Taylor, Charles, 2007. *A Secular Age*. Cambridge, Mass/London: The Belknap Press of Harvard University Press
Castoriadis, Cornelius. 1987. *The Imaginary Institution of Society*. Cambridge: Polity Press.
Gaonkar, Dilip Parameshwar. 2002. "Toward New Imaginaries: An Introduction." *Public Culture* 14 no. 1: 1–19.
Gorski, Philip S. and Ateş Altınordu. 2008. "After Secularization?" *Annual Review of Sociology* 34 no. 1: 55–85.
Hurd, Elizabeth Shakman. 2010. "Appropriating Islam: The Islamic Other in the Consolidation of Western Modernity." *Critique: Critical Middle Eastern Studies* 12 no. 1: 25–41.
Salama, Mohammad R. 2011. *Islam, Orientalism and Intellectual History: Modernity and the Politics of Exclusion since Ibn Khaldun*. London: I. B. Tauris.
Sheehan, Jonathan. 2010. "When Was Disenchantment? History and the Secular Age," in *Varieties of Secularism in a Secular Age*. ed. Michael Warner, Jonathan VanAntwerpen, and Craig Calhoun, 217–242. Cambridge, Mass: Harvard University Press.
Shelley, Percy. [1821] 2002. *Shelley's Poetry and Prose*, ed. Donald H. Reiman and Neil Fraistat. New York: Norton.
Strauss, Claudia. 2006. "The Imaginary." *Anthropological Theory* 6 no.3: 322–344.
Taylor, Charles. 1989. *Sources of the Self: The Making of the Modern Identity*. Cambridge, Mass: Harvard University Press.
Taylor, Charles. 1992. *The Ethics of Authenticity*. Cambridge: Harvard University Press.
Taylor, Charles. 2002. "Modern Social Imaginaries." *Public Culture* 14 no.1: 91–124.
Taylor, Charles. 2004. *Modern Social Imaginaries*. Durham/London: Duke University Press.
Taylor, Charles. 2010. "Afterword: Apologia pro Libro suo," in *Varieties of Secularism in a Secular Age*, ed. Michael Warner, Jonathan VanAntwerpen, and Craig Calhoun, 300–321. Cambridge, Mass: Harvard University Press.
Taylor, Charles. 2011. "Understanding the Other: A Gadamerian View on Conceptual Schemes," in *Dilemmas and Connections*, 24–38. Cambridge, Mass: Harvard University Press.
van der Veer, Peter. 2001. *Imperial Encounters: Religion and Modernity in India and Britain*. Princeton, N.J.: Princeton University Press.
Wagner, Peter. 2014. "World-Sociology Beyond the Fragments. Oblivion and Advance in the Comparative Analysis of Modernities." In *Social Theory and Regional Studies in the Global Age*, ed. Saïd Amir Arjomand: 293–311. Albany: State University of New York Press.

I. **The Potential of Taylor's Story for Various Disciplines**

Matthias Koenig
Beyond the Paradigm of Secularization?

1 Introduction

Secularization theory is today facing greater criticism than ever before. The claim that modernization would necessarily lead to a declining social significance of religion has already long been the subject of intense controversy in the sociology of religion (Ausmus 1982; Glasner 1977; Hadden 1987; Luckmann 1980; Martin 1965). But only the more recent visibility of religion as evinced in fundamentalist movements, ethno-religious conflicts, and migration-driven religious diversity has stripped secularization theory of its former status as virtually uncontested paradigm. Various intellectuals have commented upon the renaissance of religion, "de-secularization," or even a new "post-secular" condition (Berger 1999; Habermas 2001). And within specialized literatures in history, political science or sociology, many authors emphasize the necessity of moving decidedly beyond conventional versions of secularization theory (see literature reviews in Borutta 2010; Ebaugh 2002; Gorski and Altınordu 2008; Philpott 2009).

What exactly the many critics of the secularization paradigm aim to achieve is however anything but clear. Thus, while they claim that secularization theory reproduces an overly linear master narrative of modernity that overlooks the many counter-developments and historical ruptures of religious change, they sometimes draw on the very same narrative to claim that our present time represents a fundamental epochal transition.[1] Similar ambiguities can be observed among sociologists of religion, as the secularization paradigm always encompassed multiple sub-theses. José Casanova (1994: 20–39) for instance, distin-

---

This chapter is the English version of an article previously published as Koenig, Matthias. 2011. "Jenseits der Säkularisierungstheorie? Zur Auseinandersetzung mit Charles Taylor." *Kölner Zeitschrift für Soziologie und Sozialpsychologie* 63: 649–673. I acknowledge support from the Lichtenbergkolleg at the University of Göttingen as well as from the Max Planck Institute for the Study of Religious and Ethnic Diversity. An earlier version of this paper was presented at the Congress of the German Association for Sociology in Jena (2008). I am grateful to Christoph Halbig, Hans Joas, Inka-Lee Huu, Detlef Pollack, Holmer Steinfath, and the editors for helpful comments and advice.

1 Hans Joas (2004: 124) has rightly stressed that diagnoses of a 'post-secular' age should be seen as self-corrections of intellectuals' previously held positions rather than as observations of actual social change; see also Philipp 2009 and Torpey 2010 for a discussion.

guishes three sub-components: functional differentiation of religion from other social spheres; the privatization of religion; and the decline of individual religious belief (see also Dobbelaere 1981; Tschannen 1991). These different sub-theses are addressed in varying ways by critics of secularization theory. Thus, Thomas Luckmann's (1991) theory of "invisible religion" and the new religious economics promoted by Rodney Stark and others (Stark 1999; Warner 1993) – whose empirical viability is incidentally quite contested (compare Norris and Inglehart 2004; Pollack 2009) – challenge the assumption about the decline of religious belief relying on privatization and differentiation arguments in order to explain the mass-cultural form of popular religion and the supply-dependent vitality of religious practices, respectively. Casanova adds a strong criticism of the privatization theory in his analysis of "public religion" while positing the thesis of functional differentiation as valid core of secularization theory (Casanova 1994: 212). In reaction to arguments from Talal Asad (1999: 179), he has recently gone one step further in claiming that the entry of religion in the public space challenges not only arguments of privatization but also of functional differentiation; he even goes so far as to state that both sub-processes are actually difficult to separate analytically.

This state of discussion demonstrates how high the requirements for a convincing alternative to the classical secularization paradigm in sociology of religion have become. An alternative theory must fulfill the following three criteria at a minimum (compare also Gorski and Altınordu 2008). First, it must explain how 'secularity' became such an important and controversial category in the discourses of intellectual elites as well as in the mentalities of entire populations, at least in European modernity. Second, such an alternative must integrate within a coherent analytical framework the evidence accumulated during decades of empirical research on the decline of individual religiosity in Europe as well as the findings on genuinely modern forms of religious vitality within and outside of Europe as emphasized by the classical paradigm's critics. Third, this framework must enable the description and explanation of the diversity of modern differentiation patterns of religious and political orders – "multiple secularity" (Katznelson and Jones 2010: 20; see also Wohlrab-Sahr and Burchardt 2012) – in cross-national and cross-cultural perspective.

Few alternative theories are currently receiving as much attention as *A Secular Age*. Casanova praises it as "the best analytical, phenomenological, and genealogical account that we have of our modern, secular condition" (Casanova 2010: 265). Taylor's theoretical account owes its enormous resonance not least to the fact that he moves the secular self-conception of modernity to the center of the debate. According to Taylor, the concept of secularization refers not only to the differentiation of religion from other social orders and the accompanying privatization of religion (secularity 1) or to the decline of individual religious faith (secularity 2), but first and foremost to the construction of a "framework of understanding" (ASA: 3, 34), and to a cultural horizon that defines non-religious and religious practices alike (secularity 3). Taylor seeks to surpass the classic secularization paradigm by presenting it as a part and parcel of an "immanent frame" that requires hermeneutical reconstruction, and within which the other sub-processes of secularization become possible in the first place.

Such an ambitious alternative theory deserves a thorough discussion within the sociology of religion. In light of Taylor's highly selective reception of the sociological literature, the first task is to contextualize an interpretation of his theory within the wider debate in sociology of religion in order to examine to what extent his theory satisfies the aforementioned criteria. That is precisely the goal of this chapter. As a first step, I shall draw on Taylor's broader work to identify the basic concepts that allow him to adopt a reflexive stance towards the immanent frame, concepts which amount to a culturalist theory of modernity that – despite its obvious parallels to the phenomenological tradition of the discipline – explicitly keeps a certain distance from sociology (1.). In a second step I examine Taylor's theory of secularity, determining to what extent it is able to integrate the seemingly contradictory findings of secularization on the one hand and religious vitality on the other (2.). Finally, I shall discuss his contribution to the enterprise of cross-national and cross-cultural comparisons of differentiation patterns between religious and political orders. Such an intensive reading of Taylor's alternative to the conventional secularization paradigm is worthwhile not only because his reconstruction of the immanent frame tremendously enriches the secularization debate, but also because the deficits of his account point to as yet unresolved questions for sociological research on religion.

2 Secularity as cultural construction – fundamental concepts

An alternative to the classic secularization paradigm, as formulated in the first requirement above, must be able to explain how secularity became such an important and controversial category of self-interpretation of modern societies. While conceptual history and discursive genealogies have laid the groundwork for such an explanation (Asad 1993, 2003; Milbank 1990), Taylor attempts to examine the cultural horizon not only of elite intellectual discourses, but also of the mentalities of the wider population. Taylor pursues this goal in a manner quite similar to the phenomenological tradition in sociology, by introducing sparse formal anthropological prerequisites that allow for a radical historicization of modern conceptions of the natural, social, and subjective worlds. Taylor levels particular criticism at sociological secularization theories for naturalizing the immanent frame through the use of categories such as 'disenchantment' or 'rationalization,' and for obscuring the contingency of the frame's cultural construction.

2.1 Formal anthropology and cultural theory of modernity

Since his early work on Hegel (Taylor 1975), Taylor has attempted to formulate a philosophical anthropology that takes into consideration the fact that human perception is based on the senses and that humans therefore cannot fully comprehend themselves within the categories of scientific naturalism (see in particular Taylor 1992). Taylor's thought, as was repeatedly emphasized, combines a formal anthropology with a hermeneutic reconstruction of the culture of modernity (see in particular Rosa 1998: especially 24–25; Smith 2002: 7). In that, it is reminiscent of Thomas Luckmann's phenomenological sociology that articulates a phenomenological reconstruction of invariant structures of subjective meaning with the sociological analysis of historically constructed social realities (see, for example, Luckmann 2002: 51). In fact, Taylor's formal anthropology, like Luckmann's theory, builds on the phenomenological legacy (Merleau-Ponty, Husserl, Heidegger). Although he is sensitive to the paradoxes and problems of Husserl's methods of pure reduction, he simultaneously strives for a minimal definition of what it means to be human. According to Taylor, this includes the corporeal dimension of human experience, the linguistic nature of human expressiveness, and the moral orientation of human behavior according to "strong evaluations." Taylor understands these "strong evaluations" to mean the values embedded in a cultural lifestyle that, in contrast to that which we simply desire, contain that which we perceive to be desirable, and which are therefore constitutive for our personal identity.[2] These formal anthropological assumptions are important to Taylor because they place the historical-narrative reconstruction of modern culture, which he himself mainly conducted in *Sources of the Self* (Tay-

---

[2] See Joas 1997: 200 as well as Rosa 1998: 109. One could also relate Taylor's concept of 'strong evaluations' to the concept of 'ultimate values' found in Parsons's early work (1935). However, Taylor emphasizes a different aspect as evaluations do not simply exist within a cultural system, but arise from the interplay of the system with the practical experiences of the actor; see Joas 1997: 32 and 212.

lor 1994), onto the path of a *culturalist* theory of modernity (see Reckwitz 2001: 478–522).

The linkage of formal anthropology and the cultural theory of modernity also characterizes *A Secular Age*, the work in which Taylor continues his profound interest in the fate of religious traditions in modernity (see in particular Taylor 1999; 2002a; see Kühnlein 2008). Here again, he bases his arguments on a formal anthropological premise, namely the premise that humans invariably experience their lives in relation to ideas of "fullness:" "Somewhere, in some activity, or condition, lies a fullness, a richness" (ASA: 5), or, as he states elsewhere: "for *any* liveable understanding of human life, there *must* be some way in which this life looks good, whole, proper, really being lived as it should" (ASA: 600, emphasis mine). These notions, according to Taylor, play a role not only in extraordinary experiences of fullness, but also in negative experiences of loss or failure, and even in the experiences of everyday life. For Taylor, the idea that humans live their lives in some way or other oriented toward fullness is an invariable element of the human condition. How humans experience fullness, on the other hand, is extremely varied throughout history. Taylor distinguishes ideal-typically between religious "belief" and "unbelief" as two variants of the lived experience of fullness (ASA: 8). In the variant of belief, he argues, fullness of life is experienced as something received from another source while the "final goals" of life are located in transcendence, such as in the love of God. By contrast, the final goals receive a purely immanent definition in the variant of unbelief, which Taylor sees realized in "self-sufficient" or "exclusive humanism" – "a humanism accepting no final goals beyond human flourishing, nor any allegiance to anything else beyond this flourishing" (ASA: 18–19). In this type, the fullness of life is sought in "human flourishing" itself and is not experienced as received from another source but as achievable, whether via reason (Kant), emotion (Romanticism) or heroism (Nietzsche).

Taylor explicitly links the division between belief and unbelief as two idealtypes of the formal-anthropologically invariant openness of humans for experiences of fullness to the distinction between transcendence and immanence. This distinction is common in theories of religion (see Pollack 1995), but Taylor gives it a particular twist. First, in line with his critique of scientific naturalism, he firmly holds on to a theory of religion that is grounded in anthropological assumptions; this distinguishes him from sociologists who advocate moving toward a communication theory of religion and regarding the transcendence/immanence distinction as a code of communication (see Luhmann 2000: 13, 77). Second, Taylor uses a strict definition of transcendence. While Luckmann (1991) in his phenomenological analysis regards experiences of transcendence as invariant givens and hence conceives of religiosity as anthropologically given, Taylor's formal-anthropological approach posits only experiences of fullness as invariant. Religious belief as one of the variants of experiencing fullness consists not simply in moving through everyday life towards human final goals, but in transcending those human goals themselves. Taylor emphasizes not so much the cognitive assertion of a transcendental reality (such as God), but rather the normative orientation towards visions of a fulfilled life, which include goods that exist beyond human flourishing (such as the love of God) and enable the transformation of humans beyond their own perfection (ASA: 20, 510).

2.2 The immanent frame and the boundaries of sociological secularization theory

The basic concepts introduced so far help to clarify what Taylor means by "secularity 3," namely a situation in which the suspension of all goods beyond human flourishing becomes imaginable, or, put differently, a situation in which unbelief has become a real option. The secular age thus differs fundamentally from the age of belief where certain assumptions about the natural, subjective, and social worlds rendered religious belief the self-evident way of experiencing fullness. In the age of belief, the natural world was regarded as cosmos and as God's creation, the self was imagined as being open to the impact of transcendental power (the "porous self"), and the social world was structured by hierarchical relationships embedded within a higher order (the church) and time (salvation history). Taylor argues that the secular age emerged from a "disenchantment" of these three world concepts. In the secular age, the cosmos was replaced by the idea of a mechanistic universe, the concept of a "buffered self" was created, and the social world was imagined as a direct-access society in which identity was no longer conceived of as relational but as categorical (i.e. national belonging), and whose history plays out in a homogenous time with an undetermined future. According to Taylor, the disenchantment of the three world concepts led to the establishment of an "immanent frame" that enables new experiences of fullness, namely experiences of unbelief, while simultaneously making the former naïveté of belief impossible. The key feature of the secular age is hence the fact that even religious belief is experienced as an option (ASA: 14).

Up to this point it might seem that Taylor is reformulating a rather conventional secularization theory, as can be found in Peter L. Berger's sociological account (1973; 1992). His analytical distinction between three variants of secularity corresponds rather neatly to Berger's three-pronged concept of secularization as a process at the level of individual consciousness, social institutions, and cultural worldviews (Berger 1973: 103–105). Taylor's emphasis on the optional character of religious belief in the modern age is particularly reminiscent of Berger's "heretical imperative" (1992), according to which the collapse of an overarching sacred canopy and the subsequent pluralization of worldviews had rendered religious belief one among many contingent options.

Where Taylor departs from Berger, however, is in the narrative of how the secular age came about. According to Taylor, conventional secularization theories typically take the form of a "subtraction story" (ASA: 26). In that story, modern science, with its urge for rationalizing, tears apart the veil of irrationality, exposes the secrets of the magic garden, recognizes the true nature of the universe, self and society, and thereby divests religious belief of its previous plausibility.[3] Taylor's criticism centers on neo-orthodox secularization theory in sociology (Bruce 1996; 2002; Wallis and Bruce 1992). He argues that this theory, with its implicit stage-consciousness and its attitude of a neutral observer position, un-reflexively employs an epistemology that is culturally constructed (ASA: 428, 436). Upon closer examination, Taylor's critique of subtraction stories of secularization has a two-fold aim: their lack of consciousness of contingency and their reductionist theory of religion.

Taylor charges, first, that conventional secularization theory naturalizes the immanent frame while masking the contingent process of its historical construction (ASA: 556–566).

> The subtraction story gives too little place to the cultural changes wrought by Western modernity, the way in which it has developed new understandings of the self, its place in society, in space and in time. *It fails to see how innovative we have been*; its tendency is to see modernity as the liberating of a continuing core of belief and desire from an overlay of metaphysical/religious illusion which distorted and inhibited it (ASA: 573).

From Taylor's point of view, understanding the secular age requires tracing the history of the construction of the immanent frame as a collective cultural horizon, a new sacred canopy, so to speak.

Second, Taylor argues that conventional secularization theory suffers from a reductionist theory of religion. What Taylor initially does not dispute is that religious experiences of fullness, which require transcendence and aim toward a transformation of humanity, have lost plausibility as a result of the influence

---

3 This is reminiscent of the appropriation of Weber's concept of disenchantment by Habermas (1981) in his theory of communicative rationalization, which Taylor has repeatedly criticized. It should be noted, though, that Taylor himself occasionally speaks of "disenchantment" which might run counter to his own goals; see Milbank 2010: 57; on the conceptual history of 'disenchantment' see Lehmann 2009.

of the immanent frame ("secularity 2"). What he finds questionable, though, is the explanation for this loss of significance and, complementarily, the assessment of possible religious futures. Neither does Taylor regard the modernization of social structures as a sufficient condition for the decline of religious belief, nor does he regard indifference towards experiences of fullness as the inevitable end point of that process. In his view, both such claims falsely ascribe an epiphenomenal character to religion: "I don't accept what often seems to be an unspoken premise about human motivation which underlies this master narrative of secularization. In particular, I hold that religious longing, the longing for and response to a more-than-immanent transformation perspective [...] remains a *strong independent source of motivation* in modernity" (ASA: 530). From a religious-philosophical perspective, Taylor represents an anti-reductionist position whereby religious beliefs cannot be reduced to psychic or social factors, but rather are able to unfold their own motivational power.[4] Only such a position would allow one to identify instances of religious vitality within the conditions set by the immanent frame.

It is true that both of these critiques of sociology – its lack of contingency awareness and its reductionist theory of religion – are somewhat exaggerated and over-generalized. Taylor's basic concepts not only mirror those of phenomenological sociology, but also bear a resemblance to the so-called "strong program" of recent cultural sociology (Alexander 2003; Reckwitz 2001) and can easily be translated into the Weberian tradition of interpretative sociology. That tradition is known for being quite open to the motivational power of religious ideas (Schluchter 1988) and to conceive of modernity as a cultural program whose internal construction fundamentally changes the forms of religious belief (see Eisenstadt 1998; Meyer, Boli, and Thomas 1987). Nonetheless, Taylor's critique of sociology cannot simply be pushed aside. Its core challenge is that assuming a (supposedly) neutral observer's perspective from the start sets reflection upon the immanent frame on a problematic track. Expanding our ability to think through the immanent frame – which is Taylor's pragmatic goal in formulating an alternative theory – instead demands that the diversity of the religious and non-religious participant perspectives that developed during modernity be hermeneutically reconstructed on equal terms.[5] Whether sociology would

---

4 From time to time, Taylor (in particular ASA: 437 and 768) even favors the position of a theistic realism, which regards religious belief as a superior answer to a transcendental reality over exclusive humanism; on this topic, see Smith 2010: 113.

5 This specifically includes the participant's "perspective as a believer" (ASA: 437); see also his foreword in the English translation of Marcel Gauchet's *Désenchantement du monde* (Taylor 1997) and his lecture "A Catholic Modernity" (Taylor 1999). Taylor's normative purpose here

be well advised to adapt Taylor's hermeneutic position or whether the discipline should maintain its observer perspective is a question that cannot be resolved here. At a minimum, Taylor's alternative to the conventional secularization paradigm demands that we examine sociology's own ontological and normative assumptions more critically (see also Smith 2010).

In light of the above argumentation, Taylor's alternative theory does fulfill the first of the criteria mentioned at the outset of this chapter. The core of his account consists precisely of explaining the secular self-interpretation of (western) modernity in its historical emergence. It remains to be seen to what extent Taylor's hermeneutic reconstruction of the immanent frame also fulfills the two other criteria.

3 The immanent frame and the religious history of modernity

An alternative theory to the conventional secularization paradigm, as formulated as second criterion above, must be capable of integrating the empirical evidence for declining individual religious beliefs ("secularity 1") with competing findings of religious vitality. *A Secular Age* undoubtedly provides several insights as to why the immanent frame was able to bring about a decline in the plausibility of religious belief while simultaneously creating new forms of religious belief.

True to his hermeneutical intentions, Taylor reaches these insights through a narrative about how contemporary forms of experience have been culturally constructed. Such a narrative cannot restrict itself to a conventional intellectual history, but must examine the cultural horizon of modern societies in its entirety. The term *social imaginaries*, which Taylor introduced elsewhere (2002b; 2004) is of great significance in this respect. Social imaginaries such as conceptions of the market economy, the public sphere or democratic self-governance, embody implicit ideas of social order that go beyond intellectually articulated theories in three ways: They consist (a) of multiple layers of factual and normative assumptions that (b) are shared by entire societies, and (c) enable collective practices (ASA: 171; see Taylor 2004: 23). Explaining the *transformation* of social imaginaries, from which the cultural horizon of modernity arose, requires tracing how new theories come into existence, combine themselves with the limited practices of elites, then spread across diverse fields of action and finally turn into

---

is to re-articulate Christian belief to provide additional foundations for modernity's strong evaluations (see Joas 2004: 100; Smith 2002: 236).

taken-for-granted assumptions held by entire populations. In its attempt to explain this process, Taylor's secularity narrative operates on two levels that are not always easily to distinguish. At the level of articulated theories, the subject of Taylor's narrative is the establishment of exclusive humanism, through which "unbelief" became an option in the first place, at least among intellectual elites. At the level of social imaginaries, Taylor's narrative then traces how such theories enabled certain interpretations of social practices and were finally subsumed into the cultural assumptions of modern societies.

3.1 Reform, exclusive humanism and the proliferation of options

Much like in *Sources of the Self* and quite in line with the Weberian tradition in sociology (see Schluchter 1979; Eisenstadt 2003; Gauchet 1985; Meyer, Boli, and Thomas 1987), Taylor chooses Christianity as starting point of his secularization narrative. He is particularly interested in the drive for reform that began during the high and late middle ages and reached its zenith during the age of the Protestant Reformation and the Catholic Counterreformation. Basing his argumentation on historiographical literature on the medieval period (Jean Delumeau, Keith Thomas etc.), Taylor (ASA: 63) emphasizes the "rage for order" that blazed a trail within the clergy, the religious orders and heterodox movements, and which strove to overcome the contradiction between religious virtuosi and a lay religiosity characterized by magical practices and carnival-like "anti-structure" (Turner), especially by increasing the standards of orthodox faith. Activism, uniformity, homogenous organization, and rationalism are the most important elements of the drive for reform that not only advanced the process of "disenchantment" but also, particularly in the Calvinistic branch of the Reformation, created new forms of religious and social discipline (ASA: 77).[6]

Taking this as his starting point, Taylor first traces the establishment of exclusive humanism as an elaborate theory of moral order. He argues that the Christian drive for reform enabled the rise of new, educated intellectual and political elites, some of them recently liberated from the church hierarchy. Starting in the sixteenth and seventeenth centuries, these elites created new intellectual discourses in the sciences, ethics, and arts, which, as Taylor does not cease to

---

[6] In light of the importance that Taylor attributes to the juridification of social relationships in modernity, it is surprising that he does not discuss Harold Berman's legal historical works (1983; 2004) on the Gregorian Reform and its consequences.

emphasize, were initially grounded in Christian theology. Thus, he argues that the newly formed sciences' interest in nature did not stem from a rejection of but rather an orientation toward God. Taylor goes on to claim that neo-Stoicist thinking on natural law (Grotius, Locke), formulated an early version of the modern theory of moral order, which, with its principles of rights, freedom, equality and mutual benefit (ASA: 170), prepared the way for exclusive humanism, while being able to interpret the principle-based design of society as a divine task (ASA: 126–127).

The radical breakthrough to exclusive humanism, in Taylor's view, occurred in the form of deism at the turn of the seventeenth to the eighteenth century, at a time when a far-reaching anthropocentric transition was occurring in philosophical and, to an extent, in theological discourses (ASA: 222). Old ideas about God's presence through predestination, mercy or miracles were reformulated until nothing remained of them but the idea of a distant creative deity. Humans were increasingly regarded as independent, free subjects actively shaping their world, and goods beyond human flourishing completely disappeared from view. This anthropocentric transition was supported by ideas of an impersonal order in nature and particularly in society, which was no longer conceived of as based on relationships but on rules (ASA: 271, 282). Conceptions of natural or rational religion rounded off the set of deistic assumptions (ASA: 292). From these assumptions, or so Taylor's narrative goes, it was but a small step to exclusive humanism, in which goods beyond human flourishing completely disappeared from view (ASA: 245) and unbelief became a plausible option. The fact that this humanism cannot deny its origin in internal Christian transformations becomes especially obvious, in Taylor's view, in the idea of universal mutual benevolence – a version of Christian *agapè* clipped of its transcendental references. Denying this Christian origin – a denial that is essential to the self-interpretation of exclusive humanism – therefore requires an 'awareness of stages' that interprets the present as progress and any recollection of transcendence as regression, and that is made plausible through the subtraction narratives of secularization as canonized in classical sociology (ASA: 289).

Taylor regards the development of exclusive humanism as prelude to the secular age. What he emphasizes as significant to the stabilization of the immanent frame, in which belief and unbelief are experienced as options, is the constant diversification of possible worldviews. Not only Christian orthodoxy but also exclusive humanism provoked a variety of critiques and counter-critiques. Taylor traces these in detail along multiple ethical controversies in philosophy, literature, and art from the Romantic period until the late nineteenth century. The wealth of positions that ensues essentially oscillates around three poles: the religious option of faith, whether in orthodox or liberal variations; the aforementioned exclusive humanism (utilitarianism, Kant); and heroism, as introduced by Nietzsche (ASA: 636). I will not delve further into Taylor's clear-sighted discussion of the dilemmas equally encountered by these three options in their views on human flourishing, suffering, violence, and death. It suffices to note that this diversification of possible worldviews further underscores their inherently optional character.

3.2 Social imaginaries and modern forms of religion

At the second level of his narrative of emerging secularity, Taylor concentrates less on articulated theories of moral order and more on broader social imaginaries. He first discusses how denominational discipline and early modern state formation led to new practices of civility among elites, which provided fertile soil for the aforementioned anthropocentric turn and marked the beginning of a three-step transition from theories of moral order to social imaginaries (ASA: 237).

Taylor (ASA: 438) labels the first stage the Ancien Régime when new theories of order formulated by elites still coexisted with pre-modern social imaginaries. Due to the Christian drive for reform, church, state, and society became more closely linked in various programs of social discipline, such as the banning of carnivals, the bureaucratization of administration, and the increase in economic productivity, moral conformity and confessional orthodoxy (ASA: 108–112), so amply documented in historical and historical-sociological literature on the confessional age (see Gorski 2003). To account for the fact that society was still imagined as organically embedded in a church-based order, especially at the local level, Taylor sometimes refers to this stage in somewhat idiosyncratic fashion as "paleo-Durkheimian."[7] "The 'paleo' phase corresponds to a situation in which a sense of the ontic dependence of the state on God and higher times is still alive, even though it may be weakened by disenchantment and an instrumental spirit" (ASA: 455).

In Taylor's view, the second stage was achieved in the nineteenth century with the Age of Mobilization (ASA: 445), in which large groups of people were removed from their local contexts through industrialization and urbanization,

---

[7] Hans Joas (2004: here 105) has thoughtfully pointed out the problems of this terminology, which Taylor previously employed in his study of William James (Taylor 2002a). It should also be noted that Taylor misrepresents Durkheim's church concept which is formulated not in the semantic opposition of church and state, but rather as a form of moral community, see for extensive discussion in Tyrell 2008.

re-embedded in new social structures, and thus introduced to modern social imaginaries. According to Taylor's argument, the experience of new practices in the social fields of the economy, democratic rule, and public space lent plausibility to the assumptions articulated within modern theories of moral order regarding individual freedom, equality, and reciprocity. Taylor highlights that the immanent frame, which was strengthened by these experiences, did at first not lead to a decline in belief, but rather unleashed new social forms of religion. He distinguishes two types in particular. The first is "civil religion," which Robert Bellah (1967) famously discovered in representations of the American nation, but which can also be found in the Victorian equation of Christianity and civilization, so significant for the early imperialistic phase of globalization (see van der Veer 2001). The second type consists of new voluntary religious associations, as illuminated by historical research on the evangelical movement, on confessional milieus, and not least on Catholic restoration. In both variants, identity is articulated in religious language, which leads Taylor to refer to it as neo-Durkheimian: "[I]n 'neo' societies, God is present because it is his Design around which society is organized. [...]. [T]he senses of belonging to group and confession are fused, and the moral issues of the group's history tend to be coded in religious categories" (ASA: 455). Taylor thus argues that the gradual and uneven decline of older religious forms was – counter to the arguments of linear secularization theories – accompanied by intensive and publicly virulent religious mobilization.

This situation changed in the Age of Authenticity, the third stage, which in Taylor's view started with the cultural revolution of the 1960s and was characterized by expressive individualism (ASA: 473).[8] The three fields that are of particular importance for modern theories of moral order, namely the market, democracy, and public space, are here complemented by a fourth field, namely that of consumer culture (ASA: 481), whose social practices are not characterized by collective action but by mutual display. According to Taylor, the public social forms of religion previously developed – whether civil religion or denomination – were subjected to a process of de-institutionalization whose consequences were not only secularization but also the creation of "post-Durkheimian" individualized forms of religion. In what Taylor calls a "supernova effect," the fragmentation of options of belief and un-belief was transformed from an elite to a mass phenomenon (ASA: 199, 412). This did not mean that the options were reduced simply to orthodox religious or orthodox secular attitudes, but rather that highly

---

[8] Taylor had previously examined the ideal of authenticity in terms of its historical origins in the Romantic period in *Sources of the Self*; see Taylor [1991] 1995: particularly 32.

variable appropriations of religious tradition and individual forms of spirituality emerged, ones that changed from members of one generation to another as well as within individual life trajectories, and all of which were crucially also experienced as options.

3.3 A new perspective on modern religious history?

Taylor's culturalist narrative of the immanent frame goes beyond conventional secularization theories in terms of both its breadth as well as the detail of the historical materials on which it is based. He provides an account of modern religious history that accounts for the many entangled and at times contradictory developments, thereby fulfilling the second criterion stated at the beginning of this chapter. Without doubt, there are also noticeable gaps within this narrative. In particular, it is surprising that Taylor does not further discuss the well-documented invention of new concepts of 'religion' that began in the seventeenth century and reached its provisional conclusion in the nineteenth century with the intellectual construction of 'world religions' (see Asad 1993; Masuzawa 2005). Such a discussion could have shown how the creation of the immanent frame was reflected in the conceptual history of 'religion' itself (see Tenbruck 1993). Another problem lies in the fact that Taylor glosses over many complex debates about the relationship of Christianity and modernity. For example, he simply labels Blumenberg as another proponent of subtraction narratives (ASA: 294) without engaging in Blumenberg's debate with Carl Schmitt and its echo in German and French intellectual thought (see Blumenberg 1988; Monod 2002). In fact, since the nineteenth century, the process of secularization has been told not only as a subtraction or discontinuity narrative, but also as a continuity narrative. In that sense, Taylor stands in a long tradition of argument about Christian genealogies of modernity, a tradition that actually encompasses substantial parts of sociology which receive not much attention in his account.

Yet despite such objections, Taylor's reconstruction of the creation and expansion of the immanent frame is indeed able to combine the empirical evidence for a decline in religious belief ("secularity 2"), which had previously conveyed the impression of the irreversibility of secularization, with findings about religious revitalization. His narrative makes it possible to conceive of secularization processes as episodes in a volatile history of religion, in which phases of religious mobilization and phases of religious decline alternate. The religious revival movements that occurred in nineteenth-century America (Finke and Stark 2005; Thomas 1996) as well as the creation of denominational milieus in Europe during the so-called "second confessional age" (Blaschke 2000), can be interpreted as specifically modern religious forms, i.e. forms that presuppose the existence of the immanent frame. And even the use of religion for the construction of ethnic, national or civilizational identities no longer remains to be conceptualized as cultural defense (according to Bruce 2002: 31), but rather integrates well into modern social imaginaries. Taylor's depiction of the Age of Authenticity, i.e. the time period for which religious-sociological survey research has most convincingly confirmed the un-churching of Europe, joins up with the revisionist historiographies of Hugh McLeod (2007) and Callum Brown (2001), without losing its perspective on the mass cultural forms of individualized religion (see in particular Davie 2000; Hervieu-Léger 2004). Global fundamental movements can also be interpreted within Taylor's frame, namely as de-culturalized forms of religion which again presuppose the expansion of an immanent frame (on this topic see Eisenstadt 1998; Roy 2008). Less thoroughly examined in Taylor's narrative, however, are lifestyles characterized by indifference to religion, since his formal anthropology analytically privileges extraordinary experiences of fullness, whether these are transcendent or immanent in nature (see Butler 2010: 206–208).

The fact that Taylor provides a coherent narrative of the religious history of modernity does not necessarily mean that it is the best or only alternative to conventional secularization theory. Luhmann's systems-theory, for instance, provides a no-less plausible account by emphasizing religion's loss of structural support within a functionally differentiated society during modernity, while showing how religion is capable of reacting to this situation with new organizational and movement-like forms (Luhmann 2000: 285). This leads to the question of how exactly Taylor's culturalist reconstruction of the secular age is positioned in the ongoing controversy on the differentiation of religious and other social spheres.

4 The immanent frame and the controversy of differentiation

The third requirement formulated at the start of this chapter was that an alternative to the conventional secularization paradigm should be able to describe and explain the variations of differentiation patterns in modern societies. Even differentiation theory, which has long been the undisputed paradigmatic core of the secularization paradigm, is currently the subject of harsh criticism (see e.g. Casanova 2006). In contrast to unilinear concepts of increasing functional differentiation of religion and politics, the debate about multiple modernities, initiated by Shmuel N. Eisenstadt, has moved the remarkable variability of differentiation patterns within modernity to the fore (see Martin 1978; and more recently Gorski 2000; 2005; Katznelson and Jones 2010; Schwinn 2009; Spohn 2008). Current debates also give greater attention to the problem of how to explain the differentiation of religious and non-religious spheres.[9] It therefore needs to be discussed whether and how Taylor's account of the immanent frame ("secularity 3") contributes to explaining the variable differentiation patterns of religion and politics observed in modern societies ("secularity 1").

In this regard, Taylor's theory suffers from two systematic weaknesses. First, his culturalist theory of modern secularity is not fully worked out as a culturally comparative sociology of multiple secularities. Second, his theory does very little to explain the causal mechanisms that led to waves of differentiation of political and religious orders and their various institutional outcomes.

4.1 Cultural premises of differentiation

It should be emphasized at the start that Taylor's reconstruction of the immanent frame does indeed contribute to a better understanding of the differentiation of religion and politics in Western modernity. He persuasively argues that imagining historical time as separate from a salvation story, and the social sphere as liberated from church hierarchies and therefore directly accessible to all, was a necessary prerequisite for the creation of autonomous public spheres, national societies, and sovereign states. In doing so, Taylor illuminates the cultural horizon that enabled political order to differentiate itself from religious order more sharply, while simultaneously capturing the continuing cultural impregnation of various forms of political order through Christian values.[10]

However, such a culturalist reconstruction of the prerequisites of differentiation calls for a comparison with non-Western cultures. Only such a comparison would allow the idiosyncrasies of Christianity, which made the West the arena for the emergence of the immanent frame and corresponding differentiation processes, to become apparent. Yet, Taylor explicitly does *not* include non-Western cultural spheres as part of his analysis. He justifies this decision by citing not only the wealth of material to be examined, but also his hermeneutic intentions of opening up debates among various positions within Western modernity (rhet-

---

9 The call for more fine-grained explanations of differentiation applies not only to the secularization debate, but also to sociological theory in general; see in particular Schwinn 2001: 25.
10 Similar arguments can be found in Parsons (1967: in particular 391) and Schwinn (2001).

orically marked in the text as "we"). At this point, a certain tension arises between Taylor's hermeneutic intentions and his culturalist theory. On the one hand, he limits the concept of religious belief, as a variant of the interpretation of experiences of fullness oriented toward transcendence and human transformation, to the civilizational sphere of Western Christianity (ASA: 15). On the other hand, he employs this concept in a much more general and comparative sense when he argues that all traditions of the "Axial Age," meaning Confucianism, Hinduism, Buddhism as well as the monotheistic salvation religions, had opened up new possibilities for human transformation through the radicalization of transcendence (ASA: 151–153, 611).

In fact, Taylor at times directly follows the work of Eisenstadt (1982; 2003; see also Bellah 2005), who introduced the concept of the Axial Age in comparative macro-sociology – understood as the tension between transcendent and mundane spheres, between 'world' and 'world behind the world' (*Hinterwelt*), from which the given forms of order appear in need of reconstruction. Taylor's discussion of the social structural correlates of Axiality, especially the establishment of religious virtuosity as the opposite of pre-Axial mass religiosity, joins up with Eisenstadt's work at this point. The concept of Axial religions even takes on a leading role in Taylor's narrative genealogy of the immanent frame. He argues that within Christianity the tension between religious virtuosity and mass religiosity was increasingly experienced as unsatisfactory (ASA: 155). Consequently, the drive for reform, as prelude to the construction of the immanent frame, originated in attempts to overcome the tension characteristic for Axial religions more generally. But if this is the case, the question arises whether and why the breakthrough to secular modernity occurred only within Christian Axial civilization and not elsewhere. It should be obvious that such a question cannot be answered without in-depth intercultural comparisons.

Intercultural comparisons become even more important when one examines not only the historical constructions of the immanent frame and its respective differentiation patterns, but also their contemporary dynamics. Eisenstadt's concept of multiple modernities aims to address precisely that question. According to that concept, the encounter of the cultural program of Western modernity with other Axial civilizations led to highly distinctive configurations of social spheres and collective identities. Dealing with such configurations would be only a natural extension of Taylor's agenda. For despite the fact that he interprets the drive for reform and the subsequent institutionalization of the immanent frame as uniquely Christian, he claims that the social imaginaries of modernity have been globally diffused, partly as result of their inherent universalism (see Taylor 2004 in particular). However, as Casanova (2009: 98, 104) has aptly argued, such a global diffusion of the immanent frame across global society could be expected to bring about specific local variations ("secularity 3") that are potentially devoid of European stage-consciousness and generate completely different patterns of differentiation ("secularity 1") (see also Koenig 2007). While briefly alluding to such a comparative analysis, Taylor does not actually carry it out, nor does his theory take into consideration the various inter-civilizational encounters, particularly in colonial contexts, that lastingly shaped even the occidental path of secularization.

Whether the tension between Taylor's hermeneutical intentions and his appropriation of Eisenstadt's theory of Axial Age cultures can be resolved cannot be conclusively discussed at this point.[11] It is also beyond the scope of this chapter to discuss to what extent comparative civilizational analysis is a viable endeavour at all (see criticism in Breuer 1994; Knöbl 2007). What I argue here is that a sociological theory of modern secularity, its Western origins, and of its global expansion, remains deficient without incorporating cultural comparative and historical transfer analyses. Many historical and empirical questions thus remain to be answered by the sociology of religion if the aim is to go beyond the conventional secularization paradigm.

4.2 Imaginaries, institutions, and interests

The most fundamental problem of a culturalist theory of modern secularity, however, lies elsewhere. While such a theory greatly contributes to reconstructing the prerequisites for differentiation, it does little to explain the specific patterns of differentiation that are at the heart of current comparative research on the relationship between religious and political order. Starting with the *description* of the various differentiation patterns, recent typologies and categorizations have achieved a higher degree of sophistication than is present in *A Secular Age* (see Fox 2008; Madeley 2009). Even in those writings (e.g. Taylor 1996) where he distinguishes three models of 'secularization' – the "strategy of the common foundation" (Pufendorf), the "strategy of independent political ethics" (Hobbes), and the "strategy of an overarching consensus" (Rawls) – Taylor does not use them productively for comparative purposes. To the extent that he considers relationships between religious and political orders at all, he does so only in reference to questionable paleo-, neo-, and post-Durkheimian configurations.

---

[11] There is good reason for a certain skepticism, as the theory of Axial Age cultures can be seen as a late heir of the invention of 'world religions' (Masuzawa 2005) and therefore as assuming a relativizing perspective of religion as culture (Luhmann 2000), which is biased to naturalizing the immanent frame.

There, he employs Tocquevillian arguments to explain transatlantic differences by pointing to the specific situations in which modern social imaginaries became effective; thus, he claims that during the French Revolution, social imaginaries were linked with the invention of new practices, while in the American Revolution, as a result of a lack of a "paleo-Durkheimian" phase, they led to the reinterpretation of already existing social practices (see in a similar vein Casanova 2009: 102; Berger, Davie, and Fokas 2008).

When it comes to *explaining* various differentiation patterns, Taylor remains far behind developments in historical sociology that have moved the problem of effective causal mechanisms into the center of controversy (see Gorski 2000; Smith 2003). It is at this very point that Taylor's culturalist secularization narrative runs into the theoretical problems and methodological traps that strictly culturalist theories of modernity face more generally. Taylor is clearly aware of these problems, as he openly discusses the objection leveled at him that his narrative reconstruction of modern social imaginaries suffers from an idealistic bias. He attempts to dispel this objection with two arguments. He first claims that the objection is based on a false dichotomy of ideational and material factors (Taylor 2004: 31). In his view, social practices are equally riven with ideational and material dimensions (in the Wittgensteinian sense) and practices exist in a reciprocal relationship to one another; social practices become possible only through the existence of a common background, but this common background simultaneously exists only through social practices (ASA: 212–213). The other argument consists quite simply of a rejection of the requirements for strong causal explanations. Taylor asserts that the reconstruction of world views accessible "to us" does not strive for historical-sociological explanation, but rather for hermeneutic understanding (Taylor 1995: 354–355). Both these attempts to defend his theory are however not entirely convincing. Even a narrative reconstruction with primarily hermeneutic goals cannot reject the plausibility requirements demanded of historical explanations (see Smith 2002: 213). And precisely if one emphasizes the ideational-material dual character of social practices, an idealistic top-down explanation that tends to sideline power or interest constellations remains incomplete (see Rosa 1998: 282).

Recent historical-sociological attempts to explain differentiation processes focus not only on cultural but also on other factors, including interest constellations and institutionalized power configurations. Anthony Gill (2008), for example, takes a decidedly anti-culturalist position, and uses the USA, Latin America, and the post-Soviet states to develop a theoretical model that accounts for the origins of religious liberty, i.e. a specific component of the differentiation of political and religious order. The model proceeds axiomatically from the typical interests of ruling political elites (in maintaining their power), religious majorities (in regulating the religious field), and religious minorities (in deregulating the religious field), and identifies the political conditions (a stable power framework and high opportunity costs of regulation) as well as religious conditions (pluralization) under which – assuming rational action choices among all three groups of actors – the provision of religious freedom and/or the deregulation of the religious field becomes plausible. An interest-based model possesses explanatory power because it identifies not only the situation-specific conditions for the political guarantee of religious freedom, but also the social mechanisms of self-increasing differentiation. Once pluralization has achieved a critical mass, as in the American case, it increases the opportunity costs of restrictive religious politics, resulting in the gradual deregulation of the religious field, which itself enables further pluralization, and so forth. Of course, a purely interest-based model remains incomplete insofar as it assumes the identities and preferences of the actors to be exogenously given in a situation, instead of making them objects of historical analysis themselves (see Katznelson and Stedman Jones 2010: 65). The model also fails to explain the conditions under which religious freedom is institutionalized in the long-term, even in opposition to volatile interest constellations. However, it cannot be denied that an explanation of the origins of specific differentiation patterns requires analyzing the specific interests of political and religious actors, their power-configurations, and the institutional dynamics to which these give rise (also see Kuru 2009; Smith 2003).

But when one takes these explanatory problems seriously, then Taylor's culturalist secularity narrative also becomes destabilized with respect to explaining the social imaginaries *themselves* ("secularity 3"). At both levels of his reconstruction, Taylor fails to discuss the intense conflicts that accompanied the creation of the immanent frame. This applies initially to the formulation of new theories about the world, society, and the self. One cannot comprehend the dynamics of cultural creativity if one does not also take into account the internal conflicts within the intellectual field that gained autonomy after the denominational conflicts in the sixteenth century led the Catholic and Protestant churches to lose control over the means of intellectual production to the rising territorial states (see Collins 1998: 570–617; also see Wuthnow 1989). Taylor grants even less space to addressing the conflict that occurred during the transition from modern moral theories to social imaginaries of entire populations. The group of authors around Christian Smith (2003), for example, using the case of American religious history of the late nineteenth century, has provided a detailed depiction of the creation of a secular hegemonial culture as a result of intense power conflicts between Protestant elites and aspiring professional groups in the fields of education, medicine, law, media, and academia, which led to a reduction in the institutional control of the church over cultural production throughout the country. The history of cultural conflicts in Europe also shows that the hegemony of secular imaginaries was the result of intense and partially violent conflicts (Borutta 2010; Clark and Kaiser 2003; Poulat 1987). This suggests that even the historical-comparative analysis of variations of "secularity 3" requires that interests and institutional contexts be taken more thoroughly into account than Taylor's culturalist approach allows.

5 Conclusion: several questions for the historical sociology of religion

Taylor's monumental study is undoubtedly a significant contribution to the current debate on religion in modernity. In opposition to time-diagnostic prognoses of 'post-secular' societies, Taylor's work underscores how little would be won by discarding the concept of secularization entirely. Simultaneously, the work allows us to study the problems that confront the formulation of an alternative to conventional secularization theory.

Of the requirements outlined at the beginning of this chapter, Taylor's account quite clearly fulfills the first criterion, for his work as a whole seeks to reconstruct the secular self-perception of (Western) modernity. His formal anthropological cultural theory of the secular age provides a reflexive perspective for a variety of disciplines, not least for the social sciences, which have been tightly bound up in the construction of the immanent frame. Taylor not only underscores the need to examine the genealogies of both discontinuity and continuity narratives of secularization (see Borutta 2010), but also calls for a renewed clarification of the assumptions of sociological theories of religion. Secondly, Taylor succeeds in setting up an interpretative framework within which the allegedly contradictory developments of religion in modernity can be integrated. The cultural construction of the immanent frame enables secularization processes in the sense of classic secularization theorists ("secularity 2"), but also unleashes collective and individual inventions of new religious identities. A further task of religious-sociological research lies in determining the exact conditions under which the immanent frame generates one or another effect. Advancing from general statements about trends to an analysis of causal mechanisms is also the permanent task of comparative research on the differentiation patterns of religious and political order ("secularity 1"). Third, Taylor's culturalist narrative of secularization fails to convince when it comes to formulate culturally and historically comparative perspectives. His theory lacks analytical instruments to capture instances of conflict or the interest and power constellations behind them, from which not only institutional arrangements of religion and politics, but also the social imaginaries themselves emerge.

But while Taylor's alternative to the conventional secularization paradigm leaves many questions unanswered, it does raise substantial issues that historical and sociological research must address – questions that all lead away from large-scale narratives and toward fine-grained causal analysis. One may doubt whether this more modest historical-philosophical and time-diagnostic agenda can do justice to Taylor's own aspiration for a hermeneutic mediation of different internal perspectives on experiences of fullness, but one can certainly hope that it would benefit our understanding of contemporary religious controversies.

Bibliography

Alexander, Jeffrey C. 2003. *The Meanings of Social Life: A Cultural Sociology*. Oxford, New York: Oxford University Press.
Asad, Talal. 1993. *Genealogies of Religion. Discipline and Reasons of Power in Christianity and Islam*. Baltimore/London: Johns Hopkins University Press.
Asad, Talal. 1999. "Religion, Nation-State, Secularism," in *Nation and Religion: Perspectives on Europe and Asia*, ed., ed. Peter van der Veer and Hartmut Lehmann, 178–196. Princeton: Princeton University Press.
Asad, Talal. 2003. *Formations of the Secular. Christianity, Islam, Modernity*. Stanford: Stanford University Press.
Ausmus, Harry J. 1982. *The Polite Escape. On the Myth of Secularization*. Athens, Ohio: Ohio University Press.
Bellah, Robert N. 1967. "Religion in America." *Daedalus. Journal of the American Academy of Arts and Science* 96: 1–21.
Bellah, Robert N. 2005. "What is Axial about the Axial Age?" *Archives européennes de sociologie* XLVI: 69–87.
Berger, Peter L. 1973. *Zur Dialektik von Religion und Gesellschaft. Elemente einer soziologischen Theorie*. Frankfurt a.M.: Fischer.
Berger, Peter L. 1992. *Der Zwang zur Häresie. Religion in der pluralistischen Gesellschaft*. Freiburg: Herder.
Berger, Peter L. ed., 1999. *The Desecularization of the World. Resurgent Religion and World Politics*. Washington, D.C.: Ethics and Public Policy Center.
Berger, Peter L., Grace Davie, and Effie Fokas. 2008. *Religious America, Secular Europe? A Theme and Variations*. Aldershot: Ashgate.
Berman, Harold J. 1983. *Law and Revolution. The Formation of the Western Legal Tradition*. Cambridge, Mass.: Harvard University Press.
Berman, Harold J. 2004. *Law and Revolution II The Impact of the Protestant Reformations on the Western Legal Tradition*. Harvard: Harvard University Press.
Blaschke, Olaf. 2000. "Das 19. Jahrhundert: Ein Zweites Konfessionelles Zeitalter?" *Geschichte und Gesellschaft* 26: 38–75.
Blumenberg, Hans. [1966] 1988. *Die Legitimität der Neuzeit*. Frankfurt a.M.: Suhrkamp.

Borutta, Manuel. 2010. "Genealogie der Säkularisierungstheorie. Zur Historisierung einer großen Erzählung der Moderne." *Geschichte und Gesellschaft* 36: 347–376.
Breuer, Stefan. 1994. "Kulturen der Achsenzeit. Leistung und Grenzen eines geschichtsphilosophischen Konzepts." *Saeculum* 45: 1–33.
Brown, Callum. 2001. *The Death of Christian Britain*. London: Routledge.
Bruce, Steve. 1996. *Religion in the Modern World. From Cathedrals to Cults*. Oxford: Oxford University Press.
Bruce, Steve. 2002. *God is Dead. Secularization in the West*. Oxford: Blackwell.
Butler, Jon. 2010. "Disquieted History in *A Secular Age*," in *Varieties of Secularism in a Secular Age*, ed. Michael Warner, Jonathan VanAntwerpen, and Craig Calhoun, 193–216. Cambridge, Mass.: Harvard University Press.
Casanova, José. 1994. *Public Religions in the Modern World*. Chicago: Chicago University Press.
Casanova, José. 2006. "Rethinking Secularization: A Global Comparative Perspective." *The Hedgehog Review* 8: 7–22.
Casanova, José. 2009. *Europas Angst vor der Religion*. Berlin: Berlin University Press.
Casanova, José. 2010. "A Secular Age. Dawn or Twilight?," in *Varieties of Secularism in a Secular Age*, ed. Michael Warner, Jonathan VanAntwerpen, and Craig Calhoun, 265–281. Cambridge, Mass.: Harvard University Press.
Clark, Christopher, and Wolfram Kaiser, eds., 2003. *Culture Wars. Secular-Catholic Conflict in Nineteenth Century Europe*. Cambridge, Mass.: Cambridge University Press.
Collins, Randall. 1998. *The Sociology of Philosophies. A Global Theory of Intellectual Change*. Cambridge: Harvard University Press.
Davie, Grace. 2000. *Religion in Modern Europe. A Memory Mutates*. Oxford: Oxford University Press.
Dobbelaere, Karel. 1981. *Secularization. A Multi-Dimensional Concept*. London: Sage.
Ebaugh, Helen R. 2002. "Return of the Sacred: Reintegrating Religion in the Social Sciences." *Journal for the Scientific Study of Religion* 41: 385–395.
Eisenstadt, Shmuel N. 1982. "The Axial Age: The Emergence of Transcendental Visions and the Rise of the Clerics." *Archives européennes de sociologie* 23: 299–314.
Eisenstadt, Shmuel N. 1998. *Die Antinomien der Moderne. Die jakobinischen Grundzüge der Moderne und des Fundamentalismus. Heterodoxien, Utopismus und Jakobinismus in der Konstitution fundamentalistischer Bewegungen*. Frankfurt a.M.: Suhrkamp.
Eisenstadt, Shmuel N. 2003. *Comparative Civilizations and Multiple Modernities*, 2 volumes. Leiden/Boston: Brill.
Finke, Roger, and Rodney Stark. 2005. *The Churching of America: Winners and Losers*. New Brunswick: Rutgers University Press.
Fox, Jonathan. 2008. *A World Survey of Religion and the State*. Cambridge et al.: Cambridge University Press.
Gauchet, Marcel. 1985. *Le désenchantement du monde. Une histoire politique de la religion*. Paris: Gallimard.
Gill, Anthony. 2008. *The Political Origins of Religious Liberty*. Cambridge: Cambridge University Press.
Glasner, Peter E. 1977. *The Sociology of Secularization. A Critique of a Concept*. London: Routledge & Kegan Paul.

Gorski, Philip S. 2000. "Historicizing the secularization debate." *American Sociological Review* 65: 138–167.
Gorski, Philip S. 2003. *The Disciplinary Revolution. Calvinism and the Rise of the State in Early Modern Europe.* Chicago: University of Chicago Press.
Gorski, Philip S. 2005. "The Return of the Repressed: Religion and the Political Unconscious of Historical Sociology," in *Remaking Modernity. Politics, History, and Sociology*, ed. Julia Adams, Elisabeth S. Clemens, and Ann Shola Orloff, 161–189. Durham/London: Duke University Press.
Gorski, Philip S., and Ates Altınordu. 2008. "After Secularization?" *Annual Review of Sociology* 34: 55–85.
Habermas, Jürgen. 1981. *Theorie des kommunikativen Handelns*, 2 volumes. Frankfurt a.M.: Suhrkamp.
Habermas, Jürgen. 2001. *Glauben und Wissen. Rede anläßlich der Verleihung des Friedenspreises des Deutschen Buchhandels.* Frankfurt a.M.: Suhrkamp.
Hadden, Jeffrey K. 1987. "Toward Desacralizing Secularization Theory." *Social Forces* 65: 587–611.
Hervieu-Léger, Danièle. 2004. *Pilger und Konvertiten. Religion in Bewegung.* Würzburg: Ergon-Verlag.
Joas, Hans. 1997. *Die Entstehung der Werte.* Frankfurt a.M.: Suhrkamp.
Joas, Hans. 2004. *Braucht der Mensch Religion?* Freiburg: Herder.
Katznelson, Ira, and Gareth Stedman Jones. 2010. "Introduction: Multiple Secularities," in *Religion and the Political Imagination*, ed. Ira Katznelson, Ira and Gareth Stedman Jones, 1–22. Cambridge, Mass.: Cambridge University Press.
Knöbl, Wolfgang. 2007. *Die Kontingenz der Moderne. Wege in Europa, Asien und Amerika.* Frankfurt a.M./New York: Campus.
Koenig, Matthias. 2007. "Kulturelle Konstruktionen und institutionelle Varianten der Moderne in der Weltgesellschaft," in *Kulturen der Moderne. Soziologische Perspektiven der Gegenwart*, ed. Andreas Reckwitz and Thorsten Bonacker, 71–96. Frankfurt am Main/New York: Campus Verlag.
Kühnlein, Michael. 2008. *Religion als Quelle des Selbst. Zur Vernunft- und Freiheitskritik von Charles Taylor.* Tübingen: Mohr Siebeck.
Kuru, Ahmet T. 2009. *Secularism and State Policies Toward Religion. The United States, France, and Turkey.* Cambridge: Cambridge University Press.
Lehmann, Hartmut. 2009. *Entzauberung der Welt. Studien zu Themen von Max Weber.* Göttingen: Wallstein Verlag.
Luckmann, Thomas. 1980. "Säkularisierung – ein moderner Mythos." in *Lebenswelt und Gesellschaft*, 160–172. Paderborn: Ferdinand Schöningh.
Luckmann, Thomas. [1967] 1991. *Die unsichtbare Religion.* Frankfurt a.M.: Suhrkamp.
Luckmann, Thomas. 2002. *Wissen und Gesellschaft. Ausgewählte Aufsätze 1981–2002.* Konstanz: UVK.
Luhmann, Niklas. 2000. *Die Religion der Gesellschaft.* Frankfurt am Main: Suhrkamp.
Madeley, John T.S. 2009. "Unequally Yoked: The Antinomies of Church-State-Separation in Europe and the USA." *European Political Science* 8:273–288.
Martin, David. 1965. "Towards Eliminating the Concept of Secularization," in *Penguin Survey of the Social Sciences*, ed. Julius Gould, 169–182. Harmondsworth: Penguin.
Martin, David. 1978. *A General Theory of Secularization.* Oxford: Basil Blackwell.

Masuzawa, Tomoko. 2005. *The Invention of World Religions. Or, How European Universalism Was Preserved in the Language of Pluralism.* Chicago: Chicago University Press.
McLeod, Hugh. 2007. *The Religious Crisis of the 1960s.* Oxford: Oxford University Press.
Meyer, John W., John Boli, and George M. Thomas. 1987. "Ontology and Rationalization in the Western Cultural Account," in *Institutional Structure. Constituting State, Society, and the Individual*, ed. George M. Thomas, John W. Meyer, and John Boli, 12–37. Newbury Park: Sage Publications.
Milbank, John. 1990. *Theology and Social Theory. Beyond Secular Reason.* Oxford, UK/Cambridge, Mass: Blackwell.
Milbank, John. 2010. "A Closer Walk on the Wild Side," in *Varieties of Secularism in a Secular Age*, ed. Michael Warner, Jonathan VanAntwerpen, and Craig Calhoun, 54–82. Cambridge, Mass.: Harvard University Press. 54–82.
Monod, Jean-Claude. 2002. *La querelle de la sécularisation de Hegel à Blumenberg.* Paris: Vrin.
Norris, Pippa, and Ronald Inglehart. 2004. *Sacred and Secular. Religion and Politics Worldwide.* Cambridge: Cambridge University Press.
Parsons, Talcott. 1935. "The Place of Ultimate Values in Sociological Theory." *The International Journal of Ethics* XLV: 282–316.
Parsons, Talcott. 1967. "Christianity and Modern Industrial Society," in *Sociological Theory and Modern Society*, ed. Talcott Parsons, 385–421. New York: The Free Press.
Philipp, Thomas. 2009. "Gesellschaft und Religion. Eine kritische Auseinandersetzung mit Habermas' Zeitdiagnose der postsäkularen Gesellschaft." *Berliner Journal für Soziologie* 19: 55–78.
Philpott, Daniel. 2009. "Has the Study of Global Politics Found Religion?" *Annual Review of Political Science* 12: 183–202.
Pollack, Detlef. 1995. "Was ist Religion? Probleme der Definition." *Zeitschrift für Religionswissenschaft* 3: 163–190.
Pollack, Detlef. 2009. *Rückkehr des Religiösen?* Tübingen: Mohr Siebeck.
Poulat, Emile. 1987. *Liberté, Laïcité. La guerre des deux France et le principe de la modernité.* Paris: Cerf-Cujas.
Reckwitz, Andreas. 2001. *Die Transformation der Kulturtheorie.* Weilerswist: Velbrück Wissenschaft.
Rosa, Hartmut. 1998. *Identität und kulturelle Praxis. Politische Philosophie nach Charles Taylor.* Frankfurt am Main, New York: Campus.
Roy, Olivier. 2008. *La sainte ignorance. Le temps de la religions sans culture.* Paris: Seuil.
Schluchter, Wolfgang. 1979. *Die Entwicklung des okzidentalen Rationalismus.* Tübingen, Mohr.
Schluchter, Wolfgang. 1988. *Religion und Lebensführung. Studien zu Max Webers Religions- und Herrschaftssoziologie*, 2 volumes. Frankfurt a.M.: Suhrkamp.
Schwinn, Thomas. 2001. *Differenzierung ohne Gesellschaft. Umstellung eines soziologischen Konzepts.* Weilerswist: Velbrück.
Schwinn, Thomas. 2009. "Multiple Modernities: Konkurrierende Thesen und offene Fragen. Ein Literaturbericht in konstruktiver Absicht." *Zeitschrift für Soziologie* 38: 454–476.
Smith, Christian, ed., 2003. *The Secular Revolution: Power, Interest, and Conflict in the Secularization of American Public Life.* Berkeley: University of California Press.

Smith, Christian. 2010. *What is a Person? Rethinking Humanity, Social Life, and the Moral Good from the Person Up.* Chicago: University of Chicago Press.
Smith, Nicholas H. 2002. *Charles Taylor: Meaning, Morals and Modernity.* Cambridge: Polity Press.
Spohn, Willfried. 2008. *Politik und Religion in einer sich globalisierenden Welt.* Wiesbaden: VS Verlag für Sozialwissenschaften.
Stark, Rodney. 1999. "Secularization, R.I.P." *Sociology of Religion* 60: 249–274.
Taylor, Charles. 1975. *Hegel.* Cambridge: Cambridge University Press.
Taylor, Charles. 1992. *Negative Freiheit. Zur Kritik des neuzeitlichen Individualismus.* Frankfurt am Main: Suhrkamp.
Taylor, Charles. 1994. *Quellen des Selbst. Die Entstehung der neuzeitlichen Identität.* Frankfurt am Main: Suhrkamp.
Taylor, Charles. 1995. *Das Unbehagen in der Moderne.* Frankfurt a.M.: Suhrkamp.
Taylor, Charles. 1996. "Drei Formen des Säkularismus." in Kallscheuer, Otto, ed., 1996. *Das Europa der Religionen.* Frankfurt am Main: Fischer. 217–246.
Taylor, Charles. 1997. "Foreword." In Gauchet, Marcel. 1997. *The Disenchantment of the World. A Political History of Religion,* ix–xv Princeton: Princeton University Press.
Taylor, Charles. 1999. "A Catholic Modernity?" In *A Catholic Modernity? Charles Taylor's Marianist Award Lecture,* ed. James L. Heft, 13–38. Oxford: Oxford University Press.
Taylor, Charles. 2002a. *Die Formen des Religiösen in der Gegenwart.* Frankfurt a.M.: Suhrkamp.
Taylor, Charles. 2002b. "Modern Social Imagineries." *Public Culture* 14: 91–124.
Taylor, Charles. 2004. *Modern Social Imagineries.* Durham: Duke University Press.
Tenbruck, Friedrich H. 1993. "Die Religion im Maelstrom der Reflexion." in *Religion und Kultur. Sonderheft der Kölner Zeitschrift für Soziologie und Sozialpsychologie,* ed. Jörg Bergmann, Alois Hahn, and Thomas Luckmann, 31–67. Opladen: Westdeutscher Verlag.
Thomas, George M. 1996. *Revivalism and Cultural Change. Christianity, Nation Building, and the Market in the Nineteenth Century United States.* Chicago: University of Chicago Press.
Torpey, John. 2010. "A (Post-)Secular Age? Religion and the Two Exceptionalisms." *Social Research* 77: 269–296.
Tschannen, Olivier. 1991. "The Secularization Paradigm: A Systematization." *Journal for the Scientific Study of Religion* 30: 395–415.
Tyrell, Hartmut. 2008. "Kulturkämpfe in Frankreich und Deutschland und die Anfänge der Religionssoziologie." in *Religionskontroversen in Frankreich und Deutschland,* eds. Matthias Koenig and Jean-Paul Willaime, 97–181. Hamburg: Hamburger Edition.
Wallis, Roy, and Steve Bruce. 1992. "Secularization: the Orthodox Model." in *Religion and Modernization,* ed. Steve Bruce, 8–30. Oxford: Oxford University Press.
Warner, R. Stephen. 1993. "Work in Progress Towards a New Paradigm for the Sociological Study of Religion in the United States." *American Journal of Sociology* 98: 1044–1093.
Wohlrab-Sahr, Monika, and Marian Burchardt. 2012. "Multiple secularities: toward a cultural sociology of secular modernities." *Comparative Sociology* 11:1–35.
Wuthnow, Robert. 1989. *Communities of Discourse. Ideology and Social Structure in the Reformation, the Enlightenment, and European Socialism.* Cambridge, Mass./London, UK: Harvard University Press.

Günter Thomas
The Temptation of Religious Nostalgia: Protestant Readings of *A Secular Age*

1 Introduction

The thesis of this chapter is that *A Secular Age* is not just an ambitious study in the history of culture and the philosophy of religion; it is a deeply religious book, and furthermore a thoroughly Catholic project, which provokes a Protestant reading.[1]

Before substantiating why *A Secular Age* demands a Protestant reading, however, it is first necessary to discern the methodical assumptions underlying Taylor's book. I will then summarize the basic features of his master narrative which relate to its thoroughly Catholic orientation. In a third step, I will attempt to show why Charles Taylor's magnum opus demands not only a theological reading but also a specific Protestant reading. Because this critique of Taylor's proposal is intended to be a conversation, I will eventually turn to the challenges Charles Taylor's narrative poses for Protestant theology.

2 Foundational methodical assumptions

In *A Secular* Age a set of foundational assumptions are 'given'[2]. Five basic assumptions are of particular interest when exploring the Catholic nature of the project.

I would like to thank Samuel Shearn, who translated a hard-to-read German text into this much more accessible English version.

1 Charles Taylor's critique of Protestantism (both in its Lutheran and Calvinistic version) does have more detailed parallels in the philippic offered by Brad S. Gregory (2012) launched against the devastating long-term effects of the Protestant Reformation. For a lucid discussion which also draws parallels to Charles Taylor, see: http://blogs.ssrc.org/tif/the-unintended-reformation/ (last accessed July 15, 2015).
2 On reflection, this is unavoidable. The critique of a strict 'presuppositionlessness' is shared by the hermeneutic traditions (Bernstein 1983), pragmatic traditions (Stout 1981), and system-theoretical traditions (Luhmann 1990).

2.1 The concentration on Western Christianity

Charles Taylor offers an alternative to the grand narratives of modernity. In the German context one thinks of Hans Blumenberg, Max Weber, and Ernst Troeltsch; in the English-speaking world, Jonathan I. Israel.[3] It is a narrative, a history of modernity, which concentrates specifically on Western Christianity. *A Secular Age* radically limits the sources to Latin Christendom.[4] This means in practice that both Eastern Orthodoxy and minorities such as Jews in the West and the historical power of Islam in Spain and the Near East are excluded. Furthermore, the highly dynamic confrontations between Pentecostal forms of Christianity with so-called 'pre-modern' societies are beyond Taylor's scope. It is all about Western Catholic Christianity.

2.2 The self-initiated transformation of religion

There is a great affinity with Max Weber's cultural and social historical analysis of modernity, with regard to one central systematic point. Like Weber, Taylor assumes that the modern Western world, in its religious form, ultimately emerges from *inner impulses* and *self*-initiated transformations of *religion*. Philosophical emancipation movements, political upheavals, the social evolution of society, developments in the media, economic crises, crises of colonialism, and the restructuring of legal systems play no decisive role – not even rudimentarily – in Taylor's grand narrative of the fate of religion in modernity.[5] In order to reconstruct this process of transformation, Taylor, who is obviously oriented by a Right-Hegelian perspective, turns exclusively to instructive texts in the history of ideas and decisive moments *within* religious and philosophical developments. Key moments in the history of art, political philosophy, and literature become sources for the discourse, but only in so far as they mirror religious changes.[6] Taylor's analysis is 'monocausal' with regard to the historical development of Christianity. Observable religious development within the history of ideas does

---

3 See, for example, Blumenberg (1975, 1974, 1966) and Israel (2001, 2006).
4 For a pointed criticism of this limit, see Chakrabarty (2009: 393–403).
5 For the influence of the development of the media in the Reformation and for the development of modernity, see the exemplary contribution by Eisenstein (1979). But see also Giesecke (1991) and the exceptional, lucid and large study by Sandl (2011).
6 Much here is reminiscent of the Chicago Catholic theologian David Tracy: the richness of sources, the meandering course of the argument, the encyclopedic learnedness, and also his apologetic-Catholic concern.

not follow from a matrix of socio-cultural and technological factors, but rather is depicted as strictly 'self-initiated'.

2.3 The rejection of a reductionist analysis of religion

If one places Taylor's approach within the broad field of non-theological study of religion, it is striking that his method is strictly non-reductionist, although he does not explicitly formulate it as such.[7] The reality of religion is not translated into the dynamic ontology of politics or science. Religion is not the medial layer of something else, neither with regard to the powers of transformation nor – as Taylor's remarks on eschatology make clear – with regard to the reality intended by believers.[8] This approach makes a principally fruitful point of contact with theology. This can be seen very clearly in Taylor's definition of religion.

The formal distinction between transcendence and immanence is foundational for Taylor: "a reading of 'religion' in terms of the distinction transcendent/immanent is going to serve our purposes here" (ASA: 15). Nevertheless, there is more to religion than this basic formal distinction. The concept of religion must be augmented, anthropologically and functionally in the sense of a belief in the transcendent. "Every person, and every society, lives with or by some conception(s) of what human flourishing is: what constitutes a fulfilled life? what makes life really worth living?" (ASA: 16). As a Catholic and someone who knows Augustine well, the undeniable presence of this question and the need for an answer lead Taylor to see the manifestation of a reference to something transcendent, of a search for the experience of fullness. In a third step, Taylor goes beyond potentially reductionist answers by asking, "does the highest, the best life involve our seeking, or acknowledging, or serving a good which is beyond, in the sense of independent of human flourishing?" (ASA: 16). As a Christian, this means for Taylor that "Loving, worshipping God is the ultimate end" (ASA: 17). However, "we have moved from a world in which the place of fullness was understood as unproblematically outside of or 'beyond' human life [...]" (ASA: 15).

---

[7] For a short presentation of the complex problem of reductionism in the study of religion, see Thomas (2001a: 219–263); Idinopulos and Yonan (1994); and Segal (1983). For a reductionist theory of religion, see the work of Pascal Boyer (1994, 2001).
[8] On the problem of the scientific necessity to develop a perspective which diagnoses an error on the part of believers and in theology, see Hamnett (1973).

This third and last aspect of religion is for Taylor that one believes in an acting instance or power beyond immanence. It is the theistic conception of a transcendent God, who in the end enables our life to be one which goes beyond the span of birth and death and to be one which is more than immanent life. Religion is constituted for Taylor out of the connection of these three dimensions: transcendence, the life beyond as goal, and a divine agent.[9] Thus he distinguishes himself clearly from the mainstream study of religion in cultural studies and the social sciences.

2.4 The assumption of strong transcendence

> In the term 'sacred', I'm pointing to the belief that God's power is somehow concentrated in certain people, times, places or actions. Divine power is in these, in a way it is not in other people, times, etc., which are 'profane' (ASA: 76).

This conviction decisively shapes Taylor's perception of historical changes in organization in the field of religion. The foundational asymmetry or unequal distribution with regard to the presence of the divine leads to a natural affinity with a hierarchy-based management of the religious – thus the relativizing of these asymmetries and hierarchies appears on the monitor of scientific analysis as a crisis of religion. Complementary to this characterization of the holy or sacred, Taylor understands the transcendent as something "beyond life." Transcendence is the opposite of a (spatially imagined) horizontal immanence.[10] Although Taylor never finally explains the opposition of transcendence and immanence, it is intended to give an account of the fate of a faith which is characterized in two ways: "the belief in transcendent reality, on one hand, and the connected aspiration to a transformation which goes beyond ordinary human flourishing on the other" (ASA: 510). Only by means of this conceptual calibration can Taylor's criticism be of power and weight. However, this opposition of terms, shared by other analyses in the sociology of religion, should be strongly questioned.[11] It goes against foundational biblical-theological and systematic in-

---

9 I do interpret Taylor's reference to a "belief in a higher power" as implying a notion of divine agency (ASA: 20). Nonetheless, throughout *A Secular Age* Taylor considers Buddhism to be a religion (ASA: 167, 612).
10 For early observations on Taylor's concept of transcendence, see Haughton (1999). For a precise criticism from the perspective of cultural and philosophical history, see Gordon (2011).
11 For a Trinitarian theological critique of this distinction in sociology of religion influenced by Niklas Luhmann, see Thomas (2001b).

sights about the presence of God, that is, it misses the manifold and subtle interweaving of immanence and transcendence (for example, in the Spirit, in the Word and in fellowship), which help to overcome such abstract theism.[12] These completely contingent assumptions are those which determine Taylor's instruments of diagnosis for the processes of decline in modernity.

2.5 The presence of religious orientation

The fifth assumption in Taylor's method becomes clear in a specific openness and intentional lack of definition on Taylor's part. We may formulate this as a question: How, in *A Secular Age*, are theology and historical reconstruction related? *Prima facie*, Taylor is a philosopher and historian, specifically a phenomenologist and historian of ideas, i.e. he *does not* develop his narrative explicitly as a theologian. His great reputation in the academy is no doubt dependent on this external perspective on religion – a factor which becomes clear in the reception of his work. At the same time, he freely admits, with reference to Foucault, that his "writing is also shaped by a different 'unthought'" (ASA: 429), which he wants to contrast with that "unthought" contained in large parts of the secularization theory. What does it mean methodically, if Taylor expounds a religious "historicized existentialism," as John Milbank diagnoses?[13]

3 Basic features of Taylor's grand narrative

The narrative woven through the chapters of *A Secular Age* describes *four* phases in the development of religion: At the beginning, we have "early" or "pre-Axial" religion (ASA: 792, fn 4). The second phase is from the Axial Age (800–200 B.C.) until around A.D. 1250, while the third, characterized by Reform (Taylor's term), reaches into the early modern period. Growing out of Reform, there follows so-called exclusive humanism. As one might expect from an expert on Hegel, this story does not develop linearly, but with dialectical turns, and full of unintended consequences.

---

[12] On various models of transcendence, see Thomas (2007). Dietrich Bonhoeffer's theology stands for a Christological understanding of an 'immanence of transcendence in immanence'.
[13] For this characterization, which is part of a positive evaluation, see Milbank (2009: 102). The religious orientation of Taylor is discussed in the various replies in Taylor and Heft (1999).

For all further developments, the measure, the gold standard, is 'early religion,' religion before the Axial Age.[14] This is a thoroughly 'enchanted' world, full of spirits and demons, a world in which moral powers are felt and present in the events of one's life and in one's environment.[15] In contrast to later developments, religious meaning was not merely 'in the head,' but real and experienced 'out there' in the world. Even the "natural world [...] testified to divine purpose and action [...]" (ASA: 25). In an enchanted world, just about every object of everyday life can embody supernatural powers. This experience of the world is equivalent to a certain experience of subjectivity. The self cannot be experienced as separated from the world. Rather, the self is vulnerable and – as Taylor formulates in *Sources of the Self* – "porous." Within this religious cosmos, God and society are interwoven. The social connections themselves are holy. Starkly formulated this means: "God was also implicated in the very existence of society" (ASA: 25). Furthermore, "[i]n general, going against God is not an option in the enchanted world" (ASA: 41). There is a threefold embedment of people and their religion, which characterizes this epoch: 1. The embedment of people in a social order, 2. embedment in a cosmos, and 3. embedment in understandings of human salvation as natural flourishing.[16]

Taylor's early religion, with its consistently positive and undoubtedly romanticized and idealized description, undergoes a modification in the course of that phase of upheaval between 800 and 200 B.C., called the Axial Age. This modification leads to a peculiar and instable balance of opposites until around A.D. 1250. The Axial Age is particularly significant for Taylor because he says here emerged an ideal combination of 'early religion' and Christianity – a combination which profits from the best of both. It is this synthesis Taylor yearns for with considerable nostalgia, and which was dissolved, even shattered in the process of Reform, particularly through the Reformation.

Why, one could ask, is the religiosity formed by the Axial Age not already a degenerate product? Taylor sees clearly that a process of dis-embedding has

---

14 Taylor refers here to Karl Jaspers's concepts and the research of Shmuel Eisenstadt, and furthermore Robert Bellah's thoughts about religious evolution. However, the influence of Mircea Eliade on the idea of an original religion can hardly be overestimated (Bellah 2011). For recent discussion of the upheavals of the Axial Age, see Bellah and Joas (2012).
15 With a direct reference to Max Weber, Taylor claims that "[p]eople lived in an 'enchanted' world" (ASA: 25). See also Taylor (ASA: 146–158). "The Great Disembedding," starting in the Axial Age, "reaches its logical conclusion" in post-axial religions (ASA: 146).
16 "Axial religions [...] all call into question the received, seemingly unquestionable understandings of human flourishing... The highest human goal can no longer just be to flourish, as it was before" (ASA: 152). The Axial Age marks a shift in religious aims from inner-worldly flourishing to salvation, including a strong notion of transcendence.

taken place, although different religions address different embedments. He emphasizes that Christianity as well as Buddhism develop "a notion of our good which goes beyond human flourishing" (ASA: 151) and that through this notion new forms of dis-embedded religion are created – with a precarious tension between a religious search for well-being and a search for salvation. The fuller, higher good "promised a transformation in which we would find our deepest and fullest end in this higher good [...]" (ASA: 611). However, a solution developed in the midst of this tension, of which Taylor is in awe, despite occasional criticism: The breaks and oppositions in the contemporaneous pre- and post-Axial religiosities led to a "combination of strain on one hand, and hierarchical complementarity on the other" (ASA: 154). Within the Christian community there appears to have been a powerful division of labor:

> [I]n the Latin Church a (in theory) celibate clergy prays and fulfills priestly and pastoral functions for a married laity, which in turn supports the clergy. On a broader scale, monks pray for all, mendicant orders preach; others provide alms, hospitals, etc. Over time, the tension is overlaid with an equilibrium, based on a complementarity of functions (ASA: 44).

In this differentiation, a model of different religious 'speeds' emerges. While some, as a minority and elite, devote themselves to 'higher forms' of religion, the others live in ritual, social and cosmological embedments.

Taylor is undoubtedly fascinated theologically, and as a scholar of religion, by this complementarity, by "the difference between dedicated minorities of religious 'virtuosi' (to use Max Weber's term), and the mass religion of the social sacred, still largely oriented to flourishing, survived or reconstituted itself" (ASA: 154). What attracts Taylor is the remaining presence of a "pre-Axial stratum of popular Christianity" (ASA: 439).

In the third phase, the historical Fall of Christianity transpires, with far-reaching changes to the social imaginary and consequences which still wreak havoc in the present. But how does the story get off the ground? What causes the break? Which historically describable, *inner-religious* changes to religion begin the process which ends with the present, highly problematic religious culture?

The change in social imaginary Taylor wants to describe – the foundational change in Western Christianity – begins *before* the Reformation, in the thirteenth century. Taylor calls the process of transformation Reform (with a capital R). He is thinking about the Hildebrandian and Gregorian reforms of the eleventh century, initiated by Pope Gregory VII which culminate in the Fourth Lateran Council in 1215.[17] Taylor believes here a move was made to unify religious practices, in particular through the rule of a yearly confession and communion for the laity (ASA: 64).[18] From this point onward, processes started to ensure a better training of priests, with handbooks developed to standardize their work. In these measures, the attempt "to align the masses on the religion of the élites" (ASA: 64) became visible. According to Taylor, it is part of the irony of history that in the long-term this was an important step towards the weakening of traditional religiosity and the modification of various forms of faith.

The crux of this eventually destructive process of reform, which still continues in the present, is for Taylor a certain "rage for order," in a "drive to make over the whole society to higher standards" (ASA: 63) and thus an attempt to dissolve the balanced system of the two speeds of faith. This tendency was strengthened and accelerated by the Reformation. From the middle of the sixteenth century the Reformation became the main carrier of the process of Reform, which drove on the disenchantment and dis-embedment of individuals and finally the radical loss of real transcendence. "[A]ll branches of Reform push towards disenchantment, Protestants in a more radical fashion" (ASA: 266). Morally, people are trapped in consequentialist calculations and expectations of reciprocity. Taylor thinks that in particular the Reformation encouraged an "excarnation" of the remaining, still fairly "embodied" religious life (ASA: 614–615). The path from the Reformation led, via Deism and the unbelief of the elites in the eighteenth century to the a-religiosity and religious apathy of the present. At the end of this process we have individuals who are no longer "porous," but "buffered." At the end of the twentieth century and at the beginning of the 21st century, people do not understand themselves as belonging to a holistic network of institutions and ways of believing. They are no longer embedded. During the last 500 years, the secular world emerged and with it the gradual dismantling, breakdown, modification and shaking of this integrated and integrating religious society.[19]

This narrative, admittedly only rudimentarily sketched here, opens up many questions to be addressed. It is easy to see that the critiques of Taylor's descrip-

---

17 At the same time, Taylor can also work with a comparison of the years 1500 and 2000.
18 The narrative of chapter 2 is repeated with variations in chapter 8.
19 As Taylor summarizes, he has "been drawing a portrait of the world we have lost, one in which spiritual forces impinged on porous agents, in which the social was grounded in the sacred and secular time in higher times, a society moreover in which the play of structure and anti-structure was held in equilibrium; and this human drama unfolded within a cosmos. All this has been dismantled and replaced by something quite different in the transformation we often roughly call disenchantment" (ASA: 61).

tion of 'early religion,' and of culture and society in the early Middle Ages agree on at least three points:

1. Taylor undoubtedly claims to be working as a *historian of ideas*, to be working *historically*.

2. At the same time it is clear that he is working *typologically*. Only in this way can he use 'early religion' as a foil, in the mode of a "perspectival illusion" (De Vries 2009: 310). Only in this way can an earlier normality of faith be claimed, which excludes antiquity and its critique of religion. Only in this way can a specific contrast to modern society be made. And, one must add, only in this way can Taylor's picture of Protestantism be painted.

3. Furthermore, a *normative-apologetic approach* to the history of ideas is observable. To mention one prominent example, which is important for the very structure of Taylor's narrative, it is astounding that Taylor understands the Fourth Lateran Council of 1215 principally as a critical instance of increasing control over the laity and the unification of the practice of piety. However, one could undoubtedly also see the manifold rules for the priests and bishops positively as a restitution of complementarity, as the attempt to make the difference of the 'two speeds' clear.[20] Viewing it from this perspective – which incidentally has much going for it in terms of evidence – Taylor's 'Age of Religion' is revealed as no less characterized by opposing powers and critiques of religion than the 'Age of Modernity'.[21] The normative-apologetic approach of his narrative becomes particularly visible in the case of the Reformation – for both Luther and Calvin.

4 The necessity of a Protestant reading

From the perspective of systems theory, every definition demands a differentiation and – viewed from the other direction – every differentiation creates sight or

---

[20] It seems reasonable to assume that the arrangements of the Council which had bearing on the practice of the bishops and clergy had their origin in a perceived problem in their social practice. Thus it becomes clear that Taylor's model of two speeds does not take into account the problematic processes on the side of the professional clerics which also influence the religion of the age. The time before 1215 is stylized according to an ideal type. For a more nuanced analysis, see Cushing (2005). Furthermore, Moore (2000) is foundational. The decisions of the council can be found at http://www.fordham.edu/halsall/basis/lateran4.asp (last accessed January 7th 2015).

[21] William Schweiker (2010: 383) also asks whether Taylor does not "have too benign a view of the tensions underlying the medieval cooperative enterprise."

insight, while also creating a specific blindness. Until now, the fluid difference between philosophy of religion or history of religion versus theology has been mentioned. Which insights emerge if one proceeds with the differentiation of Catholic and Protestant? Which readings of *A Secular Age* impress themselves upon us? I want to emphasize four observations.

4.1 The narration of modernity as religious apologetics

Charles Taylor offers a deeply theological and unabashedly Catholic narration of modernity as an apology for religion. The reception of *A Secular Age* in the different disciplines with an interest in religion undoubtedly draws on very different aspects of the book. Nevertheless, it is surprising how little his deeply Catholic theological position is discussed in sociological, philosophical, and Cultural studies discourses.[22] Theologians recognize and emphasize more strongly the theological character of Taylor's work, for example Stephen Long (2009). However, enthusiasm for the defense of religion and also the criticism of modernity often seems to push the question about *which* religion Taylor is powerfully arguing for into the background. The Catholic sociologist Hans Joas sees in Taylor's story a clear "defense of the possibility of a monotheistic, specifically Christian and in particular Catholic faith, under contemporary intellectual assumptions" (Joas 2009: 296).[23]

Among those thinkers who respond to Charles Taylor, it is not the sociologists of religion or philosophers of religion who see most clearly, but the historians. The Harvard philosopher and historian of ideas Peter E. Gordon recognizes and names most clearly the specific perspective of the book. Gordon sees in Taylor the Catholic philosopher of modernity, who practices apologetics out of confessional obligation, and who has presented in *A Secular Age* a book with "unabashedly confessional character" (Gordon 2008: 650). The Berkeley historian Martin Jay also thinks that *A Secular Age* stands "clearly in the tradition of Catholic apologetics, which finds in the Reformation the acceleration of a slide down the slope toward faithlessness and normative anomie that accompanies it. [...] As

---

[22] An astute exception is offered by William E. Connolly (2004). The sustaining assumptions are marked relatively openly in Taylor (2010). His theological position is succinctly presented and explicit in the essay *A Catholic Modernity?* (Taylor 1999).

[23] Similarly, Graham Ward points out Taylor's basic assumption, that is: "I hold that religious longing, the longing for and response to a more-than-immanent transformation perspective, what Chantal Milon-Delsol calls a *'desir d'éternité'*, remains a strong independent source of motivation in modernity" (Ward 2010: 341).

such, it is hard to judge in strictly historical terms" (Jay 2009: 82).[24] Nevertheless, from a Protestant theological perspective, this apologetic character is not without its own rationality. However problematic apologetics – understood as the reasoned defense of religion – appears to be within Protestantism, its prominent place within the Catholic faith is understandable given the specific relationship between faith and reason in the Catholic tradition.[25]

4.2 The place of Protestantism in Reform

Although the move for Reform reaches back further than the Reformation, having emerged with post-Axial religiosity, Taylor programmatically insists that:

> The Reformation as Reform is central to the story I want to tell – that of the abolition of the enchanted cosmos, and the eventual creation of a humanist alternative to faith. The first consequence seems evident enough; the Reformation is known as an engine of disenchantment. The second is less obvious, and more indirect. It passes through the attempts to reorder whole societies which emerge in the radical, Calvinist wing of Protestantism (ASA: 77).

Protestantism and in particular the Reformed tradition is supposed to have had a fanatical urge for order. Protestantism works openly and effectively against the system of different speeds, it "abolishes the supposedly higher, renunciative vocations; but also builds renunciation into ordinary life" (ASA: 81). In this way, the three interwoven but differentiated orders are created: the order of personal relations, the new social order and finally an inner order, which is about "building the right inner attitude. Being able to avoid despair, or paralyzing melancholy, on one side, and a facile, unthinking confidence on the other" (ASA: 83).

---

24 The Berkeley historian Jonathan Sheehan similarly criticizes Taylor, detailing the thoroughly classical apologetic character of *A Secular Age*, and its implicit normative basis. See Sheehan 2010.

25 See the entries for "Apologie" and "Apologetik" in Buchberger (1993, 1: 834–847), and "Apologetics, History of" in Catholic University of America (2003, 1: 563–566). The decree *Dei Filius* of the First Vatican Council in 1870 formulates paradigmatically: "The same holy Mother Church holds and teaches that God, the beginning and end of all things, may be certainly known by the natural light of human reason, by means of created things." For a contextualization of Taylor's project, see amongst others Dulles (2005). For Protestants, the different confessional ordering of faith and reason is foundational. In contemporary Protestant theology a rejection of apologetics (in the context of a debate about nonfoundationalism) is connected with the names George Lindbeck, Hans Frei, Karl Barth – and on the philosophical side, with Jeffrey Stout.

The whole of Protestantism appears here as a destruction of the rich and vital variety of Catholic spiritual traditions, a catalyst of that questionable Reform. Furthermore, and this is particularly significant, it appears as an important preparation for the closed, autonomous and 'punctual' individual, and for so-called exclusive humanism. These two movements fostered by the Reformation in the medium and long term are, according to Taylor, unable to defend themselves against a militant anti-humanism, as the twentieth century has shown.

But can the Reformation really be interpreted as a movement driven by elites who pay homage to a rule-fetishism? Can it really be understood as the destruction of a tolerant and plural paradigm of faith?

a) Taylor suggests that the Reformation, in particular the Lutheran Reformation, dissolved the basic model of spiritual and worldly orders. However, from the perspective of Protestant research into church history, the two-speed model was already in great crisis. Thus the Reformation helped to uncover what was felt to be an unbearable double standard, for example, in the early phase through the marriage of priests.

> Similarly to fasting, celibacy represented an ordering of life demanded by the church, a standard only transgressed to the extent that it was seen to be a duty. The visibility of flagrant breaking of celibacy and the double standard of a church hierarchy which on the one hand demanded celibacy of its priests while on the other hand raising dispensation charges for the children of priests, profiting from the transgressions, created a web of moods and demands for reform, before the Reformation (Kaufmann 2009: 340).[26]

In opposition to Taylor's narrative, the Reformation reacted to an irreparable break in the Axial-age compromise of the two paths and speeds.

b) Taylor's massive objection to the Reformation does not see that Protestantism is a story of education and freedom, which cannot simply be shelved under Reform. Rather, as can be seen by the rapid dissemination of Luther's writing *On the Freedom of a Christian*, the thought of emancipation from a religious system of rules, which also saw religious acts of love yoked into a religious calculation of sanctification, was extraordinarily resonant. Furthermore, here Luther's central thought of a responsible service to one's neighbor and to society in fact *opposes* that rage for order that Taylor attributes to Reform (Kaufmann 2009: 281–284). In view of the historical and textual evidence it seems hardly possible to distort the Protestant insight into the sole efficacy of grace such that one's every-

---

[26] On more recent scholarship, see Kaufmann (2012).

day life fits into the corset of excarnation, uprooting, and regulation. It also seems implausible to see the doctrine of justification so directly and immediately as a cause, and later as mainspring, of an individual and social rage for control.[27] The Chicago ethicist William Schweiker has pleaded that we understand the Reformation as having developed another notion of 'fullness' and therefore having changed our perception of religious 'fullness.' Questions of justice, of responsibility in the world, and questions of human dignity were answered in a new way, according to new understandings of fullness (Schweiker 2010b: 372). This can be seen in the Lutheran revaluation of everyday work. The worldly professions also have in its strict sense a *vocatio dei*.[28]

4.3 Analyzing the transformation of Christianity

In contrast to Taylor, a Protestant reading of the history of Christianity in the West raises the question of the minimal demands placed on the *translation* of religious content by any philosophy of religion or history of culture which merely observes religion. A confident, self-critical theology will also test whether the translations of any philosophy of religion, which in the case of Taylor flow directly into the elementary tools of the narrative, are complex enough.[29] On the one hand it is undoubtedly good that Taylor takes the internal rationality of religion seriously. On the other hand, one can ask many questions of Taylor's theism, with respect to the tools of the narrative, and despite the overwhelming amount of material. Multidimensional tools are required in a double sense: It is not just the problematic ignoring of non-theological factors pertaining to the media, the state, or social, economic, and demographic conditions of modernity.[30] It is also his theologically weakly developed analytic tools, which, lacking a Trinitarian multi-dimensionality, make everything which does not support his specific version of theism appear as decline. Therefore while Taylor recognizes that nearly all reform movements articulate their concerns in the medium of Christology and Pneumatology, he does not allow this to enrich his dualistic tool of the distinction between immanence and transcendence. This could well be a result of the fact that religious apologetics traditionally only argues for theism. At the

---

27 For this "rage for order," see for example ASA: 63, 76, 143, 145.
28 Astute remarks about the recognition and affirmation of ordinary life through the theology of the reformers can be found in *Sources of the Self* (Taylor 1989: 215–216).
29 The philosopher Vittorio Hösle (2009: 322–327) also sees this.
30 From the theological side, with reference to the Reformation, this is offered to some degree by Kaufmann (2009); from the perspective of media studies by Sandl (2011).

same time, Taylor turns against a spiritual "excarnation," which, to formulate it with Friedrich Nietzsche and Dietrich Bonhoeffer, terminates in "faithfulness to the earth," without seeing the advantages of a productive imposition of a Christology over against his bald theistic model of transcendence. By way of Christology, a much more positive evaluation of immanent humanism would be possible. Demands for differentiation from the field of Trinitarian theology, Christology, and Pneumatology, which in various ways formed the development of both the Reformation and the spiritualities of the twentieth century, do not appear on Taylor's theory-radar.

4.4 Catholic mysticism

Which forms of hope does Taylor envisage, given "that our Christian life itself has suffered a mutilation" (ASA: 772)? In a revealing final chapter named "Conversions," he discloses where and from which traditions he expects a renewal of living faith under the conditions of the present.

Who are the people "who broke out of the immanent frame; people who went through some kind of 'conversion'" (ASA: 728)? If one follows Taylor's recommendations, it is Catholic mystics like Bede Griffith and Therese of Lisieux, above all those "influential converts" (ASA: 732) who turn to Catholicism,[31] and not least Ivan Illich, whose developments are broadly sketched and who obviously represent the most powerful inspirations and role models for Taylor.

I already mentioned the asymmetry in the distribution of the presence of the holy. It should therefore not surprise that for Taylor the present is "a world in which the fate of belief depends much more than before on powerful intuitions of individuals, radiating out to others" (ASA: 531). Taylor concedes that "all the people I have been talking about in this chapter were in one clear sense impeccably orthodox Catholics" (ASA: 765). The common denominator of this 'cloud of witnesses' is their opposition to an objectifying modernity, against social differentiation and against an objectification of nature, and their support of a romantic conception of language, a stronger connection with nature, an aestheticization of spirituality and a deep skepticism about the pluralistic character of modern societies. Here one should also not forget their support of an ethics which is deeply grounded in transcendence. Although Taylor emphasizes again and again that there can be no return to a pre-modern situation, the anal-

---

[31] Taylor refers to Jacques Maritain (1882–1973), Charles Pierre Péguy (1873–1914), and Gerard Manley Hopkins (1844–1889).

ysis and the therapy is steeped in a powerful romantic yearning and a surprisingly open nostalgia, which mourns the loss of the "enchanted world."[32] Although Taylor opaquely pleads for agapeically organized and mystically oriented communities, he finds it hard to find any gains at all for spirituality in modernity.[33] The question of how religion can be organized under the conditions of late modernity remains ignored in this variant of Romantic Catholicism. For this reason, Taylor's notion of agapeic communities – thought without the organizational and structural constraints of the established Catholic church – remain singularly undefined and pale.

A Protestant vision will have a different emphasis and move beyond Taylor's alternative of either pining for a truly Christian order or putting up with the incompatibility of immanent and transcendent order through forms of mystical spirituality. In view of the crisis-rich development of immanent humanism sketched by Taylor, the Protestant alternative will be developed in a dynamic triangle: Coming from the justification of the godless as something which has already happened, it will be about connecting the "prayer and action of the righteous," to use a phrase of Dietrich Bonhoeffer's. Without needing God, Christians participate in the effective reality of the Spirit of God in the continuing work of Jesus Christ; allow themselves to be used by God, and "seek the welfare of the city" (Jer 29:7). They participate in God's own 'faithfulness to the earth'.[34] This

---

[32] For Taylor it is Schiller's poem "Die Götter Griechenlandes" with which he exemplifies the loss of an enchanted world and the lament about a "universe in which we find ourselves [...] totally devoid of human meaning" (Taylor 2011: 115). And in the end, Taylor can also see his own narrative as a type of "subtraction story" (ASA: 530). This is why – in an ironic turning of his own method – his narrative structurally mirrors that narrative of secularization which he brands negatively as a subtraction story. Against the background of the strong romantic yearning, the results of the analysis and interpretation of Michael Kühnlein (2008) should be questioned. It is remarkable that Taylor's criticism of uniformity and Reform, of control and paternalism of vital spirituality in no place leads him to an open critical position against 'Rome'.

[33] The converts drawn upon by Taylor were mostly distinctly anti-democratic. It is not for nothing that Taylor clearly sees that the difference emphasized by these converts, between this world and its orders on the one hand and transcendence and its more extensive order on the other hand, makes two attitudes possible: First, "the more alienated from the modern age, the more fiercely one condemns it, the more likely one is to adopt the first view, and to pine for a really Christian order" (ASA: 745). Alternatively, "those that believe that there is something uniquely valuable and important about the civilization of democracy and human rights [...] will become modern civilization's 'loyal opposition' [...]" (ASA: 745) and accept the basic tension between both orders.

[34] Therefore they also recognize that immanent humanism, as Peter Gordon (2008: 667) emphasized, does not just offer a "Nietzschean self-assertion," but rather "a deepened sense of human vulnerability."

comes to pass when, in community, they spiritually celebrate the presence of Christ and at the same time work towards reconciliation and justice in their socio-cultural environment. Without the support of a worldwide legally constituted organization, Protestants rely on the many forms of the presence of the resurrected Christ through the Holy Spirit in real, communal and thoroughly plural practices of faith, hope, and love.

5 Challenges for Protestant theology

Despite all the necessary criticism of not only the details but basic shape of Taylor's narration, a Protestant reading of this magnum opus would be well advised to consider – being both unperturbed and self-critical – the formulated challenges. Which problems are displayed in Taylor's Catholic narrative which should be taken up productively? In this final section I want to note just two challenges for Protestant theology.

5.1 Protestantism and the process of modernity

Despite all the moderating qualifications, the history of religion Taylor sketches offers a fundamental critique of modernity. Modernity is not a solution, but understood as a tragic problem which, at least in its present form, has to be overcome.[35] The question that Taylor's position indirectly but forcefully asks of us, and which should be taken up by Protestant theology and Protestant churches, is: What do the traditions of Protestantism make of modernity? That is, what does liberal Protestantism, and also Bible and confession-oriented Protestantism which takes the Word of God seriously, charismatic and traditional Lutheran, and also Reformed Protestantism, make of modernity in its manifold epistemic, social, cultural and political components? Taking account of the undeniable ambivalence of modernity, what do they make of the differentiation of society, of the specific particularity of the church and of faith and of the sense in certain milieus that religion is no longer normal? And, taking into account the necessary critique of a destructive, objectifying treatment of nature, what does Christianity make of the improvements to life and to life expectancy through technology, i.e.

---

[35] In the epilogue to *A Secular Age*, Taylor points to the parallels between his own account and the criticism of modernity in a theology of Radical Orthodoxy. See for example the introductory chapter in Milbank, Pickstock, and Ward (1999: 1–20). For a pointed criticism of Radical Orthodoxy, which is also relevant to the 'theology' of Taylor, see Hankey and Hedley (2005).

also through medical and pharmacological developments? Is modernity, to put it pointedly, even God's way with the church? Which implications might such a suggestion have for a post-theistic theology of history, i.e. of the manifold (hi) stories? Without a theological ability to articulate one's stance within the field of a plural modernity, without saying something of its blindnesses, but also its stories of freedom and emancipation, a constructive theological engagement with present problematic anti-modernist approaches is impossible.[36] To stay within Taylor's language: Not every "embedment" is a cozy home. Quite a few forms of embedding are a corset or even a prison. Quite a few forms of disembedding offer gains in freedom.[37] Do 'weak religion' and an 'immanent humanism' really endanger humanity? Are they really unable to cope with a violent anti-humanist impulse?[38] Even the late Karl Barth, writing in the 1960s, in the heyday of the secularization paradigm, denied the complete unknowability of God in the world and would not allow the self-witness of the resurrected Christ be reduced to the witness of the church.[39] The different traditions of Protestantism are challenged in the medium of their theological thought, which itself shapes their spirituality, to develop a nuanced relationship to modernity. There is otherwise a danger that they will sooner or later drift into the alternative of an uncritical, naive affirmation or a vague, brash criticism of modernity.

5.2 Protestantism as a religion of redemption?

For Charles Taylor, who in relation to this question is a strong Augustinian, redemption is not simply being oriented by transcendence, but most profoundly, participating in transcendence. The real 'fullness' is not in this world, but in a

---

[36] It does not seem very convincing to respond to Taylor's critique by referring to the intellectual gains in the philosophy of religion in modernity, or to a reasonable Protestantism. This is the general line of Tobias Braune-Krickau (2011). Despite the apologetics, Taylor is not primarily interested in asking about final reasons, but about *culturally formative powers*. Despite his defense of religion, one should not overlook the fact that his project is a lucid and direct attack of any justificatory program of Protestant origin which is purely oriented by a theory of subjectivity.
[37] Just how dependent these evaluations are on one's perspective is demonstrated by the present religious (and not just internal Christian) debates about family, the emancipation of women and sexual self-determination.
[38] For an important and different evaluation of humanism, see for example Todorov (2002).
[39] On the relative godlessness of the world, see Karl Barth (1976: 187–219). That the church itself only participates in the self-witness of Jesus Christ, and is not the only witness, is one of the fundamental differences between Barth's program and that of the influential Stanley Hauerwas (2001) – despite his emphatic reception of Barth.

world beyond.⁴⁰ But is his alternative to a secular, and in a pointed sense *limited* humanism, really exhaustive? Does Taylor not overlook important positive changes in the understanding of fullness?⁴¹ After the failure of secular redemptive visions of utopia, the question remains at the beginning of the 21st century as to what 'faithfulness to the earth' aims. Charles Taylor provokes the self-critical question whether, with the exception of a few traditions of Protestantism, a strong redemptive understanding has largely morphed into a program of clever and thoughtful counsel, and a strategy for social and psychological coping, without any sense that this life is grasped by a real hope.⁴² However, in the case of Taylor it also remains unclear how the good from beyond can be brought into a productive relationship with responsibility for creation and appreciation for the traditions of freedom in modernity.

How ever one understands that "fullness" which is to be grasped by Christians, the question always remains pertinent whether transcendence is dissolved in natural, social and cultural processes within the framework of a religious naturalism, or whether one dares to think of and hope for a God whose loving kindness spans and holds this life. Will this risky, fragile and so vulnerable life be completed in God's justice?⁴³ A Protestant theology will not follow Taylor's all too abstract theism, but seek to unfold a Trinitarian theological account of creatureliness in the incarnation, the presence of God in the Spirit, the coming of the kingdom and the hope of a new creation of heaven and earth. It will seek to communicate this into a plural civil society and thereby, with this humane ethos, seek alliances with forms of immanent humanism – beyond the temptation to re-clericalize the late modern culture and beyond the temptation of religious nostalgia.⁴⁴

---

40 For the changes criticized implicitly by Taylor, see the articles in Hölscher (2007). See also Segal (2004).
41 Thus also the critique by Sheehan (2010: 227–242), from a perspective of cultural history. Similarly, from a perspective of theological humanism (Schweiker 2010b).
42 For a lucid sketch of the upheavals in the history of theology, see Osthövener (2004). Attempts to reconsider 'redemption' are offered in the volume by Thomas and Höfner (2015).
43 For thoughts in this direction, see Thomas (2009; 2013).
44 For a sketch of such an open Christian humanism, see Schweiker (2010a).

Bibliography

Catholic University of America, ed., 2003. *New Catholic Encyclopedia*. Vol. 1. Detroit: Thomson/Gale.
Barth, Karl. 1976. *Das christliche Leben. Die Kirchliche Dogmatik IV/4, Fragmente aus dem Nachlaß, Vorlesungen 1959–1961*. Zürich: Theologischer Verlag.
Bellah, Robert N. 2011. *Religion in human evolution: from the Paleolithic to the Axial Age*. Cambridge, MA: Belknap Press of Harvard University Press.
Bellah, Robert N., and Hans Joas, eds., 2012. *The Axial Age and its Consequences*. Cambridge, MA: Belknap Press of Harvard University Press.
Bernstein, Richard J. 1983. *Beyond objectivism and relativism. Science, hermeneutics, and praxis*. Philadelphia: University of Pennsylvania Press.
Blumenberg, Hans. 1966. *Die Legitimität der Neuzeit*. Frankfurt a.M.: Suhrkamp.
Blumenberg, Hans. 1974. *Säkularisierung und Selbstbehauptung. Erweiterte und überarbeitete Neuausgabe von 'Die Legitimität der Neuzeit', erster und zweiter Teil*. Frankfurt a. M.: Suhrkamp.
Blumenberg, Hans. 1975. *Die Genesis der kopernikanischen Welt*. Frankfurt a. M.: Suhrkamp.
Boyer, Pascal. 1994. *The naturalness of religious ideas: a cognitive theory of religion*. Berkeley: University of California Press.
Boyer, Pascal. 2001. *Religion explained: the human instincts that fashion gods, spirits and ancestors*. London: Heinemann.
Braune-Krickau, Tobias. 2011. "Charles Taylors religionsphilosophische Rehabilitierung der christlichen Religion in 'Ein säkulares Zeitalter'." *Neue Zeitschrift für systematische Theologie und Religionsphilosophie* 53, no. 3: 357–373.
Buchberger, Michael, Walter Kasper, and Konrad Baumgartner, eds., 1993. *Lexikon für Theologie und Kirche. Bd. 1*. 3., völlig neu bearb. Aufl., Freiburg im Breisgau: Herder.
Chakrabarty, Dipesh. 2009. "The Modern and the Secular in the West. An Outsider's View." *Journal of the American Academy of Religion* 77, no. 2: 393–403.
Connolly, William E. 2004. "Catholicism and Philosophy. A Nontheistic Appreciation." in *Charles Taylor*, ed. Ruth Abbey, 166–186. Cambridge, UK/New York: Cambridge University Press.
Cushing, Kathleen G. 2005. *Reform and the papacy in the eleventh century. Spirituality and social change*. Manchester medieval studies. Manchester: Manchester University Press.
De Vries, Hent. 2009. "Tiefendimension von Säkularität." *Deutsche Zeitschrift für Philosophie* 57, no. 2: 301–318.
Dulles, Avery R. 2005. *A history of apologetics*. Second edition. Modern apologetics library. San Francisco: Ignatius Press.
Eisenstein, Elizabeth L. 1979. *The printing press as an agent of change. Communications and cultural transformations in early modern Europe*. 2 volumes. Cambridge, UK/New York: Cambridge University Press.
Giesecke, Michael. 1991. *Der Buchdruck in der Frühen Neuzeit. Eine historische Fallstudie über die Durchsetzung neuer Informations- und Kommunikationstechnologien*. Frankfurt a. M.: Suhrkamp.
Gordon, Peter E. 2008. "The Place of the Sacred in the Absence of God. Charles Taylor's A Secular Age." *Journal of the History of Ideas* 69, no. 4: 647–673.
Gordon, Peter E. 2011. "Must the Sacred be Transcendent?" *Inquiry* 54, no. 2: 126–139.

Gregory, Brad S. 2012. *The Unintended Reformation. How a Religious Revolution Secularized Society.* Cambridge, Mass.: Belknap Press of Harvard University Press.

Hamnett, Ian. 1973. "Sociology of religion and sociology of error." *Religion* 3, no. 1: 1–12.

Hankey, Wayne J., and Douglas Hedley, eds., 2005. *Deconstructing Radical Orthodoxy. Postmodern Theology, Rhetoric, and Truth.* Aldershot/Burlington, VT: Ashgate.

Hauerwas, Stanley. 2001. *With the Grain of the Universe. The Church's Witness and Natural Theology (Gifford lectures delivered at the University of St. Andrews in 2001).* Grand Rapids, MI: Brazos Press.

Haughton, Rosemary L. 1999. "Transcendence and the Bewilderment of Being Modern," in *A Catholic Modernity? Charles Taylor's Marianist Award Lecture, with Responses by William M. Shea, Rosemary Luling Haughton, George Marsden, and Jean Bethke Elshtain,* ed. Charles Taylor and James Heft, 65–81. Oxford/New York: Oxford University Press.

Hölscher, Lucian, ed., 2007. *Das Jenseits : Facetten eines religiösen Begriffs in der Neuzeit,* Band 1. Göttingen: Wallstein.

Hösle, Vittorio. 2009. "Eine metaphysische Geschichte des Atheismus." *Deutsche Zeitschrift für Philosophie* 57, no. 2: 319–327.

Idinopulos, Thomas A., and Edward A. Yonan, eds., 1994. *Religion and Reductionism. Essays on Eliade, Segal, and the challenge of the social sciences for the study of religion,* Studies in the history of religions 62. Leiden/New York: E.J. Brill.

Israel, Jonathan I. 2001. *Radical Enlightenment. Philosophy and the making of modernity, 1650–1750.* Oxford/New York: Oxford University Press.

Israel, Jonathan I. 2006. *Enlightenment Contested: philosophy, modernity, and the emancipation of man, 1670–1752.* Oxford/New York: Oxford University Press.

Jay, Martin. 2009. "Faith-Based History." *History and Theory. Studies in the Philosophy of History* 48, no. 1: 76–84.

Joas, Hans. 2009. "Die säkulare Option. Ihr Aufstieg und ihre Folgen." *Deutsche Zeitschrift für Philosophie* 57, no. 2: 293–300.

Kaufmann, Thomas. 2009. *Geschichte der Reformation.* Frankfurt a. M./Leipzig: Verlag der Weltreligionen.

Kaufmann, Thomas. 2012. *Der Anfang der Reformation: Studien zur Kontextualität der Theologie, Publizistik und Inszenierung Luthers und der reformatorischen Bewegung.* Tübingen: Mohr Siebeck.

Kim, David K. 2007. *Melancholic Freedom. Agency and the Spirit of Politics.* Reflection and theory in the study of religion series. Oxford/New York: Oxford University Press.

Kühnlein, Michael. 2008. *Religion als Quelle des Selbst. Zur Vernunft- und Freiheitskritik von Charles Taylor.* Religion in Philosophy and Theology. Tübingen: Mohr Siebeck.

Long, Duane S. 2009. "How to read Charles Taylor. The Theological Significance of 'A Secular Age'." *Pro Ecclesia* 18, no. 1: 93–107.

Luhmann, Niklas. 1990. *Die Wissenschaft der Gesellschaft.* 1st ed. Frankfurt am Main: Suhrkamp.

Milbank, John. 2009. "A Closer Walk on the Wild Side. Some Comments on Charles Taylor's A Secular Age." *Studies in Christian Ethics* 22, no. 1: 89–104.

Milbank, John, Catherine Pickstock, and Graham Ward, eds., 1999. *Radical Orthodoxy. A new Theology.* London/New York: Routledge.

Moore, R. I. 2000. *The first European revolution, c. 970–1215.* The Making of Europe. Oxford/Malden, MA: Blackwell.

Osthövener, Claus-Dieter. 2004. *Erlösung. Transformationen einer Idee im 19. Jahrhundert.* Beiträge zur historischen Theologie. Tübingen: Mohr Siebeck.
Sandl, Marcus. 2011. *Medialität und Ereignis. Eine Zeitgeschichte der Reformation.* Medienwandel – Medienwechsel – Medienwissen. Zürich: Chronos.
Schweiker, William. 2010a. *Dust that breathes. Christian faith and the new humanisms.* Chichester, UK/Malden, MA: Wiley-Blackwell.
Schweiker, William. 2010b. "Grappling with Charles Taylor's 'A Secular Age'." *Journal of Religion* 90: 367–400.
Segal, Alan F. 2004. *Life after death: a history of the afterlife in Western religion.* New York: Doubleday.
Segal, Robert A. 1983. "In Defense of Reductionism." *Journal of the American Academy of Religion* 51 no. 1: 97–124.
Sheehan, Jonathan. 2010. "When was Disenchantment? History and the Secular Age," in *Varieties of Secularism in a secular age*, eds. Michael Warner, Jonathan VanAntwerpen and Craig J. Calhoun, 218–242. Cambridge, MA/London: Harvard University Press.
Stout, Jeffrey. 1981. *The flight from authority. Religion, morality, and the quest for autonomy.* Revisions. Notre Dame: University of Notre Dame Press.
Taylor, Charles. 1989. *Sources of the Self. The Making of the Modern Identity.* Cambridge, MA: Harvard University Press.
Taylor, Charles. 1999. "A Catholic Modernity?," in *A Catholic Modernity? Charles Taylor's Marianist Award Lecture, with Responses by William M. Shea, Rosemary Luling Haughton, George Marsden, and Jean Bethke Elshtain*, ed. Charles Taylor and James Heft, 13–37. Oxford/New York: Oxford University Press.
Taylor, Charles. 2010. "Afterword. Apologia pro Libro suo," in *Varieties of secularism in a Secular Age*, eds. Michael Warner, Jonathan VanAntwerpen and Craig J. Calhoun, 300–324. Cambridge, MA/London: Harvard University Press.
Taylor, Charles. 2011. "Recovering the Sacred." *Inquiry* 54, no. 2: 113–125.
Taylor, Charles, and James Heft, eds., 1999. *A Catholic Modernity? Charles Taylor's Marianist Award Lecture, with Responses by William M. Shea, Rosemary Luling Haughton, George Marsden, and Jean Bethke Elshtain.* New York: Oxford University Press.
Thomas, Günter. 2001a. *Implizite Religion. Theoriegeschichtliche und theoretische Untersuchungen zum Problem ihrer Identifikation.* Religion in der Gesellschaft 7. Würzburg: Ergon-Verlag.
Thomas, Günter. 2001b. "Die Unterscheidung der Trinität und die Einheit der Kontingenzformel Gott." *Soziale Systeme* 7 (2001): 87–99.
Thomas, Günter. 2007. "Transzendenz als verführerischer Begriff. Dietrich Bonhoeffer im Gespräch mit Niklas Luhmann," in *Zwischen Erziehung und Religion. Religionspädagogische Perspektiven nach Niklas Luhmann*, eds. Gerhard Büttner, Annette Scheunpflug and Volker Elsenbast, 141–153. Berlin/ Münster: Lit.
Thomas, Günter. 2009. *Neue Schöpfung. Systematisch-theologische Untersuchungen zur Hoffnung auf das 'Leben in der zukünftigen Welt'.* Neukirchen-Vluyn: Neukirchener.
Thomas, Günter. 2013. "Emergenz oder Intervention? Konstellationen der schöpferischen Treue Gottes in Auseinandersetzung mit einem theologischen Naturalismus," in *Wahrhaft Neues. Zu einer Grundfigur christlichen Glaubens*, ed. Hartmut von Sass, 151–190. Leipzig: Evangelische Verlagsanstalt.

Thomas, Günter, and Markus Höfner, eds., 2015. *Umbau oder Ende einer Erlösungsreligion?* Tübingen: Mohr Siebeck.
Todorov, Tzvetan. 2002. *Imperfect Garden. The Legacy of Humanism.* Princeton/Oxford: Princeton University Press.
Ward, Graham. 2010. "History, Belief and Imagination in Charles Taylor's A Secular Age." *Modern Theology* 26, no. 3: 337–348.

Jonathan A. Lanman
An Order of Mutual Benefit: *A Secular Age* and the Cognitive Science of Religion

1 Introduction

The cognitive science of religion (CSR) is an emerging discipline attempting to deploy the theories and methods of the cognitive and evolutionary sciences to address enduring questions about the various phenomena traditionally labeled as 'religion,'[1] from why non-physical agent beliefs and collective rituals are so widespread (Boyer 2001; Atran 2002; Barrett 2004; Whitehouse 2004) to the effects of such beliefs and rituals on social cohesion and intergroup relations (McCauley and Lawson 2002; Sosis and Alcorta 2003; Whitehouse 2004; Shariff and Norenzayan 2007; Henrich 2009; Norenzayan 2013). While Charles Taylor's *A Secular Age* addresses important issues in the humanistic study of religion, it also addresses important issues in CSR. Both *A Secular Age* and CSR, for instance, examine the impact of implicit thought processes on theism and non-theism, with Taylor focusing on implicit representations of society or 'social imaginaries' and CSR scholars focusing on a wide variety of cognitive biases and predispositions (Barrett and Lanman 2008).

Juxtaposing Taylor's story and CSR may, for some, raise questions of relevance and aptness. Are not Taylor and CSR worlds apart in terms of aims, methods, and assumptions? Have CSR scholars not understood the insights provided by Weber, Evans-Pritchard (1965), Geertz (1973), and indeed Taylor (1971), that would lead them to see the study of religion not as a search for explanation

---

Work on this chapter was supported by a Large Grant from the UK's Economic and Social Research Council (REF RES-060–25–0085) entitled "Ritual, Community, and Conflict" and an award from the John Templeton Foundation entitled "Religion's Impact on Human Life." The author is grateful to the editors for their valuable comments and suggestions.

1 Many anthropologists and historians of religion (e.g. Smith 1962; Smith 1998; Asad 1993) have convincingly argued that 'religion' is not a natural kind that can be discussed as having causes and effects, but is rather a folk and academic category dragging along with it the baggage of a peculiarly Western history. Cognitive scientists of religion recognize this (e.g. Boyer 2001; Whitehouse 2008; Whitehouse and Lanman 2014), but argue that beneath this folk category exist numerous universal (or near universal) patterns of human thought and action with distinct causes and effects, such as beliefs in the existence of non-physical agents, spirit possession (Cohen 2007), creationism (Kelemen 1999), and ritualized behaviour (Boyer and Lienard 2006).

but as a search for better interpretations of experience and action in particular contexts? Are the theories and methods of the natural sciences not inappropriate for addressing questions of human thought and action?

Not necessarily.

A great many philosophers of social science have cogently argued that a simple segregation of humanistic questions of experience and meaning from scientific questions of explanations and causal mechanisms is untenable (e.g. Lawson and McCauley 1990; Henderson 1993; Hollis 1994; Slingerland 2008). Among other reasons, such segregation is untenable because of the inescapable co-dependence of interpretation and explanation (Lanman 2007). As many constructivists have argued, scientific accounts of human behavior (from Freudian psychoanalysis to rational choice theory) bear the marks of the socio-cultural contexts from which they spring and every explanation emerging from a data set necessarily involves an interpretive leap (Barnes, Bloor, and Henry 1996; Hacking 1999). Similarly, however, interpretive accounts of the meaning of an action or event necessarily make explanatory assumptions about how human minds work, from the near universal assumption that human beings act according to internal mental states such as beliefs and desires (Baron-Cohen 1995) to the cognitive theories underlying Marshall Sahlins's and Gananath Obeyesekere's accounts of how Hawaiians interpreted the arrival of Captain James Cook in 1779 (Lanman 2007; Cohen et al. 2008). An interpretation is only as good as the explanatory assumptions underlying it.

Taylor's account, like Sahlins's and Obeyesekere's, cannot escape its assumptions about human psychology. Consequently, it is both possible and prudent to examine its assumptions in light of findings from the cognitive sciences. More specifically, both beliefs and social imaginaries are cognitive states and, therefore, are subject to the same causal dynamics as all cognitive states (Lanman 2008). Further, Taylor's argument that the rise of unbelief in the North Atlantic world can be attributed to the development of a social imaginary that views society as "an order of mutual benefit" (ASA: 170) implicitly makes a cognitive claim about the causes of theism and non-theism. While the subtraction story Taylor argues against assumes the existence of naturally rational human minds that reject religion as scientific explanations of the world become available, Taylor's story assumes that human beliefs, including those in the existence of God, are strongly influenced by implicit social imaginaries.

I will attempt to demonstrate below that establishing a dialog between Taylor and CSR on these matters can produce its own "order of mutual benefit." Taylor's story benefits in two ways: 1) an abundance of evidence in the cognitive sciences supports Taylor's rejection of the "subtraction story" of the rise of unbelief (ASA: 22), and 2) work in CSR can improve on Taylor's account of how the development of a new social imaginary (Secularity 3) and the decline of religion in the public sphere (Secularity 1) influence levels of individual belief (Secularity 2). It can do so by providing an empirically-supported causal story that allows us to explain the international patterns in theism and non-theism with which Taylor struggles. CSR benefits from Taylor's account primarily by considering the possibility that, either in addition to or in place of the beliefs and behaviors that serve as its primary objects of analysis, social imaginaries are important elements of religious cognition.

2 The subtraction story, rationality, and cognitive science

2.1 The subtraction story and Taylor's alternative

In *A Secular Age*, Taylor argues not only for a particular understanding of secularization but also explicitly against a competing understanding: the "subtraction story." According to Taylor, the subtraction story holds that individuals in the North Atlantic world over the last few centuries simply saw the truth of modern science and, for reasons of logical necessity, abandoned religious beliefs (ASA: 4, 22, 267). According to this story, human beings are naturally rational, morally oriented towards the value and well-being of individuals, and have simply been waiting throughout history for oppressive religions to be stripped away and rational human beliefs and values to emerge.

Taylor declines to name and engage with particular proponents of the subtraction story, but it can easily be found in both academic and popular realms. One need not dig too deeply to find its traces, however implicit, in the work of Marx, Freud, Frazer, Tylor, and other early scholars of religion. And one can easily find its assumptions in the discourse of many self-identified atheists and humanists, from the labeling of religious instruction as 'brainwashing' to statements of pre-modern humans 'just not knowing any better.'

For Taylor, the subtraction story is both simplistic and mistaken. He argues that there are numerous responses individuals can and did have to the emergence of modern science, including integrating it with theistic beliefs. Taylor reasons from this diverse set of responses that any strongly deterministic claims of the acceptance of scientific accounts of the age of the earth or evolution by natural selection automatically leading people from theism to non-theism are unfounded. Rather, he claims, something else besides simple rationality must have led large numbers of people to see Darwin as having "refuted the Bible" (ASA: 4).

For Taylor, that something else is the emergence of a new way of imagining what society is about and for, a new social imaginary that set the implicit "conditions of belief" under which individuals draw their conclusions about the existence of non-physical agencies (ASA: 17). Referring to the writings of Justus Lipsius, Hugo Grotius, and John Locke, Taylor outlines his own story of how "Reason" began to become privileged in Europe as a method by which to order both life and society to create an order of mutual benefit. God was still seen as important in these visions, as he was seen as the source of humanity's Reason. However, doing the will of God became not a matter of pursuing a transcendent goal but an immanent one, the remaking of society into an order of mutual benefit.

Taylor argues that this new social imaginary had important consequences for the moral judgment of religion. First, religious enthusiasm began to be rejected for over-valuing transcendent goals existing either beyond or in opposition to immanent human benefit. Second, religious beliefs began to be associated with immaturity and sentimentality, most notably in the writings of such nineteenth-century writers as John Stewart Mill and Leslie Stephen, a shift which Taylor traces through Muscular Christianity and Stoicism.

For Taylor, all of this constituted a new standpoint from which individuals thought about questions of the existence of God and other non-physical agents, even if they could not explicitly articulate this standpoint. It was this, rather than any naturally given rational faculty, that triggered the rise in unbelief. When Victorians heard the arguments of Charles Darwin concerning evolution and the use of these arguments by others to reject belief in God, they did not simply evaluate this information on the basis of Reason. Rather, they evaluated it through their normative notions concerning the proper place of rational thought and religious enthusiasm in individuals and society.

Taylor's account raises but does not directly address the psychological assumptions at the heart of the two stories. The subtraction story sees human minds as naturally rational and seeking objectivity; Taylor's story sees human minds, whatever the status of their rational abilities, as heavily influenced by how they imagine the societies in which they live. These psychological assumptions directly support the respective accounts. If human minds are shown not to be naturally rational, what becomes of the subtraction story? If implicit social imaginaries are shown to have minimal impact on theistic beliefs, what becomes of Taylor's alternative story? It is at this point, I would argue, that it is prudent to turn to the findings of the cognitive sciences, as decades of research have directly addressed such questions of rationality and implicit beliefs.

2.2 Rationality and cognitive science

On the whole, the news is good for Taylor. The cognitive sciences support Taylor's rejection of subtraction stories in that they call into question the view that human beings naturally make rational decisions and conclusions from evidence and that accepting scientific accounts naturally displaces supernatural ones. This view of mind is what philosopher Edward Stein calls the "traditional," "ideal," or "standard" picture of rationality. Under this account, people reason according to normative rational principles, except for the occasional "momentary lapse" or "performance error," and take action according to their best interests as they rationally weigh the means and ends of a given situation (Stein 1996). If standard rationality were to be an accurate description of human cognition, the subtraction story would be plausible. Our minds would operate in such a way that, without mental illness or an over-abundance of emotion clouding our judgment, our thoughts would be rational. And, further, if our minds are thinking as rationally as they naturally should, it can be argued that scientific evidence should crowd out religious belief.

Standard rationality has come under sustained assault from decades of research in the cognitive sciences, with abundant evidence demonstrating that human beings do not intuitively reason according to normative principles (Gilovich 1991; Stein 1996). Rather, they systematically deviate from them, naturally reasoning via a variety of heuristics, biases, and fallacies. Relatedly, as I outline in the following section (2.3) human minds do not appear to naturally check all thoughts for consistency, meaning that scientific and religious beliefs can easily co-exist in the same mind. Here, I briefly describe two of the innumerable heuristics and biases investigated by cognitive scientists: confirmation bias and the conjunction fallacy.

One of the biases we all possess that leads us away from rational judgment is confirmation bias. Once our minds have accepted an idea, we tend to look for evidence that confirms this idea rather than the more 'rational' act of looking for evidence that could potentially disconfirm it. This can lead to the cherry-picking of evidence so common in both popular and academic spheres.

One of the most famous demonstrations of confirmation bias is the Wason Card Selection Task (Wason 1968). In the most widely referenced version of this task, participants are shown four cards with either a single letter or number showing (D, A, 2, 5) and given the following information: "Each of these cards has a letter on one side and a number on the other. Which two cards should you turn over to allow you to decide if the following statement is true: 'If there is a D on one side, there is a 5 on the other'?" Most participants, even highly educated ones, make the mistake of selecting D and 5. While turning over D does indeed test the rule, turning over 5 seeks confirmation but does not constitute a rational test of the statement, as no matter what is on the other side of the 5 card, the rule will not be shown to be false. The most rational strategy is to select D and 2, as if there is a D on the back of the 2 card, the statement will be shown to be false.

Our minds seem naturally set up to continue the patterned association of D and 5, instead of seeking potentially disconfirming evidence. We can consciously over-ride this intuitive bias with deliberate, rational thought, but this requires us to both value deliberate rational thought and be motivated to use it.[2]

Another effect demonstrating our failure to naturally reason according to rational principles is our tendency to commit what has come to be known as the "conjunction fallacy" and reason more in accordance with cultural stereotypes and representativeness than probabilistic logic (Tversky and Kahneman 1983; Stein 1996). In a widely referenced example of the conjunction fallacy, participants are given the following information:

Linda is 31 years old, single, outspoken, and very bright. She majored in philosophy. As a student, she was deeply concerned with issues of discrimination and social justice, and also participated in anti-nuclear demonstrations.

They are then asked which of the following is more probable:

1. Linda is a bank teller.

2. Linda is a bank teller and is active in the feminist movement.

Over 80% of participants say that statement 2 is more probable than statement 1, which is irrational. The probability of two events occurring together (in "conjunction") is always less than or equal to the probability of either one occurring alone. The information about Linda provided seems more representative of a feminist rather than a bank teller, leading most individuals to select statement 2. Yet, in every scenario where 2 is true, 1 is also true; consequently, 2 cannot be more probable than 1. Further, in some conceivable scenarios (such as one in which Linda stopped being active in the feminist movement after leaving university) 1 could be true while 2 could be false.

---

2 Evolutionary psychologists John Tooby and Leda Cosmides have presented evidence suggesting that, while simply making the Wason task less abstract does little to encourage rational choices, making the task about the violation of social rules does (Cosmides and Tooby 2005). Tooby and Cosmides use this evidence to argue for the existence of an evolved 'cheater detection' module as a universal feature of human cognition.

Our minds seem naturally inclined to reason according to stereotypes and representativeness. The implication is that reasoning according to probabilistic logic requires effort, which in turn requires some degree of value and motivation.

The examples above are a very limited sample of the numerous biases, heuristics, and fallacies that characterize human cognition (see Gilovich 1991; Kahneman 2011; Kelemen, Rottman, and Stetson 2013). These biases and fallacies stem not from indoctrination or mental illness or lack of education, but from the way human minds naturally work. Reasoning according to the principles of logic established by philosophers is a struggle against many of our natural cognitive proclivities, not an uncomplicated expression of them.

2.3 The co-existence of scientific and supernatural explanations

Besides evidence of biases and fallacies in human cognition, evidence from anthropology and psychology also documents an easy cognitive compatibility between scientific and supernatural explanation. This strikes a serious blow to the subtraction story, which has as a core commitment the notion that people will naturally lose their beliefs in supernatural causation when they are scientifically educated.

In anthropology, sub-Saharan Africa has been a popular context for discussions of rationality, causation, and supernatural beliefs. This is mostly attributable to the work of British social anthropologist E.E. Evans-Pritchard, who conducted ethnographic fieldwork with the Azande in Sudan in the 1920s and wrote substantially about rationality and belief in the power of witchcraft to cause misfortune (1976).

Evans-Pritchard is clear in saying that witchcraft beliefs do not stem from any Zande ignorance of natural causes; the attribution of misfortune to witchcraft among the Azande merely fills the explanatory gap that others might leave open by reference to coincidence. In Zandeland, granaries sometimes collapse from termites eating away at the supports over a period of several years. Granaries also provide shade in the summer and, consequently, may sometimes collapse while people are sitting beneath them. When asked by Evans-Pritchard, the Azande were quick to affirm that the immediate cause of a granary collapsing was the damage caused by termites. Simultaneously, and with no hint of dissonance, they also say that one of the individuals beneath the granary must have been bewitched, as this would explain why the granary fell when it did and on the particular people it did. Rather than attribute the matter to coincidence, the

Azande believe in bewitchment. This was not out of ignorance of a physical cause, but in addition to it.

More recently, developmental psychologists Cristine Legare and Susan Gelman (2008) have documented a similar dynamic between natural and supernatural explanations for individuals contracting HIV in South Africa, where, in 2005, 30% of pregnant women tested HIV positive. Three studies examined the co-existence of natural and supernatural explanations for contracting HIV across participants from a variety of age groups. In these studies, Legare and colleagues tell participants short stories about individuals contracting HIV and ask them why these individuals have contracted the virus. They are given biological explanations (e.g. having unprotected sex, cutting oneself with a razor with "dirty blood") and witchcraft explanations (a neighbor was jealous and bewitched her), among others. For each explanation, participants are asked to answer whether or not this was why the individual contracted HIV.

What Legare and Gelman find is that receiving formal education and accepting biological explanations of disease, including HIV, has no negative impact on an individual's simultaneous acceptance of witchcraft explanations. In fact, it is among educated adults that witchcraft explanations are most frequently endorsed, as individuals formally learn biology but also informally learn about the existence of witchcraft. Bewitchment explanations here are not replaced by biological ones. Rather, both natural and supernatural explanations are learned during development and both are used to explain the same phenomenon.

Taken together (sections 2.2 and 2.3), the findings of the cognitive sciences give strong support for Taylor's rejection of the subtraction story. The subtraction story claims that human minds naturally reason rationally and, as scientific accounts of the world emerged, these rational human minds naturally gave up belief in God. The cognitive sciences problematize both of these claims. Human minds do not naturally reason in line with rational principles but must be sufficiently motivated to do so. Likewise, evidence documents that accepting scientific accounts in no way automatically leads to the loss of supernatural beliefs surrounding disease and suggests that accepting Darwin's theory of evolution by natural selection would not, on its own, result in human minds leaving religion for science. Something else, perhaps the modern social imaginary described by Taylor, would be required.

3 Secularities and the disembodiment of religion

3.1 The sociology of secularization

The cognitive sciences benefit Taylor's account of Western secularity by supporting his rejection of the subtraction story. They can also benefit Taylor's account through critique. More specifically, they can help provide a more empirically grounded account of how the altered conditions of belief (Secularity 3) and the retreat of religion from the public sphere (Secularity 1) can cause an increase in non-theism (Secularity 2).

Taylor argues that the conditions of belief created by the modern social imaginary of an order of mutual benefit help lead many to find religious beliefs and values implausible (ASA: 4). From a cognitive perspective, however, the links between these forms of secularity are unclear. How would the changed conditions of belief actually lead to changed beliefs? Through what psychological processes or mechanisms would these conditions make their impact? What evidence is there for the existence of any of these supposed processes and mechanisms?

While Taylor's hypothesis of a new social imaginary directly affecting theistic belief is plausible, it lacks empirical testing. Moreover, it is complicated by international diversity in levels of theism and non-theism. How can the changed social imaginary Taylor describes, which is presumably shared by the majority of individuals in the North Atlantic world, explain the substantial variation between North Atlantic countries in their populations of theists and non-theists (Norris and Inglehart 2004; Zuckerman 2007)? More specifically, why would well over half of the population of Scandinavian countries such as Denmark and Sweden be non-theists in comparison to only 3–9% of Americans (Zuckerman 2007)? Taylor "stabs in the dark" (ASA: 530) by suggesting that Americans are so religious because they still hold to a neo-Durkheimian concept of their society, partially because they are a hegemonic power (ASA: 528). He offers no evidence to support this explanation, however, and admits that "a fully satisfactory account of this difference, which is in a sense the crucial question facing secularization theory, escapes me" (ASA: 530).

Rather than distinct national social imaginaries, sociological evidence (which Taylor neglects in *A Secular Age*) points to the role of "existential security" in determining national differences in proportions of theists and non-theists (Gill and Lundsgaarde 2004; Norris and Inglehart 2004). As conceptualized by Norris and Inglehart, existential security is the subjective sense that one's life and livelihood are relatively secure from threats such as illness, unemployment, and conquest. Using data from the World Values Surveys and a variety of governmental reports, Norris and Inglehart show moderate to strong negative correlations between factors increasing existential security (such as high Human Development Index scores, per capita GDP, low economic inequality, high literacy rates, and access to clean water sources) and measures of religiosity (2004: 62–63). Further, they use regression analysis to demonstrate the predictive power of these factors on religiosity (2004: 66). They argue that existential security may well explain not only the differences between North Atlantic nations and other nations but also the curious case of the United States. The United States, via its high levels of economic inequality, low welfare spending, and high ethnic heterogeneity, creates a significant amount of existential insecurity among its citizens in comparison to relatively egalitarian and homogenous Scandinavian societies (Norris and Inglehart 2004; Stenner 2005; Zuckerman 2007; 2008).

Unfortunately, like Taylor, the sociologists fail to offer a convincing cognitive account connecting the environmental conditions of security to differences in theism and non-theism. Rather, they fall back on the old assumption that individuals believe in non-physical agents because of the comfort this provides them (Norris and Inglehart 2004: 19). While it is certainly the case that many religious beliefs can and do provide comfort for individuals in difficult circumstances, there is little to no evidence that the need for such comfort actually produces such beliefs in individual minds or that it can explain who becomes a theist and who does not. Psychological evidence does exist for some types of "motivated reasoning" (Kunda 1990), but little evidence exists to suggest that non-empirical entities are made believable because an individual would be comforted if they existed. Further, ethnographic evidence suggests that the non-physical agent beliefs present in existentially insecure societies often provide little comfort (Child and Child 1993; Boyer 2001; Lanman 2012) and that the supernatural beliefs present in affluent, North Atlantic countries, such as New Age discourses of personal destiny and power (Heelas 1996) and Christianities emphasizing divine love and deemphasizing divine punishment (Luhrmann 2012), often provide substantial comfort. This evidence suggests that any supposed need for comfort is not the main driving force behind non-physical agent beliefs. Consequently, we need to find another way to connect existential security to non-theism.

3.2 A cognitive science of secularization

My argument here is that CSR can provide an empirically supported account connecting the environmental conditions provided by existential security, as well as Secularities 1 and 3, to the decline in theism seen in the second half of the twentieth century in numerous European countries. This account centers on two claims: 1) that a common effect of existential security, Secularity 1, and Secularity 3 is the disembodiment of religion, and 2) this disembodiment has negative consequences for belief (Secularity 2).

Evidence from both psychology and anthropology suggests that human beings respond to the threats of insecure environments by embodying their religious beliefs and commitments. Threatening stimuli, for instance, have been shown to increase actions demonstrating commitment to ingroup ideologies (Greenberg et al. 1990; Hogg 2000; Navarrete et al. 2004; Stenner 2005). To the extent that a religious ideology serves as an ingroup ideology, perceived threats would increase religious commitment and action. Further, threatening stimuli have been shown to increase the numbers of individuals choosing to join and actively participate in religious groups for the material benefits these groups provide, as numerous Indonesians did in the wake of the financial crisis in 1997 (Chen 2010). Third, threatening stimuli have been shown to increase "superstitious" actions, such as prayer and psalm recitation, in a range of societies (Malinowski 1948; Sosis 2007). The implication of these accounts is that, in existentially secure environments, religious beliefs may still be held in individual minds but not as easily seen in individual actions.

Secularities 1 and 3, I would argue, also result in the disembodiment of religion. To say that religion has retreated from the public sphere (Secularity 1) is to say that in numerous public gatherings and social spaces, from hospitals to schools to markets, there are fewer actions referencing religious beliefs and commitments, from personal displays and greetings to architectural specifications and aesthetics. To say that individuals live their lives with a social imaginary of an order of mutual benefit (Secularity 3), rather than a kingdom under God, is to say that they act in the world in a way that reflects this imaginary. With Secularities 1 and 3 in place, religious beliefs may be professed by believers but are not as fully embodied in everyday life.

The disembodiment of religion is not without consequence. The embodiment of religious beliefs through action may, in fact, be crucial to the intergenerational transmission of religious beliefs, as human beings have a cognitive bias to attend to what have been labeled "credibility enhancing displays" or "CREDs," in forming their worldviews (Henrich 2009; Lanman 2012; Lanman and Buhrmester in press).

Human beings do not simply accept the information provided to them by others in their societies. Rather, they possess numerous cognitive mechanisms and biases that influence what information they take in from others and how they process that information. Evolutionary anthropologists interested in how the evolution of cultural capacities also led to the evolution of cognitive biases for acquiring more adaptive information from surrounding cultural models have hypothesized and found evidence for the existence of a variety of biases in belief acquisition (Henrich and McElreath 2003; Richerson and Boyd 2005). Examples of such biases in social learning include a prestige bias, which biases us towards accepting information from individuals with high levels of social prestige (Henrich and Gil White 2001), and a conformist bias, which biases us towards accepting the most common beliefs, attitudes, and practices within our ingroups (Henrich and Boyd 1998).

In 2009, evolutionary anthropologist Joseph Henrich presented a *prima facie* case for the existence of an additional bias in human psychology, one that may have significant implications for explaining why some come to believe in the existence of non-physical agents and others do not. This bias is to accept information expressed by a cultural model to the extent that this information is accompanied by what Henrich calls credibility enhancing displays or "CREDs" (2009). These are, according to Henrich (2009: 244), "displays by a model that would seem costly to the model if he or she held beliefs different from those he or she expresses verbally." We are biased, the argument goes, to believe the pronouncements of others to the extent that they "walk the walk" and not just "talk the talk" in relation to those pronouncements. The more religious ideas are embodied in the actions of those around us, the easier they are to believe. The less religious beliefs and commitments are embodied in the world we see around us, the harder they are to believe.

As an initial empirical exploration of Henrich's claim, I utilized the CREDs construct in field and survey research on atheism in Denmark, the UK, and the US. Survey and ethnographic evidence suggested that exposure to CREDs concerning non-physical agent representations may explain who, among Westerners, comes to believe in the existence of "God," broadly defined (Lanman 2012; 2013).

To better ascertain the importance of exposure to CREDs for explaining theism and non-theism, I have recently collaborated with social psychologist Michael Buhrmester to validate a CREDs exposure measure and test its predictive power in determining who becomes a theist and who becomes a non-theist. In an initial study, we surveyed over two-hundred US Americans and found that exposure to CREDs predicted theism/non-theism, certainty of belief, and religiosity, all while controlling for a more standard measure of religious socialization (Lanman and Buhrmester in press). The implication of this analysis is that a significant amount of the causal power behind religious socialization is exposure to CREDs and that actions do indeed speak louder than words in convincing individuals of the reality of non-physical agents.

If CREDs are as important to the transmission of theistic beliefs as the data suggest, this can help address weaknesses in the secularization accounts of both Taylor and Norris and Inglehart. The increase of existential security in the latter half of the twentieth century in many countries, the modern shift in social imaginaries, and the retreat of religion from the public sphere all decrease the number of theistic CREDs performed and, consequently, observed by young people forming their worldviews. Consequently, individuals growing up in such environments, on average, find theism less convincing. With lower levels of CREDs being performed, levels of theism decrease generationally, explaining the increase in Secularity 2 without recourse to subtraction stories and without unsubstantiated claims of neo-Durkheimian imaginaries or comfort-seeking.

4 Bringing social imaginaries to mind

4.1 Social imaginaries

While work in CSR benefits Taylor's account by discrediting the subtraction story and causally connecting the various secularities, Taylor's account can also provide benefits to CSR. Generally speaking, CSR focuses on the causes and effects of objects of analysis commonly labeled 'religion,' such as beliefs in the existence of non-physical agents, creationism, spirit possession, and ritualized behavior. Taylor's work suggests that social imaginaries may be relevant objects of analysis in the study of religious cognition, either to be placed alongside such constructs as 'belief' or, more radically, to replace them.

In *A Secular Age*, Taylor's central argument is that the decline in religious belief seen in the North Atlantic world (Secularity 2) resulted from a change in the commonly held social imaginary (Secularity 3). In "Modern Social Imaginaries" (2002) Taylor gives a more detailed description of what he means by the term "social imaginary," which can be described as the implicit representations individuals have of the normative, ontological, and chronological elements of their social worlds.

Taylor states:

> What I'm trying to get at with this term is something much broader and deeper than the intellectual schemes people may entertain when they think about social reality in a disengaged mode. I am thinking rather of the ways in which people imagine their social existence, how they fit together with others, how things go on between them and their fellows, the expectations that are normally met, and the deeper normative notions and images that underlie these expectations.

> I want to speak of social imaginary here, rather than social theory, because there are important – and multiple – differences between the two. I speak of imaginary because I'm talking about the way ordinary people imagine their social surroundings, and this is often not expressed in theoretical terms; it is carried in images, stories, and legends. (2002: 106)

Taylor continually emphasizes that social imaginaries are implicit imaginaries. A social imaginary is "not a set of ideas; rather it is what enables, through making sense of, the practices of a society" (2002: 91). These implicit imaginaries, for Taylor, necessarily involve normative, ontological, and chronological components: a "moral order is more than just a set of norms; it also contains what we might call an 'ontic' component, identifying features of the world that make the norms realizable" (2002: 95). This might involve the existence of a heaven, hell, and a moralizing God for the social imaginary of complementary hierarchy that characterized pre-modern Europe or the existence of rational human minds for the social imaginary of an order of mutual benefit. Moreover, Taylor emphasizes that this normative and ontological scheme does not exist separately from notions of time but rather within and through narratives of mythic history, from founding ancestors to the French Revolution.

Taylor is, of course, not the first to argue that individuals possess schematic representations of their societies and their normative implications. Similar claims have a long history in the social sciences and humanities (e. g. Durkheim 1912; Bourdieu 1977; Giddens 1984; Castoriadis 1998). Perhaps uniquely, however, Taylor argues that these representations have important causal effects on theistic beliefs, such that a shift in social imaginary can have direct effects on theism.

4.2 Social imaginaries in mind

Whatever else social imaginaries may involve, they undoubtedly involve cognition. Taylor may prefer to minimize any discussion of psychology, but it is only with a mind that such imaginaries can, in fact, be imagined. Perhaps unknowingly, Taylor himself suggests as much as he describes the implicit nature of social imaginaries: "The understanding expressed in practices stands to social theory the way that my ability to get around a familiar environment stands to a literal map of this area" (2002: 108). Here, Taylor directly compares social imaginaries to the implicit mental maps that help give us our ability to move around a familiar environment and which constitute a substantial topic of interest in cognitive psychology (e. g. Jacobs and Schenk 2003).

Many of the individual aspects of Taylor's conception of social imaginaries reflect established research programs in the cognitive sciences (e.g. implicitness, normativity, non-physical agent beliefs). What is unclear from a cognitive perspective is whether these various elements are linked together to form something like a social imaginary or if "social imaginary" is simply humanist shorthand for a hodgepodge of distinct cognitive processes and representations. Either way, Taylor's work raises interesting questions about the relevance of these implicit social representations on theism and presents an opportunity for CSR.

Throughout CSR and the other cognitive sciences, for instance, a substantial amount of evidence suggests that much of our thinking, including our thoughts about non-physical agents, is implicit (Barrett and Keil 1996; Chaiken and Trope 1999; Boyer 2001; Barrett 2004). Further, a growing body of work in CSR addresses morality and values (Shariff and Norenzayan 2007; Sibley and Bulbulia 2014), though the emphasis of most of this work is on moral behavior as an outcome of particular beliefs (Shariff and Norenzayan 2011), practices (Wiltermuth and Heath 2009), and norms (Chudek and Henrich 2011). Similarly, a substantial portion of work in CSR concerns ontologies, both the "intuitive ontologies" that underlie arguments of supernatural representations being "counter-intuitive" and, consequently, better remembered than other types of representations (Boyer and Ramble 2001) and the non-physical agent beliefs that help form explicitly held religious ontologies (Boyer 2001; Barrett 2004; Cohen 2007; Norenzayan 2013). Little of this work, however, looks beyond the causes and effects of isolated beliefs, whether implicit or explicit, to networked representations of social and religious worlds.

While examining these elements in isolation has been helpful in the development of CSR, the possibility that these isolated elements are accompanied by or, in fact, represented together as more networked "imaginaries" has not been investigated. There are, however, a few lines of thinking within CSR that might serve as a foundation for such an investigation. One of these is anthropologist Harvey Whitehouse's modes of religiosity/cohesion theory (2004). The modes theory proposes that particular types of ritual practice (low frequency/high arousal rituals vs. high frequency/low arousal rituals) produce qualitatively different bonds between individual identities and social identities (Whitehouse and Lanman 2014). The specification of what social identities are and how they are represented in individual minds is discussed through reference to the literature in social psychology on social identity theory (Tajfel and Turner 1979) and identity fusion theory (Swann et al. 2009; Gomez et al. 2011; Whitehouse and Lanman 2014), but this work is still in its infancy. It is not beyond the realm of possibility that social identities are cognitively represented along the lines Taylor assumes.

Perhaps the closest approach to Taylor's (and the furthest from mainstream CSR) is Maurice Bloch's argument for the importance of what he calls a "transcendental social" (2008; 2013). Bloch (2008: 2056) argues that humans have a cognitive adaption to "imagine other worlds." Rather than simply keeping track of the "transactional social" world of dominant individuals and temporary coalitions, as non-human primates do, humans imagine a world of the "transcendental social," composed of a system-like set of essentialized roles and groups that transcend the individuals inhabiting them and help determine more specific norms. Bloch goes on to argue the more radical point that the transcendental social should not just be examined alongside beliefs and norms in CSR but, in fact, replace them as an object of analysis, as the transcendental social represents a true universal while religious 'belief' is a Western construct.

Unfortunately, neither Bloch nor Taylor provides much detail on how a science of social imaginaries or transcendental socials would proceed. There are other projects in the cognitive sciences, however, that might serve as resources for such an effort. For example, cognitive schema theory (Strauss and Quinn 1997; Shore 1996) has been applied to social knowledge in such a way as to cognitively ground Bourdieu's account of *habitus* (Strauss and Quinn 1997: 44–47). Further, moral psychologist Jonathan Haidt and colleagues have argued that societies construct moral frameworks and virtuous individuals out of innate and universal "moral foundations" (e.g. care/harm, fairness/cheating, loyalty/betrayal, authority/subversion, and sanctity/degradation) through the use of narrative (Haidt and Joseph 2004; Graham et al. 2013), echoing Taylor's statement that social imaginaries are represented through story and image. In addition, Edward Slingerland (2003) has utilized Lakoff and Johnson's conceptual metaphor theory (1980; 1999) to offer an account of how the ancient Chinese ideal of *wu-wei* (effortless action) becomes cognitively represented and extended to numerous domains of life.

Despite the existence of these potential resources, it remains to be seen whether the notions of social imaginary or transcendental social can help CSR establish a viable research program that tests hypotheses (such as Taylor's central claim in *A Secular Age*) in a systematic way. Numerous research paradigms in CSR benefit from the fact that key objects of analysis such as non-physical agent belief, teleological bias, and altruism can be operationalized in both laboratory and survey research. It is unclear at this point whether "social imaginaries" or "transcendental socials" can be effectively operationalized and investigated quantitatively. It is only through such an investigation that we would be able to speak about their place in the causal matrix of the phenomena commonly labeled as 'religion.' If successful, however, a cognitive investigation of social imaginaries would allow us to better test Taylor's claims, add an important object of analysis to the cognitive study of religion, and develop a better understanding of human life.

Conclusion

While *A Secular Age* and CSR may initially appear as unrelated enterprises, both offer accounts of the causes of theism and non-theism in the contemporary world and can benefit from mutual engagement. Above, I have argued that Taylor's story can benefit in two ways from engagement with the cognitive sciences. First, Taylor's argument against subtraction stories of the development of widespread non-theism in the North Atlantic world can be substantially supported by cognitive science's rejection of the standard picture of rationality. The standard picture of rationality is a central assumption of subtraction stories and has been thoroughly discredited through painstaking empirical and interdisciplinary research. Second, the cognitive sciences can help construct an empirically substantiated account of how the retreat of religion from the public sphere and the change of social imaginaries described by Taylor can influence theistic beliefs. This account centers on the role of credibility enhancing displays in the vertical transmission of theistic beliefs and can add to or even replace the less empirically supported accounts centered on social imaginaries and comfort seeking.

I have also argued that Taylor's rich account of differing secularities can benefit the cognitive study of religion by hypothesizing the existence and importance of social imaginaries. While most research in CSR focuses on relatively isolated beliefs and behaviors, Taylor's story suggests that religious ideas and practices may be represented in individual minds not merely as isolated 'beliefs' but as part of networked representations of social worlds involving normative, ontological, and chronological dimensions. An interdisciplinary investigation of how such imaginaries are, in fact, imagined, and how this might affect research on the causes and effects of 'religion' within CSR would be a welcome development and, perhaps, a demonstration of an order of mutual benefit between the sciences and the humanities.

Bibliography

Asad, Talal. 1993. *Genealogies of Religion: Discipline and Reasons of Power in Christianity and Islam*. Baltimore: JHU Press.
Atran, Scott. 2002. *In Gods we Trust: The Evolutionary Landscape of Religion*. Oxford: Oxford University Press.
Barnes, Barry, David Bloor, and John Henry, eds. 1996. *Scientific Knowledge: A Sociological Analysis*. Chicago: University of Chicago Press.
Baron-Cohen, Simon. 1995. *Mindblindness: An Essay on Autism and Theory of Mind*. Cambridge, MA: MIT Press.
Barrett, Justin L. 2004. *Why Would Anyone Believe in God?*. Walnut Creek: AltaMira Press.
Barrett, Justin L., and Frank C. Keil. 1996. "Conceptualizing a Nonnatural Entity: Anthropomorphism in God Concepts." *Cognitive Psychology* 31, no. 3: 219–247.
Barrett, Justin L., and Jonathan A. Lanman. 2008. "The Science of Religious Beliefs. *Religion*, 38, no. 2: 109–124.
Bloch, Maurice. 2008. "Why Religion is Nothing Special but is Central." *Philosophical Transactions of The Royal Society B: Biological Sciences* 363, no. 1499 : 2055–2061.
Bloch, Maurice. 2013. *In and Out of Each Other's Bodies: Theories of Mind, Evolution, Truth, and the Nature of the Social*. Boulder, Colorado: Paradigm Publishers.
Bourdieu, Pierre. 1977. *Outline of a Theory of Practice*. Cambridge: Cambridge University Press.
Boyer, Pascal. 2001. *Religion Explained: The Evolutionary Origins of Religious Thought*. New York: Basic Books.
Boyer, Pascal, and Pierre Liénard. 2006. "Why Ritualized Behavior: Precaution Systems and Action Pasing In Developmental, Pathological, and Cultural Rituals." *Behavioral and Brain Sciences* 29, no. 06: 635–641.
Boyer, Pascal, and Charles Ramble. 2001. "Cognitive Templates for Religious Concepts: Cross Cultural Evidence for Recall of Counter-Intuitive Representations." *Cognitive Science* 25: 535–564.
Calhoun, Craig, Mark Juergensmeyer, and Jonathan VanAntwerpen, eds. 2011. *Rethinking Secularism*. Oxford: Oxford University Press.
Castoriadis, Cornelius. 1998. *The Imaginary Institution of Society*. Cambridge, Mass: MIT Press.
Chaiken, Shelly, and Yaacov Trope, eds. 1999. *Dual-process Theories in Social Psychology*. New York: Guilford Press.
Chen, Daniel L. 2010. "Club Goods and Group Identity: Evidence from Islamic Resurgence During the Indonesian Financial Crisis." *Journal of Political Economy* 118, no. 2: 300–354.
Child, Alice B., and Irvin Long Child. 1993. *Religion and Magic in the Life of Traditional Peoples*. Engelwood Cliffs, NJ: Prentice Hall.
Chudek, Maciej, and Joseph Henrich 2011. "Culture–Gene Coevolution, Norm-psychology and the Emergence of Human Prosociality." *Trends in Cognitive Sciences* 15, no. 5: 218–226.
Cohen, Emma. 2007. *The Mind Possessed: The Cognition of Spirit Possession in an Afro-Brazilian Religious Tradition*. New York: Oxford University Press.

Cohen, Emma, Jonathan A. Lanman, Harvey Whitehouse, and Robert N. McCauley. 2008. "Common Criticisms of the Cognitive Science of Religion—Answered." *Bulletin of the Council of Societies for the Study of Religion* 37, no. 4: 112–115.

Cosmides, Leda and John Tooby. 2005. "Neurocognitive Adaptations Designed for Social Exchange." *The Handbook of Evolutionary Psychology*, ed. David Buss, Hoboken: Wiley: 584–627.

Durkheim, Emile. 1912 [1995]. *The Elementary Forms of Religious Life.* Trans. Karen Fields, NY: Free Press.

Evans-Pritchard, Edward E. 1937. *Witchcraft, Magic, and Oracles among the Azande.* Oxford: Clarendon Press.

Evans-Pritchard, Edward E. 1965. *Theories of Primitive Religion.* Oxford: Clarendon Press.

Geertz, Clifford. 1973. "Religion as a Cultural System," *The Interpretation of Cultures*, 87–125. New York: Basic Books.

Giddens, Anthony. 1984. *The Constitution of Society: Outline of the Theory of Structuration.* Berkeley, CA: University of California Press.

Gill, Anthony, and Erik Lundsgaarde. 2004. "State Welfare Spending and Religiosity A Cross-National Analysis." *Rationality and Society* 16, no. 4: 399–436.

Gilovich, Thomas. 1991. *How We Know What Isn't So: The Fallability of Human Reason in Everyday Life.* New York: Simon and Schuster.

Graham, Jesse, Jonathan Haidt, Sena Koleva, Matt Motyl, Ravi Iyer, S. Wojcik, and Peter H. Ditto. 2013. "Moral Foundations Theory: The Pragmatic Validity of Moral Pluralism." *Advances in Experimental Social Psychology* 47: 55–130.

Gómez, Angel, Matthew L. Brooks, Michael D. Buhrmester, Alexandra Vázquez, Jolanda Jetten, and William B. Swann Jr. 2011. "On the Nature of Identity Fusion: Insights into the Construct and a New Measure." *Journal of Personality and Social Psychology* 100, no. 5: 918–933.

Greenberg, Jeff, Tom Pyszczynski, Sheldon Solomon, Abram Rosenblatt, Mitchell Veeder, Shari Kirkland, and Deborah Lyon. 1990. "Evidence for Terror Management Theory II: The Effects of Mortality Salience on Reactions to Those who Threaten or Bolster the Cultural Worldview." *Journal of Personality and Social Psychology* 58, no. 2: 308–318.

Hacking, Ian. 1999. *The Social Construction of What?* Cambridge, MA: Harvard University Press.

Haidt, Jonathan, and Craig Joseph. 2004. "Intuitive Ethics: How Innately Prepared Intuitions Generate Culturally Variable Virtues." *Daedalus* 133, no. 4: 55–66.

Heelas, Paul. 1996. *The New Age Movement.* Oxford: Blackwell.

Henderson, David. 1993. *Interpretation and Explanation in the Human Sciences.* Albany, N.Y.: SUNY Press.

Henrich, Joseph. 2009. "The Evolution of Costly Displays, Cooperation and Religion: Credibility Enhancing Displays and their Implications for Cultural Evolution." *Evolution and Human Behavior* 30, no. 4: 244–260.

Henrich, Joe, and Robert Boyd. 1998. "The Evolution of Conformist Transmission and the Emergence of Between-group Differences." *Evolution and Human Behavior* 19, no. 4: 215–241.

Henrich, Joseph, and Francisco J. Gil-White. 2001. "The Evolution of Prestige: Freely Conferred Deference as a Mechanism for Enhancing the Benefits of Cultural Transmission." *Evolution and Human Behavior* 22, no. 3: 165–196.

Henrich, Joseph, and Richard McElreath. 2003. "The Evolution of Cultural Evolution." *Evolutionary Anthropology: Issues, News, and Reviews* 12, no. 3: 123–135.

Hogg, Michael. 2000. "Subjective Uncertainty Reduction through Self-categorization: A Motivational Theory of Social Identity Processes." *European Review of Social Psychology* 11: 223–255.

Hollis, Martin. 1994. *The Philosophy of Social Science: An Introduction.* Cambridge: Cambridge University Press.

Jacobs, Lucia F., and Françoise Schenk. 2003. "Unpacking the Cognitive Map: the Parallel Map Theory of Hippocampal Function." *Psychological Review* 110, no. 2: 285–315.

Kahneman, Daniel. 2011. *Thinking, Fast and Slow.* London: Penguin Books.

Kelemen, Deborah. 1999. "Why Are Rocks Pointy? Children's Preference for Teleological Explanations of the Natural World." *Developmental Psychology* 35, no. 6: 1440–1452.

Kelemen, Deborah, Joshua Rottman, and Rebecca Seston. 2013. "Professional Physical Scientists Display Tenacious Teleological Tendencies: Purpose-based Reasoning as a Cognitive Default." *Journal of Experimental Psychology: General* 142, no. 4: 1074–1083.

Kunda, Ziva. 1990. "The Case for Motivated Reasoning." *Psychological Bulletin* 108, no. 3: 480–498.

Lakoff, George, and Mark Johnson. 1980. *Metaphors We Live By.* Chicago: University of Chicago Press.

Lakoff, George, and Mark Johnson. 1999. *Philosophy in the Flesh: The Embodied Mind and its Challenge to Western Thought.* New York: Basic Books.

Lanman, Jonathan A. 2007. "How 'Natives' Don't Think: The Apotheosis of Overinterpretation." *Religion, Anthropology, and Cognitive Science.* Eds. Harvey Whitehouse and James Laidlaw. Durham: Carolina Academic Press: 105–132.

Lanman, Jonathan A. 2008. "In Defence of 'Belief': A Cognitive Response to Behaviorism, Eliminativism, and Social Constructivism." *Issues in Ethnology and Anthropology,* Beograd 3, no. 3: 49–62.

Lanman, Jonathan A. 2012. "The Importance of Religious Displays for Belief Acquisition and Secularization." *Journal of Contemporary Religion* 27, no. 1: 49–65.

Lanman, Jonathan A. 2013. "Atheism and Cognitive Science," in *The Oxford Handbook of Atheism,* ed. Stephen Bullivant and Michael Ruse. Oxford: Oxford University Press: 483–496.

Lanman, Jonathan A. and Michael Buhrmester. In press. "Religious Actions Speak Louder than Words: Exposure to CREDs Predicts Theism." *Religion, Brain, and Behavior.*

Lawson, E. Thomas, and Robert N. McCauley. 1993. *Rethinking Religion: Connecting Cognition and Culture.* Cambridge: Cambridge University Press.

Legare, Cristine H., and Susan A. Gelman. 2008. "Bewitchment, Biology, or Both: The Co-existence of Natural and Supernatural Explanatory Frameworks Across Development." *Cognitive Science* 32, no. 4: 607–642.

Luhrmann, Tanya M. 2012. *When God Talks Back: Understanding the American Evangelical Relationship with God.* New York: Random House.

Malinowski, Bronislaw. 1948. *Magic, Science, and Religion and Other Essays,* ed. Robert Redfield. Glencoe, Ill: Waveland Press.

McCauley, R. N., and Lawson, E. T. 2002. *Bringing Ritual to Mind: Psychological Foundations of Cultural Forms.* Cambridge: Cambridge University Press.

Navarrete, C. David, Robert Kurzban, Daniel MT Fessler, and Lee A. Kirkpatrick. 2004. "Anxiety and Intergroup Bias: Terror Management or Coalitional Psychology?." *Group Processes & Intergroup Relations* 7, no. 4: 370–397.
Norenzayan, Ara. 2013. *Big Gods: How Religion Transformed Cooperation and Conflict*. Princeton: Princeton University Press.
Norris, Pippa, and Ronald Inglehart. 2004. *Sacred and Secular: Religion and Politics Worldwide*. New York: Cambridge University Press.
Richerson, Peter J., and Robert Boyd. 2005. *Not by Genes Alone: How Culture Transformed Human Evolution*. Chicago: University of Chicago Press.
Shariff, Azim F., and Ara Norenzayan. 2007. "God is Watching You: Priming God Concepts Increases Prosocial Behavior in an Anonymous Economic Game." *Psychological Science* 18, no. 9: 803–809.
Shariff, Azim F., and Ara Norenzayan. 2011. "Mean Gods Make Good People: Different Views of God Predict Cheating Behavior." *The International Journal for the Psychology of Religion* 21, no. 2: 85–96.
Shore, Bradd. 1996. *Culture in Mind: Cognition, Culture, and the Problem of Meaning*. New York: Oxford University Press.
Sibley, Chris G., and Joseph A. Bulbulia 2014. "How Do Religious Identities and Basic Value Orientations Affect Each Other Over Time?." *International Journal for the Psychology of Religion* 24, no. 1: 64–76.
Slingerland, Edward. 2003. *Effortless Action: Wu-wei as Conceptual Metaphor and Spiritual Ideal in Early China*. Oxford: Oxford University Press.
Slingerland, Edward. 2008. *What Science Offers the Humanities*. New York: Cambridge University Press.
Smith, Jonathan. 1998. "Religion, Religions, Religious.," in *Critical Terms for Religious Studies*, ed. Mark Taylor. Chicago: University of Chicago Press: 269–284.
Smith, Wilfred Cantwell. 1962. *The Meaning and End of Religion*. Minneapolis, MN: Fortress Press.
Sosis, Richard. 2007. "Psalms for Safety: Magico-religious Response to Threats of Terror." *Current Anthropology* 48: 903–911.
Sosis, Richard, and Candace Alcorta. 2003. "Signaling, Solidarity, and the Sacred: The Evolution of Religious Behavior." *Evolutionary Anthropology: Issues, News, and Reviews* 12, no. 6: 264–274.
Stein, Edward. 1996. *Without Good Reason: The Rationality Debate in Philosophy and Cognitive Science: The Rationality Debate in Philosophy and Cognitive Science*. Oxford: Clarendon Press.
Stenner, Karen. 2005. *The Authoritarian Dynamic*. Cambridge: Cambridge University Press.
Strauss, Claudia, and Naomi Quinn. 1997. *A Cognitive Theory of Cultural Meaning*. Cambridge: Cambridge University Press.
Swann Jr, William B., Angel Gómez, D. Conor Seyle, J. Morales, and Carmen Huici. 2009. "Identity Fusion: the Interplay of Personal and Social Identities in Extreme Group Behavior." *Journal of Personality and Social Psychology* 96, no. 5: 995–1011.
Tajfel, Henri, and John C. Turner. 1979. "An Integrative Theory of Intergroup Conflict." *The Social Psychology of Intergroup Relations* 33, no. 47: 33–47.
Taylor, Charles. 1971. "Interpretation and the Sciences of Man." *The Review of Metaphysics*: 3–51.

Taylor, Charles. 2002. "Modern Social Imaginaries." *Public Culture* 14, no. 1: 91–124.
Tversky, Amos, and Daniel Kahneman. 1983. "Extensional Versus Intuitive Reasoning: The Conjunction Fallacy in Probability Judgment." *Psychological Review* 90, no. 4: 293–315.
Warner, Michael, Jonathan VanAntwerpen, and Craig J. Calhoun, eds., 2010. *Varieties of Secularism in a Secular Age*. Cambridge: MA: Harvard University Press.
Wason, Peter C. 1968. "Reasoning About a Rule." *The Quarterly Journal of Experimental Psychology* 20, no. 3 : 273–281.
Whitehouse, Harvey. 2004. *Modes of Religiosity: A Cognitive Theory of Religious Transmission*. Walnut Creek: CA: Altamira.
Whitehouse, Harvey. 2008. "Cognitive Evolution and Religion: Cognition and Religious Evolution." *The Evolution of Religion: Studies, Theories, and Critiques*, ed. Joseph Bulbulia et al. Santa Margarita, CA: Collins Foundation Press: 31–41.
Whitehouse, Harvey, and Jonathan A. Lanman. 2014. "The Ties That Bind Us: Ritual, Fusion, and Identification." *Current Anthropology* 55, no. 6: 674–695.
Wiltermuth, Scott S., and Chip Heath. 2009. "Synchrony and Cooperation." *Psychological Science* 20, no. 1: 1–5.
Zuckerman, Phil. 2007. "Atheism: Contemporary Numbers and Patterns," in *The Cambridge Companion to Atheism*, ed. Michael Martin. New York: Cambridge University Press: 47–65.
Zuckerman, Phil. 2008. *Society Without God: What the Least Religious Nations Can Tell Us about Contentment*. New York: NYU Press.

II. The Story's Normative Implications

Guido Vanheeswijck
The Ambiguity of "Post-Secular" and "Post-Metaphysical" Stories: On the Place of Religion and Deep Commitments in a Secular Society

1 Introduction

On October 15, 1989, Vaclav Havel was awarded the Peace Prize of the German Booksellers Association.[1] In his acceptance speech, entitled "A Word about Words," he underlined the great impact that words can have, all over the world. As a dissident author from Eastern Europe, he directed this message in the aftermath of the Cold War to a mainly Western European audience:

> At the beginning of everything is the word. It is a miracle to which we owe the fact that we are human. But at the same time it is a pitfall and a test, a snare and a trial. More so, perhaps, than it appears to you who have enormous freedom of speech, and might therefore assume that words are not so important. They are. They are important everywhere.
>
> The same word can be humble at one moment and arrogant the next. And a humble word can be transformed easily and imperceptibly into an arrogant one, whereas it is a difficult and protracted process to transform an arrogant word into one that is humble.

Both Jürgen Habermas and Charles Taylor are very sensitive to the subtleties of words. As leading critics of Western modernity, they have been focusing on the exact significance of the word 'modern'. Perceptive to its potential pitfalls, they conclude that the project of modernity is still unfinished. Furthermore, they have delved deeply into the repercussions of this 'unfinished modernity' on how to define the words 'religious' and 'secular' and, in particular, on how to cope with the tensions between the advocates of religion and secularity.

At first sight, Habermas and Taylor seem to share a common view of all these topics in our contemporary age. The Western societies we are living in have to be, ideally, loci of compromise and complementary learning processes so as to find an 'overlapping consensus.' Since both believers (in different religions) and secular citizens belong to the same society, they share a common citizenship against

---

[1] This text was subsequently translated into English and published in *The New York Review of Books*, 18 January 1990.

the backdrop of different worldviews. Therefore, both Taylor and Habermas invite believers and non-believers alike to deliberate in the public sphere so as to adjust to the continued existence of religious communities on the one hand and to an increasingly secularized environment on the other.

However, their interpretations of how to live up to this ideal of a deliberative consensus are different. Whereas Habermas describes contemporary western society as 'post-secular' and pleads for a form of 'post-metaphysical' thinking in terms of a re-articulation of reason as procedural, Taylor explicitly rejects the former term in *A Secular Age* and implicitly renounces the latter. This difference of opinion is mainly due to a deeper dissensus: their different views of the project of modernity itself. While Habermas believes that its *execution* has remained incomplete, Taylor's claim is that the *conception* of the project has been defective.[2]

What is the central difference between these two interpretations of the word 'modernity'? Habermas more or less equates modernity with the heritage of Enlightenment. At the same time, he claims that the original and emancipatory project of Enlightenment has been dispensed with prematurely, i.e. when Kant's definition of Enlightenment was abandoned by the development of post-Kantian and in particular Hegelian idealism. Since the original program of human and political emancipation has been retarded by Hegel's metaphysical and pseudo-religious theory, Habermas's original aim was to restore the emancipatory spirit of Enlightenment by dispelling metaphysics and religion from the public sphere. Admittedly, since 2001 he has given much more room to the role of religion in the public sphere, albeit always subordinate to the dominant and even decisive role of procedural reason. Habermas's use of the words 'post-secular' and 'post-metaphysical' must be understood in this specific context (Habermas 2008; Mendieta 2010).

By contrast, Taylor considers modernity as a field of tension between at least two different waves: Enlightenment and Romanticism. He defines modernity as a continuous event, which has been and still is transforming the relation between the cosmos, its transcendent source and its human interpreter (cf. Dupré 1993: 249). By taking this twofold background into account, Taylor can demonstrate how and why Enlightenment's implicit awareness of internal tensions and strains between subject and object, finitude and infinity, became manifest in Romanticism as a search for the Absolute, or the transcendent, which had disappeared in Enlightenment. But that search could only be executed by the human subject that, as heir to Enlightenment, had emancipated itself from a pre-

---

[2] Here, Taylor finds company in Louis Dupré's recent writings (cf. Dupré 2008: 37–38; Dupré 2004: 16–17).

scribed belief in the Chain of Being which had been dominating classic and medieval philosophy. Against that backdrop, Taylor criticizes the use of the words 'post-secular' and 'post-metaphysical'.

In this essay, my intention is to focus on these two words, coined by Jürgen Habermas, and to raise the question of whether they are still humble words or already surreptitiously transformed into arrogant ones. Admittedly, the discussion about the exact definition of 'religion' and 'secularity' is an old one. But in *A Secular Age* Taylor gives that discussion a new and unexpected twist. It is surely no coincidence that Taylor's opus magnum on the relation between belief and unbelief is entitled *A Secular Age*, and not *A Post-Secular Age*. Neither is it insignificant that he has often chided 'post-metaphysical' authors for not making explicit their constitutive goods (Taylor 1994: 212) and raised the 'metaphysical' question of "whether our moral or ethical life, properly understood, can really be captured by the accounts which fit with our favoured ontology" (ASA: 609). Whereas Habermas framed the words 'post-secular' and 'post-metaphysical' as humble expressions of a balanced position in this discussion, Taylor considers them to be dependent on the hegemony of the mainstream narrative of secularization that needs to be challenged. (ASA: 534–535). To that end, Taylor presents an *alternative story* about the genesis and evolution of the secular age in *A Secular Age*.

Explaining and assessing the implications of that alternative narrative for an alternative approach to the contemporary relation between secularity and religion is the main objective of this contribution. Since the words 'post-secular' and 'post-metaphysical' are not innocent and their interpretation is likely to determine the view on the place of deep metaphysical commitments, including religious ones, that will prevail in contemporary society, a painstaking interpretation of both words is important.

Inspired by Taylor's position in *A Secular Age* and in subsequent essays, I will trace the consequences of divergent interpretations of these two words as to the role of religious (part 2) and metaphysical arguments or 'deep commitments' (part 3) in the current debate on the place of religion in the public sphere. Next, I will suggest that the controversy around the interpretation of both words is not only due to different epistemological premises, but to divergent political stances as well (part 4). Finally, I will claim that achieving mutual respect and tolerance in this regard is less amenable to the neutrality of procedural rationality than to the imaginative force of subtle words (part 5).

2 Post-secular

Habermas's repeated use of the word 'post-secular' after 2001 undoubtedly illustrates an evolution in his thinking. As a proponent of Enlightenment, his initial attitude towards religion was rather negative. He designated it as a remnant of pre-modern culture or, at best, as a transitory phase in the process towards modernization. In the early nineties, he began to grant religion a more positive status. Already in *Post-metaphysical Thinking* (1988), Habermas had acknowledged the existential (mainly comforting) role of religion in the lives of individuals. But he was hardly interested in its public role. Only after 2001 (partly owing to 9/11), did he claim that modernity and secularization were not equivalent. He began to appreciate the possibly positive role of religion in the public sphere, but with the proviso that its inspirational force was translatable into rational and secular terms.

This apparent evolution as to the role of religion was no rupture in his thought, as it is often suggested. On the whole, Habermas has been defining philosophy as an ongoing rationalizing process of inspirational experiences and ideas introduced by – among others – the Axial religions. But whereas his original feeling was that philosophy, by transforming religious sources into rational ideas, eventually would make religions redundant, after 2001, he admitted that the philosopher's task to translate religious traditions into rational terms was a never ending story. Thus, Habermas's post-secular story functions as an interesting, nuanced and thoughtful counterbalance to the stance of so-called new 'radical' atheists like Richard Dawkins, Daniel Dennett and Christopher Hitchens. Equally taking the ideals of Enlightenment as their starting-point but interpreting them in 'hard' naturalist terms, they come to a quite different conclusion: that religion was utterly unreasonable and socially dangerous.

But the nuanced word 'post-secular' (as coined by Habermas) is not a neutral term either. It actually presupposes a classic interpretation of the term secular, i.e. a narrative in which secularization is synonymous to the disappearance of religion. Moreover, not only does the word 'post-secular' presuppose a classic interpretation of the word 'secular'; it is exclusively applicable to those societies which have gone through the process of secularization. Put differently, the background of a secular society is the necessary condition of possibility for the development of a post-secular society:

> A 'post-secular' society must at some point have been in a 'secular' state. The controversial term can therefore only be applied to the affluent societies of Europe or countries such as Canada, Australia and New Zealand, where people's religious ties have steadily or rather

quite dramatically lapsed into the post-War period. These regions have witnessed a spreading awareness that their citizens are living in a secularized society (Habermas 2008: 17).

It should not be forgotten that Habermas's definition of a secularized society is deeply embedded in his concept of Enlightenment: under the guidance of procedural rationality, Enlightenment has transformed initially religious societies into secular ones, replacing God's authority with that of a procedural, democratic process of rational deliberation. Consequently, a post-secular society, in which religions which possess the power to articulate ethical sensitivities and intuitions of solidarity may play a role again, must remain within the framework of a secular society, i.e. a society in which religious intuitions are welcomed, if and only if they are translatable into procedural rational terms. In that light, the words 'rational,' 'secular' and 'neutral' are synonymous.

As already stated, it is surely no coincidence that Taylor's opus magnum on the relation between belief and unbelief is entitled *A Secular Age* and not *A Post-Secular Age*. Even more, only once in the whole book does he make use of the term 'post-secular:'

> Perhaps something analogous [to "minimal religion"] can be said about the situation in "post-secular" Europe. I use this term not as designating an age in which the declines in belief and practice of the last century would have been reversed, because this doesn't seem likely, at least for the moment; I rather mean a time in which the hegemony of the mainstream master narrative of secularization will be more and more challenged. This I think is now happening. But because, as I believe, this hegemony has helped to effect the decline, its overcoming would open new possibilities (ASA: 534–535).

Obviously, the word 'post-secular' in this quotation does not refer to a new period in our culture, following that of a secular age, but to an *alternative story* about the genesis and evolution of the secular age. If this alternative story, as told in *A Secular Age*, is accepted as a more reliable genealogical account of our secular age, then it implies as well an alternative approach to the contemporary relation between secularity and religion. Presenting that alternative approach, by developing some salient aspects of Taylor's approach in *A Secular Age* in dialogue with Habermas's procedure, is the main objective of this contribution.

The quintessence of this alternative approach is indicated on the very last page of *A Secular Age*. Taylor states there that in the account he is offering "there is no place for unproblematic breaks with a past which is simply left behind" (ASA: 772). Following Robert Bellah, he believes that with regard to people's past imaginaries and convictions "nothing is ever lost." In order to understand the specific predicaments of a secular age, he equally warns us for the lure of completely breaking with a so-called problematic past. Since all endeavors to supersede the past may give rise to the repetition of its horrors in our own way, Taylor instead is opting for an alternative approach, where a fusion of past and present horizons may take place. Especially in the domain of human affairs, where "understanding the other" (the historical and the geographical other alike) is at stake, this model of a "fusion of horizons" has to replace the classic model of scientific theory that stems from the epistemological tradition and is adequate to explaining the behavior of objects. Put differently, the model of a fusion of horizons is related to the art of telling stories rather than to the construction of scientific theories.

This plea for a "fusion of horizons" – the expression is borrowed from Gadamer – and for alternative normative stories is equally applicable to the modern secular era and, in particular, to the contemporary relation between religious and secular stances. Both Gadamer's and Taylor's accounts of the challenge of the other and of the "fusion of horizons" do not only apply to understand past epochs and alien societies. They first and foremost form a challenge to our own identity in the contemporary secular age we are living in, demanding for an equilibrium between acknowledging completely different ways of being human on the one hand and still being capable of living our own way on the other (Taylor 2011b: 33–38).

Now, Taylor's genealogical story about the relation between religion and secularization in *A Secular Age* is such an alternative normative story that differs in at least two central points from the classic secularization thesis. While the classic story presents the phenomenon of secularization as a logical outcome of western rationality's advancement, Taylor shows that a host of fundamental changes within religious culture itself has been shaping countless aspects of modern society and eventually has led to the secularization of our contemporary lifeworld.[3] Moreover, Taylor's alternative master narrative in *A Secular Age* argues that religion has not disappeared, as the classic story claims, but that it has become more fragile, an embattled option among other options.

Against the backdrop of these different genealogies of contemporary culture, there are two different interpretations of the role of religious accounts vis-à-vis secular arguments in the public sphere. Habermas's and Taylor's interpretations

---

3 As to this point, the resemblance between Marcel Gauchet's analysis and Taylor's is striking. See Gauchet 1985. This book was translated into English with a preface by Taylor; see Gauchet 1997. As generally known, this genealogical analysis of modernity was introduced in the writings of Max Weber, Karl Löwith and Hans Blumenberg. See: Weber [1920]1988; Löwith 1949; Blumenberg 1973. A selection from more recent books depicting the phenomenon of secularization as the product of an internally religious development: Dupré 2008; Gillespie 2008; Gregory 2012. See for a historical survey of this topic: Monod 2002.

of the word 'post-secular' form, indeed, part of the debate between so-called exclusionists and inclusionists (Mendieta, VanAntwerpen 2011). On the one hand, exclusionists take the position that only secular arguments and motives count in the public debate and that, consequently, religious argumentation has to be excluded (Audi 2000). Inclusionists, by contrast, claim that there is no need of a proviso regarding the public use of religious arguments, even not if a religious majority can take public decisions on the basis of religious argumentation alone (Weithmann 2002; Wolterstorff 1997). Habermas and Taylor take mid-positions between those of exclusionists and inclusionists. But, due to their divergent interpretations of the concepts 'secular' and 'post-secular', their positions as to the role of religious and secular language in the public sphere and to a possible 'fusion of horizons' are divergent as well (Habermas 2008; Mendieta and VanAntwerpen 2011).

Habermas is an inclusionist in the informal sphere and an exclusionist in the formal sphere of institutional bodies. Convinced that religious concepts and intuitions preserve indispensable semantic potentials for enriching the public debate, he claims that public deliberation has to include religiously inspired voices. But at the same time he insists that, since the appearance of religious language in the formal sphere of institutional political bodies may violate the principle of Church-State separation, religious citizens are obliged, if they wish to argue in the formal public sphere, to filter their arguments by translating them into generally accepted secular terms.

Taylor, however, rejects this 'epistemic break' between secular reason and religious thought. Of course, he accepts that there are zones of a secular state where neutral language has to be used. But these zones, situated on the formal, institutional level of *formulating* legislation must be clearly distinguished from the level where legislation is *justified* on the basis of religious and non-religious argumentation:

> This zone can be described as the official language of the state: the language in which legislation [...] and court judgments must be couched. It is self-evident that a law before Parliament couldn't contain a justifying clause of the type: 'Whereas the Bible tells us that...' [...] But this has nothing to do with the specific nature of religious language. It would be equally improper to have a legislative clause: 'Whereas Marx has shown that religion is the opium of the people' or 'Whereas Kant has shown that the only thing good without qualification is a good will.' The grounds for both these kinds of exclusions is the neutrality of the state (Taylor 2011a: 50).

Like Habermas, Taylor distinguishes two levels of deliberation: the level of an 'overlapping consensus' about the basic principles of a secular state, and the underlying level of their *justification*. At the first level, the 'overlapping consensus' must be universally respected and described in a neutral, official language. At the second level, the *justification* of these basic principles might be divergent and couched in different languages, secular and religious alike. But unlike Habermas, for whom neutral and secular languages are synonymous, Taylor does not put neutral language on a par with secular language. Based on the distinction between 'neutral' and 'secular', Taylor opts for the use of neutral, official language at the level of formulating legislation and for the use of secular and religious arguments alike at the second level of institutional deliberation (Mendieta and VanAntwerpen 2011: 66–67).

Thus, even as a member of parliament, a Christian or Muslim may justify the application of fundamental human rights by invoking the idea that every human being is a child of God, as much as a Kantian rationalist may bring up that each individual is a rational being, or a utilitarian that everyone is entitled to the highest form of happiness, etc. (MacLure & Taylor 2011: 11–12). Consequently, there is no contrast between the idea of shared citizenship, implying the universal recognition of constitutionally anchored ethical basic principles, and the idea of diversity as to the justification of these principles.

What is more, Taylor's dismissal of the claim that religiously informed reasoning is less rational than secular thought has both an explicit epistemological and an implicit political ground. Indeed, two premises underlie the claim that only secular reasoning is genuinely rational: first, that reason is to be articulated as procedural, since only procedural reason – in contrast to religion – has universal validity (epistemological) and second, that religion with its particular claims is often seen as a possible threat to peaceful coexistence (political). In order to assess the first premise, I shall focus in the next part on the different layers of meaning of the word 'post-metaphysical'. Subsequently, I evaluate the second premise based on a (much too concise) historical reconstruction of the fear of religious menace and its accompanying feelings of fanaticism and enthusiasm.

3 Post-metaphysical

It may come as no surprise that the controversy around the concept 'post-secular' and its implications is strongly related to the controversy surrounding the concept 'post-metaphysical.' The term 'post-metaphysical' (as coined by Habermas) is not a neutral term either. This term equally presupposes a certain – classic – interpretation of the term metaphysics, i.e. as a logically coherent view of reality as a whole. Since this kind of metaphysics has become untenable in the post-Hegelian era, Habermas (and others) characterizes our era as 'post-metaphysical.'

The implication of this labeling is not only that metaphysics has become outmoded as a philosophical discipline but equally that metaphysical views ('deep convictions'), if they still play a role in the process of democratic decision-making, must be subjected to the formal procedures and rules of argumentative rationality. So, within Habermas's ideal of argumentative dialogue based on procedural rationality, the significance of the word 'post-metaphysical' amounts to that of 'non-metaphysical'. Taylor – albeit implicitly – rejects this term as well in *A Secular Age*. But before going into that debate, I shall first try to clarify the complexity of the term 'post-metaphysical' by relating its genealogy to two different interpretations of the status of metaphysics in Kant's philosophy.

3.1 Post-metaphysical and the Kantian heritage

According to Habermas, Kant is the very first 'post-metaphysical' thinker. His transcendental dialectic, indebted to late-medieval nominalist revolution and devaluing not only the philosophical proofs of God's existence but all kinds of essentialist statements, introduced a distinction between practical and theoretical reason which in the long run led to a clear-cut separation between a hermeneutical approach and an objectifying scientific description of reality (Mendieta 2010: 3). In brief, due to Kant's heritage, metaphysical statements were replaced by scientific statements in the field of nature and by hermeneutical interpretations in the domain of human experiences.

After 2001, it remains Habermas's intention to purify the debate in the public sphere from all metaphysical appeals and ontological commitments (Mendieta 2012: 309–311). Because post-secular reason is in his perspective synonymous to sheer procedural, post-metaphysical reason, he even radicalizes Kant's original position. Whereas Kant could still derive the validity of legislation from his moral imperative, for Habermas the validity of legislation cannot be deduced – not even indirectly – from moral imperatives, let alone metaphysical convictions. Doing that would be tantamount to violating the formal procedures of the democratic decision process. Thus, if metaphysical convictions, analogous to moral and religious convictions, can still play a role in the formal process of decision-making, it is only on the condition that they are translated into procedural, argumentative language. Even if Habermas deliberately conceives post-secular rationality as more than means-end rationality in view of a moral-practical finality, it equally functions in the latter perspective as merely procedural.

One of Habermas's main objections to the direct use of metaphysical viewpoints in the public sphere is that it underestimates the finite and historical dimensions of human language and argumentation. Already in *Post-metaphysical*

Thinking he had formulated his extreme aversion to metaphysics in technical terms: since post-metaphysical thinking includes the dimensions of contingency and finiteness, it is fully aware of its dependence on language (linguistic turn), of the historicity of reason (detranscendentalization of the subject) and its embeddedness in everyday praxis (deflating the extra-ordinary) (Habermas 1994: 28– 112). Not only did he refute the Hegelian project of historical metaphysics, he even opposed the basic possibility of any metaphysics to do justice to the contingent vicissitudes of history:

> A history that takes the self-formative processes of nature and spirit up into itself, and that has to follow the logical forms of the self-explication of this Spirit, becomes sublimated into the opposite of history. To bring it to a simple point, that had already irritated Hegel's contemporaries: a history with an established past, a pre-decided future, and a condemned present is no longer *history* (Habermas 1994: 133).

Countless reactions, from different angles, to Habermas's concept of post-metaphysical thinking have occurred. I select only two of them. Common to these two critical reactions is that they blame Habermas himself for not taking into account the daily vicissitudes of history. But whereas in the former case this critique leads to a full rejection of metaphysics, the outcome in the latter is a rehabilitation of metaphysics, albeit in the shape of a drastic reform.

The first reaction is exemplified by Gianni Vattimo. He utterly rejects Habermas's concept of procedural rationality as a manual for genuine communication, because it still bears the traces of metaphysics deep in itself. In his perspective, Habermas's belief in the very possibility of transparent communicability heavily relies on his belief in the existence of an 'inter-subjective essence' of the subject. That is to say that the transcendental subject does not really disappear, but that it makes room for a transcendental inter-subjectivity. In Vattimo's eyes, Habermas's inter-subjective constitution of the subject does neither do justice to the contingent finiteness of the subject nor to that of a genuine process of deliberation and decision making. Instead, by introducing a transcendental inter-subjectivity he remains deeply indebted to the classic metaphysical ideal of knowledge as the description of objectively given structures.[4]

Therefore, Vattimo bluntly dismisses an ethics of communication in favor of an ethics of interpretation, where all remnants of metaphysics have disappeared and an attitude of friendship is more important than a search for truth. He is pleading for a historical hermeneutics which, by doing away with the belief in

---

[4] Vattimo 1992: 112 : "Habermas's intersubjective I is wholly the I of modern metaphysics-science. It is the object of the human sciences and the equally ahistorical subject of the laboratory"

truth as the mirror of reality and the possibility of communicative consensus based on transcendental inter-subjectivity, heralds the coming epoch of the end of metaphysics and ontology. Only by effacing all metaphysical and ontological traces will hermeneutics or 'weak thought' recognize its nihilistic destiny (Vattimo 1992: 105–120).

The second reaction equally recognizes our thought and language as inherently historical. But taking a Kant-interpretation as their starting-point, which is different from Habermas's, scholars like Dieter Henrich or Vincent Descombes wish to rehabilitate a reformed metaphysical position. They believe Habermas's post-metaphysical Kant-interpretation is wide of the mark, since Kant repeatedly underlines the importance of the metaphysical need and therefore considers metaphysical questions as inevitable. (Van Eekert 2005) In their view, Kant is not the herald of the end of metaphysics, but the originator of a reformed metaphysics.[5]

Henrich and Descombes are not the only scholars who reject a post-metaphysical interpretation of Kant. In the wake of the so-called 'meta-critics' of Kant (Herder and Hamann in Germany; later Collingwood and Berlin in England), who did not reject but historicized the Kantian transcendental approach, contemporary Anglo-Saxon authors like Stephen White and Charles Taylor equally object to Habermas's approach. In their view, the ineradicable metaphysical need inevitably leads to metaphysical answers, however tentative and inherently historical these answers might be.

3.2 Taylor's position

Consequently, Taylor and White alike claim that metaphysics has not disappeared, but has become more fragile. We cannot but think within frameworks which are at the same time vulnerable to potential revisions. But these frameworks or basic presuppositions are, one way or another, ontologically inspired:

> We treat our beliefs, theories, as over against reality, to be related to these frameworks. But all this goes on within a larger context of presumed contact with reality. The presumption can be erroneous, but never totally (Taylor 2013: 76).

It is against this 'meta-critical' backdrop that, in answer to Habermas, Taylor (and White) articulate the central role of metaphysical arguments ('deep commit-

---

[5] Descombes 2000; Heider 1999; Henrich 1987: 11–43; 1988: 17–25. For more information see: Van Eekert 2005: 17–65.

ments') within the current debate on ethical, religious and political issues in the public sphere. (Taylor 1995: ix; Taylor 2015: 30fn3) In their eyes, that debate is much more complex than is assumed by Habermas's procedural discourse ethics. Disagreement and controversy hardly ever arise from procedural argumentation, but are mostly, if not always, the outcome of discord at the level of basic presuppositions ('deepest convictions') about humans, world and God. It is, therefore, impossible to purify the public debate from metaphysical appeals and to dispense with all metaphysical and ontological commitments by converting them into procedural, argumentative language.

Put differently, the central notions of 'frameworks', 'forms of life', 'strong evaluation', 'hypergoods' or 'background of sources' in Taylor's main writings testify to the fact that our fundamental conceptions of the self, other and world are – in their diversity – necessary and unavoidable for an adequately reflective discussion on ethical and political issues. Even if we are aware that they always remain contestable and liable to revision, that they may be refined, improved and even revised, their mutual differences can never be obliterated by transposing them into argumentative terms. (Taylor 2005: 40). In other words, this 'meta-critical' position of White and Taylor rejects any form of 'strong ontology', inherent in pre-Kantian metaphysics, in favor of what is defined as 'weak or historical ontology', an ontology in which metaphysical positions are at the same time necessary and revisable.[6]

> [...] There is space to stand between a "Platonist" mode of moral realism, which would see the goods as standing quite independent of human existence, and as capable of formulation in a public language, on one hand, and mere subjectivism on the other. I am trying to stand in that space, which is why any equation of moral realism with Platonism seems to me to obfuscate things (Taylor 1994: 211).

In *A Secular Age,* Taylor had only implicitly drawn the contours of that ontological space. It was waiting until 2015, when, together with Hubert Dreyfus, he elaborated on this topic of moral realism, that was neither analogous to Platonic realism nor reducible to mere subjectivism in their book, *Retrieving Realism.* The position they defend in this book is no longer characterized as 'weak ontology' or 'philosophical anthropology', as in Taylor's earlier writings, but as 'pluralistic robust realism:'

> Our position could then be characterized as *pluralistic robust realism*. That is, there may be (1) multiple ways of interrogating reality (that's the "plural" part), which nevertheless (2)

---

[6] Taylor 2005: 35–42; White 2005: 11–25. For the difference between Taylor's and White's concept of "weak ontology" and Vattimo's 'weak thought: see White 2009: 808–816.

reveal truths independent of us, that is, truths that require us to revise and adjust our thinking to grasp them (and that's the robust realist part), and where (3) all attempts fail to bring the different ways of interrogating reality into a single mode of questioning that yields a unified picture or theory (so they stay plural) (Taylor 2015: 154).

Contrary to Habermas, Taylor believes that in the domain of human affairs, where "understanding the other" is at stake, the aim of a "fusion of horizons," as understood by Gadamer, cannot be achieved within the procedural boundaries of a discourse ethics. The model of a fusion of horizons, related to the art of telling stories, must be informed by a belief in the possibility of contact with reality. If we assume that stories, in forming our cultural worlds, mediate our contact with other people, and that we may be able to situate these stories in relation to other stories so as to elaborate common reference points, we have to add inevitably that these stories do not exhaust that contact with reality.

This plea for a fusion of horizons, based on the contact theory inherent in pluralistic robust realism, is equally applicable to the contemporary relation between religious and secular stances. In Gadamer's and Taylor's accounts, the perspective of a 'fusion of horizons' remains always fragile and subject to everlasting challenge. Like Habermas, Gadamer and Taylor alike know that attempts to such a fusion may completely go wrong and that only time and constant effort can tell us what is achievable. There are no a priori assurances available. (Taylor 2015: 129–30) But unlike Habermas, Taylor believes that:

> prior to, and as a condition of, any attempted fusion, comes the kind of understanding of the initially strange other, which is grounded in our common ability, as human, linguistic animals, to learn. A "principle of charity" does emerge from this condition, properly understood. It is grounded in a contact theory, and reposes finally on an unproblematic "realism." It can allow for the striking gaps and incommensurabilities which actually show up between human cultures, while making it understandable that we can in fact often come to straddle them, even if we can't go beyond this to fuse them (Taylor 2015: 130).

To sum up. Contemporary philosophers, taking a shared rejection of classic metaphysics and a Hegelian view of metaphysics in particular as their starting-point, have been following different paths. On the one hand, there are the 'post-metaphysical' philosophers who reject or at least marginalize all metaphysical and ontological claims or convictions in the public debate. This anti-metaphysical attitude has many fathers: (neo)positivism, (neo)pragmatism, inter-subjective discourse ethics, nihilistic hermeneutics, etc.. On the other hand, there are a host of philosophers who intend to rehabilitate metaphysics in a reformed shape, i.e. fully aware of the historical, fragmented and fragile character of its views on man, world and God, but at the same time attentive to its inevitable nature.

Those who reject metaphysics in this reformed shape consider the post-metaphysical public sphere either as a neutral space, where procedural rationality functions as the only judge in the public debate (Habermas) or as a playing-field for interpretative dialogue, without any prospect of truth-claims (Vattimo, Rorty). Those who believe that our "deepest convictions," albeit often unconsciously, form the basis of discord in the public space, consider the contributions of procedural rationality or sheer interpretative dialogue as insufficient to arrive at a consensus. In their view, procedural rationalists drastically undervalue the deeper anthropological and ontological sources out of which discord actually arises. Therefore, they propose, instead of a procedural or mere dialogical stance, a position that they either define as 'weak ontology' (White) or as 'pluralistic robust realism' (Taylor, Dreyfus).

4 On fanaticism and enthusiasm

So far, I have tried to demonstrate that what is applicable to the word 'post-secular' is equally applicable to the word 'post-metaphysical.' Neither religion nor metaphysics have disappeared from the public sphere; only their status has become more fragile. On the level of *justification* of basic principles, our deepest convictions or our metaphysical claims continue to play a decisive role. Instead of blotting out their mutual differences and delivering the search for consensus at the mercy of procedural rationality, we have to recognize and articulate them in their diversity and fragility. They form, by definition, the starting-point of the debate in the public sphere, on the informal and formal level alike.

Now, if this position has any plausibility, then its consequences are twofold. On the one hand, there is no ready-made formula available for a definite solution to all our controversies, nor a consensus based on procedural and rational discourse alone. Belief in such a ready-made formula is tantamount to accepting, as Vattimo suggests, the existence of a transcendental subjectivity, even if conceived in terms of inter-subjectivity. On the other hand, the meta-critical position makes us sensitive to hidden forms of metaphysics, lurking beneath concepts like 'secular neutrality' and 'procedural rationality'. Philosophers, who are congenial to Taylor, such as R.G. Collingwood, Ludwig Wittgenstein and Hans-Georg Gadamer have drawn attention to the 'unconscious' and 'unreflective' character of central basic assumptions. More often than not, we do not realize that – to use Taylor's metaphor that he borrows from Wittgenstein – a "picture holds us captive" (cf. Taylor 2015: 1–26; ASA: 557, 565, 575).

As a matter of fact, the epistemological status of basic assumptions – they form the building stones of the 'picture that holds us captive' – has always been controversial. Analytic (neo)positivists neglected or refuted their existence and considered all talk about them as senseless or idle. Of course, Habermas's position is much more nuanced: he acknowledges their existence and their possible influence. But, his intention is to subject them to procedural, rational criticism by their translation and transformation into non-metaphysical terms. Now, the main objection to Habermas's position is that basic assumptions or presuppositions about man, world and God can never be fully translated into propositions, liable to verification or procedural argumentation. Presuppositions are not verifiable or logically deductive propositions. (Collingwood 1998; Wittgenstein 1975) They do not function as conclusions of an argument, but rather as the subtle – often unconscious – framework within which these arguments and their conclusions are developed.[7]

But there is more at stake than only this epistemological controversy. Previously, I referred to Taylor's remark that the distinction between rational and religious / metaphysical argumentation is not only related to epistemological but also to political and historical issues. Since it is often suggested that religious and metaphysical convictions with their particular claims might be a possible threat to peaceful coexistence, it might be the case that Habermas's (and many others') reticence about the role of deep convictions in the public debate is partly due to an age-old history of fear of the (presumed) undermining force of religious (and metaphysical) controversies for the public order.

In academic circles and in public opinion alike, the essentially secular character of Enlightenment and of the rise of modern public sphere is often – unconsciously – taken for granted. Habermas's classic book *The Structural Transformation of the Public Sphere* (1962) is an influential example that illustrates this point. And it is undoubtedly true that a secular, anti-clerical branch of 18th-century philosophy has marked Enlightenment in Holland, England and surely in France (Israel 2001). But Enlightenment was a movement of religious thinkers as well. How to explain then that Enlightenment is seen generally as basically and even exclusively secular?

Of course, the European religious wars belong to a remote past. But even the distant past is not without influence on attitudes that are taken for granted today. (Gregory 2012) During the sixteenth and seventeenth centuries, the controversy around religious and metaphysical convictions had devastating consequences. These deep convictions were mostly inseparable from feelings of *enthu-*

---

[7] This epistemological discussion is part of a much broader discussion, i.e. that about the role of propositional logic and its relation to the logic of question and answer (Collingwood, Gadamer) and its embeddedness in forms of life (Wittgenstein).

siasm and *fanaticism* – terms used in seventeenth century England to characterize Puritans who continued to insist on what was revealed by 'inner light' and therefore rejected any compromise. Consequently, in the public sphere, which began to take shape in that period, it was not only the views of religious moderates, but those of religious fanatics as well that found support.

Taylor argues convincingly in *A Secular Age* that enlightened authors like David Hume, Lord Shaftesbury and Edward Gibbon, who were driven by their aversion to religious fanatics and at the same time were convinced of the public sphere's essential significance for modern society, defined their own approaches in terms of resistance to enthusiasm. Consequently, their ideal view of how to discuss in the public sphere was intimately related to attitudes of detached aloofness and (ironical) suspicion towards too strong passions and dynamism (ASA: 239 – 241).[8] And because enthusiastic dynamism and fanatic relentlessness mostly accompany deep (religious and metaphysical) convictions, more and more voices were calling to exclude these convictions from the public debate. Hence, the emphasis on cool detachment and (ironical) distance, motivated by fear of violent derailments, has been gradually undermining the belief in the transformative force of religious and deep convictions, even in the case of those people who still called themselves religious.

The deist alternative to the religious belief in the transformative force of divine inspiration is an unmistakable illustration of this surreptitious evolution. Since the concept of a deist God was the outcome of a rationalist trade-off rather than the source of religious inspiration, enthusiasm and fanaticism not only proved to be uncontrollable feelings and attitudes. In the deists' eyes, they equally gave rise to uncontrollable deep convictions, easily crossing the borders between belief and superstition.[9] Gradually, not only feelings of enthusiasm and fanaticism were castigated as dangerous, even deep convictions themselves accompanying these feelings were banned from the public sphere as being unreli-

---

[8] ASA: 241: "The version of polite culture embodied by Gibbon and Hume is not only averse to 'enthusiasm' in the sense the term had, but also to what the term means today. Politeness and refinement entailed also a stance of cool and ironic distance from the heated, ugly, and frequently cruel and destructive actions of those in the grips of religious fervour. Though plainly their condemnation of these acts was strong, these writers expressed the superiority of their civilized stance by maintaining a cool distance from their object, laced periodically with ironic wit."

[9] ASA: 238: "Further, insofar as the figure of Christ, as divine, stands behind claims to sacral authority, while the issue whether Jesus was God or simply a great prophet or teacher is not relevant to the question whether God is the designer of the order of mutual benefit, there is a temptation to abandon either the question or the doctrine of Christ's divinity, to slide towards Socianism, or Deism; or else to adopt a skeptical stance towards such questions."

able and seen as obstacles to the neutral role the state actually had to play (ASA: 286–287).

Of course, there is a real danger to stubbornly sticking to one's deep convictions. But in reaction to this danger, there are at least two strategies. First, we can bracket our deepest convictions and their accompanying feelings of inspired enthusiasm. Already in *Sources of the Self*, Taylor described such a strategy as the prudent strategy. Maybe this strategy was the only possible one in the 18th century, when the religious wars were still fresh in memory:

> The prudent strategy makes sense on the assumption that the dilemma is inescapable, that the highest spiritual aspirations must lead to mutilation or destruction (Taylor 1989: 520–521).

However, that assumption is only an assumption, i.e. it might be applicable to certain eras and contingent situations, but it is not universally applicable to all periods and all circumstances. On the verge of the 21st century, living in the North Atlantic world with its age-long tradition of freedom of speech, Taylor proposes a second strategy as an answer to the challenge of an open confrontation between different religious and metaphysical convictions. He does not accept the dilemma 'that the highest spiritual aspirations must lead to mutilation or destruction' as our inevitable lot.

> The dilemma of mutilation is in a sense our greatest challenge, not an iron fate (Taylor 1989: 521).

In order to face that challenge head on, it is not necessary to fall back on attitudes of detachment and neutral distance and to neutralize our deepest (religious and metaphysical) convictions. On the contrary, Taylor's suggestion is that we have to rely on alternative attitudes of empathy and wisdom. In particular at the justificatory level of our viewpoints, this attitude of empathy is appropriate, if accompanied by a sensitivity to the use of subtler languages (Taylor borrows this term from Shelley). The force of subtle words which refer to our deepest convictions is not reducible to terms tailored to the criteria of empirical verifiability or logical deduction. Subtle language is no neutral instrument to rationally convince the other of one's own position. Its empathic force is rather akin to the evocative force of poetical images than to the argumentative force of logical concepts. Put differently, it is related to a form of reason that makes appeal to our implicit understanding of our own ways of life and simultaneously to the belief that our ways of reasoning may reveal truths that are independent of us (cf. Taylor 1995: 34–60; Taylor 2015: 154).

As an illustration of the inaptitude of mere detached and neutral logical deduction in coping with ethical dilemmas, Richard Dawkins's defense against the many critical reactions to his recent famous tweet on the right and even the duty to abort Down's syndrome fetuses is a case in point. His defense against the objections to his position was that he was only "approaching moral philosophic questions in a logical way." Bur such a retort only exposes his complete neglect of the gap between the justificatory level of our deepest convictions and the descriptive level of objective and measurable data. Ultimately, Dawkins's reaction proves his insensitivity to the difference between the role of fragile, subtler languages in the former domain and the use of neutral descriptive words in the latter. In the domain of existential questions, propositional logic cannot play the role of a neutral judge.

Believing in the neutral role of logic is not only an illusion, a 'category mistake' of confusing two levels; above all, it shows as well a lack of subtlety to what is really at stake. In the discussion on the duty to abort Down's syndrome fetuses, the central issue is not first and foremost whether a fetus is a human person or not (a propositional statement). Discord in this discussion mainly has to do with personal (often implicit) views on the role of suffering in life, on dealing with handicap, on the significance of human life and the meaning of embodied subjectivity. Only by articulating these implicit understandings that are given marginal importance in apodictic logical argumentation, a genuine reasonable discussion about divergent moral positions is possible.

5 The illusion of neutrality and the importance of articulation

So far I have argued that neutrality in personal affairs is a strategy that will end up in a deadlock. In this section, I would like to situate the genesis and inadequacy of this neutral attitude within the broader historical context of modern Western philosophy and illustrate it by means of a small essay, written by the Israeli novelist Amos Oz.

Societies and states have always been formed by communities of people. Since there are no neutral human beings, there is no neutral society or state either. Therefore, the state's mandate is not to adopt an attitude of neutrality (as is often proclaimed) but to adopt *an attitude of impartiality*. This attitude implies that the state's members cannot be reduced to neutral robots – not even its public servants – but that they are expected, without putting aside their own strong convictions and commitments, to treat others respectfully and without discrimination. Thus, a *culture of impartiality* is completely different from a *culture of neutrality*.

Neutrality is a concept typical of Enlightenment, generally related to the names of René Descartes and those of the British empiricists. It is embodied in the typical views on subjectivity, described by Taylor as 'disengaged subjects' (Descartes) and 'punctual selves' (Locke). Precisely the latter view of man led David Hume to the conclusion that a stable self is an illusory idea. If one becomes a person through the process of registering and assimilating impressions, such a neutral person can, by definition, never become a stable self, perhaps not a self at all. Because every individual is fully dependent on data and stimuli provided by the outer world and because registering changing stimuli is the only knowledge source of the outer world, the individual eventually coincides with the stimuli.

It was this view that woke up Immanuel Kant from his 'dogmatic slumbers'. In answer to Hume's skepticism, he claimed that we do not just register stimuli from the outer world but that we order them into a whole in which we can recognize ourselves and with which we organize our world. But, Kant added, the way these stimuli are ordered is universal, i.e. identical for everyone. It was on this universally valid possibility to organize stimuli that he founded our human capacity to do scientific research. Scientific results are universally applicable to all cultures, precisely because they bracket all cultural differences. They arise from a 'neutral' core with which anyone in all circumstances is gifted so as to arrive at universal, objectively valid statements.

In Western philosophy, this neutral core was granted the enigmatic name of 'transcendental subject'. Kant made it clear that we must not confuse a transcendental subject with a concrete, empirical subject like you and me. But the two concepts of subjectivity are not as completely separated as Kant wished them to be: indeed, we are only able to discover transcendental subjectivity if all contents related to the empirical subject's concrete life course are purified by subjecting them to the formal judgment of procedural rationality.

It is common knowledge that Romanticism reacted against this enlightened concept of a transcendental subject and that its major thinkers soon began to undermine the transcendental subject's universal claims. Sensitive to each human being's individual character, they rejected an 'empty' view of man (conceived as a transcendental subject) and the accompanying possibility of formal purification. Opposing the neutralization of the subject, romantic meta-critics of Kant (Hamann, Herder, Humboldt) highlighted the fact that every human being has a particular core, shaped by descent, education and tradition. It is at this very juncture that the already mentioned controversy around the unfinished project of Enlightenment is to be situated.

Habermas believes that the *execution* of the project of Enlightenment has remained incomplete. His intention is to amend its one-sidedness by emphasizing, along with instrumental rationality, the importance of communicative, argumentative rationality in the public sphere. He continues to believe in the possibility of a formal consensus based on inter-subjective argumentation and shared by all empirical subjects involved. But, as already stated, his main critics argue that the *concept* of Enlightenment itself is incomplete. It must be liberated from its belief in the conceptual 'reality' of a transcendental subject by relating it to the heritages of Humanism and Romanticism alike.

Against this background, Taylor's position, as elaborated in *A Secular Age*, is of utmost significance. Already in his Hegel-book did he claim that the search for a situated inter-subjectivity, freedom and tolerance remains the main challenge in contemporary society. Since Hegel's ontology of the Absolute Spirit seems to deny the very problems as we now experience them, we are facing the philosophical challenge to look for a new ontology, with the help of what he coins as "subtler languages" (Taylor 1975: 570–1). Taylor has taken up this challenge, from *Ethics of Authenticity* over *Sources of the Self* to *A Secular Age*. As already indicated, he developed that position more in detail in *Retrieving Realism*, characterizing it as 'pluralistic robust realism.'

Now, it is not my intention to repeat the whole history of the complex and complicated relations between Romanticism and Enlightenment, as depicted in all these writings, and its repercussions for our current view of man. Nor do I want to go into all the vicissitudes of our western epistemological predicament and the divergent efforts of overcoming epistemology, as magnificently outlined by Taylor and Dreyfus in *Retrieving Realism*. Rather, I would like to consult a contemporary novelist from Israel, Amos Oz in order to shed light on the same topic, i.e. the complexity of 'living together' and looking for a "fusion of horizons."

Like all great novelists, Oz is extremely sensitive to the subtlety of words. And it goes without saying that, living in the spiritual no man's land between Jews and Palestinians, he is extremely sensitive to the stealthy danger of fanaticism and enthusiasm as well. But unlike thinkers from the 18th century who, stamped by the scars from religious wars, propagated an attitude of cool detachment and a neutralization of deepest convictions as an antidote to fanaticism, Oz, tried and tested by the vicissitudes of the Jewish people in modern European culture, proposes another attitude. Disclaiming the traditional view that the fanatic has too much 'self,' he sees him as someone who is destitute of a 'self.' Put in a more familiar terminology, the fanatic has no 'sources of the self.'

There are, indeed, different ways of being fanatic. As a rule, fanaticism is linked to the danger of enthusiastic belief in the unshakable truth of a conviction. During the last centuries, we have deservedly become sensitive to guarding against its threatening danger. But there is another form of fanaticism, which is much less visible, because it presents itself – paradoxically enough – as an antidote to fanaticism. This – mostly hidden and hardly recognizable – form of fanaticism is interwoven with marginalizing our 'deepest convictions', either by discrediting them as potentially dangerous or by tailoring their contents to a procedural format. In this perspective, any idea of a human person's deep core, to which he or she wishes to remain loyal, is seen as illusory and likely dangerous.

Even if Oz in his essay, *How to cure a fanatic*, does not explicitly distinguish both forms of fanaticism, he arrives at the apparently paradoxical conclusion that the fanatic is generally a 'most unselfish creature', a great altruist. In the absence of a 'self', he is mostly focused on the other:

> The fanatic wants to save your soul, he wants to redeem you, he wants to liberate you from sin, from error, from smoking, from your faith or from your faithlessness, he wants to improve your eating habits, or to cure you of your drinking or voting habits. The fanatic cares a great deal for you; he is always either falling on your neck because he truly loves you or else he is at your throat in case you prove to be unredeemable. And, in any case, topographically speaking, falling on your neck and being at your throat are almost the same gesture. One way or another, the fanatic is more interested in you than in himself, for the very simple reason that the fanatic *has very little self or no self at all* (Oz 2006: 57–58; italics mine).

Indeed, the fanatic has no self at all. Whether clinging to his fundamentalist belief in the truth of his own worldview or taking a detached, empty, so-called neutral point of view, the fanatic feels that he must liberate the other from the ballast of his traditions and convictions, which he deems as either unimaginably stupid and hopelessly outmoded or as extremely dangerous. Only by breaking free from these oppressing shackles can the other liberate himself.

But Oz wants to cure the fanatic. To that end, on the very last pages of his essay he puts forward an alternative definition of the person as a pensinsula

> half attached to the mainland, half facing the ocean – one half connected to family and friends and culture and tradition and country and nation and sex and language and many other things, and the other half wanting to be left alone to face the ocean (Oz 2006: 69–70).

Genuine tolerance is only possible, Oz writes, when we are "allowed to remain peninsulas." As a matter of fact, we all belong to a family, a culture and a worldview, a country and a language. We have not chosen these after a long process of deliberation. Instead, we have received them from earlier generations. Forgetting this peninsular quality makes us easily susceptible to proselytism: the lurking will to convert the other, while forgetting that the other – like myself – is equally attached to his own part of the mainland:

> The essence of fanaticism lies in the desire to force other people to change (Oz 2006: 57).

Do we hear an echo of a conservative plea for securing tradition and rejecting critical reflection? Not at all. Even if you are aware of your deep attachment to a host of customs and traditions, nothing prevents you from looking over the ocean, facing its infinitude, comparing your own background with other traditions and customs and finally adjusting your attitude, modifying your position, changing your view. Facing the ocean, empathy with another does not have to be in conflict with recognition of your own quality of peninsula. An attitude of imaginative empathy can help you feel that the other is equally a peninsula and that every peninsula is, by definition, contingent:

> And in my own personal background, in my own personal life story and family story, I can't help thinking, very often, that with a slight twist of my genes, or of my parents' circumstances, I could be him or her, I could be a Jewish West Bank settler, I could be an ultra-orthodox extremist, I could be an oriental Jew from a Third World country; I could be anyone. I could be one of my enemies. Imagining this is always a helpful practice (Oz 2006: 68).

The predominant belief in the neutral force of procedural rationality makes us often fail to remember the presence of this peninsula quality in each of us. Yet that peninsula quality is interwoven with our deepest convictions, our basic choices in life, our cherished values, the persons we feel attached to. If we neutralize that quality, it is as if nothing really matters. Evading potential frictions by converting the contents of divergent opinions into sheer procedural terms seems then the only 'prudent' strategy left to combat fanaticism. But a person with outspoken opinions is not, by definition, fanatic. A person becomes a fanatic when he forgets that we are all peninsulas, not empty cabinets or unwritten pages.

6 Conclusion

I return to my starting-point. Are the words 'neutrality,' 'post-secular' and 'post-metaphysical' the most appropriate words to create a tolerant society, to bring together people from different backgrounds, cultures, religions, convictions, colors? Why demand that people bracket their deepest convictions or, at best, translate them in procedural terms? I reformulate these crucial questions in yet another way: is the demand not to show diversity, to neutralize its versatility and richness or, at least, to marginalize those things – is that demand really the best way to live up to the ideal of diversity?

Of course, Habermas's and other thinkers' appeal for a procedural translation of convictional frictions is set up as a deliberate and well-intentioned effort to be honest and decent. But a well-thought and honest stance implies self-knowledge, an empathic attitude towards others and the acceptance of the peninsula that we all represent; it does not require blotting out your own identity. To turn the danger of fanaticism in the direction of more tolerance and reciprocal respect, a neutral stance – if such an attitude is possible at all – remains ineffective. Rather, we need an attitude that demands more nuance and subtle sensitivity, an attitude which is always vulnerable and, therefore, immensely valuable:

> A sense of humor, the ability to imagine the other, the capacity to recognize the peninsular quality of every one of us may be at least a partial defense against the fanatic gene that we all contain (Oz 2006: 71).

Perhaps neutrality is applicable in exact and positive sciences. But it is to no avail within human relations. Moreover, experience itself is the best teacher here: people with different convictions and worldviews – sharing and articulating an honest and vulnerable stance and reciprocal interest – can become friends and even soul-mates. Attitudes of empathy and wisdom, averse to ideological hair-splitting or quibbling, are likely to generate mutual respect and deep understanding.

Admittedly, procedural rationality is needed so as to establish a certain form of social cohesion and political stability. But its real effect will remain a dead letter if it is not embedded in an ethics of respect and attention for our deepest convictions. Even more, it will remain a dead letter if it is not embedded in the stronger 'pluralistic robust realist' sense "that all exercises of reflective, conceptual thought only have the content they have situated in a context of background understanding which underlies and is generated in [our] everyday coping [with reality]" (Taylor 2015: 54).

Words like 'post-secular' and 'post-metaphysical' are important words today. They were, undoubtedly, meant as humble words. But humble words can easily change into arrogant words. Arrogant words that – perhaps unwillingly and unwittingly – are bracketing our deepest convictions and thus threaten to destroy the largest part of the peninsula that we are. The deepest core of our self is not translatable into procedural terms; only subtle words are able to touch that deep, often hidden core, operative beyond the level of procedures and exclusively rational regulations.

Reasoning about our deepest convictions is possible; articulating them is necessary. By the same token, we ought never forget that our deepest convictions are neither the outcome of logical arguments nor the subject of empirical propositions; they are operating in a different way. As the framework of basic presuppositions within which logical arguments are developed and propositional statements are propounded, they neither build easy consensus nor simply lead to utter dissent. They are living from the humble force of subtle words. They function in the public sphere as

> a basis for radical challenges and radical questions; they bring enthusiasm, passion, indignation, outrage and love. If enthusiasm is sometimes harnessed to unreflective conviction, passion is also vital to critical engagement with existing institutions and dangerous trends. [...] The public sphere is a realm of rational-critical debate in which matters of the public good are considered. It is also a realm of cultural formation in which argument is not the only important practice and creativity and ritual, celebration and recognition are all important. It includes the articulation between deep sensibilities and explicit understandings and it includes the effort – aided sometimes by prophetic calls to attention – to make the way we think and act correspond to our deepest values or moral commitments (Calhoun 2011: 132–133).

I write these lines at the very moment that a murderous attack on the editorial offices of *Charlie Hebdo* in Paris takes place. At such moments, we experience all philosophical efforts to create mutual respect as extremely vulnerable. Charles Taylor's zig-zag account of the relation between religion and secularity, as elaborated in *A Secular Age*, reminds us of that vulnerability. Taylor's position in *A Secular Age* makes us, living in a secular age and facing our contemporary predicament, realize that we are dwelling in an uncharted area. For perhaps the first time in our history, we are challenged to legitimate our ethics of solidarity, indissolubly related to the *formal* values of Western culture, on divergent *substantive* positions.

So far, the ethical stances of confessional and non-confessional societies alike were based on one single foundation. First, Western culture was founded on Christianity. Subsequently, Enlightenment dreamed of a universal secular philosophy – a 'civil religion' – as the only reliable and secure foundation of a tolerant society. But one single foundation is no longer able to uphold our contemporary multicultural society: "We are societies that, in our tremendous diversity, are powered by a great many different engines of commitment to our common ethic, and we cannot afford to switch off any of these engines. All these together are what keep our societies going as viable, equal, democratic, and solidary societies" (Taylor 2010: 8).

Such an attitude – open to a diversity of sources at the level of legitimation – is related to a belief in the ability to shape a society based on solidarity:

> The sense of solidarity in a society can only be sustained if all the different spiritual families that make up that society find it in them to recreate their sense of dedication to it: if the Christians see that as central to their Christianity, if the Muslims see that as central to their Islam, if the various kinds of lay philosophies see that as central to their philosophy (Taylor 2010: 8).

But such an attitude is also rooted in a sensitivity for the fact that we are not imprisoned in our own minds, that we may remain open to a shared world and that the things we cherish most are somehow related to an independently existing reality.

I opened this article with a quote from Havel's acceptance speech on the fragility of words. I end this contribution by quoting him again. Taylor selected this very quote of Havel in his article, "Ethics and Ontology" in order to demonstrate the fragile, albeit indispensable, relation between our ethical attitude and its ontological background:

> I have often asked myself why human beings have any rights at all. I always come to the conclusion that human rights, human freedom, and human dignity have their deeper roots somewhere outside the perceptible world. These values are as powerful as they are because, under circumstances, people accept them without compulsion and are willing to die for them, and they make sense only in the perspective of the infinite and the eternal. I am deeply convinced that what we do, whether it be in harmony with our conscience, the ambassador of eternity, or in conflict with it, can only finally be assessed in a dimension that lies beyond that world we see around us. If we did not sense this, or subconsciously assume it, there are some things that we could never do.[10]

Of course, such an ethical attitude is not easy to maintain and its result cannot but remain vulnerable and unpredictable. Every 'modus vivendi' directed towards tolerance and mutual respect between people and cultures with divergent 'deep convictions' will always remain fragile. However, if working with *A Secular Age* may teach us one lesson, it is that we will have to learn to live with this fragility. Failing to appreciate that fragility is tantamount to forgetting the 'otherness' of the other. Articulating the implicit background of our own beliefs and reasoning about them with people with different backgrounds will always remain a 'lotta continua.' If there is one precarious challenge in our contemporary society, it is to maintain the paradoxical effort to search for the horizon of mu-

---

[10] Vaclav Havel, *The New York Review of Books*, xlvi, 10 (June 10, 1999), 6. Quoted in Taylor 2003: 317. Cf. ASA: 728–730.

tual respect and understanding along with facing the atmosphere of tensions and strains inherent in that effort.

Bibliography

Audi, Robert. 2000. *Religious Commitment and Secular Reason*. New York: Cambridge University Press.
Blumenberg, Hans. 1973. *Die Legitimität der Neuzeit* (erweiterte und überarbeitete Neuausgabe). Frankfurt: Suhrkamp Verlag.
Calhoun, Craig. 2011. "Religion's Many Powers," in *The Power of Religion in the Public Sphere*, ed. Eduardo Mendieta and Jonathan VanAntwerpen, 118–134. New York: Columbia University Press.
Collingwood, Robin George. 1998. *An Essay on Metaphysics*. Ed. Rex Martin. Oxford: Clarendon Press.
Descombes, Vincent. 2000. "Latences de la métaphysique," in *Un siècle de philosophie. 1900–2000*, ed. Karl Otto Apel and Jonathan Barnes, 11–52. Paris : Gallimard.
Dupré, Louis. 1993. *Passage to Modernity. An Essay in the Hermeneutics of Culture and Nature*. New Haven: Yale University Press.
Dupré, Louis. 1993. "Postmodernity or Late Modernity?" *Review of Metaphysics* 47 (December: 277–295).
Dupré, Louis. 2004. *The Enlightenment and the Intellectual Foundations of Modern Culture*. New Haven: Yale University Press.
Dupré, Louis. 2008. *Religion and the Rise of Modern Culture*. Indiana: University of Notre Dame Press.
Dupré, Louis. 2013. *The Quest of the Absolute. Birth and Decline of European Romanticism*. Indiana: University of Notre Dame Press.
Gauchet, Marcel. 1985. *Le désenchantement du monde. Une histoire politique de la religion*. Paris: Gallimard.
Gauchet, Marcel. 1997. *The Disenchantment of the World. A Political History of Religion*. Translated by Oscar Burge. Princeton, N.J.: Princeton University Press.
Gillespie, Michael. 2008. *The Theological Origins of Modernity*. Chicago: The University of Chicago Press.
Gregory, Brad. 2012. *The Unintended Reformation. How a Religious Revolution Secularized Society*. Harvard: The Belknap Press.
Habermas, Jürgen. 1988. *Nachmetaphysisches Denken: philosophische Aufsätze*. Frankfurt: Suhrkamp.
Habermas, Jürgen. 2008. "Notes on a Post-Secular Society." *New Perspectives Quarterly* 25 no. 4: 17–29.
Habermas, Jürgen. 2009. *Geloven en weten, en andere politieke essays*. Amsterdam: Boom.
Habermas, Jürgen. 2011. "'The Political': The Rational Meaning of a Questionable Inheritance of Political Theology," in *The Power of Religion in the Public Sphere*, ed. Eduardo Mendieta, Jonathan VanAntwerpen, 15–33. New York: Columbia University Press.

Habermas, Jürgen, 2011. "Jürgen Habermas & Charles Taylor: Dialogue," in *The Power of Religion in the Public Sphere*, ed. Eduardo Mendieta and Jonathan VanAntwerpen, 60–69. New York: Columbia University Press.
Heider, Placidus Bernhard. 1999. *Jürgen Habermas und Dieter Henrich. Neue Perspektiven auf Identität und Wirklichkeit*, Freiburg-München: Alber.
Henrich, Dieter. 1987. "Was ist Metaphysik – was Moderne? Zwölf Thesen gegen Jürgen Habermas," in *Konzepte. Essays zur Philosophie in der Zeit*, 11–43. Frankfurt, Suhrkamp.
Henrich, Dieter. 1988. "Warum Metaphysik?," in *Metaphysik nach Kant? Stuttgarter Hegel-Kongress 1987*, ed. Dieter Henrich and R.P Horstmann, 17–25. Stuttgart: Klett-Cotta.
Israel, Jonathan. 2001. *The Radical Enlightenment*. Oxford: Oxford University Press.
Lilla, Mark. 2007. *The Stillborn God. Religion, Politics and the Modern West*. New York: Vintage Books.
Löwith, Karl. 1949. *Meaning in History. The Theological Implications of the Philosophy of History*, Chicago: University of Chicago Press.
Maclure, Jocelyn & Taylor, Charles. 2011. *Secularism and Freedom of Conscience*. Cambridge: Harvard University Press.
Mendieta, Eduardo and VanAntwerpen Jonathan, eds., 2011. *The Power of Religion in the Public Sphere*. New York: Columbia University Press.
Mendieta, Eduardo. 2003. "A Postsecular World Society? On the Philosophical Significance of "Postsecular Consciousness and the Multicultural World Society. An Interview with Jürgen Habermas" (translated by Matthias Fritsch), http://blogs.ssrc.org/tif/2010/02/03 (last accessed February 19, 2015).
Monod, Jean-Claude. 2002. *La querelle de la secularisation. Théologie politique et philosophies de l'histoire de Hegel à Blumenberg*. Paris: Librairie philosophique J. Vrin.
Oz, Amos. 2006. *How to Cure a Fanatic?* Princeton: Princeton University Press.
Taylor, Charles. 1975. *Hegel*. Cambridge: Cambridge University Press.
Taylor, Charles. 1989. *Sources of the Self. The Making of the Modern Identity*. Cambridge: Cambridge University Press.
Taylor, Charles. 1992. "Reply to Commentators," *Philosophy and Phenomenological Research* 54 no.1: 203–213.
Taylor, Charles. 1995. *Philosophical Arguments*. Cambridge: Harvard University Press.
Taylor, Charles. 1997. "Foreword," in Marcel Gauchet: *The Disenchantment of the World. A Political History of Religion*. Translated by Oscar Burge, ix-xv. Princeton: Princeton University Press.
Taylor, Charles. 2003. "Ethics and Ontology," *The Journal of Philosophy* 100 no. 6: 305–220.
Taylor, Charles. 2005. "The 'Weak Ontology' Thesis," *The Hedgehog Review* 7 no. 2: 35–42.
Taylor, Charles. 2010. "Solidarity in a Pluralist Age," IWMpost, n.104, *Religion in a Secular Age*, April–August: 1–8.
Taylor, Charles. 2011a. "Why We Need a Radical Redefinition of Secularism," in *The Power of Religion in the Public Sphere*, ed. Eduardo Mendieta, Jonathan VanAntwerpen, 34–59. New York: Columbia University Press.
Taylor, Charles. 2011b. *Dilemmas and Connections. Selected Essays*. Cambridge: The Belknap Press of Harvard University Press.
Taylor, Charles. 2013. "Retrieving Realism," in *Mind, Reason, and Being-in-the-World. The McDowell-Dreyfus Debate*, ed. Joseph K. Schear, 61–90. Abingdon: Routledge.

Taylor, Charles and Dreyfus, Hubert. 2015. *Retrieving Realism*. Cambridge: Harvard University Press.
Van Eekert, Geert. 2005. "De moderne natuurwetenschappen en de onttroning van de prima philosophia," in *De koningin onttroond. De opkomst van de moderne cultuur en het einde van de metafysica*, ed. Herbert De Vriese, Geert Van Eekert, Guido Vanheeswijck, Koen Verrycken,17–65. Kapellen: Pelckmans.
Vattimo, Gianni. 1992. *The Transparent Society*. Cambridge: Polity Press.
Weber, Max. [1920] 1988. "Die protestantische Ethik und der Geist des Kapitalismus," in *Gesammelte Aufsätze zur Religionssoziologie I*, 1–206. Tübingen: J.C.B. Mohr (Paul Siebeck) Verlag.
Weithman, Paul. 2002. *Religion and the Obligations of Citizenship*. Cambridge: Cambridge University Press.
White, Stephen K. 2005. "Weak Ontology: Genealogy and Critical Issues," *The Hedgehog Review*, 7 no. 2: 11–25.
White, Stephen K. 2009. "Violence, Weak Ontology, and Late-Modernity," *Political Theory*, 37 no. 6: 808–816.
Wittgenstein, Ludwig. 1975. *On Certainty / Über Gewissheit*. Ed. G. EM. Anscombe and G. H.von Wright. Oxford: Blackwell.
Wolterstorff, Nicholas. 1997. "The Role of Religion in Decision and Discussion of Political Issuesm," in *Religion in the Public Square*, ed. Robert Audi and Nicholas Wolterstorff, 67–120. London: Rowman and Littlefield.

Aurélia Bardon
Liberal Pluralism in a Secular Age

> Was the universe designed by God? That's up to everyone in this country to decide for themselves because the framers of our Constitution believed that if the people were to be sovereign and belong to different religions at the same time, then our official religion would have to be no religion at all. It was a bold experiment then, as it is now. It wasn't meant to make us comfortable. It was meant to make us free.
>
> Matt Santos, *The West Wing*

1 Introduction

The most important characteristic of the secular age, as described by Charles Taylor, is pluralism: our secular age "is a pluralist world, in which many forms of belief and unbelief jostle, and hence fragilize each other" (ASA: 531). The idea of pluralism is the common and uncontested starting point of contemporary liberal political theory. Taylor's discussion of belief and unbelief and of their epistemological consequences sheds light on the fact that this pluralism is twofold: it is a moral pluralism about what is the good life or what is the right thing to do, but it is also an epistemological pluralism concerning conditions of knowledge of moral matters.

As Taylor describes it, our secular age is not neutral: it is not independent of controversial normative assumptions but rather builds upon specific foundations.[1] My argument in this chapter supports that contention, though from a dif-

---

Research for this chapter was funded by European Research Council (ERC) Grant 283867 on "Is Religion Special?"

1 Neutrality is an ambiguous term, and is only used in this chapter as referring to independence from all controversial philosophical principles. More recently, Taylor has associated secularism with a different meaning of neutrality (Taylor 2011; Maclure and Taylor 2011). When he argues that secularism "must be understood within the context of the more general ideal of neutrality" (Maclure and Taylor 2011: 19), he uses neutrality as referring to an impartial, even-handed treatment of all faiths and of all religious and non-religious citizens. When he says however that "the immanent frame isn't simply neutral" (ASA: 555), he means that it is not a freestanding

ferent angle. My goal is to show why the liberal pluralism characteristic of our secular age is itself not neutral: the commitment to moral and epistemological pluralisms suggested by Taylor reveals the fact that the immanent frame, which lays the foundation for the emergence of a liberal society, is in fact based on specific normative and epistemological assumptions, *i.e.* a commitment to basic liberal norms and to a limited version of epistemological skepticism. Only these assumptions can explain why we expect and accept both moral and epistemological pluralisms; at the same time, they help explain why both are strictly limited. Taylor acknowledges explicitly the normative assumptions of his liberal pluralism and I argue that his description of the immanent frame also reveals implicitly that he accepts a specific epistemological assumption: only a weak epistemological skepticism can guarantee the possibility of both belief and unbelief and that they are both equally valid options.

I first distinguish between moral and epistemological pluralisms (2). I then show why the liberal commitment to these pluralisms is based on specific normative and epistemological assumptions (3). These assumptions, however, are themselves limited and cannot include certain metaphysical claims: in other words, the liberal commitment to moral and epistemological pluralisms is not and cannot be based on the validity of metaphysical pluralism (4). This is why I describe Taylor's account as skeptical.

2 Moral pluralism and epistemological pluralism

The nature and depth of the pluralism that characterizes secular societies is brought to light through Taylor's focus on the choice between belief and unbelief. Secularity, according to Taylor, describes a change "which takes us from a society in which it was virtually impossible not to believe in God, to one in which faith, even for the staunchest believer, is one human possibility among others" (ASA: 3). In a secular society, belief and unbelief are both valid options that are "followed by a multiplication of both believing and unbelieving positions" (ASA: 531). Each option is associated with specific *moral beliefs*, but also with a specific understanding of conditions of validity of moral beliefs, or *moral epistemologies*. This means that there are two types of pluralism that are combined in secular modern societies: a moral pluralism and an epistemological pluralism.

---

view but rests on specific normative assumptions. In *A Secular Age*, as in this chapter, these issues of secularism and of neutrality as impartiality are left aside.

Moral pluralism is a pluralism of moral beliefs. In this sense, moral beliefs refer to all the beliefs that individuals can have concerning moral issues, for example the belief that all human beings deserve equal respect, the belief that one should not harm others on purpose, or the belief that the interests of other individuals, including future generations of individuals, should be taken into account to evaluate the desirability of particular actions.[2] Moral pluralism tells us that individuals disagree on moral, religious or philosophical issues. This pluralism focuses on what moral philosophers call the first-order view of morality, i.e. the question of whether a certain thing is good or not (or right or not).

Epistemological pluralism refers to disagreements about the nature and conditions of validity of moral statements.[3] It corresponds to a second-order view of morality, i.e. questions concerning the status and nature of moral statements and what it means to say that it is true that a certain thing is good. The immanent frame itself is characterized by epistemological pluralism: Taylor's focus on different epistemological perspectives (ASA: 539–593), what he calls a "closed" and an "open" perspective, is an expression of this epistemological pluralism.[4] The opposition of closed and open perspectives is based on the relation to transcendence. The open perspective is the perspective of transcendence; it is the perspective of religious believers, though not only them; the closed perspective is the perspective of immanence, and it is the perspective of those who are not religious believers, and those who subscribe to what Taylor calls "exclusive humanism." Both perspectives are related to and distinct from the immanent frame, which all individuals have in common. The immanent frame is what we all share, but it "leaves the issue open whether, for purposes of ultimate explanation, or spiritual transformation, or final sense-making, we might have to invoke something transcendent" (ASA: 594). It does not take sides between the closed and the open perspectives and considers them both as valid options. Epistemological pluralism corresponds to the fact that we consider both perspectives as equally plausible options for living a meaningful life. There can however be

---

[2] The way in which I use "belief" here therefore differs from the way in which Charles Taylor uses the concept of belief to refer to the belief in God. Moral beliefs, in my sense, include the belief in the existence of God, but they also include the belief in the non-existence of God (which Taylor labeled as "unbelief").
[3] Epistemological pluralism as I treat it here is limited to moral issues; it does not extend to the nature and conditions of validity of scientific statements.
[4] Taylor's "closed" and "open" perspectives are not only epistemological positions, they are also about what he "ha[s] called 'strong evaluation,' whereby we distinguish good and evil, noble and base, virtuous and vicious, and the like, that it distinguish between terms, one (or some) of which are in some way incommensurably higher than the other(s)" (ASA: 544). I am however singling out the epistemological dimension of these perspectives here.

"spins" of closure or openness (ASA: 550), which refer to ways of "convincing oneself that one's reading is obvious, compelling, allowing of no cavil or demurral" (ASA: 551). Taylor claims, for instance, that the spin of closure has become dominant in our contemporary societies. He criticizes this secularist spin because it "implies that one's thinking is clouded or cramped by a powerful picture which prevents one seeing important aspects of reality" (ASA: 551). Furthermore, spins of both closure and openness threaten the immanent frame and its epistemological pluralism. Respecting the epistemological pluralism of the secular age means that one should not dismiss the perspective of others, even when one is personally convinced of the truth of one's own perspective.

Both moral and epistemological pluralisms are here understood as expressing normative doctrines rather than as being simply descriptive statements. As a descriptive statement, pluralism refers to a fact: it is used to describe situations in which people actually happen to disagree about what is good (descriptive moral pluralism) as well as about how to know what is morally true (descriptive epistemological pluralism). As a normative doctrine, pluralism is the idea that such disagreements should be respected. But descriptive pluralism does not necessarily entail normative pluralism: one can accept descriptive pluralism and acknowledge that disagreements exist, and at the same time one might reject normative pluralism and claim that such disagreements should not be tolerated. Although it is expected that moral and epistemological pluralisms will exist as a matter of fact in contemporary liberal societies, *i.e.* that there will be disagreements, the more important dimension of the liberal commitment to pluralism is that these disagreements should, to a certain extent, be accepted and tolerated: liberal pluralism is both descriptive and normative. This however does not entail that liberalism is committed to metaphysical pluralism, *i.e.* to the belief that such disagreements are explained by the nature of things, by the fact that there are different moral goods that cannot be ranked or compared, and that not every moral question has a single true answer. Moral and epistemological pluralisms imply both that disagreements exist as a fact and that they should be respected, but they do not imply any claim about the nature of morality. Contrary to what the term "fact" would suggest, what Rawls (1993: 63) calls the "fact of reasonable pluralism" refers to both the descriptive and the normative versions of pluralism.[5] But beyond Taylor's immanent frame and Rawls's fact of reasonable pluralism, I believe liberalism itself is characterized by a combination of

---

5 Using "the fact of reasonable pluralism" instead of simply "pluralism" might have been motivated by the need to distinguish this view from the metaphysical version of pluralism, or value pluralism. This metaphysical pluralism is discussed later in this chapter.

both moral and epistemological pluralisms: liberals regard disagreements not as errors but as the inevitable consequence of freedom.

3 The assumptions and limitations of liberal pluralism

That modern secular societies are committed to pluralism is not very surprising: the expected response to moral and epistemological disagreements in liberalism is respect for diversity, toleration, and recognition, not repression or persecution. Pluralism is not something to be fixed.

More problematic is how liberalism justifies its commitment to pluralism. A radical and unlimited pluralism is obviously incompatible with the objective pursued by liberal political theory of a stable and fair society. Liberalism, consequently, is only committed to limited versions of pluralism: moral pluralism is limited by the normative assumptions of liberalism, and epistemological pluralism is limited by the epistemological assumptions of liberalism. These specific normative and epistemological assumptions are the basis of liberalism and they limit the ambitions of neutrality that are sometimes attached to it.

The normative dimension of liberalism is obvious: all political conceptions are moral theories. Rawls insisted however on a difference in scope between a liberal and political conception of justice and other moral conceptions: the former is limited to "the main institutions of political and social life," while the latter can extend to "the whole of life" (Rawls 1993: 175) This is why, although liberalism is committed to moral pluralism and protects the freedom of individuals to have a great range of different moral beliefs, certain moral beliefs are considered incompatible with liberal basic norms. The liberal state cannot prohibit directly any kind of beliefs, but it does prohibit certain types of practices or behaviors that are based on illiberal beliefs. This, however, does not entail that liberal basic norms are considered as being true in any sense. We might consider them as valid because they are shared by the majority of the population in our societies, because they are the result of our particular cultures, or because we think they fit well with how we subjectively understand the good life.

The same kind of limitation applies to epistemological pluralism. Just as not all moral beliefs are compatible with liberal moral beliefs, not all moral epistemologies are compatible with liberal moral epistemology. However, both liberal moral beliefs and liberal moral epistemology are very limited. In the case of liberal moral beliefs, there is a set of basic norms that are considered as being shared by all, although they are not enough to design any full understanding of the good life. In the case of the liberal moral epistemology, what is required is not the imposition but the rejection of a specific moral epistemology. The liberal commitment to (limited) moral pluralism is only possible if liberalism itself is based on a specific epistemological assumption: moral epistemologies that do not accept moral pluralism are considered as invalid from the perspective of the liberal state. Or, in Rawls's words, we should accept the burdens of judgment and "recognize the practical impossibility of reaching reasonable and workable political agreement in judgment on the truth of comprehensive doctrines"(Rawls 1993: 63).

Some commentators on Rawls have convincingly argued that the burdens of judgment are not neutral or uncontroversial. Leif Wenar, for example, has claimed that some religious believers might reject these burdens of judgment:

> The difficulty is that religious doctrines typically deny that the burdens of judgment obtain. This, on reflection, should not be surprising. The burdens of judgment are meant to explain (among other pluralisms) why some people believe in one faith, while others believe in other faiths, and still others are agnostics and atheists. The explanation essentially says that questions about religion – about which is the truth faith, if any have truth at all – are hard to think through even under the best of conditions. [...] By contrast, a religious doctrine – as a purportedly authoritative guide to moral requirements and/or salvation – characteristically presents itself as universally accessible to clear minds and open hearts (Wenar 1995: 43–44).

Although Wenar is right to point out the conflict between liberal epistemological assumptions and certain moral epistemologies, his focus on religion is misleading: in fact, some religious doctrines might accept the implications of the burdens of judgment and some secular doctrines might not.

There is however one specific moral epistemology that is always incompatible with the liberal epistemological assumptions. This moral epistemology is a combination of monism, *i.e.* the belief that there is only one single moral truth, with moral anti-skepticism, *i.e.* the belief that moral knowledge is possible. Let's call this moral epistemology anti-pluralism: the implication of the combination of monism with anti-skepticism is that moral or epistemological pluralism can never be justified. Those who are anti-pluralists reject all moral beliefs that are not supported by their anti-pluralism: for example if they believe that x is morally wrong, they will consider that they know this to be true, that it is therefore also true for everyone else and that disagreements about this belief should not be accepted. They apply to morality what we commonly apply to science: when I have knowledge about something, I am not expecting any disagreement about it. There can be no reasonable disagreement about my belief that water boils at 100 degrees Celsius at sea level, because I am actually justified in holding this belief, and I can provide the adequate evidence to support my belief. Whoever rejects this belief is not merely disagreeing with me, he is actually wrong. With the same reasoning, moral anti-pluralists believe there can be no reasonable disagreements about moral beliefs, because they have knowledge of them and because there cannot be several true answers to a single moral question. For the same reason, they reject all moral epistemologies that are incompatible with monism or with moral anti-skepticism.

Some might argue that liberalism is based on an epistemological abstinence rather than on a specific and contestable epistemological assumption, that it is a "freestanding view" (Rawls 1993: 10): why would the liberal state necessarily rely on the invalidity of anti-pluralism? Why isn't it enough to abstain from assessing its validity, the same way that the immanent frame abstains from choosing between belief and unbelief? Because "not choosing" is in itself a choice or, in the words of the fictional character quoted at the beginning of this chapter, saying that there is no official religion is in fact in itself not neutral towards religion: it is not simply that we disagree, but rather that we agree to disagree. If neutrality means independence from particular normative or epistemological claims, then putting belief and unbelief on the same level and claiming that "justice requires that a modern democracy keep an equal distance from different faith positions" (ASA: 532) is far from being a neutral claim. The necessity to consider that anti-pluralism, from the perspective of liberalism, is invalid, comes from the fact that it is incompatible with the idea that different faith positions, or moral beliefs, should be treated equally: liberalism rejects anti-pluralism because anti-pluralism implies that we disagree to disagree. Consequently, although the recognition that liberalism is based on controversial normative and epistemological assumptions does rightly put into question the extent to which liberalism can claim to be neutral, there can be no alternative to this. This foundational breach of neutrality is not a flaw; it is a necessary feature of any possible version of liberalism.

4 The difference between liberal and metaphysical pluralisms

The challenge for liberalism is to find the right balance between its controversial assumptions and its commitment to pluralism. The only acceptable controversial assumptions are precisely those that make its commitment to pluralism possible. But there are several ways to justify liberal pluralism: which one is the most appropriate for liberalism?

Liberal pluralism starts from the idea that moral and epistemological disagreements are the logical consequence of freedom because human beings are unable to reach agreement about moral beliefs and about moral epistemologies. This inability can result from any of the following three hypotheses about morality:

(1) There are many different things that are morally true: this plurality of incommensurable moral goods explains that there is no single true answer to every moral issue. It is possible to know what these goods are, but there is no correct way to rank them and therefore, whenever they conflict, there will be disagreements among individuals about how to reconcile them or prioritize them. This is the pluralistic hypothesis, defended by many liberals such as Isaiah Berlin, Charles Larmore or Joseph Raz.

(2) There is no such thing as moral knowledge, and therefore moral beliefs are neither true nor false. Morality is not an objective reality, it is something that is created by human beings and therefore varies from one situation to the other, depending on different individuals, cultures, etc. This is the relativistic hypothesis, defended by Richard Rorty.

(3) Even if there is a moral truth, even if there is one single true answer to every moral question we have, the limits of human understanding are such that we can never demonstrate or prove that a moral statement is true. We are unable to have knowledge about morality because it is a feature of morality itself that it cannot be objectively known in the way we can have knowledge about scientific or factual statements. This is the skeptical hypothesis, defended by Brian Barry. I argue that this is also the hypothesis put forward by Rawls and by Taylor,[6] although both might reject the term "skeptical."

The first hypothesis, although it is also called pluralism, is different from the moral and epistemological pluralisms identified earlier. Moral and epistemological pluralisms were normative claims; this new type of pluralism is a metaphysical and meta-ethical claim, usually referred to in philosophy as value pluralism. George Crowder defines this value pluralism as "a thesis about the nature of value, the idea that values cannot be reduced to any single hierarchy or frictionless system, but are on the contrary irreducibly multiple and permanently liable

---

6 There are obviously many differences between Rawls and Taylor. Their main area of agreement is justified by their shared commitment to the core claims of liberalism (that the main political objective is the protection and guarantee of equal individual liberties and that government should therefore be limited). It is because of this commitment that they their conceptions of justice start from a similar kind of skepticism. This is however compatible with the fact that they then develop diverging understandings of liberalism.

to come into conflict with one another" (Crowder 1994: 293). It is true that moral and epistemological pluralisms follow logically from metaphysical pluralism: if disagreements are explained by the way morality really is, there can be nothing we can do to obtain agreements about moral issues under conditions of freedom. The deeply controversial character of metaphysical pluralism is however obvious, even for those who, like Charles Larmore, think it is a valid metaphysical claim:

> Indeed, value pluralism is itself the sort of philosophical view about which reasonable people are bound to be divided. It may well be correct (I count myself among its adherents), but certainly many religious and philosophical doctrines, having their own plausibility, will continue to oppose it, seeing the human good as fundamentally a matter of a single and ultimate end, such as serving God, exercising reason, or enjoying pleasure (Larmore 2008: 142).

As Larmore has noted, such a metaphysical pluralism is bluntly incompatible with many religious and philosophical doctrines[7] that reject the idea that there is more than one single morality and one true answer to each moral question. Because metaphysical pluralism is so divisive, Larmore rightfully concludes that "liberalism must aim to make its guiding principles independent of it" (Larmore 1996: 155): it follows that the justification for the liberal commitment to moral and epistemological pluralisms must be found elsewhere.

The two remaining hypotheses to justify the liberal commitment to moral and epistemological pluralisms are relativism and skepticism. It is important to explain the difference between both terms. Relativism and skepticism are sometimes considered as being very close: Catriona McKinnon defines relativism as a form of what she calls metaphysical skepticism.[8] Admittedly, both are based on the idea that there can be no objective knowledge of morality. In the way I use these terms, skepticism is however only an epistemological claim about the impossibility of knowledge of morality, whereas relativism is always a metaphysical claim concerning the inexistence of a moral reality. Skepticism is about what we can know, while relativism is about how things are. Metaphysical skepticism is therefore a form of relativism, since it "relates to *what there is*, morally speaking,

---

[7] "Whether true or false, pluralism is an eminently controversial doctrine. It has been, as Berlin has emphasized, a peripheral view in the history of Western thought. It is incompatible with the religious orthodoxies that have sought in God the single, ultimately harmonious origin of good." (Larmore 1996: 154)

[8] She writes that "metaphysical ethical skepticism can be divided into at least two further camps: subjectivism and relativism." (McKinnon 2006: 35) Based on the distinction that I use, skepticism and relativism are different and subjectivism is a form of relativism.

and what we mean when we talk about what exists in the moral universe" (McKinnon 2006: 35).

Because it is a metaphysical claim, relativism is as problematic as value pluralism as a basis for the commitment to pluralism: not only is it rejected by anti-pluralists, but it is also rejected by value pluralists. It is too divisive and, like value pluralism, it cannot be the reason why liberalism accepts moral and epistemological pluralisms.

The argument defended in this chapter is that the liberal commitment to pluralism is based on the assumption of epistemological skepticism. Rawls and many other liberal political theorists have claimed that liberalism does not entail skepticism.[9] I believe however that this is because of a confusion between epistemological and metaphysical versions of skepticism and that a limited version of epistemological skepticism can be found in Rawls's political liberalism like in Taylor's immanent frame.

The epistemological skepticism that I am defending here is different in two ways from Rawls's understanding of the concept of skepticism. First, it does not entail that there is no moral truth, since this would be a metaphysical claim. Second, and following from the first point, it also does not imply that we should stop considering that our moral beliefs can be true. This means that we should acknowledge that we will never have the adequate evidence[10] to establish this truth and therefore obtain an agreement among all individuals about it. In other words, epistemological skepticism entails that we are unable to show to all other citizens why our moral belief is true, but it does not entail that we should "be hesitant and uncertain, much less skeptical, about our own beliefs" (Rawls 1993: 63), that we should question the fact that certain moral beliefs can be true.

Let's take the example of Mary. Mary is Catholic: she was raised in the Catholic faith, she shares the beliefs that are characteristic of Catholicism and she tries as much as possible to live her life according to what she believes is the way in which God wants her to live her life. Mary is absolutely certain that her religious beliefs are true. However, there are many individuals in her society who do not agree that these beliefs are true. Mary is aware of the existence of

---

9 "Skepticism must be avoided" (Rawls 1993: 62); "none of the varieties of skepticism considered here clearly provides a successful justification of toleration." (McKinnon 2006: 50)
10 The first item on the list of Rawls's burdens of judgment is that "the evidence – empirical and scientific – bearing on the case is conflicting and complex, and thus hard to assess and evaluate." (Rawls 1993: 56) The other items on this list seem to all be, to some extent, the consequence of this. For this reason, I believe that Rawls's burdens of judgment are a version of the weak epistemological skepticism identified here.

such disagreements: she sees that there is a plurality of moral beliefs in her society. But beyond this mere recognition of this moral diversity, Mary understands why certain people disagree with her: they had a different life, a different childhood, different kinds of experiences and particular events that led them to hold different beliefs. Besides, she believes that she is unable to prove the truth of the existence of God: she understands her Catholic faith as being based on belief, precisely because her religion cannot be objectively demonstrated. This however does not entail that she should give up her beliefs, or that she should hold them with less certainty. Mary still believes that her specific moral beliefs are true, she still believes that anyone disagreeing with her religious beliefs is wrong, but she also accepts that she is unable to prove them wrong. This distinction between moral truth and the demonstration that there is a moral truth, which is what is required by knowledge, is what characterizes epistemological skepticism.

The same epistemological moral skepticism is found in Taylor's description of the immanent frame:

> My understanding of the immanent frame is that, properly understood, it allows of both readings, without compelling us to either. If you grasp our predicament without ideological distortion, and without blinders, then you see that going one way or another requires what is often called a "leap of faith" (ASA: 550).

This is Taylor's response to those who believe that "the immanent frame calls out for one reading," a closed one, and present that reading as being "natural, logically unavoidable" (ASA: 500). In fact, Taylor argues, the immanent frame does not take sides in the diversity of perspectives: it is even characterized by the fact that it would be impossible to justify the validity of one of them. The illusion that the immanent frame pushes us more toward one position than toward the other is therefore something Taylor worries about: whether the "spin" (ASA: 551) is secularist or not, the problem is that it violates the epistemological skepticism of the immanent frame.

Epistemological skepticism does not entail the claim that there is no moral truth. In fact, although both Rawls and Taylor seem to share the epistemological assumptions of this weak version of skepticism, they are not themselves skeptics: both personally hold the belief that there are moral truths, that moral statements can appropriately be described as being more or less true or correct. However, these metaphysical hypotheses shared by both philosophers are incompatible with the ambitions of the liberalism they both defend. They are therefore excluded from the set of liberal assumptions: appealing to such metaphysical hypotheses in an argument aiming at the justification of political authority would mean abandoning the liberal framework.

5 Concluding remarks

The analysis of the implications of the kind of pluralism characterizing the secular age leads us to acknowledge the specific moral and epistemological assumptions that justify the liberal commitment to pluralism. Liberalism, however, being committed to the largest range of moral and epistemological beliefs possible, cannot be based on metaphysical claims: such claims are too divisive, and they are not necessary to justify pluralism. Liberalism rests instead on normative and epistemological assumptions that are more limited in scope than metaphysical claims. Although liberalism is not neutral, in the sense that it is not independent from all controversial claims (normative, epistemological and metaphysical), it is at least more impartial than any other political doctrine because it is non-metaphysical or, at least, weakly metaphysical.[11]

This impartiality is, however, itself justified by the normative and epistemological assumptions of liberalism: in other words, there is no neutral justification for it. For this reason, the liberal state is not expected to treat equally practices that respect liberal basic norms and practices that do not. The limits of toleration are set by specifically liberal assumptions. Such assumptions might be rightfully considered as controversial claims, and some will reject the idea of equality or the idea that certain disagreements should be accepted: those people cannot expect to benefit from an impartial treatment, since impartiality itself is based on the specific claims they reject.

There are also in our liberal societies many individuals who reject the epistemological assumptions of liberalism: they are anti-pluralists and believe that disagreements about morality are never justified. Such anti-pluralists include for example many religious believers but also those who believe in certain versions of positivism and utilitarianism.[12] Should all citizens acknowledge the validity of the liberal epistemological assumption that makes pluralism possible? Rawls and many other liberals believe they should: acknowledging the burdens of judgment is part of what he calls being reasonable.[13]

---

[11] I do not want to make any claim in this chapter about whether liberalism can be *completely* independent from metaphysical claims.
[12] Religious doctrines, positivism and utilitarianism are however not necessarily anti-pluralist: many believe that although there is one single moral truth, it cannot always be known with absolute certainty or at least that this truth cannot always be demonstrated and established.
[13] "The first basic aspect of the reasonable, then is the willingness to propose fait terms of cooperation and to abide by them provided others do. The second basic aspect, as I review now, is the willingness to recognize the burdens of judgment and to accept their consequences for the

But this raises the question: what happens if I do not accept such consequences? What if I am convinced that pluralism is not justified and that disagreements are simply the result of errors of reasoning or ignorance?

The answer is that nothing actually happens to the individuals who reject pluralism. The combination of monism and moral anti-skepticism is in fact a moral epistemology that is itself tolerated in the name of epistemological pluralism: it cannot be recognized as valid from the impersonal and abstract perspective of liberalism, but there is no reason that the same should apply to individuals themselves. However, since liberalism itself is based on the rejection of this anti-pluralism, the institutions of the liberal society should also reflect this rejection and the liberal commitment to moral and epistemological pluralism. At no point in the process of making and justifying decisions is it ever justified to question liberal pluralism. This is why "the language of some public bodies, for instance courts, has to be free from premises drawn from one or other position" (ASA: 532): the immanent frame has to remain a frame in which different options are considered as valid, and therefore it should "avoid favoring or disfavoring not just religious positions but any basic position, religious or nonreligious" (Taylor 2011: 37).[14] If we want to take liberal pluralism seriously, then our official position has to be no position at all.

Bibliography

Barry, Brian. 1995. *Justice as Impartiality*. Oxford: Oxford University Press.
Crowder, George. 1994. "Pluralism and Liberalism." *Political Studies* 42 no. 2: 293–305.
Larmore, Charles. 1996. *The Morals of Modernity*. New York: Cambridge University Press.
Larmore, Charles. 2008. *The Autonomy of Morality*. Cambridge: Cambridge University Press.
Maclure, Jocelyn, and Charles Taylor. 2011. *Secularism and Freedom of Conscience*. Cambridge: Harvard University Press.
Matravers, Matt, and Susan Mendus. 2003. "The reasonableness of pluralism," in *The Culture of Toleration in Diverse Societies*, ed. Catriona McKinnon and Dario Castiglione, 38–53. Manchester: Manchester University Press,
McKinnon, Catriona. 2002. *Liberalism and the Defense of Political Constructivism*. Basingstoke: Palgrave Macmillan.

---

use of public reason in directing the legitimate exercise of political power in a constitutional regime." (Rawls 1993: 54)

14 It is important to note, however, that Taylor believes this independence from different particular and controversial positions is only necessary for the liberal state itself, for "the language in which legislation, administrative decrees, and court judgments must be couched" (Taylor 2011: 50). It does not imply that there is a moral duty for citizens to refrain from appealing to such positions, as in Rawls's public reason (Rawls 1993: 212–254).

McKinnon, Catriona. 2003. "Toleration and the character of pluralism," in *The Culture of Toleration in Diverse Societies*, ed. Catriona McKinnon and Dario Castiglione, 54–70. Manchester: Manchester University Press.

McKinnon, Catriona. 2006. *Toleration: A Critical Introduction*. London: Routledge.

Rawls, John. 1993. *Political Liberalism*. New York: Columbia University Press.

Raz, Joseph. 1990. "Facing Diversity: The Case of Epistemic Abstinence." *Philosophy & Public Affairs* 19 no.1: 3–46.

Taylor, Charles. 2011. "Why We Need a Radical Redefinition of Secularism," in *The Power of Religion in the Public Sphere*, ed. Eduardo Mendieta and Jonathan VanAntwerpan, 34–59. New York: Columbia University Press.

The West Wing. Episode no. 136 "Mr. Frost," first broadcast 16 October 2005 by NBC. Directed by Andrew Bernstein and written by Aaron Sorkin.

Wenar, Leif. 1995. "Political Liberalism: An Internal Critique." *Ethics* 106 no.1: 32–62.

Marian Burchardt
Does Religion need Rehabilitation? Charles Taylor and the Critique of Secularism

1 Introduction

Between 2006 and 2014, Quebec – Charles Taylor's home – has witnessed some of the fiercest political debates about secularism and public religion in recent history. In this chapter, I explore how *A Secular Age* is related to the normative claims made in these debates and to Taylor's own political interventions in them. Similar to other Western societies, contestations about secularism in Quebec are characterized by the fact that they drew on divergent understandings of 'the secular.' In other words, participants in these discourses crafted divergent versions of secularism as a "problem-space" (Agrama 2012). As I will show, centered on the notion of emancipation from religion on the one hand and respect for religious diversity on the other, these discourses feed on collective memories that were mobilized to buttress the claims made in their name.

While recognizing the legitimacy of open versions of secularism and liberal nationalism, Taylor argues that strong versions of secularism, based on the idea of emancipation from religion, reify secularism as a goal and institutional arrangement in its own right while in reality it should be subservient to promoting the values of liberty, equality, and solidarity. Interestingly, whereas in powerful traditions of European thought religion was viewed as playing an ambiguous, if not detrimental, role in the promotion of these values, these assumptions are currently being reassessed and sometimes reversed. Therefore, I begin by examining Taylor's contribution to the project of religion's intellectual rehabilitation and suggest sociological perspectives on it. The second part of this essay explores how in public discourse in Quebec this rehabilitation underwrites the project to respect and promote religious diversity, and how this project clashes with historically shaped and competing notions of secularity as a lever of national unity and progress.[1]

---

[1] My use of the concepts 'secularism' and 'secularity' slightly differs from Taylor's use. I explain my definitions at length on p. 149–150.

2 Secularism in *A Secular Age*

In *A Secular Age*, Taylor distinguishes among three understandings of secularity: (1) the differentiation of religion from other institutional spheres and its concomitant privatization; (2) the decline of belief in God and the decrease in participation in collective religious life; and (3) the construction of what he calls a "framework of understanding," by which he means a particular cultural horizon that shapes both non-religious and religious practices and subjectivities. It is this third dimension that interests Taylor the most. This is the "context of understanding in which our moral, spiritual or religious experience and search take place" (ASA: 3), which he refers to as the "conditions of belief." The novelty here is the evolution of an immanent frame within which belief is experienced as an option.

With its focus on the emergence of the immanent frame and the changes in the conditions of belief it spawns, *A Secular Age* is in an important sense a philosophical critique of sociological secularization narratives. It provides a phenomenological account of how belief came to be experienced as an option against the backdrop of a world in which a purely immanent understanding of human flourishing, captured by Taylor in the notion of "exclusive humanism," as all "there is" (ASA: 7), and in which this understanding is not only possible but widely taken for granted. Certainly, in *A Secular Age* Taylor also addresses the relationship between cognitive concerns over religion as belief and political concerns over religion as church and community. He argues that the emergence of autonomous public spheres, national communities, and sovereign states all presupposed the construction of a historical time that was independent of the higher times of God, as well as a social space that would be accessible to people independently from church hierarchies, and he traces these transformations to the drive to "Reform, with a capital R" (ASA: 62) as one of the key sources of modern secularity.

While the book is not primarily a story about secularism as a "principle of statecraft" (Casanova 2009: 1049), it does provide some clues that feed into, and hence help us understand, Taylor's normative stance in the debates over secularism in Quebec. There are three points I deem central. First, Taylor focuses on the question of how secularity could become such an extremely important category of self-understanding, self-description, and interpretation within the modern West. This is, in a fundamental sense, different from the usual sociological exercise of observing aspects of religious life and 'defining' changes as 'amounting to' the rise of secularity. By adopting this reflexive mode, which for the study of secularity was first developed by Talal Asad (2003) and scholars in critical religious studies (Masuzawa 2005), Taylor gives further impetus to a way of construing secularity that was in fact pioneered in theorizations of modernity. These intellectual movements are epitomized in Peter Wagner's book *Modernity as Experience and Interpretation* (2008), which turns on the ways in which people come to see, or aspire to see, themselves as modern – mainly through their ways of being positioned in particular historical events.

Secondly, Taylor consciously writes from an engaged point of view as a practicing Catholic (ASA: 437). While recognizing the power of the immanent frame, he expresses the clear intuition (if that oxymoron is permissible) that the life of the believer has a somewhat richer and deeper level of experience, perhaps by virtue of the believer's realization of her or his dependence on a higher power enforcing a commitment to goals that transcend human flourishing alone, and her or his *openness* to these goals. This is different from exclusive humanism, which Taylor describes as underpinned by "closed world structures" (ASA: 507). There is thus, in Taylor, a preferential option for belief.

Thirdly, Taylor insists that the perspective of disengagement is itself historically constructed, emerging precisely from the drive to reform and the subsequent stages of what he calls the "Ancién Regime," the "Age of Mobilization," and the "Age of Authenticity" with its "expressive revolution" (Parsons 1973). Disengagement makes possible claims to neutrality, but according to Taylor it also largely prefigures and *constrains* the analysis of the immanent frame. What is more, the notion of neutrality hinges on the historical construction of disengaged reason: "The sense that we have reached maturity in casting aside faith can be played out in the register of disengaged reason, and the need to accept the deliverances of neutral science, whatever they may be" (ASA: 588). A more complete account of the modern age, Taylor insists, requires an emphatic engagement with both religious and nonreligious perspectives. He criticizes sociological accounts because they are, by virtue of their commitment to the ethics of neutrality, inclined towards secularity. (He feels especially offended by those, like Weber, who claim that certain kinds of religion may in the last instance not stand up intellectually to rational science, or at least only stand up at the price of terrible intellectual dilemmas and inconsistencies to be paid by those who cannot bear the fate of times.) As we will see, Taylor's criticism of Quebecois secularists is partially borne from the same idea, namely that secularists falsely claim to occupy the grounds of universal reason and neutrality, while in reality the secular argument in favor of a public sphere emptied of religious signs is itself particularistic.

In another publication, Taylor (2011a) explicitly called for "a radical redefinition of secularism." Here, he argues that secularism can be explored from the point of view of its three goals, "which we can class in the three categories of the

French Revolutionary trinity: liberty, equality, fraternity" (2011a: 34). One of the key problems with secularism as it is understood in contemporary politics and social science in the West is according to Taylor the fetishization of a particular historically inherited institutional arrangement, namely the separation of church and state. Instead of being an end in itself, Taylor suggests, secularism should always be a means to the realization of these values. I agree with these arguments, but I am not confident that Taylor's conclusion is based on an adequate reading of the sociological debate. In order to better appreciate Taylor's partisan scholarship, I will briefly reconsider how it relates to its normative dimensions.

3 Objects of critique

The critique of classical secularization theory, as affirmed by Taylor, can be crystallized into three fundamental objections concerning respectively (a) its alleged universalism, (b) its underlying teleology and evolutionism, and (c) its modernist normative bias. Importantly, however, these critiques are themselves highly normative. While the secularization paradigm is often considered Eurocentric and antireligious, recent research generally fashions itself as sympathetic towards religion. Many studies create the impression that there is not only a 'natural' religiosity among populations worldwide but also an ideological secularism founded on an alliance between political and academic elites (Hjelm 2014). This idea underpins, for instance, Peter Berger's widely used notion of "The De-secularization of the World" (1999), in which he argued that secularity as a worldview was largely limited to the "faculty club" and that it was secularity, not religious vitality, that was in need of sociological explanation.

However, in Berger and others empirical description is often confounded with, or motivated by, pro-religious politics. More precisely, compared to earlier debates recent contributions engender an inversion of the subject and object of the critique: whereas secularism used to be regarded as a means of liberation from the constraints of traditional and religious authority, religion now appears as a space of freedom, and secularism as an instrument of regimentation and exclusion (Mahmood 2006; 2010). The heightened awareness of secularism's articulation with power relations and knowledge regimes, including the production of religious forms of subjectivity and expression that are compatible with liberal modernity, leads to one-sidedness when it downplays the autonomy associated with modernity and secularity. The triumphalism with which some scholars have generally endorsed the new significance and visibility of religion is closely associated with the symbolic rehabilitation of their research subject and its presumed ability to question social boundaries in new ways. More importantly still, for some it is associated with the notion that the rehabilitation of religion feeds into new forms of empowerment of the oppressed (critically see Tugal 2007). In the debates on religion and immigration (Levitt 2007), religion and democracy (Ranger 2008), and religion and development (Deneulin and Bano 2009), religious identities and forms of association are construed in these terms.

In this context, it seems to me that the contemporary sociological and anthropological critique of power and the state is understood better if it is viewed less through the angle of its object than its subject. In sociology, critical social theory and research suffered heavily from the end of the Cold War and the end of the socialist dream. While some critical energy was channeled into the support of new social movements, especially those of the World Social Forum variety, it was also directed to supporting religious groups viewed as suffering at the hands of oppressive secularist and undemocratic states that act to curtail individual and collective freedoms in order to secure their sovereign power (Bader 2007). Within sociological and anthropological discourse and its enthusiasm for religion's emancipation, state power over religion came to be taken for granted; meanwhile the power of religion over people was largely obliterated as a field of concern. This seems to hold even if we take the critical scholarship on fundamentalism into account. As a critical concept, fundamentalism has for many reasons largely disappeared from scholarly debates, while the most extreme manifestations of its subject matter, such as violent religious radicalism, are now mostly treated as lying outside the realm of religion proper; terrorism now comes under the purview of security studies, for example.

Today, the diverse political imperatives behind the promotion of religious diversity are accompanied by the confluence of diverse culturalized strands of identity politics on the one hand (European Christian conservative, Islamic), and the rise of religion as a category of legal protection against discrimination in western judicial politics and minority rights, and human rights discourses more broadly, on the other. These imperatives powerfully remind us of earlier shifts from the politics of redistribution to that of recognition that Nancy Fraser began analyzing more than two decades ago (Fraser 1995; 2009). As claims in the name of religion have acquired greater legitimacy (Koenig 2005), in religiously diverse liberal polities people are increasingly incited to understand themselves as religious beings and to construe their participation in society in terms accruing from religious membership: interfaith forums acquire greater visibility and political traction as representations of society (Griera 2012); the incorporation of migrant groups qua religious communities in the public institutions of state and civil society within the framework of religious diversity is deemed increasingly important for social cohesion (Bowen et al. 2013; Burchardt and Michalowski 2014); simultaneously, native Europeans, and Quebeckers too as I will show below, are called to recall and identify with their Christian, or 'Judeo-Christian', culture in discourses that turn religious patrimony into cultural heritage (van den Hemel 2014; Zubrzycki 2012).

Beaman (2013) calls this discursive assemblage "the will to religion," which should be analyzed in terms of "obligatory religious citizenship." In a similar vein, and with regard to Islam specifically, Tezcan (2007) noted how religion is being increasingly conceptualized as a resource in liberal governmentality in an effort to secure the social order. Such transformations can be observed in the practices of "government through community" (Tezcan 2007: 59) and the rise of interreligious dialogues, which prefigure the shift from "race" to "faith" and are premised on the construction of a *Homo Islamicus* of sorts.[2] In the field of urban policy (Eade 2011) and discussions about the presumed failure of multiculturalism (Grillo 2010) as well, the discourses and categories of religion replace the language of race. In order to understand these shifts, which run in parallel to the transformation of "community" from natural spontaneous social units into a mode of governance, it is important to recall their links with the premises of liberal governmentality. "Individuals are to be governed through their freedom," as Rose (1996: 41) noted from a Foucauldian perspective a while ago, "but neither as isolated atoms of classical political economy, nor as citizens of society, but as members of heterogeneous communities of allegiance."

If one wishes to gain a better understanding of the power and significance of religion today while at the same time reflexively and critically exploring the *doxa* of the construction of religion as a research subject, one should scrutinize the ways in which not only the secular state but religion itself is implicated in technologies of governmentality and of categorizing, classifying, naming, and rendering legible people through and with religion.

The project of the "rehabilitation of religion" in scholarly and academic debate, that is, the exorcizing of what remained of Weberian intellectualist arrogance, has in the meantime advanced in a way that appears to take some of the wind out of Taylor's sails. Contrary to what Taylor suggests in *A Secular Age*, the rejection of secularization has *already* turned into a new orthodoxy, not only analytically but normatively as well. One of the consequences of this is that, with very few exceptions, scholars rarely explore religion in terms of power and authority other than in triumphalist ways (as typically in research on global Pentecostalism). Taylor too only mentions religious domination as an aspect of past history (2011a: 48). In a few important ways, his account there-

---

[2] On the British variant of this story, see Schönwälder (2007).

fore misses some of the turns the debate has taken over recent years (see also Koenig in this volume).

I concur with Taylor that in their specific variations, secularities are very likely outcomes of sometimes latent, sometimes overt and ongoing social conflicts between different groups, which cannot but sustain the institutionalized and public interfaces of religion and other social spheres (Wohlrab-Sahr et al. 2008). What is more, in some sense the entanglements of religion and secularity, as manifested, for instance, in public discussions, with their multiplicity of religious and non-religious voices, do not disprove but *confirm* the notion of the "secular/religious divide" (Beyer 2013), or religious-secular distinctions. It is in and through these controversies that the boundaries between religion and secularity are established, contested, negotiated and recomposed (Göle 2010: 44; Schenk et al. 2015).

In addition, it is certainly necessary to dismantle some of the public myths and narratives about secularism in Europe and elsewhere, of which ideas about the internal connections between secularism, modernity, progress and democracy, as well as the notion of secularism as providing *per se* equal opportunities and equitable religious freedoms, are the most powerful ones. Simultaneously, however, from a sociological point of view the entanglements of religion and politics as we find them in state regulations and the policing of religion are hardly surprising. They are in fact an inevitable component of the religious–secular divide, which is why they cannot obliterate it. A long time ago, Georg Simmel ([1909]1994) cogently and felicitously captured the simultaneity of connection and separation through the metaphors of the door and the bridge. "There is no real unity in space," Simmel wrote; "[o]nly man, as opposed to nature, has the faculty of binding and unbinding, and in this specific manner: that one is always the presupposition of the other. By disengaging two things from the undisturbed state of nature, in order to designate them 'separate,' we have already related them to each other in our awareness. We have differentiated them both, together, from everything that lies between them" (5). Contrary to Stark (1999) and others, I am therefore highly sympathetic to Casanova's insistence that abandoning the notions of secularization and the secular would impoverish the sociological study of religion and that these notions continue to be useful "as an analytical framework for a comparative research agenda that aims to examine the historical transformations of all world religion under conditions of modern structural differentiation" (2006: 19).

More generally, empirical and analytical critiques of secularization theories as inaccurate or reductive have been enmeshed with normative critiques of secularism as oppressive, partial, and particularistic. Together they have formed an anti-secularist affect in contemporary academia that produces narratives that are sometimes as contradictory as the secularist pretensions they are seeking to dismantle (Gourgouris 2008: 453). On the one hand, the secular is seen as vanishing, either empirically through global religious revivals (Berger 1999), or conceptually through the genealogical deconstruction of its epistemological assumptions. On the other hand, especially in governmentality-inspired accounts of the powers of the secular modern, secularism is seen as omnipotent in shaping and regulating "religious subjectivities, practices, and forms of life" (Mahmood 2008: 464), as well as in producing religious sensibilities that are compatible with sovereign state power under the regime of political liberalism. In many of these accounts, this power is rooted in Christianity, which "turned against itself in a complex and ambivalent series of parallel movements, continuous gestures and rituals, reformist and counterreformist, or revolutionary and not so revolutionary upheavals and reversals while slowly coming to name that to which it ultimately claimed to oppose itself: religion. [...] Christianity [...] reincarnated itself as secular" (Anidjar 2006: 59–60). In these analyses, religious identities, practices and expressions are always already products of the alignments of secularism, state power and empire, rendering the historical variations of secularism negligible in both form and degree.[3] In this perspective, even US foreign policy under George W. Bush, with its explicit Christian legitimizing formulae of military interventions, becomes a secularist project (Mahmood 2006). Are these the powers of the secular-modern?

The first of these perspectives, the idea that secularity vanishes through religious revivals, misses the point that religion rather becomes contemporaneous with the secular modern (Göle 2010: 44). Governmentalist perspectives, meanwhile, sometimes underestimate the internal variations of secularism or fail to capture and theorize the multiple resistances to secularist state power, the indigenizations and transmutations of secularism outside the western world, as well as the manifold pragmatic compromises between religious and secular claims (Casanova 2006). I now turn to the analysis of these clashes and compromises in Quebec.

4 Contesting secularism in Quebec: cultural memory and religious diversity

Like many other western societies, Quebec has experienced heated debates about the appropriate place of religion in society. Especially since 2006, these

---

[3] For this criticism see also Casanova (2006).

debates have been framed in the language of secularism, and it was generally assumed that they were mainly responses to new forms of migration-driven religious diversity. In modern Quebec, there is a powerful tradition of the participation of public intellectuals in such controversies. With regard to concerns over religion, this could be witnessed in the case of the school commission that was tasked with preparing the secularization of the public schools system, and more especially with the appointment in 2007 of Charles Taylor and sociologist Gerard Bouchard to head a commission to investigate practices of "reasonable accommodation" that had triggered a major media uproar in the preceding period. In their report entitled "Building the Future" (2008), Taylor and Bouchard promoted a balance between individual rights to freedom of religion and the need for secular state authorities. Similarly, with regard to majority-minority relationships, Taylor and Bouchard supported the position of liberal nationalism that accepts the right to cultural precedence of the majority, as expressed through the privileged position of the French language, while simultaneously granting minorities the right to express their culture in public institutions. The report also stated that the presumed "crisis of secularism" was largely a "crisis of perception" driven by biased media coverage.

However, the conflicts surrounding secularism in Quebec reached a new climax when, in September 2013, after several announcements and leakages of information, first informally and later in a near-perfect, spin doctor-driven fashion, the then-government of Pauline Marois and her Parti Quebecois presented its ideas for a "Charter of Quebec Values" to Quebec's parliament. In doing so, it took a first step in fulfilling promises made during the electoral campaign in the run-up to the provincial elections in September 2012 to ban all ostentatious religious symbols for public-sector employees, whether judges or nursery teachers, if they were voted into office. During the campaign the project was still called the "Charter of Secularism."

In response, numerous civil-society organizations and initiatives started to challenge the moral and political premises of this proposal and to campaign against it. The involvement of intellectuals became crucial in shaping these debates. Taylor was one who became very active in these campaigns, giving interviews to TV stations, signing petitions and manifestos, writing articles in the press, and speaking at public demonstrations. In these contributions Taylor emphatically rejected and condemned the proposed limitation on religious signs as discriminatory, socially divisive, and an unjustifiable infringement of religious freedom. The discussions came to a halt with the defeat of the Parti Quebecois in the provincial elections in March 2014.

Taylor's political activism, including his leadership of the Bouchard-Taylor Commission and his public pronouncements during the debates on the Charter

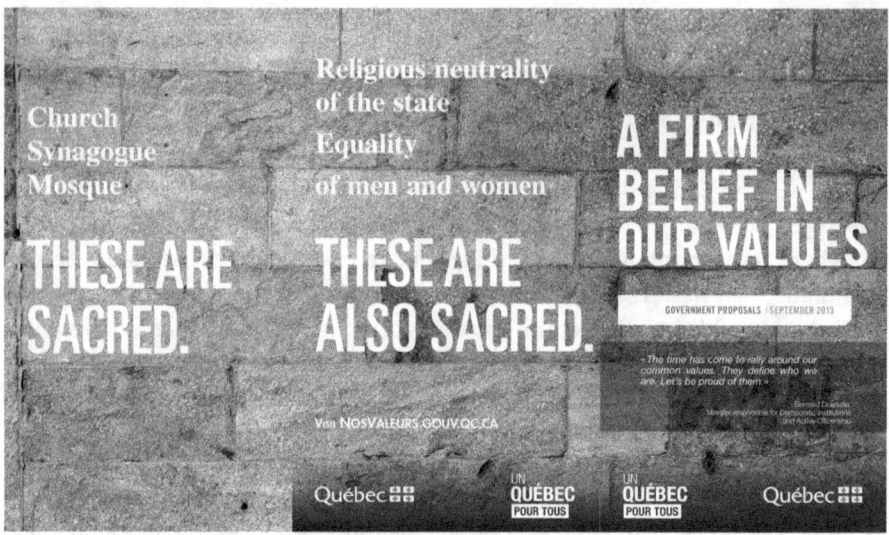

Figure 1: Billboard Poster advertising the Charter of Quebec Values

of Quebec Values, raises intriguing questions about how his active political approach relates to the normative implications of his philosophical writings on religion and secularity. Taylor is indeed very interesting to think and work with in this regard, since, together with Jürgen Habermas, José Casanova, and David Martin, he is one of the few social theorists who have explored both sociological questions of secularization *and* political-ethical questions of secularism.

While generally viewed as a milestone in sociological discussions about secularization and modernity, *A Secular Age* has been received as confirming secularization theories by some observers but as refuting them by most. Meanwhile, discussions of secularity inevitably center on particular dimensions of religious life. Taylor's key notion of "conditions of belief" seems to favor a rather cognitive reading of religion, as does his work on William James and his theory of social imaginaries as something enabling shared social practices and institutions. In *A Secular Age* Taylor compares social imaginaries to Kantian transcendental schemes. In his earlier book on the particular social imaginaries of modernity (Taylor 2004: 2), he distinguished social imaginaries from both ideas and institutions and characterized them as the deep proto-social inner side of social practices. Some sociologists (Nelson and Gorski 2014, Casanova 2010), in responding to Taylor, have emphasized conditions of belonging over conditions of belief. They suggest that the reproduction of religion depends more on collective ritual than on belief. Here I will address a third dimension, namely "forms of distinction" between religious and secular spheres of society. I draw on the notion of "multiple secularities" (Wohlrab-Sahr and Burchardt 2012) to address this third dimension. In Quebec, the contestations around different versions of *laïcité*, namely *laïcité ouverte* and *laïcité fermée*, indicate that competing rationales must be understood as competing cultural memories vying for hegemony in the public sphere.

What has happened in the contestations around secularism in Québec today has only partially to do with "religion-as-belief." Certainly that is the case for one particular group, namely secular humanists, atheists, rationalists, and their associations, who have been very vocal in campaigns in favor of the secularist Charter and even had meetings with the minister in charge of the project to present their ideas and demands. These groups focused on the intellectualist question of religion and religion's presumed epistemological errors. They tried to bring this understanding of religion into the public sphere and thus sought to manipulate circulating notions of secularity in the direction of an understanding of secularity as basic ontological ground, as the 'real' from which to draw epistemological certainty. This is expressed, for instance, in their campaigns to help people identify as atheists, especially their insistence that every non-churchgoer is a non-believer and hence an atheist.

When I talked to the Parti Quebecois government's legal advisers, in some sense the masterminds behind the party's plans for institutional secularity, they would usually state that beliefs don't matter, that beliefs are actually a private affair, and that the law is indifferent to what people believe. One may, of course, argue that it is the privilege of the non-believer to mobilize the standpoint of disinterestedness and that the presumed irrelevance of religious belief for politics is the necessary fiction of privilege, as is 'state neutrality' in all other political matters in unequal societies. At the same time, indifference towards religion is indeed much more widespread than self-conscious atheism or ethically charged secular humanism. This implies that religion is in socially, legally, and politically complex ways simultaneously private, as affirmed by Luhmann (2000) and public, as Casanova (1994) stresses.

This is not to say that belief and belonging do not matter. But I would argue that secularity as a category of modern self-understanding, a notion with which to think through and make sense of one's place in the world, acquires its particular sociological traction through the ways it articulates concerns over demarcating the religious and secular spheres, in other words, forms of distinction. Taylor too has explored the ways in which the secular figures in categorical distinctions and conceptual dyads, as well as their multiple historical transformations in the axial and postaxial period (Taylor 2011b: 32). But whereas he is mainly concerned with these distinctions in terms of conceptual history, I am interested in how such distinctions play out in political mobilizations.

With regard to political controversies over religion, Taylor (2011a: 36) has observed that "We think that secularism (or *laïcité*) has to do with the relation of the state and religion; whereas in fact it has to do with the (correct) response of the democratic state to diversity." In my view, Quebec is an excellent case with which to demonstrate that this perspective might be too narrow to account for the multiple meanings of secularism and their historical roots. From the perspective of "multiple secularities," diversity is just one reference problem of secularity among many, albeit an extremely important one. The idea of "multiple secularities" is meant to capture the structured diversity of forms in which such practices of distinguishing religious and nonreligious spheres are played out. Secularity refers to practices of drawing boundaries between these spheres, boundaries that are inevitably porous and shifting and that simultaneously redefine the meanings of religion.

To put it differently, what we need to study are the different purposes for which the category of the secular is mobilized. During the demonstrations on the streets of Montreal in the autumn of 2013, it was striking to see that both the supporters and the opponents of the Charter project defended their aims in the name of *laïcité*. In other words, the *laic*, or the secular, was mobilized for different ends. Both camps had invested deeply in the emotive power of the discourse around the secular, but contested its practical political and legal meanings.

We can use the notion of 'secularity' to capture the institutionally, culturally, and symbolically anchored forms and arrangements of differentiation between religion and other social spheres (see Asad 2003). Secularity is therefore, as Taylor has also noted, more encompassing than secularism in that it also captures the at times latent, taken-for-granted, and implicit forms of demarcating religion. Importantly, secularity as a *social practice* is linked to problems different from those of the philosophical discourse of secularism. Often, however, secularity is socially legitimized through guiding ideas that set the basic terms for practices of distinction. The idea of culturally grounded distinctions defining the conditions and the appropriate scopes, spaces and times of religious expression is obviously associated with sociological theories of differentiation, which is what Taylor terms *secularity 1*. However, in contrast to these theories, I see symbolic boundary drawing as inevitably contested, historically and culturally contingent, and reversible. This historical and cultural contingency is expressed in the idea of *multiple* secularities. Just as Shmuel N. Eisenstadt's concept of "multiple modernities" (Eisenstadt 2000) offered a way out of the crisis of modernization theories, the concept of multiple secularities could stimulate new ways of thinking about the relationships between religion and secularity in modernity beyond secularization theories.

Figure 2: Demonstrators demanding *laïcité* in a protest against the Charter of Quebec Values. Photo taken by the author in September 2013.

Secularities acquire different shapes in different countries or regions; they function according to different cultural logics that document specific social histories of conflict, as well as characteristic configurations of competing notions of secularity. Such ambivalent configuration may be among the consequences of colonial encounters or immigration. Furthermore, secularities "respond" to imagined or real problems as their reference problems and offer "solutions" to them. Obviously, these problems arise with different degrees of urgency and at different points in time.

Based on both theoretical and empirical considerations, we identify four such reference problems: (1) the problem of individual freedom in relation to dominant social units, be they groups or the state; (2) the problem of religious heterogeneity and the resulting potential or actual conflict; (3) the problem of social or national integration and development; and (4) the problem of the independent development of institutional domains (Wohlrab-Sahr and Burchardt 2012). These four problems constitute motives and provide motifs for institutionalizing distinctions between religious and non-religious social spheres. As latent motives and practices, they can certainly coexist; as overt motives and motifs, they may compete with each other. It seems, however, that under specific circumstances one of them can become dominant by being associated with a guiding idea, thereby pushing the other motifs, at least temporarily, into the background. As the case of Quebec shows, these motifs are often highly contested.

We use the formula "secularity for the sake of..." to designate such basic types. Articulating social problems, I distinguish between the following forms: (1) secularity for the sake of individual rights and liberties; (2) secularity for the sake of balancing religious diversity; (3) secularity for the sake of social integration and national development; and (4) secularity for the sake of the independence of institutional domains. The four forms are associated with different guiding ideas: (1) the ideas of freedom and individuality; (2) of tolerance and respect; (3) of progress and enlightenment; and, finally, (4) of rationality, efficiency and institutional autonomy.

In Quebec, claims made in the name of secularity arose from two fundamentally different historical and social experiences and the way they were articulated through the mobilization of collective memories. On the one hand, for the supporters of the Charter project, the meaning of secularity emerged from the history of emancipation from the domination of the Catholic Church that is stored in the memory of the modernization period starting in the late 1950s. On the other hand, for opponents of the project, secularity meant individual rights to freedom of religion and equality and drew on the discourse of inclusiveness and multiculturalism.

When investigating forms and codes of collective memory in Quebec, it is important to keep in mind that, like many European societies, processes of secularization and migration-driven religious diversification are happening at the same time. Secularization refers to institutional separations between the Catholic Church and Quebec society as well as the dimension of religious participation, which has fallen dramatically since the 1960s as part of a wider process of cultural change and modernization.[4] In public discourse, this process is understood to be part of a wider package of national emancipation and the building of a modern welfare state and is widely referred to as the "Quiet Revolution." Significantly, it is emphatically framed as a process of cultural emancipation. According to some revisionist historiography (Baum 1991; Cristiano 2007), this revolution happened "quietly" and not "loudly" because it was carried out not against the church but with its active participation, and its roots are now traced back to earlier periods in the twentieth century.

---

4 Interestingly, participation in some Catholic rituals fell more dramatically only during the past decade.

Simultaneously, the Quiet Revolution is increasingly being turned into a 'national myth,' in fact one of the most powerful national myths of Quebec in the twentieth and twenty-first centuries. This myth suggests that Quebec's national identity is born from its own secularization, particularly the nation's exit from historical "darkness."[5] For supporters of *laïcité fermée*, being a Quebecer means having gone through the school of modernity and enlightenment and, with pride, drawing on this aspect of collective subject formation. This is, for example, apparent in the very detailed presentation of the history of the Quiet Revolution in the National Museum of Civilization in Quebec City, which functions as the museum of national history. The Quiet Revolution and the process of secularization are explicitly made the subjects of historical explanation, and the entire history after the Second World War is presented from this perspective, just next to the overriding concern with independent statehood. The Quiet Revolution is thereby rendered an object of contemplation, a thing to be looked at – it is, in other words, historiographically objectified.

The periods when I did field research in Quebec, in 2012 and 2013, were rather busy times for secular activists in Quebec. "Secular activists" are people who are either members of or inhabit the cultural vicinity of associations such as Coalition Laïcité Québec, the Mouvement laïque québécois, Association humaniste du Québec, Les Intellectuels pour la laïcité, Libres penseurs athées but also feminist groups such as Éditions Sisyphe. All of the activists I interviewed are linked through either direct experiences of, or intimate connections to, the Quiet Revolution. The understanding of these experiences is often forged through anecdotes in which religion, usually Catholicism, appears as oppressive and divisive, irrational and immoral; essentially it is viewed as something belonging to the past.

Many pro-Charter activists had already participated in the hearings of the Bouchard-Taylor Commission and had later also written, discussed and submitted memoirs during the civil-society participation process surrounding "Bill 94," an earlier attempt to ban face-veils from public service interactions. In the years of my research they were then busy reading, commenting upon and signing declarations and manifestos on secularism, as well as meeting and discussing ideas and strategies surrounding the Charter of Secularism, which saw the light of day during the electoral campaigns of the Parti Quebecois in the summer of 2012. It was thus a time when the narratives and discourses of secularism were very present and very much in the (re-)making.

---

5 Related to this, see the discourse on "la grande noirceur."

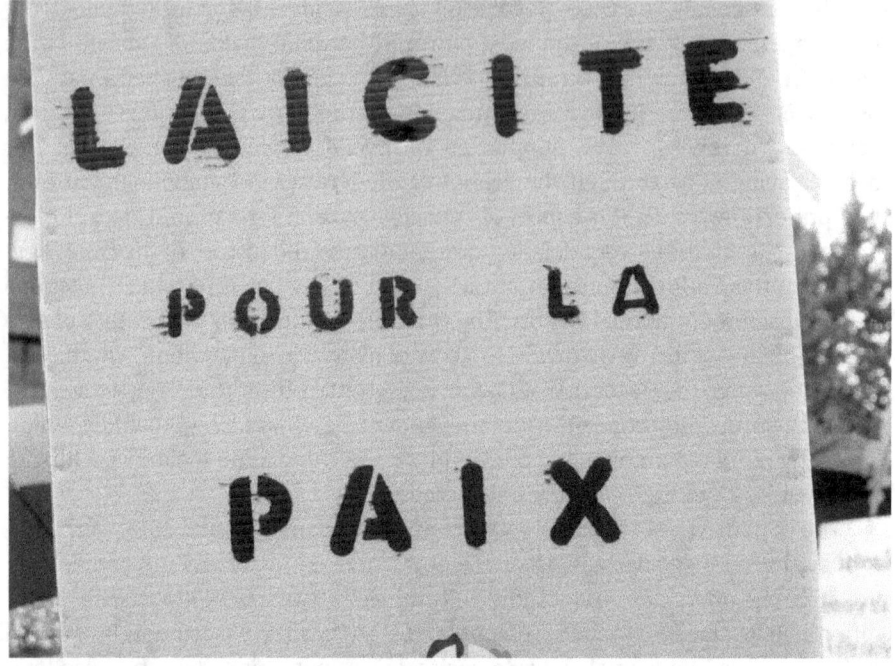

Figure 3: Demonstrators demanding *laïcité* in a street campaign in support of the Charter of Quebec Values. Photo taken by the author in Montreal, September 2013.

It is worth quoting at length from the Declaration of Intellectuals for Secularism, which was released in 2010 and is one of the most important documents of intellectual intervention. Among other things it states that:

> Secularism is part of the history of Quebec. In Quebec, the defense of secular ideals is not new. They are evidenced by the work of Fleury Mesplet for the dissemination of the Enlightenment in Canada in the late eighteenth century. The idea of separation of state and church was also included in the Declaration of Independence of 1838 proclaimed by the Patriots. The principle was subsequently defended by the Canadian Institute with Papineau, Dessaulles, Doutre and Buies. Later, Premier Adelard Godbout, supported by Minister Télesphore Damien Bouchard, was to head to the Catholic Church by granting the rights of women to vote and adopting a law on compulsory education. Criticizing the religious yoke then found its way to the heart of the manifesto "Refuse Global," which prefigured the Quiet Revolution. In the 60s, the secular movement promoted the French language claiming secular public schools. In 1975, Quebec adopted the Charter of Rights and Freedoms that recognizes the freedom of conscience and equality of religions, two essentially secular notions. And recently, the de-confessionalization of school structures was complet-

ed. If the idea of a secular state is prior to the Patriots[6], we cannot say that secularism is a defensive reaction to recently immigrated minority communities. The secularization of public institutions is made in the name of freedom of conscience and pluralism. Efforts to put an end to prayers in municipal assemblies and remove crucifixes from courts, municipal halls and the National Assembly are also based on these principles. In no event shall the rights of minorities be threatened by this secularization; on the contrary, many immigrants who fled authoritarian and theocratic regimes are strong advocates of secularism. Secularism is thus part of the Quebec historical landscape and the recent achievements that characterize it.[7]

It becomes immediately obvious that for secularists history matters. One of the first things to note, however, is that, while secular modernity usually operates as a discourse of rupture or breakthrough (Wagner 2002; 2008), here the focus is on *continuity*. In discussions among secularists, it is common to reject the idea that until the 1960s the Quebecois were steeped in Catholicism and subject to religious authority. The most important point of reference for them instead is the Patriot rebellion that occurred during the 1830s. These rebellions, which aimed at casting off the shackles of British domination, are typically portrayed as republican *and* by implication secular in spirit. In an interview, a former president of the Mouvement laïque québécois explained to me that, before the repression that followed the defeat of the Patriots, the republicans had already installed public schools that were religiously neutral and where instruction would be given by trained teachers, not priests. Such arguments echo, of course, not only the centrality of secular schools for French-style *laïcité*. They are also meant to corroborate the idea that Quebec's history was fundamentally distorted through British domination, that history actually proceeds as the gradual emancipation from this distortion, and that Quebec's place as a part of Canada is a continuation of colonial domination by different means. Secularists see the confessional school system as one of the extreme manifestations of colonially-induced abnormalities and its dismantling as only occurring, as mentioned above, towards the end of the 1990s as another step in emancipation from it. The deconfessionalization of the public school system, just as the desired implementation of a more rigid form of secularism more broadly, is therefore understood not only as a logical continuation of the Quiet Revolution and a necessary

---

6 The notion of the "Patriots Rebellion" refers to a series of political uprisings against British colonial domination during the 1830s that articulated anti-colonialism with republicanism.
7 See http://www.ledevoir.com/societe/actualites-en-societe/285021/declaration-des-in tellectuels-pour-la-laicite-pour-un-quebec-laique-et-pluraliste; accessed 30 January 2015; translation mine.

step on the way to its historical completion as secularization, but also in terms of emancipation from Canada.

It is important to note, however, that not all secularists are also sovereignists. When I asked people about the "national question" they would often emphasize that there are a variety of positions and opinions in the movement and that secularism was the goal that actually unified people across the sovereignist/federalist divide. However, my impression was that sovereignists were in the majority and that federalists tended to be upper middle-class people with clear reservations about the leftist leanings that are presumed to be part of the independentist project. At the same time, it became very obvious that, within secularist collective memory, secularist and nationalist arguments feed into one another.[8] Here, anticlericalism invariably doubles as resistance against British colonial domination, organized, as it was, through the instrumental participation of Catholic clergy in British colonialism.

The controversy over the Quebec Charter of Values reflects longstanding contestations between the notion of *secularity for the sake of progress and enlightenment* on the one hand, and the notion of *secularity for the sake of accommodating religious diversity* on the other. The first concept grows out of the historical experiences especially of the baby-boom generation, who routinely justified *laïcité fermée* as the consummation of the Quiet Revolution and *their* project of liberation and secular emancipation. The second concept grows out of contemporary discourses on diversity and human rights and the historical experiences of those social groups that closely identify with the multicultural (and also the intercultural) project, and it has typological similarities to other historical scenarios in which the accommodation of diversity is of overriding concern, as for instance in India (Burchardt and Wohlrab-Sahr 2013).

Interestingly, both discourses on secularity make claims about individual liberties, although for both, individual liberty does not constitute so much as support their cases – of progress for supporters and of diversity for opponents of the Charter project. On the one hand, for the supporters of *laïcité fermée*, the power given to religious communities in controversial cases of reasonable accommodation restrains individual liberties. For the proponents of *laïcité ouverte*, on the other hand, the proposed limitations on religious signs in the public sphere and the spheres of the state are limitations on individual freedom and must be rejected in the name of freedom of religion and non-discrimination. They clearly engage with *laïcité* with a view to protecting individual liberties,

---

[8] The connections between secularism and sovereignism are much more direct in the discourse and strategies of the Parti Quebecois.

while in some instances this approach also comes into conflict with more group rights-oriented theories of multiculturalism. We thus see that the different positions in the Quebec controversy neatly map on to the normative concerns that are raised in sociological and legal debates on secularism such as human rights, especially freedom of religion, equality, non-discrimination and the state's neutrality. Meanwhile, issues such as the use of religious argument in public deliberation, which are widely discussed by political philosophers like Habermas and Rawls, rarely mattered.

Ultimately, I suggest that *A Secular Age* is helpful and extremely inspirational when it comes to understanding the ideational roots and historical emergence of secularity in terms of "conditions of belief" in secularized societies and the ways in which these are *transformed into* the conditions in which people draw distinctions between religion and the secular in times of contestation. In a broad sense, *A Secular Age* charts a path towards the cognitive and practical framework from which Quebeckers view the place of religion in their society and new forms of migration-driven religious diversity, though sometimes this framework undoubtedly creates new dilemmas with regard to human rights and social coexistence. In her study of power and freedom in late modernity, Wendy Brown (1995: 8) pointed to the "paradox in which freedom responds to a particular practice of domination whose terms are then often reinstalled in its practice. When institutionalized, freedom premised upon an already vanquished enemy keeps alive, in the manner of a melancholic logic, a threat that works as domination in the form of an absorbing ghostly battle with the past." We cannot fail to see in some moments of the contestations over secularity in Quebec such ghostly battles with the past. At the same time, the question of freedom *of*, *from*, and *inside* religion has never disappeared. The issue today is really how questions of the articulation of religion and freedom are posed, how the quest for freedom is formulated within different cultural logics of secularity, and whether there can be a practice of freedom that satisfies a diversity of religious and secular claims.

Bibliography

Agrama, Hussein A. 2012. "Reflections on secularism, democracy, and politics in Egypt." *American Ethnologist*, 39 no. 1: 26–31.
Anidjar, Gil 2006. "Secularism." *Critical Inquiry*, 33 no. 1: 52–77.
Asad, Talal. 2003. *Formations of the Secular: Christianity, Islam, Modernity*. Stanford: Stanford University Press.
Bader, Veit. 2007. *Secularism or Democracy? Associational Governance of Religious Diversity*. Amsterdam: Amsterdam University Press.

Baum, Gregory. 1991. *The Church in Quebec*. Outremont, Québec: Novalis.
Beaman, Lori G. 2013. "The will to religion: obligatory religious citizenship." *Critical Research on Religion*, 1 no. 2: 141–157.
Beckford, James A. 2012. "SSSR presidential address public religions and the postsecular: critical reflections." *Journal for the Scientific Study of Religion*, 51 no. 1: 1–19.
Berger, Peter L. 1967. *The Sacred Canopy*. Garden City, NY: Doubleday.
Berger, Peter L, ed., 1999. *The De-secularization of the World*. Washington D.C.: Ethics and Public Policy Center.
Bouchard, Gerard, and Charles Taylor. 2008. *Building the future. A time for reconciliation. Report of the Consultation Commission on Accommodation Practices Related to Cultural Differences*. Montreal: Government of Quebec.
Bowen, John R., Christophe Bertossi, Jan W. Duyvendak, and Mona L. Krook, eds., 2013. *European States and their Muslim Citizens*. Cambridge: Cambridge University Press.
Brown, Wendy. 1995. *States of Injury. Power and Freedom in Late Modernity*. Princeton: Princeton University Press.
Burchardt, Marian, and Ines Michalowski. 2014. "After integration: Islam, conviviality and contentious politics," in *After integration: Islam, conviviality and contentious politics in Europe*, ed. Marian Burchardt and Ines Michalowski, 3–16. Wiesbaden: Springer Fachmedien.
Burchardt, Marian, and Monika Wohlrab-Sahr. 2013. "Von Multiple Modernities zu Multiple Secularities: kulturelle Diversität, Säkularismus und Toleranz als Leitidee in Indien." *Österreichische Zeitschrift für Soziologie*, 38 no. 4: 355–374.
Burchardt, Marian, Monika Wohlrab-Sahr and Matthias Middell, eds., 2015. *Multiple Secularities beyond the West: Religion and Modernity in the Global Age*. Boston and Berlin: de Gruyter.
Casanova, José. 1994. *Public religions in the modern world*. Chicago: The University of Chicago Press.
Casanova, José. 2006. "Secularization Revisited: A Reply to Talal Asad," in *Powers of the Secular Modern. Talal Asad and His Interlocutors*, ed. David Scott and Hirschkind, Charles 12–30. Stanford: Stanford University Press.
Casanova, José. 2007. "Immigration and the new religious pluralism: a European Union/United States comparison," in *Democracy and the new religious pluralism*, ed. Thomas Banchoff, 59–83. Oxford: Oxford University Press.
Casanova, José. 2009. "The Secular and Secularisms." *Social Research*, 76 no. 4: 1049–1066.
Casanova, José. 2010. "A secular age: dawn or twilight?," in *Varieties of Secularism in a Secular Age*, ed. Michael Warner, Jonathan VanAntwerpen and Craig Calhoun, 265–281. Cambridge: Harvard University Press.
Casanova, José. 2011. "Cosmopolitanism, the Clash of Civilizations and Multiple Modernities." *Current Sociology*, 59 no. 2: 252–267.
Christiano, Kevin. 2007. "The trajectory of Catholicism in twentieth-century Quebec," in *The church confronts modernity: Catholicism since 1950 in the United States, Ireland, and Quebec*, ed. Leslie Woodcock, 21–61. Washington, DC: Tentler The Catholic University of America Press.
Deneulin, Séverine, and Masooda Bano. 2009. *Religion in Development: Rewriting the Secular Script*. London and New York: Zed Books.

Eade, John. 2011. "From Race to Religion: Multiculturalism and Contested Urban Space," in *Postsecular Cities: Space, Theory, and Practice*, ed. Justin Beaumont and Christopher Baker, 154–167. London: Continuum.
Eisenstadt, Shmuel N. 2000. "Multiple Modernities." *Daedalus*, 129: 1–29.
Fraser, Nancy. 1995. "From redistribution to recognition? Dilemmas of justice in a 'post-socialist' age." *New Left Review* 212 (July/August): 68–93.
Fraser, Nancy. 2009. *Scales of justice: re-imagining political space in a globalizing world.* New York: Columbia University Press.
Göle, Nilüfer. 2010. "Manifestations of the Religious-Secular Divide: Self, State, and the Public Sphere," in *Comparative Secularisms in a Global Age*, ed. Linell E. Cady and Elizabeth Shakman Hurd, 41–53. New York: Palgrave Macmillan.
Gourgouris, Stathis. 2008. "Detranscendentalizing the Secular." *Public Culture*, 20 no. 3: 437–445.
Griera, Mar. 2012. "Public policies, interfaith associations and religious minorities: a new policy paradigm? Evidence from the case of Barcelona." *Social Compass*, 59 no. 4: 570–587.
Grillo, Ralph. 2010. "British and others: From 'race' to 'faith'," in *Multiculturalism Backlash: European Discourses, Practices and Policies*, ed. Steven Vertovec and Susanne Wessendorf, 50–71. New York and London: Routledge.
Hjelm, Titus. 2014. "Understanding the New Visibility of Religion." *Journal of Religion in Europe*, 7 no. 3–4: 203–222.
Koenig, Matthias. 2005. "Incorporating Muslim migrants in Western Nation States: A Comparison of the United Kingdom, France, and Germany." *Journal of International Migration and Integration*, 6 no. 2: 219–234.
Koenig, Matthias. 2011. "Jenseits des Säkularisierungsparadigmas?." *Kölner Zeitschrift für Soziologie und Sozialpsychologie*, 63 no. 4: 649–673.
Levitt, Peggy. 2007. *God needs no passport: Immigrants and the changing American religious landscape.* New York: New Press.
Luhmann, Niklas. 2000. *Die Religion der Gesellschaft.* Frankfurt a. M.: Suhrkamp.
Mahmood, Saba. 2006. "Secularism, Hermeneutics, and Empire: The Politics of Islamic Reformation." Public Culture 18, no. 2: 323–347.
Mahmood, Saba. 2008. "Is critique secular? A symposium at UC Berkeley." *Public Culture*, 20 no. 3: 447–452.
Mahmood, Saba. 2010. "Can Secularism be Other-wise?," in *Varieties of Secularism in a Secular Age*, ed. Warner, Michael, Jonathan VanAntwerpen, and Craig Calhoun, 282–299. Cambridge, Mass: Harvard University Press.
Masuzawa, Tomoko. 2005. *The invention of world religion, or, How European universalism was preserved in the language of pluralism.* Chicago: University of Chicago Press.
Nelson, Samuel, and Philip S. Gorski. 2014. "Conditions of religious belonging: Confessionalization, de-parochialization, and the Euro-American divergence." *International Sociology*, 29 no. 1: 3–21.
Parsons, Talcott and Gerald M. Platt. 1973. *The American University.* Cambridge, Mass: Harvard University Press.
Ranger, Terence O., ed., 2008. *Evangelical Christianity and Democracy in Africa.* Oxford: Oxford University Press.

Rose, Nikolas.1996. "Governing Advanced Liberal Democracies," In *Foucault and political reason: liberalism, neo-liberalism, and rationalities of government*, ed. Andrew Barry, Thomas Osborne, and Nikolas Rose, 37–64. New York: Routledge.

Schenk, Susanne, Marian Burchardt, and Monika Wohlrab-Sahr. 2015. "Religious Diversity in the Neoliberal Welfare State: Secularity and the Ethos of Egalitarianism in Sweden." *International Sociology* 30 no. 1: 3–20.

Schönwälder, Karen. 2007. "Gesellschaftlicher Zusammenhalt und kulturelle Differenz: Muslime und Debatten über Muslime in Großbritannien." *Soziale Welt*. Sonderband 17: 241–260.

Simmel, Georg. 1994 [1909]. "Bridge and door." *Theory, Culture & Society*, 11 no. 1: 5–10.

Stark, Rodney. 1999. "Secularization, R.I.P." *Sociology of Religion*, 60 no. 3: 249–273.

Tezcan, Levent. 2007. "Kultur, Gouvernementalität der Religion und der Integrationsdiskurs." *Soziale Welt*. Sonderband 17: 51–76.

Taylor, Charles. 2004. *Modern Social Imaginaries*. Durham: Duke University Press.

Taylor, Charles. 2011a. "Why we need a radical redefinition of secularism," in *The Power of Religion in the Public Sphere*, ed. Eduardo Mendieta and Jonathan VanAntwerpen, 34–59. New York: Columbia University Press.

Taylor, Charles. 2011b. "Western Secularity," in *Rethinking Secularism*, ed. Craig Calhoun, Mark Juergensmeyer and Jonathan VanAntwerpen, 31–53. Oxford and New York: Oxford University Press.

Tugal, Cihan. 2009. *Passive revolution: absorbing the Islamic challenge to capitalism*. Palo Alto: Stanford University Press.

Van den Hemel, Ernst. 2014. "(Pro)Claiming Tradition: The 'Judeo-Christian' Roots of Dutch Society and the Rise Conservative Nationalism," in *Transformations of Religion and the Public Sphere*, ed. Rosi Braidotti, Bolette Blaagaard, Tobijn de Graauw, and Eva Midden, 53–76. New York: Palgrave Macmillan.

Wagner, Peter. 2002. *A Sociology of Modernity: Liberty and Discipline*. London: Routledge.

Wagner, Peter. 2008. *Modernity as Experience and Interpretation. A New Sociology of Modernity*. Cambridge: Polity Press.

Wohlrab-Sahr, Monika, Thomas Schmidt-Lux, and Uta Karstein. 2008. "Secularization as Conflict." *Social Compass*, 55 no. 2:127–139.

Wohlrab-Sahr, Monika, and Marian Burchardt. 2012. "Multiple Secularities: Toward a Cultural Sociology of Secular Modernities." *Comparative Sociology*, 11 no. 6: 875–909.

Joyce Dalsheim
Other Sovereignties in Israel/Palestine: The Limited Imaginings of a Secular Age

> Tell me a story, great-aunt,
> so that I can sleep.
> Tell me a story, Scheherazade,
> so you can live ...
> Ursula LeGuin (1980)

1 Introduction

We all tell stories to ourselves to explain the way things are, how they got this way, who we are, or what we believe (Dalsheim 2003). Sometimes we tell stories to engage the imagination, to garner support for our cause, or just to distract. But the stories we tell are never completely innocent. There once was a storyteller who stayed up for many, many long nights to tell a story in such great detail that it would occupy many people's minds for months and years. Because of the fame of this storyteller, men and women from near and far were attracted to it, or distracted by it. This storyteller writes from a cold place in the north, and imagines his story is a very important one indeed. How could he think otherwise? Readers have awarded him precious prizes and his story has led to gatherings of all sorts of very smart people who discuss his story, and write about it over and over again. Indeed, this storyteller and his tale are the subject of this book.

Despite the prizes and the fame – or maybe because of them – we might wonder what makes this particular story so important. Charles Taylor tells an especially long and detailed story about the way things came to be as they are in what he describes as the contemporary "secular age." He is convinced that his attention to detail will help his story replace another one; what he calls the "subtraction story" of secularization. What I find most remarkable about Taylor's story lies less in its details and whether or not he's gotten them right, but rather

---

I would like to express my thanks to the conference organizers and editors of this volume for their comments and suggestions and for their skill and professionalism throughout the process of actualizing this edited volume. I am also grateful to the series editors and external reviewers for their helpful comments. Many thanks to my colleagues who read earlier or different versions of this piece, especially Gregg Starrett, Jonathan Boyarin, and Gil Anidjar.

his conviction that what requires explanation is that "belief in God, or in the transcendent in any form, is contested: it is an option among many [...]. Five hundred years ago in our civilization," he writes, "it wasn't so" (Taylor 2010: 304). Belief in God or the transcendent as optional clearly does not describe the experience of many people in the contemporary world. Indeed, Charles Taylor does not deny this. Instead he says it describes "Western modernity." But what that admission occludes is the work accomplished through the *idea* of a secular age;[1] the work of producing as enemies those who do not fit neatly into the "we" it describes.[2]

The story Taylor tells is a particularly powerful one – not necessarily correct, but hegemonic. Taylor often seems to be reflecting on the cultural norms of a group to which he belongs; telling his own culture like a native informant. When anthropologists listen to native informants, questions of historical accuracy are less relevant than native beliefs, how widely shared those beliefs are, and how they work. Thus, my concern is not with the historical accuracy or inaccuracy of Taylor's tale, but with how this conceptualization works to discipline certain ways of being and believing. In particular, I am concerned with who takes comfort in the story he tells and who is cast out from it. Those who live in the shadows of the hegemonic secular moral order Taylor describes can be vilified or demonized and produced as enemies of the order itself. The production of such enemies is especially important in contemporary attempts at peacemaking.

This chapter provides a glimpse into some of the disciplining force of conventional or liberal peacemaking, by focusing briefly on three examples of those who are in some ways cast out from the moral order of a secular age. I take Taylor's description of a secular age to be a depiction of a powerful modern discourse that marginalizes, silences or ignores that which falls outside its normative bounds. I present three brief ethnographic depictions which reveal challenges to some of the assumptions of the hegemonic secular age that are foundational to contemporary peacemaking, including the idea of the "buffered self" and the idea of the autonomous individual which forms the basis of human sovereignty, particularly popular sovereignty. Although my concern in this chapter is

---

[1] Here I distinguish between the book and the idea itself. The social imaginary that Taylor describes is one others have called "modernity" or "liberalism." The work accomplished by this idea is vast. Here my interest is in one component of its work.

[2] The "we" is synonymous with what Taylor calls "modern Westerners" (Taylor 2010: 300). Of particular relevance for this essay is Taylor's explanation that "a general feature of our modern self-understanding" is the "self-ruling 'people'" indicative of a new mode of "collective agency [...] among the most striking features of Western modernity and beyond; we understand ourselves after all to be living in a democratic age"(ASA: 181).

with conventional peacemaking, which shares a set of presuppositions with Taylor's depiction of a secular social imaginary, this analysis could surely be expanded to many other social and political processes in the secular age.

2 Peacemaking

Conventional peacemaking, or what is sometimes called liberal peacemaking (Campbell, Chandler, and Sabaratnam 2011; Mullin 2010; Paris 2010; Roberts 2011), takes place within the moral order or "modern social imaginary" (Taylor 2002) in which human beings are considered "rational, sociable agents" who can collaborate in peace to their mutual benefit. An important part of this imaginary is the idea of "the sovereign people" (ASA: 196–207), which has to do both with the constitution of "a people" and with an underlying presumption about *human* sovereignty itself. Whether or not most people put their faith in human political authority with no final authority elsewhere, the idea of human sovereignty is crucial to Taylor's story, foundational to the contemporary norm of collective self-determination through self-rule in a democratic state, and hegemonic in international peacemaking efforts. Indeed, some political analysts claim that sovereignty is one of the "implicit international norms" that should guide the ethics of foreign policy (Telhami 2004: 84; see Sassen 1996: 2).

The order of sovereign democratic nation-states is premised on the idea that individuals enter into a contract in which they receive freedom and security while granting the sole right to violence to the state. This order is supposed to create international stability because a general consensus is required to go to war, and most people will be reluctant to do so. Most readers will recognize this idea that emerges from Immanuel Kant's writing on "Perpetual Peace" in the eighteenth century. Kant wrote that "if the consent of the citizens is required in order to decide that war should be declared, [...] nothing is more natural than that they would be very cautious in commencing such a poor game, decreeing for themselves all the calamities of war" ([1795] 1903: 122). Not only would the citizens have to fight, they would also bear the costs of the war and of reconstruction afterward. The citizens, Kant writes, "having painfully to repair the devastation war leaves behind, and, to fill up the measure of evils, load themselves with a heavy national debt that would embitter peace itself and that can never be liquidated on account of constant wars in the future" ([1795] 1903: 121–123). Since rational citizens would be loath to enter into a state of war for all it would cost them in life and livelihood, peace should be the expected norm in a world of democratic nation-states. This is one of the primary reasons justifying Western powers' attempts at state building around the world. In the case of conflict resolution, peace is expected to last when parties to conflict take their place in the world order of nation-states, where they will have sovereignty over their own territory and act in their own interests. Thus, order, and specifically the order of nation-states, is foundational to liberal peace processes.

The narrative of the state foundational to liberal peacemaking "is that the modern state system is a European construct [...] which put an end to the religious conflicts of the late 16th and 17th centuries in Europe" (Mullin 2010: 531; see ASA: 164–165). According to this narrative, it was the elimination of God from the realm of politics that paved the way for modern sovereignty. Taylor qualifies this idea, suggesting that human action in the realm of politics was thought to be the fulfillment of God's will. It was this secular sovereignty based on a set of principles including individualism and personal pursuits of liberty and happiness that ultimately became foundational both to free markets and to the international order of nation-states. Taylor explains that "ordered, peaceful, productive [...] activity has become the model for human behaviour, and the key for harmonious co-existence" (ASA: 167); the key to peace in the secular age.³

Moving away from rule by a dictator or a monarch endowed by God with the power to rule, or away from rule by a foreign power or colonizer to self-rule, is often considered the best means currently available to achieve liberation. And the belief in a natural order of nations means that the character and essence of the nation is best guaranteed and also best expressed through participation in the polity. It is a value so fundamental that it seems counterintuitive to contemplate arriving at peace without such sovereignty.

3 Sovereignty

> We know sovereignty when we see it—at least we think we do. Post- nineteenth-century definitions of sovereignty highlight the ambition to control what and who crosses borders as well as the power to make laws to regulate what happens within them. State sovereignty and national sovereignty are terms that have lodged themselves in our political vocabulary to such a degree that they appear to have no logical substitutes. Yet we also know that sovereignty is more a myth than a reality, more a story that polities tell about their own power than a definite quality they possess (Benton 2010:279).

The idea of human sovereignty underlies a faith in popular sovereignty, which in turn constitutes the norm for [liberal] peacemaking in the contemporary world.

---

3 Here Taylor refers to John Locke's influence on contemporary thought.

Because the work of peacemaking often depends on the telling and recognition of narratives of national history, stories form an important part of the work of gaining and contesting sovereignty (Dalsheim 2014). The stories I will tell here come from the case of peacemaking and its "outsides" in Israel/Palestine.[4] In Israel and Palestine, as in all conflicts, there are a number of accounts of how the conflict came into being, who is at fault, and what happened along the way. Depending on how its story is told, the case of Israel/Palestine has come to stand for intractable conflict, a tragedy of right against right, or a late case of anti-colonial liberation. But no matter how it is told, the moral conclusions drawn from all the major narratives rely in one way or another on some form of popular sovereignty.

Each narrative, as Hayden White (1990) argues, is necessarily partial and selective, expressing a particular moral imperative as it guides the teller and the audience to a particular conclusion or solution in the case of conflict. If for example, we narrate the conflict as a tragedy of two national groups vying for the same piece of territory, we might conclude that each deserves its own nation-state, and we label this a "two-state solution." Or we might conclude that they must share power in the same territory, and we label this "one democratic secular state for all its citizens." We might also tell the story as a post-colonial struggle in which the colonizers must give up sovereignty to the rightful owners of the place. Alternately, it might be seen as a different post-colonial struggle in which some local residents are identified as temporary squatters who have to give up sovereignty to the rightful owners of the place. Yet, despite the endless ways one might imagine of telling the past and the present, all the stories about the situation in Israel/Palestine that have come to matter in international politics narrate two parties to the conflict, producing themselves and being produced as separate and distinct from each other, subsuming both internal differences and also commonalities across the ethno-national divide.

All currently powerful ways of narrating the conflict express both the problem and the possible solutions in ways that link the idea of ethno-national identity to the very notion of humanity itself. In the words of Herbert Kelman (2004: 122), director of the Program on International Conflict Analysis and Resolution at Harvard, resolution requires that each group must acknowledge "the other's nationhood and humanity." In the meta-narrative of nation-states that structures contemporary frameworks of peacemaking, there appears to be no way to con-

---

[4] These stories are part of a larger ethnographic project, which involves research carried out in Israel/Palestine since the early 1980s. The issues that arise in this chapter are dealt with in greater detail in my two books (Dalsheim 2011; 2014).

ceive of the conflict except as the story of two competing national groups that will culminate in triumph for one and tragedy for the other, or in a statist political/territorial compromise between them. The idea of sovereignty that forms part of the social imaginary Charles Taylor narrates, has come to be most powerful in international politics and peacemaking not only because of its repetition, but also because of its duration (Caton 2014).[5]

And yet, some people on the ground in Israel/Palestine have begun thinking and acting in ways that pose challenges to the "sovereignty" component of the episteme of people/territory/sovereignty that underlies the modern nation-state (Dalsheim 2014). These challenges – or what Foucault ([1978] 2007) called forms of "counter-conduct" – are sometimes considered unconventional, sometimes crazy. Sometimes these kinds of actions are called visionary, but other times they are categorized as criminal or treasonous. I will focus on just three examples – each of which poses a different challenge to what is generally thought of as popular sovereignty.[6] Those who pose these challenges fall outside the norms of the modern social imaginary Taylor represents, and outside the boundaries of conventional peacemaking. They pose threats to the modern order of nation-states in which peace is expected to take place and may therefore be considered "spoilers" of peace.

I tell these stories not to suggest they provide preferable solutions for arriving at peace in Israel/Palestine, but because they mark the borders of the moral order in which conventional or liberal peacemaking is carried out: the borders[7] of the moral order of a secular age.

---

[5] Anthropologist Steve Caton (2014) writes about thinking with Henri Bergson's concept of "duration" during his fieldwork in Yemen, demonstrating the relationship between temporality, conflict and its mediation.

[6] I present these examples as anonymous characters, leaving them unnamed because I am convinced that the ideas and practices that each one represents stand for more than each individual character. These are only three examples, which I think fit into a broader range of beliefs and actions in Israel/Palestine.

[7] I do not mean to suggest particular geographical borders or a demarcation of the difference between "the West" and its others, as Taylor would have it. The idea of a secular age is one social imaginary that overlaps and interferes with others. It is powerful and limited, but, contra Taylor, its boundaries do not fall "outside the West." As a powerful imaginary it marginalizes and delegitimizes particular ways of being and believing, certain acts and ideas.

4 The Sheikh

I begin with a story about a Palestinian Sheikh who erected a peace tent near Hebron in the Israeli-occupied West Bank. There he hosted local Jewish settlers who lived in homes generally seen as having been built on land taken from Palestinians, as well as several right-wing politicians from Europe. Calling a meeting where enemies can talk peace with international observers present is similar to officially sanctioned negotiations between political leaders or diplomats. Yet the Sheikh and his peace tent have been denounced by Palestinian officials as not representative of the Palestinian people or their national interests, and it has been suggested that the Sheikh is nothing more than a traitor to his people, a collaborator.

This sheikh is the leader of a large Palestinian community near a city considered one of the most contentious places where Israeli settlers terrorize Palestinians, squat in their homes and cause their places of business to be shut down. By most accounts, the Sheikh should consider those settlers his archenemies, yet he has invited them and their supporters into a special tent on the outskirts of town, furnished with soft cushions and hand-woven carpets where he offered them strong black coffee. When they were seated and comfortable, he spoke about being neighbors and about living together in peace.

Taken together, the Sheikh's visitors are supporters of the right of Israel to expand territorially and for Jews to settle in that expanded territory. They are promoters of land theft that squeezes Palestinians out of their homes. If land is necessary for life, then struggles and negotiations over land can be contests over life itself (Wolfe 2013). But this sheikh has no interest in dividing up the land between Israelis and Palestinians. He is convinced that Muslims may *never* part with Muslim territory. Someone who takes such a stance might be considered an uncompromising hardliner; such ideas might be expected from Hamas or Islamic Jihad. And yet some of the Jewish settlers who came from communities where fear and hatred of Arabs is said to be rampant, said this sheikh was a good man, a friend, and a man of peace.

This sheikh has been denounced by Palestinian officials and by mainstream peacemakers as little more than a collaborator and traitor to the nationalist cause. But he reportedly feels betrayed in turn by those who claim authority to speak for him and is frustrated by what he describes as a corrupt Palestinian Authority (PA) that has done little to help his native Hebron. He is not alone in that sentiment. Many Palestinians express frustration with the PA, which raises questions about the extent to which elected officials can ever actually represent the populace.

This Sheikh might have traded protection of Jewish holy sites for permits or other privileges for himself and for those local people he represents. Exchanges of this sort are not unusual. It is easy to find all sorts of ways that people cooperate for economic benefit, or for protection, or for humanitarian reasons. But this kind of cooperation can trouble the epistemology of a secular age that is so foundational to the nation and nationalism (Appadurai 1993). Insofar as the Sheikh rejects the legitimacy of Palestinian Authority claims to represent the interests of "the Palestinian people," he calls into question the idea of "popular" in popular sovereignty.

5 The Rabbi

Next I'd like to tell you about a Rabbi who believes that the Jews have a right and a responsibility to God to live in the Land of Israel, which includes living in the Palestinian territories under Israeli military occupation. Yet this Rabbi also meets with Palestinian Muslim clerics to talk about what pious Jews and Muslims have in common as he seeks ways of living together. This rabbi cried about the evacuation of Israeli settlements from the Sinai in the 1980s and from the Gaza Strip in 2005, and held tight to the Torah when synagogues were closed as the result of these evacuations. But he has also brought Qur'ans to a mosque after Jewish settlers' vandalism. He mourns the deaths of Israeli settlers killed by Palestinian gunfire, but also attends the funerals of Palestinians killed by Israeli soldiers and settlers. He is passionate about the Holy Land, but not concerned about owning it. He believes Jews have to live in the Land of Israel to fulfill God's promise, but is indifferent to Jewish political sovereignty, because the very idea of *human* sovereignty is pure hubris. There already is a Sovereign of the Universe. The Muslim clerics with whom he has met share his deep belief in God as the only true Sovereign. And this, he contends, can be the basis for living together in the Holy Land, albeit each according to his own practices. He expressed a hope that Jewish settlers can take the role of what he calls an "outstretched hand" toward the Palestinians. This seems like a very strange idea since so many incidents of clench fists or other violent behavior have been reported between settlers and Palestinians. But according to the Rabbi it is important to let go of the reins of human sovereignty and understand that we are all guests on this earth and all guests in the Land of Israel. The Lord can allow us to stay or remove us, and if the Jewish people are to be a "light unto the nations," the Rabbi explains, it will be through the ways in which they live on the land together with the people God has placed them with.

The belief in human sovereignty rests on an underlying understanding of human agency, the ability to act freely in the world, an ability that is ambiguous at best in both religious and secular contexts.[8] If we know that religious texts and interpretations represent human agency as restricted in particular ways, we also know that social scientists do the same. Consider, for example, the following biblical excerpts:

> See this day I set before you a blessing and a curse: blessing, if you obey the commandments of the Lord your God that I enjoin upon you this day; and curse, if you do not obey [...] (Deuteronomy 11: 26–28)

> See, I set before you this day life and prosperity, death and adversity [...] I have put before you life and death, blessing and curse. Choose life – if you and your offspring would live [...] (Deuteronomy 30: 15–19)

And recall the words of Karl Marx ([1852] 1978: 595) in *The Eighteenth Brumaire of Louis Bonaparte:*

> Men make their own history, but they do not make it as they please; they do not make it under self-selected circumstances, but under circumstances existing already, given and transmitted from the past. The tradition of all dead generations weighs like a nightmare on the brains of the living.

From Adam Smith's invisible hand to Karl Marx's ideas about how people make history but not exactly as we might please, to Foucault's ideas about governmentality –readers can probably name their favorite theory. In any case, the Rabbi, like the modern social scientist, calls into question another way of defining the idea of "popular;" i.e., that it has to do with people. There is no sovereignty of the people because there is no human sovereignty in a world subject either to God's commands or to "the forces of history."

6 The Intellectual

Finally, I'd like to tell you about a Palestinian intellectual who recently wrote a book asking what a Palestinian state is worth.[9] It was a surprising book because

---

[8] See Michael Sandel (1990) on the difference between freedom of conscience and freedom of choice.

[9] Sari Nusseibeh is a well-known Palestinian intellectual, professor of philosophy and past president of Al Quds University in Jerusalem. I have chosen not to use in-text citations for his book, *What is a Palestinian State Worth* because, in this essay, Nusseibeh is a kind of allegorical

this intellectual was known for his earlier efforts to promote a Palestinian state alongside an Israeli state. Now he asks whether such a state is worth the high price of Palestinian suffering. Is the establishment of an independent Palestinian state really the answer to all their dreams? Is it worth the ongoing violence and destruction, the seemingly hopeless struggle? "How much has our killing of each other for so many years moved us toward peace?" he asks. He wonders what a state would be *for*, anyway, suggesting that what Palestinians need is an end to the restrictions imposed by military rule, which is not necessarily dependent upon the establishment of their own state.

Beyond the question of whether the state for which Palestinians have been struggling for decades is still worth fighting for, this Palestinian intellectual made an alternative suggestion that makes some people think he's crazy like the Rabbi, and makes others think he's a traitor like the Sheikh. Still others think he's just making this suggestion in order to shock people into realizing its absurdity.

The Intellectual has suggested that Palestinians live in an Israeli state *without* full citizen's rights. All of the territory that now makes up Israel, Israeli occupied territory, the Palestinian Authority, and Gaza could become Israel. Palestinians would be granted many of the rights and privileges provided by the state. They would be able to live wherever they could find housing without geographic restrictions. Likewise, there would be no restrictions on where they could work. They would benefit from social welfare, health insurance, and state services like education and infrastructure. However, they would not have the right to vote.

Voting is what scares Israeli Jews and their leaders, he says.[10] They fear the possibility of being outnumbered demographically and outvoted in their own state. So, he suggests, at least temporarily, Palestinians would forego the right to vote. And in so doing he suggests they give up the coveted right to self-rule, because thinking in terms of sovereignty is an impossible burden, and may be unnecessary for achieving an end to Palestinian suffering.

In the past the Intellectual recommended two states, one Israeli and one Palestinian, side by side. The idea of two states for two peoples has become the most popular solution in international politics and diplomacy. By some accounts it continues to be the solution most Israelis and Palestinians favor. However, many analysts contend that it is too late for the two-state solution because of the growth of Israeli settlements beyond the Green Line. It now seems impossible

---

character like the Rabbi and Sheikh even though all three are very real people. Charles Taylor might be equally allegorical.

[10] This idea of circumventing the demographic threat is approached by LeVine and Mattias (2014) through the suggestion of what they call parallel states.

to divide the land, and with it the population groups, into neatly separated national communities. And now, this Intellectual reverts to fundamental philosophical questions about life itself and what gives it meaning: "one of the most morally challenging dilemmas facing all of us, whoever we are wherever we might be." He asks if the value of human life is intrinsic to it, or if its value is produced by something external to it. Does the value of life depend on "a meaning without which life would be worthless?" And does such meaning derive from larger sets of beliefs and allegiances, like religious beliefs or national affiliation?[11] In other words, he asks what sorts of meanings are worth fighting, suffering, and dying for. Although he never says so in so many words, this Intellectual implies that the *ends* of popular sovereignty are a myth.

7 Other sovereignties

Sovereignty assumes agency – the possibility to act, to decide, to choose. It presumes the ability of human beings to rule their own lives, or in the very least, the perception of such agency. According to Taylor, this is a primary feature of the contemporary secular age.[12] If the Sheikh is frustrated with those who are supposed to represent his interests in the PA, is he any different from Israelis and their Knesset members, or US citizens and their Congress? We know that political power turns on the support of wealthy people and large international corporations more than the ballots of individual voters (Asad 2003: 4; Sassen 1996).[13] The belief that modern individuals have "free agency" is thus continuously undermined.

Referring to "modern Westerners" as opposed to "our ancestors of five hundred years ago," Taylor writes, "One of the big differences between us and them is that we live with a much firmer sense of the boundary between self and other. We are 'buffered' selves'" (2010: 303). The "buffered self" is closely related to the unencumbered self of a Rawlsian theory of justice (Rawls 1971). Rawls is more interested in aspects of identity than in whether we experience life as interwoven with forces beyond our individual control. But when Rawls employs the concept

---

[11] Here we might think about such value in terms of what Taylor calls "fullness" (ASA:7).
[12] Taylor writes that "free agency" is central to the way modern individuals or ("buffered" selves) perceive themselves in the moral order of the secular age (ASA: 169–170). This, of course, presumes an unencumbered self, foundational to liberal thought. See Asad (2011) on the problem of thinking in terms of "buffered" selves.
[13] See Talal Asad's critique of Charles Taylor on the relationship between secularism and the modern nation-state (2003: 2–5).

it is part of a thought experiment, in which he postulates that people blinded to their own identity and place in a social order would have the greatest chance of agreeing on a set of basic principles that make up a just society. Whether or not one agrees with the outcomes Rawls arrives at, this postulate should not be confused with actual experience in the world. In Taylor's story, on the other hand, the buffered self, the self-reliant, self-contained individual is not postulated as part of a thought experiment. It is part of a Taylorian social imaginary, part of how Taylorians experience themselves in the world, as reported by this native informant (ASA: 134–135; 2010: 302–303).

While both the Rabbi and the Sheikh seem to clearly fall outside the parameters of Taylor's buffered self, they are also marginalized by it. Although it is beyond the scope of this essay to examine in greater detail, I would suggest that the idea of "buffered selves" is a mythical component of the Taylorian social imaginary. There are no buffered selves. Even Charles Taylor is not unaffected by forces beyond his self. What is important then, is how this mythical idea can have a disciplining force.

The so-called crazy Rabbi's ideas are echoed in social science, anthropology, history and philosophy. We have learned well that human beings are not sovereign; we the people do not govern ourselves. So why should the ideas expressed by the Rabbi, Sheikh and the Intellectual seem unusual or problematic? Is it because they are forms of conduct that challenge some of the sacred principles of a secular age?

If we think of each of the characters in the stories told in this chapter as semi-allegorical, representing broader social networks and moral orders, then Charles Taylor is surely also such a character. All four are very real people, each representing his own experiences and interpretations from a particularly situated position. One of the important differences between them is the difference of power. That the stories of the Sheikh, the Rabbi, and the Intellectual each seem somehow unusual and problematic is symptomatic of the power of the secular (Asad 2003; 2006) and how its norms can be imposed in international politics and peacemaking.

The Sheikh, the Rabbi, and the Intellectual present just a few examples of the many ways in which people on the ground in Israel/Palestine are moving away from, or acting outside of, some of the secular age's metanarratives, conceiving of and producing other spaces through different forms of counter-conduct that might be best understood as the other sides of multiple, overlapping and scattered hegemonies (Grewal and Kaplan 1994; Dalsheim 2014). Each story, taken on its own, seems strange, defiant or crazy. Unlike the story Charles Taylor tells, each of these falls beyond what are generally considered acceptable norms in conventional (or liberal) politics and peacemaking. What this suggests is that Taylor's tale represents a hegemonic moral order with a disciplinary power. It presumes an unencumbered self that pre-exists the social order and produces a belief in human agency, choice, and sovereignty that limits social and political possibilities by marginalizing and delegitimizing beliefs and actions that fall beyond its parameters.

As I write, the headlines are dominated by stories and analyses of ISIS, the self-proclaimed Islamic State currently fighting in Iraq and Syria. The United States is now heading a coalition of states to fight against ISIS as part of what President Obama called a "comprehensive strategy to degrade and ultimately destroy the terrorist group."[14] The call to arms against ISIS came following video footage depicting the beheadings of US and other Western citizens. However, I would suggest that it is not necessarily the particular acts of violence committed by the group called the Islamic state that is so threatening, but the fact that they disturb the order of states. A commentator on the PBS News Hour said exactly that on September 8, 2014: Hussein Ibish of the American Task Force on Palestine exclaimed with horror that they threaten the Westphalian order we have known for centuries:

> It's not a state that wants to join the state system. It's a state that posits itself as an alternative, not to Syria and Iraq, but to the whole Westphalian state system. I mean, it's just – it's a threat to the international structure as we have known it for hundreds of years.[15]

Here the "we" to whom Ibish refers seems to overlap with the Taylorian "we" of a secular age, the same "we" for whom the Sheikh, the Rabbi, and the Intellectual are, at least partially, outsiders. Their ideas or actions are thus forms of "counter-conduct," a term which Foucault ([1978] 2007) found more useful than "dissident" because it allows us to see the many ways in which people act against "processes implemented for conducting others" (201–202). These three characters are not meant to be seen as heroes, outstanding individual actors whose brave acts change the course of human history. Instead, I present them here as representative of a broader range of everyday ideas and practices, of making do and finding meaning in one's experiences given available resources and opportunities.

The Taylorian "we" represents a social imaginary so powerful or so deeply entrenched that even some of the most creative political theorists seeking

---

[14] For the full text of Obama's speech see: http://www.whitehouse.gov/blog/2014/09/10/president-obama-we-will-degrade-and-ultimately-destroy-isil (last accessed July 19. 2015).
[15] http://www.pbs.org/newshour/bb/can-islamic-state-group-destroyed/ (last accessed July 19. 2015).

peace in Israel/Palestine have not managed to move beyond reshuffling its parameters.[16] For example, Ian Lustick (2013) has been the focus of a great deal of controversy for daring to suggest in *The New York Times* the idea of shifting who will count as "the people" in the Westphalian idea of people/territory/sovereignty to include Israelis and Palestinians as citizens of one state. And, most recently Mark LeVine and Mathias Mossberg (2014) have edited a volume recommending a scenario in which Israelis and Palestinians will each have their own sovereignty over the same territory in what they call "parallel" states.

However, as this chapter begins to demonstrate, if we can think beyond the parameters of a hegemonic order and that which threatens it, we might find patterns that reveal subtle changes in everyday practices that point toward other ways of living together, beyond the seemingly intractable conflict that characterizes Israel/Palestine today.

Bibliography

Appadurai, Arjun. 1993. "Patriotism and Its Futures." *Public Culture* 5:411–429.
Asad, Talal. 2003. *Formations of the Secular: Christianity, Islam, Modernity*. Stanford, California: Stanford University Press.
Asad, Talal. 2006. "Responses," in *Powers of the Secular Modern: Talal Asad and His Interlocutors*, ed. David Scott and Charles Hirschkind, 206–242. Stanford: Stanford University Press.
Asad, Talal. 2011. "Thinking about Religious Beliefs and Politics," in *The Cambridge Companion to Religious Studies*, ed. Robert A. Orsi, 36–57. New York: Cambridge University Press.
Benton, Lauren. 2010. *A Search for Sovereignty: Law and Geography in European Empires, 1400–1900*. Cambridge: Cambridge University Press.
Campbell, Susana, David Chandler, and Meera Sabaratnam, eds. 2011. *A Liberal Peace? The Poblems and Practices of Peacbuilding*. London/New York: Zed Books.
Caton, Steven C. 2014. "Henri Bergson in Highland Yemen," in *The Ground Between: Anthropologists Engage Philosophy*, ed. Veena Das et al., 234–253. London: Duke University Press.

---

16 While the idea of popular sovereignty has become problematic, even undone within in critical social thought, it still seems to frame the way critical thinkers often conceptualize particular arguments. See my article in *Theory, Culture and Society* (Dalsheim 2013) on how this happens and on why it is so difficult to think beyond the idea of the nation. Yehuda Shenhav (2012) is notable for his critique of the failure of the Westphalian system for Israel/Palestine, but has not offered a specific alternative.
This chapter draws on my book, *Producing Spoilers: Peacemaking and the Production of Enmity in a Secular Age* (2014, Oxford University Press) where these issues are dealt with in much greater detail.

Dalsheim, Joyce. 2003. *Uncertain Past, Uncertain Selves? Israeli History and National Identity in Question*. Doctoral Dissertation, Anthropology, Graduate Faculty of Political and Social Sciences of the New School for Social Research, New York.

Dalsheim, Joyce. 2011. *Unsettling Gaza: Secular Liberalism, Radical Religion, and the Israeli Settlement Project*. New York: Oxford University Press.

Dalsheim, Joyce. 2013. "Anachronism and Morality: Israeli Settlement, Palestinian Nationalsim, and Human Liberation." *Theory, Culture & Society* 30, no. 3:29–60.

Dalsheim, Joyce. 2014. *Producing Spoilers: Peacemaking and the Production of Enmity in a Secular Age*. New York: Oxford University Press.

Foucault, Michel. 2007. *Security, Territory, Population: Lectures at the College de France 1977–1978*. Translated by G. Burchell; edited by M. Senellart. New York: Picador.

Grewal, Inderpal, and Caren Kaplan, eds. 1994. *Scattered Hegemonies: Postmodernity and Transnational Feminist Practices*. Minneapolis and London: University of Minnesota Press.

Kant, Immanuel. [1795] 1903. *Perpetual Peace: A Philosophical Essay*. London: George Allen and Unwin LTD.

Kelman, Herbert C. 2004. "Reconciliation as Identity Change: A Social-Psychological Perspective," in *From Conflict Resolution to Reconciliation*, ed. Yaacov Bar-Simon-Tov, 111–124. Oxford: Oxford University Press.

LeGuin, Ursula. 1980. "It Was a Dark and Stormy Night; Or Why are We Huddling about the Campfire?" *Critical Inquiry* 7, no. 1:191–199.

LeVine, Mark, and Mathias Mossberg, eds. 2014. *One Land, Two States: Israel and Palestine as Parallel States*. Berkely: University of California Press.

Lustick, Ian. 2013. "Two-State Illusion." *The New York Times*, http://www.nytimes.com/2013/09/15/opinion/sunday/two-state-illusion.html?pagewanted=all&_r=0 (last accessed July 19. 2015).

Marx, Karl. [1852] 1978. "The Eighteenth Brumaire of Louis Bonaparte," in *The Marx-Engels Reader*, ed. Robert C. Tucker. New York: W.W. Norton and Company: 594–617.

Mullin, Corinna. 2010. "Islamist Challenges to the 'Liberal Peace' Discourse: The Case of Hamas and the Israel-Palestine 'Peace Process'." *Millennium- Journal of International Studies* 39, no. 2:525–546.

Nusseibeh, Sari. 2011 *What is a Palestinian State Worth?* Cambridge, Mass./London: Harvard University Press.

Paris, Roland. 2010. "Saving Liberal Peacebuilding." *Review of International Studies* 36:337–365.

Roberts, David. 2011. *Liberal Peacebuilding and Global Governance: Beyond the Metropolis*. London/New York: Routledge.

Sandel, Michael J. 1990. "Freedom of Conscience of Freedom of Choice?," in *Articles of Faith, Articles of Peace: Religious Liberty Clauses and the American Public Philosophy*, ed. James Davison Hunter and Os Guiness, 74–92. Washington, DC: Brookings Institution.

Sassen, Saskia. 1996. *Losing Control? Sovereignty in the an Age of Globalization*. New York: Columbia University Press.

Shenhav, Yehouda. 2012. *Beyond the Two-State Solution: A Jewish Political Essay*. Cambridge: Polity Press.

Taylor, Charles. 2002. "Modern Social Imaginaries." *Public Culture* 14 no. 1: 91–124.

Taylor, Charles. 2007. *A Secular Age*. Cambridge, Mass./London: Belknap Press of Harvard University Press.

Taylor, Charles. 2010. "Afterword: Apologia pro Libro suo," in *Varieties of Secularism in a Secular Age*, ed. Michael Warner, Jonathan VanAntwerpen, and Craig Calhoun: 300–321. Cambridge, Mass./London: Harvard University Press.

Telhami, Shibley. 2004. "Between Faith and Ethics," in J. Bryan Hehir et al.: *Liberty and Power: A Dialogue on Religion and U.S. Foreign Policy in an Unjust World*, 71–94. Washington, DC: Brookings Institute Press.

White, Hayden. 1980. "The Value of Narrativity." *Critical Inquiry* 7 no. 1:5–27.

Wolfe, Patrick. 2013. "The Settler Complex: An Introduction." *American Indian Culture and Research Journal* 37 no. 2:1–22.

Reinhard Schulze
The Quest for the West in an Era of Globalization: Some Remarks on the Hidden Meaning of Charles Taylor's Master Narrative

1 Introduction

Since the 1980s narrativity has become an influential theorem to analyze how human beings make sense of themselves. This highly controversial concept has traveled from psychology (Erik Erikson) via literary criticism (Frank Kermode, Northrop Frye, Hayden White, Eugene Vance) and film studies (Christian Metz) to philosophy and history. It is to the merit of Alasdair MacIntyre (1981), Paul Ricoeur (1983–1985), Jerome Bruner (1986), Charles Taylor (1989) and others that this theorem was introduced to philosophical identity studies. By restoring temporality as represented in narratives as part of philosophical interpretations, they reconciled history and ontology. Narrativists like Charles Taylor and Alasdair MacIntyre argue strongly in favor of "a normative, ethical claim: we ought to live our lives narratively, or as a story" (Strawson 2004: 428), or as Anthony Paul Kerby puts it: "Only narratives, Taylor maintains, can offer a coherent answer to the persistent questions concerning our identity" (1991: 59). Indeed, Taylor has accentuated this ethical normative aspect of narrativity: "It has often been remarked that making sense of one's life as a story is also, like orientation to the good, not an optional extra; that our lives exist also in this space of questions, which only a coherent narrative can answer" (Taylor 1989: 47). Anti-Narrativists, like Galen Strawson, radically criticized the validity of narrativity as a universal ideal (Strawson 2004). Evidently, after the wave of post-structural criticism, narrativity has reacquired its prominent position in order to justify a moral and social order. As a single narrative can never claim universal validity, a landscape of competing narratives have arisen; some are simply called a secular age, others, for example, Islam.

The social function of narrativity is evident: "Bringing narrativity to identity thus provides the conceptual sinews that produces a tighter, more historically sensitive coupling between social identity and agency" (Somers 1994: 635). Typ-

---

I would like to thank Florian Zemmin for his valuable comments on this chapter.

ically narratives share at least five properties: They "are (i) an optional medium for articulating some of our implicit self-interpretations and strong evaluations. Narratives alone enable us to (ii) care about our lives as temporal wholes and to (iii) interpret our orientations, successes and failures in a moral space. Further, narrative thinking is a way to provide concordance to (iv) diachronous and (v) synchronous dissonances in our strong evaluations" (Laitinen 2008: 146). In fact, the renewed justification of the use of narratives coincides with an ethical turn and a parallel culturalization of social worlds. Narratives, culture, and values create an evaluative framework which intertwines identity, subjectivity, and morality. The emplotment itself must be selective and constructivist and must have a constant and consistent theme. Themes such as the evolution of the "primacy of the individual which defines our culture" (ASA: 94) or, more generally speaking, of the "self" determine "how events are processed and what criteria will be used to prioritize events and render meaning to them" (Somers 1994: 617). One such important criterion or strategy is to subjectify the narrative. "My identity is defined by the commitments and identifications which provide the frame or horizon within which I can try to determine from case to case what is good, or valuable, or what ought to be done, or what I endorse or oppose. In other words, it is the horizon within which I am capable of taking a stand" (Taylor 1989: 27).

The renewed narratives of Western identity are certainly not pure and innocent. Even though they claim to give meaning to the Western world only – and in Taylor's case to a realm which may be historically linked to a "Europe of the cathedrals" (Duby 1966) – they indeed exercise power over other competing narratives. Hardly any other narrative which construes a social imaginary can avoid the discursive power exerted by narratives of the West. Indeed, even non-Western publics which seclude themselves from the ambit of the West now 'narrate' their identity. They may adopt the common validity claim of narrativity as the primary tool to justify a moral social order by weaving identity, subjectivity, and morality into a web of meaning: this has become an important discursive strategy of many value-oriented and conservative Islamic groups, such as the Muslim Brotherhood. Or they may radically dissociate themselves from emploting such a claim, as contemporary ultra-Islamic trends tend to do.

In this chapter, I tackle Charles Taylor's *A Secular* Age as an eminent instance of the quest for identity showing up in the reemergence of narratives. I am well aware that I can do full justice neither to the nuances of Taylor's rich work itself, nor to the numerous discussions it has provoked. I will instead merely try to expose a hidden meaning in Charles Taylor's Master Narrative, which, I claim, signifies a resurgence of a 'theology of society.'

2 The art of story telling

On May 22, 2008, Charles Taylor and the sociologist and historian Gérard Bouchard published their final report on behalf of the Consultation Commission on Accommodation Practices Related to Cultural Differences, which had been set up by the Québec Government in February 2007. The Bouchard-Taylor Commission had been asked to respond to public discontent concerning "reasonable accommodation" of religious and cultural practices. Although their mandate was relatively specific, Bouchard and Taylor scrutinized fundamental issues to which liberal democracies are exposed and which are conventionally labeled with expressions like "cultural integration," "collective identity," "church-state relations," and "cultural and religious harmonization" (Tremblay 2009). After having taken stock of governmental harmonization practices in Québec and having analyzed the Québec practices in a comparative perspective, the commission formulated recommendations for the government. The report suggested a strategy of harmonized practices within an order called "open secularism," framing a society based on networks, and accommodated to four principles: moral equality of persons, freedom of conscience and religion, state neutrality towards religions and the separation of church and state (Bouchard and Taylor 2008: 134–137).[1]

In September 2007, Harvard University Press published Charles Taylor's book *A Secular Age*. It may be by pure chance that both publications appeared almost simultaneously. Yet the report of the Bouchard-Taylor-Commission sheds some light on the broader meaning of *A Secular Age*. Implicitly, the book proposes a detailed justification for a social and political order built upon the principles of moral equality of persons, freedom of conscience and religion, state neutrality towards religions, and the separation of church and state. In the report, Bouchard and Taylor (2008: 20) advocated an "open secularism," which "seeks to develop the essential outcomes of secularism (first and second principles [the moral equality of persons and the freedom of conscience and religion]) by defining institutional structures (third and fourth principles [the separation of Church and State and state neutrality in respect of religious and deep-seated secular convictions]) in light of this objective." In *A Secular Age*, Taylor – although cautiously and with reservation – relates the quality of openness, which reminds us of Karl Popper's definition of an "open society" (Popper 1945),[2] to a moral virtue

---

[1] For earlier views see Taylor 1994.
[2] Taylor does not mention Popper in *A Secular Age*.

of Christianity, maintaining that "faith in our [...] theistic sense, is peculiar to a certain kind of stance of openness in the immanent frame" (ASA: 551).[3] As Taylor does not use the expression "open secularism" in *A Secular Age*, it seems more likely that the term primarily serves to valorize a specific public opinion. Nonetheless, it gives us an impression of the political ideal that may be considered the valued endpoint of *A Secular Age*.

Although the academic discussion of *A Secular Age* has taken into account its political implications as expressed in the Commission report (Mahmood 2010: 297; McGoldrick 2011: 453; Burchardt this volume), the debate on *A Secular Age* has clearly focused on the story that Taylor wrote, as if it was an answer to the deep "sigh" he uttered in *Sources of the Self:* "We who think and see have a glimpse of how deep the roots are of our fragile consciousness, and how mysterious and strange its emergence is. This spiritual attitude is in flat contradiction to the Cartesian" (Taylor 1989: 347). Any reading of *A Secular Age* should consider not only this "sigh," but also Taylor's relief at being freed from the assumed constraints of naturalism, which he suspects hides behind formalist epistemology (Taylor 1985). Richard Rorty (1994: 32) put this relief into words:

> Taylor and I both pride ourselves on having escaped from the collapsed circus tent of epistemology – those acres of canvas under which many of our colleagues are still thrashing aimlessly about. But each of us thinks that the other is still, so to speak, stumbling about among the tangled guy-ropes, rather than having escaped altogether. Taylor thinks that once one gets out from under epistemology one comes to an 'uncompromising realism.' I think one comes to a position in which the only version of 'realism' one has left is the trivial, uninteresting and common-sensical one which says that all true beliefs are true because things are as they are.

In light of these fundamental discussions, we first have to embark on an exploration of Taylor's Canadian idealism and its sometimes implicit, sometimes explicit Hegelianism (Meynell 2011) before we can turn to discuss the meaning of *A Secular Age* in detail. Yet until today the reception of *A Secular Age* has not truly integrated this issue. We can classify the criticism directed at *A Secular Age* thus far into five groups:[4] (1) Criticism of his use of conventional concepts (such as religion, secularity, modernity, secularism, belief, faith, transcendence, immanence, enchantment); (2) criticism of his metaphors and hermeneutical notions (such as buffered self, porous self, immanent frame, social imaginary, op-

---

3 The concept 'open secularism' was already used by liberal Protestant theologians in the tradition of Paul Tillich in the early 1960s and often applied to the Indian context, cf. Thomas 1962 and Thomas 1974: 19.
4 I heavily draw on the bibliography established by Zemmin (this volume).

tion, immediacy, Intellectual Deviation Story, agape, historical self, fullness, nova effect, closed world structures); (3) criticism of the story told (by referring to its assumed parochialism and reductionism, by asking whether a certain historical context would fit into *A Secular Age*, by reproaching Taylor with neglecting the role of colonialism and orientalism, by questioning his historical reconstruction of early modernity); (4) criticism of his attitude as well as his intent (such as idealism, romanticism, religious nostalgia, Catholic stance, Christian apologetic, intention to recover pre-modern spirituality) and (5) criticism of Taylor's reading of the present (with respect to the empirical reality and the normative expectations). Taylor's story bounces off all these criticisms (Taylor 2010a; 2010b; 2011). The strength of Taylor's highly sophisticated text lies in the fact that it tells a story which is based on bringing together hundreds of pieces of evidence to support the prima facie case of his own account. The dramatic composition and representation of the main elements immunize his story against each of the five fields of criticism just mentioned. As a consequence, critiques tend to interpret the whole story through just a few words. The German sociologist Matthias Koenig (in this volume) crystalizes his criticism by calling *A Secular Age* a "culturalist secularization narrative."

Taylor (2010b: 300) himself justifies his story-telling by stating:

> My book lays out, unashamedly, a master narrative. The adverb bespeaks the view I hold, that we can't avoid such narratives. The attempt to escape them only means that we operate by an unacknowledged, hence unexamined and uncriticized, narrative. That's because we (modern Westerners) can't help understanding ourselves in these terms.

Historians have again and again questioned the validity of narratives not only of secularization, but as such of history as well. The old conflict between 'plain history' and 'metahistory'[5] is still alive. Many historians have used the term 'metahistory' disparagingly, especially when dealing with Arnold Toynbee (Underhill 1951). Edward Whiting Fox (1963: 110) for example argued:

> Mr. Toynbee proposes the method of enlarging the context in an effort to find like phenomena in a larger field. Here we can anticipate his escape from history to metahistory or from the study of national states to civilizations and higher religions. The human attribute of self-consciousness, to him, carries an intimidation of Reality which exceeds the powers of reason.

Yet there were others who radically defended the importance of metahistory. In 1951, the Catholic historian Christopher Dawson argued that Tocqueville's great

---

5 For early uses of the concept 'metahistory' see Ritter 1986.

masterworks of history succeeded "not in spite of [metahistorical] principles but because of them, [...] since concern with the ultimate meaning and pattern of history imparted an element of 'profundity'." Contrary to Alan Bullock, whom he radically criticized, Dawson was convinced that "[t]he only conclusion that I can draw from this is that metahistory is not the enemy of true history but its guide and friend, provided always that it is good metahistory" (Dawson 1951: 12). Taylor (2007: 733) said that both Dawson and T. S. Eliot shared the view that "the deepest sources of European culture were in Christianity, and that this culture must lose force and depth to the extent that moderns departed from it." This was of course not Charles Taylor's intellectual forebear.[6] Yet, criticizing the attacks of "a certain trendy 'post-modernism'" against grand narratives – Taylor takes Jean-François Lyotard as an example – he (ASA: 717) comes to a conclusion that seemingly echoes Dawson:

> Running through all these attacks is the spectre of meaninglessness; that as a result of the denial of transcendence, of heroism, of deep feeling, we are left with a view of human life which is empty, cannot inspire commitment, offers nothing really worth while, cannot answer the craving for goals we can dedicate ourselves to. Human happiness can only inspire us when we have to fight against the forces which are destroying it; but once realized, it will inspire nothing but ennui, a cosmic yawn.

Since Hayden White's studies of "metahistory" (White 1973; 1987), the techniques of writing or telling academic narratives have become transparent. The start point of a successful story consists of establishing a valued endpoint, or as Alasdair MacIntyre (1997: 141) stressed: "Narrative requires an evaluative framework in which good or bad character helps to produce unfortunate or happy outcomes."[7] The next step requires the selection of events relevant to the endpoint, the ordering of these events, keeping the stability of identity, providing casual linkage and employing clear demarcation signs (Gergen 2005). Obviously, Taylor's narrative meets all these criteria.

The result could be what Donald P. Spence once called "narrative truth" (Spence 1982; 2005). Though having been built upon evidence, such a narrative truth has no factual one-to-one correspondence with reality. A narrative truth is coherent, comprehensive and consistent, that fulfills the requirements Habermas (1973: 218) defined in the following manner: "Truth we call the assertive claim we connect with the constative speech act. A statement is true if the assertive claim

---

[6] On Dawson see Caldecott and Morrill 1997; Russello 1998; Carter 2008; from an apologetic point of view Thornhill 2008–2009.
[7] Cf. MacIntyre 1981.

of the speech acts with which we use the clauses claiming that statement is justified."[8] The justification which a narrative truth represents is based on its argumentative usefulness for establishing a meaning, or as the Swedish historian Robert Thorp (2014: 28) wrote:

> [A]n ability to contextualise history and historical accounts can make the individual aware that history and the sense we make of it are contextually contingent, something that in turn will allow the individual to make metahistorical analyses and regard history and its accounts as representations of historical facts rather than historical facts in and of themselves. This ability is illustrated by the term historiographic gaze according to which the individual regards all matters as contextually contingent, even the meaning she creates herself, an ability that will allow individuals to make genetic uses of history.

Taylor of course accepts the fact that multiple master narratives of modernity exist. In *A Secular Age*, he defines a master narrative in simple terms: "A Master Narrative is an account which embeds the events it makes sense of within some understanding of the general drift of history. This in turn is intimately linked with a certain view of the gamut of human motivations" (ASA: 818n27). However, some master narratives are, as Taylor says, more convincing than others. He bases his own narrative on the conviction "that modern culture, in breaking with the structures and beliefs of Christendom, also carried certain facets of Christian life further than they ever were taken or could have been taken within Christendom. In relation to the earlier forms of Christian culture, we have to face the humbling realization that the breakout was a necessary condition of the development" (Taylor 1999: 16). The plot and valued endpoint of Taylor's narrative is based on a conviction. He confirms that the "attempt in this book has been to offer another [account of the rise of modern secularity], I think [a] more convincing one" (ASA: 573).

So what does Taylor mean when he says that a narrative should be convincing? An argument seems to be convincing if it fits with the experiences that its public audience has had and if it helps to justify the moral judgment that the public has developed and upheld. Accordingly, a narrative, as a bundle of arguments, aims at strengthening a set of beliefs and rules which govern acts, the application of which is always connected to the possibility that new doubts will come to mind regarding the suitability of the action schemes in question. Meanwhile, doubt (which must for its part lead to a new behavioral habit) arises when a conviction is questioned by a surprising event so that the hitherto undisputed validity of the specific action habit changes into a state of being an irregular ac-

---

8 Translation by Lohnstein 2014: 24; also cited in Cantarini, Abraham, and Leiss 2014: 4.

tivity (Pierce 1877; Prechtl 2008). A narrative is not a theory, as Taylor himself stresses: "This is not to say that I will be offering my own such general theory [of religion]. On the contrary, it would perhaps be better at the outset to come clean, and say that I doubt very much whether any such general theory can even be established" (ASA: 679). The difference between a narrative and a theory of wide reach lies in the fact that a narrative can be convincing or doubtful, whereas a theory can be verified or falsified. The purpose of a narrative is to convince an audience, whereas the purpose of a theory is for example to create a complete, general, consistent and precise recording of a sector of reality, being based on logical statements and theses on how this object came into being, how it is structured, how it works and how its parts cohere with the 'whole.' By critically uncovering the narrative strategy of the current theories of secularization, Taylor does not simply create an alternative narrative but simultaneously demonstrates that any genealogical narrative of a secular age is limited. Thus he factually invites us to read his narrative in a Taylorian way. So we may ask: of what does Taylor's narrative wish to convince us?

Taylor's narrative, or in his own words his "story,"[9] primarily offers a meaningful, perhaps even sensible justification. The object of this justification is twofold: first, it refers to being religious without deriving justification from a set of normative rules belonging to a certain/specific religion; second it esteems being religious as a moral value and as an epistemic order which is simply built upon the notion 'belief.' Taylor's narrative has been very successful at translating a validity claim called 'religion' into a rational argument.[10]

Yet Taylor does not contend that his narrative is 'correct' or even 'true.' For John Milbank, the privilege of narrativity not having to be true was a welcome result of postmodernism: "With this ending [i.e. of modernity], there ends also the modern predicament of theology. It no longer has to measure up to accepted secular standards of scientific truth or normative rationality" (Milbank 1991: 225).

Since the decline of poststructuralist criticism, master narratives have come into fashion again. Fredric Jameson (2007: 64) even argued that the return of master narratives was itself part of the poststructuralist paradigm:

---

9 Only in two places in *A Secular Age* does Taylor describe his story as "my narrative" (608, 768). He prefers to simply call it "my story"" (59, 85, 115, 735, 771, 773).
10 Typically, he does not explain what he means when speaking of belief and faith. He obviously uses these words in an ordinary sense, but it is never clear whether he means a certain feeling, conviction, confidence or trust. In *A Secular Age*, Taylor uses more than 1000 times the words belief and faith and their derivation. In fact, it is a book on belief and unbelief and on "the meaning and end of religion" in modern times, to quote the famous expression of Wilfred Cantwell Smith (1962), whose name does not appear in the book. Cf. Asad 2001.

> [Lyotard's] most famous statement on postmodernism is that it should prepare the return of the great modernisms. Now does that mean the return of the great master narratives? Is there not some nostalgia at work here? [...] All one has to do is look at the reemergence of religious paradigms, whether it is in Iran or in liberation theology or American fundamentalism. There are all kinds of master narratives in this world, which was supposed to be beyond narrative.

Already in 1996, the American art critic and historian Hal Foster proposed that the adieu to master narratives as proposed by poststructuralism was often understood "as the latest proper name of the West, now melancholically obsessed with its postcolonial decline" (Foster 1996: 206). Of course, master narratives never faded out, so they have not returned but rather re-emerged as a meaning-producing force. They are dominated by three themes, namely the inevitability of market economics as the historically dominant form of human progress, "biological essentialism under the cover of genetics and new evolutionary biology and psychology" (Braidotti 2006), and the anthropology of religion and ethics. Within these big histories, the Modern Age tends to become described as a new Axial Age. Already in the late 1970s many authors were in fact convinced that narrativity was loosing its structure-preserving map along with its stability of identity. In *The Postmodern Condition*, Jean-François Lyotard ([1979] 1984: xxiv) stated:

> Simplifying to the extreme, I define postmodern as incredulity toward metanarratives. This incredulity is undoubtedly a product of progress in the sciences: but that progress in turn presupposes it. To the obsolescence of the metanarrative apparatus of legitimation corresponds, most notably, the crisis of metaphysical philosophy and of the university institution which in the past relied on it. The narrative function is losing its functors, its great hero, its great dangers, its great voyages; its great goal. It is being dispersed in clouds of narrative language elements – narrative, but also denotative, prescriptive, descriptive, and so on.

Most of the poststructuralist thinkers were positive about destroying metanarratives, meta-discourses, grand narratives or master narratives. They identified them as simple formulas or "scripts" that we often use when telling stories, or as the story that produces other stories. Master narratives, it was said, embodied our expectations about how things work. Typically, they were based on actual experience. The term, borrowed from literary criticism (Genette 1972: 239: "le métarécit est un récit dans le récit") identified those stories that generate all the other stories.

Lyotard, who had analyzed two master narratives of modernity (the master narrative of the emancipation of the rational subject[11] and the master narrative

---

11 Lyotard [1979] 1984: xxiii.

of the history of the universal spirit[12]) advocated what he termed a kind of Wittgensteinian language game (*petits récits*)[13] and called for a multiplicity of theoretical standpoints[14] which would be instrumental in eroding the hegemony of master narratives.[15] The poststructuralist skepticism towards the master narratives of progress, Enlightenment, or secularism and of the ideological justification of master narratives by means of Marxism or liberalism was at the height of its popularity from the collapse of ideologically justified political and social orders in Eastern Europe until the events of 9/11.

As a matter of course, poststructuralist criticism did not destroy the use and meaning of master narratives in late modernity (one need only think of Francis Fukuyama's *End of History* [1992] or of Samuel Huntington's *The Clash of Civilizations* [1996]). Still, contrary to the old set of master narratives of the nineteenth and early twentieth century, which had created the cultural imagination of the West, poststructuralism now contributed to the fact that these new master narratives had to be justified for *being* master narratives.

3 The re-emergence of narratives

After 9/11, this incredulity or skepticism vanished, and since then a multitude of new master narratives have emerged which forgo any justification. Many of them deal with specific so-called cultural concepts, often in the popularized form of "short histories." So there are short histories of "God," "religion," "violence," "humanity," "time," "world history," "the West," "love," and even "secularism" (Smith 2007). Many of them are anthropological in the sense that they portray the genealogy of the respective concept as part of a grand story of the human condition. Taylor's narrative coincides with two major current trends: a) with the trend to define the *conditio humana* in general, and b) with the shift from the social to the cultural.

Taylor's genealogy of secularism, of course, does not fall into the category of these histories: it is anything but short, and it does not tell the story of the *human condition*, but rather of the Christian condition of modernity or of Christian secularity (he does not use this expression in *A Secular Age*). Thus, the historical scope is much smaller and covers only some 700 years. In principle, how-

---

12 Lyotard [1979] 1984: 32.
13 Lyotard [1979] 1984: xxiv.
14 Lyotard [1979] 1984: 57.
15 Lyotard and Thébaud [1979] 1985: 59.

ever, Taylor's quest for a genealogy of secularity or secularism clearly shares the current endeavor to ascertain the normative *Eigensinn* of modernity (Kluge, Negt 1993). Here, I intentionally use the German term *Eigensinn*, a concept that, with its double meaning of resistance and proprietary, does not readily translate into English, but could perhaps best be described as an obstinacy in self-referentiality and self-demarcation.[16]

So, what is the meaning of retelling the genealogy of modernity, that is, of the relation of religion and society? Apart from the fact that Taylor's learned and masterful genealogy is in many respects extremely enjoyable to read and that Taylor has told a very suggestive story, *A Secular Age* fulfills a cultural want and seems to be in accordance with a desire to secure the hallmark(s) of Western excellence.

Obviously, Taylor's narrative makes sense, even if many critics have suggested alterations to certain chapters of his story. Working with *A Secular Age* often simply implies discussing the meaning of one of Taylor's many telling metaphors, such as "fullness," "buffered self," "enchantment," and so on; to question the historical validity of certain descriptive events with which Taylor has furnished his narrative; or to change the main characters which govern the story. But even these sometimes-meticulous critical interventions only deepen the forceful meaning of this narrative. In a way, it looks like a relief story after 9/11, although Charles Taylor of course had already written on secularism in his earlier works. With that said, his earlier books, chapters, and articles were known primarily to specialists only. After 9/11, however, the situation changed dramatically. In view of what had happened in New York and Washington, there obviously was a renewed need for contemporary forms of Western self-assurance and of rationalizing the Western *Eigensinn*.

Taylor's narrative coincides with this need, and this may explain why it garners such wide-ranging attention. The narrative technique of developing an argument has turned out to be very instrumental as an adequate response to the challenges to which many think the West is exposed. Even scholars, who formerly had elaborated their argument along historical, analytical and/or hermeneutic traditions of epistemology, took up narrativism as a distinct form. Consider the following statement of Jürgen Habermas (2001: 175):

> Egalitarian universalism, from which the ideas of liberty and solidary co-existence, of autonomous life-style and emancipation, of individual morals of conscience, human rights and democracy stem, is an unmediated heir of the Jewish ethics of justice and the Christian ethics of love. Being in substance unchanged, this heritage had been critically appropriated

---

16 Pavsek (1996) translated Negt's and Kluge's term "Eigensinn" as "obstinacy."

again and again and newly interpreted. There is no alternative to it to this day. Also in view of the current challenges of a post-national constellation, we still live on this substance. Everything else is postmodern ramblings.

No wonder that the contemporary trend toward narrativity coincides with a renewal of heritage discourses.[17] At the same time, however, critics tend to transform part of the narrative structure into analytical terms. So Taylor's metaphors, which in my view produce meaning only within the framework of *his* story, have been discussed as if they were analytical categories which could be theorized independently. In this case the metaphor develops a life of its own and then becomes the object of investigation, as if there was a correspondence between the metaphor's meaning and reality.

Now, there are many ways to re-assure the West of its inherent meaning. The boom in historical novels is in itself telling. *A Secular Age*, of course, is not a novel or an epic, but what I would call an example of *argumentative narrative genealogy*. The privilege of such a genealogy lies in the fact that in "the argumentative imagination, argument is also narrative – the argument emerges from the narrative, and the narrative is part of the argument" (Myerson 1992: 179). Thus, narrative and argument are indissolubly bound together. Habermas (1990: 124) insisted that "to *contradict*, to negate, has only the sense of 'wanting to be different'." We can certainly circumscribe the purpose of a master narrative to establish this "wanting to be different," keeping in mind that as much as contradicting and negating, a master narrative also confirms and enforces the *Eigensinn* of modernity.

The broad influence of Taylor's master narrative indicates that many in the West feel more and more uncomfortable with the idea that they have been interpreted as post-modern, as the proposed fragmentation of epistemic orders inevitably leads to a loss of clear demarcation signs. The need for an *argumentative narrative genealogy* of the Western *eigensinn* surely fits within the current debates over the 'end of postmodernism.' The American sociologist Norman Kent Denzin had, for instance, already predicted in 1997 that after the end of postmodernism qualitative research will contribute to a new "scientific spirituality" and will thereby leave its mark on the morals of the society of the future (Denzin 1997: 20–21).

This in some way characterizes *A Secular Age*. The book – and in saying "book," I include its reception and influence – illustrates a painful subject,

---

[17] ASA: 370: " Exclusive humanism has inherited both the allegiance to the moral order, and the affirmation of ordinary life." In *A Secular Age*, the concept of heritage, however, is still rather seldom used, whereas it has become the basic conceptual notion in Cook 2014.

namely the quest for the West in an era of globalization. This quest is not *In Search of Lost Time* or the *Remembrance of Things Past*, it is rather a modus by which the West tries to justify its being the West. Taylor has tried to give a new meaning to the West. Earlier, the West had been the place in the world where Enlightenment, technology, and rationalization had produced a societal and political order which represented the civilizational ideal for mankind. In this context, Orientalism had been instrumental to discursively justify the factual hegemony of European powers over the world order. Put simply, Orientalism explained to the public why a particular order should have universal validity and be vested with the power to govern the universal realm of its particularity, whereas the participation in the legitimacy of its universal validity should be restricted to the West. The discursive practices linked to Orientalism still needed this difference in order to give meaning to the West.

Now, with the end of the post-modern condition, the West obviously requires new and adjusted narratives that digest not only modern orientalism but also poststructuralist criticism. It is one of the strengths of *A Secular Age* that it fits perfectly with exactly these preconditions. First, it radically refrains from dealing with anything beyond the Latin Christian West. Taylor seldom deals with competing traditions that have also been used to express modernity, such as Judaism, Islam or Buddhism. As an example, we read (ASA: 676):

> I have been trying to describe the conflicted field of debate between belief and unbelief in Western culture today. I characterized this first, as a field under cross pressure between extreme positions, represented by orthodox religion on one hand (that is, originally by Christianity and Judaism, but now more and more joined by Islam, Hinduism, Buddhism, and other faiths), and hard-line materialistic atheism on the other.

Yet Taylor also makes the following assessment: "[T]he modern secular world emerged from and out of the more and more rule-bound and norm-governed Reform of Latin Christendom" (ASA: 741–742). So, what is Taylor's "modern secular world"? He uses this expression only twice in his book (ASA: 742, 772), and nowhere does he explain to where the confines of that world called Latin Christendom should extend. Given the fact that quite a large number of Indian, Arab, Chinese or African writers *do* "experience moral fullness," *do* "identify the locus of their highest moral capacity and inspiration, without reference to God, but within the range of purely intra-human powers" (ASA: 244–245), we have to ask how it became possible that they nowadays (and in fact since the nineteenth century) live within the confines of that modern secular world. Look at Akeel Bilgrami, Salman Rushdie and many other writers and scholars from Bombay, or Sadik J. al-Azm from Damascus, ʿAbdallah al-Qasimi from Riyad, ʿAli Ahmad Saʿid Adonis from Qassabin in Northern Syria, who all explicitly have *chosen not* to believe in God. True, many of them have preferred to live in Western countries, as they feared social marginalization or even political persecution in their homelands. Nevertheless, their writings and public appearances attest to the fact that they are all sharing in the search for fullness, and the ideal of an exclusive humanism and the order of choice. Is it then sufficient to identify these writers as participants in a secularist elite subculture?

A simple answer would be that they have been socialized within the confines of a modern secularity built up by the colonial order. This, however, does not explain how these writers and scholars entered the immanent frame without having accepted the validity of the Christian genealogy of secularism first. Does one have to become a Christian first before becoming a legitimate heir of secularism? Does one really have to become a Christian first, before becoming an atheist, as Michel Onfray (2007: 55–58) proclaimed? No wonder then that some Muslim authors have been discrediting secularism as a hidden form of Christianity; the Egyptian professor of agriculture, Faraj Foda, who had advocated secularism, was accused of apostasy and finally was killed by two members of al-Jamaʿa al-Islamiyya on June 8, 1992. For them, secularism was a Christian project, allegedly proven by the fact that the Arabic term for 'secularism' is of Christian origin.

Or, should the genealogy of the modern secular world, with all its implications, be extended beyond the West? Peter van der Veer (forthcoming), Dipesh Chakrabarty (2009), Tomoko Masuzawa (2005), Saba Mahmood (2010), Elizabeth Hurd (2008) and others have forcefully shown that the West has never existed in a vacuum and that its secularity deeply depended on the interaction with the so-called non-Western world. True, but are there any other affirmative genealogies of secularism apart from that in Western form? Some authors, like the Berkeley historian Jonathan Sheehan, reply that we should dismiss such affirmative genealogies in general, as they are nothing but apologetics, a combination of theological argument and historical framework (Sheehan 2003; 2005; 2006; 2010). Sheehan of course is right that a master narrative offering a genealogy of the *eigensinn* of the modern can never be a historical reconstruction of complex social and cultural processes. Due to the fact that narratives represent a genealogy affirming and justifying the validity of a given modern order, they also propose a different type of interpretation. In addition, they serve a different purpose, which Hans Joas (2003: 11) explains as follows: "It is not about a pure narration of contingent coherences, which does not even search for a way to universal validity, but about a remembering reconstruction of experiential coherences out of which our loyalty to these values emerged."

Narrators of these narratives have set themselves the task of giving *back to moral values* their motivating and guiding force. This form of affirmative genealogy is reconstructive. It differs in principle from negative deconstructive genealogies as for example related by Michel Foucault. Affirmative genealogies are not historical novels but novelistic histories, and of course an affirmative genealogy is not, as Nancy Levene (2014) puts it, simply "fiction." Yet narratives cannot be proven right or wrong, correct or false. They do not correspond to a real world, but are instead consistent with a particular set of beliefs that people actually hold. Thus, a narrative could only be true under the condition of a coherent theory of truth. In this case the particular set of beliefs which produce such truth must themselves be justified? In the case of *A Secular Age*, why is it just a set of Christian sentences, propositions and beliefs that can specify secularism?

4 On the far side of the West

Thus it is not very helpful to transpose the narrative into a historical account and then to criticize it for not having considered contrary developments or for having generalized its pieces of evidence according to its plot and *telos*. The same is true for Max Weber's work, which as we all know cannot be regarded as history but as an ideal-typically conceived semantic realm of understanding reality. The only way to criticize Taylor and Weber is (a) to ask whether they produce a convincing account, (b) whether they offer a coherent interpretation and (c) whether the information upon which the narrator has developed his story is fictitious or related to a historical imaginary shared by the audience.

Now, some other authors try to expand Taylor's master narrative beyond the West. Florian Zemmin (this volume) rightly points out that this project first of all means "testing Taylor's concepts for individual cases," be they in the West or beyond the West. But even if the result of such a testing yields a certain concept that does not make sense, let us say in an Islamic context, this would, as Zemmin convincingly put it, "not make Taylor's story meaningless, for it still speaks to us," – and, I would like to add, speaks also to a Muslim audience. Strictly speaking, this means that we can only compare stories or parts of stories, as it is the stories that represent a view of the facts within an analogy. This seems plausible. But still there remains the problem that Taylor uses metaphors such as "immanent frame," "fullness," or "social imaginary" which are by definition implicit analogies and which work only in the context of *his* story. I deem it rather difficult to translate the metaphorical meaning of these terms into objective 'phenomena' which could be compared. Nevertheless, Zemmin's approach seems to me more promising than simply placing "Islam in Conversation with *A Secular Age*," as Elizabeth Barre (2012) tries to do. Barre misreads Taylor's narrative as providing a theoretical framework for a universal historical process. She focuses on Taylor's three social imaginaries, the age of the *Ancien Régime*, the

Age of Mobilization and the *Secular Age*. The actual Secular Age or the *Age of Authenticity* is said to have come into the world only after the 1960s; during the Age of Mobilization, stretching from the earliest drives to reform the Church in the fifteenth century to the "era after the Second World War" (ASA: 445) religious forms of the *ancien régime*-type suffered decay, but new forms emerged that met the needs of the age and "recruited and mobilized people on an impressive scale" (ASA: 471). Now, Barre (2012: 142) identifies the social imaginaries of the contemporary Muslim world with Taylor's *Age of Mobilization:*

> for most Muslims the moral life is primarily, if not exclusively, about living in accord with the divine law, or shari'ah. Moreover, if there is anything the Qur'an makes clear, it is that Allah—like the God of the Protestant reformers—will hold each of us responsible for whether we have done so on an ultimate day of judgment.

In addition, she argues that "the Muslim imaginary also mirrors the Age of Mobilization in its willingness to admit of denominations within the larger religious-moral order." Yet instead of preparing the ground for a shift to an Age of Authenticity, the Muslim World supposedly is even "witnessing a move in the opposite direction (from a modern moral order to something closer to the Ancien Régime)" (Barre 2012: 144).

This reading of Taylor's novelistic history is highly problematic for four reasons. First, it handles Taylor's narrative as if it was a theoretical model. Second, it generalizes Islamicity as if it was a uniform way of giving meaning to the world through the use of Islamic traditions. Third, it '– again (Schulze 2010) – equates Islam to the normative conceptualization of Protestantism. And fourth, it creates the idea that there is a "Muslim imaginary." Taylor himself surely would have been very cautious about such a framing of the Muslim world. He himself never speaks of a "Christian imaginary" – which indeed would not have made any sense within his story – and he would never accept the idea that there is a time lag between the West and other "worlds."

Thus, despite Taylor's focus on the history of the Christian West and his explicit protests to the contrary, is the argument of *A Secular Age* – in both its descriptive and normative forms –ultimately universal in its scope? After all, not only would his claims about the transcendent make little sense were they confined to a particular part of the world at a particular point in history, but because he himself betrays this universalism in numerous passages.

However, if the *argument* of *A Secular Age* really were universal in its scope, then Taylor's narrative would have lost its sense as an affirmative genealogy of modernity as experienced by "the West." Instead, it would be more accurate to say that Taylor's narrative shares a universal trend to construe validity through affirmative genealogies. In fact there is a worldwide consensus that normative validity nowadays has to be justified by recourse to convincing affirmative genealogies of moral values. In the academic world this has been mirrored by neo-pragmatism and by the now widely discussed "ethical turn," a label proposed by Peter Baker (1995).

The applicability of Taylor's narrative to so-called non-Western contexts is thus stretched to its limits. Certainly, the confines of the validity of this narrative are construed within the narrative itself. In its self-limiting aspect, *A Secular Age* radically differs from earlier master narratives, such as the great bundle of modernization theories, which openly claimed universal validity. This restraint leaves the floor open for competing narratives to affirm the moral order of a social imaginary. The main question then is whether or not these forms of justification refer to social imaginaries of the same kind, which can all be assembled under the umbrella term of "secularity." Because Taylor's narrative does not offer an analytical global theory of secularity, and indeed criticizes older theories of secularity, we would need a theory that adequately generalizes worldwide experiences of contemporary secularity. In other words, the meaning of secularity should be established beyond *A Secular Age*, that is, beyond those particular master narratives which serve to justify a particular moral order.

Taylor's narrative masterfully addresses a *state of affairs*, which does not maintain the ontology of secularity and does not necessarily correspond to the factuality of a social order. In a nominalist sense, secularity is primarily a normative order which justifies and safeguards liberty, or in other words a plurality of options. Calling this order "secular," however, relates it to Christianity, and the narration of the genealogy of secularity justifies its being Christian.

5 On semanticizing difference

We have to keep in mind that all theories of secularity are based on a semantic transposition of the notion "secular." The term "secular" originally was used by religious actors to characterize a societal order. It was only in the 1840s that George Jacob Holyoake (1817–1906) dared to introduce an affirmative meaning of "secular" in order to define the autonomous state of society independent from any order of the church.

The negative use of the term was still predominant when, in the 1840s, the phrase "Secular Age" became a widely used *topos*, particularly in the context of the "Second Awakening." In 1841, Alexander Campbell (1788–1866), a prominent figure of the American Restoration Movement, stated in a short report on his travels to Ohio (Campbell 1841: 226):

> This is truly a secular age. The political and commercial spirit seems to pervade all society. It enters the sanctuary of religion and carnalizes the very worship of God. It profanes the family altar, and seems to mingle its sordid counsels and ceaseless croakings with the most sanctified schemes of piety and benevolence. It inhibits the retirements of the closet, the moral culture of children, the proper sanctification of the Lord's day, and that preparation of heart essential to the profitable enjoyment of the ordinances of religion.

No wonder that by the 1850s, religious actors stressed that they lived not in a secular but in a *religious age*. Likewise, societal actors grew to mistrust religion more and more, fearing its hegemony. Holyoake (1896: 50), who had at least popularized, if not indeed invented, the term *secularism*, related a discussion that took place in London in 1853 (Grant, Holyoake 1853):

> Our adversary[18] had been appointed with clerical ceremony, on a 'three year's mission' against us. He had wit, readiness, and an electric velocity of speech, boasting that he could speak three times faster than any one else. But he proved to be of use to us without intending it, 'his acid words turned the sweet milk of kindness into curds', whereby he set many against the cause he presented. He had the cleverness to see that there ought to be a 'Christian Secularism', which raised Secularism to the level of Christian curiosity.

Five years after this discussion, George Holyoake's ally John Watts (1834–1866) noted: "Orthodox ministers, indeed, have begun to proclaim a 'Christian Secularism,' which means attention to human as well as to spiritual affairs" (Watts 1859: 146).[19] Despite Holyoake's efforts, the term "secular" only very slowly turned into an affirmative category describing the state of society as a normative order. In fact, societal actors turned religious actors' pejorative ascription into a positive self-description. Initially, this discourse was restricted to the Anglo-Saxon world. In German, the notion "säkulare Gesellschaft" (secular society) became common only in the late 1950s. The preferred expression still was "religious age" or "modern age." In 1912, the Austrian author and artist Hermann Bahr (1863–1934) for example, who advocated a modernized form of Catholicism, was still convinced that he lived in a *religious age* and pointed at the importance of William James, Henri Bergson and Rudolf Eucken. The first German language use of "a secular age" that I have found is in a book by Hermann Sauer, the Berlin minister and representative of the so-called German Church (1938: 459). In

---

18 Rev. Brewin Grant (1821–1892), until 1853 a Congregational minister in Birmingham, had been engaged in a mission against Secularism until 1868. In 1868 he retired as a pastor and devoted himself to a campaign against what he called "Ritualism" and a "Catholic revival in England" (Grant 1869: 237–244).
19 John Watts was the brother of Charles Watts (1836–1906), who later became one of the leading figures of the free thought movement in Britain. See Royle 1974: 6, 283.

1961 Otto Dibelius (1880–1967), then president of the Protestant Council of Churches in Germany, was still denouncing the secular age as responsible for transforming the gospel into an "unrealistic affair" (Dibelius 1961: 319),[20] and Jürgen Moltmann, a German Reformed theologian, identified the change from productive to skeptical tolerance as a common trait of the secular age (Moltmann 1975: 178). The date of the shift towards an affirmative use of the term "säkular" may be symbolically dated with the deliberations of the Fifth Section of the General Assembly of the World Council of Churches in Uppsala in 1968 where for the first time the secular age was defined as a positive frame for German Protestantism (Müller 1971).[21]

As for the Arabic public, the equivalent notion "secular age" (al-ʿaṣr al-ʿalmānī or less often al-ʿaṣr al-dunyawī [al-ʿArawi 1978]) and the expression "secular society" (al-mujtamaʿ al-ʿalmānī ['Uthman 1969] or al-mujtamaʿ al-dunyawī [al-Turabi 1974]) was not used affirmatively before the 1960s. The best example is Nasif Nassar, who stated in 1970: "The historical dialectical movement in which the Lebanese people live expresses by itself the necessity of the transformation of a religious society [mujtamaʿ dīnī] into a secular society [mujtamaʿ ʿalmānī]" (Nassar [1970]) 1995: 176). So the German as well as the Arabic public showed the same reservation in using the attribute "secular" as an affirmative category.

The same semantic transposition is true for the concept that societal actors used to characterize religion, namely the word 'culture,' which religious actors then adopted in the nineteenth century. This leads us to a principle question: is it meaningful to use (polemical or affirmative) concepts of self-interpretation that arose within a given normative order as analytical categories? Knowing that both the secular and the cultural are merely ascriptions of the two normative orders called religion and society, wouldn't it be more appropriate to analyze "religion and society" and ask to what extent and how these two orders have been shaping the human world?

We would thus need a theory that models the common history of the epistemic order that configured the pair religion and society. We may even look at a common history of semanticizing this twin couple by means of the Christian pair secular and cultural, for these latter concepts have become common to all traditions that are used to give meaning to a nation state. The emergence of the religion-and-society order can be reconstructed historically for many coun-

---

[20] This skeptical view was prominent until the late 1960s. See, for example, Vicedom 1969: 60–63.

[21] The expression "Gottesdienst in einem säkularisierten Zeitalter" stems from Dietrich Bonhoeffer, see Bethge [1968] 1990: 340–359; Novák 1968: 193–197. Often, theologians resigningly accepted secularism as a general frame, for example Friese 1967: 60.

tries worldwide. Both terms do not describe an extra-human fact but normative orders which grow out of a differentiation within the epistemic mode of dealing with the world. In my view this theory could be modeled in form of a genealogy that follows Foucault's vision: "Genealogy does not oppose itself to history as the lofty and profound gaze of the philosopher might compare to the molelike perspective of the scholar; on the contrary, it rejects the metahistorical deployment of ideal significations and indefinite teleologies. It opposes itself to the search for 'origins'" (Foucault 1977: 140). Genealogy in this radical anti-foundationalist sense is not a quest for the origins of the Secular Age. It rather questions the strategies that justify a normative order through the use of history. This strategy, of course, is part of the bulwark of modernity and of its *Eigensinn*.

Thus, genealogy is in principle critical of any form of historical fundamentalism. In the Foucauldian sense it unearths the social and cultural remnants by means of which the *Eigensinn* of Western modernity justifies its hegemony. But as Foucault (above quote) writes, "it opposes itself to the search for 'origins'." In other words, the genealogy of the modern self or of modern social imaginaries does not hunt for an ultimate "origin," but explains why and how the modern self reassures itself through the use of history and why, in general, the modern self needs to reassure its *Eigensinn*.

Now, Taylor's way of representing this *Eigensinn* in the form of a narrative, which Martin Seel (1991: 49) has called an affirmative genealogy, raises the danger of it being read as 'real history.' But as soon as 'real history' does come in, the formerly meaningful and coherent narrative disintegrates into parts. Thus we should keep in mind that when translating Taylor's narrative into other traditions, for example into an Islamic one, we should be aware that we do reshuffle the meaning of the narrative, and in two respects: First we transform the narrative into 'history,' and second, simultaneously, we create a new narrative.

Martin Kavka, for example, has translated the *telos* of Taylor's narrative into a Jewish context and created a new narrative according to which "a vision of the divine law that is divine because of its effects in society, namely the promotion of human welfare, can mend the relations between varying kinds of believers and unbelievers in a way that Taylor thinks is impossible" (Kavka 2012: 123). Defining "a God who commands laws [as] a God who inaugurates an 'anthropocentric shift' long before current understandings of secularization see it beginning," Kavka (2012) focuses on a trope of the modern *eigensinn*, namely the quest for "what is human being?," and traces its origin by means of an affirmative narrative. This, of course, is meaningful in that it adds to the "religious law" *a moral value* which justifies the presence of "religious law" in the modern world.

As I said earlier, there are at least two possibilities for applying *A Secular Age* to a world beyond the West: Either one completely dissolves the confines of a

Secular Age. This would ultimately result in globalizing *A Secular Age*. Or one consequently qualifies *A Secular Age* as a particular narrative. Then, a Secular Age can only become meaningful by being embedded into specific traditions. *A Secular Age* narrated within a multitude of traditions, however, cannot avoid the hegemony of the master narrative as told in *A Secular Age*. The *telos* of this narrative remains the common ground upon which local narratives are construed. Thus, for example, a Muslim author were to narrate the genealogy of secularism in so-called Muslim societies he or she might use the concept of *secularism* as the common denominator of all social imaginaries, even if he/she knows very well that secularism is the *telos* of a very specific local narrative, namely a Latin-Christian narrative. But he/she may argue that in fact secularism has become globalized and that, as a result, there is a need to justify the secular moral order by means of local narratives. That is why he/she may construe an Islamic version of *A Secular Age*. Again there are two possible forms of narration: either the author may say that the scope of the Secular Age-narrative should be broadened by including Islamic or Jewish traditions; or he/she may argue that the Islamic context requires an independent local narrative which affirmatively justifies the secular moral order. Indeed, both ways have been pursued.

While the first solution works with *A Secular Age* by dissolving its confines, the second option is built upon the argument that because *A Secular Age* is a local Christian narrative, secularity cannot be the *telos* of narratives justifying other moral orders. Thus, partisans of this view favor translating the *meaning* of *A Secular Age* into other local narratives without using the *telos* of secularity as a common ground. They imply a transcultural perspective based on the interpretation of family resemblances between the various modern narratives worldwide, which all share the purpose of historically framing a theological argument by means of affirmative narratives. All the options I have just described in very short terms have been used in Arabic, Persian or Turkish discourses since the nineteenth century.

This basic structure, namely the historical framing of a theological argument, limits the possibility of participation. As I am participating neither in an Islamic nor in a Christian discourse, it would be morally unjustifiable if I proposed an Islamic narrative of the modern moral order. What I can do, as an observer, is analyze and interpret narratives of the genealogy of modernity, respective of the *religion and society-order*, or in other words, I can discuss the genealogy of these narratives in a Foucauldian sense, and describe a historical model which could be used as a backdrop for understanding these narratives.

As for the historical model, I will restrict myself to the following observations:

1. From a historical point of view, the religion/society divide that created a normative twin order and eventually constituted modernity is valid for most great traditions.
2. This divide grew out of a unified normative order which had related the world in its totality to a transcendental truth. It evolved into two self-sufficient autonomous orders, the first of which, namely religion, was the first to be named. The conceptualization of its twin partner as 'society' came at a later date.
3. Both orders presuppose each other. This divide, which gradually evolved with the ordering of transcendence, framed what would later be called Early Modernity.
4. This divide preconditions an order of transcendental truth, but not all orders of transcendental truth evolved into the binarity of religion and society.

As this divide took place within the old order of transcendental truth, the twins 'religion and society' were always expressed by use of that tradition which had been employed to construe a transcendental truth. Within the Christian tradition, *society* reached some sort of conceptual autonomy only during the *Sattelzeit* (c. 1750–1850), in which "a major horizon shift in the meaning of social concepts occurred, and when old words acquired new meaning" (Marchart 2007: 52) or perhaps this occurred only at its tipping point around 1850 (Koselleck 1967: 82; 1979; 1986; 1989; Heilbron, Magnusson, and Wittrock 1998).

One of the most important features of the emerging religion was the re-semanticization of the notions 'belief' and 'faith.' Within the order of transcendental truth, both notions had translated the post-classical Latin sense of *fidēs*, that is, fidelity or loyalty. As an expression of religion, however, *fidelity* was newly interpreted as an inner-personal, internalized mental process, motivated by conscience and personal conviction. Practice now became an expression of this internal mental reality and lost its character as a manifestation of loyalty and fidelity. Simultaneously, virtue and morality emerged as the markers of the religious order, leaving the sphere of law to the secular world (or nature). As a matter of fact, the evolution of a concept of religion as an autonomous self-governing order based on belief (or faith) which does not need the world to verify its validity claim can be traced just as well in Christian (Feil 2000) as in Jewish (Batnitzky 2011), Islamic (Schulze 2008) or even Mongolian traditions (Kollmar-Paulenz 2007; 2012).

This divide affected most great orders of transcendental truth from the fifteenth to the nineteenth century. It profoundly reconfigured the use of traditions (Jewish, Christian, Islamic, etc.) and finally defined "religion" as a global standard. In all these traditions religion now claimed autonomy, but simultaneously all "religions" now recognized a societal order as a twin. The way these two orders were related to each other was always part and parcel of the history of their specific environments (Luhmann 2000).

This model does not qualify the way the divide has been addressed. There is no possibility for one master narrative to give meaning to all of the processes reproducing this historical model. Charles Taylor's narrative is just one version of the history of this divide within the Latin-Christian world. It is what I call a cultural imaginary. There are of course many cultural imaginaries that give meaning to the religion-and-society divide. There are cultural imaginaries that proclaim the hegemony of either religion or society and there are academic strategies that claim one twin over the other as an explanatory force: the sociology of religion and the theology of society. In this respect, Charles Taylor's narrative can be read as a work of theology of society.

6 In lieu of a conclusion

Some children are sitting in a sandbox. All of them are building structures in the sand. For whatever reason, one child exclaims:

"You over there, you are just copying my castle!"

And perhaps the child would add:

"You may build such castles, but you have to accept me as the architect, for I designed the castle."

Perhaps then some children would try to fix a border between their castles and that of the self-styled architect and perhaps they would tell the story that they built their castles according to their own construction plan. They would point at differences between their castles and that of the self-appointed architect, and they would say that their castle is built upon these differences and that their buildings do not represent castles at all. The first child would certainly accept this, as it implicitly recognizes the validity claim that only this first child built a castle. But perhaps another child would say:

"Look, we all built our castles out of sand. All our castles depend on the fact that they are made out of sand, so in a way, there is no reason to assume that any one of us is the only designer. In reality, it is the sand that designed our castles."

Bibliography

al-'Arawi, 'Abdallah. 1978. *Azmat al-Muthaqqafin al-'Arab – Taqlidiyya am Tarikhiyya?* Cairo: al-Mu'assasa al-'Arabiyya li-l-Dirasat wa-l-Nashr.
Asad, Talal. 2001. "Reading a Modern Classic: W. C. Smith's The Meaning and End of Religion." *History of Religion* 40: 205–222.
Bahr, Hermann. 1912. "Religion," in Hermann Bahr, *Inventur*, 61–73. Berlin: S. Fischer.
Baker, Peter. 1995. *Deconstruction and the Ethical Turn*. Gainesville, Flo.: University Press of Florida.
Barre, Elizabeth A. 2012. "Muslim Imaginaries and Imaginary Muslims: Placing Islam in Conversation with A Secular Age." *Journal of Religious Ethics* 40: 138–148.
Batnitzky, Leora. 2011. *How Judaism Became a Religion: An Introduction to Modern Jewish Thought*. Princeton: Princeton University Press.
Bethge, Eberhard. 1990. "Gottesdienst in einem säkularen Zeitalter, wie Bonhoeffer ihn verstand. Vortrag der Ökumenischen Arbeitsgemeinschaft in Herrenalb am 30. Januar 1968 zum Thema der Sektion V 'Gottesdienst in einem säkularen Zeitalter' der Vierten Vollversammlung des Ökumenischen Rates in Uppsala 1968," in *'Religionsloses Christentum' und 'nicht-religiöse Interpretation' bei Dietrich Bonhoeffer*, ed. Peter H. Neumann, 340–359. Darmstadt: Wissenschaftliche Buchgesellschaft.
Bouchard, Gérard and Charles Taylor. 2014. *Building the Future. A Time for Reconciliation. Report*. [Québec, Qué.]: Commission de consultation sur les pratiques d'accommodement reliées aux différences culturelles, 2008, http:/collections.banq.qc.ca/ark:/52327/bs1565996 (last accessed December 12, 2014).
Braidotti, Rosi. 2006. "The Return of the Masters' Narratives," http:/www.commissie-meijers.nl/assets/e-quality/publicaties/e-quality.final.rosi.braidotti-1.pdf (last accessed December 12, 2014).
Bruner, Jerome. 1986. *Actual Minds, Possible Worlds*. Cambridge, Mass/London: Harvard University Press.
Caldecott, Stratford and John Morrill, eds., 1997. *Eternity in Time: Christopher Dawson and the Catholic Idea of History*. Edinburgh: T. and T. Clark.
Campbell, Alexander. 1841. "Excursions No. 1." *The Millennial Harbinger. A Monthly Publication Devoted to Primitive Christianity* 5: 224–227.
Cantarini, Sibilla, Werner Abraham, and Elisabeth Leiss. 2014. "Introduction," in *Certainty-uncertainty – and the Attitudinal Space in Between*, ed. Sibilla Cantarini, Werner Abraham, and Elisabeth Leiss, 1–26. Amsterdam: John Benjamins.
Cantwell Smith, Wilfred. 1962. *The Meaning and End of Religion*. Minneapolis: Fortress Press.
Carter, Stephen G. 2008. "The 'Historical Solution' versus the 'Philosophical Solution': The Political Commentary of Christopher Dawson and Jacques Maritain, 1927–1939." *Journal of the History of Ideas* 69: 93–115.
Chakrabarty, Dipesh. 2009. "The Modern and the Secular in the West: An Outsider's View." *Journal of the American Academy of Religion* 77: 393–403.
Cook, Michael. 2014. *Ancient Religions, Modern Politics: The Islamic Case in Comparative Perspective*. Princeton, N.J.: Princeton University Press.
Dawson, Christopher. 1951. "The Problem of Metahistory: the Nature and Meaning of History and the Cause and Significance of Historical Change." *History Today* 1: 9–12.

Denzin, Norman K. 1997. *Interpretive Ethnography: Ethnographic Practices for the 21st Century*. Thousand Oaks, CA: Sage.
Dibelius, Otto. 1961. *Ein Christ ist immer im Dienst: Erlebnisse und Erfahrungen in einer Zeitenwende*. Stuttgart: Kreuz.
Duby, Georges. 1966. *L'Europe des cathédrales, 1140–1280*. Geneva: Skira.
Feil, Ernst. 2000. *On the Concept of Religion*. Binghamton: Global Publ.
Foster, Hal. 1996. *The Return of the Real: The Avant-garde at the End of the Century*. Cambridge, Mass: MIT Press.
Foucault, Michel. 1977. "Nietzsche, Genealogy, History," in Michel Foucault, *Language Counter-memory, Practice. Selected Essays and Interviews*, ed. Donald F. Bouchard, trans. Donald F. Bouchard and Sherry Simon, 139–164. Ithaca: Cornell University Press.
Fox, Edward Whiting. 1963. "The Divine Dilemma of Arnold J. Toynbee." *The Virginia Quarterly Review* 39: 104–131.
Friese, Joachim. 1967. *Die säkularisierte Welt: Triumph oder Tragödie der christlichen Geistesgeschichte*. Frankfurt am Main: Schulte-Bulmke.
Fukuyama, Francis. 1992. *The End of History and the Last Man*. London: Hamish Hamilton.
Genette, Gérard. 1972. *Figures III*. Paris: Éditions du Seuil.
Gergen, Kenneth J. 2005. "Narrative, Moral Identity and Historical Consciousness: a Social Constructionist Account," in *Narration, Identity, and Historical Conciousness*, ed. Jürgen Straub, 99–119. New York: Berghahn.
Grant, Brewin and Holyoake, George Jacob. 1853. *Christianity and secularism. Report of a public discussion between Brewin Grant and George Jacob Holyoake, Esq. Held in the Royal British Institution, London, commencing Jan. 20 and ending Feb. 24, 1853*. London: Ward.
Grant, Brewin. 1869. *The Dissenting World. An Autobiography*. New York: The American News Company.
Habermas, Jürgen. 1973. "Wahrheitstheorien," in *Wirklichkeit und Reflexion: Walter Schulz zum 60. Geburtstag*, ed. Helmut Fahrenbach, 211–265. Pfullingen: Neske.
Habermas, Jürgen. 1990. *The Philosophical Discourse of Modernity. Twelve Lectures;* trans. Frederick Lawrence. Cambridge: Polity Press.
Habermas, Jürgen. 2001. *Zeit der Übergänge. Kleine Politische Schriften IX*. Frankfurt am Main: Suhrkamp.
Heilbron, Johan, Lars Magnusson and Björn Wittrock. 1998. "Introduction," in *The Rise of the Social Sciences and the Formation of Modernity: Conceptual Change in Context, 1750–1850*, ed. Johan Heilbron, Lars Magnusson and Björn Wittrock, 1–33. Dordrecht: Kluwer.
Holyoake, George Jacob. 1896. *English Secularism: A Confession of Belief*. Chicago: The Open Court Publishing Co.
Huntington, Samuel. 1996. *The Clash of Civilizations and the Remaking of World Order*. New York: Simon and Schuster.
Hurd, Elizabeth Shakman. 2008. "Review of A Secular Age by Charles Taylor." *Political Theory* 36: 486–491.
Jameson, Fredric. 2007. *Jameson on Jameson. Conversations on Cultural Marxism*. Durham, NC: Duke University Press.

Joas, Hans. 2003. "Menschenwürde achten – die Freiheit wahren. Gedanken zum Ökumenischen Kirchentag III," *Salzkörner / Materialien für die Diskussion in Kirche und Gesellschaft* 9: 10–11.

Kavka, Martin. 2012. "What is Immanent in Judaism? Transcending A Secular Age." *Journal of Religious Ethics* 40: 123–137.

Kerby, Anthony Paul. 1991. *Narrative and the Self*. Bloomington: Indiana University Press.

Kermode, Frank. 1979. *The Genesis of Secrecy: On the Interpretation of Narrative*. Cambridge, Mass: Harvard University Press.

Kluge, Alexander and Oskar Negt. 1993. *Geschichte und Eigensinn*. 3 vols. Frankfurt am Main: Zweitausendeins/Suhrkamp.

Kollmar-Paulenz, Karénina. 2007. *Zur Ausdifferenzierung eines autonomen Bereichs Religion in asiatischen Gesellschaften des 17. und 18. Jahrhunderts: Das Beispiel der Mongolen*. Bern: SAGW.

Kollmar-Paulenz, Karénina. 2012. "Aussereuropäische Religionsbegriffe," in *Religionswissenschaft*, ed. Michael Stausberg, 81–94. Berlin: De Gruyter.

Koselleck, Reinhart. 1979. "Einleitung," in *Historische Semantik und Begriffsgeschichte*, ed. Reinhart Koselleck, 9–16. Stuttgart: Klett-Cotta.

Koselleck, Reinhart. 1967. "Richtlinien für das Lexikon politisch-sozialer Begriffe der Neuzeit." *Archiv für Begriffsgeschichte: Bausteine zu einem historischen Wörterbuch der Philosophie* 11: 81–99.

Koselleck, Reinhart. 1986. "Sozialgeschichte und Begriffsgeschichte," in *Sozialgeschichte in Deutschland. Entwicklungen und Perspektiven im internationalen Zusammenhang*, vol. 1, ed. Wolfgang Schieder and Volker Sellin, 89–109. Göttingen: Vandenhoeck & Ruprecht.

Koselleck, Reinhart. 1989. "Sprachwandel und Ereignisgeschichte." *Merkur* 43: 657–673.

Laitinen, Arto. 2008. *Strong Evaluation without Moral Sources: On Charles Taylor's Philosophical Anthropology and Ethics*. Berlin: Walter de Gruyter.

Levene, Nancy. 2014. "A Secular Age: Commentaries on our age," *The Immanent Frame. Secularism, religion, and the public sphere*. http://blogs.ssrc.org/tif/2010/07/08/commentaries-on-our-age/, posted on Thursday, July 8th, 2010 (last accessws December 12, 2014).

Lohnstein, Horst. 2014. "Verum focus," in *Handbook of Information Structure*, ed. Caroline Féry and Shinichiro Ishihara, 1–29. Oxford: Oxford University Press.

Luhmann, Niklas. 2000. *Die Religion der Gesellschaft*; hg. von André Kieserling. Frankfurt a.M.: Suhrkamp.

Lyotard, Jean-Francois. [1979] 1984. *The Postmodern Condition: A Report on Knowledge*, trans. Geoff Bennington and Brian Massumi. Minneapolis: University of Minnesota Press.

Lyotard, Jean-Francois and Jean-Loup Thébaud. [1979] 1985. *Just Game*, trans. Wlad Godzich. Minneapolis: University of Minnesota Press.

MacIntyre, Alasdiair. 1981. "Ideology, social science and revolution." *Comparative Politics* 5: 321–341.

MacIntyre, Alasdiair. 1981. *After Virtue*. Notre Dame: University of Notre Dame Press.

MacIntyre, Alasdiair. 1997. "Epistemological Crises, Dramatic Narrative, and the Philosophy of Science," in *Why Narrative?: Readings in Narrative Theology*, ed. Stanley Hauerwas and L. Gregory Jones, 138–158, Eugene: Oregon: Wipf and Stock.

Mahmood, Saba. 2010. "Can Secularism be Other-wise?" in *Varieties of Secularism in a Secular Age*, ed. Michael Warner, Jonathan VanAntwerpen, Craig J. Calhoun, 282–299. Cambridge, Mass.: Harvard University Press.
Mammen, Madathilparampil Thomas. 1962. "Editorial." *Religion and Society* 9: 1–5.
Marchart, Oliver. 2007. *Post-Foundational Political Thought – Political Difference in Nancy, Lefort, Badiou and Laclau*. Edinburgh: Edinburgh University Press.
McGoldrick, Dominic. 2011. "Religion in the European Public Square and in European Public Life–Crucifixes in the Classroom?" *Human Rights Law Review* 11: 451–502.
Masuzawa, Tomoko. 2005. *The Invention of World Religions: Or, How European Universalism Was Preserved in the Language of Pluralism*. Chicago: University of Chicago Press.
Meynell, Robert. 2011. *Canadian Idealism and the Philosophy of Freedom: C.B. Macpherson, George Grant, and Charles Taylor*. Montreal & Kingston: McGill-Queen's University Press.
Milbank, John. 1991. "'Postmodern Critical Augustinianism': A Short Summa In Forty-two Responses to Unasked Questions." *Modern Theology* 7: 225–237.
Moltmann, Jürgen. 1975. *Kirche in der Kraft des Geistes: ein Beitrag zur messianischen Ekklesiologie*. München: Kaiser.
Müller, Karl Ferdinand, ed., 1971. *Gottesdienst in einem säkularisierten Zeitalter eine Konsultation der Kommission für Glauben und Kirchenfassung des Ökumenischen Rates der Kirchen in deutscher Sprache mit einem Vorwort von Lukas Vischer und einem Konsultationsbericht*. Kassel: J. Stauda
Myerson, George. 1992. *The Argumentative Imagination: Wordsworth, Dryden, Religious Dialogues*. New York: St. Martin's Press.
Nassar, Nasif. [1970] 1995. *Naḥhwa Mujtamaʿ Jadid – Muqaddimat Asasiyya fi Naqd al-Mujtamaʿ al-Taʾifi*. Beirut: Dar al-Taliʿa.
Novák, Antonín. 1968. "Gottesdienst im säkularen Zeitalter." *Communio viatorum* 11: 193–197.
Onfray, Michel. 2007. *Atheist manifesto: the case against Christianity, Judaism, and Islam*. New York: Arcade Publishing.
Pavsek, Christopher. 1996. "History and Obstinacy: Negt and Kluge's Redemption of Labor." *New German Critique* 68: 137–163.
Pierce, Charles S. 1877. "The Fixation of Belief." *Popular Science Monthly* 12 no. 11: 1–15.
Popper, Karl R. 1945. *The Open Society and Its Enemies*, vol. 1–2. London: Routledge.
Prechtl, Peter. 2008. "Überzeugung/Zweifel," in *Metzler Lexikon Philosophie*, ed. Peter Prechtl and Franz-Peter Burkhard, 632. Stuttgart: Metzler.
Ricoeur, Paul. 1983–1985. *Temps et recit*, 3 vols. Paris: Seuil.
Ritter, Harry. 1986. *Dictionary of Concepts in History*. Westport, Con.: Greenwood Press.
Rorty, Richard. 1994. "Taylor on Truth," in *Philosophy in an Age of Pluralism: The Philosophy of Charles Taylor in Question*, ed. James Tully and Daniel M. Weinstock, 20–33. Cambridge/New York: Cambridge University Press.
Royle, Edward. 1974. *Victorian Infidels: The Origins of the British Secularist Movement, 1791–1866*. Manchester: At the University Press.
Russello, Gerald J. 1998. "[Review of] Eternity in Time: Christopher Dawson and the Catholic Idea of History." *The Catholic Historical Review* 84: 697–698.
Sauer, Hermann. 1938. *Abendländische Entscheidung: arischer Mythus und christliche Wirklichkeit*. Leipzig: Hindrichs.

Schulze, Reinhard. 2008. "Islam und andere Religionen in der Aufklärung," *Jahrbuch des Simon-Dubnow-Instituts* 7, ed. Dan Diner, 317–340. Göttingen: Vandenhoek & Ruprecht.
Schulze, Reinhard. 2010. "Islam und Judentum im Angesicht der Protestantisierung der Religionen im 19. Jahrhundert," in *Judaism, Christianity, and Islam in the Course of History: Exchange and Conflicts*, ed. Lothar Gall, Dietmar Willoweit, 139–164. München: Oldenbourg.
Seel, Martin. 1991. "Die Wiederkehr der Ethik des guten Lebens." *Merkur* 45: 41–49.
Sheehan, Jonathan. 2003. "Enlightenment, Religion, and the Enigma of Secularization: A Review Essay." *The American Historical Review*, 108: 1061–1080.
Sheehan, Jonathan. 2005. *The Enlightenment Bible*. Princeton: Princeton University Press.
Sheehan, Jonathan. 2006. "Sacred and Profane: Idolatry, Antiquarianism and the Polemics of Distinction in the Seventeenth Century." *Past and Present* 192: 35–66.
Sheehan, Jonathan. 2010. "When was Enlightenment?" in *Varieties of Secularism in a Secular Age*, ed. Michael Warner, Jonathan VanAntwerpen, Craig J. Calhoun, 224–266. Cambridge, Mass: Harvard University Press.
Shibl, Fu'ad Muhammad. 1974. *al-Fikr al-Siyasi – Dirasa Muqarana li-l-Madhahib al-Siyasiyya wa-l-Ijtima'iyya*. Cairo: al-Hay'a al-Miṣsriyya al-'Amma li-l-Kitab.
Smith, Graeme. 2007. *A Short History of Secularism*. London: I. B. Tauris.
Spence, Donald P. 1982. *Narrative Truth and Historical Truth. Meaning and Interpretation in Psychoanalysis*. New York: W. W. Norton.
Spence, Donald P. 2005. "Narrative truth and identity formation: Abduction and abuse stories as metaphors," in *Narration, Identity, and Historical Consciousness*, ed. Jürgen Straub, 120–131. New York: Berghahn.
Strawson, Galen. 2004. "Against Narrativity." *Ratio* (new series) 17: 428–452.
Taylor, Charles. 1985. "Interpretation and the sciences of man," in Charles Taylor, *Philosophy and the Human Sciences. Philosophical Papers Volume 2*, 15–57. Cambridge: Cambridge University Press.
Taylor, Charles. 1989. *Sources of the Self. The Making of the Modern Identity*. Cambridge, Mass.: Harvard University Press.
Taylor, Charles. 1994. "The politics of recognition," in *Multiculturalism: Examining the Politics of Recognition*, ed. Amy Gutmann, 25–73. Princeton, NJ: Princeton University Press.
Taylor, Charles. 1999. *A Catholic Modernity? Charles Taylor's Marianist Award Lecture*. Edited and with an Introduction by James L. Heft. New York/Oxford: Oxford University Press.
Taylor, Charles. 2010a. "Challenging Issues about the Secular Age." *Modern Theology* 26: 404–416.
Taylor, Charles. 2010b. "Afterword: Apologia pro Libro Suo," in *Varieties of Secularism in a Secular Age*, ed. Michael Warner, Jonathan VanAntwerpen, Craig J. Calhoun, 300–321. Cambridge, Mass.: Harvard University Press.
Taylor, Charles. 2011. "Response." The Australian Journal of Anthropology 22: 125–133.
Thomas, Abraham Vazhayil. 1974. *Christians in Secular India*. Cranbury, NJ.: Associated University Press.
Thornhill, John. 2008–2009. "An Introduction to Christopher Dawson's Interpretation of History." *Australian eJournal of Theology* 11.1–14.1. http://aejt.com.au (last accessed December 12, 2014).

Thorp, Robert. 2014. "Towards an epistemological theory of historical consciousness." *Historical Encounters: A journal of historical consciousness, historical cultures, and history education* 1: 20–31.
Tremblay, Luc B. 2014. *The Bouchard-Taylor Report on Cultural and Religious Accommodation: Multiculturalism by Any Other Name?* EUI Working Paper LAW 18. Fiesole: European University Institute http:/cadmus.eui.eu (last accessed December 12, 2014).
al-Turabi, Hasan. 1974. *al-Iman – Atharuhu fi Hayat al-Insan*. Cairo: Dar al-Qalam.
Underhill, Frank. 1951. "Arnold Toynbee: Metahistorian." *The Canadian Historical Review* 32: 201–219.
'Uthman, Fathi. 1969. *al-Fikr al-Islami wa-l-Tatawwur*. Kuwait: al-Dar al-Kuwaytiyya li-l-Tiba'a wa-l-Nashr wa-l-Tawzi'.
van der Veer, Peter. Forthcoming. "Is Confucianism Secular?" in *Secularism Outside of Latin Christendom: Essays in Response to Charles Taylor*, ed. Akeel Bilgrami. New York: Columbia University Press.
Vicedom, Georg Friedrich. 1969. *Mission in einer Welt der Revolution: Vorträge über die Aufgaben der Mission in einer Zeit der sozialen Erneuerung*. Wuppertal: Theologischer Verlag Brockhaus.
Watts, John. 1859. *Secularism 'the one thing needful'*. London: Holyoake.
White, Hayden. 1973. *Metahistory. The Historical Imagination in Nineteenth-Century Europe*. Baltimore: The Johns Hopkins University Press.
White, Hayden. 1987. *The Content of the Form: Narrative Discourse and Historical Representation*. Baltimore: The Johns Hopkins University Press.

III. The Story's Subtler Languages

Colin Jager
Language within Language: Reform and Literature in *A Secular Age*

1 Introduction

In *A Secular Age*, Charles Taylor dwells on the contrast between a pre-modern world in which it was "impossible not to believe in God" (ASA: 25), and our modern "expanding universe of unbelief" (ASA: 352), characterized by reflexivity and fragilization. Friedrich Schiller, a romantic-era thinker whom Taylor cites a number of times in his book, made a similar distinction. Schiller called it the difference between "naïve" and "sentimental" poetry. Naïve poets were conscious of no rift between themselves and their environment; sentimental poets, by contrast, were conscious of precisely this rupture; indeed, it often became the very subject of their writing. Most modern writers, Schiller thought, were sentimental: they had lost a sense of direct contact with the world, and so tried to develop techniques for finding their way back to it. Like Schiller, Taylor is interested in how the languages of romantic and post-romantic art register the turn from a self deeply embedded in its world to a situation in which we are poised "between two stances, in which everyone's construal shows up as such." Taylor describes this poise or suspension as, variously, a "neutral zone," a "free space," and a "space in which people can wander" (ASA: 14, 351, 352, 351).

Drawing on Taylor's discussion of the languages of art, this chapter looks closely at several examples of how aesthetic languages register the nuances of the secular age. I turn first to the emergence of the gothic genre in the mid-eighteenth century and then to the work of Friedrich Schiller and Percy Shelley, two romantic-era writers on whom Taylor draws in his own account of the phenomenology of the secular age. In both cases I will be modifying Taylor's own interpretations of these moments so as to suggest a more political rendering. This revised description of the romantic terrain of Taylor's project prepares the ground for a more plural and politically resonant account of the secular age.

2 The politics of disenchantment

Why seek a more politically-pointed account of the secular? We can begin by contrasting Taylor's account with two other possible narratives. The first, familiar from Coleridge ([1829] 1976) and Arnold ([1869] 2009), and criticized by Marx

([1843] 1972) and Bourdieu (1984) among others, sees a capacious sense of nineteenth-century "Culture" (including music, literature and visual art) replacing "Religion" as the chief ideological bulwark against modernity. In this version of secularization, both Christianity and Culture are forces for order and civilization, ranged against the secular immanence of exclusive humanism.[1]

A second possible narrative begins with the same observation about Culture replacing Religion but sees such blurring of the lines as a category mistake. The modern critic James Wood, for example, writes that "Fiction, being the game of not quite, is the place of not-quite-belief. Precisely what is a danger in religion is the very fabric of fiction" (Wood 1999: xiv). Wood's argument is that one cannot believe in both – the real of fiction and the real of religion – because they operate in different modalities: fiction is tentative, while religion is confident; fiction hesitates, while religion asserts. When writers forget this, they behave as if the truths of religion can somehow be preserved by the fictional mode of "not quite." The only result is what Wood calls "futile poetry" (1999: 243), namely writing that is still trying to have it both ways, not yet prepared to admit that belief in the divine is no longer supportable.

Both of these accounts – of Art replacing Christianity, or of Art confusing itself with Christianity – draw upon the narrative of secularization that Taylor names the "subtraction story" (ASA: 22). This is the idea that the secular age comes about by the draining away of religion from an already-existing secular, so that what was once hidden can now emerge. The great and over-arching thesis of Taylor's book is that this is the wrong story (though one very comforting to those who tell it). For Taylor the modern secular dispensation in the West was not in fact revealed but built, often unintentionally, by forces that understood themselves to be acting in the name and service of Christianity.

A critic like Wood can therefore help us to grasp what is at stake in Taylor's description of aesthetics as a place of ontological suspension. Wood has a powerful sense of the distinction between aesthetic and religious belief; the temptation to blur the two categories is, he thinks, bad for both: "Once religion has revealed itself to you, you are never free. In fiction, by contrast, one is always free to choose not to believe, and this very freedom [...] is what helps to constitute fiction's reality" (Wood 1999: xiv). This is very much like what Taylor says of modern poetics when he writes of it as a "free space" (ASA: 352), and yet Wood's

---

[1] Although it arises at roughly the same time, this Arnoldian "Culture" is different from the anthropological sense of "culture" as the location of difference. See Schulze, this volume, for an argument that this latter definition of culture involves the repositioning of religion. At the same time, it should be noted that *both* senses of culture have their roots in the romantic period, or what Taylor (1989) calls the "expressivist turn" (368–390).

point is very nearly the opposite of Taylor's: that to model religious belief on aesthetic belief is to empty religion of all that makes it *religion*. Taylor's argument, by contrast, is that aesthetics helps to *build* our modern sense of what religion looks and feels like, since even the staunchest modern believer lives with the fragilization and potential loss of meaning that characterizes the secular age.

So the first point to be gleaned from Taylor's discussion of romantic and post-romantic aesthetics is that we can turn to the languages of art in order to learn what the secular age is like. This is already a step beyond the more familiar idea that aesthetic practices simply reflect or trail behind already-existing cultural and historical changes. But Taylor takes a further step as well, for his rhetoric of "open" and "free" space outlines a participatory role for the languages of art. Post-romantic aesthetics does not only give us a window onto the social world; it actually helps to *create* that world through the constitutive power of language itself. Through such language, we grasp something that we would otherwise have been unable to grasp; in the more Heideggerian idiom that Taylor occasionally favors, the world *discloses itself* through language. Here I take "language" in the broad sense of "expression," though elsewhere Taylor also has specific things to say about the constitutive powers of human language.[2] Taken in either its narrow or its broad sense, however, Taylor's discussion of what he calls the subtler languages of art is a crucial part of his general romantic commitment to the creative and normative possibilities of expression itself.

Yet it may be that such languages participate nonetheless in an ultimately provincial construction of the secular. One charge sometimes leveled at *A Secular Age* is that it remains too caught up within the normative dimensions of Christianity, so that even its laudable invocation of inter-religious dialogue remains blind to the power imbalances between the rest of the world and a Western secularism that owes its conceptual contours to Christianity. This is the kind of critique likely to come out of post-colonial studies; perhaps its most pointed version is that offered by Saba Mahmood, who suggests that Taylor "depoliticizes" the secular by telling it as a story internal to Christianity without attending to Christianity's own historical self-constitution in relation to religious difference: "If the task of contemporary Christianity is to become open to others, would it not need to begin with an internal accounting of how this historical privilege structures the possibility of communication across difference?" she asks (Mahmood 2010: 298; see also Sheehan 2010; Asad 2012; Schulze, this vol-

---

2 On Taylor's romanticism in *A Secular Age*, see Jager 2010. For a book-length exposition of Taylor's theory of language, much influenced by the romantic tradition, see *The Language Animal* (2016).

ume). On this account, the story of the secular is one of asymmetrical relations between Europe and its others. And one cannot tell the story of those relations from within the exclusive boundaries of a Latin Christendom conceived as analytically separable from the other traditions that, from the very beginning, helped to shape its self-understanding. In attempting to do so, Mahmood suggests, Taylor underplays the work of secular power in creating, forming, and maintaining subjectivities and the categories through which we apprehend them: western, Christian, primitive, non-modern, and so on.

This call for Christianity to internalize its own historical relation to its others is a complex one, and certainly cannot be answered quickly. But I do think that there are resources within Taylor's own story of the secular that make possible the kind of "internal accounting" for which Mahmood calls. For although "power" is not one of Taylor's keywords, it is possible to read *A Secular Age* as a story of asymmetrical power relations – not, to be sure, between Europe and its others but within a supposedly hegemonic "Latin Christendom" itself. Christendom's own internal fracturing, not simply its self-reform, is central to Taylor's story. The splintering that he emphasizes is not the usual one of Protestant ideological and denominational conflict but a prior faultline running between elite and common. "Again and again," Taylor writes,

> Semi-refractory masses were forced to shape up to a new regime, sometimes rudely, sometimes by gentle persuasion [...]. They are dealt with by being organized, taken in hand, disciplined, sometimes semi-incarcerated (ASA: 85).

Cutting across theological and doctrinal disputes, this "work of Reform" was an effort at social control in which laity were either encouraged or forced to accept a more rigorous moral discipline and a more rational faith. As an analytic category, "Reform" thus shifts attention away from doctrine and belief (Catholic vs. Protestant, the "wars of religion," and so on) and away from secularization (did it happen, how should it be defined, and so on). It focuses instead on a different kind of process: the withdrawal of elites from popular culture – their withdrawal, we might say, from a commitment to a reciprocal social order. This allows Taylor to make two points often missed in discussions of secularism: first, that the secular age was *built* (sometimes deliberately, often not) rather than discovered or uncovered; second, that secularism is not only about religion but about many other things as well – or, to put the point more strongly, that there is no 'religion' before its invention as a problem in the early modern period.

As elites withdrew from participation in the popular practices that had marked an older, reciprocal social order, they became more willing to countenance reform movements aimed at policing sexuality, controlling prostitution, and increasing productivity. In this way, self-consciousness distributed along an axis of power became central to secularism's identity. Here we can discern the outlines of the immanent frame, inflected less through competing ideas than through competing regimes of power.

This argument aligns Taylor with a broad cross-section of scholars who in the past decades have reminded us that religion is not some 'thing' in the world but rather a mobile discourse answerable to particular needs at particular historical moments; that for Europe the crucial moment was an early modern crisis of authority within Christianity; that a new, more cognitive definition of religion as belief in propositional statements was one answer to that crisis; and that this answer in turn made it possible to invent 'religions,' in the plural, as a set of customs and, later, beliefs, typical of those on Europe's periphery (Smith 1979; Harrison 1990; Asad 1993; Masuzawa 2005). This does not, of course, fully address the charge of provincialism; it does, however, re-politicize what can at times seem like an account of the secular that dwells too much on ideas and aesthetics rather than historical and social causes.[3] My goal in the remainder of this chapter is to demonstrate that Taylor's own account of aesthetics can be likewise re-politicized.

3 Reform and the gothic novel

Despite Taylor's emphasis on Reform in the early going, readers can miss its importance because social history recedes into the background as the book progresses. Taylor seems to suggest that by the end of the eighteenth century there is no ordinary experience that has not already been shaped by the movement of secular reform; he turns therefore to literary (or, more broadly, aesthetic) evidence in his search for the phenomenology of the secular age. While it is possible to interpret this turn as an escape from the political and historical narrative of the book's first section, this is unlikely given Taylor's own affinities for theories of art and language that make normative and not merely descriptive claims. Indeed, it is more likely that Taylor's turn to art in *A Secular Age* is intended as a way of carrying forward the earlier analysis of Reform – though now under newer conditions that no longer allow for its direct manifestation. In the aftermath of Reform, that is to say, politics and history move in a fugitive space: in the languages of art, with their ability not simply to register ontological suspen-

---

[3] See Bender and Koenig, this volume, for the charge that Taylor does not provide a causal account.

sion but to identify places of weakness or tension that might shadow forth a different relation to the dominant order.

An important part of Taylor's argument is that the widespread social changes he names "Reform" came to manifest themselves at the level of the individual. Here Taylor joins thinkers in the tradition of Schiller and Marx who analyzed the relationship between large-scale social changes and individual perception. Taylor's own key concept is the "buffered self," a phrase that invokes a specific picture of the subject's detached relation to the world. For the buffered self, "the only locus of thoughts, feelings, spiritual élan is what we call minds; the only minds in the cosmos are those of humans; and minds are bounded, so that these thoughts, feelings, etc. are situated 'within' them" (ASA: 30).[4] In Taylor's version it is not science or humanism or industrialization (though all these are part of the story) but Reform that brings about the buffered self. Where before humans lived with a sense of openness to the world of spirits and powers ("the porous self"), we now live in the immanent frame, with a metaphysics that makes firm distinctions between the natural and the supernatural, between mind and world. The relations among mind, body, and world, then, are not merely philosophical matters but are caught up in various forms of social control, developed perhaps by elites but proliferating widely thanks to various institutions, including the church, court, prison, and school. Reform and the buffered self are part of a single package. As terms, they pick out different aspects of the same secular age.

In Taylor's account, it was not until the middle of the eighteenth century that European culture began to take stock of these developments. Not coincidentally, it was around the same time that a new literary mode arrived on the scene: the gothic novel, which emerged quite suddenly in the middle years of the eighteenth century, reached a highpoint in the early years of the nineteenth, and then scattered its influence across the literary landscape, from the Brontës and Poe to Dracula and Flannery O'Conner and the current explosion of vampire and zombie fiction (Hogle 2002; Punter 2012; Nelson 2012). With its celebration of irrationality and its exploration of fractured and threatened identities, the gothic mode gave voice to many of the anxieties that characterized what we have too-easily termed the "Age of Reason." Moreover, in its celebration of non-normative modes of spirituality, the gothic mode anticipates current sociological discus-

---

4 There is an important continuity here with the theory of alienation that Marx developed in the *Economic and Philosophic Manuscripts* of 1844. Marx did not view disenchantment as the primary cause of the self's felt detachment from the world, but that should not obscure the deep continuity between Taylor and Marx on the consequences of such objectification. See Bilgrami 2014: 150 for a similar claim about the connection between Marx and Gandhi.

sions of new religious movements: the shamanic drummers, astrologers, yoga practitioners, neopagans, homeopathic healers, telepathers, theosophists, and UFO enthusiasts who have caught the attention of academics and pundits alike (Bruce 2002; Bender 2010).[5] Indeed the gothic mode itself, and its sustained popularity across genres and platforms to this day, offers excellent evidence for Taylor's claim that "we are now living in a spiritual super-nova, a kind of galloping pluralism on the spiritual plane" (ASA: 300).

Toward the end of *A Secular Age*, Taylor tries to give some philosophical heft to this galloping pluralism. And it is easy to see why he finds modern spirituality philosophically interesting. By linking it to the experience of "fullness" at the center of his analysis of the secular age, he rescues contemporary spiritual seekers from being dismissed as mere symptoms of late capitalist narcissism. In Taylor's hands they become instead guides to life in the secular age, with its proliferating spiritual options and lack of institutional interpretive control. Unlike those living with a thoroughly buffered self, seekers are open to the multidimensional fullness that others miss, the lines of connection and meaning that escape what Taylor following Walter Benjamin calls the "empty, homogenous time" of the modern state (ASA: 54; Benjamin 1968: 261).

Along similar lines, critics have written of the gothic as a reaction to the confluence of enlightenment, secularization, and finance capital in the eighteenth century (Clery 1999). Others have written of it as a mode poised on the cusp of the transition into a modern age, casting a backward glance at the old enchantments while also imagining new modes for the secular future (Miles 2010; Hoevelaar 2010). Supplementing these analyses with Taylor's account of Reform and the buffered self, however, suggests an interpretation of gothic writing that is less about what immanence opens up than what it closes down. As an example, we can turn to Horace Walpole's *The Castle of Otranto* (1764), widely considered to be the first gothic novel. It ends with these words: "Theodore's grief was too fresh to admit the thought of another love; and it was not till after frequent discourse with Isabella, of his dear Mathilda, that he was persuaded he could know no happiness but in the society of one with whom he could

---

[5] Sociologists disagree about whether the rise of new religious movements and non- or newly institutionalized spiritual practices confirm or challenge narratives of secularization. For Steve Bruce, new religious movements are symptomatic of secularization; even if we agreed to count these movements as "religion," their growth hardly counteracts the decline in mainstream denominations (Bruce 2002). For Grace Davie, by contrast, the phenomenon of "believing without belonging," far from indicating that belief lags behind practice, suggests that "as institutional disciplines decline, belief not only persists, but becomes increasingly personal, detached, and heterogeneous particularly among young people" (Davie 2002: 8; see also Davie 1994).

forever indulge the melancholy that had taken possession of his soul" (Walpole 1964: 110). Theodore's first love, Mathilda, had been killed accidentally; here, Theodore is granted an equally eligible substitute in whom he shows no erotic interest. For a text credited with producing an entire genre of writing, Theodore's melancholy and lack of interest in his new bride seems a gloomy, non-productive note upon which to end. This is a fiction whose primary plot device is the absence of an heir, so Walpole's decision to let the problems of paternity and inheritance linger beyond the text is a remarkable one. But the air of melancholy is pervasive in this novel, extending from its rejection of the normative heterosexuality and conjugal family whose establishment had been one of Reform's primary tasks to the images, paintings, and statues that seem to live and move only to be subjected, in the end, to naturalistic explanation. The debris that slowly piles up – literal dead bodies, but also smashed idols, broken passageways, and, at the end, much of the castle itself, which collapses in spectacular fashion – makes the melancholy Theodore something like Walter Benjamin's famous angel of history, helplessly gazing upon the wreckage of the past as he is propelled into a future (of marriage, paternity, and upright behavior) that he cannot face (Benjamin 1968: 257). Whatever possibilities were represented in the now-dead Mathilda remain as only vague intimations of a different order of things never realized and now definitively foreclosed upon.

Melancholy is one example of the reflexivity that characterizes the secular age. Taylor writes that the premodern link between black bile and melancholy was intimate: black bile doesn't *cause* melancholy, it *is* melancholy, and thus the experience is redolent with meanings, and with a sense of vulnerability to forces beyond one's control: "The emotional life is porous here again; it doesn't simply exist in an inner, mental space" (ASA: 37). By contrast, when we moderns feel melancholic (or more likely, depressed), we get a medical explanation for its causes, perhaps a drug or other treatments, and thereby "take a distance from this feeling, which is ipso facto not justified. Things don't really have this meaning; it just feels this way, which is the result of a causal action utterly unrelated to the meanings of things" (ASA: 37). But this, in turn, can lead to a different and peculiarly modern sort of melancholy, or malaise. The old melancholy was a specific condition of the soul, but its presence did not threaten the overall ontic ground upon which humans stood. In a secular age the poles are reversed: we can take a distanced, third-person stance in regard to our own selves, but the very nature of things seems drained of meaning: "this malaise is specific to the buffered identity, whose very invulnerability opens it to the danger not just that evil spirits, cosmic forces or gods won't 'get into' it, but that nothing significant will stand out for it" (ASA: 303).⁶ In Theodore's case, the dead Mathilda stands in for this larger sense of significance; indeed, Walpole shows little interest in developing any erotic attraction between the two when Mathilda is alive, which is one reason why Theodore's melancholy seems so under-determined in the novel. He is mourning something larger than Mathilda, something for which she is a symbol only.

It should be stressed that Taylor is *not* arguing that the modern sense of ennui or malaise is *right*. He is agnostic about whether modern malaise hooks onto something that is objectively true about the world. Many critics of *A Secular Age* have taken Taylor to be saying that modern life is inherently less meaningful than life in a medieval parish. But this is not his argument: his point is rather that the *worry* about lack of meaning is a specifically modern worry. This can arise only once the shift from porous to buffered identity has taken place.

Taylor's analysis thus allows us to see that what a character like Theodore mourns is something very like the movement of Reform itself, those civilizing imperatives that cleaned up unruly common practices, privatized devotion, death, and other bodily activities, and narrowed and deepened the experience of both religious and sexual privacy. Melancholy is a feeling that doesn't go anywhere; it cannot be put to use or made productive. Theodore's refusal of a destiny limited to merely human flourishing limns his stubborn sense that there must be more to life – even though that "more" is located somehow behind him, in a past life that he never quite lived. In its extravagant destructiveness, moreover, *Otranto* makes this kind of melancholy a social phenomenon, a register of what happens when a reciprocal culture that balanced varied demands through well-developed but informal mechanisms is replaced by the immanent frame. The result is a particularly secular form of haunting, a gothic alternative to official culture that arises when a reforming elite withdraws from a social compact that had once upon a time made space for popular culture.

In this way, the return of the repressed, captured in literary form, not only provides evidence for Taylor's claim that "subtraction stories" of secularization are too simple and linear. It also casts doubt on the claim that Taylor's story, its twists and turns notwithstanding, offers an "affirmative genealogy" of Western secular self-identity (Schulze, this volume). The spectral history of the gothic suggests that the autonomy celebrated by such affirmation may not be the real story

---

6 Freud gives voice to one important aspect of this more modern alienation when he develops his own theory of melancholy as the unfinished process of grieving: when a "person has to give up a sexual object, there quite often ensues an alteration of his ego which can only be described as a setting up of the object inside the ego," Freud writes (1960: 29).

at all; it may simply be secularism's way of misinterpreting its own psychic and libidinal investments.

4 Stepping backward into freedom

The gothic may register, then, a protest at the narrative of disenchantment, a protest whose melancholy is powerful enough to destabilize linear or affirmative accounts of the secular age. But Taylor's story is much more interested in Romanticism, the movement that immediately succeeds the gothic, taking over many of its interests in expression, vulnerability, and pathological uncertainty. "The salient feature of the modern cosmic imaginary," Taylor writes,

> is not that it has fostered materialism, or enabled people to recover a spiritual outlook beyond materialism, to return as it were to religion, though it has done both of these things. ... The most important fact ... is that it has opened a space in which people can wander between and around all these options without having to land clearly and definitively in any one (ASA: 351).

"The creation of this free space," Taylor continues, "has been made possible in large part by the shift in the place and understanding of art that came in the Romantic period" (ASA: 352).

In order to understand this shift, Taylor makes reference to two key terms from the romantic period: the "subtler language," a phrase he adapts from Percy Shelley (by way of the literary critic Earl Wasserman), and "play," which he adapts from Friedrich Schiller. I will begin with Schiller, who like many of his contemporaries felt he was confronting the consequences of the widespread disenchantment of the world brought about by modernity. If nature was stripped of intrinsic meaning, what of human beings? Some, like Spinoza and Hobbes, thought that humanity could be folded into a larger materialist framework. In Germany, the most important response to this unsettling possibility came from Immanuel Kant, for whom the self's freedom from determination made possible the autonomy of will, morality, and reason from material conditions. But Kant's proposed solution created its own problems, for his picture of the will imposing itself on our refractory desires internalized and recapitulated the problem of modernity without solving it.

Schiller's contribution, like that of Rousseau before him, was to historicize this problem. In his telling, it was *civilization itself* that had created the divisions between reason and feeling, subject and object, self and other:

> It was civilization itself which inflicted this wound upon modern man. Once the increase of empirical knowledge, and the more exact modes of thought, made sharper divisions between the sciences inevitable, and once the increasingly complex machinery of the State necessitated a more rigorous separation of ranks and occupations, then the inner unity of human nature was severed too, and a disastrous conflict sets it harmonious powers at variance (Schiller 1988: 130).

Schiller's terms for these opposed tendencies are the form-drive (*Formtrieb*), which seeks to impose moral and conceptual clarity on the world, and the material-drive (*Stofftrieb*), which is sensual and largely concerned with self-gratification. Left to its own devices, each of these drives is destructive: form is empty and lifeless; sense is chaotic and disorganized. Schiller's solution is the famous "play-drive" (*Spieltrieb*), where, as Taylor puts it, "the moral and the appetitive are perfectly aligned in us" (ASA: 313). When we are playing, what we ought to do and what we want to do are the same. This is the characteristic mode of artistic activity, where form and content merge and we experience ourselves not as free *from* the world but as free *within* it.

That feeling of freedom is articulated in romantic "languages of art" (ASA: 359), and Taylor's favored term for this is the "subtler language." Subtler languages, he writes, are the languages of the immanent frame; they acknowledge our continued need for transcendence or for transcendence-substitutes in a world now conceived as immanent and bounded. The paintings of Caspar David Friedrich, for example, are "trying to say something for which no adequate terms exist and whose meaning has to be sought in his work rather than in a preexisting lexicon of references" (ASA: 354). Taylor gets the concept of "subtler language" from the literary critic Earl Wasserman (ASA: 353, 357; cf. 771), who borrowed it from Percy Shelley and employed it in an influential reading of romantic poetry published in 1968. By "subtler language" Wasserman meant languages developed poetically over the course of early modernity in order to capture the new sensibility of an age in which the old verities were losing their grip:

> Until the end of the eighteenth century there was sufficient intellectual homogeneity for men to share certain assumptions.... the Christian interpretation of history, the sacramentalism of nature, the Great Chain of Being, the analogy of the various planes of creation [...].
> By the nineteenth century these world-pictures had passed from consciousness. [...] Now [...] an additional formulative act was required of the poet [...]. Within itself the modern poem must both formulate its cosmic syntax and shape the autonomous poetic reality that the cosmic syntax permits (Wasserman 1968: 10–11).

This account nicely matches the one in *A Secular Age*, where the disenchantment that attends Reform and the buffered self culminates in the Romantic recognition that the new age will require a different vernacular. The subtler languages of art have, writes Taylor, "unhooked themselves from intentional objects [...]. The ontic commitments are very unclear" (ASA: 356). Again, the contrast with Kant is obvious, for in Kant's aesthetics we borrow the idea of beauty's purposiveness from our own reason, thus keeping the aesthetic subordinate to the moral. Kantian beauty ("purposiveness without a purpose") is still very much *about* the world (see Kant 1987: 65). By contrast, Taylor suggests something quite different. If in modern aesthetics the ontological commitments are unclear, then the aesthetic is a mode of knowledge and a manner of proceeding *particular to itself*; it creates, as Wasserman (above quote) writes, "its own cosmic syntax," not one borrowed from another faculty. It is thus unclear what art so conceived delivers knowledge *of*. The dilemma is less the epistemological one of how the mind hooks onto the world than the ontological one of which world is the right world.

Romanticism in Taylor's account therefore functions both as a remarkable *critique* of the developing secular consensus brought about by Reform, and as a *symptom* of these same processes.[7] For the sense of wandering among options, searching for fulfillment but without a strongly motivated sense of what the right choices might be – this is for Taylor the central phenomenological experience of the secular age. "The languages of art," as he puts it, have "enabled people to explore these meanings with their ontological commitments as it were in suspense" (ASA: 351).

On the face of it, this sense of exploration and existential uncertainty is a long way from the quasi-Foucauldian political story of Reform and discipline that Taylor offers in the first section of *A Secular Age*. Indeed, his account of a disenchanted world where it is up to the sensitive soul to make her own meaning may contribute to the charge that Taylor's account of the secular is depoliticized. The Romantic story, that is, seems to offer ideal solutions to material problems and thus to slide easily into a mere symptom or even ideology of modernity. And it seems to assume that any proffered alternative to the present order will be personal, even idiosyncratic, and thus to preclude a collective response to the rise of secular modernity.

But this is just where a more detailed account of Schiller's *Aesthetic Education* and of Shelley's poetry can help us. Schiller's tale about the rise of civilization and its consequent effects on psyche and society is quite similar, in outline, to the sorts of historical accounts that thread their way through *A Secular Age*. Though Schiller's point of reference is Greek civilization rather than medieval Europe, his contrast between then and now works to the same effect by evaluat-

---

7 For a much fuller development of this idea, see Jager 2015.

ing a contemporary sensibility against the postulated harmony of an earlier time. The *Letters*, much like Rousseau's *Discourse on Inequality*, are a utopian volume that deploys a narrative of decline in order to gain leverage on a contemporary situation. *A Secular Age*, too, though less obviously utopian, uses its historical narrative as a way to help us recognize modern alienation – and thus to suggest, by way of contrast, what a fuller and more plentiful life might look like.

When Schiller looks at the modern condition, he sees a people divided from nature and from each other. He also sees a subject divided against itself. Like the early Marx, Schiller focuses on an individual rather than a collective solution to these divisions, and this places him, like Taylor himself, in the broadly Romantic camp. But as Fredric Jameson suggests in his classic account of Schiller in *Marxism and Form*, the internal alienation that is Schiller's primary focus must be read as a translation of the wider social, historical, and political alienations that surrounded him. Schiller wrote his book in 1793/94, as the initial promise of the French Revolution degenerated into the hardened polarities of counter-revolution and Terror. The *Letters* operate, then, as a translation of social divisions into "the inner functioning of the mind [...] a spiritual deformation which is the exact equivalent of the economic alienation in the social world outside" (Jameson 1971: 87). In Schiller's text, the analysis of freedom, in whose name the Revolution had been staged, appears no longer in a discussion of politics but in a discussion of beauty – which achieves perforce a politics of its own. "Schiller aims," writes Jameson, "at giving a description of the artistic process such that its protopolitical character will remain visible, even for the citizens of a world fatigued by politics" (1971: 86).

A clue to such "protopolitics" appears in Schiller's description of modern alienation and its Kantian hypostatization. Once intuition and speculation withdraw to separate corners, Schiller writes, "we have given ourselves a master within, who not infrequently ends by suppressing the rest of our potentialities" (1988: 130). How to destroy this internal master and release those potentialities? We glimpse a possibility in the notion of play itself, where, as Taylor writes, "we achieve full freedom, since one side of us is no longer forced to submit to the demands of the other, and in which we experience the fullness of joy" (ASA: 358). But what is the politics of such play? How do we render fullness as a political rather than "merely" aesthetic posture?

It is hardly an accident that Taylor's keyword "fullness" appears in his summary of Schiller – nor that the corresponding image of freedom sounds like his description of carnivals and feast days in the earlier sections of *A Secular Age*. The implication is that the aesthetic realizes under modern conditions the kind of fullness earlier experienced in carnival. This suggests a certain backward glance. That it is not merely nostalgia is made clear in the history that Schiller himself outlines in the *Letters* (and that, incidentally, Taylor's own zig-zag story of Reform confirms).[8] This is the history of how *Formtrieb*, in its various manifestations as instrumental reason, capitalism, good behavior, and the demystified metaphysics of Newtonian science, has outstripped *Stofftrieb* to the extent that a simple rebalancing of the scales by way of *play* is no longer possible. The modern dominance of Form is indeed the very work of Reform that Taylor describes in the first section of *A Secular Age*; its formal equivalent on the individual level is the development of the buffered self – or, as Schiller calls it, the "master within." Form and sense may have at one time operated in rough equilibrium, but the story of modernity is the story of the former's increasing dominance. As I've already suggested, the trauma of Reform's success is a large part of the story that Taylor tells (its equivalent in psychoanalysis is the traumatic break from the mother imposed by the father). This indeed is what brings about, albeit unintentionally, the secular age whose existential groundlessness is finally measured and described, in Taylor's story, by Romanticism itself. And this is also why Taylor acknowledges that the forms of aesthetic self-fashioning that he analyzes toward the end of the book are a long way from the freedom of Schiller's *Spieltrieb*, or indeed from carnival itself. The panoply of modern spiritual "options" in the West may make Form tolerable, but they hardly point a different way forward.[9] In the first part of this essay I interpreted the rise of the gothic mode in the eighteenth century as an early warning sign of this imbalance, a marker and symptom of the elite withdrawal from popular culture and that culture's consequent condemnation, banalization, and sensationalization. The gothic became a register of bits and pieces, of what was left of carnival in the aftermath of Reform's triumph, remade now as entertainment and spectacle rather than a vision of a different world.

If "play" is to be more than a temporary compensation for the buffered self – if it is, rather, to function as a critique of the historical processes that have produced that self – it cannot simply follow in this gothic mode. It will require a slightly different description. Given that what Schiller calls the "master within" and Taylor calls the "buffered self" have the upper hand, a political account of their dominance requires an overhaul of the senses, a return to something like carnival, to the celebration of fullness over form. A clue, again, may be found in what I described above as Taylor's "backward glance" in his account

---

[8] Here I am resisting the tendency to read Schiller progressively, as though play/beauty is a mere synthesis or neutralization of the twin drives toward form and sense.

[9] In *Eros and Civilization*, a book with a more than passing resemblance to *A Secular Age* in its appeal to Schiller, Herbert Marcuse calls such attempts to make modernity tolerable "repressive desublimation."

of Schillerian beauty. But the real guide is Schiller himself. For when Schiller turns in the *Letters* to the location of human freedom, he describes a curious two-step process. We begin, he writes, as "nothing but life, in order to end by becoming form [...].The sensuous drive, therefore, comes into operation earlier than the rational, because sensation precedes consciousness, and it is this *priority* of the sensuous drive which provides the clue to the whole history of freedom" (Schiller 1988: 140).

Why is the priority of sense such an important clue? Because it means that the development of the human being is not simply a matter of form replacing sense, or even growing naturally from it. Rather, sense had first to be destroyed so that form could emerge: "Man cannot pass directly from feeling to thought," Schiller writes. "He must first *take one step backwards*" (1988: 141). Because of this, there is a moment when sense has been erased and form has not yet been imposed, when we are "free of all determination whatsoever" (Schiller 1988: 141). This is the backwards step into what Schiller calls a "negative state" (1988: 141). At the beginning of life, this negative state of "pure determinability" is without content because nothing has yet made an impression upon the senses. In adult life, we revisit this earliest of states by means of the aesthetic, a "real and active determinability" (Schiller 1988: 141) which recalls for us the phenomenology of that first, long-lost moment of freedom, but now with the whole of our human powers at our disposal. The aesthetic is thus the *memory of the backward step into freedom.*

This doubled movement – freedom as a backward step, and the aesthetic as its phenomenological accounting, the bringing to adult consciousness of that long-ago moment when we first experienced what freedom was, when we were liberated from sense and not yet determined by form – can give us a richer and more politically robust reading of the emptiness that Taylor describes as the ontological ground of romantic and post-romantic art. Art unhooked from intentional objects is less a striving for a new language than the phenomenological return of the repressed. It is a "negative state" less concerned with the loss of the intentional object than with the feeling of freedom itself and its cost: with the erasure, that is to say, of the first, sensuous experience of life, and then of life's overcoming by form and Reform. This suggests a way to redeem Taylor's history of disenchantment as a political accounting of a loss that we cannot bear to remember.[10] It becomes the loss of that primal fullness and *jouissance*

---

[10] As Jameson writes about Schiller's "unrealistic" historical speculations, perhaps that judgment stands "as a judgment upon us, rather than on the Utopian speculation that we are unable to take seriously. What if our judgment were itself a measure and a symptom of our own incapacity to support such thinking?" (Jameson 1971: 90).

that Freud placed at the heart of his theory and that Herbert Marcuse, channeling both Freud and Schiller, turned to political ends in *Eros and Civilization*. "If memory moves into the center of psychoanalysis as a decisive mode of *cognition*," Marcuse wrote in 1955,

> this is far more than a therapeutic device; the therapeutic role of memory derives from the *truth value* of memory. Its truth value lies in the specific function of memory to preserve promises and potentialities which are betrayed and even outlawed by the mature, civilized individual, but which had once been fulfilled in his dim past and which are never entirely forgotten (Marcuse 1955: 18).

5 Fullness and subtler languages

With this reading of the potentially emancipatory role of memory, and thus of art, we are ready for a discussion of the subtler languages. As mentioned above, Taylor borrows the term from Earl Wasserman, who himself borrows it from Percy Shelley's 1817 poem *Laon and Cythna*. Partway through that long poem, Cythna, the poem's heroine, is trapped in a cave by the sea, brooding over the failure of the nonviolent revolution that she has helped to lead. A sea eagle carries food to Cythna in her imprisonment, and she first tries to instruct the eagle to bring her ropes so that she can escape:

> And long in vain I sought
> By intercourse of mutual imagery
> Of objects, if such aid he could be taught;
> But fruit, and flowers, and boughs, but never ropes he brought.
> (Shelley 2012: lines 3087–3090)

To recur to Taylor's terminology, Cythna's attempt at a new language must construct both a new reality and a new syntax in which to express it. Fighting madness, and with only her own resources and memories to sustain her, Cythna seems the prototypical modern subject, poised on the cusp of a new world, creating not only her own meaning but the very conditions of its intelligibility. (Like Schiller's *Letters*, this is a text written in the shadow of the French Revolution.) Her initial goal is ambitious: ropes, which would enable her to climb to freedom. But the project fails. "We live in our own world, and mine was made / From glorious phantasies of hope departed" she concludes (Shelley 2012: lines 3091–3092).

Then she tries another tack:

> And on the sand would I make signs to range
> These woofs, as they were woven, of my thought;
> Clear, elemental shapes, whose smallest change
> A subtler language within language wrought (Shelley 2012: lines 3109–3112)

This is a subtler language *within language*. It is not heroically self-generated nor wholly new but contingent and interstitial, finding room in the gaps and spaces of a dominant language (Keach 1984: 39). This is a point that Taylor, following in Wasserman's footsteps, misses. Cythna's gender matters here. So too does her marginal location and the fact that Shelley sets his allegory of the French Revolution in an exotic eastern clime, with an Orientalized version of Islam, rather than Christianity, in the background. The notion of the subtler language reminds us of the historical conditions and social arrangements out of which all dominant formations emerge. Memory, as Marcuse says, preserves the promises overwritten by the imposition of Form. Or, to put the point another way, there was a time when such things were not and this means that no dominant form is ever so dominant that other voices cannot become manifest within it.

For example, Cythna locates her subtler language not in the future but in the past, first in "The key of truths which once were dimly taught / In old Crotona" and then, more fulsomely, in "sweet melodies / Of love" (Shelley 2012: lines 3109–3115), namely her memories of an earlier time together with Laon, her fellow revolutionary leader.[11] There is a politics to this memory that goes far beyond its content. Earlier in the poem, when both are much younger, Laon had described Cythna as "A second self, far dearer and more fair" (Shelley 2012: line 875). "Communion with this purest being / Kindled intenser zeal" (Shelley 2012: lines 946–947), he declares. There is a muted eroticism in these childlike scenes, but as so often in Shelley it is directed less toward a particular person than toward a vision of the world in general as a place of bounty, peace, and harmony, of "intenser zeal" distributed among all living things. Laon and Cythna are brother and sister, and the poem's references to incest caused Shelley to withdraw it almost immediately. But incest has a powerful political resonance here, for when the siblings meet again much later, Cythna remembers her childhood time with Laon as one of plenitude and gratification:

> Thy songs were winds whereon I fled at will,
> As in a winged chariot, o'er the plain

---

11 Although Shelley is influenced by Plato at various points in his thinking, Cythna's memories bear no relation to the Platonic doctrine of recollection. Cythna is recalling an experience that exists in time and is fully embodied.

> Of crystal youth; and thou wert there to fill
> My heart with joy, and there we sate again
> On the grey margin of the glimmering main,
> Happy as then but wiser far [...] (Shelley 2012: lines 3118–3123)

"Happy as then but wiser far" could be the one-line formula for Shelley's revolutionary thinking. Like Schiller's backward step, it beautifully anticipates the bliss Marcuse cites as evidence of revolutionary eros: the backward step into a prior, now lost, state of childlike play that becomes a blueprint for an alternative future. "The memory of gratification," Marcuse writes, "is at the origin of all thinking" (1955: 18; 29). With this phrase Marcuse means to indicate that the only order worth fighting for is an order of abundance, and that contrary to all merely progressive narratives of civilization we have experience of that abundance already. What is required is the willingness to recover it – to recover what freedom felt like, though now in a more mature idiom: "happy as then, but wiser far."

"Fullness," which is Taylor's word for this same phenomenological feeling, can here take on a new kind of political charge, far removed from merely psychological, subjective, or ideational inflections. So conceived, "fullness" recaptures the political energy of the first sections of *A Secular Age*, and allows us to see these sections as the two-part story that Taylor intends: the remaking both of an entire society to higher standards of behavior and the remaking of individual senses and instincts so as to block access to an entirely different order of things. Under the influence of form, the senses become merely raw material to be organized. By contrast, the romantic bet, which is also Taylor's bet, is that the senses must be liberated again. "Play" would be the picture or image of that liberation, a language of art that reveals what a world remade might be.

6 Conclusion

I began this chapter by considering the charge that *A Secular Age* remains too caught up within the normative dimensions of Christianity, that it is analytically inattentive to the power imbalances between the rest of the world and a Western secularism that owes its conceptual contours to Christianity.

My accounts of the gothic novel and of some of Taylor's romantic sources suggest two things about the subtler languages. First, there is really no such thing as a *new* language of art: all such languages develop in relation to the world, in relation to other languages, and in relation to the histories that have gone before them. Cythna's subtler language gives up on the languages of freedom and revolution so prevalent at the turn of the nineteenth century; instead, her language *within language* alters materials already available. It is written on the sand and energized by prior voices of love and communion: it will change, disappear, reappear in new forms. And when it does so, it reactivates an earlier language of plenitude.

Second, conceiving romantic aesthetics as a neutral zone balanced among spiritual options is not perhaps quite the right image, for it suggests a freedom largely on the model of capitalist modernity. (That Taylor conceives of secularism as a principle of equidistance from religious options is not unrelated to this kind of spatial imagery [Taylor 2011]). I have been arguing, by contrast, that the languages of aesthetic freedom have an ontological relation to prior moments of fullness – fullness denied and then recaptured as melancholy absence in the gothic, or fullness reformed and than recaptured as aesthetic play in romanticism. Such moments exist in time rather than space. There is no such thing as a truly open space, and real freedom is both more nuanced and more politically resonant than the image of open space suggests, for real freedom depends upon the emancipatory power of memory. Learning to remember plenitude, which means learning to remember its erasure and denial, makes the past into an image of a possible future distinct from the present reality and from the downward pressure that reality exerts on all who wonder if things could be otherwise. Sometimes, as with Theodore, such memory may yield an almost unbearable melancholy; at other times it can become the key of a new language. Such freedom does not mean choice but rather the capacity to act. And for that, art's subtler languages may be very good training indeed.

Bibliography

Arnold, Matthew. [1869] 2009. *Culture and Anarchy*, ed. Jane Garnett. Oxford: Oxford University Press.
Asad, Talal. 2012. "Thinking About Religion, Belief, and Politics," in *The Cambridge Companion to Religious Studies*, ed. Robert A. Orsi, 36–57. New York: Cambridge University Press.
Bender, Courtney. 2010. *The New Metaphysicals: Spirituality and the American Religious Imagination*. Chicago: University of Chicago Press.
Benjamin, Walter. 1968. *Illuminations: Essays and Reflections*, ed. Hannah Arendt. New York: Schocken Books.
Bilgrami, Akeel. 2014. *Secularism, Identity, and Enchantment*. Cambridge, Mass: Harvard University Press.
Bourdieu, Pierre. 1984. *Distinction: A Social Critique of the Judgement of Taste*. Trans. Richard Nice. Cambridge, Mass: Harvard University Press.
Bruce, Steve. 2002. *God Is Dead: Secularization in the West*. Malden, Mass.: Blackwell.

Clery, E. J. 1999. *The Rise of Supernatural Fiction, 1762–1800*. Cambridge: Cambridge University Press.

Coleridge, Samuel Taylor. [1829] 1976. *On the Constitution of Church and State. The Collected Works of Samuel Taylor Coleridge*, ed. John Colmer. Volume 10. Princeton: Princeton University Press.

Collings, David. 2009. *Monstrous Society: Reciprocity, Discipline, and the Political Uncanny, 1780–1848*. Lewisburg, PA: Bucknell University Press.

Davie, Grace. 2002. *Europe, the Exceptional Case: Parameters of Faith in the Modern World*. London: Darton Longman & Todd.

Davie, Grace. 1994. *Religion in Britain Since 1945: Believing Without Belonging*. Oxford: Blackwell.

Freud, Sigmund. 1960. *The Ego and the Id*. Vol. 19 of *The Standard Edition of the Complete Psychological Works of Sigmund Freud*. Ed. and Trans. James Strachey. 24 vols. London: Hogarth, 1953–1970.

Hoeveler, Diane Long. 2010. *Gothic Riffs: Secularizing the Uncanny in the European Imaginary, 1780–1820*. Columbus: Ohio State University Press.

Hogle, Jerrold E., ed., 2002. *The Cambridge Companion to Gothic Fiction*. Cambridge: Cambridge University Press.

Jager, Colin. 2015. *Unquiet Things: Secularism in a Romantic Age*. Philadelphia: University of Pennsylvania Press.

Jager, Colin. 2010. "This Detail, This History: Charles Taylor's Romanticism," in *Varieties of Secularism in a Secular Age*, ed. Michael Warner, Jonathan VanAntwerpen, and Craig Calhoun, 166–192. Cambridge, Mass/London: Harvard University Press.

Jameson, Fredric. 1974. *Marxism and Form*. Princeton: Princeton University Press.

Kant, Immanuel. [1790] 1987. *Critique of Judgment*. Trans. Werner S. Pluhar. Indianapolis: Hackett.

Keach, William. 1984. *Shelley's Style*. New York/London: Methuen.

Marx, Karl. [1843] 1972. "On the Jewish Question," in *The Marx-Engels Reader*, ed. Robert C. Tucker, 24–51. New York: W. W. Norton.

Mahmood, Saba. 2010. "Can Secularism Be Other-wise?," in *Varieties of Secularism in a Secular Age*, ed. Michael Warner, Jonathan VanAntwerpen, and Craig Calhoun. Cambridge, Mass/London, 282–299. Harvard University Press.

Miles, Robert. 2010. "Romanticism, Enlightenment, and Mediation: The Case of the Inner Stranger," in *This is Enlightenment*, ed. Clifford Siskin and William Warner, 173–188. Chicago: University of Chicago Press.

Nelson, Victoria. 2012. *Gothicka: Vampire Heroes, Human Gods, and the New Supernatural*. Cambridge, Mass: Harvard University Press.

Punter, David, ed., 2012. *A New Companion to the Gothic*. Malden, Mass/Oxford: Wiley-Blackwell.

Schiller, Friedrich. [1793–4] 1988. *On the Aesthetic Education of Man, in a Series of Letters*, in *The Origins of Modern Critical Thought: German Aesthetic and Literary Criticism from Lessing to Hegel*, ed. David Simpson. 129–147. Cambridge: Cambridge University Press.

Sheehan, Jonathan. 2010. "When was Disenchantment? History and the Secular Age," in *Varieties of Secularism in a Secular Age*, ed. Michael Warner, Jonathan VanAntwerpen, and Craig Calhoun, 217–242. Cambridge, Mass/London: Harvard University Press.

Shelley, Percy Bysshe. 2012. "Laon and Cythna; or, The Revolution of the Golden City: A Vision of the Nineteenth Century," in *The Complete Poetry of Percy Bysshe Shelley*, ed. Donald H. Reiman, Neil Fraistat, and Nora Crook. Vol. 3, 109–322. Baltimore: The Johns Hopkins University Press.

Taylor, Charles. 1992. *The Ethics of Authenticity*. Cambridge, Mass/London: Harvard University Press.

Taylor, Charles. 1989. *Sources of the Self: the Making of the Modern Identity*. Cambridge, Mass: Harvard University Press.

Taylor, Charles. 2011. "Why We Need a Radical Redefinition of Secularism," in *The Power of Religion in the Public Sphere*, ed. Jonathan VanAntwerpen and Eduardo Mendieta. 34–59. New York: Columbia University Press.

Taylor, Charles. 2016. *The Language Animal*. Cambridge, Mass: Harvard University Press.

Wasserman, Earl. 1968. *The Subtler Language*. Baltimore: Johns Hopkins University Press.

Wood, James. 1999. *The Broken Estate: Essays on Literature and Belief.* New York: Random House.

Oane Reitsma
Musical Works as 'Higher Times': Concert Culture in a Secular Age

1 Introduction

In *A Secular Age*, Charles Taylor outlines four salient features of modern culture: "The [1] buffered identity of the disciplined individual moves in [2] a constructed social space, where [3] instrumental rationality is a key value, and [4] time is pervasively secular" (ASA: 542). This chapter examines the meanings and implications of three of these features in relation to modern concert culture. I will examine 'buffered identity,' 'constructed social space,' and the secular experience of time from the viewpoint of studies concerning the development of classical concert culture since 1800 (e.g. Goehr 2007; K. Hamilton 2008; Smithuijsen 2001; Benson 2003). I will elaborate the three topics as follows: first the perception of the identity of a musical work, second the concert hall as a social space, and third the secular experience of musical time.

Modern concert culture does not only form an example that clarifies Taylor's description of Reform in Western society. Taylor's features also function as an analytical tool to understand modern musical culture.[1] Indeed, there is an analogy between Taylor's conception of identity and the reform of social structures, and the way musicologists describe the development of Romantic and modern concert culture. Nevertheless, the main intention of this chapter is to explore whether music in the secular age might shed light on Taylor's search for "a way of maximal demand." Taylor develops this idea as an escape from what he conceives as a deadlocked conflict among exclusive humanism, neo-Nietzscheanism, and orthodox belief. His aim is to do justice to the immanent without rejecting a search for the transcendent: "After all, Plato in the *Republic* seemed quite prepared to sideline the (in his culture too) central human desires to form families, own property, and hand this to one's children; all in the name of a higher, fuller harmony of the state" (ASA: 640; see also 636–637). For the modern age, Taylor mentions Nelson Mandela and Desmond Tutu as examples of such an "imma-

---

This article is largely derived from Chapter 3 of my PhD dissertation, which has been published in Dutch (Reitsma 2014: 85–121).

[1] When talking about 'concert culture', I am pointing at the listening practice of western art music culture, as developed since approximately Beethoven's era (see e.g. Goehr 2007: passim).

nent counter-Enlightenment," who transfigure the "madness of violent categorizations" by showing a higher dimension of reconciliation and trust against the satisfactions of retribution, in the light of an eschatological dimension (ASA: 706–707, 710).

Apart from this ethical component which allows one to escape from the malaise of immanence, there is also an aesthetic dimension, more contemplative in character, which has the power to make a vertical connection with the transcendent (ASA: 757, see also 355). Taylor states that in music history, the development of 'absolute music' since 1800 "has helped create a kind of middle space, neither explicitly believing, but not atheistic either, a kind of undefined spirituality" (ASA: 360). "People began to listen to concerts with an almost religious intensity," he concludes (ASA: 360). In the final section of this chapter a musical example from the Estonian composer Arvo Pärt will illustrate the role of music in the vertical connection to the beyond.[2] While Taylor sees absolute music as a kind of neutral middle space, Pärt offers something closer to a maximal demand by showing how the immanent can be connected with the transcendent in a modern way, founded in immanence but acknowledging the value of a new world beyond mere human capacity.

2 Buffered identity

According to Taylor, individualism is an exclusive feature of modern society. It has its origin in a "long process of Reform in Latin Christendom" (ASA: 675). Taylor understands Reform in a broader sense than the ecclesiastical and theological developments of the Reformation and Counter-Reformation. He points to cultural, scientific and ethical aspects of the Renaissance and Enlightenment that strove to remake European society over to a higher standard (ASA: 61–75, 85–88). In order to grasp the effects that Reform has had on our notions of subjectivity, Taylor contrasts the pre-modern world of 1500 with modern society in the year 2000. In 1500 the hierarchy of feudal society was ontologically founded in the transcendent. The whole of the cosmos was perceived as a closed system, in which God was the highest thinkable entity (ASA: 25, 32–35, 40–41). The boun-

---

[2] In line with Martin, I am looking here for a way to get out of the binary of sacred and secular music. "It is here that we touch on what may be a fourth tradition in which music is capable of abolishing the distinction between sacred and secular," Martin (2002: 63) writes. In trying to do so, this 'fourth tradition,' in addition to (1) the understanding of music as sonic aspect of prayer, (2) a 'demotic' understanding of music and (3) the understanding of the expression of music as a religious phenomenon, has a strong similarity with Taylor's own 'fourth way.'

daries around the cosmos were closed – there was nothing imaginable outside an immanent transcendent reality.[3] On the other hand, the boundaries *within* this worldview were porous. The boundaries among faith, science, and magic were not clear, nor were the boundaries between the immanent and the transcendent. Finally, human identity was mainly defined by the greater connections of family, community, and history (e.g. ancestors). Taylor's keyword for this last is "the porous self" (ASA: 31–33, 38, 41, 137).

The secular age reverses this situation. Whereas the concept of the individual used to be articulated in terms of a major whole – whether understood contemporaneously or historically, horizontally or vertically – in the 21st century the individual is perceived as a singular and autonomous entity. The universe is open, boundless and endless (ASA: 79). At the same time, the perception of the individual and the human self-image is no longer dependent on the community, nor is God's existence a prerequisite for the perception of the individual. The human subject is able to untie itself from its context. It can be defined on the basis of its own being. Taylor's term for this perception of the individual is the "buffered self" (ASA: 36–38, 41–43).

Taylor does not relate the development from the porous to the buffered self and from a closed cosmos to an open universe in a causal way. But exactly this is, in my judgment, the key to the application of his thesis to other areas of study, such as musicology. This is because he is starting with human *perception*. And perception of a musical piece lies at the heart of musicology. Both shifts, from 'closed' to 'open' and from 'porous' to 'buffered,' seem to relate in a paradoxical way at first sight. Nevertheless, I believe that these shifts pre-suppose each other. In a closed cosmos the understanding of the self can permit openness to external forces. But after the universe had come to be figured as 'without end,' the buffers of human existence needed to be reformulated. The boundaries of imagination had to be redefined, and the human subject had to define itself over against the boundless world.

3 The work of music as a buffered self

Around 1800, musical works began to be perceived differently.[4] From this point onward, the so-called 'work concept' came into being. Neither Palestrina nor Vi-

---

[3] For this term, see: Stoker (2012).
[4] Goehr (2007: 148, 2, passim) argues that Beethoven is the starting point. Johnson mentions 1770 as a starting point (Johnson 1995: 53–70). Smithuijsen locates the shifting attitude of the

valdi nor Bach composed musical 'works' in the way modern art culture perceives such compositions. By contrast, Beethoven's orchestral symphonies are a most striking example of 'absolute music'—works, in Goehr's words, of a 'purely instrumental' or 'absolute' sort" (2007: 2).[5] The perception of music is no longer lead by extra-musical aspects, such as religious, social, scientific, domestic or profane purposes. The music does not serve its context anymore, such as the liturgy or at a celebration or festival, but the sound serves the magical power of music itself, which is called 'absolute' (A. Hamilton 2008: 66–94). Goehr relates this development in the perception of music directly to modern concert culture.

Musical works thus are more and more perceived as clearly defined entities,[6] which withdraw from the common, every-day and worldly. They are perceived from the point of view of aesthetic judgement in the abstract and artificial silence of the concert hall[7] – as 'objects' exposed, like paintings in a museum, apart from their context. This separability principle (Goehr 2007: 157–159)[8] resembles Taylor's buffered identity in two ways. In the first place identity is caught in definition and becomes autonomous over against the context of the world. Secondly, this fixed identity is created by the *perception* of modern man.

Kenneth Hamilton underlines Goehr's analysis by focusing on piano recitals in the nineteenth and twentieth centuries. The growing focus on a note-perfect performance exactly according to the score, he writes, lead to an "aesthetics of perfection" (Hamilton 2008: 193–199; see also Smithuijsen 2001: 100–111). Moreover, a historicizing fixation on the *Urtext* or even on the one historical moment of an original performance, the *Uraufführung*, suggests that musical cultural witnesses an even stronger shift to Taylor's notions of rationalization and buf-

---

audience in a broader development of the urbanization of society in Western Europe since 1600. He mentions the rivalry between the private court concerts of the nobility and the public musical gatherings of the civil aristocracy as a starting point (Smithuijsen 2001: 88–99, 112–123).

5 Although Goehr's clear explanation of 'absolute music' serves here as an introduction to the topic, she herself criticizes the ontological view of this concept in a fundamental way as non-historical, because the metaphysical connotations of this abstraction are not reasonable. She quotes Dahlhaus: "The idea that music is exemplified in works [...] is far from self-evident" (Goehr 2007: 13).

6 In the tradition of Nelson Goodman and others this 'definition' is formulated in the score, of which the sound should be an exact resemblance (Goodman 1969).

7 Smithuijsen (2001: 113) coins the term "purpose-rational silence." See note 12.

8 Gadamer (1990: 93) calls this the "ästhetische Unterscheidung," which he rejects for the same reasons as Goehr does.

fered identity, in this case to a very strict definition formed by the (unapproachable) original performance – a superhuman ideal.[9]

According to Hamilton, this development is radicalized by the growth of the twentieth-century recording industry.[10] The 'Recording Age' after 1940 captures and furthers a concert culture that exhibited musical pieces in a sterile environment, excluded all spontaneity, and prescribed a decorum of absolute silence.[11] The earlier period, or what Kenneth Hamilton (2008) terms the 'recital age' (26) had granted the performing artist more freedom in combining fragments of several pieces, improvising interludes, adding notes and chords, and changing rhythms (218–223).[12] "'Strict adherence to the letter of the score' likely meant something very much more flexible to a nineteenth-century (or earlier) musician and critic—even to the most literal-minded—than its broadly accepted meaning nowadays," Hamilton concludes (2008: 21–22). At the same time, audiences were much noisier in those earlier performances. The shift into the recording age can be explained best by the terms "original" and "recreation." Whereas 'originality' in the recital age meant entertaining (recreating) the audience in an 'original' way, in the recording age the strict adherence to the 'original' score, which should be re-created, became more important (see also Begbie 2000: 155). This shift in re-creating the original shows the shift in perceiving the identity of a musical work, which is no longer brought into being by a subjective interpretation of the pianist; instead, the pianist tries to do justice to the 'objective' entity of the piece.

In relation to Taylor's notion of 'buffered' identity, we can see an analogy in the perception of a musical work, which is perceived now as an autonomous and fixed entity, an identifiable opus. This development is a consequence of modernity, where a formerly porous world is gradually rendered as a series of buffered segments. One of the segments of social space is the concert hall. In this space

---

9 In Hamilton's view the historicizing obsession with the composer's autographs and *Uraufführung* is profoundly *un*historical (Hamilton 2008: viii).
10 Smithuijzen also shows that non-aesthetical motives play a role as well in this development, for example commercial reasons (Smithuijsen 2001: 91).
11 Smithuijsen mentions this as a 'purpose-rational silence' (doelrationele stilte), which even regards coughing and sneezing negatively (Smithuijsen 2001: 90, 93–95, 114). In his opinion the rise of radio and grammophone influences the listening discipline still in an other way: afraid for the loss of its function on the profit of the electronica, the concert hall was propagandized as the only place where classical music could be heard in a justified way.
12 Hamilton sees two parallel developments, one in the direction of a concert as social gathering and the other in the direction of a concert as an art performance, which regards the music as piece of art from an aesthetic perspective. In the twentieth century the latter developments wins out over the former.

music does not form an organic unity with its context anymore. Music is not in service to the open cosmos of liturgy, nor is it accompanying a celebration at court or at a public happening, but in the modern concert hall music becomes the centre itself, perceived as an object: a "work."[13]

4 Constructed social space

The perception of a piece of music as a "work" was of course related to its immediate context, the modern concert hall. Whereas pre-modern society was hierarchically structured, viewing the existence of God as fundament and goal of a closed cosmos, the main characteristic of the new order was a horizontally-based democratic structure of equality, manifested in social spaces, economies, and political structures. Along with "drawing rooms, coffee houses, salons, and [...] more (authoritatively) 'public' places, like Parliament" (ASA: 186), the concert hall can be added to this group of constructed social spaces that together make up the public sphere. Here attendees can discuss the music and their musical taste in relative equality, either as *connoisseurs* or consumers.

Taylor starts his explanation of the development from vertical structure to horizontal structure with the Reformation. Divine salvation was no longer reached only by an elite group of people living a celibate life, but rather became directly accessible to the people, who could read the Scriptures themselves. This is an important step in a broad process of rationalization in society as a whole. Taylor states that according to the ideals of the (Calvinist) Reformation the rules and disciplinary life in the monasteries changed to discipline for all individuals in the whole society (ASA: 85–86, 146–158). 'Holiness' is no longer the property only of an elite minority. The perception of the transcendent changes with this broadening of the direct relationship between the divine and the people. The 'higher religion' shifts to secular time and its immanent horizontal order. Taylor summarizes the developments of rationalization, discipline, and neutralizing the sacred with the term 'disenchantment' (ASA: 77, 86, 266, 272). Disenchantment does not mean that the notion of the transcendent disappears in favor of the immanent. That is exactly what Taylor denies over against the 'subtraction story' that characterizes the usual secularization theory. Rather, the relationship be-

---

[13] Benson (2003: 132) chooses to use the older term "piece of music" instead of "musical work," because "in contrast to the notion of the work, the idea of a *piece* implies something that is connected to a contextual whole." In doing so, he exactly reflects the difference that Taylor identifies between the pre-modern conception of the "porous self" and the modern conception of the "buffered self."

tween the immanent and the transcendent is changing: "The process of disenchantment is the disappearance of [the world of spirits, demons, moral forces which our predecessors acknowledged], and the substitution of what we live today: a world in which the only locus of thoughts, feelings, spiritual élan is what we call minds; the only minds in the cosmos are those of humans" (ASA: 30 – 31). This does not mean that God has disappeared from society, but rather that the approach to the beyond now follows a multifarious range of ways, where the immanent relates differently, often more directly, to the transcendent than in orthodox forms of faith.[14] As a result religion does not disappear, but changes into a broad, secular phenomenon. No one Church is the only gateway to the truth, but many churches and denominations appear. Later on truth is sought in the collective, democratic, public conversations, which Taylor calls 'metatopical spaces.' How do we locate the concert hall and the art of music amidst these transformations?

5 The concert hall as a constructed social space

Three features of the above transformations appear in the phenomenon of the concert hall as it has developed after 1800.[15] In the first place the concert hall is an exponent of democratic public space. Relative equality comes into being in the concert hall. Whereas recitals were originally attended by *connoisseurs* from the nobility, the concert hall became more and more accessible for middle class citizens.[16] An important example for this development is the chair, fixed to the floor with screws – all the seats for the audience become equal and standardized, without distinctions (Smithuijsen 2001: 114). Next to equality, discipline is the second feature of the secular age which appears in the concert hall. The performance requires silence, to which all attendees must adjust. A recital is no longer a noisy sociable gathering; refreshments are banned to the foyer outside the performance hall, to be consumed after the concert or during the break

---

14 Stoker (2012) tries to grasp this transformation in terms of "shifting transcendence" and specifies four types: radical transcendence, immanent transcendence, radical immanence, and transcendence as alterity.
15 From this time on the musician also becomes an autonomous artist and the modern view of "fine arts" arises (A. Hamilton 2008: 68 – 69; Goehr 208 – 211).
16 According to Kenneth Hamilton, in the first half of the nineteenth century both practices existed next to each other. But during this period, the practice of the concert hall, with a broad audience, slowly won out over the salon with its select group of listeners (K. Hamilton 2008: 38, 61, 82).

(Smithuijsen 2001: 96). The highly standardized and formalized fixed order of the modern concert, starting with applause, followed by silence, careful attentive listening and again applause, demands a strong discipline from the concert visitors. This type of listening almost reaches the state and discipline of contemplation. The discipline is ordered by the music and makes its demands equally of all audience members.

Along with equality and self-discipline, however, the modern concert hall manifests a sacred aspect. Taylor argues that in the "Modern Moral Order" the sacred is embodied in the profane; the transcendent is understood in the immanent. On the one hand one could say that music culture wants to replace religion in a disenchanted universe. This happens especially in the *Kunstreligion* (literally: art-as-religion), a nineteenth-century understanding in which art is sacralized rather than pointing to a beyond. The music scene becomes a religion in itself, with ambitions to reach the divine in the music itself, with the performer as a demiurge and the music as the "Absolute." But such aesthetic experience with no reference to the divine should be contrasted with another possibility in which music opens its horizon to a kind of spirituality that does not deny the existence of God.[17]

Taylor emphasizes in this respect the fact that poetry and music cannot rely any longer on traditional symbols. "[F]or a couple of centuries we have been living in a world in which these points of reference no longer hold for us," he writes (ASA: 352). Music does not point any longer to external meanings, but has to shape its own meaning: "where formerly poetic language could rely on certain publicly available orders of meaning, it now has to consist in a language of articulated sensibility" (ASA: 353). On the one hand this means that art is unhooked from pre-modern ontological commitments, because the traditional symbols and accepted conventions do not make sense anymore to the public. On the other hand it implies that the arts need to develop subtler languages than the traditional ones. Here music perhaps has an advantage. For whereas poetry still has to deal with words and their meanings, music, phenomenologically speaking, exists as pure sound. Thus it can more easily develop into an art in its own right. What Taylor calls "resemanticisation" (ASA: 355) thus matches pure instrumental music even more than text-related music, because pure instru-

---

[17] Taylor gives an example from post-Romantic literature, where he says: "One might say that the ontological indeterminacy of the "subtler languages" of post-Romantic literature allowed for three kinds of position. One could remain with the indeterminacy [...]; one leaves the issue undecided, to what extend one is invoking an extra-human spiritual reality, or rather pointing to something wholly within experience. But one can also firmy disambiguate one's position" (ASA: 404). To explain Pärt's music later on in this chapter, I choose the first of the three options.

mental music (like 'absolute' music) simply cannot refer to any textual meaning. "Subtler languages which have taken this "absolute" turn, unhooked themselves from intentional objects [...], are moving in a new field. The ontic commitments are very unclear" (ASA: 356). Nevertheless this is not the weak point of absolute music. On the contrary, Taylor makes the plausible argument that "this means that such art can serve to disclose very deep truths which in the nature of things can never be obvious, nor available to everyone, regardless of spiritual condition" (ASA: 356). Although Taylor argues that absolute music, with its unclear ontic and ontological commitments, can only reflect "the mystery of anthropological depth" (ASA: 356, see also 359), I want to emphasize that modern music has the ability to open a new spirituality: probably the best example in the twentieth century is formed by the oeuvre of Olivier Messiaen, also mentioned by Taylor (ASA: 360).

In doing so, I connect to what Taylor (ASA: 360) calls "a kind of middle space, neither being explicitly believing, but not atheistic either." This ambiguous space "on the one hand draw[s] towards unbelief, while on the other, feel[s] the solicitations of the spiritual – be they in nature, in art in some contact with religious faith, or in a sense of God which may break through the membrane [of modern buffered identity]" (ASA: 360). Even more than Messiaen's compositions, which refer to a rather fixed understanding of orthodox (Catholic) faith, Arvo Pärt's works reflect this middle space in their spiritual unclearness. In this unclearness his works refuse to reject an understanding of the beyond. On the contrary, they form a continuous attempt to break through the membrane.

This twentieth-century music moves a step beyond the 'absolute music' of the nineteenth century, which is the main object of discussion in this section. Nevertheless, I see Messiaen's and Pärt's works as an outcome of one of the possible options opened up by absolute music. Absolute music developed an understanding of music as a sheer immanent phenomenon of organized sound, in which all religious and spiritual possibilities are sought within the immanent. Music is no longer a means to approach the divine, conceived as transcendent, but it is about the divine *in* or *of* the music itself. Here one can clearly see what Taylor means when he talks about disenchantment. But the next step is that the immanent sound without any particular meaning is the starting point for a subtle language, which tries to make a vertical connection with the transcendent again. Arvo Pärt's work, of which the last section gives an example, reflects that "[t]he dimension of profundity is entered through art, whose subtler language can open us to mystery, but with its ontic commitments suspended and undefined" (ASA: 411).

We have been tracing the shift from mimesis to absolute. Music no longer refers to an external, whether transcendent (in the liturgy) or worldly (in memorial or festival). Like the closed space of the concert hall, absolute music forms a cosmos in itself. It denies the surrounding world and replaces it by building its own realm. The music comes to the fore, appearing out of an unnatural silence, as a *creatio ex nihilo* in which composer and performer are the divine creators. What had been a (servile) medium before, now becomes a genre in its own right (A. Hamilton 2008: 155). This is exemplified by the fact that the annotation 'string quartet' starts to appear as a title of a work instead of only a description of instrumentation, like Mozart's *String Quartet no. 14 in G Major* or, for example, Beethoven's *Piano Sonata no. 32*. The title descriptions suggest that what used to be "form" now becomes "content," and the means becomes the goal. This is because the instrumentation no longer serves to reach a certain musical effect, but the musical composition serves the specialities and limitations of the instrument(s). The concert hall creates ritual, communal spirit and common worship in its own way – indeed it becomes an exponent of secular society.

6 Secular and higher times[18]

We have discussed the buffered identity and the closed social space of the concert hall; the third aspect of western art music is to be found in the understanding of music as "higher times." In a certain way, this forms a path to the solution of the problem of the identity of music as a closed sphere.

According to Taylor, following Bergson, premodern peoples made a distinction between "ordinary time" and "higher time." Ordinary time is secular time. It is the time of day-to-day life. What Taylor calls "kairotic" moments, by contrast, are those moments that "gathered, assembled, reordered, punctuated profane, ordinary time" (ASA: 54). These higher times connect events that are temporally far removed from one another. "Good Friday 1998 is closer in a way to the original day of the Crucifixion than mid-summer's day 1997" (ASA: 55). What has changed in the modern age is that secular time is no longer grouped around such moments.

According to Taylor, the idea of "higher times" has been borrowed from Plato, for whom the unchangeable Ideas are elevated above time and time is "a moving image of eternity" (ASA: 55). What happens in time is thus less perfect than what happens in Plato's unchangeable world. This thinking also displays cyclical elements because ultimately everything will return once again to its fixed, unchangeable form. Christianity's view was somewhat different precisely

---

18 This topic is also elaborated in: Reitsma 2012.

because what happened in history was important for Christianity. Salvation history occurs, after all, according to a linear process and not according to a cyclical concept of time. The present is always related to the past and the future. These three are constantly giving meaning to one another and are gathered in the "now." "There is a kind of simultaneity of the first note with the last, because all have to sound in the presence of the others in order for the melody to be heard" (ASA: 56).

Taylor also introduces a third concept of higher time, namely the "time of origin" (ASA: 57), a term he borrows from Mircea Eliade. This time of origin is not a concept that has arisen in philosophical or theological thinking but in folk traditions. It concerns an idea of a Great Time in which things were formed. Creation, gods, Exemplars, Lawgivers: these are entities larger than we are, who preceded us but are also always present "above us" and to whom we are related through our movement through history, either by coming closer to or by moving further away from what happened in the beginning.

All three views of "higher time," Platonic, Christian, and Originary, have in common that they order secular time by means of a vertical connection. According to Taylor, what is unique about the modern experience of time is that the vertical component has been banished or even denied. This happens due to a shift from "place" to "space," wherein objects that were once marked or filled become empty shells or even a vacuum.[19] The modern concept of time is likewise characterized by homogeneity and emptiness. We now "measure and organize time as never before in human history" (ASA: 59). The stable factor is no longer eternity but the measurable regularity of time. My discussion of the horizontal democratic structure of the concert hall as a public space to be "filled" has already suggested some implications of this way of thinking in relation to music. The experience of time has become homogeneous because all points of time are equidistant from eternity. Or as Taylor puts it, "[t]he long time horizon of modern reconstruction is linear, and it is made up of 'homogeneous, empty time'" (ASA: 129).[20]

---

[19] In relation to music, Cobussen (2008: 7, 149) deconstructs the phenomenon of music as a "non-place," an "*a*-topos," a "*para*-site;" an undefined space which is "not (t)here."
[20] Gadamer (2001: 132) explains the concept of empty time in the same way, when he points to time as a tormenting and boring presence.

7 Music as 'higher times'[21]

I would now like to argue that musical works can nonetheless fulfil a kairotic function in a secular age because they can draw us out of our daily trek through existence and evoke existential experiences by means of time. Because music in modern time is experienced as an independent phenomenon with its own intrinsic value, it opens a path to the "higher times." Above, I criticized the distance between audience and work caused by the separability principle and the space of the modern concert hall. Yet it is exactly this conception of absolute music that gives music the opportunity to transform, and in doing so, to transcend ordinary time. When music is no longer in service to external factors, the central place of the music itself as an autonomous composition makes it inevitable that the music requires an *internal* ordering of secular time. The order can no longer be borrowed externally from hierarchical social contexts. Time, experienced as an empty shell or even as a vacuum, has to be given new punctuation – but now by the composition itself. This is only possible when music is phenomenologically defined as a "transformation of time by means of sound and rhythm" (Reitsma 2014: 110, 165).[22] The characteristic of music to order and punctuate by its own internal musical means – sound and rhythm – connects secular time and higher time, because it is time itself that is transformed. Music is in this sense the art of time itself. Every piece of music shapes its own idiosyncratic time experience, which happens to be irreplaceable by any other medium.

It is in this way that music can function as Taylor's "fourth path," next to the other three of traditional faith, humanism, and anti-humanism. Taylor calls this alternative the way of "maximal demand," which "defines our highest spiritual or moral aspirations for human beings, while showing a path to the transformation involved which doesn't crush, mutilate or deny what is essential to our humanity" (ASA: 639–640). Music can become an exponent of this way because it has the capacity to break through the immanent frame, not by a force from outside, but by its own means. Nothing other than phenomenological rootedness in time enables music to do so. By transforming ordinary temporal experience, music becomes expressive of the higher times in a pluralist age.

---

[21] Hermsen (2010: 62) elaborates the concept of 'other times' in relation to modern time experience. For an aplication of this concept to music, see: Reitsma (2014: 108–109).

[22] Implicitly I refer here to Begbie, who states that music "is connected [...] to the temporalities of the physical world at large in which all [...] temporalities participate" (Begbie 2000: 55, see also 31). Rooted in this physical and temporal world, music overcomes this world by transforming time.

Thus, on the one hand, modern music culture locks music into a conception of the absolute work. But music can liberate itself from that role by manipulating horizontal "empty" time experience into a time filled with sounds which open new horizons. It expels time, experienced as an empty shell or even as a vacuum, and creates the capacity to host a vertical breakthrough and to open up the relationship with the unknown by its purely phenomenological being (see ASA: 758). Because it is a complex art, music has a variety of means for doing so. Rhythm, harmony, timbre, and tempo provide variation, while several voices or several groups of instruments can create multiple atmospheres at the same time. Slow and fast can be heard at the same time, as can loud and soft. That makes it possible for music to break through its own buffered identity and constructed social context into a beyond. Indeed, in performance music can even "transcend" itself. In an excellent performance an unknown aspect of a composition can be revealed, which even the composer did not envisage. A piece of music is always open to a new form of being, which is realized in every new performance of the piece. In performance, the piece comes into a new being again, which completes its identity temporarily, until it is performed again.

8 Arvo Pärt's *Annum per annum*

The way in which music breaks through the immanent frame is fully dependent on the character of the musical forms used in a composition.[23] Perhaps all music has this potential, but to really become a way of *maximal* demand depends on what the composer envisages and what means he uses. An example from the oeuvre of the Estonian composer Arvo Pärt can help to make this clear. My analysis will suggest that Pärt redeems the strenuousness of the listening experience, rescuing the listener from the strain of the world and bringing the listener into a spiritual realm. This piece therefore is rightly an example of *subtle* language.

The theme of Pärt's organ composition *Annum per annum* ('Year by year') is explicitly connected with the overarching theme of time.[24] The composition consists of two parts, or actually two 'types' of music. A calm part with a melodic character in a soft timbre is bracketed by an introduction and coda in which a fifth chord is repeated continuously in a long-short rhythm, played in a rapid tempo. The introduction starts with the full volume of the organ, which dies

---

[23] Elsewhere I give examples exposed by works of Olivier Messiaen, Kaikhosru Sorabji, and Simeon Ten Holt (Reitsma 2012).
[24] For a short description of the piece, see: Hillier (1997: 173–174).

away slowly into total silence. In contrast, the tempo does not die but keeps up the same rapid pace (long-short, long-short) until the sound is gone. Motion goes on, that is, but the listener leaves the busy world of this restless sound and steps into another world. Likewise, the end of the coda comes abruptly, as if the music can start again from the beginning, which gives the piece as a whole a cyclical character. It is, as the title suggests, time repeating itself over and over again, through the years.

Meanwhile, the calm middle segment forms the core of the piece. It exists in five sections, which bear the letters K, G, C, S, A – referring to the ordinary parts of the Catholic mass. Each section is a variant on the same theme, which is revealed in its most simple way in the last of the five sections. At the same time, this last section is the longest, because the eight musical phrases of the first four parts are extended into ten. One could say that it reaches closer to eternity, because the theme is extended and simplified at the same time. The listener learns to grasp the theme better, and its essence is revealed only at the end. But also the middle part as a whole expresses a breakthrough of eternity into restless worldly experience, as if entering the liturgy lifts us up from the busy world. On the basis of sheer musical forms, we see here a clear suggestion of higher time – whether religious or not.

Following Taylor, one could state that every work of art has the potential ability to break through the ordinary. But in this case, we see a breakthrough within the piece itself. The middle part forms a contrast with the surrounding parts, which in their turn already form a contrast with the silence of the concert hall. Moreover, the middle part contains some aspects that demand more attention. First is the element of repetition. In the five sections, there is a clear continuum in melody and atmosphere. Although the modus changes – from d minor to D major in part C, for example – the continuity remains much stronger than the discontinuity. The atmosphere intensifies because the timbre changes in every section – it appeals to a broad palette of listening abilities. On top of that, the experience of listening intensifies, because the modus changes from minor to major and the structure of the notes becomes simpler, so that one could speak of a reversed climax. The piece grabs the ear of the listener more and more, until, at the end, only the essential remains. Yet the removed parts of the melody and the harmony still resound in the consciousness of the listener – the joyous cadence is so strong that it never entirely leaves the listener's ear. This suggestion is reinforced by the fifth section, which simplifies the theme and extends the number of repetitions of the theme compared to the previous sections, so that essence of the musical theme lasts the longest in the ear of the listener.

All in all, there is no connection between the intensive middle part and the two surrounding parts of the piece; indeed there is a little silence in between, both before the start and at the end of the middle part. At the same time, in spite of the title and the reference to the mass, there is no clear religious reference or connotation external to the music itself in the melody. The indeterminate melody seems to refer more to agnosticism. The ontological reference remains unclear. But it is exactly this ontological suspension which transforms the listening experience into "an extra-human spiritual reality" (compare ASA: 404). Over against the intensive strain of the two surrounding parts the listener is left in a relaxed state that becomes, paradoxically, more and more intense. The listener is drawn out of everyday strenuousness and brought into a subtle realm of peace of mind.

Annum per annum reflects clearly what Taylor tries to express with the idea of the subtler languages. This is not because of the punctuation of musical climaxes as such. The measure and tempo are quite flat, even throughout the middle part. This recalls an almost "horizontal" experience, rather than the gathering of higher time. But this experience of otherness, which is produced by the manipulation of time by means of sound, becomes nevertheless an experience of breakthrough towards another realm, though without denying the restlessness of the everyday world. Pärt depicts a realm parallel to everyday reality; ordinary and higher times coexist, without denying or mutilating each other. At the same time, there is little connexion with traditional musical forms derived from classical religious music. *Annum per annum* thus seeks a genuinely new way for people to orient their lives.

Bibliography

Begbie, Jeremy S. 2002. *Theology, Music and Time*. Cambridge: Cambridge University Press.
Benson, Bruce Ellis. 2003. *The Improvisation of Musical Dialogue: A Phenomenology of Music*. Cambridge, Mass: Cambridge University Press.
Cobusen, Marcel. 2008. *Thresholds: Rethinking Spirituality Through Music*. Aldershot/Burlington: Ashgate.
Gadamer, Hans-Georg. 1990. *Wahrheit und Methode: Grundzüge einer philosophischen Hermeneutik. Gesammelte Werke* Bd. 1. *Hermeneutik I*. Tübingen: J.C.B. Mohr (Paul Siebeck).
Gadamer, Hans-Georg. 2001. "Die Aktualität des Schönen: Kunst als Spiel, Symbol und Fest," in *Kunst als Aussage. Gesammelte Werke* Bd. 8. *Ästhetik und Poetik I*, 94–142. Tübingen: J.C.B. Mohr (Paul Siebeck).
Goehr, Lydia. 2007. *The Imaginary Museum of Musical Works: An Essay in the Philosophy of Music*. Oxford: Oxford University Press.
Goodman, Nelson. 1969. *Languages of Art: An Approach to the Theory of Symbols*, London: Oxford University Press.
Hamilton, Andy. 2008. *Aesthetics & Music*. London/New York: Continuum.

Hamilton, Kenneth. 2008. *After the Golden Age: Romantic Pianism and Modern Performance*, Oxford: Oxford University Press.

Hermen, Joke J. 2010. *Stil de tijd: Pleidooi voor een langzame toekomst.* Amsterdam/Antwerpen: Arbeiderspers.

Hiller, Paul. 1997. *Arvo Pärt*, Oxford/New York: Oxford University Press.

Johnson, James H. 1995. *Listening in Paris: A Cultural History*, London/Berkeley/Los Angeles: University of California Press.

Martin, David. 2002. *Christian Language and its Mutations: Essays in Sociological Understanding*, Aldershot/Burlington VT: Ashgate.

Reitsma, Oane. 2012. "Some Time for Timelessness: Performance Time of Works by Messiaen, Sorabji, and Ten Holt," in *Looking Beyond? Shifting Views of Transcendence in Philosophy, Theology, Art, and Politics*, ed. Wessel Stoker and W.L. van der Merwe, 487–504. Amsterdam/New York: Rodopi.

Reitsma, Oane. 2014. *Klank als religieuze presentie: de muzikale gestalte in een seculiere tijd belicht vanuit werk van Messiaen*, Amsterdam: VU University Press.

Reitsma, Oane. 2015. "Religious Music as Child's Play: Gadamer's Hermeneutics and Instrumental Music," in *Music and Transcendence*, ed. Férdia J. Stone-Davis, 177–193. Farnham/Burlington VT: Ashgate.

Smithuijsen, Cas. 2001. *Een verbazende stilte: Klassieke muziek, gedragsregels en sociale controle in de concertzaal.* Amsterdam: Boekmanstudies.

Stoker, Wessel. 2012. "Culture and Transcendence: A Typology," in *Looking Beyond? Shifting Views of Transcendence in Philosophy, Theology, Art, and Politics*, ed. Wessel Stoker and W.L. Van der Merwe, 5–28. Amsterdam/New York: Rodopi.

Thomas A. Carlson
Secular Moods: Exploring Temporality and Affection with *A Secular Age*

1 Introduction

In *A Secular Age*, Charles Taylor productively contends that modern secularity is not simply the neutral and natural result at which we arrive once an objective scientific rationality destroys and leaves behind the unfounded superstitions of traditional religious belief. Modern secularity entails rather its own newly developed moral and spiritual sensibilities. Among those sensibilities, I suggest in what follows, we can note distinctive turns of human affection largely overlooked by theories of secularization that focus on modern rationalities in scientific, technological, political, bureaucratic, and related domains. In attending, however, to the affective turns that we might understand, or feel, as distinctive to the experience of *time* in modern thought and culture, we should see therein not only Taylor's version of secular time, the homogenized and objectified time of instrumental calculation on the part of disciplined individuals with buffered identities and masterful projects.[1] We should see also a quite different – more modest and vulnerable, but no less affirmative and meaningful – experience of time and of its mortal condition. This latter sense of time, I argue, while meaningfully construed as secular, stands at odds not only with the masterful aspirations of Taylor's buffered selves in *their* secular time but also with the Christian-Augustinian thinking about time that resonates in Taylor's critique of that secu-

---

I extend my warm thanks to Enno Rudolph for his most insightful and generous response to the first public version of this paper at "Working with *A Secular Age*," University of Bern, March, 2014, as well as to Colin Jager and Jonathan VanAntwerpen for their challenging questions and extended conversation; to Birgit Meyer and Ernst van den Hemel for organizing a lively and rewarding seminar discussion of a later draft at the Centre for the Humanities and the Department of Philosophy and Religious Studies at Utrecht University in September, 2014; and to the students and faculty participating in the Religious Studies Colloquium at the University of California, Santa Barbara, who read and debated the paper in November, 2014.

1 This summarizes Taylor's much discussed "immanent frame." "The predominance of instrumental rationality, and the pervasiveness of secular time go together," he writes. "So the buffered identity of the disciplined individual moves in a constructed social space, where instrumental rationality is a key value, and time is pervasively secular. All of this makes up what I want to call 'the immanent frame'" (ASA: 542).

lar time and in his response to the crisis of meaning he believes it to yield – most acutely in love's encounter with death.

2 Secular time, the crisis of death, and the meaning of love according to Taylor

Linked intimately to the processes of "disenchantment" in which Max Weber (with Leo Tolstoy) saw the question of death's meaning, and thus of life's meaning, grow troublesome,[2] Taylor's "secular time" poses a crisis of meaning insofar as it cannot sustain the kinds of gathering and fullness that are achieved, on Taylor's view, by what he calls the "higher times" of traditional religion. Just as modern Western civilization's "progress" threatens for Weber and Tolstoy to render the individual death – and hence life – meaningless because the individual in it never reaches any culminating fulfillment, but simply passes away within time's ongoing flow, so Taylor's secular time constitutes an empty, homogenous stream wherein our individual lives and achievements are dissolved and forgotten. As coming to light especially in his treatment of death, however, Taylor's contrast between secular time (as empty and dispersive) and the higher times of religion (as gathering unto fullness and wholeness) finally concerns not so much time as eternity – which alone satisfies, in Taylor's thinking, the desire for meaning that presses upon us when we face the apparent crisis of death.

In answer to the criticism (which is not mine here) that religious "yearning for eternity" is a "trivial and childish thing," Taylor argues that such yearning much rather "reflects an ethical insight [...] that death undermines meaning" (ASA: 722). On this view, death signals the extreme of a dispersive power that Taylor sees at work already in the "secular time" he critiques, and religious yearning for eternity constitutes the extension and consummation of a gathering

---

2 See Weber 1946: 139–140. "All of [Tolstoy's] broodings," Weber writes, "increasingly revolved around the problem of whether or not death is a meaningful phenomenon. And his answer was: for civilized man death has no meaning. It has none because the individual life of civilized man, placed into an infinite 'progress,' according to its own immanent meaning should never come to an end; for there is always a further step ahead of one who stands in the march of progress. And no man who comes to die stands upon the peak which lies in infinity [...]. [Civilized man] catches only the most minute part of what the life of the spirit brings forth ever anew, and what he seizes is always something provisional and not definitive, and therefore death for him is a meaningless occurrence. And because death for him is meaningless, civilized life as such is meaningless; by its very 'progressiveness' it gives to death the imprint of meaninglessness" (trans. modified).

work that he counts as already essential to love. "One of the things which makes it very difficult to sustain a sense of the higher meaning of ordinary life, in particular our love relations, is death," Taylor writes. "It's not just that they matter to us a lot, and hence leave a grievous whole in our lives when our partner dies. It's also because just because they are so significant, they seem to demand eternity. A deep love already exists against the vicissitudes of life, tying together past and present in spite of the disruptions and dispersals of quarrels, distractions, misunderstandings, resentments. By its very nature it participates in gathered time. And so death can seem a defeat, the ultimate dispersal which remains ungathered" (ASA: 720). If the work of love is a gathering that repairs rupture and loss, love's logical extreme for Taylor is the ultimate gathering of an eternity where time's seeming dispersion is overcome. In this thinking, desire for eternity – "a desire to gather together the scattered moments of meaning into some kind of whole" (ASA: 720) – is only the extension of love's core logic.

This refusal of death spoken in religious yearning for eternity entails, furthermore, not just the desire that life should continue; it goes more deeply, Taylor thinks, to an essential link between our "happiness" and "meaning:" "the deepest, most powerful kind of happiness, even in the moment, is plunged into a sense of meaning. And the meaning seems denied by certain kinds of ending. That's why the greatest crisis around death comes from the death of someone we love" (ASA: 721). Here, for Taylor, is the real sense of Friedrich Nietzsche's pronouncement that *"Alle Lust will Ewigkeit:"* "not just because you might want it to go on and on, as with any pleasant experience. Rather, all joy strives for eternity, because it loses some sense if it doesn't last" (ASA: 720). Despite the citation of *Thus Spoke Zarathustra*, however, Taylor's appeal here to eternity seems more in tune with Augustinian than with Nietzschean sensibilities.

3 Augustine and Heidegger in Taylor's analysis of time

In first sketching out his understanding of secular time and its contrast with the "higher times" that point to eternity, Taylor emphasizes that the "secular" is a temporal category – referring in its Christian, especially Augustinian, contexts to "the life of ordinary time" by contrast to a life "turned away from this in order to live closer to eternity" (ASA: 55). Rightly signaling the temporal and Christian derivation of the term, Taylor goes on, more problematically, to equate his version of "secular time" with "our" understanding and experience of time as such. "'Secular time' is what to us is ordinary time, indeed to *us* it's just time, period. One thing happens after another, and when something is past, it's past. Time placings are consistently transitive. If A is before B and B before C, then A is before C" (ASA: 55). While "secular time" for Taylor consists in such an empty, homogeneous flow, where successive points arise and pass away in a movement whose dispersion defies gathering, the "higher times" of religion are defined by a logic that finds exemplary expression in Book XI of Augustine's *Confessions*, where what would otherwise remain a meaningless multiplicity of fleeting moments is gathered into the unified and sustained temporality of memory, attention and anticipation. "Augustine in his famous discussion in *Confessions* XI examines lived time. His instant is not the 'nun' of Aristotle, which is a limit, like a point, an extensionless boundary of time periods. Rather it is the gathering together of past into present to project a future. The past, which 'objectively' exists no more, is here in my present; it shapes this moment in which I turn to a future, which 'objectively' is not yet, but which is here qua project. In a sense, Augustine may be thought to have foreshadowed the three ekstaseis of Heidegger" (ASA: 56).

In light of this apt linkage of Augustine to Heidegger, one should note that Heidegger's position within Taylor's treatment of secular time proves ambiguous. On the one hand, Taylor suggests that Heidegger represents one of the more important responses to the modern crisis of time consciousness induced by the reign of secular time; like Bergson's before him, Heidegger's work stems in large part for Taylor from the "need to rediscover a lived time beneath or beyond the objectified time-resource of the disciplined order of civilization" (ASA: 72). On the other hand, however, while noting that Heidegger aims to articulate a lived temporality differing from the secular time that Taylor critiques, Taylor nonetheless situates Heidegger still on the side of Taylor's "secular time:" "The step to emptiness is part of the objectification of time which has been so important a part of the outlook of the modern subject of instrumental reason. Time has been in a sense 'spatialized.' Heidegger has mounted a strong attack on this whole conception in his understanding of temporality; see especially *Sein und Zeit*...Division 2. But distinguishing secularity from the objectification of time allows us to situate Heidegger on the modern side of the divide. Heideggerian temporality," Taylor asserts without elaboration or explanation, "is also a mode of secular time" (ASA: 798fn45). Although Heidegger rejects the homogenization and objectification of time typical of Taylor's secular modernity, arguing that it represents a derivative and fallen conception of time that, while based in a more primordial ecstatic temporality, denies or flees from the essence and implications of such temporality through the effort to render temporal existence calculable and controllable; and although Heidegger rejects, correlatively, any understanding of time as an indifferent container "in" which humans somehow "find" themselves, insisting instead that human being (as *Dasein*) is in its very being temporalizing; and although he does all of this within an affective-ecstatic conception of time according to which time essentially "gathers" along lines deeply akin, and moreover indebted, to Augustine; Heidegger nonetheless falls for Taylor – for reasons not developed – on the side of "secular time" and thus presumably remains, and leaves "us," at a loss before the crisis of meaning that secular time, and mortality, entail. This relegation of Heidegger to the side of secular time relates, I think, to the different ways in which Taylor and Heidegger inherit Augustinian thinking about time. While Taylor's analysis reflects an Augustinian construal of time that sees transience and loss – as experienced most pointedly in mortality – to be at odds with true (lasting and thus "full") meaning and happiness, which is to say at odds with love's most fundamental intention, Heidegger draws on Augustine to develop an understanding of human temporality – as affective and ecstatic – that would receive mortality as a condition rather than contradiction of whatever meaning, and happiness, human love, and life, may entail.

4 Love and mortal temporality in light of Heidegger: a differing reception of Augustine

Heidegger suggests to my reading a manner of thinking, and living, secularity that would derive neither from modern rationality's subtractions nor from the positive projects of techno-scientific modernity's buffered selves but from an affective and temporal turn that diverges as much from the (Augustinian) desire that love's happiness be eternal, and thus secure, as from modernity's (often strikingly similar) techno-scientific quest for the certainty and security of instrumental calculation. And while surely responding critically to tendencies within modern thought and culture that threaten to "flatten" the world and eclipse all "mystery," the affective turn at stake in Heidegger diverges also, on my reading, from the Romantic appeal to "subtler languages," insofar as these, on Taylor's account, follow a compensatory logic and aspire still to "restoring our lost unity" (ASA: 359).

Heidegger's critique of Western modernity's calculative and instrumental rationality is widely referenced in academic circles, and that critique seems in key ways consistent with Taylor's critical analysis of "secular time." Just as secular time and its homogenous flow exclude hope for any ultimate gathering or meaning, so the calculating rationality of modernity effectively cancels, according to Heidegger, any meaningful sense of futurity, and thus any meaningfully temporal, or genuinely historical, existence for human Dasein.[3] No less relevant but less often noted (and not attended to by Taylor) is that Heidegger signals an alternative to such calculating rationality in what he calls a logic of the heart. While the former – calculating reason – is preoccupied with the controlled fabrication and rapid consumption of objects that prove endlessly replaceable[4] (in a kind of perverse copy of the Augustinian eternity where nothing dear is lost), the latter – a logic of the heart – inclines toward things in their fragility and toward persons in their native mortality:

> At nearly the same time as Descartes, Pascal discovers the logic of the heart [*die Logik des Herzens*] as over against the logic of calculating reason. The inner and invisible domain of the heart is not only more inward than the interior that belongs to calculating representation, and therefore more invisible; it also extends further than does the realm of merely producible objects. Only in the invisible innermost of the heart is man inclined toward what there is for him to love: the forefathers, the dead, the children, those who are to come (Heidegger 1971: 127–128 = Heidegger 2003: 306).

While he evokes Pascal, and thus Augustinian tradition, in drawing this contrast between the logics of heart and calculation, Heidegger's debt to Augustine can be seen more directly through a glance both toward *Being and Time* and toward Heidegger's later writings on technology in light of his 1930–1931 seminar on the question of temporality in Book XI of Augustine's *Confessions*. This latter provides rich textual grounds on which to explore and elaborate the proximity of Heidegger to Augustine that Taylor himself points to, while signaling also significant differences between the paths that Taylor and Heidegger each might open for thinking about love and mortal temporality in relation to the secular.[5]

---

[3] Along these lines, what Taylor calls a "closed world structure" seems close kin to what Heidegger calls the "one-track thinking" of modern metaphysics.

[4] See, for example, "Wozu Dichter?" in Heidegger 2003: 308, translated as "What Are Poets For?" in Heidegger 1971: 129–130: "As long as man is wholly absorbed in nothing but purposeful self-assertion, not only is he unshielded, but so are things, because they have become objects. In this, to be sure, there lies also a transmutation of things into what is inward and invisible. But this transmutation replaces the frailties of things by the thought-contrived fabrications of calculated objects. These objects are produced to be used up. The more quickly they are used up, the greater becomes the necessity to replace them even more quickly and more readily. What is lasting in the presence of objective things is not their self-subsistence within the world that is their own. What is constant in things produced as objects merely for consumption is: the substitute – *Ersatz*."

[5] Published in 2012 in Martin Heidegger, Gesamtausgabe, Vol. 83: Seminare Platon-Aristoteles-Augustinus (Frankfurt am Main: Vittorio Klosterman, 2012).

Just as *Being and Time* calls forth the world-disclosing role both of mood and of practical life, which precede and found any theoretical cognition[6], so Heidegger's 1930–1931 seminar highlights the priority of affection and everyday practice within an understanding of time that, according to Augustine, we inhabit prior to – and despite the stumblings of – any theoretical cognition or definition of time. As Heidegger emphasizes, Augustine works toward this affective construal of time through a mode of questioning that is itself driven by affection in at least two senses. First, Augustine *feels* that he knows what time is insofar as, in the practice of everyday life, he does effectively measure and compare its various spans of duration – even though he remains at a loss when, upon reflection, he cannot define or comprehend time theoretically. Second, in turn, the feeling that he knows what time is, even though he faces theoretical aporia, leads him to persist in a questioning about time that turns him also affectively toward God. Thus highlighting the role of affection both in Augustine's questioning about the nature of time and in his eventual response to that question, Heidegger arrives with Augustine at an understanding both of time and of philosophical questioning as themselves movements of affection or, indeed, of love – and, in turn, at an understanding of love as a fundamental mood of philosophy.[7] Citing the oft-cited claim of Augustine that "I do (or make) this (confession) out of love for your love," Heidegger takes its "authentic meaning" to be that we miss the essential, and "we are mistaken about the essence of being" insofar as "in philosophizing we do not intend and let rule the fundamental mood" – going on then to sum up "this fundamental mood of philosophizing out of the essence of man: letting-be, *questioning releasement*, gathered restraint of the heart [Seinlassen, *fragende Gelassenheit*, gesammelte Verhaltenheit des Herzens] [...]." [8]

Heidegger's appeal here to love as a fundamental mood of philosophical questioning seems to me important background for the later appeal I've signaled

---

6 Taylor too highlights Heidegger's critique of the priority given to matters of epistemology in modern philosophy. See, for example, ASA: 558–559.
7 Time is, as Heidegger puts it, "the possibility of the standing and of the hold where what I love gives itself [*die Möglichkeit* des *Stehens* und des Haltes, wo *sich das gibt*, quod *amo*]," and "my asking-after-time," he continues, is "the *possibility* of the *gathered stretching-out-from-oneself* toward the one, eternal, that love itself is (amor amoris tui) [die *Möglichkeit* des *gesammelten Sichhinausstreckens* zum Einen, Ewigen, der die Liebe selbst ist (amor amoris tui)]." Heidegger here goes on to cite a favored understanding of love that he attributes to Augustine: "Amo...volo ut sis," then immediately glossing: "the letting be of being gives me *the* being that is, that *authentically* is [*Volo ut sis:* Seinlassen des Seienden gibt mir *das* Seiende, das ist, das *eigentlich* it]," in Heidegger 2012: 73, 78, 78, respectively. The translations are my own.
8 Heidegger 2012: 80, 80–81, 81, respectively.

to a logic of the heart that diverges from modernity's calculating rationality. In *Being and Time*, Heidegger had already distinguished between a temporality of expectation or awaiting [*das Erwarten*], based in the calculation of now-time according to ontic possibility, and a temporality of anticipation [*das Vorlaufen*], based in the irreducibly open, ontological possibility of primordial, ecstatic temporality, which, as coming to light notably in the fundamental mood of anxiety before death, remains incalculable.[9] This distinction comes to expression in the Augustine seminar as that between, on the one hand, the "inauthentic awaiting" [*uneigentliches Erwarten*] of measuring as calculating, which – much like Taylor's empty secular time (or Augustine's sinful temporality of dispersion) – entails "running after, losing one's way. Forgetting," and, on the other hand, a gathering and readiness of the heart in my experience of love as "fundamental mood." [10] But how might we understand anxiety before death in relation to this gathering of the heart? And might that relation suggest an alternative to Taylor's way of thinking about the interplay of love and mortality in a secular mood?

In a fascinating letter dated May 13, 1925, to his student and lover Hannah Arendt, Heidegger describes love in terms strikingly similar to those he deploys two years later, in *Being and Time*, to describe Being-toward-death:

> Thank you for your letters – for how you have accepted me into your love – beloved. Do you know that this is the most difficult thing a human is given to endure? For anything else, there are methods, aids, limits, and understanding – here alone everything means: to be *in* one's love = to be forced into one's ownmost existence [*in der Liebe sein = in die eigenste Existenz gedrängt sein*]. Amo means volo, ut sis, Augustine once said: I love you – I want that you be what you are (Arendt and Heidegger 2004: 21 = Arendt and Heidegger 1998: 31).

---

[9] On the distinction between expectation and anticipation as relating to the (ontological) possibility of Being-toward-death, see Heidegger 1962: 306 = Heidegger 1986: 262: "To expect something possible is always to understand it and to 'have' it with regard to whether and when and how it will be actually present-at-hand. Expecting is not just an occasional looking-away from the possible to its possible actualization, but is essentially a *waiting for that actualization* [*ein Warten auf diese*]. Even in expecting, one leaps away from the possible and gets a foothold in the actual. It is for its actuality that what is expected is expected. By the very nature of expecting, the possible is drawn into the actual, arising out of the actual and returning to it. / But Being towards this possibility [of the impossibility of my existence], as Being-towards-death, is so to comport ourselves towards *death* that in this Being, and for it, death reveals itself *as a possibility*. Our terminology for such Being toward this possibility is *'anticipation' of this possibility* [...]. In this kind of coming close [...] one does not tend towards concernfully making available something actual [...]. *The closest closeness which one may have in Being towards death as a possibility, is as far as possible from anything actual.*"

[10] "Beim Messen bewege ich mich für '*Rechnen.*'/ Statdessen *Sammlung – Bereitschaft – amo – Grundstimmung*," in Heidegger 2012: 68.

My own-most or "authentic" existence – to which I am opened in *Being and Time* most (in)famously through the anticipatory resoluteness of my Being-toward death, which unsettles and resists the kinds of falling and flight-from-self that are sustained by inauthentic expectation and its calculations – is given to me here, rather, through the "most difficult" experience of being "in my love." While some might question the evocation of such personal correspondence for philosophical purposes, [11] the fact is that we now have in the public record of Heidegger's teaching, along with the same (not quite exact) citation of Augustine, the same claim about love – which Heidegger describes in the seminar not only as fundamental mood in which the self is gathered temporally and pulled out of its "inauthentic expectation" but indeed, as the "deepest fundamental experience" [*tiefste Grunderfahrung*], which corresponds to the "highest difficulty" [*Höhepunkt der Schwierigkeit*] that calls to, and for, thought (Heidegger 2012: 55).

If the analysis of temporal affection in the Augustine seminar yields in terms of love a construal of existence, and of thinking, accessed in *Being and Time* more notably through mortality, perhaps we can suspect likewise, contrary to common assumption and assertion, that *Being and Time*'s analysis of our mortal Being-in-the-world and its temporality entail already, also, a fundamental role for love. Such a role can be seen, I think, both in Heidegger's analysis of "solicitude," or care for the other person (*Fürsorge*, which other readers, such as Jean-Luc Nancy, Giorgio Agamben, and Françoise Dastur have likewise seen as a thinking of love[12]) and in the far less noted contention by Heidegger that our most basic state as Dasein, our Being-*in*, is itself already a form of diligence (from *diligo*: I love). It is not quite true, in spirit or even strictly, that *Being and Time* mentions love only once, and in a footnote.[13] In fact, in *Being and*

---

11 As does George Pattison in a brief response to my article "Notes on Love and Death in Augustine and Heidegger," in Carlson 2012, which covers, without the aid of the 1930–1931 seminar, much of the terrain I am revisiting here with that aid. See Pattison 2013: 126fn30. In a larger study of which the current analyses will form a part, I build a response to Pattison's objection not by accepting its premises (and thus turning, as I do here, to the published record of Heidegger's academic writing and teaching) but by exploring the extent to which the movement of loving, and erotic, address operative in such personal, epistolary relation may prove fundamental also both to relations of teaching and learning (which epistolary relations can also be) and, inseparably, to the nature and task of thinking as Heidegger understands it.
12 See Nancy 1983; Agamben 1999; and Dastur 1992.
13 This is a widely made and accepted claim, as much among critics like Hannah Arendt's biographer Elisabeth Young-Bruehl as among more constructive heirs to Heidegger like Giorgio Agamben. The charge that *Being and Time* excludes love has a long history going back to Wilhelm Koepps, Ludwig Binswanger, and Karl Jaspers.

Time's earliest elucidation of what "Being-in" means for that being – *Dasein* – who is defined essentially by its Being-in-the-world, Heidegger notes in the etymological ground of the German and English preposition "in" a verbal form that means both dwelling and loving: "'In' is derived from '*innan*' – 'to reside,' '*habitare*,' 'to dwell.' '*An*' signifies 'I am accustomed,' 'I am familiar with,' 'I look after something.' It has the signification of '*colo*' in the senses of '*habito*' and '*diligo*'" (Heidegger 1986: 54 = Heidegger 1962: 80). If I dwell essentially *in* the world (*habito*), this means also, fundamentally, that I love (*diligo*). Like my being "in" time, my being "in" the world is not the spatialized relation of one thing present-at-hand inside another; it is rather the affective opening of my world as such.

And if my Being-in is already an aboriginal kind of diligence or affective opening, my relations with others bear that out. One can read *Being and Time*'s analysis of the two positive forms of my care for the other person, my solicitude or *Fürsorge*, not only as a reflection on love but indeed as a reflection whose scheme closely parallels, and likely draws on, Augustine's analysis of two directions that love can take. Heidegger's two directions of positive solicitude – one that leaps *in* for the other and *takes over* her concern (as relating to an ontic possibility amenable to actualization and management), in order then to hand it back to her as already realized or dealt with, and one that leaps *ahead* of the other to enable her *care*, which only she can live (as a matter of ontological possibility, never convertible as such into manageable or calculable actuality)[14] – echoes and extends Augustine's distinction between a love that dominates and consumes the beloved, on the one hand, and, on the other, a love that enables and frees the beloved for her existence.[15] While likely drawing thus on Augustine, Heidegger's analysis of solicitude should be seen also to diverge from him, insofar as Heidegger's thinking would have us translate the Augustinian distinction into a thinking and sensibility – finally foreign to Augustine – where love's truth and mortality not only do not stand at odds but belong together essentially. While for Augustine I can truly (which means happily) love the other, and will her being, only to the degree that I love her in God's eternity, where no one dear is lost, and while for Taylor, echoing this Augustinian sensibility, death threatens to undermine the meaning and happiness of love, whose logic demands eternity, here the mortality of beloved and lover alike would not contradict but condition love's meaning and happiness, giving to them, in each singular case, their full weight.

---

14 On this contrast, see Heidegger 1986: 122; 1962: 158.
15 In Heidegger 1995: 291–292 = Heidegger 2004: 220–221.

There is surely a paradox here, understandably difficult for most of us *not* to overlook or avoid, and one that seems relevant also to Heidegger's later distinction between the calculating rationality of modern metaphysics (which yields reproducible and hence ever replaceable objects) and a logic of the heart (which attends to the frailties of things and the mortality of persons, both irreducible to calculation and replacement): if my beloved is mortal and finite, then to will her existence must mean to will or affirm that finitude and mortality, which means also her singular and separated being – something that appears through my acknowledging that I cannot take over for her, or take from her, the mortal being that is hers. Even more, I fool myself when I believe that I would want to annul her mortality, for such would negate the very nature of her being. While critics of Heidegger find in his emphasis on the "non-relational" character of each individual's Being-toward-death a sign of erotic and/or ethical disconnection and failure, I read it instead as signaling that which allows me – a separated and singular being, non-replaceable – to respond to, care for, and love the other not as every or any old other but as the separated and singular being that she likewise is, in *her* (mortal) existence.

In the midst of life, we could note, the paradox operative here is perhaps more commonly and readily accepted, or perhaps not as pointedly seen or reflected on: I affirm, for example, the growth and aging of my child, even though doing so means not only gain and good but also exposure to, and experience of, unspeakable loss; I take joy in my child's childhood and its various stages and changes, even while suffering, and mourning, their transience. This intuition of paradox grows deeper and more acute if we reflect on the experience of human conception, gestation, and birth within the modern medical apparatus: On the one hand, out of a sense of responsibility, or love, and their concern to ensure so far as possible the safety, health, and well-being of mother and child in the course of pregnancy, labor, and delivery, we might be inclined to make use of whatever available scientific knowledge and technological power would seem best able to assist us – and to ignore such knowledge and forego such power might well be judged irresponsible or unloving. On the other hand, if we were actually and fully to achieve that toward which such science and technology seem to tend in their basic logic – if we were to attain a scientific knowledge that was complete, and a corresponding technological power that was absolutely secure, such that we could calculate precisely ahead of time and subsequently execute with unshakeable certainty each and every stage of pregnancy and delivery, excluding from these any possible surprise or danger – then we would have transformed human birth into something more like industrial or mechanical (re)production. Similarly, the subjection of dying to the security of management – either in the direction of rendering the death process absolutely programmatic, or in the direction of controlling death to the point of erasing it – seems in fact a horror, or at the very least a contradiction of what many may well accept more widely than is perhaps acknowledged by a thinker like Taylor: that death is inherent to the meaning of life, which does not for its happiness need, or desire, eternity.

5 Secular mood and temporalities of anticipation and recollection: contrasting receptions of Augustine in Taylor and Heidegger

Heidegger's analysis of temporality in *Being and Time*, which helps considerably to elucidate the conditions of the paradox I have just sketched out, seems to me all the more relevant here insofar as it entails an inheritance of Augustine that contrasts as I believe it does with the resonance of Augustine one can hear in *A Secular Age*. To sketch the main lines of this contrast, we might begin by noting a favored illustration in Augustine, referenced by Taylor, for the gathering work of time: the singing or recitation of a psalm.

In Book XI, Ch. 28, of the *Confessions*, Augustine analyzes the logic at work in the recitation of a psalm in order to illustrate how our mind's expectation, memory, and attention constitute through their interplay a meaningful temporality. For meaning to be realized and sustained through the movement of a psalm's recitation, multiple and transient individual moments must somehow be retained and unified even as they pass, for otherwise such movement would yield not any meaning, which requires unity and stability, but only an endless, un-gathered, and thus meaningless passage or dispersion (akin to the empty flow of Taylor's secular time, itself echoing the dispersion of sinful, fallen time in Augustine himself). Such unity and stability are achieved insofar as the fulfillment of expectation and the completion of memory are realized and sustained in and through each other. Right as we begin a psalm's recitation, then, all is expectation, the whole is implicitly present but not yet explicitly realized; in the midst of the recitation, we are divided between expectation of the future, which diminishes as we move forward, and recollection of the past, which grows until the projected future is fully realized, and all movement is converted into memory. All has thus passed and is *past* – but not simply gone by, in unregistered and thus meaningless dispersion, but held together now, and effectively kept present, in a unified, meaningful whole. As tied essentially to such wholeness, meaning is achieved insofar as expectation is consummated or exhausted (since nothing of its *telos* remains outstanding) and (really the same thing from a different angle) insofar as memory is filled out and secured. Within the singing of a psalm, the transience of multiple parts (sounds, syllables, words, sentences, etc., and eventually the recited psalm itself) serves the stable meaning of a greater unified whole, which alone endows those parts, otherwise sheerly multiple and transient, with their meaning. In this way the structure and movement of our psalm experience mirrors that of all meaningful temporal movement as Augustine understands it – both for the individual life (where individual moments pass but are retained within the greater meaningful whole) and for the broader history of humanity (where individuals and generations pass but are maintained in the greater whole assured ultimately by God's eternity). From syllables themselves, sentences and psalms, through a single man's life, to the time or age – the *saeculum* – of humankind as a whole, the consummation of expectation in memory, or time's closure back upon itself, allows time to mirror the fullness, wholeness, and stability of the eternal (and thus it allows history to follow and fulfill God's providential plan, from which any deviation is in the end merely apparent[16]).

Taylor alludes to the Augustinian analysis I've just summarized within his own initial sketch of secular time and its contrast with Augustine's higher times. The gathering of past, present, and future within Augustine's lived time, on Taylor's reading, "creates a kind of simultaneity between the components of an action; my action knits together my situation as it emerges from my past with the future I project as a response to it. They make sense of each other. They cannot be dissociated, and in this way there is a certain minimum consistency in the now of action, a minimal thickness, below which time cannot be further dissected without disaggregating the coherence of action. This is the kind of coherence we find in a melody or a poem, favourite examples of Augustine. There is a kind of simultaneity of the first note with the last, because all have to sound in the presence of the others in order for the melody to be heard" (ASA: 56).

---

[16] This is the Augustine whose Hegelian translation into modern thinking about historical progress is central to Karl Löwith's secularization hypothesis in *Meaning in History*, which could be taken to describe the logic of Taylor's position when Löwith writes that "there would be no search for the meaning of history if its meaning were manifest in historical events. It is the very absence of meaning in the events themselves that motivates the quest. Conversely, *it is only within a pre-established horizon of ultimate meaning*, however hidden it may be, *that actual history seems to be meaningless*. This horizon has been established by history, for it is Hebrew and Christian thinking that brought this colossal question into existence." See Löwith 1949: 4 (my emphasis). Given the importance of the question of time and meaning in *A Secular Age*, and, more pointedly, of the contribution of Augustine to Taylor's treatment of that question, all within the frame of investigating the secular, it is puzzling that Löwith's work does not play a greater role in Taylor's discussion.

And just as Augustine will note that this temporal logic holds as much for humanity's collective history as for the individual life, so Taylor will find the meaning of intergenerational temporality in a gathering whose logic points again to the eternal: "Part of what it has normally meant for the patterns and cycles of my life to have meaning and validity for me," Taylor writes, " is that they are those of my forebears. These patterns are one with theirs, in the sense of qualitatively the same. But not only this, they are continuous with theirs, segments of the same story. It was part of their life pattern that they handed this on to me; it is part of my life pattern that I honour them through re-enactment, that I remember them in reliving the pattern, and that I hand them on. These different enactments are not discontinuous. They connect; they gather into an unbroken story" (ASA: 719). The logic of tradition that Taylor here posits is characterized by continuity and identity. He needs the intergenerational story – if it is to remain "meaningful" – to remain securely gathered, unified, unbroken. This need (or desire) relates directly to his contention that meaning, like happiness, demands eternity: "That the repeatable cycles of life connect over time and make a continuity is an essential condition of a life having meaning. Just this kind of connection was assured by earlier modes of gathering in the eternal; as it is also provided by strong modern narratives of human self-realization. But where the credibility and force of these narratives weaken, the unity comes under threat" (ASA: 719). Insofar as we lack the ultimate gathering of an eternity like Augustine's – or some analogue such as we might see in a modern narrative like that of Hegel – we fall into the emptiness of secular time and its attendant crisis of meaning.

The Hegelian would be an especially relevant version of the kind of modern narrative Taylor points to here insofar as its conception of temporal gathering – through the interplay of expectation and recollection – constitutes another major Augustinian inheritance with which Taylor stands in notable continuity – and from which Heidegger, as I read him, departs.

The temporality through which I exist most fundamentally, Heidegger argues, is not the commonly assumed stream of "now" time, where time is construed in terms of a future present or "now" that is not yet here but coming toward me; a present present that "now" is here but constantly slips away; and a past present, where all the once present nows go once they have streamed by. The primordial temporality of my existence consists rather in my always already "standing-out" from myself, that is, existing, in terms of my "having-been" or past-ness (which, irreducible to any past present, structures and accompanies my temporal being through and through); my "to be" or futurity (likewise irreducible to any future present, ever keeping open the defining possibility of my Being); and the present that always emerges for me in terms of the essential interplay between my (distinctive) having-been and my ever open to-be. No one mode of this "equiprimordially" threefold ecstatic temporality, nor the whole of their interplay, is ever completed or consummated in some actuality, filled out or exhausted by the mortal individual who exists through it – according to the irreducibly open structure and movement of the ontological possibility that defines Being-in-the-world (by contrast to the various delimited "ontic" possibilities, grounded in the ontological, that are amenable to actualization or completion and the kinds of calculation and expectation that these enable).

If love means to will the existence of the beloved, and if that existence is temporalized through this irreducibly open interplay of her having-been, her to-be, and her being-present, then the incompletion of the beloved's being, its unfinished and also ever vulnerable possibility, is at the heart of what I affirm; I do not will that she be eternally – and securely, or certainly – what and how she now actually is; I will rather that she take up her existential possibility so as to become whoever she is to become – unforeseeably, uncertainly, in all of her capability and weakness alike. Resistant to the kind of consummation that is essential to the Augustinian (or Hegelian) temporality and history that resonate in Taylor, this temporality's "fullness" – that is, its meaning and weight, its joy and sorrow alike – would depend on just this openness and incompletion. My relation to the beloved's 'presence,' then, like hers to mine, entails always a movement not only of reception and attention but also of anticipation that can never be met or fulfilled in the manner of some determinate expectation, and of recollection, which can never be completed. The power of our presence one to another is conditioned by the openness of its possibility, by that fact that it is never fully actualized in any given present.

What holds true along these lines for love relations between individuals (whose logic we can elucidate as much on the basis of *Being and Time* as on the basis of Heidegger's correspondence with Arendt) would hold likewise for a love – such as that noted in "What are Poets For?" – that binds us intergenerationally, under the conditions of our mortality and natality. When we love the ancestors, the dead, the children, and those to come, which means also when we dwell (as we inevitably do) *in* our tradition(s), we recall anticipations and we anticipate recollections through a temporality that defies any consummation of one through the other; that is, we recall anticipations, and we anticipate recollections, whose exact shape and direction we can and will never exhaustively comprehend or (re)present. This is so because we never coincide with one another, or indeed with ourselves, in our dying – which means, inseparably, in our being born and existing. Within this outworking of the temporality and love that I take Heidegger's thought to illuminate, death would constitute neither, as Taylor entertains, "a denial of the significance of love" (ASA: 726), nor, as he likewise suggests (as a reading of Heidegger's Being-toward-death), "the privileged perspective, the paradigm gathering point for life," "the paramount vantage point in which life shows its meaning" (ASA: 726). On both counts, I read Heidegger to suggest nearly exactly the reverse, and each in relation to the other: far from denying, our mortal being conditions love's significance, and it does so in the (measureless) measure that it disallows any ultimate gathering or final vantage – such as the God's-eye view of eternity – where life would make its meaning fully and finally present, whether for individuals or for communities and their traditions.

To work out an understanding of secularity in the terms of love and mortal temporality that I have been exploring here would mean drawing not only on the Heidegger I have been calling to the fore but also on a broader sweep of modern and postmodern thinking and sensibility – from Nietzsche[17] himself (or Emerson) through Freud[18] to Jacques Derrida (or Stanley Cavell) – that diverges as

---

17 Although Taylor cites Nietzsche in positing a human desire, or indeed a need, for eternity, the Augustinian logic and tone of Taylor's analysis seem to me largely at odds both with Nietzsche's death of God and, correlatively, with his thought of eternal recurrence. If in the former we can hear a claim that we need, and should, not appeal to the unity and eternity of any "true being" "beyond" in order to embrace and affirm and celebrate the becoming – that is, the arising *and passing away* – of life in its multiplicity and flux, then we might suspect that the thought of eternal recurrence entails something quite other than a desire that happiness, and thus meaning, endure permanently. Indeed, in thinking through what Nietzsche may be after in his notion of eternal return, one might explore further than I think Taylor's reading does the possibility that the thought of eternal return involves not any claim that transience and loss compromise the joy or meaning of life (which without eternity would be deprived of its joy and meaning), but rather a challenge: that to affirm any moment of joy demands that we affirm not only its return but also the return of every sorrow bound with it – in a life and world where all is interwoven, without any outside – that is, any God's-eye view – from which some part (like the beloved's death) would be judged or condemned, or excepted or extracted, as an objection against life.

18 While for Taylor Freud (along with Weber) can seem to stand as poster-boy of the scientific, or scientistic, arrogance that would condemn religious belief and its desire for eternity as immature, the "education to reality" that Freud encourages may well be concerned far less with belittling religious sensibility as childish (a charge about which Taylor is notably touchy) and far more with advancing – as Freud does for example in his short, rich piece "On Transience," and in a tone or mood of deep modesty and vulnerability – the sense that the beauty, joy, and meaning of life are not contradicted but conditioned by loss. For a powerful reading of Freud's modesty, see Jean-Luc Nancy's "Freud – pour ainsi dire," in Nancy 2010. The question of modesty, along with Freud, plays an important role also in Peter E. Gordon's astute reading and critique of *A Secular Age*; see Gordon 2008. For a critique of Taylor's Augustinianism in light of an inquiry into the overlooked role of humility in shaping modern political thought, see Cooper 2013: 29 – 38.

much from the (Augustinian) desire that love's happiness be eternal, and thus secure, as from modernity's (often strikingly similar) techno-scientific quest for the certainty and security of instrumental calculation. In abandoning the desire for eternity or its analogues, however, it loses neither meaning nor happiness; rather, it finds these, through an affective shift, nowhere else than in the experience of our natively mortal temporal life. Perhaps no writer captures this shift as I sense it, and the secular mood attendant to it, more succinctly than Derrida, when in the near-last words of his last published interview he states, "I am never more haunted by the necessity of dying than in moments of happiness and joy. To feel joy and to weep over the death that awaits are for me the same thing" (Derrida 2005: 55). But to evoke such a secular mood, we need not confine ourselves to one who passes for an atheist. We could instead cite Wendell Berry's Sabbath Poem XII from 2000:

> 1.
> We follow the dead to their graves
> and our long love follows on
> beyond, crying to them, not
> "Come back!" but merely "Wait!"
> In waking thoughts, in dreams
> we follow after, calling "Wait!
> Listen! I am older now. I know
> now how it was with you
> when you were old and I
> was only young. I am ready
> now to accompany you
> in your lonely fear." And they
> go on, one by one, as one
> by one, we go as they have gone.
>
> 2.
> And yet are we not all gathered
> in this leftover love,
> this longing become the measure
> of a joy all mourners know,
> have known, and will know?
> An old man's mind is a graveyard
> where the dead arise.[19]

---

[19] In Berry 2006.

Bibliography

Agamben, Giorgio. 1999. "The Passion of Facticity," in *Potentialities*, trans. Daniel Heller-Roazen. Stanford: Stanford University Press.
Arendt, Hannah, and Heidegger, Martin. 1998. *Briefe 1925–1975*. Frankfurt am Main: Vittorio Klostermann.
Arendt, Hannah, and Heidegger, Martin. 2004. *Letters 1925–1975*, ed. Ursula Lutz, trans. Andrew Shields. New York: Harcourt.
Berry, Wendell. 2006. *Given: Poems*. Berkeley, CA: Counterpoint.
Carlson, Thomas A. 2012. "Notes on Love and Death in Augustine and Heidegger." *Medieval Mystical Theology* 21 no. 1: 9–33.
Cooper, Julie E. 2003. *Secular Powers: Humility in Modern Political Thought*. Chicago: University of Chicago Press.
Dastur, Françoise. 1992. "Phénoménologie et thérapie dans les Zollikoner Seminare," in *Figures de la subjectivité: Approches phénoménologiques et psychiatriques*, ed. Jean-François Courtine, 165–177. Paris: Editions du Centre National de la Recherche Scientifique.
Derrida, Jacques. 2005. *Apprendre à vivre enfin*. Paris: Galilée.
Derrida, Jacques. 2007. *Learning to Live Finally*, trans. Pascale-Anne Brault and Michael Naas. Hoboken, NJ: Melville House.
Gordon, Peter E. 2008. "The Place of the Sacred in the Absence of God: Charles Taylor's 'A Secular Age'," in *Journal of the History of Ideas* 69 no. 4 (October, 2008): 647–673.
Heidegger, Martin. 1962. *Being and Time*, trans. John Macquarrie and Edward Robinson. Oxford: Blackwell.
Heidegger, Martin. 1971. "What Are Poets For?" in *Poetry, Language, Thought*, trans. Albert Hofstadter. New York: Harper.
Heidegger, Martin. 1986. *Sein und Zeit*. Sechzehnte Auflage. Tübingen: Max Niemeyer Verlag.
Heidegger, Martin. 1995. *Gesamtausgabe*, Vol. 60: *Phänomenologie des religiösen Lebens*, ed. Matthias Jung, Thomas Regehly, and Claudius Strube. Frankfurt am Main: Vittorio Klostermann.
Heidegger, Martin. 2003. "Wozu Dichter?" in *Holzwege*. Frankfurt am Main: Vittorio Klostermann.
Heidegger, Martin. 2012. *Gesamtausgabe*, Vol. 83: *Seminare Platon-Aristoteles-Augustinus*. Frankfurt am Main: Vittorio Klosterman.
Heidegger, Martin. 2004. *The Phenomenology of Religious Life*, trans. M. Fritsch and J. A. Gosetti-Ferencei. Bloomington: Indiana University Press.
Löwith, Karl. 1949. *Meaning in History*. Chicago: University of Chicago Press.
Nancy, Jean-Luc. 1983. "L'amour en éclats," in *La communauté désoeuvrée*. Paris: Christian Bourgeois.
Nancy, Jean-Luc. 2010. *L'Adoration, Déconstruction du christianisme*. Tome II. Paris: Galilée.
Pattison, George. 2013. *Heidegger on Death: A Critical Theological Essay*. Surrey, England: Ashgate.
Weber, Max. 1946. "Science as a Vocation," in *From Max Weber: Essays in Sociology*, ed. Hans Heinrich Gerth and C. Wright Mills. New York: Oxford University Press.

Samuel Shearn
Charles Taylor, Nietzsche and Theology in *A Secular Age*

1 Introduction

> I am making war with this theologian-instinct: I found its trace everywhere. Whoever has theologian's blood in the body, relates from the outset to all things falsely and dishonestly (Nietzsche 1988: 175).

The history of theological responses to Nietzsche is awash with contradictory approaches, from theologians denouncing his nihilistic corruption of the youth to theologians celebrating his Dionysian liberation from a false pharisaical gospel. Taylor is another voice among Christian voices that give Nietzsche a role in their story and attempt to respond to his challenge.

Indeed, Nietzsche is conspicuously *present* in Taylor's narratives. At the end of *Sources of the Self*, Taylor characterizes "the major point elaborated" (Taylor 1989: 520): that people of all outlooks, believing and unbelieving, find themselves stuck between their highest moral ideals and a sense that these ideals may stifle something of their lives. This, suggests Taylor, is a dilemma Nietzsche articulated exceptionally well. Furthermore, "[o]nly if there is such a thing as agape, or one of the secular claimants to its succession, is Nietzsche wrong" (Taylor 1989: 516). A few pages later he suggests that "Judaeo-Christian theism" may offer some hope in "its central promise of a divine affirmation of the human, more total than humans can ever attain unaided" (Taylor 1989: 521).

My contention is that part of Taylor's normative purpose in *A Secular Age* is to address the question of whether Christian theism indeed offers any hope in light of the Nietzschean dilemmas we face. Because Taylor's re-imagination of Christianity in a secular age takes place in dialogue with Nietzsche, a focus on this engagement is highly instructive for understanding Taylor *per se*. It also demonstrates

---

Research for this essay was made possible by an Ertegun Graduate Scholarship in the Humanities at the University of Oxford, thanks to the visionary generosity of Mica Ertegun. I also want to thank the editors for their valuable comments.

that Taylor is thinking theologically about culture, and that he has an apologetic interest.[1]

In what follows I begin by sketching out the kinds of Christian theological responses to Nietzsche one may encounter. Two thinkers, Merold Westphal and Giles Fraser, represent examples of positive and negative responses. This provides the background upon which I later plot Taylor's contribution to Christian theology. In the next two sections I show first that Taylor's characterization of Nietzsche as deeply insightful but peculiarly inhuman, and then describe how Taylor employs Nietzsche in his apologetic strategy. Taylor's message uses Nietzschean critique to raise difficulties for the norms of humanism. In particular, he claims, the public commitment to universal equality, justice, and the reduction of suffering needs powerful moral sources—resources he finds lacking in traditions of exclusive humanism.

In the fifth section I describe Taylor's theological response to Nietzsche. Taylor holds out hope that a vision of the divine affirmation of the world provides the best sustenance for life together in the 21st century. Yet he concedes the continuing strength of Nietzsche's critique and insight for Christianity. I am not attempting here to intervene in the impressive industry of Nietzsche scholarship, though Taylor's selective reading and presentation of Nietzsche may be of critical interest to that party. I am interested in two things: the light that Taylor's Nietzsche sheds on our understanding of Taylor, and the usefulness of Taylor's response to Nietzsche for Christian theology. In the concluding part of my essay I offer reflections on Taylor's contribution, with recourse to the parable of the prodigal son.

2 Nietzsche and Theology

2.1 Nietzsche as ancilla theologiae

Since Nietzsche wrote a *Gesetz wider das Christenthum* it is not surprising that several Christian thinkers build Nietzsche into their narratives as a foil – to show that modernity is a dead-end street ending with bestial Nietzsche (MacIntyre 2007), that life is meaningless without God (Craig 2008), or that without God one is left with an ontology of violence (Milbank 2006). Yet there has also been a

---

[1] I therefore agree with previous characterizations of Taylor's work as rehabilitation of theism (Kühnlein 2008: 1) or Christianity (Braune-Krickau 2011: 358).

steady tradition of theologians who see Nietzsche as helpful for authentic Christian theology.²

Often Nietzsche is cast as the patron saint of 'post-metaphysical,' 'anti-ontotheological' Christianity (Altizer 1966; Jüngel 1978; Caputo 2001; Marion 2001; Hovey 2008). Or he is valued as an honest and insightful expositor of human fallenness (Deane 2006) and the Church's tendency to *ressentiment* (e. g. Dietrich Bonhoeffer, Merold Westphal).³ The Catholic theologian Hans Urs von Balthasar saw an affinity between the Dionysian and the Christian (Von Balthasar 1998).

Merold Westphal is a good example of someone who values Nietzsche as a resource for theology. He sees Nietzsche's perspectivism and hermeneutics of suspicion as prophetic protests against theology's idolatry, in particular the idolatry of ontotheology (Westphal 1997). Westphal thinks that many readers give the death of God, the vision of the *Übermensch*, and the doctrine of eternal return too much attention because of their shock factor. Nietzsche's opposition to the hypocrisy of Western morality is in fact a more central concern. For Nietzsche, the fundamental human drive is the will to power though this drive is made opaque by "systematic self-deception" (Westphal 1998: 246). When Nietzsche rejects neighborly love, for example, he means that "what is passed off as neighbor love is sometimes nothing more than low self-esteem" (Westphal 1998: 248). In like manner, through pity "I can belittle the other and elevate myself to a place of moral superiority" (Westphal 1998: 261). Such Pharisaism is the corollary of being good. Westphal concludes that Nietzsche's drive for honesty should be admired by Christians (Westphal 1998: 236–237). "[N]o piety is exempt from scrutiny," he concludes (Westphal 1998: 287).

---

2 Giles Fraser offers an excellent and concise overview (Fraser 2002: 3–22). For the early 20th Century, see Bailey 1989; Mourkojannis 2000; Kleffmann 2003: 333–354. See also Booth 1992, Wiley 2009, and Köster 1982 (reprinted with further essays in Köster 2003).
3 One should not think of Bonhoeffer as a pro-Nietzschean thinker, despite his indebtedness to Nietzsche's insight (Fraser 2002: 4–8). See Stephen Williams' excellent discussion of the relationship between Bonhoeffer and Nietzsche (Williams 2006: 241–250). Merold Westphal's *Suspicion and Faith* understands Ricoeur's 'masters of suspicion,' Freud, Marx, and Nietzsche, as inadvertent help to authentic Christian faith (Westphal 1998).

2.2 Nietzsche, Antichrist

The attempt to make Nietzsche useful for theology has its critics.[4] Giles Fraser is a recent example of someone who thinks that Nietzsche, as an enemy, is to be overcome.[5] His study *Redeeming Nietzsche: The Piety of Unbelief* identifies Nietzsche as a primarily soteriological thinker attempting to face up to the truth that the world is a dark and cruel place and live creatively with that truth (Fraser 2002: 45–71).

Following a careful account of the development, influences and soteriological character of Nietzsche's thought, Fraser criticizes Christian theologians such as Thomas Altizer and Eberhard Jüngel for celebrating the 'death of God' as an iconoclastic liberation of theology from the clutches of a Cartesian, sub-Christian God. He also chides 'postmodern' theologians such as Westphal and Graham Ward for too enthusiastically welcoming Nietzsche as a deconstructor of oppressive ways of doing theology. Nietzsche, Fraser insists, did not just attack bland theism, ontotheology and heteronomy *per se*, but specifically the Christian God, the God of the Bible and Christian worship: "What Nietzsche hates above all, is the cross and the Christian story of redemption" (Fraser 2002: 21). Nietzsche renounces metaphysics because of its ability to transport a weakening and imprisoning story of self-hatred, and not the other way around.

Fraser's response to Nietzsche draws on many thinkers including Karl Barth, Dietrich Bonhoeffer, René Girard, John Milbank, Martha Nussbaum and Stanley Cavell. His central claim is that unlike Christianity, Nietzsche's soteriology is incapable of facing the horror of human suffering. Fraser polemically amplifies Nussbaum's characterization of Nietzsche as an armchair philosopher of bourgeois suffering:

> [T]he idea of the *Übermensch*-as-redeemer may seem plausible from within the fantasy world of Nietzsche's adventures, but would one trust the *Übermensch* to shoulder the horrors of AIDS? (Fraser 2002: 98).

To wake up all-too-academic readers, Fraser insists on calling such suffering "shit." The shit of the Holocaust is contrasted with the "*kitsch*" of Nietzsche's celebration of the *Übermensch*. Kitsch "is insufficiently honest ... it prefers, wher-

---

[4] Köster says too many theologians seek proximity to Nietzsche which is only possible with "interpretory acrobatics" (Köster 1982: 684).
[5] Many other theologians would be worth interacting with – and they have received detailed study in other places. On Karl Barth see for example Peter 1994 and Kleffmann 2003: 500–559.

ever possible, sentimental fantasy to painful reality" (Fraser 2002: 126).[6] Nietzsche's "pale and self-obsessed" account

> takes suffering away from its locatedness in particular contexts and stories, thereby rendering it kitsch. When Zarathustra ascends to his mountain top he leaves the shittiness of the world far behind (Fraser 2002: 138–139).[7]

A Nietzsche who exhibits this kind of "disloyalty to the earth" (Fraser 2002: 153) hides his peculiar weakness in the cloth of Stoic "hardness" which will not acknowledge human limitations (Nussbaum 1994: 160; Fraser 2002: 152). Nietzsche rejects compassion and ordinary life out of his sense of isolation and "desire for self-authoring, for self-salvation" (Fraser 2002: 159) – thus fundamentally out of fear: "an unwillingness fully to face the pains and disappointments of his own humanity" (Fraser 2002: 164).

Against the backdrop of this character assassination, Fraser intermittently sketches the Christian alternatives. Christ crucified is realism about horrors, the place where God and shit coincide (Fraser 2002: 140); repentance is facing up to the past rather than running away from it (Fraser 2002: 104); community relationships are the place where one learns to face up to one's own vulnerability and dependence (Fraser 2002: 164–166).

3 Taylor's characterization of Nietzsche

It is striking how frequently Nietzsche is mentioned in *A Secular Age*. On average one has to read only 12 pages before one finds a reference to Nietzsche.[8] The great contrast between Fraser's and Westphal's approach to Nietzsche – the difference between attack and appreciation – illustrates something of the range of

---

[6] Though Nietzsche claims to disparage sentimentality and mass appeal Fraser says he is guilty of "'high-brow' kitsch" (Fraser 2002: 134).
[7] The attack on Nietzsche's kitsch – glossing over the reality of suffering – resembles theological anti-theodicy by giving a voice to the sufferers of horrendous evils.
[8] I counted 66 pages where Nietzsche is mentioned at least once. Yet there are extremely few direct quotes. Striking exceptions include one very long excerpt from the close of *The Will to Power* celebrating the doctrine of the eternal return (ASA: 587) and a particularly gruesome depiction of Nietzsche's idealized ruthless warriors from *The Genealogy of Morality*, albeit hiding in an endnote (ASA: 841fn52). Besides these two works, only *Thus Spake Zarathustra* is mentioned. As a comparison, Kant or Kantianism is mentioned at least once on around 50 pages and Hegel on only 10 pages.

responses to Nietzsche available from within Christian theology. How does Taylor compare?

Taylor's Nietzsche is insightful. Firstly, he recognizes the dark side of humanity: he exhibits a post-Schopenhauerian anthropology, of "belief in our reliance on the forces of irrationality, darkness, aggression, sacrifice" (ASA: 346). This insight exposes the paucity of modern notions of happiness which exchange heroism for bland equality (ASA: 319, 379). Such a shallow view of life "reduces us by enclosing us in a too-rosy picture of the human condition, shorn of tragedy, irreparable loss, meaningless suffering, cruelty and horror" (ASA: 338). In contrast, maturity for Nietzsche means being brave enough to "face the void, and to be energized by it to the creation of meaning" (ASA: 589).

Secondly, Nietzsche recognizes the oppressive potential of orders of meaning and morality. These hinder our self-realization, threatening "our spontaneity, or our creativity, or our desiring natures" (ASA: 599, 313). Nietzsche saw that giving us the responsibility to create meaning can appear as "the ultimate emancipation" (ASA: 587). And he protested against life lived under conformity to rules (ASA: 312), because when we are in touch with our desires, we truly live (ASA: 613).

Despite this praise for Nietzsche's insight, Taylor also sees a most unwelcome dark side. Nietzsche's stance is ultimately inhuman because, firstly, he rejects an ethic of benevolence. Nietzsche "wanted to jettison [...] pity, the relief of suffering, democracy, human rights" (ASA: 626; see also 373). In this, Nietzsche is unrepentantly elitist: "Only the excellent truly count" (ASA: 683).

Secondly, Nietzsche celebrates violence, cruelty, and aggression. Bestial urges are not condemned because he "wants to rehabilitate destruction and chaos, the infliction of suffering and exploitation, as part of the life to be affirmed" (ASA: 373). His Übermenschen "have to fight off the temptation of pity. [...] [T]heir answer to the power of evil [...] is to internalize it, and baptise it, as it were, consecrate it to the striving for excellence [...]" (ASA: 683).

In *Sources of the Self*, Taylor's Nietzsche is committed to an affirmation of life, an affirmation entailing the heroic rejection of universal benevolence. Nietzsche is far more the 'people's philosopher' removing obstacles to self-affirmation, "releasing nature and desire from a stultifying thraldom" (Taylor 1989: 343). But in *A Secular Age*, Nietzsche is portrayed as standing in elitist, cruel, and sadistic opposition to all that modern secular liberals should hold dear.[9]

---

[9] This portrait of a more troubling Nietzsche is already present Taylor's lecture *A Catholic Modernity?* (Taylor 1999: 27–28). Indeed, several paragraphs on Nietzsche are later lifted verbatim into *A Secular Age*.

Nietzsche's anti-humanist rebellion "chafes at the benevolence, the universalism, the harmony" (ASA: 373) of the modern moral order. The aesthetic affirmation of all things means saying "yes" to "the wild dimensions" (ASA: 672) of life, finding beauty in "sacrifice, suffering, and a kind of indifferent cruelty" (ASA: 665).[10]

4 Taylor's employment of Nietzsche

The methodological foundations of Taylor's story in *A Secular Age* are laid in his earlier work, in particular *Sources of the Self*. Taylor believes that *hypergoods*[11] emerge in a process of supersession. One paradigm (e. g. a warrior ethic) is superseded by a better account, one with more explanatory power and attraction (e. g. the hypergood of a commitment to universal benevolence – justice for all). "Practical reasoning" does not have to start from nothing, but "is a reasoning in transitions. It aims to establish, not that some position is correct absolutely, but rather [...] that this transition is an error-reducing one" (Taylor 1989: 72).[12]

Taylor credits Nietzsche with insight and skill with regard to reasoning in transitions: this is another way of describing Nietzsche's *Umwertung aller Werte* (Taylor 1989: 65). Nietzsche is effective because of his genealogical method: he does not merely tell the story of the genesis of an idea, but rather makes the story itself critical to a given idea's success. To take Nietzsche's most famous example, we have learned to think of good and evil in the way that we have not because kindness is intrinsically good and power intrinsically evil, but because of the persuasiveness of a particular story about those concepts. We are led to love, or disdain, the position being described. And it therefore becomes the job of the critical genealogist to investigate why and how a particular story has become so persuasive.

---

10 Given Taylor's emphasis on Nietzsche's celebration of violence and cruelty, it is no surprise that on several occasions he discusses Nietzsche or Nietzscheanism in connection with Fascism or Nazism (ASA: 256, 373, 418–419, 683). Taylor insists that he does not intend "to score off neo-Nietzscheanism, as some kind of antechamber of Fascism" (ASA: 373–374). However, says Taylor, "Nietzsche's influence was not entirely foreign" (ASA: 373) to Fascism.
11 A hypergood is Taylor's word for the (often unarticulated) basis of discrimination between the various *strong evaluations* which sit in judgement upon our immediate desires, and may be orienting frameworks for life.
12 For a helpful overview of Taylor's epistemology and method of argumentation in his earlier works, see Yi 2014: 160–162.

For Taylor the essential aspect of the art of genealogy is that it engages us emotionally. *Sources of the Self* is a genealogy by design, because only through the articulation of certain values, a presentation of them open to *affective* appreciation, could we be led to accept these values (Taylor 1989: 72–74). Thus, although Taylor is not as explicitly *critical* as Nietzsche, Nietzschean genealogy nevertheless provides something of a methodological foundation for Taylor's narrative.[13]

At least as far back as 1996, when he presented the lecture eventually published as "A Catholic Modernity?," Taylor has been picturing contemporary Western culture as a "three-cornered battle" of humanism, anti-humanism, and belief in transcendence – that is, belief in some good beyond life, beyond human flourishing (Taylor 1999: 29).[14] In *A Secular Age*, this agonistic triangle provides the framework for the dialectics of the whole book.[15] As Taylor puts it, "[a]ny pair can gang up against the third on some important issue" (ASA: 636).[16] Nietzsche's role in this battle is to play the part of the ultimate anti-humanist, who, unlike his gone-soft descendants, still drank his whiskey straight (ASA: 599–600).

Wrapped up in Taylor's methodological use of Nietzsche, then, is the normative vision of his story. If Nietzsche's genealogy aimed to discredit both Christianity and humanism, so Taylor's genealogy in *A Secular Age* would call into question contemporary exclusive humanism, in part by using Nietzsche as an

---

13 Colin Jager argues that "it is precisely that [Nietzschean] tradition's interest in genealogy that would sharpen [Taylor's] analysis; without it, his sometime impulse to criticize the secular age is deprived of a methodological foundation" (Jager 2010: 183). Jager's target is Taylor's reading of Romanticism, which he believes is overly nostalgic, and does not appreciate just how subversive (genealogical) the immanent counter-Enlightenment is for any account of transcendence. Attention to that particular subversion, he claims, would show Taylor's method – in particular the over-simplistic distinction between a romantic, "nostalgic desire for something more" and a "Nietzschean aristocratic contempt for ordinary human flourishing" – to be problematic, and make his criticism of exclusive humanism weaker for it. (Jager 2010: 182–183). The point I am making is related: Taylor does not want that famous star of the immanent counter-Enlightenment, Nietzsche, to be the subversion or replacement of Christianity, but rather an ally in the (genealogical) fight against Enlightenment-inspired exclusive humanism. This role I explain below.
14 Taylor's concept of transcendence is designed to include Christian, theistic and non-theistic religious perspectives (in particular, Buddhism). However, Taylor's point of reference is usually theistic, and Christian.
15 Nietzsche's role as the prime example of an anti-humanist is also already underlined in Taylor's (rather forgotten, because barely accessible) essay *Nietzsche's Legacy* (Taylor 1993: 179).
16 Taylor thinks there may be four corners, with two versions of Christianity – one set on repristination and one acknowledging the achievements of modernity (Taylor 1999: 29). Taylor sees himself in the latter category.

ally. And, as we have seen from the sketch in section 3, his genealogy would also present the unbelieving alternative to secular humanism – Nietzscheanism – in such an unpalatable light that a return to Christianity, or at least belief in some transcendent good beyond human life, seems the most attractive option. For *A Secular Age* is also a call to Christian faith, and Taylor presents Christianity as a potentially more promising option than its two secular counterparts, humanism and anti-humanism. Taylor's work is detailed and descriptive on an historical level, and it would be wrong to reduce him to an apologist, not least because of the distinctly non-triumphant finale of *A Secular Age*. But this apology is one important aspect of what is going on. Taylor's method is in one sense Nietzschean, precisely because he attempts to out-narrate his opponents.[17]

Already in *Sources of the Self*, without the notion of an agonistic triangle, Taylor uses Nietzsche to give weight to the post-Schopenhauerian crisis of affirmation: the basis of affirming humanity and being concerned for the reduction of human suffering comes under threat when we are aware of the "murkier depths of human motivation" that Nietzsche expounded in his genealogies (Taylor 1989: 517). In *Sources of the Self*, Nietzsche also underlines the "dilemma of mutilation" (Taylor 1989: 521): high moral ideals seem to hinder our self-realization; we feel we have to choose between being moral and being a creative, desiring human. This is not only a "high price" (Taylor 1989: 499, see also 518) to pay at the personal level: we live in an age of unprecedented high moral standards which leads to inevitable conflict between will and desire (Taylor 1989: 515).

Many years later in *A Secular Age*, Taylor builds on the work of *Sources of the Self* in highlighting the high standard of benevolence we (at least) assent to in the West, and suggests this level cannot be sustained, that we should not be surprised when benevolence gives way to the "hardening of feeling against the impoverished and disfavoured in many Western democracies" (ASA: 695). Nietzsche's insight into the dark side of humanity, the paucity of modern understandings of happiness, the blandness and flattening effect of egalitarianism, the oppres-

---

17 In *Sources of the Self*, Taylor directs one significant strand of critique against Neo-Nietzschean writers such as Derrida and Foucault. He sees in Neo-Nietzschean thought a superficial relativism concealing a hypergood of "unconstrained freedom" (Taylor 1989: 489). Taylor acknowledges a tension between Nietzsche's (apparently relativistic) emphasis on "interpretation as an imposition of power" (Taylor 1989: 488) and his (non-relativistic) affirmation of the will to power, but he deems the latter pole central. Thus Taylor thinks Neo-Nietzscheans should acknowledge their debt to Nietzsche expressed in their hypergood of unfettered freedom, and concede the point that they are indeed oriented by a vision of the good life, indeed have a framework with which they live and act.

sive potential of morality and meaning, and the negative motivation of (and *ressentiment* in) modern morality highlights problems with exclusive humanism.

From the perspective of exclusive humanism, says Taylor, the unease we feel, or the guilt which high moral demands impress on us, is no longer part of the human spiritual condition but something to be cured (ASA: 622). Violence and aggression are redescribed as primitivism. Anything which does not conform is a sign of underdevelopment, lack of rational thinking, or mental illness (ASA: 672). In these stiflings, humanism expects too much of humanity and endorses attempts at change that will end up over-burdening and destroying human life (ASA: 624). Furthermore, a Nietzschean reading suggests that humanism can be negatively motivated. Even "a peace-loving, egalitarian, liberalism" (ASA: 743) can become complicit in a self-righteous violence against those who will not convert.

5 Taylor's theological response to Nietzsche

In Taylor's characterization and employment of Nietzsche we have learned more about Taylor's apologetic strategy. However, there is a sense that Taylor has held Nietzsche at arm's length. He praises Nietzsche's insight and deploys his critique of humanism, but also portrays him in a manner so off-putting that Nietzsche ceases to be a serious option (Connolly 2010). Can more be said for the case of Christianity than that Nietzsche is horrible and exclusive humanism unsustainable?

In *Sources of the Self*, Taylor introduces a response to the crisis of affirmation in what he calls *transfiguration*, "a doctrine of affirming power" (Taylor 1989: 455). This makes use of a late Romantic (and Nietzschean) insight into the power of imagination, but takes its cue from the book of Genesis to articulate a theistic affirmation of being. Here, says Taylor:

> The goodness of the world is not something quite independent from God's seeing it as good. His seeing it as good, loving it, can be conceived not simply as a *response* to what it is, but as what *makes* it such (Taylor 1989: 449; emphasis original).

Taylor suggests that human affirmation of the goodness of creation is analogous to God's 'seeing as good,' which means "a seeing which also helps effect what it sees" (Taylor 1989: 449). Transfiguration is an *effective seeing-as*.

Taylor finds such a notion of affirmation through transfiguration in Kierkegaard, and in Nietzsche, but dwells in particular on Dostoyevsky.[18] In Dostoyevsky, Taylor sees affirmation arise from the *transfiguration that grace affords*. For Dostoyevsky, openness to grace is connected to openness to the world. Paradoxically, one can close oneself to grace (the greatest sin) for the loftiest reasons, as in the example of Ivan Karamazov, because "the more noble and sensitive and morally insightful one is, the more one is liable to feel this loathing [...] for ourselves and for this world" (Taylor 1989: 451).

But to reject the world is to be cut off from grace. This is hubris since we refuse to understand ourselves as belonging to the problem:

> What will transform us is an ability to love the world and ourselves, to see it as good in spite of the wrong. But this will only come to us if we can accept being part of it, and that means accepting responsibility. ... Loving the world and ourselves is in a sense a miracle, in face of all the evil and degradation that it and we contain. But the miracle comes on us if we accept being part of it. Involved in this is our acceptance of love from others. We become capable of love through being loved [...] (Taylor 1989: 452).

The contrast between nobility and being given grace, or between hubris and the conviction of sin, is clear. The mere observer of the evil in the world can become a sin-confessing participant in the world. Note also the role of acceptance of love in contrast to the (grace-less) nobility of the one who would reject the offer of compassion. Taylor says we are able to love our fellow creatures when we enter into the stream of God's love for and affirmation of creation. Our affirmation of the world participates through grace in God's love which sees the world as good and as such effects its goodness (Taylor 1989: 516).

Taylor's move here is intriguing because he is using an insight which Nietzsche would be open to – the creative power of the imagination – to overcome the Schopenhauerian vision which Nietzsche, in his own way and with his anti-pessimistic opposition, endorsed. Nietzsche, it is implied, could have found a way to affirm the world without rejecting benevolence. Affirmation is possible with *agape*, the love of God which by grace enables us to love. But is this possible, or will Christian spirituality also stifle?

---

[18] Bruce K. Ward's thoughtful reflections on Dostoyevsky's role in Taylor's narrative deserve attention (Ward 2014).

5.1 Responding to the dilemma of mutilation in *A Secular Age*

The dilemma of mutilation is a shared human predicament, suggests Taylor. We are looking for a way to "define our highest spiritual or moral aspirations for human beings, while showing a path to the transformation involved which doesn't crush, mutilate or deny what is essential to our humanity" (ASA: 639–640). Taylor calls this the "maximal demand" (ASA: 640) that we place on our conception of a good human life because of our desire to be whole. A solution according to this maximal demand would lift us out of the dilemma of mutilation which Nietzsche so keenly felt and articulated.[19]

Can a re-imagined Christianity meet the maximal demand? Such a Christianity will need to resist what Taylor calls *excarnation:* the great change in religious life in a secular age understood as a process of moving from embodied religious practices to those more cerebral (ASA: 554). It will also need to resist hegemony. Already in "A Catholic Modernity?" Taylor had warned of the dangers of misunderstanding what it means to be united:

> Our great historical temptation has been to forget the complementarity, to go straight for the sameness, making as many people as possible into "good Catholics" – and in the process [...] failing wholeness; unity bought at the price of suppressing something of the diversity of humanity that God created; unity of the part masquerading as the whole (Taylor 1999: 14).

But Taylor does not only confess the sins of the church. He would like to make a positive case for transcendence: that it in fact does not stifle like other positions. Thus he offers a Christian hermeneutic of violence as a response to the dilemma of mutilation but also against the claim that Christianity bowdlerizes reality.

This hermeneutic depends upon what Taylor calls "God's pedagogy" (ASA: 669):

> [H]umans are born out of the animal kingdom, to be guided by God; and the males (at least the males) with a powerful sex-drive, and lots of aggression. [...] Being guided by God means some kind of transformation of these drives; not just their repression, or suppression [...] but some real turning of them from within, conversion, so that all the energy now goes

---

19 Taylor thinks Nietzsche is also not free from the charge of stifling. Those such as Nietzsche "are full of exhortations to 'self-overcoming': would want us to stifle pity [...] would hardly leave us as we are, with our list of goods and excellences unimpaired" (ASA: 630). This criticism of Nietzsche is not developed at any length, although it is implicit in the many instances where Taylor simply assumes that his readers will be sympathetic to humanism and an ethic of benevolence.

along with God; the love powers agape, the aggression turns into energy, straining to bring things back to God, the energy to combat evil (ASA: 668).

Taylor sees this process of revelation reflected in the biblical narrative, with humanity exhibiting just this mix of violence and redirection of violence toward God's ends: from a merely bloodthirsty lust for violence to ritualized human sacrifice as ordered violence turned back toward divinity. Then from human sacrifice to the *rejection* of human sacrifice as the practice of the pagan "other," to whom one still responds with holy war, albeit without pleasure in battle for its own sake. Each revelation "comes with a gift of power" which can be misused (ASA: 669).

In Christ, God as the victim provides a new paradigm for the connection between violence and divinity. In Christendom this achievement is reversed because there remains a sanctioned violence against those outside of the community of the faith. But violence was also redirected toward the overcoming of sinful acts and attitudes (ASA: 669–670): "We might see God as the supreme tennis player, who responds to our bad moves with new ways of countering them" (ASA: 671).

In this sketch, progress is made in God's slow pedagogy. We think human sacrifice is bad, says Taylor, but think of it as a step in the right direction, compared to unfettered blood-lust. I find the image of a divine tennis player to be a breathtakingly awkward anthropomorphism. However, we may be able to see beyond the image. Taylor is talking of God's pedagogy as an immanent dialectical process and struggle between the use and misuse of divine power in the creature in which it is possible to hear the divine calling upon one's life. This dialectic is progressive in Scripture and history.

Taylor thinks that the Christian hermeneutic of violence he has offered opens "a perspective of transformation" (ASA: 673) which is not a conditioning program and has more explanatory power than secular alternatives. Rather than pathologization or celebration of violence, and rather than its reification as mere biological necessity, "transformation is much more mysterious, and involves offering another spiritual direction" (ASA: 673). The appeal to mystery suggests a weak critical moment in Taylor's cumulative case. But to his credit, he admits that dilemmas remain.

5.2 Anticipatory confidence

The agonistic triangle of humanism, anti-humanism and belief in transcendence has exposed the difficulty that unbelieving variants have in getting us beyond the dilemma of mutilation. Secular humanism cannot meet the maximal demand because its high ideals also stifle, and Nietzschean anti-humanism, by Taylor's lights, simply gives up the quest for a solution, jettisoning high ideals other than the ideal of unrestricted freedom and self-expression. But, according to Taylor, there should be no Christian triumphalism, only anticipatory confidence. Taylor's apologetic has not proved secular understandings to be demonstrably wrong, and cannot hand out easy solutions. He is conciliatory, wanting to remove the barriers of labels which cover a shared heritage and predicament, and introduce a note of humility to proceedings:

> [I]t's not an accident that "Christians" fall into similar deviations to those of "secular humanists." As I have tried to show throughout this book, we both emerge from the same long process of Reform in Latin Christendom. We are brothers under the skin (ASA: 675).

In Christianity there are only "intimations" of how to move past the dilemma of mutilation, and these "are not of the kind which could be decanted into a general code or programme" (ASA: 674–675). Moreover, a Biblical perspective would problematize any attempt to purify humanity of vice if "the wheat [virtues] and the tares [vices] are so inextricably interwoven that the latter cannot be ripped out without also damaging the former" (ASA: 646; square parentheses original).

Taylor shares with Westphal the belief that the chief concern of Nietzsche's thought is his critique of modern morality. Furthermore, just as Westphal sees a continued role for Nietzsche's genealogy in keeping Christian love genuine, so Taylor acknowledges an enduring relevance of Nietzsche's challenge through his admission of the continuing force of the dilemma of mutilation. Finally, like Westphal, Taylor emphasizes that both subtle and explicit forms of violence plague the history of Christendom (ASA: 684):[20]

> Many believers (the fanatics, but also more than these) rest in the certainty that they have got God right (as against all those heretics and pagans in the outer darkness). They are clutching onto an idol, to use a term familiar in the traditions of the God of Abraham (ASA: 769).

Taylor wants to rehabilitate Christianity as an option, even an attractive option. At the same time, he sees too much material in Christian past and present to make a full-blown defense of Christianity honest or tenable: "religious faith

---

20 Taylor makes references several times to the persecution of "witches" (ASA: 43, 89, 456, 688) and also heretics, most notably in the Inquisition (ASA: 89, 638, 688).

can be dangerous" (ASA: 769). There is too much insight in Nietzsche's position to curtly dismiss it.

5.3 Overcoming Nietzsche?

Michael Kühnlein asks why Taylor does not critique Nietzsche's view that Christian morality is driven by resentment. Kühnlein draws attention to Max Scheler's characterization of Christian love as the opposite of the Greek conception, where the lower strives towards the higher. Christian love is the attending of the higher, the stronger, to the needs of the weaker. Self-loathing need not be the source of this love. Such love may also be the expression of a vital power, an overabundance of the ability to love, which the person consumed with *ressentiment* could never attain (Scheler 1923: 107; see discussion in Joas 1997: 45–46).

Kühnlein regrets Taylor's apparent reluctance to press this point home (Kühnlein 2008: 126). Instead, he says, Taylor resorts to the blank statement of hope that there is indeed something like *agape* which would make Nietzsche wrong, when he could instead make clear the very great difference between the "sovereignty and power of Christian loving action" and "aristocratic nobility [*Vornehmheit*]" (Kühnlein 2008: 130).

Why does Taylor not take this route? Perhaps, as Kühnlein implies, he does not know Scheler (Kühnlein 2008: 127).[21] However, even if he did not, there are good reasons why Taylor does not attempt something like a defense of Christian love. First, he sees too many counterexamples in the history of Christianity for a defense to not beg questions. Second, he thinks Nietzsche has a point. As we saw, Taylor is open to the possibility that we may not be able to entirely separate our virtues from our vices (ASA: 675). Third, Taylor thinks that only communities of genuine *agape* could be the refutation of Nietzsche's genealogy. To be Christian is to have faith, anticipatory confidence that one is "standing *among others* in the stream of love which is that facet of God's life we try to grasp, very inadequately, in speaking of the Trinity" (ASA: 701, emphasis mine). Being inspired by such love in community is "the path towards a much more powerful and effective healing action in history" (ASA: 703). Attempts to overcome the Nietz-

---

[21] This is possible. The only time Taylor mentions Scheler I am aware of is in connection with Scheler's description of the modern understanding of natural science as "Leistungswissen" (ASA: 113, 543).

schean predicament can "only point to the exemplary lives of certain trail-blazing people and communities" (ASA: 643).²²

Fraser also emphasizes community as a Christian solution but does not only point in this direction. Fraser wants to overcome Nietzsche in a way Taylor does not attempt. The attack on Nietzsche's kitsch is paralleled to some extent in Taylor's portrayal of Nietzsche's inhumanity, but there is great difference in tone. The difference between (religious or non-religious) humanism and anti-humanism is for Taylor a real dilemma, not an easy choice that can be reduced to "Nietzsche is cruel."²³ Despite Taylor's portrayal of Nietzsche as inhuman, Nietzsche's challenge and purgative role remains.

6 Attending to the prodigal

In the parable of the prodigal son (Luke 15), the father gives the younger son his inheritance early and the son blows it on wild living, only to end in the (ritually unclean) pigpen. The parable comes in a set of three spoken to Pharisees who disapprove of Jesus's morally questionable, spiritually 'lost' crowd. The parables emphasize lost things – sheep, a coin, and a son. In each case, joy over lost things now found births a community of celebration.

Nietzsche is a lost son – even if he does not return. This son of the Lutheran church found the expectations of his Lutheran milieu oppressive to the point of spiritual sickness, and, at least metaphorically, went abroad in hope of escaping his home. What should theologians do with Nietzsche? If we see Nietzsche as such a prodigal, then Christian attempts to appropriate Nietzsche in the service of the gospel see his flight as an understandable reaction to life under the shadow of the older moralizing brother of the parable. Westphal stands for a theological response to Nietzsche which grants that Christianity mediated through the life of the older brother is a Christianity from which one should flee. Westphal understands the younger son's rebellion, chides the older brother and perhaps imagines the father setting up a new farm with conceptual input from the prod-

---

22 It is an interesting feature of Taylor's mention of communities of faith that his ecclesiology does not appear to be distinctively Roman Catholic. His emphasis on communities in the plural points more obviously to examples far removed from the magisterium, like Jean Vanier's diaconic community, or even Protestant Pietist welfare societies.
23 "What makes me impatient are the positions which are put forward as conversation-stoppers: I have a three-line argument which shows that your position is absurd or impossible or totally immoral" (Taylor 2010: 318).

igal. But one might worry that the new business plan would prove the new domicile so unlike the father's house as to be unrecognizable.

Fraser has time for what we imagine to be the prodigal's disdain for his older brother's miserly spirituality, but his analysis ends with a view of Nietzsche that puts Nietzsche and Christianity at great odds. Nietzsche, who has spent so much time pouring scorn on and deconstructing his father's house, is now portrayed as a man far off in a pigpen, consumed by fear and self-loathing, a delusional weakling. As such he may be vanquished, but at the cost of Christian compassion. It is truly Nietzschean to gain power over Nietzsche by explaining the ethic of the *Übermensch* as a function of *ressentiment*, but does it help the lost son come home?

Fraser's full-frontal attack on Nietzsche's character may be satisfying for Christians, given Nietzsche's own vitriol; *revenge* may indeed always be satisfying. Taylor's irenic tone appears anemic in comparison. Like Lessing's parable of the ring in Nathan the Wise, Christians have to wait until the eschaton to find out which faith will not stifle.[24] But, one could say, Christian communities do not simply wait for the eschaton: they are missionary, they proclaim. Does not Taylor's generous stalemate lack the fire of conviction?

Perhaps, but the father in the parable *waits* for the prodigal. Would not the father pass on offering a public character-assassination of his wayward son? Arguably, "we live in a human world in which language is an expression of will to power, the word a weapon of self-assertion" (Ward 2014: 285). Would then the power of having explained Nietzsche in terms of his lower motives really be preferable?

It may be that Fraser, for all his perceptive and instructive critique, becomes too much like his opponent. Fraser's critique bears some fruit for Christian theologians in helping to defend against Nietzsche's own bombast. But Fraser's response needs augmentation by a further move toward pastoral theology that does not remain content with psychologizing Nietzsche. The danger with reducing Nietzsche to his fears and inabilities is that we obscure the likelihood that these fears and inabilities are for Nietzsche wounds inflicted by Christianity. We should talk with him, and not just about him.

Taylor's theological response to Nietzsche, against the background of Westphal and Fraser, makes an important contribution in this regard and offers a way forward for theologians responding to Nietzsche. Taylor does not merely occupy

---

[24] William Hart understands and articulates well Taylor's insistence that "[u]ntil the eschaton, the *fact* that one has evaded the horns of the dilemma and met the maximal demand is a matter of faith and the faithful prefiguring of the kingdom within exemplary communities and lives" (Hart 2012: 155).

some odious middle ground, or Hegelian synthesis; he maintains that Nietzsche is cruel and elitist, and would presumably agree with much of Fraser's analysis. Rather, the contribution is the way Taylor approaches the prodigal. He lets him voice concerns and insights while suggesting paths back home through a hermeneutic of violence and perspective of transformation, and by offering an invitation to join communities envisioned by divine affirmation. Perhaps such communities are like an incarnate "subtler language" that "opens new paths, 'sets free' new realities" (ASA: 758).

Taylor has Nietzschean confidence in his genealogical account of exclusive humanism, which in his account resembles the older brother of pharisaical Christianity. Taylor feels he knows the weaknesses and hypocrisies of that tradition well enough to make any thoughtful secular liberal think twice about rolling out any self-congratulatory narratives. Yet this Nietzschean confidence does not translate into an over-confident Catholic Christianity. There are facile critiques which can be laughed off. But some Nietzschean critiques get under one's skin, even trouble one's conscience. When the prodigal is welcomed back, the father's house will not remain the same.

Some theologians will find Taylor's approach entirely wrong-footed in conceding so much to the enemy. And at the other end of the spectrum, Nietzsche would be unimpressed with Taylor's concern to avoid misanthropy, or suggest that a renewed vision of God's love is the answer. Nevertheless, Taylor's irenic apologetic, which emphasizes common ground and would rather sublate than defeat its opponents, is suitable for a church taught to remember to ask for forgiveness alongside its daily bread.

Bibliography

Altizer, Thomas J.J. 1966. *The Gospel of Christian Atheism*. Philadelphia, PA: Westminster.
Bailey, Charles E. 1989. "Nietzsche: moralist or immoralist? The verdict of the European Protestant Theologians in the First World War." *History of European Ideas* 11: 799–814.
Booth, David. 1992. "Nietzsche's Legacy in Theology's Agendas." *Nietzsche-Studien* 21: 290–307.
Braune-Krickau, Tobias. 2011. "Charles Taylors religionsphilosophische Rehabilitierung der christlichen Religion in Ein säkulares Zeitalter." *Neue Zeitschrift für Systematische Theologie und Religionsphilosophie* 53 no. 3: 357–373.
Caputo, John D. 2001. *On Religion*. New York: Routledge.
Connolly, William E. 2004. "Catholicism and Philosophy. A Nontheistic Appreciation," in *Charles Taylor*, ed. Ruth Abbey, 166–186. Cambridge: Cambridge University Press.
Craig, William L. 2008. "The Absurdity of Life without God," in *Reasonable Faith. Christian Faith and Apologetics*, Third edition, ed. William Lane Craig, 65–90. Wheaton, IL: Crossway.

Deane, David. 2006. *Nietzsche and Theology. Nietzschean Thought in Christological Anthropology.* Aldershot: Ashgate.
Fraser, Giles. 2002. *Redeeming Nietzsche. The Piety of Unbelief.* London: Routledge.
Hart, William D. 2012. "Naturalizing Christian Ethics. A Critique of Charles Taylor's A Secular Age." *Journal of Religious Ethics* 40 no. 1: 149–170.
Hovey, Craig. 2008. *Nietzsche and Theology.* London: T & T Clark.
Jager, Colin. 2010. "This Detail, This History. Charles Taylor's Romanticism," in *Varieties of Secularism in A Secular Age,* ed. M. Warner, J. Vanantwerpen and C. Calhoun, 166–192. Cambridge, MA: Harvard University Press.
Joas, Hans. 1997. *Die Entstehung der Werte.* Frankfurt am Main: Suhrkamp.
Jüngel, Eberhard. 1978. *Gott als Geheimnis der Welt. Zur Begründung der Theologie des Gekreuzigten im Streit zwischen Theismus und Atheismus.* 3rd edition. Tübingen: Mohr Siebeck.
Kleffmann, Thomas. 2003. *Nietzsches Begriff des Lebens und die evangelische Theologie. Eine Interpretation Nietzsches und Untersuchungen zu seiner Rezeption bei Schweitzer, Tillich und Barth.* Tübingen: Mohr Siebeck.
Köster, Peter. 1982. "Nietzsche-kritik und Nietzsche-rezeption in der Theologie des 20. Jahrhunderts." *Nietzsche-Studien* 10: 615–685.
Köster, Peter. 2003. *Kontroversen um Nietzsche. Untersuchungen zur theologischen Nietzsche-Rezeption.* Zürich: Theologischer Verlag Zürich.
Kühnlein, Michael. 2008. *Religion als Quelle des Selbst.* Tübingen: Mohr Siebeck.
MacIntyre, Alasdair. 2007. *After Virtue. A Study in Moral Theory.* 3rd edition. London: Duckworth.
Marion, Jean-Luc. 2001. *Idol and Distance. Five Studies.* Chicago, IL: Fordham University Press.
Mourkojannis, Daniel. 2000. *Ethik der Lebenskunst. Zur Nietzsche-Rezeption in der evangelischen Theologie.* Münster: LIT Verlag.
Milbank, John. 2006. *Theology and Social Theory. Beyond Secular Reason.* 2nd Edition. Oxford: Blackwell.
Nietzsche, Friedrich. 1988. *Der Antichrist,* Vol. 6, *Kritische Studienausgabe,* 2nd edition ed. Giorgio Colli and Mazzino Montinari, 165–254. Berlin/New York: Walter de Gruyter.
Nussbaum, Martha. 1994. "Pity and Mercy: Nietzsche's Stoicism," in *Nietzsche, Genealogy, Morality,* ed. Richard Schacht, 139–167. Oakland, CA: University of California Press.
Peter, Niklaus. 1994. "Karl Barth als Leser und Interpret Nietzsches." *Zeitschrift für neuere Theologiegeschichte* 1 no. 2: 251–264.
Scheler, Max. 1923. "Das Ressentiment im Aufbau der Moralen," in *Vom Umsturz der Werte. Abhandlungen und Aufsätze,* Band 1, 2nd Edition, ed. M. Scheler, 47–233. Leipzig: Der Neue Geist Verlag.
Taylor, Charles. 1989. *Sources of the Self: The Making of the Modern Identity.* Cambridge, MA: Harvard University Press.
Taylor, Charles. 1993. "Nietzsche's Legacy." *Lonergan Review* 2: 171–187.
Taylor, Charles. 1999. "A Catholic Modernity?" in *Catholic Modernity? Charles Taylor's Marianist Award Lecture,* ed. J.L. Heft, 13–37. Oxford: Oxford University Press.
Taylor, Charles. 2010. "Afterword: Apologia pro Libro suo," in *Varieties of Secularism in a Secular Age,* ed. M. Warner, J. VanAntwerpen and C. Calhoun, 300–321. Cambridge, MA: Harvard University Press.

Von Balthasar, Hans Urs. 1998. *Apokalypse der deutschen Seele. Studien zu einer Lehre von letzten Haltungen. Bd. II. Im Zeichen Nietzsches* (1939), Einsiedeln: Johannes Verlag.

Ward, Bruce K. 2014. "Transcendence and Immanence in a Subtler Language. The Presence of Dostoevsky in Charles Taylor's Account of Secularity," in *Aspiring to Fullness in a Secular Age. Essays on Religion and Theology in the Work of Charles Taylor*, ed. Carlos D. Colorado and Justin D. Klaasen, 262–290. Notre Dame, IN: University of Notre Dame Press.

Westphal, Merold. 1997. "Nietzsche as a Theological Resource." *Modern Theology* 13 no. 2: 213–226.

Westphal, Merold. 1998. *Suspicion and Faith: The Religious Uses of Modern Atheism*. New York: Fordham University Press.

Wiley, Craig. 2009. "I Was Dead and Behold, I am Alive Forevermore: Responses to Nietzsche in 20th Century Christian Theology." *Intersections* 10: 507–517.

Williams, Stephen N. 2006. *The Shadow of the Antichrist: Nietzsche's Critique of Christianity*. Grand Rapids, MI: Baker Academic.

Yi, Zane. 2014. "Disclosure and Disruption. Charles Taylor's Post-Metaphysical Philosophy of Religion," in *Groundless Gods. The Theological Prospects of Post-Metaphysical Thought*, ed. Eric E. Hall and Hartmut von Sass, 159–184. Eugene, OR: Pickwick.

Courtney Bender
"Every Meaning Will have its Homecoming Festival:" *A Secular Age* and the Senses of Modern Spirituality

1 Introduction: Two Gifford Lectures

In the final decade of the nineteenth century Harvard Divinity School student Edwin Starbuck conducted a novel psychological survey. He asked numerous rank and file Protestants to respond in writing to a battery of questions about "the feelings of divine presence" and "actual feelings of the sense of communion during the ceremony of communion." The survey asked them to describe their experiences in detail. Starbuck intended his scientific survey to assay the qualities of various religious conversion experiences. It caused quite a stir among Cambridge's educated elite, many of whom rejected his scientific approach to religious experience outright. They bristled that this intimate and holy moment could be subjected to the cold scrutiny of science. Even Starbuck's advisor William James expressed such concern. "This is New England! ... People here will not reply to an inquisitorial document of that sort." But Starbuck persevered and, as those who have read the footnotes to *The Varieties of Religious Experience* will know, James would come to draw liberally from Starbuck's collected accounts in his Gifford lectures of 1901.[1]

Neither James nor Starbuck were purely in the business of dissecting religious experiences with scientific method, nor were they disinterested in probing the relationships between religious experience and text. Of the two, Starbuck's interests were explicitly ministerial and scientific. He understood the survey instrument he administered as a mechanism that could heighten religious awareness for those who responded. He expected that it would also "awaken ... certain immediate reactions. He hoped that 'what came forth spontaneously would be

---

An earlier version of this essay was originally prepared for the conference "Varieties of Secularism" at Yale University, April 2008. The author thanks the organizers of that conference, Jonathan VanAntwerpen, Craig Calhoun and Michael Warner for the impetus to write, and Colin Jager for the invitation to revisit, this essay.

[1] Christopher White (2008) chronicles Starbuck's research program, its reception and his relationship with William James. He notes that James draws on Starbuck's surveys 37 times and quotes from his published material another 26 times, more than from any other single source.

the most vital and essential elements of the experience.'" James did not share Starbuck's overtly pastoral mission, but he nonetheless also wrote *The Varieties* in a way that might "elicit emotional responses or somehow give off traces of their intensity" (White 2008: 137). *The Varieties* is thus not only a scientific work that lifts religious experiences from their contexts in order to identify the contours of a psychological concept. It is also a pedagogical instrument in which listeners and readers encounter the residue of other people's strongly resonant, singularly authoritative experiences. Readers therefore encounter religious experiences in at least two ways through this text. A century after its publication, this doubleness makes James' book a curious, ever-adaptable *magnum opus*.

Charles Taylor's *A Secular Age* invites a comparison with James' book in many ways.[2] Both originated as Gifford Lectures, both display staggering erudition and a similar authorial loquaciousness. Beyond these superficial aspects, both also share the kind of doubleness mentioned above: they are simultaneously analytic works of the highest caliber and pedagogical texts designed to elicit certain responses in their readers. Whereas James's text seeks to place readers within a milieu that provoked religious experience, Taylor's seeks to situate readers within an historical plotline of loss that will provoke a desire for recovery and struggle. In retelling a well-trod historical narrative of disenchantment, Taylor calls upon his readers (or rather, those who find themselves able to identify with his persistent "we" and "us") to feel the quandaries of "the immanent frame" and seek out "spiritual/moral fullness." He does so, moreover, by invoking James at multiple points within his historical narrative, even calling the open spaces of the immanent frame, "where you can feel the winds pulling you, now to belief, now to unbelief" a "Jamesian open space" (ASA: 549).

The invitations to compare the two texts also highlight some of the stronger divergences in both authors' approaches to their own contemporary moment, or what Taylor calls the "supernova" of "religion today." Where James and his peers developed a range of ways to consider the continued circulation of spirits and ghosts in the turn-of-the-century United States, the continued appeal of Mesmerism and mediumship, and the rise of various "healthy-minded" activities that had new and challenging relationships to "religion," Taylor plots these actions and ideas into a larger European story that shapes such activities and practices as an index of Western civilization's transformation into a disenchanted, secular

---

[2] Taylor likewise encourages this comparison, see for example Taylor 2002: 58–60 (compare ASA: 549).

world.³ By considering the contrasting approaches that these doubly-directed texts take to understanding contemporary religion, readers can observe the power and the limits of *A Secular Age*'s doubleness and situate Taylor's *magnum opus* as an exemplum within a richer field of religious and secular production. This essay proceeds with a reinterpretation of Taylor's much debated depiction of disenchantment and the characteristics of "religion today," drawing on cases that disturb Taylor's representation of modern secularity as fully disenchanted. Questioning the ways that *A Secular Age* renders "modern enchantments" as weak forms of prior experiences, I focus on two American cases ("wilderness" and "automatic writing") which suggest a more diffuse and flourishing space of enchantment in American contexts, wherein both enchantment and disenchantment are social effects, created with our own modern efforts. These observations do not lead me to suggest that the narrative of *A Secular Age* is false, but rather to position the volume and its arguments *within* the processes and efforts of enchantment and disenchantment. As such, I call attention to the narrative gaps and interpretive frames required to produce the powerful effects of *A Secular Age*, and which render its narrative so valuable and so convincing for its many readers.

2 Tales of enchantment

As is well known to readers of *A Secular Age*, Charles Taylor's argument is shaped within a rich and complex narrative of transformations in the modern West. Central to this narrative are changing "conditions of belief," wherein belief comes to be a central axis of religion (or irreligion) in a new secular age, and wherein an ability for individuals to choose belief or unbelief marks secular experience. These changing conditions are charted through transformations in the social imaginary, which is in Taylor's view the background "social condition" through which ordinary people "imagine their social existence, how they fit together with others, how things go on between them and their fellows, the expectations which are normally met, and the deeper normative notions and images which underlie these expectations" (ASA: 171). In Taylor's story, a new theory of modern order, developing in the halls of law and theology (and eventually philosophy and literature as well) "gradually *infiltrates* or *penetrates* and transforms our social

---

3 Taylor says, "[...] this whole book is an attempt to study the fate in the modern West of religious faith in the strong sense. The strong sense I define, to repeat, by a double criterion: the belief in transcendent reality, on one hand, and the connected aspiration to a transformation which goes beyond ordinary human flourishing on the other" (ASA: 510).

imaginary" (ASA: 175).[4] As a consequence, people are changed from naïve and porous selves who encounter an enchanted world to choosing and buffered subjects who encounter a disenchanted array of options for belief and unbelief.

Put succinctly, this is the story of the modern West's movement "from a society in which it was virtually impossible not to believe in God, to one in which faith, even for the staunchest believer, is one human possibility among others. ... Belief in God is no longer axiomatic. There are alternatives" (ASA: 3). Taylor notes that the arbiters of these changes came from within religion – that is, from religious actors throughout Europe who found magical thinking unsavory and sought to transform religion (Christianity) from within. Thus secularity

> ... came to be along with the possibility of exclusive humanism, which thus for the first time widened the range of possible options, ending the era of naïve religious faith. Exclusive humanism in a sense crept up on us through an intermediate form, Providential Deism; and both the Deism and the humanism were made possible by earlier developments within orthodox Christianity. Once this humanism is on the scene, the new plural, non-naïve predicament allows for multiplying these options beyond the original gamut (ASA: 19).

Taylor is clear that the result is that "we" no longer have the *capacity* to naïvely believe in God or the transcendent, thanks to the transformation in our social imaginary. To use William James's language, we are all twice born. A prior time of naïve belief, marked by an absence of organized doubt about the presence of enchanted things and transcendent order, is lost to us. We have also lost access to the "porous" selves of that earlier era, wherein people encountered spirits, forces, and other free-floating agents that impinged upon the soul, the mind, and the body.

In the modern social imaginary, by contrast, we confront and live within a different way of being that situates religion as a question of belief or, perhaps better, of varieties of belief. Secularity does not offer a position within a social-religious world where norms guide our beliefs naively, or where we experience our life as given to us. We are likewise no longer able to feel and experience

---

[4] Taylor's overall understanding is that ideas flow and penetrate in one direction (from theology, law and philosophy to ordinary people) but he does not present an explication of the mechanisms for such flows, nor does he consider the possibility of a more complicated sociology of knowledge with various interactions and influences. In contrast, sociological analyses of knowledge production often highlight the elasticity of culture and the relationships among different fields of knowledge and ideology production, power, and daily life. For a few representative examples, see Schudson 1989; Wuthnow 1989; Sewell 1999. A similar set of theoretical and methodological questions have preoccupied religious studies scholars and historians, for example Hall 1996; Orsi 2005; Griffith 1997.

our prior, naïve worlds or the touch of true porousness. We can grope toward these experiences in the varieties of fictions and religious activities that characterize the modern and the secular – going to a film, perhaps.⁵ Taylor calls such activities "subtler languages." He writes movingly of the enchanted "world we have lost, one in which spiritual forces impinged upon porous agents, in which the social was grounded in the sacred and secular time in higher times, a society moreover in which the play of structure and anti-structure was held in equilibrium; and this human drama unfolded within a cosmos. All this has been dismantled and replaced by something quite different" (ASA: 61).

While this is a rich and complex story, it has troubled scholars who question the depiction of rupture that Taylor presents between the pre-secular "enchanted" and the secular "disenchanted" world in which we live now. Historians have focused largely on the issue of whether pre-secular "western" (or contemporary non-Western cultures) societies or cultures were ever as enchanted and porous as Taylor's narrative assumes, and some anthropologists have likewise bristled at the suggestion that non-western peoples remain enchanted. And literary scholars, anthropologists and sociologists who similarly question a story of rupture ask whether the enchantments of modern life may share more with earlier forms of experience and enchantment than Taylor's story of rupture allows.⁶

2.1 Brooklyn Bridge and Brooklyn Ferry

Taylor's critics ask: What would happen to the narrative of secularism if the "great divide" were not as self-evident or untroubled as *A Secular Age* suggests? What, then, could we say about secularity? Taking into account that real changes have happened in the world, and that we can still speak about living in a world shaped by something designated as secularizing processes, what happens to enchantment? The very packaging of the book itself raises this question, obliquely,

---

5 Taylor describes the way that it must have felt to be so enchanted, so as to help us imagine and feel the distance between us and them. He presents various comparisons through the book: he says that our forebears would look on in actual horror as we feel the frisson of horror when we watch the movie *Titanic*; he states that enchanted people could not distance themselves from their melancholia and that we in contrast gain comfort in the ability to say that the depression or other diseases we have are separate from us (ASA: 36–38; see also Taylor 2002: 39–40).
6 For example, see Jay 2009, Butler 2010, Sheehan 2010, and various responses to *A Secular Age* at The Immanent Frame, http://blogs.ssrc.org/tif/secular_age/ (last accessed 31 July 2014). In a different yet related vein, see Bruno Latour's (2010) critique of modern narratives of rupture and enchantments.

by inviting readers to consider the photograph of Brooklyn Bridge which graces its cover. The bridge's cables and coils stretch into space, signaling the cross-cutting, akimbo networks that characterize modern cities and their social worlds.

Taylor says little directly about urban experience and life in *A Secular Age*, although he has written elsewhere that urban life is lived horizontally and without transcendence. Urban existence is exemplary of and a container for buffered and disenchanted modern experience. It has encouraged "[a] new, more individualized pursuit of happiness, loosening some of the ties and common lifeways of the past, the spread of expressive individualism and the culture of authenticity, the increased importance of these spaces of mutual display, all these seem to point to a new way of being together in society." In the city, people appear as "[u]rban monads [who] hover on the boundary between solipsism and communication [...]" (Taylor 2002: 86–87).

This rendering of urban life's immanent zones becomes an important background (or backdrop) in Taylor's depiction of nineteenth-century European Romanticism. As he argues, the wilderness becomes an important literary motif, emerging as a critique and check against the "self-absorption" of modern life that is itself suited to buffered selves of the new secular age: "[t]he moral meaning of the sublime can vary with the different views about what is our higher purpose, but in its general form it fits into the self-perception of buffered selves engaged with merely human goods .... The sight of 'Excess', vast, strange, unencompassable, provoking fear, even horror, breaks through this self-absorption" (ASA: 338–339). As Taylor notes, the value of the wilderness "in the period after 1700 is not that it offers us an alternative way of life." On the contrary, "[p]art of the sublimity of wilderness consisted in its otherness, its inhospitableness to humans; in the fact that you *couldn't really live there*. But opening to it makes it possible for you to live properly outside of it" (ASA: 339, 341).

The Romantic embrace (even the distanced embrace) of the sublime wilds furthermore embeds within it a critique of the "anthropocentrism" of Providential Deism emerging in the eighteenth century. Romanticism is a "reaction to the shallowness and anthropocentrism" of the theological articulations of God as designer and instead locates God "in the vastness of space and the abyss of time" (ASA: 343). The wilderness breaks us out of self-absorption, connects us with the "universal current of life" in which "we can conceive of giving [...] moral meaning to the wilderness with us – this is only comprehensively within the world animated by the modern cosmic imaginary. This is one which relates to a universe which is not necessarily structured and limited by a rational, benign plan, one where we cannot touch bottom, but which is nevertheless the locus of our dark genesis" (ASA: 346).

It may well be that the "wilderness" operated in these ways in European contexts, but they do not comprise the whole of nineteenth century uses of and claims upon "the wilderness." From the beginning of the North American colonial project and into the turn of the twentieth century, wilderness was a real place, one where a transplanted European settler *must* live. The "wilderness" was not imagined but rather a political, protean force that continued to act on civilization. No mere metaphor, no mere vista, seventeenth and eighteenth century American colonists and their offspring did not find themselves standing at a remove from the wilderness, and while they may have experienced it as their own personal terra incognita, it certainly was not empty. The wilderness was populated. Native peoples, strange creatures, spirits and ghosts alike inhabited the wilderness, coexisting with settlers or going to war with them. Even third generation settlers in the Massachusetts Bay colony lived "surrounded by an invisible world of spirits as well as by a natural world of palpable objects," *both* of which "communicated God's messages" (Norton 2003: 295; see also Castiglia 1996.)

For the American settlers whose progeny would eventually become readers of Taylor's volume, God's messages were written out in many ways in this American wilderness, frequently in violent and often inexplicable encounters. In the same year (1845) that Thoreau moved to Walden Pond (which was by then a second-growth woods on the outskirts of a sizeable town), the United States Congress voted to pursue more aggressive American expansion to the West, annexing Texas, fighting for Oregon territory with Britain, and making real the story of manifest destiny and America's prized place in God's plan. In that same year Mormons began to move into Utah Territory, promulgating Joseph Smith's arch-American sacralized reading of the American landscape and encounters with its Native American denizens as evidence not only of Providence but of the reclamation of the enchanted world. For all these reasons, even Thoreau's transcendental engagements with the forests around Walden Pond should be read as richly populated spaces of encounter (for both good and ill, peace and violence), in dialogue with written reports of borderland encounters circulated in news reports and pamphlets and in the testimony of Americans returned from "the West." In these many places, God's calling and God's "manifest destiny" for the nation's expansion were not merely read in the wilderness' leaves of grass but in the decisiveness of warfare, brutal hunger, heat and cold, the real and imagined fear of captivity, and the ongoing expulsion of peoples.

And yet, even as the American wilderness continued to figure in Americans' "social imaginary" as connecting national expansion to a transcendent order (where time was expansive not abyssal) its denizens began to "return" to the new urban centers as spirits and emanations that inhabited the bodies of urban dwellers. The complexities of wilderness offered ways for urbanites in New York and Boston to interpret the life that they began to experience in their teeming, burgeoning cities (New York's population quintupled in the middle decades of the nineteenth century). With the advent of Spiritualism and other sundry metaphysical religions, northeastern cities were inundated with civilized and uncivilized spirits, invited and not. Even the skeptical attested to feeling the touch of ghosts across their brows and palms. Spirits manifested in urban parlors and sitting rooms. They penetrated the civilization of the city, inhabiting both its spaces and its residents, showing both to be porous, enchanted, and uncontrollable (Albanese 2006; Cox 2003). Where the Romantic wilderness that Taylor reads is evidence of a shift of consciousness where human beings inhabit (for the first time) "a nature of deep time and unfathomable spaces, [...] a universe which is in many ways strange and alien, and certainly unfathomable" (ASA: 347), the wilderness of America remained filled with spirits who forced upon settlers an experience of their own porosity. While the sublime of the European Romantics was disenchanted, invoking an "inhuman, violent, disordered" universe, the spirits who returned from the beyond to speak through the porous American bodies of mediums attested to the orderliness (and even democratic character) of the worlds beyond. The various Indian guides who inhabited the physical bodies of middle class mediums thus made clear to those who would listen that despite the chaos that appeared in the city, it was ultimately organized, assembled through sympathies, energies, and connections that were invisible to humans but evident to the spirits who lived fully within these energetic networks (Schmidt 2005; Modern 2011).

It would be misleading to suggest that cities were *only* inhabited by spirits and ghosts, newly arriving spectral immigrants from the receding American wilderness. City dwellers also found themselves mystified and overwhelmed, sometimes quite literally, by the circulating energies of the cityscape itself. They felt in its strangely common synchronicities and electric encounters with others the touch of danger and eros. Walt Whitman wrote that city life "completely satisf[ies] my senses of power, fullness, motion, etc. and gives me, through such senses and appetites [...] a constituted exaltation and absolute fulfillment." He continued: "I realize (if we must admit such partialism) that not Nature alone is great in her fields of freedom and the open air, in her storms, the shows of night and day, the mountains, forests, sea – but in the artificial work of man too is equally great – in this profusion of teeming humanity – in these ingenuities, streets, goods, houses, ships – these hurrying, feverish electric crowds of men, their complicated business genius (not least among geniuses), and all this might, many-threaded wealth and industry concentrated here" (Quoted in Thomas 1982: 377). Whitman's cityscape emerges as fearsome and uncontrollable: it might be "the artificial work of man" but it is within this "many-threaded"-ness and concentration that fullness is realized.

Whitman did not live to see the metal cables of the Brooklyn Bridge join Brooklyn to Manhattan. He took the Brooklyn Ferry. Nevertheless, standing on the water between the two cities he found himself bound to the entire metropolis, to its denizens, to the masts in the harbor. The city's energies, human made but prompting a form of connectivity that resonates with transcendence, emerges in this literature – not as a sublime replacement of traditional theism but as a modern, layered coursing through the city and through Whitman's porous body:

> I too lived – Brooklyn, of ample hills, was mine;
> I too walk'd the streets of Manhattan Island, and bathed in the waters around it;
> I too felt the curious abrupt questionings stir within me,
> In the day, among crowds of people, sometimes they came upon me,
> In my walks home late at night, or as I lay in my bed, they came upon me.
> I too had been struck from the float forever held in solution;
> I too had receiv'd identity by my Body;
> That I was, I knew was of my body – and what I should be, I knew I should be of my body.

The kinds of enchantments evoked (and invoked) by the view from the Brooklyn Ferry – and in time, from the Brooklyn Bridge[7] – resonate with an ongoing American experience wherein selves are porous, and where uncanny presences continue to orient the actions of groups and individuals who are deeply embedded in urban landscapes. In this the poets are ahead of the philosophers. The latter have yet to account fully for the emergent expressions and experiences of sociality carried forward in imagined and realized networks, enchanted associations and lines of sympathy. It is this understanding of American religious life that informs a growing number of studies by historians and religious studies scholars, including my own.

---

[7] The best known examples of Brooklyn Bridge poetry beyond Whitman's "Crossing Brooklyn Ferry" would include Vladimir Mayakovsky's "Brooklyn Bridge," Marianne Moore's "Granite and Steel," Jack Kerouac's "Brooklyn Bridge Blues," and Hart Crane's "To Brooklyn Bridge." One can also add visual arts to this list, including Joseph Stella's "Brooklyn Bridge." The bridge is the site of a yearly pilgrimage organized by Poet's House and described on their website thus: "Just before sunset, scores of poetry lovers gather on the Manhattan side of the bridge and walk across en masse while reading poems about the bridge and the city. Once the group reaches the Fulton Ferry Landing, they listen to the entirety of "Crossing Brooklyn Ferry" read aloud as the sun sets behind the stunning arc of the bridge." http://www.poetshouse.org/programs-and-events/poetry-walk/poetry-walk-across-brooklyn-bridge-0 (last accessed July 31, 2014).

3 "Religion Today"

My inquiry in *New Metaphysicals* (Bender 2010) was prompted by dissatisfaction with the sociological analyses of "spirituality" from which Taylor draws liberally in his chapters on "religion today." Taylor is certainly in good company when he argues that spirituality in America and western Europe is characterized by quests for authenticity and individualized, self-focused concepts of religious experience.[8] In numerous volumes, sociologists have described spirituality as something other than (and less than) religion – its pale shadow, its last gasp, or its secular translation. Where religion has authority, transcendence, historical connections, and community, spirituality appears to be a "condition" – something that emerges within the individual and organizes the search for the religious – rather than a set of traditions and ideologies in its own right.

As I learned, my respondents (all "mystics" or "spiritual but not religious" types) at least partially agreed with the view that spirituality was not religion, but their arguments ran in a different and more enthusiastic direction. Most, for example, told me that "spirituality" was not religion because while it had always existed, it was more akin to science (organized, that is, around laws and systems) rather than religion (which was organized around appeals to tradition). Unlike religion, they said, spiritual forces were real, and they operated independently of whether anyone believed them. Spiritual laws were like gravity – people ran into trouble when they thought that they did not live by its rules, and would find themselves more at peace if they conformed to them.

All the same, their theological claims about spirituality (and religion) were embedded in a tradition that had developed and thrived in Cambridge, Massachusetts, the site of my field work. In other words, while my respondents made claims about the timeless and porous realities of energy and spirit, they did so from seats within the parlors and basements of the Swedenborgian Chapel, the Theosophical Society or the Spiritualist Temple. These venerable organizations opened their buildings to various spiritual groups which they viewed as linked, either sympathetically or historically, with their own longlasting metaphysical interests. These older groups' understandings of relationships between old and new spiritualities subtly challenged and altered many of the newer groups' claims to their own newness, pointing rather to their deep roots in Amer-

---

[8] For a review of some of the voluminous literature that identifies spirituality in this way see the introduction of Bender 2010. For discussions of the political effects of these framings of spirituality, see Sullivan 2014 and Lofton 2011.

ican metaphysical, harmonial religious traditions.[9] More than that, however, these relationships confounded the oft-repeated sociological claim that 21st century "spirituality" is mediated only through the individual and the market rather than through lineages and traditions.

Most of my respondents and informants were relatively uninterested in the longer histories of their practices, to be sure. Taylor would suggest that their ahistoricism (or anti-historicism) is symptomatic of the "supernova" of options that took shape in the post-World War II period, when ideas about self-actualization and fulfillment were detached from particular social settings or practices. He argues that the individualism that marks the "age of authenticity" fractures the need for external authority, and the attendant range of religious and spiritual "options" becomes recast likewise as an undifferentiated mass of ways to work on the self. When Taylor labels the age of authenticity "post-Durkheimian," he means precisely that spiritual longing is not oriented toward the interests or demands of pleasing or submitting to *any* group or identity, but takes place in full service of the self (ASA: 487–489). As Taylor puts it, we live in a "pluralist world, in which many forms of belief and unbelief jostle, and hence fragilize each other. It is a world in which belief has lost many of the social matrices which made it seem 'obvious' and unchallengeable." And he continues: "We could say that this is a world in which the fate of belief depends much more than before on powerful intuitions of individuals, radiating out to others" (ASA: 531).

Such analysis of the state of contemporary spiritual life assumes that the rhetoric of spiritual practice employed by practitioners reflects an accurate portrait of spiritual "community." That is, if the practitioners say that what they do has no important history or lineage, then this must be so. Even leaving aside the larger methodological question of how particular situations of social embeddedness structure claims to spiritual experience, we can still seek to understand the various ways that a social practice's past meanings and the claims through which they are made can be revived or reinterpreted, in ways that work as a kind of enchantment. Paying attention to various modes of transmission, including the intersection of popular-textual and embodied transmissions, illuminates a different set of claims to authority and authenticity that eclipse (or stand apart

---

[9] Numerous studies abound; many tell the story of developing and changing histories of new age and occult religions (Hanegraaff 1998), American transcendentalism (Albanese 1977; Versluis 1993); debates about the boundaries between medicine, science and religion (Moore 1977; Schmidt 2000; Fuller 1989). A developing body of recent research seeks to link these histories with mainstream currents in American religious, cultural, and political thought and expression (Griffith 2004; Satter 1999; Schmidt 2005, and Albanese 2006).

from) issues of belief, and do not map easily onto the trajectories and histories of belief foregrounded in *A Secular Age*.

3.1 Automatic writing

The writing habits of my Cambridge respondents offer a concise example.[10] Many wrote regularly, in journals, correspondence, unpublished essays, and on-line blogs. Spiritualized or not, writing was the thing to do in Cambridge's hyper-textual orbit. One homeopath told me that there was too much text in Cambridge. When she asked her new clients for "a timeline of their lives, they xerox their diaries. I get wheelbarrows full. [Or, they say], I happen to be writing the story of my life, let me download it for you. – Welcome to Cambridge!" While at first these practices did not attract my attention, I learned that for many, writing (and reading) was a complex site of porosity, where they *could sometimes* encounter the divine, manifested within their bodies and texts.

Marcy, for example, was a Catholic and a yoga teacher who also regularly taught courses on *The Artist's Way*, a book by Julia Cameron that recommends ways to release the "artist within" and find the "spiritual path to higher creativity." Cameron provides a number of practical suggestions and disciplines through which people can connect with the "creative" part of themselves, but first among them is an exercise that she calls writing "morning pages." This exercise consists of daily, solitary longhand writing: Cameron suggests a minimum of three pages and recommends that people should put down on the page whatever comes. She says, "these daily morning meanderings are not meant to be art. Or even writing. [...] Pages are meant to be, simply, the act of moving the hand across the page and writing down *whatever* comes to mind. Nothing is too petty, too silly, too stupid, or too weird." Cameron further suggests, "It may be useful for you to think of the morning pages as meditation... It is impossible to write morning pages for any extended period of time without coming into contact with an unexpected inner power. Anyone who faithfully writes morning pages will be led to a connection with a source of wisdom from within. When I am stuck in a painful situation or problem that I don't think I know how to handle, I will go to the pages and ask for guidance" (Cameron 1992:10 – 11, 15 – 16).

---

10 Spiritual writing practices are not limited to the "spiritual not religious" but also are practiced and taught in various American religious communities across the denominational spectrum (see Bender 2008).

Marcy's description of writing is quite in line with Cameron's. She told me, "I wake up, feed the cat, make some tea, and then do my journaling. [...] It became the ritualistic way that I wake up every day and make myself do my journal writing." Marcy explained to me that writing morning pages "is really about the process of excavating: What do I want to do with my life? What can I change in my life?" At first, she said, she liked writing because it allowed her to "do something that is completely nonproductive" but she soon discovered that it was in fact productively allowing her to "get back in touch with herself." And now, writing is primarily "a time of connection. [...] I would pray sometimes, in the writing, sometimes it was prayer that I was writing. It became a sacred practice to me. So I began to embrace sacred ritual – that's really what happened, actually." At some point Marcy began to ask for "wisdom" about the next steps in her life through her journal. She had been journaling for a year, and "by that point I was pretty much ingrained in a practice of daily journaling, and that's where a lot of truths were being heard. Sometimes it was a laundry list, but often times, answers would come to questions, things I was dealing with – really answers to prayer. So I journalled for a while about this decision, and, in my mind I was thinking, maybe I would temp or do some more freelance. Within a week I had all this work – all over the place. Stuff was literally falling into my lap – money and work and good co-workers."

Marcy's hope that "answers would come" in the pages of her notebook resonates with Cameron's suggestion that it is not only one's inner monologue that comes to the surface in these pages but also the words of the divine, or something outside the self. Cameron counsels her readers that they should not see themselves as the authors of their journals, but rather as "the instruments" of divine creativity. The divine becomes present *within* the practice of writing and is encountered there. Writing and language is far from flattened out; it becomes, rather, a source, expression, and material evidence of divine presence in the details of life.

Neither Cameron's claim about the "divine" as the active source of writers' creative effervescence nor her view that "divine creativity" is manifest within passive, open-ended flow writing are new ideas. They in fact resonate with the styles and practices of earlier metaphysical writing and mediumship. For example, Cameron's rules for "morning pages," share a number of direct similarities with Charles Hammond's instructions for mediums first published in 1852 and attached to a volume of messages he received from his dead sister through automatic writing. Hammond suggests that readers who follow the printed rules will be able to receive messages just as he did. The techniques can be learned and practiced. But they take effort. To have contact with the dead, one must "sit one hour each day where no noise will attract attention." Calmness and passivity are necessary, Hammond writes, for the spirit will communicate when it wants to, "without aid." Mediums should not resist or doubt when their hand starts moving, Hammond instructs, because "when mediums resist, nothing reliable can be written." Hammond adds that it is best to meditate on spirits who are "capable of instructing in the knowledge of God," rather than the darker spirits who (presumably) know less about truth. Nonetheless, the clear instruction is not to question or resist what comes but to give up attention, to let things "flow."

Deceased people continue to contact Spiritualists and trance channelers through writing, even today (Brown 1995). But as we observe in Cameron's book, the practices of passive, open writing have not always carried spirits with them. These practices have expanded and transformed in other settings, including into the growing commercial world of popular "entertainment" (enter the Ouija Board) and also into the orbit of psychological research. By the late nineteenth century, psychologists hypothesized that automatic writing presented evidence for "dissociated consciousness" or "double consciousness," and brought the tools of mediumship, including the planchette (the free-hanging board on which mediums rested their arms) into their laboratories. American psychologists' interests in automatic writing soon dwindled, but not before a young Gertrude Stein assisted in William James's laboratory experiments and co-authored two academic papers on the phenomenon.[11]

In the same year (1897) that Stein published her first psychology paper on automatic writing, Ralph Waldo Trine published his New Thought classic *In Tune with the Infinite*. Not surprisingly, his spiritual guidebook also claimed that writing could help people get "in tune." Trine encouraged readers to practice mental discipline "In order for your higher inspirations to come through [...] you must open your soul, you must open it fully to the Supreme Source of all inspiration [...]." But opening one's soul takes place through a variety of practices that are generally viewed not as "disciplines" but as "returning the body" to its natural state. Writing is one of many such practices, where rules and codes are eschewed in favor of the "freedom" that comes from writing naturally. Trine writes: "Be true. Be fearless. Be loyal to the promptings of your own soul. Remember that an author can never write more than he himself is. If he would write more, then he must be more. *He is simply his own amanuensis.*" Yet

---

11 Stein coauthored two academic papers on automatic writing (Solomons and Stein 1896; Stein 1898) based on research conducted in William James' and Hugo Münsterberg's laboratories. Stein's investigations into writing automatically have been a perennial subject of debate since the 1930's, but Barbara Will (2001) argues convincingly that Stein privileged genius as the "surplus" of the normal mechanics of writing, and that genius was possible as a type of detached observation of writing as the process occurred.

Trine also suggests that the source of one's writing ultimately emanates from elsewhere: "I had rather be an amanuensis of the Infinite God, as it is my privilege literally to be, than a slave to the formulated rules of any rhetorician, or to the opinions of any critic" (Trine 1897: 159, 163, 174. Emphasis added). These claims are nonetheless often accompanied by rules and practices for being cathartic.

Such hesitations between freedom and discipline rest at the core of all automatically-written texts. One of the clearest examples of this productive questioning appears in Jane Revere Burke's 1922 volume, *The One Way*. Burke was an Episcopalian woman who published several volumes of automatic writing in the first decades of the twentieth century, all consisting of spirit messages from notable men. *The One Way* records the spirit-world ruminations of none other than William James (d. 1910), with whom Burke recorded long "conversations" about the nature of spirit writing and the value of her books. Burke has the great fortune of finding the answers to her questions about automatic writing in her pen: as she tells her readers, she writes questions on the page and then allows James to answer. "Why do I know what the pencil is going to write?" she asked James. The answer came, "You know that the language you and I use is the thought language, and you perceive the thought before the pencil gets it down." Burke continues to dwell on the actual position of the spirit's control, and wonders whether it resides in her body, her pencil, or her mind. She determines that James and the other spirits whom she contacts "think" thoughts to her and that she then translates these unformed words onto the page. "The experience of automatic writing is an absolutely extraordinary one," she writes. "No one who has been through it can question the certainty of a control outside themselves. [...] I feel sure that the contact between the amanuensis and the control can be wholly spiritual, and that though it may be only psychic it is never material" (Burke 1922: xv-xx).[12]

While the spirits might "think thoughts" and Burke has some ability to choose how to convey them, she disavows any authorial role. Instead, she claims for herself the role of medium or channel. She also argues that William James's spirit is likewise a kind of medium, insofar as he is not the author of her book. Fending off any criticism that she was possessed by a spirit, she claims that the source of her knowledge is none other than "[...] the one old channel of Jesus Christ." Had she not encountered the idea of automatic writing she could have

---

[12] Burke published several volumes recounting messages of recently departed luminaries, including Mark Twain, William James, and Andrew Jackson Davis. One reviewer drolly reported: "[a] reader who is familiar with James' writings might wonder why his famous literary style does not appear in his messages from the spirit world" (Scarf 1935: 186).

published the book just as she had, "without realizing that it was being done by automatic writing – simply believing that I was inspired" (Burke 1922: xii). Burke's dialogic depictions of James's influence and Christ's inspiration suggests that identifying the "actual" origin and mechanisms of writing are of less interest than her observations that such inspiration is possible. Like Hammond and Trine, Burke emphasizes her passivity. Authority comes not through the active work of shaping ideas but rather by letting go, writing (as Trine demands) "from the heart" rather than from convention, or as Cameron encourages, writing whatever comes, and refusing to think it over.[13] "Letting go" in all of these cases means eschewing what has been learned or handed down as the proper way to write. It inspires the creative moment "itself" as the true nub or core of the proper practice and of its power.

There is more that can be said about how the religious worlds of contemporary people are shaped along these boundaries. Contrary to arguments that contemporary spiritual practices are just picked up by chance, or through encounters with a "spiritual marketplace," we find that they are structured and reproduced across a range of settings, in a field of social action and language that includes writing workshops, journaling clubs, Sunday school classes, and popular media. These settings appear in the background, but they also support each other, and the resonance among them invites robust reflection as well. They encourage those who use them to consider questions of external and even transcendent authority through embodied experiences. They place individuals in worlds that they encounter as porous. In order to understand how secular, religious, and spiritual people today (in all their varieties) find enchantments, divinity, and transcendence coursing through the modern world we need to pay more attention to the ways that these "conditions" of experience and enchantment – or disenchantment and immanence – are worked out now and in the past.

Widening the frame of social practices under investigation to include both theorized and untheorized, naïve and reflexive practices – and not incidentally to include both those that are coordinated along lines of belief and those organized differently – can offer not only a stronger sense of the experience of "religion today," but also can help us to grasp the experiential effects of scholarly arguments, including those of *A Secular Age*.

---

[13] Such writing practices were further developed in the 1960s and 1970s in the field of composition and education (for example Elbow 1963), which in turn influenced guides to journaling, writing and meditation (for example Goldberg 1986).

4 "Every meaning will have its homecoming festival"

Does disturbing *A Secular Age*'s claims for a disenchanted world lead us to reconsider its doubleness, or to imagine *A Secular Age* as itself participating in a kind of practice of enchantment (one that it does not identify)? I considered this question as I pondered Taylor's footnoted admission of modern ineffability: "I am acutely aware of how inadequate *all* words are," he writes, to describe "the condition we aspire to" (ASA: 780fn8). What does this particular kind of invocation mean, and what does it make possible? *A Secular Age* is a complex offering of recovery – or at least, of an ability to see clearly through the mists while we stand in the "open spaces." Yet we can also see that even as its narrative brings this object of recovery to our attention, it has also done the work of rendering its object missing. At this moment, Taylor's claim that he is "acutely aware of how inadequate *all* words are" to describe "the condition we aspire to" takes on a different cast. We confront it not only as a claim about the difficulty of his project, but also as a gesture toward the textual condition he has crafted to help readers experience disenchantment, and to experience it as their own.

Ineffable or inadequate as words may be, *A Secular Age* nonetheless ends with a claim that "nothing is ever lost" (ASA: 772), a phrase that resonates strongly with a passage in Mikhail Bakhtin's late work that reads:

> At any moment in the development of the dialogue there are immense, boundless masses of forgotten contextual meanings, but at certain moments of the dialogue's subsequent development along the way they are recalled and invigorated in renewed form (in a new context). Nothing is absolutely dead: every meaning will have its homecoming festival (Bakhtin 1986: 170).

Disenchantment is one of the stories modernity tells about itself. It does the work of shaping our understandings of our place and role in world history and politics, in relation to a story of our own enchanted past and to others' enchanted present.[14] My argument in the foregoing pages has been that the secular is

---

14 As Mary Douglas stated over thirty years ago, "Everything [about theories of modernization] is wrong because the stereotype of premoderns is wrong. It has been constructed to flatter prejudged ideas, primary among them already given differences" (Douglas 1982: 18). The same claim is echoed in numerous essays and monographs since then about secularization theories. As a consequence, we know that we cannot read a narrative of disenchantment unpolitically, that is, as a story of historical "fact" that does not work in specific ways to render certain religious formations as less than fully religious.

marked not by disenchantment but by an *oft-repeated claim* that we have been disenchanted (Weber 1958). "We" believe that the enchantments we feel now are not like those of our forebears: we believe that we are (for good or ill) living with nothing but a faint shadow of something that is now gone, something that was real. But if we take a cue from the historians who question this very move, then we can no longer assume that modern enchantments are so shadowy, or that we are haunted by nothing but the faint traces of a past cut off from us.

Which helps to explain, at last, why this essay begins with Edwin Starbuck's investigations. Noting the doubleness of his research (or the doubleness of James's or Taylor's) does not lead us to a position where a reader can state that an interpretation is untruthful. To call attention to doubleness is not to call out "It's a lie!" – as one nameless Cantabridgian shouted out at the end of one of Starbuck's lectures. Indeed, such a tack misses the point entirely. Rather, my point is just to say that above all else, *A Secular Age* shows us, in great complexity and in magisterial story, that what it tells is true insofar as its narrative becomes part of the story that we tell about our selves. That stories like those offered in *A Secular Age* are reinforced both within the biographies and yearnings of many (although not all) Christians, and also within the bibliographies of working theorists, theologians or historians is not so much a surprise or a shock as a clear call to ask about the effects of such claims.

And therefore we cannot leave it at that. Indeed, it is imperative that we do not. For if secularization narratives render a range of things that people do in a secular age, and which sustain our collective capacities to touch the transcendent and be touched by it, as invisible, fragmentary, limited, and shadowy, then we need to work toward a better rendering of what this secularity is, and what its mechanisms and projects are. To do so would mean embarking on a study of the narratives and moreover the social and cultural processes (so infrequently considered in *A Secular Age*) through which we seek and experience fullness, some of which may have nothing at all to do with belief.

Such are the practices and memories that bind us together while sloping at all angles – neither transcendent nor immanent, but all akimbo, perhaps much like the taut cables of the Brooklyn Bridge. They make possible forms of American politics that are rendered as spiritual and diffuse. These worlds need not evade our attention, and indeed we will only suffer if they do. For, insofar as they are also sustained by scholarly projects that render them as apparitions, their powers only increase. Bringing these spirits to share in our secular story will shape a different kind of meaning and, perhaps, a different type of homecoming.

Bibliography

Albanese, Catherine. 1977. *Corresponding Motion: Transcendental Religion and the New America*. Philadelphia: Temple University Press.
Albanese, Catherine. 2006. *Republic of Mind and Spirit*. New Haven: Yale University Press.
Bakhtin, Mikhail. 1986. *Speech Genres and Other Late Essays*. Austin: University of Texas Press.
Bellah, Robert. 2007. "Secularism of a New Kind." *The Immanent Frame*. http://blogs.ssrc.org/tif/2007/10/19/secularism-of-a-new-kind/ (last accessed August 7, 2014).
Bender, Courtney. 2008. "How Does God Answer Back?" *Poetics: A Journal of Empirical Research on Culture, the Media and the Arts* 36: 476–492
Bender, Courtney. 2010. *The New Metaphysicals: Contemporary Spirituality and the American Religious Imagination*. Chicago: University of Chicago Press.
Bender, Courtney. 2013. "Practicing Religion," in *The Cambridge Companion to Religious Studies*, ed. Robert Orsi, 273–295. Cambridge: Cambridge University Press.
Berger, Peter. 1967. *The Sacred Canopy*. Garden City, New York: Doubleday.
Bourdieu, Pierre, 1990. *The Logic of Practice*. Palo Alto, CA: Stanford University Press.
Brown, Wendy. 1995. States of Injury. Power and Freedom in Late Modernity. Princeton: Princeton University Press.
Burke, Jane Revere. 1922. *The One Way*. New York: Dutton.
Bynum, Caroline Walker. 2001. *Metamorphosis and Identity*, New York: Zone Books.
Cameron, Julia. 1992. *The Artist's Way: A Spiritual Path to Higher Creativity*. New York: Tarcher Putnam.
Camic, Charles. 1986. "The Matter of Habit." *American Journal of Sociology* 91:1039–1067.
Castiglia, Christopher. 1996. *Bound and Determined*, University of Chicago Press.
Cox, Robert S. 2003. *Body and Soul: A Sympathetic History of American Spiritualism*. Charlottesville: University of Virginia Press.
Daston, Lorraine and Katharine Park. 2001. *Wonder and the Order of Nature 1150–1750*. New York: Zone Books.
Douglas, Mary. 1982. "The effects of modernization on religious change." *Daedalus*. 1–19.
Elbow, Peter. 1963. *Writing Without Teachers*. New York: Oxford University Press.
Fuller, Robert C. 1989. *Alternative Medicine and American Religious Life*. New York: Oxford.
Goldberg, Natalie. 1986. *Writing Down the Bones: Freeing the Writer Within*. New York: Shambhala Press.
Griffith, R. Marie. 2004. *Born Again Bodies: Flesh and Spirit in American Christianity*. Berkeley: University of California Press.
Hammond, Charles. 1852. *Light from the Spirit World : Comprising a Series of Articles on the Condition of Spirits*. Rochester, NY: Dewey.
Hanegraaff, Wouter. 1998. *New Age Religion and Western Culture*. Albany, NY: SUNY Press.
Jay, Martin. 2009. "Faith-based History." *History and Theory* 48:76–84.
Kessel, Reuben. 1954. "Price Discrimination in Medicine," *Journal of Law and Economics* 1:20–53.
Klassen, Pamela E. 2007. "Radio Mind: Protestant Experimentalists on the Frontiers of Healing," *Journal of the American Academy of Religion* 75:651–683.
Latour, Bruno. 2010. *On the Modern Cult of the Factish Gods*. Durham, NC: Duke University Press.

Lofton, Kathryn. 2011. *Oprah: Gospel of an Icon*. Berkeley: University of California Press.
Modern, John Lardas. 2011. *Secularism in Antebellum America*. Chicago: University of Chicago Press.
Moore, R. Laurence. 1977. *In Search of White Crows*. New York: Oxford University Press.
Norton, Mary Beth. 2003. *In the Devil's Snare*. New York: Vintage.
Owen, Alex. 2007. *The Place of Enchantment British Occultism and the Culture of the Modern*. Chicago: University of Chicago Press.
Peters, John Durham. 1999. *Speaking into the Air: A History of the Idea of Communication*. Chicago: University of Chicago Press.
Ramaswamy, Sumathi. 2004. *The Lost Land of Lemuria: Fabulous Geographies, Catastrophic Histories*. Berkeley: University of California Press.
Satter, Beryl. 1999. *Each Mind a Kingdom: American Women, Sexual Purity and the New Thought Movement, 1875–1920*. New York: Oxford University Press.
Scarf, R.C. 1935. "Book Review: Burke's *One Way*." *American Journal of Psychology* 47:186.
Schmidt, Leigh. 2000. *Hearing Things: Religion, Illusion, and the American Enlightenment* Cambridge, MA: Harvard University Press.
Schmidt, Leigh. 2005. *Restless Souls: the Making of American spirituality*. San Francisco: HarperSanFrancisco.
Schmidt, Leigh. 2011. "History and the Historyless" *The Immanent Frame*. http://blogs.ssrc.org/tif/2011/01/14/history-and-the-historyless/ (last accessed August 7, 2014).
Schudson, Michael. 1989. "How Culture Works." *Theory and Society* 18:153–180.
Sheehan, Jonathan. 2010. "When Was Disenchantment? History and the Secular Age" in *Varieties of Secularism in a Secular Age*, ed. Michael Warner, Jonathan VanAntwerpen, and Craig Calhoun, 217–242. Cambridge, MA: Harvard University Press.
Sewell, William H. Jr. 1999. "The Concept(s) of Culture" in *Beyond the Cultural Turn*, ed. Victoria Bonnell and Lynn Hunt, 35–61. Berkeley: University of California Press.
Solomons, Leon M. and Gertrude Stein. 1896. "Normal Motor Automatism." *Psychological Review* 3:492–512.
Stein, Gertrude. 1898. "Cultivated Motor Automatism: a A Study of Character in its Relation to Attention." *Psychological Review* 5:295–306.
Sullivan, Winnifred Fallers. 2014. *A Ministry of Presence*. Chicago: University of Chicago Press.
Taylor, Charles. 2002. *Varieties of Religion Today: William James Revisited*. Cambridge, MA: Harvard University Press.
Thomas, M. Wynn. 1982. "Walt Whitman and Mannahatta-New York." *American Quarterly* 34: 362–378.
Trine, Ralph Waldo. 1897. *In Tune With the Infinite*. New York: Dodd, Mead and Company.
Versluis, Arthur. 1993. *American Transcendentalism and Asian Religions*. New York: Oxford University Press.
Viswanathan, Gauri. 2000. "The Ordinary Business of Occultism." *Critical Inquiry* 27:1–20
Weber, Max. 1958. "Science as a Vocation," in *From Max Weber: Essays in Sociology*. Transl., ed. and with an Introduction by H. H. Gerth and C. Wright Mills, 129–156. New York: Oxford University Press.
White, Christopher. 2008. *Unsettled Minds: Psychology and the American Search for Spiritual Assurance 1830–1940*. Berkeley: University of California Press.

Will, Barbara. 2001. "Gertrude Stein, Automatic Writing and the Mechanics of Genius." *Forum for Modern Language Studies* 37:169–175.

Wuthnow, Robert. 1989. *Meaning and Moral Order: Explorations in Cultural Analysis.* Berkeley: University of California Press.

Wuthnow, Robert. 1989. *Communities of Discourse.* Cambridge, MA: Harvard University Press.

IV. Islamic Stories

Florian Zemmin
A Secular Age and Islamic Modernism

1 Introduction

Why use *A Secular Age* for research on modern Islamic self-understandings?[1] After all, Taylor explicitly limits his story to what he imagines to be the West. The problems with this imagination as well as with the conceptual pairing of 'Islam' and the 'West' have been stressed in the introduction to this volume and need not be repeated.[2] What is important here is that modernity, even though it only evolved in the encounter among different regions, came to be epitomized by the West; that is, the understanding of modernity (self-)ascribed to the West became hegemonic for, or even conflated with, the understanding of modernity at large. Studies pointing to the power mechanisms at work in the construction and perpetuation of this Western hegemony are of course important. However, whether we deplore the fact or not, we cannot write power out of history.

Critiquing the hegemony of an imagined West as reflected in *A Secular Age* thus does not solve another, larger problem resulting from this hegemony: research on Islamic contexts is continuously forced to resort to Western theories and self-understandings, for there are no equally powerful Islamic versions of modernity or secularity. Simply assuming the validity of Western accounts beyond their original context is obviously not an option. Yet, the potential alternative, of inductively establishing Islamic (hi)stories of modernity via historical and empirical research, has a long way to go – due largely to a sheer lack of workforce and the vastness of the empirical field. A temporary solution to this dilemma is to use Western theory, history, or, in our case, self-understandings as a heuristic tool to shed light on Islamic contexts. It is in this sense that *A Secular Age* can fruitfully be applied to Islamic self-understandings.

For their remarks on various versions of this chapter, I would like to thank Colin Jager, Junaid Quadri, Frank Peter, Reinhard Schulze, and Johannes Stephan. Ariel Pate very much improved the English of this text.

1 Previous works using *A Secular Age* for research on Islamic and other non-Western contexts are Appleby (2011) and Madsen (2011). See soon: Bilgrami (forthcoming); Künkler, Madeley, and Shankar (forthcoming).
2 See pages 14–15.

In the second section of this chapter I elaborate why and in what sense I take *A Secular Age* to be a promising tool for research on modern Islamic self-understandings, and why I consider Taylor's story advantageous over other accounts. Briefly, it is because Taylor grasps the most profound background understandings of modernity – that is, background understandings common not only to believers and non-believers in the West but possibly also to non-Westerners. After all, as section three of this chapter suggests, Islam may be absent from *A Secular Age*, but it is very much present in our common secular age. If we agree that the endpoint of Taylor's narrative is sufficiently shared, then an understanding of developments in Islamic (hi)stories via Taylor's story becomes plausible. The general considerations of sections two and three also prepare the ground for the following case studies by Junaid Quadri and Johannes Stephan.

My own case study offers some first observations on the concept of 'society' in Islamic modernism. As I argue in section four, the broader relevance of these observations lies in the concept of 'society' reflecting the meta-norm of Taylor's modern social imaginaries, which underlie our self-understanding as living in a secular age. The Arabic term most pertinent for expressing the modern meaning of 'society' is *mujtamaʿ*. Section five analyzes the usage of *mujtamaʿ* in the journal *al-Manar* (Cairo, 1898–1940), widely considered to be the mouthpiece of Islamic modernism. I show that, contrary to previous assumptions, 'society' was already the dominant meaning of *mujtamaʿ* in the first issue of *al-Manar*. Moreover, familiarity with European thought greatly facilitated the usage of *mujtamaʿ* in this meaning. In turn, the authors writing regularly for *al-Manar* and especially the journal's editor, Rashid Rida advanced terms from within the Islamic discursive tradition as alternatives to *mujtamaʿ*, most conspicuously *umma*.

In the epilogue I suggest that the asymmetric power constellations of colonialism, with the West's claim of exclusivity for its version and genealogy of modernity, have generally made it harder for Muslim intellectuals to bring forward their own stories. This is why the authors of *al-Manar*, while understanding themselves historically, resorted to expressing distinctly modern understandings via the allegedly timeless essence of Islam.

2 *A Secular Age* as a heuristic tool

Two peculiarities of working with *A Secular Age* in general also apply to research on modern Islamic self-understandings: Firstly, *A Secular Age*, being the impressively rich and complex work that it is, can only be approached selectively. Working with instead of working on *A Secular Age* simply cannot do justice to all the complexities of Taylor's story. Thus the interdisciplinary task is not about getting

Taylor right (in all his details); it is rather about using *A Secular Age* to get one's primary object of study 'right,' that is, to grasp it more adequately and portray it more comprehensibly. Such an approach might sound unsatisfactory to participants in theoretical debates, who strive for consistency and systematization. However, because research on Islamic contexts must generally resort to theories elaborated in and for a Western context, sticking to these theoretical models wholeheartedly runs the danger of distorting one's own object of research. For this reason I advocate a pragmatic and selective usage of such theories as means, not ends unto themselves. Of course, not distorting the theory out of its original shape is desirable in order to facilitate conversation with other usages of this theory and possibly contribute to circumscribing the potentials and limits of the theory itself. Secondly, one also needs to address the fact that *A Secular Age* is not a theory in the conventional sense; it is a story containing both a descriptive and a normative level.

A major advantage of *A Secular Age* over most accounts of secularization and theories of secularity lies in Taylor's magisterial deconstruction of the oft-presumed binary between religion and secularism and between religious and secular stances.[3] Taylor convincingly shows what religious and secular modern Westerners fundamentally share: the idea of an immanent frame, which some – those believing in God – read as open and others – those believing that the immanent frame is all there is – as closed (ASA: 543–544; Taylor 2010a: 306–307). In this vein Scott Appleby (2011) has depicted Islamic fundamentalists as upholding an "open spin" of the immanent frame. Considering that the modern character of fundamentalists is often exclusively illustrated by their use of technology and media, this application of Taylor's concept offers a more foundational reading. A similarly powerful concept, which also shows the commonalities between seemingly adversarial positions, is the "fullness" to which all humans aspire (ASA: 5–12).

Both concepts, "the immanent frame" and "fullness," have been extensively criticized for their underlying Christian bias (Gordon 2008; Schweiker 2009; Connolly 2010; Sheehan 2010). Indeed, in the end Taylor does conceive of the immanent frame so that its "closed spin" appears as deficient, and fullness can only be truly achieved when it involves striving for something beyond this world. So Taylor is not speaking from nowhere – but who is? Taylor rightfully points to academia as the milieu where unbelief most clearly became the hegemonic option,

---

3 I am using 'secularization' for the process of making or becoming secular, 'secularity' as the description of the outcome of this process, and 'secularism' for normative positions advocating secularization.

with most academics reading the immanent frame as closed. This reading is even more dominant when it comes to theory-making, where personal beliefs are expected to be put aside: if one wants to presume an open reading, one has to do theology.

The secular bias of most academic disciplines has been acknowledged by secular theorists themselves, who saw it leading to blindness to religious phenomena, and therefore to a misconception of reality. However, these theorists, of whom Jürgen Habermas is a prominent example, trying to find more adequate theoretical models is not accompanied by abandoning their own personal stances, which still are discernable from their remodeled theoretical conceptions.[4] From the side of *believing* academics, meanwhile, reality certainly will not be portrayed more adequately by trying to subsume all secular knowledge production under a theological framework.[5] Here Taylor's book offers a far more constructive, integrated account that actually complements secular theories. Rejecting a religiously-informed conception, like Taylor's, due to its underlying bias – a charge that can, of course, go both ways – would prematurely inhibit this complementary potential. Secular research on religious topics in particular can benefit from resorting to Taylor's ideas, as they make the phenomena at hand more intelligible. In short, Taylor's depiction of modernity and secularity allows for the integration of religious phenomena – including Islamic ones – into a common framework of understanding.

Logically, there are four possible explanations for commonalities between Western and Islamic contexts: a) similar understandings[6] which have evolved autonomously in both contexts and then converged; b) an understanding evolved in mutual contact and exchange; c) hegemony of the Western understanding in an Islamic context; and d) vice versa. In reality, these explanations are not always clearly separable. At least since colonial times we would primarily expect a mixture of b) and c). For example, the idea of an 'us' living in an immanent frame evolved in distinction from a supposed Islamic other; yet, once this idea had became hegemonic, Muslim thinkers, too, had to at least refer to the immanent frame, even if in negation of it respectively of its closed spin. Thus, the immanent frame might not only be common to believers and unbelievers in the West, as Taylor has it, but also to Westerners and non-Westerners.

---

4 See the debate between Habermas and Taylor (2011).
5 See Milbank (1991) for a prominent example.
6 These possibilities would also hold true for historical phenomena; I use 'understanding' here because *A Secular Age*, and especially my usage of it here, is concerned less with empirical reality than with self-understandings.

Having shown the desirability of using *A Secular Age* as a heuristic tool for research on Islamic contexts, it remains to establish the plausibility of doing so. The less the secular age is confined to the West, the more similarities between Western self-understandings as depicted in Taylor's story and Islamic self-understandings we may suspect. And, indeed, I will now argue that while Islam is absent from the genealogy of secularity Taylor narrates, it is present in our common secular age.

3 Islam as absent from *A Secular Age* but present in the secular age

"Above all, I have neglected the way in which Western understandings of religion were informed through the pre-colonial and then the colonial encounter with other parts of the world [...]" (Taylor 2010a: 301). With this statement, Taylor early on in the debate on *A Secular Age* acknowledged a central criticism directed at the book, namely that the story of Latin Christian secularization can't be told without taking into account the contributions of Latin Christendom's others, both within and beyond the North Atlantic world. This point has been most forcefully argued by Saba Mahmood (2010). Mahmood advances another point of criticism, namely that the civilization Taylor limits his story to, which he alternately designates as "North Atlantic world," "Latin Christendom," or "the West," is not a given but itself a historical construction. This is why, "[t]he boundary Taylor draws around Latin Christendom is difficult, if not impossible, to sustain for both historical and conceptual reasons" (Mahmood 2010: 296). Taylor indeed rather uncritically adopts discursive categories that evolved from and strengthen Western hegemony; however, to be fair, he did not invent 'the West,' nor its hegemony, himself.

What is more, Taylor's intention in drawing a boundary around Latin Christendom is less to exclude others but rather to isolate this previously constructed civilization with the aim of better understanding it. Taylor advocates the idea of multiple modernities, according to which crucial features of modernity, most profoundly secularity, are constituted and expressed differently in different "civilizations" (ASA: 21; Taylor 2011a). He defends his decision to limit *A Secular Age* to the West as wanting to avoid premature universalization; only after an in-depth study of one civilization could one attempt comparisons with other contexts (ASA: 21; Taylor 2011a: 36–37). Taylor is quite consistent in his self-imposed limitation: there are only few allusions to the non-West on the pages of *A Secular Age*, most remarkably parallels between Christianity and Buddhism. The few times Islam is mentioned in Taylor's story, it is both as a counter-example (ASA: 102, 283, 419) and to illustrate commonalities (ASA: 154, 608, 781fn19). Unlike many contemporary debates on secularity, the central counter-foil to our contemporary Western societies in *A Secular Age* is not Islam but the West's own past,[7] and Taylor explicitly criticizes the othering of Islam for the sake of assuring one's own secularity (ASA: 770, 834fn19).

Then again, Taylor's interest in an understanding of a secularity allegedly specific to the West goes along with an exclusion of the non-West, including Islam. At the beginning of *A Secular Age*, Taylor names two common characterizations of secularity, secularity 1, the "emptying" of public spaces of God, or what more commonly would be termed social differentiation; and secularity 2, "the falling off of religious belief and practice" (ASA: 1–2). According to the latter understanding, the United States, Pakistan, and Jordan – exemplary cases for the West and the non-West – would be classed "as the same" (ASA: 3), and this is not the secularity of his interest. Taylor is interested in an understanding of secularity that brings out the specifics of Western societies, with Muslim societies serving as contrast cases. To him, the West's specific secularity (secularity 3) consists of the asserted fact that belief in God is no longer axiomatic but has become a mere option. If these supposedly *specific* characteristics then serve as the benchmark for whether "an age or society" is "secular or not" (ASA: 3), the answer is a given – only 'we'[8] are secular. Therefore, while Taylor names characteristics of secularity extending to the non-West, he advances an understanding that turns 'secularity' into a placeholder for 'our' alleged exclusivity.

However, while less obvious than regarding secularity 1 and 2, Taylor's own characterization is not all that exclusive to the West, either. One can hardly doubt the predominance of "secularity 1" throughout the Islamic world. Gudrun Krämer, in an article that also draws on Taylor, leaves no doubt that this is a historical fact: "A close look at modern political thought and practice (including notably Islamic discourse), economics, law, art and education would reveal that secularization processes form an integral part of Middle Eastern history and society" (Krämer 2013: 630). As Krämer notes, the question is rather how Muslims position themselves towards this factual secularity. Regarding secularity 2, the decline of religious beliefs and practices, Taylor himself has stated that the United States (as a crucial example of the West) is on the same level as Islamic countries Jordan and Pakistan (ASA: 3). The issue is indeed less clear regarding secularity

---

7 That is why Taylor cannot acknowledge historians' empirical claims that complicate his picture of past societies as holistically and harmoniously grounded in transcendence (Gordon 2008; Sheehan 2010).

8 For a complication of Taylor's "we," see Tester (2010).

3, the optionality of belief. Taylor of course has not settled on this understanding without reason, pointing out Muslim societies as clear counter cases. Yet even in Islamic societies, belief is no longer axiomatic; these societies might instead appear as counter cases because belief is the hegemonic *option*.

Let us approach this argument from its least controversial side: Nilüfer Göle has indisputably shown that migrant Muslims, especially in a European setting, use Islam as a means for *individual* "self-fashioning" (Göle 2010: 261).[9] As argued by Krämer (2013: 635), the spread of new media might also multiply the options available in Muslim majority societies. But unbelief as an option has not become available only recently. Samuli Schielke (2012: 302) reminds us that "nonreligion and atheism have long had supporters among Muslim peoples too." These supporters may be few in number, but contemporary Islamic revival movements should not deceive one into thinking that belief is axiomatic. Rather, these very movements testify to belief being an option, and, through failing to deliver on their comprehensive agenda, may even motivate people to embrace unbelief (Schielke 2012: 302). True, in Muslim majority societies, even fewer people are put in that "Jamesian open space" (ASA: 549, 551, 592) than in the West. But at least since the colonial era, a naive, unreflective belief has become unavailable to many milieux in Islamic societies.[10] Since then, religion as a basis for society has been disputed even more profoundly, with secularism, nationalism, and socialism representing major competitors to religious agendas.

This rough sketch suggests that while Islam is absent from Taylor's story, it does participate in our common secular age as conceived of in *A Secular Age*. The background understandings which, according to Taylor, made possible and continue to support the secular age, and which are more fundamental than the degree to which belief is an option, can therefore be used as heuristic tools for research on Islamic contexts. Interestingly, Taylor himself tentatively suggests Islam as the one tradition next to Western Christendom that produces a crucial landmark of his story, namely the division between a natural and a supernatural order (ASA: 781fn19). In the following two chapters of this volume, two other landmarks are addressed: Junaid Quadri shows the convergence of the Arabic term *dīn* with the modern concept of 'religion,' and Johannes Stephan identifies the idea of civilization and immanent progress in nineteenth century Arabic literature. My own case study offers observations on the concept of 'society' in Islamic modernism. The broader relevance of these observations lies in the con-

---

9 One could fully attribute this fact to the European environment; however, for cultural accounts stressing the importance of religious traditions, like Taylor's, Muslims within European societies are relevant signifiers of an Islamic self-understanding.
10 This is not only true for urban areas (Loeffler 1988).

cept of 'society' reflecting of the meta-norm of Taylor's modern social imaginaries.

4 Modern social imaginaries and the concept of 'society'

Working with *A Secular Age* in an Islamic context requires greater caution than in the Western context for which Taylor elaborated his story; still, most of Taylor's concepts and descriptions require testing for the West as well. This concerns fundamental concepts like the distinction between immanence and transcendence as well as empirical descriptions like the contemporary hegemony of secular stances.[11] It should be clear that such testing is only feasible for individual cases and not for the West or Islam in general. However, as I see it, counter-examples do not make Taylor's story meaningless, for it still speaks to us.[12] Remember that the landmarks of Taylor's story are not really situated on the level of empirical reality but rather capture a certain self-understanding. Taylor (2010a: 314) describes himself not as a historian but as "a mapper of social imaginaries."

A social imaginary consists of the most profound background understandings of how we make sense of ourselves and of our relations with others. While this background, which is normative insofar as it is regulating social life, cannot be clearly delimited, "one way of defining a social imaginary is as the kind of collective understanding that a group has to have in order to make sense of their practices" (2010a: 315). To Taylor it is different social imaginaries that most profoundly account for cultural differences across regions and ages. Taylor's multiple modernities are in the end due to multiple social imaginaries, with the modern Western imaginary differing from all previous imaginaries and from all non-Western imaginaries. It is the difference in imaginaries which allegedly makes 'us' secular and 'them' not. Discerning the modern Islamic social imaginary might therefore take Taylor's depiction of the West's allegedly specific imaginary (Taylor 2004; ASA: 159–211) as a starting point.

But before getting to the specifically modern social imaginary, I suggest departing from Taylor's general usage of the concept in two points: Firstly, Taylor

---

[11] Taylor (2010b: 411), in response to Hauerwas and Cole (2010), acknowledged that he portrayed immanence and transcendence in too binary a way. For an empirical questioning of Taylor's assessment of the dominance of secularism, see Miller (2008); Abbey (2010).
[12] Of course, not every Westerner sees her self-understanding adequately expressed by Taylor.

distinguishes social imaginaries from theories, for he aims to analyze the unreflectively-held background understandings of whole societies rather than only the reflective theories of elites. Yet surely the latter also hold a certain social imaginary – even when writing theories. This is to say, texts written by elites (and for most of human history, that is all texts) are valid sources for discerning a social imaginary. In the end, Taylor mainly relies on such texts too, positing that the modern social imaginary originated in theory.[13] Secondly, Taylor, in line with his broad focus on Western civilization at large, tends to speak of *the* social imaginary held by a society or "the Western social imaginary" (Taylor 2010a: 314). However, as tentatively acknowledged by Taylor himself in the discussions following *A Secular Age* (Taylor 2010c: 677–678; 2011b: 128), we can hardly expect a uniform imaginary throughout the West – nor, obviously, for all Muslims (but compare Barre 2012). A first attempt at discerning the modern Islamic imaginary should therefore limit itself to a rather specific group of people as the actual carriers of that imaginary (see Strauss 2006) and not claim validity for the Islamic civilization at large.

A promising starting-point for this attempt is a history of concepts: The usage and plausibility of concepts containing a normative dimension, whether explicitly defined or not, is supported by and depends on a social imaginary. As such, concepts provide a fruitful access point to intellectual history. My understanding of a concept follows Ophir's (2011) pragmatic approach, according to which we can turn any word into a concept by problematizing its meaning. Of course, some words as concepts are more fruitful than others. The immense potential of 'society' lies in the fact that it contains the meta-norm of Taylor's modern social imaginaries.

Taylor regards the Christian quest for a civilized order as crucial to the evolution of the modern social imaginary at large – which he illustrates via the three more specific imaginaries of the public sphere, market economy, and democratic self-rule. Beyond what its originators hoped for, the Christian quest for order made possible the idea of a purely immanent good order (Taylor 2010a: 305– 306). This immanent, self-sufficient order was seen as composed "of rights-bearing individuals, who are destined (by God or nature) to act for mutual benefit" (Taylor 2010a: 305). Taylor maintains that this new self-understanding was equally important for the rise of modern society as the social changes pointed out by Benedict Anderson, whose work on the construction of nations as "imagined communities" ([1983] 2006) has greatly influenced Taylor: "Modern society also required transformations in the way we figure ourselves as societies" (Taylor

---

13 On this aspect, see also the contribution by Bender in this volume (286fn4).

1998: 42). To this I wish to add that not only "the way" but the very fact *that* "we figure ourselves as societies" is specifically modern – hence the potential of the concept 'society' for discerning the modern imaginary.

Indeed, society is equally as imaginary as nation, whose evolution and spread Anderson has so brilliantly analyzed. The historicity and normativity of 'society' might be more obscure than with 'nation' due to the fundamental role society plays in our background understandings. We can hardly imagine our lives not taking place in society, and tend to project the concept of 'society' back across ages. Yet, rather than imaging their society differently, pre-modern people did not imagine their collectivity as society at all. For what Mary Poovey (2002: 125) has shown for 'the social' is equally true for 'society' as an abstract entity: it "has become thinkable [only] as part of the long history of reification that we call modernity." Phil Withington (2010) traces the origins of 'society' in sixteenth century England, a formative period for modernity at large (and indeed the evolution of 'society' was intrinsically connected with the evolution of 'modern' itself). The normative core of the concept of 'society' was to be a "voluntary and purposeful association" (Withington 2010: 12, 105) of free individuals. This normative core was maintained when the scope of 'society' was widened from individual corporations to society as an all-encompassing social sphere.

Thus the normative core of 'society' mirrors the meta-norm of Taylor's three social imaginaries, which consists of free individuals, voluntarily and purposefully assembling for mutual benefit. Indeed, Taylor once (ASA: 156) defines the social imaginary itself as "the ways we are able to think or imagine the whole of society." In this sense, *A Secular Age* is the story of the shifting background understandings about society, whose specifically modern understanding, I then add, is expressed by the concept of 'society.' In other words, what Taylor characterizes as specific for modern societies is in fact characteristic of 'society' *tout court*.

5 'Society' in *al-Manar*

As stressed above, one can hardly aim at discerning the modern social imaginary of Muslims at large, but only that of a specific group of people. The latter can, however, be selected so as to be representative of more general trends. This is the case with the group of authors around the journal *al-Manar*, which I have selected as the corpus of the following analysis for four reasons: Firstly, *al-Manar*, published in Cairo from 1898 to 1940, witnessed a formative period of modernity and distinguished itself from the vast number of short-lived newspapers and journals by virtue of its duration. Secondly, *al-Manar* presumably addressed the concept of 'society,' since the subtitle of the journal's first issue read, "a journal for the philosophy of religion and the affairs of human society and of civilization" (majalla fī falsafat al-dīn wa-shu'ūn al-ijtimāʿ wa-l-ʿumrān). Thirdly, al-Manar came to be widely acknowledged as *the* mouthpiece of Islamic modernism. The influence of *al-Manar* beyond Egypt and to the present day is well documented (see, for example, Azra 2008; Burhanudin 2005; Hamzawy 2004). According to their self-description, the Islamic modernists of *al-Manar* aimed at harmonizing or combining Islam and (Western) modernity. The perpetuation of this normative claim by secondary literature in seemingly neutral descriptions is not unproblematic, but for present purposes it is useful, as it suggests Islamic modernism as a location where we might find a vision of an Islamic modernity which interweaves aspects of European modernity and secularity with the Islamic discursive tradition. The fourth advantage of *al-Manar* is of a practical nature: the journal is available in an electronic version,[14] which allows for a comprehensive term search of its nearly 30,000 pages.

Before getting to this search, let me briefly outline the relevant setting of *al-Manar*. Clearly the authors of *al-Manar* were confronted with secularist claims. Some were of a practical nature, especially in the fields of politics, law, and education, not least because Egypt was occupied by England in 1882; but others were of an ideological nature, since European secularist, nationalist, and socialist ideas were present to and in fact adopted by Arab thinkers.[15] The Islamic modernists, at least in their writings, did not uphold secularist stances but were part of a secular situation insofar as their voices were among many in an increasingly diverse public sphere. This pluralization of stances is best mirrored by the diversification of newspapers and journals in the last decades of the nineteenth century (Ayalon 2010). Within this arena, *al-Manar* was clearly the most prominent "Islamic journal," a label by which it was known at the time (al-Hadi 1905). One recalls here the importance Benedict Anderson ([1983] 2006) attributes to print capitalism for the emergence of modern nations. Newspapers facilitate a sense of belonging and solidarity among people who have never met;

---

[14] The electronic version is available from al-Maktaba al-Shamila: http://shamela.ws/index.php/book/6947 (last accessed September 13, 2013); for information on this website, see Gilet (2010). This version proved reliable, except that it does not include the Qur'an commentary (*tafsīr*), which accounts for more than a fifth of the journal's overall content. I filled this gap by using an electronic version of the *tafsīr*, which was published separately later. This electronic version is available here: http://shamela.ws/index.php/book/12304 (last accessed October 28, 2013). I have crosschecked all passages identified via the electronic versions against the printed versions and quote only the latter. The printed version of the *tafsīr* I used is Rida (1948–1961).
[15] For the spread of leftist ideologies in *al-Manar*'s rival journals, see Khuri-Makdisi (2013).

they not only greatly support the nation as an imagined community, but also as a society.

Now, attempts to discern the specifically modern notion of society in *al-Manar* are facilitated by the fact that an Arabic term gained prominence to express this concept: *mujtamaʿ*. Talal Asad, with his ingenious grasp of epistemological shifts in the development of modernity, has pointed to the significance of the evolution of *mujtamaʿ*. He has written, in regards to the 1899 court reforms proposed by Muhammad ʿAbduh, the greatest modern Muslim reformist and a protagonist of *al-Manar*, that: "The modern Arabic word for society (*mujtamaʿ*) [was] not yet linguistically available, nor [was] the modern concept to which it now refers" (Asad 2008: 229). However, while a conceptual history of *mujtamaʿ* is still missing, there are hints that the term had already evolved to express the modern European concept of 'society' by the end of the nineteenth century: A series of Arabic encyclopedias, which provide examples for the usage of key terms and list Arabic expressions for European terms, do not list *mujtamaʿ* in the volume covering the years 1700 to 1890 (Dughaym 2000: 1365). This changes in the volume covering the years 1890 to 1940, which roughly coincides with the life span of *al-Manar*. Here, *mujtamaʿ* is listed as an expression of 'society' and its French pendant *société* (al-ʿAjm 2002: 1219). A telling example is given from a book by Ameen Rihani, a Lebanese emigrant to the United States, who wrote in 1910, "*al-Mujtamaʿ! Irfaʿūhu ʿalā al-ḥukūma wa-l-ḥukkām* [Society! Elevate it over the government and the rulers]" (al-Rihani 1956, 1: 190, taken from al-ʿAjm 2002: 944). The normative usage of society in this instance hardly requires elaboration. Ameen Rihani wrote in both English and Arabic, and his particular cultural position "between the 'West' and the 'East'" (Schumann 2008) might partially explain why we find an Arabic expression of 'society' in his works. Indeed, familiarity with European thought greatly facilitated the usage of *mujtamaʿ*, as the following analysis of *al-Manar* will demonstrate.

The search for *mujtamaʿ* in *al-Manar* produced a total of 358 instances. Not all of these, however, refer to society as an overall social sphere. Since these other cases are relevant for establishing the semantic range of *mujtamaʿ* and specifying which authors popularized the modern meaning of *mujtamaʿ* as 'society,' I will briefly summarize them here: In 19 cases the reference is to an assembly of something other than people, for example stars in a zodiac (al-Tunisi 1921: 218/21)[16] or a confluence of water (Rida 1898a: 176/11; 1930: 50/14); eight times a specific club or association is addressed, for example student clubs (Rida 1907: 933/21) or welfare organizations (Sidqi 1905: 778/22); twelve times

---

[16] References to instances of *mujtamaʿ* in *al-Manar* are by page/line.

mujtama' means 'place of assembly' (Rida 1899: 285/2) and 58 times it refers to the assembly itself, either to a gathering or get-together (Rida 1898b: 81/15–16, 82/7,9; 1902: 702/13); in 13 instances it is not clear which of the last two meanings is intended (Rida 1898c: 115/9; 1928: 468/3). Regarding an increase or decrease of the different usages over the lifespan of *al-Manar*, the only noteworthy trend is a declining usage of *mujtama'* in the sense of 'gathering.' For the meaning of 'society' no significant diachronic trend can be discerned;[17] however it is remarkable that 'society' was already the dominant meaning of *mujtama'* in the first issue of *al-Manar*. Moreover, as the term was used without any explanation, the authors seem to have assumed the readers' familiarity with its meaning society. This meaning continued to dominate throughout the journal's publication: in 138 cases *mujtama'* refers to (human) society in general, and in 110 cases a particular society or societies are addressed. I formed a separate category for these last cases, as here the specifically modern meaning becomes most obvious.

A first look at the authors[18] using *mujtama'* reveals a most interesting finding: *al-Manar*'s editor, Rashid Rida, who also wrote most of the journal's articles, accounts for 66 percent of the instances in which *mujtama'* does not mean society; his share of *mujtama'* as society in general is only 27 percent, and it drops to ten percent in cases when a particular society is addressed. Moreover, Rida's usages of *mujtama'* are of a rather scattered nature, as his 38 references to society in general are spread over 30 articles; and nowhere does Rida offer an explicit definition of *mujtama'*. The latter holds true for the other authors of *al-Manar*, too. Although not explicitly defined, the broader outlooks of the authors using *mujtama'* to mean 'society' suggests that the term *mujtama'* was embedded in and expressive of a broader social imaginary containing normative implications. One should add that while Rida used *al-Manar* for disseminating his own Islamic reformist ideas, he allowed for a variety of stances to be expressed in his journal and included articles that had been previously published elsewhere.

The one article (Muhaysin 1928) which most frequently uses *mujtama'* in the sense of society *in general* – 14 times – was first published in the journal *al-Siyasa*, the mouthpiece of the Liberal Constitutionalist Party (Hizb al-Ahrar al-Dusturiyin). This is also the only article to include *mujtama'* in its title. There are

---

17 Though one could interpret the declining usage of *mujtama'* as 'gathering' as an indicator that *mujtama'* came to mean 'society' more exclusively.

18 I defined the authorship of an occurrence of *mujtama'* as follows: The case is clear in an article originally written in Arabic and whose author uses *mujtama'* in his own words. I also attributed the term to the author of an article when he (all authors referred to here were male) used it while paraphrasing someone else. In cases of direct quotes, I assigned the instance to the writer being quoted.

25 instances in which *mujtamaʿ* is found in translations of European works. Most remarkable of these are the eleven cases to be found in the translation of *l'Émile du dix-neuvième siècle* (The Émile of the Nineteenth Century) by French writer and politician Alphonse Esquiros (1869). Esquiros was imprisoned in France in 1841 due to allegedly anti-religious views, yet the entire translation of his book on education, whose title draws on Rousseau's *Émile*, was published by *al-Manar*. Its translator, ʿAbd al-ʿAziz Muhammad, also once used *mujtamaʿ* to mean a particular association, rendering *l'Académie des sciences* as *al-mujtamaʿ al-ʿilmī* (*akadīmiyā*) (Muhammad 1901: 778/1–2; Esquiros 1869: 168). While this illustrates the different possible meanings of *mujtamaʿ*, Muhammad seems to have identified *mujtamaʿ* most closely with the meaning of society as overall social sphere since he chose the Arabic term *mukhālaṭa* when the French *société* referred to the company of people one is with (Muhammad 1901b: 741/12; Esquiros 1869: 159). The translation of Esquiros's *Émile* also accounts for ten of the 110 instances in which *mujtamaʿ* refers to a *particular* society or societies in the plural.

Particular societies referred to by the authors and worth mentioning here are "the modern civilized society" (*al-mujtamaʿ al-madanī al-ḥadīth*), "the Turkish society" (*al-mujtamaʿ al-turkī*), "the Arab society" (*al-mujtamaʿ al-ʿarabī*), "the European society" (*al-mujtamaʿ al-ūrūbī*), "Western societies" (*al-mujtamaʿāt al-gharbiyya*), and "the Islamic society" (*al-mujtamaʿ al-islāmī*). Again the authorship of these instances is remarkable: The reference to a specifically modern society is most clearly elaborated in an article by the Indian Muslim reformer Amir ʿAli, which was originally written in English and translated for Egypt's leading daily newspaper *al-Muʾayyad*, after which it was reprinted in *al-Manar* (ʿAli 1913). The concept of an Arab society first appears in *al-Manar* in 1919, in a translation of excerpts from the work *Psychologie politique* by French philosopher and sociologist Gustave Le Bon (Le Bon 1912; 1920). The only author who originally wrote in Arabic and referred to an Arab society or societies is ʿAbdallah ʿAnan in 1927. He also speaks of "Turkish society," "European society," "Western societies," and "Islamic society." All these instances appear in two articles first published in *al-Siyasa*. It certainly is no coincidence that ʿAnan translated the doctoral thesis of Taha Husayn, which was written under supervision of Émile Durkheim, a founding father of sociology (Husayn 1917; 2006 [1925]). The term *société* appears on every other page of Husayn's text. Whenever *société* is used to refer to society as an abstract entity (which mostly is the case), ʿAnan translated it as *mujtamaʿ*. Yet he prefers the Arabic term *jamāʿa*, when *société* refers to a specific group or organization (for example, Husayn 1917: 68–69; 1925: 58–59). This establishes the distinct meaning *mujtamaʿ* had acquired in circles familiar with European social thought in the first decades of the twentieth century.

With one exception (al-ʿAzm 1899: 867/24), the authors who regularly wrote for *al-Manar* refer to only one particular society by name: "the Islamic society." This composite occurs sixteen times in *al-Manar*,[19] with two instances originated by Rida. In one of those (Rida 1900: 757/9), Rida picks up a central topic of his overall writing when he portrays nationalism (*al-jāmiʿa al-waṭaniyya*) as a threat to the body of the Islamic society (*jism al-mujtamaʿ al-islāmī*) and to the religious bond (*al-rābiṭa al-dīniyya*). The one regular author who comes closest to defining features of an Islamic society is Hasan al-Banna. In 1928, al-Banna (1906–1949) founded the Muslim Brotherhood, the most influential movement of political Islam to date, under whose auspices the last volume of *al-Manar* appeared after Rida's death. In this volume from 1940, al-Banna tackles the relation between men and women in society. He stresses that Islam regards the mingling of men and women outside marriage as dangerous, since: "the Islamic society is a segregated society, not a joint society [*al-mujtamaʿ al-islāmī mujtamaʿ fardī/infirādī lā mujtamaʿ zawjī/mushtarak*]" (al-Banna 1940:767/7–8, 768/7–8). That we come closest to a definition of *mujtamaʿ* as society in the last volume of *al-Manar* suggests that the term was increasingly a focal point for debates about social order. However, immediately following this quote, al-Banna uses *mujtamaʿ* to mean gatherings or places of assembly, indicating that the term continued to hold multiple layers of meaning.

While these other meanings of *mujtamaʿ* should not be overlooked, the more important finding of this analysis remains that society was already the dominant meaning of *mujtamaʿ* in the first issue of *al-Manar* in 1898. Remember that according to Talal Asad, who ingeniously pointed to the epistemological shift expressed by the evolution of *mujtamaʿ*, the term did not acquire the meaning of society until later.[20] It is certainly true that the authors of *al-Manar* did not yet debate and argue over *mujtamaʿ* as a central concept. Nevertheless the authorship of the term as 'society' clearly indicates the channels through which this meaning gained prominence in Arabic. This suggests that the term was associated with implicit normative connotations, most likely those associated with 'society' in European languages, namely, a reified entity, autonomous from the state, in which free individuals interact for mutual benefit.

---

[19] There are two other occurrences of *al-mujtamaʿ al-islāmī*, however these refer to an Islamic association or assembly.
[20] Relying on dictionaries, Asad (2008: 198fn24) mentions the 1930s as the period when *mujtamaʿ* gained prominence.

That *al-Manar*'s editor and its most productive author, Rashid Rida, barely used *mujtama'* to mean 'society' could be read as his non-participation in the modern social imaginary expressed by the term. However, other facts speak against this reading: The turn to, and even primacy of, societal affairs has long been recognized as a central trait of Rida's reform efforts (Adams 1933: 187; Arslan 1933: 636/17; Haddad 2008). And Rida does stand out in his mostly positive references to sociology in *al-Manar*, accounting for 99 of the 132 occurrences of *'ilm al-ijtimā'*, the Arabic term for 'sociology.' I would therefore like to hypothesize that Rida expressed the modern social imaginary in terms other than *mujtama'*, most interestingly, *umma*.

We do know (Ayalon 1987: 26 – 28; Rebhan 1986: 24 – 35) that *umma* in the nineteenth century acquired the meaning of 'nation,' alongside its established meaning of 'community of believers;' yet before *mujtama'* was firmly established, *umma* might also have served to express the modern concept of society. Clearly, *umma* was a very flexible term at the turn of the twentieth century: Ahmad Fathi Zaghlul, in his translation of Demolins's *A quoi tient la supériorité des Anglo-Saxons* from 1899, indiscriminately uses *umma* for the original terms *nation, communauté, société*, and even *race* (Demolins 1897; 1899). In *al-Manar*'s first volume, Rida states that *mujtama'* and "civilized *umma*" (*al-umma al-mutamaddina*) are synonyms for the meaning of *al-sha'b* (the people) (Rida 1898d: 220/17). And in the same year, Rida twice writes that "the *umma* comes into existence (*tatakawwan*) by rallying around the beneficial (*al-ijtimā' 'alā l-intifā'*) and uniting to obtain what is desired (*al-ittiḥād 'alā l-murād*)" (Rida 1898e: 328/17 – 18). For Rida, *umma* might have provided an alternative discursive means for speaking about society. In other words, Rida did participate in the modern social imaginary, yet articulated it in an Islamic discourse. From within this discourse, of which *umma*, contrary to *mujtama'*, traditionally forms a part, Rida advocated an Islamic modernity that related an increasingly autonomous worldly sphere to a transcendental reality.

The foregoing exploration had two aims: Firstly, to show the potential of Taylor's modern social imaginaries to illuminate the fundamental commonalities between seemingly adverse positions. Secondly, to illustrate the potential of concept analysis for a preliminary grasp on these imaginaries. Of course, the more detailed contours of the modern social imaginary held by Rida and other Islamic modernists require a more specific analysis of their writings. An example of such an analysis is Richard van Leeuwen's (2008) analysis of Rida's theory of miracles. Translated into Taylor's framework, van Leeuwen shows how Rida aimed at clearing society's immanent frame of magic and transcendental interference, relegating religion to an autonomous sphere of its own. Further establishing the participation of Islamic modernists in our common secular age goes along with another question, namely whether the Islamic modernists, like Taylor, resorted to story-telling as a mode of advancing their particular vision of modernity.

6 Epilogue: Fundamentalism as a mode of appropriating modernity

Why does Charles Taylor tell a story? On the normative side he wants to show the Christian roots of our secular age, thereby rendering plausible the existence of a transcendent reality and strengthening the option of belief in a Christian God today. In regards to the underlying epistemology, Taylor's reason for resorting to story-telling is the assumption that "we (modern Westerners) can't help understanding ourselves in these terms [i.e. via master narratives]. I'm not claiming this for all human beings at all times" (Taylor 2010a: 300). Indeed, the Islamic modernists at the turn of the twentieth century did not narrate a continuous, autochthonic genealogy of modernity. Yet this was due less to a different epistemology than to colonial power structures. After all, why *can* Taylor tell the story he is telling? Why does his exclusivist Western story work, despite its lack of attention to the historical role of the non-West in shaping our present self-understandings? It only does work because of the West's political, economical, and cultural hegemony and seeming self-sufficiency.

Try to imagine being a modernist Muslim intellectual at the beginning of the twentieth century, like Rashid Rida, who wants to tell an exclusivist genealogy of an autochthonic Islamic modernity. He can't. That is, his story won't be very plausible or convincing, since Europe's contribution to the present state of affairs is too obvious to ignore. The potential alternative, telling a common story – which would probably best mirror historical reality – was inhibited by colonialists' exclusivist claims to modernity. Colonialists mainly upheld what Taylor terms "subtraction stories," the logic being that in Christendom reason has emancipated itself from the bonds of religion and this must happen in Islam, too. In Egypt, it was a minority of secularist thinkers who wholeheartedly embraced the Europeans' path and story of secularity as presented to them. At the other end of the spectrum, traditionalists did not pursue participating in modernity in the first place. The Islamic modernists, meanwhile, wanted to participate in modernity, but wanted their own Islamic version instead of following the allegedly areligious European model. In so doing they were buying into European subtraction stories when they maintained that in Christendom, the liberation from religious bonds was necessary to achieve modernity. They then argued that this was not true for Islam since its fundamentals, mainly the Qur'an, already contained all the positive aspects of modernity.

Rashid Rida and Muhammad 'Abduh, the protagonists of *al-Manar*, played a key role in the modern process of reification, which enforces focusing on the fundamentals or the alleged core of a religion (Tayob 2009; Jung 2011). In their search for appropriate answers to contemporary questions, they rejected the bulk of tradition, that is, of historically contingent elaborations, and instead focused on an alleged universal essence of Islam, which they saw embodied mainly in the Qur'an. In the Qur'an they distinguished between verses to be taken literally, especially those concerning matters of worship (*'ibādāt*), and verses in which God illustrated his intentions by clothing them in historically contingent examples. The latter concerns the vast realm of social affairs (*mu'āmalāt*), in which human reason was to elaborate answers appropriate for the present in light of God's underlying intentions. For this, the Sunna, the deeds and sayings of the prophet Muhammad, mainly served to elucidate the Qur'an. A third point of reference next to the Qur'an and Sunna were the pious forefathers of Islam (*al-salaf al-ṣāliḥ*), who allegedly alone truly enacted the word of God and lived the spirit of Islam. Due to their reference to the *salaf*, the Islamic modernists 'Abduh and Rida are also known as protagonists of the *salafiyya* (Lauzière 2010: 370). And in turn, this focus on the fundamentals of Islam earned some Islamic modernists, especially Rida, the label of 'fundamentalist.'

What might sound contradictory at first actually brings to light the Islamic modernists' mode of legitimizing and critiquing modernity: all the positive elements of modernity were already present in the fundamentals of Islam; the negative aspects of Western modernity are however absent. In other words, the Islamic fundamentals embody modernity in perfection. The envisioned modernity is most profoundly characterized by harmonizing religion and reason, spiritually guided ethics and material progress. Whereas in Christendom, reason had to free itself from religion, in Islam reason had always been free within a religious framework. Whereas Christianity did indeed necessitate secularization, Islam neither allows for nor requires secularization, as it has always been secular. 'Abduh (1313 h [1905/1906]), in a book first serialized in *al-Manar*, offers an elaborated version of this oft-recurring argument – although he, unlike contemporary Muslim reformers (Ramadan 1998: 59–61, 76–81, 114–115; 2001: 89–90, 261, 332–333), does not yet use the term 'secular' or its Arabic equivalent, *'almānī*. Now, this argument, which buys into the subtraction stories criticized by Taylor, is of course ahistorical and apologetic; yet it is also a way of appropriating modernity. Equally important, the Islamic modernists' use of Islamic points of reference and an Islamic discourse to address both religious and secular domains makes it harder to see the factual secularity of their thinking. Taylor (ASA:

736) refers to a similar problem regarding Christian thinkers turning to worldly affairs: "It became hard for many to answer the question, what is Christian faith about? The salvation of humankind, or the progress wrought by capitalism, technology, democracy?"

The fact that the Islamic modernists appropriated modernity via the Islamic fundamentals and thereby negated the supposed need for secularization – that is, for history – might support Taylor's consideration that story-telling is not a culturally universal mode. However, while the modernists were negating the need for one history (secularization) and one story (subtraction), they painted at least the contours of another story, which to pick up Taylor's term (ASA: 774), might be called an "Intellectual Deviation" story. The modernists needed an explanation for why, if the Islamic fundamentals had always contained modernity in perfection, Muslims were now lagging behind Europeans in so many fields. The answer was that Muslims had been betraying the Islamic message and teachings: even directly after the pious forefathers, political strife corrupted the Islamic community; and intellectual life came to a standstill in the thirteenth century, with most scholars blindly following tradition. Colonialism then arguably served as a wake-up call to return to the core teachings of Islam. While even in its longer version this narrative of deviation and its envisioned remedy does not match the complexity of Taylor's Reform Master Narrative, it does suggest that the Islamic modernists also resorted to (hi)story-telling to make sense of themselves and their present state of affairs.

Taylor and the Islamic modernists offer different narratives; they also differ on the aim of such narration, on the state of modernity itself, and on what an alternative modernity might look like. Nonetheless, there are remarkable commonalities between the two. Compare Taylor's intention to show the religious roots and essence of the present secular age with how Aziz al-Azmeh (1996: 106) summarized the basic goals of Islamic Reformism, of which modernism forms part: "Islamic Reformism was founded on the postulation of a possible equivalence between the reality of a secular age and normative religion: theorizing that, given its innate nature, normative religion preceded the reality of today, and consequently should reclaim today as its very own." If we hypothetically picture Rashid Rida walking into a book store with Taylor's story and a subtraction story on display, it seems rather clear which of the two he would have spent his money on, and which would have resonated more with his own understanding of modernity – that story may thus serve as a heuristic tool to better grasp this understanding today.

Bibliography

Abbey, Ruth. 2010. "*A Secular Age:* The Missing Question Mark," in *The Taylor Effect. Responding to a Secular Age*, ed. Ian Leask, Eoin Cassidy, Alan Kearns, Fainche Ryan, and Mary Shanahan, 8–25. Newcastle upon Tyne: Cambridge Scholars Publishing.
'Abduh, Muhammad. 1323 h [1905/1906]. *al-Islam wa-l-Nasraniyya maʿa al-ʿIlm wa-l-Madaniyya*. Cairo: Matbaʿat al-Manar.
Adams, Charles. 1933. *Islam and Modernism in Egypt. A Study of the Reform Movement Inaugurated by Muḥammad ʿAbduh*. London: Oxford University Press.
al-ʿAjm, Rafiq, ed., 2002. *Mawsuʿat Mustalahat al-Fikr al-ʿArabi wa-l-Islami al-Hadith wa-l-Muʿasir*, al-juzʾ al-thānī [vol. 2]: *1890–1940*. Beirut: Maktabat Lubnan Nashirun.
ʿAli, Amir. 1913. "al-Marʾa qabl al-Islam wa-baʿduhu." *al-Manar* 16: 933–941.
Anderson, Benedict. [1983] 2006. *Imagined Communities. Reflections on the Origin and Spread of Nationalism*, revised edition. London/New York: Verso.
Appleby, Scott R. 2011. "Rethinking Fundamentalism in a Secular Age," in *Rethinking Secularism*, ed. Craig Calhoun, Mark Juergensmeyer, and Jonathan VanAntwerpen, 225–247. Oxford: Oxford University Press.
Arslan, Shakib. 1933. "Kalimatan fi al-Shaykh Muhammad ʿAbduh wa-l-Sayyid Rashid Rida." *al-Manar* 33: 635–638.
Asad, Talal. 2008. *Formations of the Secular: Christianity, Islam, Modernity*. Stanford: Stanford University Press.
Ayalon, Ami. 1987. *Language and Change in the Arab Middle East: The Evolution of Modern Political Discourse*. New York: Oxford University Press.
Ayalon, Ami. 2010. "The Press and Publishing," in *The New Cambridge History of Islam*, vol. 6: *Muslims and Modernity; Culture and Society since 1800*, ed. Robert W. Hefner, 572–596. Cambridge: Cambridge University Press.
[al-ʿAzm, Rafīq.] 1899. "Man al-Masʾul, al-Hukuma am al-Shaʿb." *al-Manar* 1: 866–872.
al-Azmeh, Aziz. 1996. *Islams and Modernities*. London/New York: Verso.
Azra, Azyumardi. 2008. "The Transmission of *al-Manār*'s Reformism to the Malay-Indonesian World: the Case of *al-Imām* and *al-Munīr*," in *Intellectuals in the Modern Islamic World. Transmission, Transformation, Communication* ed. Stéphane A. Dudoignon, Komatsu Hisao, and Kosugi Yasushi, 143–158. London/New York: Routledge.
al-Banna, Hasan. 1940. "al-Marʾa al-Muslima (2)." *al-Manar* 35: 765–773.
Barre, Elizabeth A. 2012. "Muslim Imaginaries and Imaginary Muslims. Placing Islam in Conversation with *A Secular Age*." *Journal of Religious Ethics* 40 no. 1: 138–148.
Bilgrami, Akeel, ed., forthcoming. *Secularism Outside of Latin Christendom: Essays in Response to Charles Taylor*. New York: Columbia University Press.
Burhanudin, Tajat. 2005. "Aspiring for Islamic Reform: Southeast Asian Requests for *Fatwās* in *al-Manār*." *Islamic Law and Society* 12 no. 1: 9–26.
Connolly, William E. 2010. "Belief, Spirituality, and Time," in *Varieties of Secularism in a Secular Age*, ed. Michael Warner, Jonathan VanAntwerpen, and Craig Calhoun, 126–144. Cambridge, Mass: Harvard University Press.
Demolins, Edmond. 1897. *A quoi tient la supériorité des Anglo-Saxons*. Paris: Firmin-Didot.
Demolins, Edmond. 1899. *Sirr Taqaddum al-Injliz*, tarjamat [transl.] Ahmad Fathi Zaghlul. Cairo: Matbaʿat al-Maʿarif.

Dughaym, Samih, ed., 2000. *Mawsuʿat Mustalahat al-Fikr al-ʿArabi wa-l-Islami al-Hadith wa-l-Muʿasir*, al-juzʾ al-awwal [vol. 1]: *1700–1890*. Beirut: Maktabat Lubnan Nashirun.
Esquiros, Alphonse. 1869. *L'Emile du dix-neuvième siècle*. Paris: Librairie Internationale.
Gilet, Julien. 2010. "al-Maktaba al-Shamela." *Aldébaran, Collections numériques*, http://aldebaran.revues.orf/6597 (last accessed 30 September 2013).
Göle, Nilüfer. 2010. "The Civilizational, Spatial, and Sexual Powers of the Secular." in *Varieties of Secularism in a Secular Age*, ed. Michael Warner, Jonathan VanAntwerpen, and Craig Calhoun, 243–264. Cambridge, Mass: Harvard University Press.
Gordon, Peter E. 2008. "The Place of the Sacred in the Absence of God: Charles Taylor's 'A Secular Age'." *Journal of the History of Ideas* 69 no. 4: 647–673.
Habermas, Jürgen, and Charles Taylor. 2011. "Dialogue," in Judith Butler, Jürgen Habermas, Charles Taylor, and Cornel West, *The Power of Religion in the Public Sphere*, edited and introduced by Eduardo Mendieta and Jonathan VanAntwerpen; afterword by Craig Calhoun, 60–69. New York: Columbia University Press.
Haddad, Mahmoud. 2008. "The Manarists and Modernism. An Attempt to Fuse Society and Religion," in *Intellectuals in the Modern Islamic World. Transmission, Transformation, Communication*, ed. Stéphane A. Dudoignon, Komatsu Hisao, and Kosugi Yasushi, 55–73. London: Routledge.
al-Hadi, Shaykh bin Ahmad. 1905. "al-Manar al-Islami wa-l-Liwaʾ al-Watani." *al-Manar* 8: 478–479.
Hamzawy, Amr. 2004. "Exploring Theoretical and Programmatic Changes in Contemporary Islamist Discourse: The Journal *al-Manar al-Jadid*," in *Transnational Political Islam. Religion, Ideology and Power* ed. Azza Karam, 120–146. London/Sterling, Virginia: Pluto Press.
Hauerwas, Stanley, and Romand Coles, "'Long Live the Weeds and the Wilderness Yet': Reflections on *A Secular Age*." *Modern Theology* 26 no. 3: 349–362.
Husayn, Taha. 1917. *La philosophie sociale d'Ibn-Khaldoun*. Paris: A. Pedone.
Husayn, Taha. 1925. *Falsafat Ibn Khaldun al-Ijtimaʿiyya: Tahlil wa-Naqd*, trans. Muhammad ʿAbd Allah ʿAnan. Cairo: Matbaʿat al-Iʿtimad.
Jung, Dietrich. 2011. *Orientalists, Islamists and the Global Public Sphere: a Genealogy of the Modern Essentialist Image of Islam*. Sheffield/Oakville: Equinox.
Khuri-Makdisi, Ilham. 2013. "Inscribing Socialism into the *Nahḍa: al-Muqtaṭaf, al-Hilāl*, and the Construction of a Leftist Reformist Worldview, 1880–1914," in *The Making of the Arab Intellectual (1880–1960): Empire, Public Sphere and the Colonial Coordinates of Selfhood*, ed. Dyala Hamzah. 63–89. London: Routledge.
Krämer, Gudrun. 2013. "Modern but not Secular: Religion, Identity and the *ordre public* in the Arab Middle East." *International Sociology* 28 no. 6: 629–644.
Künkler, Mirjam, John Madeley, and Shylashri Shankar, eds., forthcoming. A Secular Age Beyond the West.
Lauzière, Henry. 2010. "The Construction of Salafiyya: Reconsidering Salafism from the Perspective of Conceptual History." *International Journal of Middle East Studies* 42: 369–389.
Le Bon, Gustave. 1912. *La Psychologie politique et la Défense sociale*. Paris: Ernest Flammarion.
Le Bon, Gustave. 1920. "Namudhaj min Kitab *al-Falsafa al-Siyasiyya*," tarjamat [trans.] ʿAbd al-Basit Efendi Fath Allah al-Bayruni. *al-Manar* 21: 345–53.

Loeffler, Reinhard. 1988. *Islam in Practice: Religious Beliefs in a Persian Village*. New York: State University of New York Press.
van Leeuwen, Richard. 2008. "Islamic Reformism and the Secular: Rashid Ridâ's Theory on Miracles," in *Religion and Its Other. Secular and Sacral Concepts and Practices in Interaction*, ed. Heike Bock, Jörg Feuchter, and Michi Knecht, 64–78. Frankfurt am Main: Campus.
Madsen, Richard. 2011. "Secularism, Religious Change, and Social Conflict in Asia," in *Rethinking Secularism*, ed. Craig Calhoun, Mark Juergensmeyer, and Jonathan VanAntwerpen, 248–269. Oxford: Oxford University Press.
Mahmood, Saba. 2010. "Can Secularism Be Other-wise?" in *Varieties of Secularism in a Secular Age* ed. Michael Warner, Jonathan VanAntwerpen, and Craig Calhoun, 282–299. Cambridge, Mass: Harvard University Press.
al-Manar. Cairo: Matbaʿat al-Manar, vols. 1 (1315 h [1898]) – 35 (1358 h [1940]).
Milbank, John. 1991. *Theology and Social Theory: Beyond Secular Reason*. Cambridge: Blackwell.
Miller, James. 2008. "What Secular Age?." *International Journal of Politics, Culture, and Society* 21 no. 1: 5–10.
Muhammad, ʿAbd al-ʿAziz. 1901a. "Amil al-Qarn al-Tasiʿ ʿAshar." *al-Manar* 3: 771–788.
Muhammad, ʿAbd al-ʿAziz. 1901b. "Amil al-Qarn al-Tasiʿ ʿAshar." *al-Manar* 3: 737–743.
Muhaysin, Hamid Mahmud. 1928. "al-ʿUquba fi al-Islam laysat Taqriran li-Nazariyyat al-Intiqam: al-Mujtamaʿ la budda li-Nizamihi min Tashriʿ al-ʿUqubat." *al-Manar* 29: 299–308.
Ophir, Adi. 2011. "Concept." *Political Concepts – A Critical Lexicon* 1, http://www.political concepts.org/2011/concept (last accessed February 12, 2014).
Poovey, Mary. 2002. "The Liberal Civil Subject and the Social in Eighteenth-Century British Moral Philosophy." *Public Culture* 14 no. 1: 125–145.
Ramadan, Tariq. 1998. *Les musulmans dans la laïcité: responsabilités et droits des musulmans dans les sociétés occidentales*. Lyon: Tawhid.
Ramadan, Tariq. 2001. *Islam, the West and the Challenges of Modernity*, trans. Saïd Amghar. Leicester: The Islamic Foundation.
Rebhan, Helga. 1986. *Geschichte und Funktion einiger politischer Termini im Arabischen des 19. Jahrhunderts (1798–1882)*. Wiesbaden: Otto Harrassowitz.
Rida, Rashid. 1898a. "al-Shiʿr wa-l-Shuʿaraʾ." *al-Manar* 1: 170–177.
Rida, Rashid. 1898b. "al-Mawalid aw al-Maʿarid." *al-Manar* 1: 79–87.
Rida, Rashid. 1898c. "Kayfa al-Sabil?!." *al-Manar* 1: 112–119.
Rida, Rashid. 1898d. "Sayhat Haqq." *al-Manar* 1: 217–225.
Rida, Rashid. 1898e. "Mashruʿ Sikkat Hadid bayna Bur Saʿid wa-l-Basra." *al-Manar* 1: 318–331.
Rida, Rashid. 1889. "Athar ʿIlmiyya Adabiyya: al-Kitaban al-Jalilan." *al-Manar* 2: 282–286.
Rida, Rashid. 1900. "al-Hayra wa-l-Ghumma wa-Manashiʾuhuma fi al-Umma." *al-Manar* 2: 753–758.
Rida, Rashid. 1902. "Bab al-Asʾila wa-l-Ajwiba." *al-Manar* 5: 699–703.
Rida, Rashid. 1907. "Khutbat al-Duktur Diyaʾ al-Din Ahmad," *al-Manar* 9: 933–939.
Rida, Rashid. 1928. "Haqaʾiq fi ʿAdawat Malahidat al-Turk li-l-Islam." *al-Manar* 29: 464–474.
Rida, Rashid. 1930. "Fatawa al-Manar," *al-Manar* 31: 46–58.

Rida, Rashid. 1948–1961. *Tafsir al-Qur'an al-Hakim, al-Mushtahar bi-Tafsir al-Manar*, 12 vols. Cairo: Maktabat al-Qahira.
al-Rihani, Amin. [1910] 1956. *al-Rihaniyyat*, 2 vols. Beirut: Dar al-Rihani li-l-Tiba'a wa-l-Nashr.
Schielke, Samuli. 2012. "Being a Nonbeliever in a Time of Islamic Revival: Trajectories of Doubt and Certainty in Contemporary Egypt." *International Journal of Middle East Studies* 44: 301–320.
Schumann, Christoph. 2008. "Within or Without? Ameen Rihani and the Transcultural Space between the 'West' and the 'East'," in *Liberal Thought in the Eastern Mediterranean: Late 19th Century until the 1960s*, ed. Christoph Schumann, 239–266. Leiden/Boston: Brill.
Schweiker, William. 2009. "Our Religious Situation: Charles Taylor's *A Secular Age*." *American Journal of Theology & Philosophy* 30 no. 3: 323–329.
Sheehan, Jonathan. 2010. "When Was Disenchantment? History and the Secular Age," in *Varieties of Secularism in a Secular Age*, ed. Michael Warner, Jonathan VanAntwerpen, and Craig Calhoun, 217–242. Cambridge, Mass: Harvard University Press.
[Sidqi, Muhammad Tawfiq.] 1905. "al-Din fi Nazr al-'Aql al-Sahih (6)." *al-Manar* 8: 771–783.
Strauss, Claudia. 2006. "The Imaginary." *Anthropological Theory* 6 no. 3: 322–344.
Tayob, Abdulkader. 2009. *Religion in Modern Islamic Discourse*. London: Hurst.
Taylor, Charles. 1998. "Modes of Secularism," in *Secularism and Its Critics*, ed. Rajeev Bhargava, 31–53. New Delhi: Oxford University Press.
Taylor, Charles. 2004. *Modern Social Imaginaries*. Durham/London: Duke University Press.
Taylor, Charles. 2010a. "Afterword: Apologia pro Libro suo," in *Varieties of Secularism in a Secular Age*, ed. Michael Warner, Jonathan VanAntwerpen, and Craig Calhoun, 300–321. Cambridge, Mass: Harvard University Press.
Taylor, Charles. 2010b. "Challenging Issues about the Secular Age." *Modern Theology* 26 no. 3: 404–416.
Taylor, Charles. 2010c: "Charles Taylor replies [to Tester (2010)]." *New Blackfriars* 91 no. 1036: 677–679.
Taylor, Charles. 2011a. "Western Secularity," in *Rethinking Secularism*, ed. Craig Calhoun, Mark Juergensmeyer, and Jonathan VanAntwerpen, 31–53. Oxford: Oxford University Press.
Taylor, Charles. 2011b. "Response." *The Australian Journal of Anthropology* 22: 125–133.
Tester, Keith. 2010. "Multiculturalism, Catholicism and Us." *New Blackfriars* 91 no. 1036: 665–676.
[al-Tunisi, Muhammad al-Khidr]. 1921. "al-Khayal fi l-Shi'r al-'Arabi (2)." *al-Manar* 22: 218–227.
Withington, Phil. 2010. *Society in Early Modern England. The Vernacular Origins of Some Powerful Ideas*. Cambridge/Malden: Polity.

Junaid Quadri
Religion as Transcendence in Modern Islam: Tracking "Religious Matters" into a Secular(izing) Age

1 Introduction

In his remarkably erudite account of the intellectual wellsprings of this, our secular age, Charles Taylor rightly notes that any attempt to describe the modern world's secularity necessarily runs up against the question of how to define its complement, 'religion.' For his part, Taylor settles on defining religion through the concept of the transcendent, in which an individual's quest for "fullness" is oriented towards something beyond the self, and indeed beyond human life altogether (ASA: 15).[1] The secular age, for Taylor, is precisely the period in our history when this sensibility ceases being uncontroversial background, and instead becomes one among a range of options, a range already heavily conditioned by its being situated within the "immanent frame" that structures our modern life.

In offering this definition for 'religion,' however, Taylor is keen to point out that he restricts his analysis to the Western (or North Atlantic, or Latin Christian) world. This decision, taken in the spirit of a certain intellectual humility and a keen awareness of the specificity of his study, has the virtue of allowing Taylor to avoid undue and historically fraught generalizations of what constitutes religion elsewhere.

His reticence in this regard, however, has been criticized by a number of commenters who find in his characterization of 'the West' a hermetically sealed and self-sufficient unity that belies its involvement in other parts of the world, especially through missionary and colonial adventure. Saba Mahmood, for example, has observed, "Not only did the discovery of and subsequent knowledge produced on other religious traditions serve as the mirror against which European Christianity fashioned itself, but the very concept of 'religion' – its conceptual

---

For their comments on this paper, I would like to thank Alexandre Caeiro, Bilal Ibrahim, Colin Jager, Nermeen Mouftah, Nathan Spannaus, and Florian Zemmin.

1 For a critique of the straight-forward identification of "religion" and "transcendence" as anachronistic, see Casanova 2010: 274–275.

contours, its classificatory system and attendant calculus of inferior and superior civilizations – was crafted within the crucible of this encounter" (2010: 286). Similarly, José Casanova points out that "the very pattern of Western secularization cannot be fully understood if one ignores the crucial significance of the colonial encounter in European developments" (2010: 277). Even stronger is the claim made by Markus Dressler and Arvind-Pal S. Mandair, who find that Taylor's genealogy does not simply draw an untenably impermeable border between civilizations, but is in fact invested in a "Western imaginary ... [which] hinges on the belief that there is an essential historical difference between the West and the non-West" (2011: 4).

That Taylor posits a difference between the two, and attends insufficiently to their mutual entanglement, is no doubt an important point, and it is one that has been ably, and amply, made. Indeed, Taylor himself has responded to these criticisms by conceding this as a gap in what is otherwise a sprawling genealogy of our modern subjectivities (2010: 301). This paper, however, considers what else may be sidelined by Taylor's editorial decision to bracket out the 'non-West.' Like Taylor's critics, I too want to re-insert the colonial experience into his account, though I wish to do so 'on the other end,' so to speak – by tracing what sort of conceptual reconfiguring this momentous intellectual shift in the West proceeded to make possible, or indeed necessary, for colonized peoples and knowledge traditions. To use Taylor's language, I am interested in investigating the changes in the "context of understanding" experienced by colonized peoples as a result of encounters with this specific notion of religion-as-transcendence, and the way in which it formed the basis for modern Muslim understandings of their own tradition. It is no doubt true, as Peter van der Veer (2001) has argued, that the modern category of 'religion' was formed in no small part through the Western encounter with certain constitutive others, but it is no less significant that this conceptual terrain found its way from the Western cultural complex, where it came to unparalleled prominence, to other societies, where it often supplanted – or at least heavily conditioned – other, older ways of thinking about the spheres of life we today associate with religiosity.[2] As Casanova has

---

[2] Van der Veer prefers to speak in the language of transformations as a result of interaction between metropole and colony, rather than the replacement of the "ancient East" by the "modern West." I share with him his interest in examining how older vocabularies and resources get deployed in new ways to make room for a modern concept of religion, and also use the word "transformations" as a descriptor for the conceptual shifts I study. However, because I find that these vocabularies and resources were subjected to new knowledge regimes as a result of a lopsided power imbalance that shifted the very ground on which these discussions were

noted, "one of the most important global trends is the globalization of the category of 'religion' itself and of the binary classification of reality, 'religious/secular,' that it entails" (2011: 62).[3] Put simply, then, I am interested in the question of how well Taylor's account travels to the Muslim world.

Using his conception of religion "in the secular age" as being concerned with transcendence in a world increasingly dominated by immanence, I track the changing meanings of the category of the *umūr dīniyya* – which we may provisionally translate as "religious matters," noting that it is precisely the instability of the term 'religious' that is of concern to us in the paper – in Islamic legal writing into the modern period. This approach draws inspiration, too, from Talal Asad's suggestion that the most fruitful way of coming to an understanding of terms as slippery as 'religion' and 'secular' is by "attend[ing] more closely to the historical grammar of concepts and not to what we take as signs of an essential phenomenon" (2003: 189).[4]

2 Immanence and transcendence in Islamic law: pre-modern conceptions

In the fall of 1910, the Khedive of Egypt, ʿAbbas Hilmi II (r. 1892–1914), received a telegram from Aswan informing him that a local judge had authenticated a testimony claiming that the crescent had been sighted, signalling the end of the fasting month of Ramadan. The Khedive, in turn, sent word to Muhammad Bakhit al-Mutiʿi (d. 1935), the head of the shariʿa court in Alexandria, asking him for his learned opinion on the appropriateness of acting upon a telegraph report in such a matter. Bakhit responded that it should indeed be acted upon, and after further consultation with the head judge in Cairo, cannons were sounded declaring the end of fasting and the beginning of the Eid festival.

Though it seems to have been a matter of consensus within the judicial establishment, this decision nevertheless gave rise to a minor controversy in Egypt,[5] motivating Bakhit to write a treatise justifying his position.[6] His argu-

---

being had, speaking of them also as supplantations rather than as shared ventures does not seem to me inappropriate.
3 See also Casanova 2010, 277.
4 See also his insistence in an earlier work on understanding the concept of religion by attending to its location within history and fields of power instead of as "a transhistorical and transcultural phenomenon" (Asad 1993: 28).
5 According to Bakhit, the same controversy was also current "in a region of India" at the time, prompting a separate request for guidance from a prominent Egyptian businessman in cosmo-

mentation in this treatise, in turn, permits us a window through which to better understand the changing connotations of the term *dīn* (from which we get the *umūr dīniyya* mentioned above) in Islamic legal thinking. In particular, the text reveals a shift from a complex notion of *dīn* as understood in terms of both transcendent and immanent concerns, to one defined exclusively in terms of transcendence.

In order to understand how this shift occurs in the thought-world of Islamic law (*fiqh*), it is important to take a step back and think about an intriguing distinction made by some pre-modern Muslim jurists, in particular those who, like Bakhit, were associated with the Ḥanafī school of jurisprudence (*madhhab*).

Virtually any conveying of a message is classified in *fiqh* works as a "report" (*khabar*). The two major sub-divisions subsumed by this category are (i) narrations (*riwāyāt*), the pre-eminent exemplars of which are the Prophetic traditions famously known as hadiths; and (ii) in-court testimonies (*shahādāt*), which, in a legal system that was (at least in theory) suspicious of written documentation, encompassed much of the proceedings of a court: statements by a witness, but also confessions, claims, advisory opinions (fatwas) and even legal verdicts. These two subtypes were mutually exclusive, and though they did not constitute opposites in the strict sense of the word, they were often framed as contraries, placed in opposition to one another because the validity of each depended on conditions which were explicitly portrayed as being in contradistinction to those of the other. For a narration to be accepted, the only requirement was that the narrator be morally upright, while testimonies demanded the fulfillment of a series of conditions, namely that they be given in court by at least two free males who had not been previously punished for slander, specifying a particular claim in formulaic language. Scholars who tried to systematize these loose descriptions by defining an "essence" for these categories were often met with frustration. The famous jurist al-Qarafi (d. 1285), for example, laments that he spent eight years trying to determine the precise nature of the distinction between narrations and testimonies without being satisfied with the answers given him (1998, 1:12–13).[7]

---

politan Medina who had encountered expatriates from this region disputing over the matter (Bakhit [1911] 2000, 16–17).

6 This is the *Irshad Ahl al-Milla ila Ithbat al-Ahilla*, first published by Matbaʿat Kurdistan in Cairo (1911), and recently edited by Hasan Ahmad Isbir (Beirut: Dar Ibn Hazm, 2000).

7 He criticizes as unsatisfactory responses to his attempts to figure out "the essence of this distinction" which simply list the different conditions for each. Listing the conditions, he says, "is subsidiary to the conceptualization [of the category itself] ... If we know the rulings and effects

In the Ḥanafī school, however, these two types did not exhaust the set of *khabar*s. There existed also a little-used hybrid category which was thought not to be adequately captured by either of the first two, though it "resembled" both of them in certain aspects. This is the category in which we find the *umūr dīniyya* ("religious matters"), the most prominent example of which was a claim by an individual that he or she had sighted the new moon that signalled the onset of the month of Ramadan. (Note that this is different than the case that confronted Bakhit in 1910, in which he was asked to pronounce on the *end* of Ramadan, and the beginning of the new month of Shawwal. This is a significant difference, as these latter reports were categorized as testimonies and not "religious matters" by pre-modern scholars, a characterization that, as we will see below, was disputed by Bakhit.)

Pre-modern Ḥanafī jurists envisioned the Ramadan case as being a "religious matter" which participated in each of the two main sub-categories discussed above. It was a narration in that it demanded a certain moral probity of the narrators involved, and it was a testimony insofar as the entire process was regulated through the legal authority of courts: the claim was to be presented before a judge (qadi), who was authorized to assess and pronounce on its validity. So, as opposed to other schools, which did not recognize the intermediate category whatsoever and so thought of such reports as simply narrations that circulate, like hadiths, outside the courts, the role of the judge was central in the Ḥanafī school, and could only be sidestepped in exceptional cases. Indeed, this is why leading scholars of other schools sometimes mistook the Ḥanafī position to simply be an uncontroversial instance of the standard legal process (al-Subki 2000: 59).[8]

Deeming the sighting of the Ramadan moon a "religious matter" incorporates two important semantic ranges of the term *dīn*. On the one hand, pre-modern dictionaries prominently include words for a legal judgement, ruling or sentence (*al-qaḍāʾ, al-ḥukm*) under *dīn*.[9] This, as Wilfred Cantwell Smith has pointed out, is an ancient Semitic root with a long history in the Middle East (1964: 94).[10] At the same time, *dīn* is also connected to the notion of proper conduct, obedience or ritual worship (*ʿibāda, ṭāʿa, waraʿ*) (Smith 1964: 94; Glei and Reichmuth

---

[attached to the category], which cannot be known before one knows [the category itself], we have circularity (*al-dawr*)."

8 For an extended reading of Subki's confusion on the matter of whether these reports are thought by Ḥanafīs to be within the ambit of the qadi's judgement (*dukhūl taḥt al-ḥukm*), see Quadri 2013: 148–154.

9 See, for example, al-Thanawi 1899, s.v., *dīn*; Firuzabadi [1925?], s.v., *dīn*.

10 See also Glei and Reichmuth, 2012: 250.

2012: 251). Thus, the connection between the sighting of the new moon and the initiation of the ritual act of fasting means that the former can easily be subsumed under the meaning of *dīn* as pertaining to ritual worship. On this reading, the *umūr dīniyya* could be understood as incorporating (though, as we will see below, not exhausted by) transcendence in the sense that they were oriented towards God and the afterlife – the technical term *diyāna*, derived from the same root as *dīn*, was often explained by the phrase "that which is between man and God" (*mā baynahu wa-bayna Allāh*) (al-Tahanawi, 1899). In contrast to this, *shahādāt*-reports were concerned with adjudicating between rival parties (*khuṣūma*) on "worldly" (*dunyawī*) matters.[11]

This long-standing Ḥanafī distinction between the 'other-worldly' and 'worldly' is one that should be familiar to modern ears. In the field of law, it provided the ground for the distinction drawn by pre-modern jurists between the moon-sightings at the beginning and end of Ramadan, respectively. The sighting on the eve of the month was, as we have indicated, associated with ritual concerns directed towards God's pleasure and rewards in the afterlife; whereas the one marking the end of the month was traditionally taken to be a simple *shahāda*-report either because it signified a licence to engage in the "worldly benefits" prohibited during Ramadan daylight hours: eating, drinking, sexual activity; or because it pertained to "the rights of people (*ḥuqūq al-ʿibād*)" (al-Sarakhsi, n.d., 3:139).

Importantly, however, this characterization of the Ramadan moon-sighting as one of the *umūr dīniyya* was not understood by the Ḥanafīs as a reason to exclude it from the mundane regulation of the courts. Indeed, for Ḥanafīs, the meanings for *dīn* that signified legal process and judgement (*al-qaḍāʾ*) seemed to be no less a constituent element of what was nonetheless considered a "religious matter." Because of their hybrid resemblance to both narrations and testimonies, the *umūr dīniyya* on this older understanding, were no less concerned with the immanent ("within human life," on Taylor's formulation) as they were with the transcendent.

Consider, for example, the following question of jurisdiction regularly mentioned in the books of the Ḥanafī school for centuries. The dominant position was that a sighting of the crescent in a given city was binding upon all people, even those who lived in other cities. The classic statement of the school can be found in the fifteenth-century text, *Fath al-Qadir:* "The sighting of the people in the West obligates the people of the East [to follow it] according to the dominant

---

[11] For a characterization of the *shahādāt* in this manner, see Ibn al-Shatt, *Idrar al-Shuruq ʿala Anwaʾ al-Furuq* on the margins of al-Qarafi 1998: 20.

position of the school" (Ibn al-Humam, n.d., 2:313–314). Even before the invention of the telegraph, however, this position inescapably gave rise to the question of how the transmission of this sighting was to be authenticated. At least for the Ḥanafīs, the report that conveyed the original sighting of the "people in the West" had to satisfy a strict procedure of transmission structured around testimonies offered in court settings. This was known as the *ṭarīq mūjib* ("the method that legitimately obliges"). Ibn al-Humam (d. 1457), the author of *Fath al-Qadīr*, specifies very precisely what this procedure looks like:

> Had [at least two witnesses] testified that two people had in turn testified, in the presence of the judge of the other town, to sighting the new moon, and that that judge had ruled in favour of their testimony, it would have been permissible for *this* judge [in *this* town] to also rule in favour of their testimony. This is because the ruling of a judge is a conclusive proof, and [this second group] has borne witness to it. (2:314)

Transmissions that did not satisfy these stringent procedures could be easily dismissed as mere "accounts," not proper testimonies, and so were to be disregarded. Indeed, what emerges from a reading of the pre-modern tradition is that the judge was empowered to discount all sorts of reports for reasons of procedure, even in cases where there were good reasons to judge the content of the report as true.[12] The *umūr dīniyya*, then, though they were directed towards the transcendent, were still governed by a logic of immanence.[13]

---

12 Indeed, Ibn al-Humam has precisely such a situation in mind when he lays out the acceptable procedure in the quote above. Consider the case in which two localities begin Ramadan on different days because one sighted the new moon a day before the other, the latter initially unaware of the former's decision. Towards the end of the month, news reaches the latter town of the earlier sighting: "Those who saw the new moon later are only obliged to act [on the earlier sighting] if it is established among them by way of a *ṭarīq mūjib*. This, to the extent that if a group of people testify that the people of such-and-such a city saw the new moon of Ramadan a day before you ... if [the town receiving the news] does not sight the Shawwal crescent that night, it is not permissible for them to [celebrate] the Eid the next day" (2:314).

13 A note about Taylor's terminology may be warranted here. In Taylor's discussions, the opposed terms of transcendence and immanence are invoked within the context of his characterization of the secular age as that in which religious belief in a transcendent power has become but one among a number of options to locate what he calls "fullness." This language is very much about a life journey oriented towards gaining proximity towards the site of this fullness in order to imbue one's life with meaning. There is something of a gap between this specific context and the manner in which I invoke these concepts, and the distinction between them, to speak of a rather mundane legal problem. I am, as will have been evident, not as interested in questions of belief as Taylor, but rather of conditions of experience that this way of looking at the problem opens up. This latter is Taylor's central concern in the book. Furthermore, even by Taylor's lights, it is too restrictive to imagine these categories as concerned exclusively with

3 Semantic and conceptual shifts in the modern period

By the time Bakhit revisited this question in 1910, however, circumstances had changed considerably. Egypt had been under British occupation since 1882, and colonial administrators felt a keen responsibility to remake Egypt into a productive, orderly state, a burden that is well-captured in their writings. For figures like Lord Cromer, British agent and consul-general from 1883 to 1907, the prevailing legal system was one of the central targets of reform.[14] Cromer was particularly concerned that Islam "crystallises religion and law into one inseparable and immutable whole, with the result that all elasticity is taken away from the social sphere" ([1908] 2000: 135). This preoccupation resulted in a re-organization of the Egyptian court system in accordance with secular presumptions – a truncation of the jurisdiction of shari'a courts to personal status and religious endowments, and the introduction of a parallel system of Native Courts to adjudicate civil, commercial and criminal cases based on newly constructed legal codes.

It is noteworthy that, for Cromer, the task of the colonial apparatus in Egypt was "to rule without having the appearance of ruling" (126). This meant that the reform of the shari'a was to be carried out by natives, and it is indeed in the internal discourse among Muslim thinkers that the imprint of the colonial encounter is most deeply felt.

There had been, among Egyptians, considerable interaction with European ideas for almost a century before the British presence.[15] As early as the Napoleonic occupation of Egypt from 1798 to 1801, the future rector of al-Azhar university Hasan al-'Attar (d. ca. 1835) was engaging French scholars who had accompanied the military invasion in order to study the newly invaded territory. Not long after, the Egyptian government began sending student delegations to study in France. The most famous member of these delegations, Rifa'a al-Tahtawi (d. 1871), stayed on in Paris for five years, recording his impressions of the place

---

questions of belief and spiritual or moral meaning. Indeed, such things also have to do with the authority exerted by these sources of fullness upon people such that they are moved to act in certain ways. Thus, immanence is also concerned with action and the governing of proper conduct in the world.

14 For an important biography of Cromer, see Owen 2004.
15 For the history of the period, see Vatikiotis 1991: 169–248; Reid 1998; and Daly 1998. For Arab intellectuals' attitudes and involvements with Europe, the classic work is Hourani 1970.

and admiration for European learning in his famous *Takhlis al-Ibriz ila Talkhis al-Bariz*.[16]

Encounters like these between Europe and the Islamic world gave rise to vigorous debates about the nature of religion, its compatibility with the modern sciences, and the status of Islam in particular. An early salvo in this debate was Jamal al-Din al-Afghani's *Refutation of the Materialists*.[17] Al-Afghani is well known to those familiar with modern Islam as the itinerant anti-imperialist preacher and public intellectual who travelled the Muslim world encouraging pan-Islamic sentiments. At the same time, he is recognized just as widely as the father of an important strain of Islamic modernism. His legacy in this latter regard was particularly important in Egypt, where his student Muhammad 'Abduh made significant headway in promoting a vision of Islam that offered a critique of prevailing Islamic thinking while constructively engaging European ideas.[18] In his *Refutation of the Materialists*, al-Afghani positioned himself as a critic of what he thought was a far too concessionary stance taken up by Sir Sayyid Ahmad Khan in British India. Decrying the materialism of what he called the *neicheri* (naturalist) sect, al-Afghani was interested in re-asserting the role of religion in a world he saw as being increasingly dominated by material considerations. Al-Afghani is himself a complex figure, and his scattered writings have often given rise to contradictory readings of his work.[19] What is clear from this text, however, is that al-Afghani's notion of religion relies upon the positing of an opposition between it, on the one hand, and the impious focus on nature to the exclusion of the divine, on the other. As Abdulkader Tayob has remarked, for al-Afghani, "Religion in this regard was the antithesis of naturalism; its essence lay in the existence of a higher reality" (2009: 54).

Taylor has commented that the obviousness of the distinction between the natural and supernatural (or immanent/transcendent) is a peculiar feature of modern life, and that this holds true whether or not one believes in the supernatural (transcendent). As he says,

> the hiving off of an independent, free-standing level, that of 'nature', which may or may not be in interaction with something further or beyond, is a crucial bit of modern theorizing, which in turn corresponds to a constitutive dimension of modern experience. (ASA: 14)

---

16 For an analysis of this work, see the chapter by Johannes Stephan in this volume.
17 For a translation of this work, see Keddie 1968.
18 For more on 'Abduh, see the contribution by Florian Zemmin in this volume.
19 In addition to Keddie, see also Kedourie 1966, who maintains that al-Afghani was simply an atheist who sought to harness Islamic sentiment for political ends; and Kohn 2009, who argues the discrepancy can be explained by the influence on al-Afghani's thinking of Ibn Khaldun and Francois Guizot.

This seems to characterize quite well the unspoken background of the debate between al-Afghani and Khan. That is to say, despite al-Afghani's condemnation of Khan for what he sees as a system of thought that effectively alienates Muslim society from the divine, he shares with him an ontology in which the distinction between natural and supernatural is intelligible.

As we move into the modern period, then, figures like al-Afghani provide us with evidence that religion was coming to be increasingly understood among Muslims as that which pertains to a transcendent realm conceptually distinct from nature. Bakhit himself studied philosophy with al-Afghani, and though he later expressed opposition to certain modernist ideas, he was far from untouched by the changes in the basic categories of thought that structured Muslims' engagements with their own tradition.[20]

When it comes to his intervention in the case of the moon-sighting controversy, Bakhit's contribution is to eliminate altogether the insistent Ḥanafī concern with court procedure. Importantly, this shift is made natural – and not just possible – because of the underlying transformation in the very conception of *dīn*, which heavily conditioned Bakhit's understanding of the *umūr dīniyya*. Bakhit is himself rather clear on this point: New-moon sightings are "religious reports (*al-akhbār al-dīniyya*). Thus, they resemble the narration (*riwāya*), and so it is impossible that any of them are subject to the qadi's judgement" ([1911] 2000: 76). Notably, it is precisely the description of the reports as being "religious" that now disqualifies them from the qadi's regulatory control – a radical departure from the prevailing Ḥanafī tradition. This secularizing move has the effect that the *umūr dīniyya*, which previously partook in both immanence and transcendence, have now been entirely removed from the world by Bakhit and placed squarely into the realm of transcendent religion.

While Bakhit's Ḥanafī predecessors would not disagree that "religious reports" resemble the narration, we have seen that they also thought them to resemble testimonies in some way. Thus, Bakhit's use of "resemblance" in the quote above must be read as an appropriation of the pre-modern language in the service of positing an identity, and not just similarity, between the *umūr dīniyya* and the category of narrations (*riwāyāt*). If "religious matters" were previously governed by a logic of immanence, Bakhit now insists rather matter-of-factly that "the mode of conveying [such reports] is *the same* as the mode of relating Prophetic reports" (151, emphasis added).[21] Whereas his predecessors had a difficult time imagining that such reports could have any standing independ-

---

20 For other examples, see Quadri 2013.
21 Recall that Prophetic reports (hadiths) are the ideal exemplars of narrations.

ent of the validating authority of the qadis, Bakhit finds this a nonsensical proposition. For him, the central criteria to be considered is not the integrity of the procedural mechanisms which had defined Ḥanafī thinking on the issue for so long, but rather the truth content of the report itself as judged by the likelihood that it may be tainted by error or lies (*maẓannat al-ghalaṭ aw al-kidhb*). This, significantly, is a move that removes us from a primary occupation with the mediation of the courts, and the materiality and authority of the bodies that inhabit them, towards the abstract realm of individual minds.[22] Importantly, this cognitive turn is thought to be justified – and indeed commonsensical – simply because the reports in question have traditionally been labelled *dīniyya* ('religious'), a descriptor which has come to have a new meaning in a new age. In effect, the previously distinct category of the *umūr dīniyya* has been assimilated entirely to the category of narrations precisely because the former are "religious matters," and so opposed in this binary scheme to the 'worldly' concerns of testimonies. To be 'religious' is now not only to be ritualistically oriented toward the transcendent, but also to be governed by a logic that properly belongs to the realm of the transcendent.

4 Secularities and the telegraph

I have previously argued that this shift should be understood in terms of the emergence of what Casanova has called "functional differentiation:" namely the separation of "secular" spheres of life from the "religious" sphere, and the specialization of the latter as being governed by its own private rationality, distinct from the public and objective modes of adjudication associated with secular spheres (1994: 19). This characterization corresponds roughly, despite some important differences, to secularity 1 on Taylor's understanding, the "emptying" of the public sphere of appeals to God or religious beliefs (ASA: 2).

---

[22] Ebrahim Moosa has pointed out that, for Cromer, chief among Islam's faults was that "it lacked a concrete inward subjectivity" (164). In this, he followed Hegel, for whom "the specific role and sensate nature of rituals in both Judaism and Islam ... [was] a definite indicator that these traditions were underdeveloped, unlike Western Christianity which aspired to inwardness and pure thought" (164). It would seem Cromer, writing a mere three years before Bakhit did not fully appreciate the extent to which the patterns of "Western Christianity" had begun to make significant headway among Egyptian Muslim jurists.

The drawing of a hard line between the two categories of 'religious' and 'non-religious' should be rather evident in Bakhit's argumentation above.[23] Indeed, not only was Bakhit keen to distinguish strongly between "religious matters" and others, he expanded the former category to include not only reports that had previously been considered *umūr dīniyya*, but also the end-of-Ramadan moon-sighting, which was expressly not. This indicates the emergence of a rather robust notion of religion which brought under its ambit not only ritual worship, but also the observance of the divine command to celebrate the Eid festival by refraining from fasting. So, not only are matters that were considered *dīnī* in the past made exclusively transcendent, other matters too are deemed "religious" because they are framed in terms of obedience to the transcendent divine, rather than in more mundane terms.

Casanova's definition, however, includes a further element, which maps equally well onto Bakhit's intervention. "Religious matters" after Bakhit are governed by their own private rationality, principally their circulation among individual minds unimpeded by the constraints of the courts. They are no longer concerned with law, but rather ethics which, Talal Asad has pointed out, are "a matter of following one's conscience, not of obeying externally-given commands. The individual, private character of ethical decisions must stand free equally of the power of the state and the demands of one's community" (2006: 14). This is evocative of the sort of individualism Taylor has noted as characteristic of religion in the secular age – an interiorized self who undertakes a personal commitment to God to act properly (ASA: 541). Consider Bakhit's explanation of the way the process of report-transmission should be thought to unfold:

> If a witness reports [a sighting of the new moon] to someone else, and he is morally upright, the truth of the reporter with regards to his report becomes epistemologically preponderant for the recipient. Then, it becomes as if the recipient saw the new moon himself, so fasting becomes obligatory on him ... It is not that the report of the witness obliged anyone else, but rather that the witness, based on his sighting of the new moon, is obliged to fast due to the existence of the proof of obligation within him (*'indahu*). If he then informs someone else of that, the proof is now also found ... in this other person. (30)

This serves as a remarkable contrast to the pre-modern jurists, for whom the *umūr dīniyya* were not only a category concerned with immanence – imbricated in the very structures of a life-world and embedded within the materiality of so-

---

[23] Western theorists of secularity have increasingly blurred this distinction, though it retains remarkable staying power in the public imagination.

cial, political and communal institutions – but also understood in terms of relationality – inextricably linked to relationships with not only God, but also other humans who contributed towards its regulation and ordering.

This is indeed one way to think about the emergence of certain secular forms in the Muslim world. However, Taylor's project of trying to understand the secular age in terms of secularity 3 – namely what changes in the "context of understanding" are at play underlying these moves – help us deepen our understanding of this period. I have argued in this paper that the shift to a notion of religion as having to do exclusively with transcendence is an important element of this story in the Muslim world.

This point can perhaps be clarified and strengthened if we think back to the original context of Bakhit's engagement with this issue, namely what to do with a report of a new-moon sighting transmitted through the telegraph. The telegraph proliferated in Egypt thanks, first, to modernization efforts by Khedive Isma'il (r. 1863–1879), and then the British interest in connecting the various parts of their empire. The telegraph has, of course, long been recognized as a technology that shrank the world, bringing people closer together. It certainly did do this in Egypt, leading, in the words of one historian, to "an implosion of Egypt's social geography" (Cole 1999: 112).

However, the telegraph also enabled certain ways of thinking. Timothy Mitchell has commented that, in the nineteenth century, the telegraph came to be the paradigmatic representative of a new ontology which distinguished not only between body and mind, but also introduced a third layer, a metaphysical realm of meaning having an "ideal existence" to which symbols in the mind pointed or referred, or more properly, which they represented. Mitchell quotes Michel Bréal of the Collège de France who, in 1897, noted approvingly that, "Words are signs. They have no other existence than the signals of the wireless telegraph." Language, then, came to be "thought of as something more, existing apart from words themselves... Linguistic meaning was to be found, then, neither within the material of the words themselves nor simply within the mind of the individual. It lay outside both, as a 'structure' with an 'ideal existence'" (1988: 140–141).

It is clear that Bakhit had signed on to this theory of language. In his discussion, the telegraph emerges as an inert medium that does not impinge on the epistemological status of the report. In terms of validity, telegraph reports are for Bakhit just as valuable as in-person spoken communication, the medium long exclusively favoured by Islamic law. This tendency of Bakhit to conceive of the transmission of reports as transcending all sorts of materiality – whether the stipulated procedures, modes of regulation and documentation of the courts, or the mediation of technology – relies heavily on a notion of language as abstract, immaterial and communicable between otherwise private minds.

It is noteworthy that Bakhit should think religious reports, by virtue of their being religious, belong properly to this model. The idea of an ideal realm outside of the world (both mind and body) fits well with the conception of religion I have been discussing above. "Religious matters" (*umūr dīniyya*), then, came to represent for jurists precisely those issues that, like telegraph reports, transcended materiality: they were ineligible for adjudication and regulation by courts, and unperturbed by their relationship to the world. They came to be conceived by their very nature as abstractions whose locus was the minds of private individuals, and so the private "religious" sphere of society in general. In this, they came to fit well with Taylor's notion of modern religion as characterized by transcendence.

5 Conclusion

Some fifteen years after Bakhit was confronted with the question of what to do about the telegram reporting the new-moon sighting in Aswan, the Muslim scholarly establishment in Egypt faced another controversy, this one much more dramatic and, so, much better known to students of modern Islam. In 1925, the Azhar-trained scholar and judge 'Ali 'Abd al-Raziq published a book, *Islam and the Foundations of Political Power*, which advanced a forthright argument for the separation between religion and state in Islam.[24] One contemporary Egyptian writer has characterized it as "the first attempt to Islamicize secularism, to claim that Islam is secular" ('Imara [1989] 1997: 8). For the views he expressed in this work, 'Abd al-Raziq met with strong opposition from his Azharite colleagues, and was eventually expelled from the community of 'ulama by the Council of Senior 'Ulama (*Hay'at Kibar al-'Ulama*).[25]

Most interesting for our purposes is that among 'Abd al-Raziq's most vocal critics was none other than Muhammad Bakhit, who not only served on the Council but also wrote a lengthy rejoinder to 'Abd al-Raziq's arguments (Bakhit

---

24 'Abd al-Raziq has been often studied, most recently in a monograph by Ali 2009, and in a dissertation by Broucek 2012. An English translation of the work has appeared in the past few years ('Abd al-Raziq 2012); and an older French translation has existed for some time ('Abd al-Raziq 1994).
25 Broucek 2012 studies the reasons for this resistance. A thorough summary of the history of this episode and a presentation of the relevant documents, including the text of the Council's verdict, can be found in 'Imara [1989] 1997.

1925). It is evident from his response that, in the immediate aftermath of the abolition of the Ottoman caliphate in 1924, Bakhit, like his colleagues, was severely opposed to the sort of hard political secularism that denied a role for Islamic normativity in affairs of state. This paper has argued, however, that thinking about the secular in the terms proposed by Taylor allows us to speak in more nuanced ways about developments in the Muslim world in this period. Despite his impassioned objections to 'Abd al-Raziq, Bakhit did not remain untouched by the shifts in the context of understanding witnessed by his era, which, if not yet secular, was secularizing in particular ways under the specter of colonial presence. One of these shifts was the assigning of 'religion' to a compartmentalized space in the world, and the characterization of it entirely in terms of transcendence – that is to say, concerned in all aspects exclusively with the other-worldly. The colonial encounter, then, forged the intellectual groundwork for a deeper and more fundamental form of Muslim secularity than we are accustomed to expect.

Bibliography

'Abd al-Raziq, 'Ali. 1994. *L'Islam et les Fondements du Pouvoir*. Translated by Abdou Filali-Ansary. Paris: Éditions La Découverte; Cairo: CEDEJ.
'Abd al-Raziq, 'Ali. 2012. *Islam and the Foundations of Political Power*. Translated by Maryam Loutfi. Edited by Abdou Filali-Ansary. Edinburgh: Edinburgh University Press.
Al-Qarafi, Ahmad b. Idris. 1998. *al-Furuq, aw Anwar al-Buruq fi Anwa' al-Furuq*, ed. Khalil Mansur. 4 vols. Beirut: Dar al-Kutub al-'Ilmiyya.
Al-Sarakhsi, Shams al-Din. n.d. *Al-Mabsut*. 31 vols. Beirut: Dar al-Ma'rifa.
Al-Subki, Taqi al-Din. 2000. "Al-'Alam al-Manshur fi Ithbat al-Shuhur," in *Arba'a Rasa'il fi Hilal Khayr al-Shuhur*, ed. Hasan Ahmad Isbir, 9–62. Beirut: Dar Ibn Hazm.
Al-Tahanawi, Muhammad 'Ali b. 'Ali. [1899 or 1900]. *Kashshaf Istilahat al-Funun*. Al-Astana: Matba'at Iqdam bi-Dar al-Khalifa.
Ali, Souad T. 2009. *A Religion, Not a State: Ali 'Abd al-Raziq's Islamic Justification of Political Secularism*. Salt Lake City: University of Utah Press.
Asad, Talal. 1993. *Genealogies of Religion: Discipline and Reasons of Power in Christianity and Islam*. Baltimore, Johns Hopkins University Press.
Asad, Talal. 2003. *Formations of the Secular: Christianity, Islam, Modernity*. Stanford, CA: Stanford University Press.
Asad, Talal. 2006. "Thinking About Law, Morality, and Religion in the Story of Egyptian Modernization." *Journal of the Interdisciplinary Study of Monotheistic Religion (JISMOR)*. Special Issue:13–24.
Bakhit al-Muti'i, Muhammad. 1911. *Irshad Ahl al-Milla ila Ithbat al-Ahilla*. Cairo: Matba'at Kurdistan.
Bakhit al-Muti'i, Muhammad. 2000. *Irshad Ahl al-Milla ila Ithbat al-Ahilla*. Edited by Hasan Ahmad Isbir. Beirut: Dar Ibn Hazm.

Bakhit al-Muti'i, Muhammad. 1925. *Haqiqat al-Islam wa-Usul al-Hukm*. Cairo: al-Matba'a al-Salafiyya.
Broucek, James. 2012. "The Controversy of Shaykh 'Ali 'Abd al-Raziq." PhD diss., The Florida State University.
Casanova, José. 1994. *Public Religions in the Modern World*. Chicago: University of Chicago Press.
Casanova, José. 2011. "The Secular, Secularizations, Secularisms," in *Rethinking Secularism*, ed. Craig J. Calhoun, Mark Juergensmeyer, and Jonathan VanAntwerpen, 54–74. New York: Oxford University Press.
Casanova, José. 2013. "A Secular Age: Dawn or Twilight," in *Varieties of Secularism in A Secular Age*, ed. Michael Warner, Jonathan VanAntwerpen, and Craig Calhoun, 265–281. Cambridge, MA: Harvard University Press.
Cole, Juan. 1999. *Colonialism and Revolution in the Middle East: Social and Cultural Origins of Egypt's 'Urabi Movement*. Cairo: American University in Cairo Press.
Cromer, The Earl of (Evelyn Baring). [1908] 2000. *Modern Egypt, Part 2*. Reissued as vol. 6 of *Orientalism: Early Sources*, ed. Bryan W. Turner. London and New York: Routledge.
Daly, M.W. 1998. "The British Occupation, 1882–1922," in *The Cambridge History of Egypt*, vol. 2, "Modern Egypt from 1517 to the end of the twentieth century", ed. M.W. Daly, 239–251. Cambridge: Cambridge University Press.
Dressler, Markus, and Arvind-Pal S. Mandair, eds., 2011. *Secularism and Religion-Making*. Oxford and New York: Oxford University Press.
Firuzabadi, Muhammad b. Ya'qub. [1925]. *Al-Qamus al-Muhit*. 4 vols. Cairo: Al-Matba'a al-Misriyya.
Glei, Reinhold, and Stefan Reichmuth. 2012. "Religion between Last Judgement, law and faith: Koranic *dīn* and its rendering in Latin translation of the Koran." *Religion* 42: 247–271.
Hourani, Albert. 1970. *Arabic Thought in the Liberal Age: 1798–1939*. London: Oxford University Press.
'Imara, Muhammad. [1989] 1997. *Ma'rikat al-Islam wa-Usul al-Hukm*. Cairo: Dar al-Shuruq.
Ibn al-Humam, Kamal al-Din. n.d. *Fath al-Qadir*. 10 vols. Beirut: Dar al-Fikr.
Keddie, Nikki R. 1968. *An Islamic Response to Imperialism*. Berkeley: University of California Press.
Kedourie, Elie. 1966. *Afghani and 'Abduh: An Essay on Religious Unbelief and Political Activism in Modern Islam*. New York: Humanities Press.
Kohn, Margaret Kohn. 2009. "Afghānī on Empire, Islam, and Civilization." *Political Theory* 37: 398–422.
Mahmood, Saba. 2013. "Can Secularism Be Other-Wise?," in *Varieties of Secularism in A Secular Age*, ed. Michael Warner, Jonathan VanAntwerpen, and Craig Calhoun, 282–299. Cambridge, MA: Harvard University Press.
Mitchell, Timothy. 1988. *Colonising Egypt*. Berkeley: University of California Press.
Moosa, Ebrahim. 2009. "Colonialism and Islamic Law," in *Islam and Modernity: Key Issues and Debates*, ed. Muhammad Khalid Masud, Armando Salvatore, and Martin van Bruinessen, 158–180. Edinburgh: Edinburgh University Press.
Owen, Roger. 2004. *Lord Cromer: Victorian Imperialist, Edwardian Proconsul*. Oxford and New York: Oxford University Press.

Quadri, Junaid. 2013. "Transformations of Tradition: Modernity in the Thought of Muḥammad Bakhīt al-Mutīʿī, PhD diss., McGill University.
Reid, Donald Malcolm. 1998. "The ʿUrabi Revolution and the British Conquest," in *The Cambridge History of Egypt*, vol. 2, "Modern Egypt from 1517 to the end of the twentieth century", ed. M.W. Daly, 217–238. Cambridge: Cambridge University Press.
Smith, Wilfred Cantwell. 1964. *The Meaning and End of Religion: A New Approach to the Religious Traditions of Mankind*. New York: The New American Library.
Taylor, Charles. 2013. "Afterword: Apologia pro Libra suo," in *Varieties of Secularism in A Secular Age*, ed. Michael Warner, Jonathan VanAntwerpen, and Craig Calhoun, 300–324. Cambridge, Mass: Harvard University Press.
Tayob, Abdulkader. 2009. *Religion in Modern Islamic Discourse*. London: Hurst & Co.
Van der Veer, Peter. 2001. *Imperial Encounters: Religion and Modernity in India and Britain*. Princeton: Princeton University Press.
Vatikiotis, P. J. 1991. *The History of Modern Egypt: From Muhammad Ali to Mubarak*. Baltimore: Johns Hopkins University Press.

Johannes Stephan
Reconsidering Transcendence/Immanence. Modernity's Modes of Narration in Nineteenth-Century Arabic Literary Tradition

1 Introduction

The classical approach to the question of modernity in the Arab world traces its moments and sources of inception (Abu Lughod 1963; Khoury 1983; Yared 2002). This reflects an understanding of modernity in terms of political thought as an option to 'tradition.' In this view, Arab modernity[1] is usually generated only by a process of adoption from the West. In contrast Charles Taylor, tackling anew the question of modernity in his *A Secular Age,* carries forward an interpretation of history that is based on the conviction that modernity is more than a set of political beliefs that can be adopted.

Taylor, however, does not try to define modernity in *A Secular Age.* I read his long narrative as an argument that modernity is our condition of life, which we can only approach by means of storytelling. The main storyline of modernity according to *A Secular Age* encloses a major historical shift from an understanding in which the world is intertwined with transcendence to an understanding in which the world is conceived of largely as self-contained in its immanence. This major shift within the transcendence/immanence dichotomy is reflected in "modes of narration," as Taylor (2004: 175) has elaborated in an earlier attempt to characterize Western modernity. As examples of the "modes" that Westerners use to make sense of their modernity, he mentions "revolution," "progress," and "nation" (2004: 177).

I am very grateful to Florian Zemmin for his critical and thorough reading of this chapter, his valuable advice, and for sharing a few references with me. I also wish to thank Reinhard Schulze, Adrien Zakar, and Feriel Bouhafa for several corrections and suggestions.

[1] Recent scholarship on the Arabic literary tradition uses this expression and thus counters the traditional understanding of modernity as a purely Western import (e.g. Sheehi 2004; El-Ariss 2013). One of the first comprehensive attempts to challenge euro-centric historiography of the Arab world was Gran's *Islamic Roots of Capitalism* (1979).

Grasping modernity as reflected in storytelling, I suggest, is a valid attempt to approach the issue of Arab modernity, for this helps us understand modes of narration in accordance with and in difference to Western modernity. Hence, I argue that during the nineteenth century the Arabic literary tradition also developed new modes of narration. These are found in attempts to imagine the course of history as ruled by the universal principles of progress (*taqaddum*) and civilization (*tamaddun*). With stories of human progress Arab thinkers did not necessarily overturn transcendence, but they reconsidered its impact on human society. This also included a pragmatic function: by promoting progress and *tamaddun* and conceiving of them historically, Arab thinkers were able to share and compare their history with Western history. Thereby the history of Western civilization became part of their new story about the world.

The two examples of this new story I shall tackle in this chapter are neither works of social theory nor historiographical projects. As short narrative digressions these examples form part of the prominent literary works of the nineteenth century reform movement called *nahḍa*, the "Arab Renaissance." The first is from the Egyptian Rifaʿa al-Tahtawi's account of Paris from 1834, *Talkhis al-Ibriz fi Takhlis Bariz* (*The Extraction of Pure Gold in the Abridgement of Paris, Takhlis*). My second example is drawn from a utopian allegoric novel from 1865 by the Syrian author Fransis Marrash, *Ghabat al-Haqq* (*The Forest of Truth*). Although neither of the accounts forms part of a larger historiographical project, as stories about progress and *tamaddun*, both express new modes of narration that had an impact on such larger historiographical projects.

To apply Taylor's transcendence/immanence dichotomy to the Arabic literary tradition poses a challenge that has to do with the nature of Taylor's own story in *A Secular Age* as being another story about Western modernity. I shall first discuss this problem and thereby elaborate on how Taylor's basic assumption can be productively applied. I then dedicate my main focus to the aforementioned examples that encompass new modes of narration. Part of these new modes is also a certain image of historical circularity in which the West is granted a decisive role. I will conclude this chapter with a summary of modes of narration of Arab modernity and a remark on conceiving of the secular age in the Arab world.

2 Transcendence/immanence

The problem of *A Secular Age*'s normative implications as a risk of excluding other stories from the secular age has been distinctly addressed in this volume as well as elsewhere (Mahmood 2010). Therefore, in the following I limit myself to the challenge of applying concepts in Taylor's work to traditions, including the Arabic literary tradition, that are not included in *A Secular Age*.

The most obvious problem one needs to address has to do with the nature of Taylor's approach, which he bases explicitly on his Christian worldview. Taylor cannot be reproached for this at all, since his aim was to regenerate a self-reflection about the West's anchorage in traditions emerging from "Latin Christendom" (ASA: 21). If we depart from this perspective, a big part of *A Secular Age* provides a specific hermeneutical means with which to understand a major transformation in the social order in Western Europe. Taylor describes this shift by means of the transcendence/immanence dichotomy, which he deems "tailor-made for our culture" (ASA: 16). Although this dichotomy serves as an interpretative pattern in a Western Christian context, its application to the Arab context seems possible and worthwhile to me. Hence, I want to support this point with two detailed remarks – each of a distinct nature. The first refers to a hermeneutical dilemma, the second is a historiographical argument.

First, drawing the transcendence/immanence dichotomy from the intellectual tradition of Latin Christendom, Taylor tries to grasp the emergence of modernity, or more specifically the secular age. Although Taylor (2010a: 412), when reacting to his reviewers, does not consider this dichotomy "watertight" for all ages, he deems it indispensable to understand "our dominant social imaginary," in other words the social world in which we live.[2] He thus still assumes a certain constancy of this dichotomy, and it is not a clear-cut historical fact. Rather it is to be seen as *a priori*, allowing for his specific perspective on modernity as being "our age." This perspective cannot only be explained by Taylor's personal beliefs or his particular choice of sources.[3] *A Secular Age* reveals anew the very problem of how to approach modernity from the viewpoint of modernity, or how to approach it in difference to something else that comes to the fore when dealing with the evolution of distinctly *modern* concepts like "nation," "progress," and "revolution." By approaching modernity with the transcendence/immanence dichotomy as embedded in shorter stories (biographies) as well as "master-narratives of secularization" (Taylor 2010b: 300), Taylor's perspective suggests a way out of this hermeneutical dilemma.

Taylor's story about transcendence/immanence is thus only one particular perspective on modernity. Instead of reading this relation as a theological claim, in this chapter I suggest reading it as a hypothetical premise for my spe-

---

[2] Here Taylor responds to comments of Hauerwas and Coles (2010).
[3] Sheehan (2010) argues that Taylor's work is not history in a stricter sense that is directed by empirical evidences. Rather Taylor lays out a theological argument within a historical framework as known from Christian apologetic literature.

cific purpose. Thus, in this chapter I understand it as a first distinction in order to put into context Arab thinkers' (his)stories, which they brought forward to make sense of their world. Hence, reading Arab modernity as a reconfiguration of storytelling around this basic distinction also helps reconsider the secular age in terms of a global secular age.

Putting into question *A Secular Age*'s historiographical restriction, this last aspect leads to my second argument. According to Saba Mahmood's critique of *A Secular Age* (2010), scholarship on Arab modernity needs to consider the historical proximity of the Western to the non-Western world. Intellectual similarities to Western modern thought are not surprising for the thinkers I deal with: Fransis Marrash from the Syrian city of Aleppo is known to have originated from a wealthy Arab, mainly melkite Catholic bourgeoisie that had established contacts with Western merchants, missionaries, and scholars from at least the eighteenth century onwards (Wielandt 1992: 119–123; Masters 2001: 98–118; Patel 2013: 38–58). Marrash also makes many references to the Catholic thought that was certainly part of his education in his hometown before he travelled to Paris in 1867 (Wielandt 1992: 128, 141; Hulw 2006: 56–58).[4]

Along with the engagement with the Catholic Church we need to account for the complexity of the Ottoman context. Most Arabs, that is speakers of Arabic, were subject to the Ottoman Empire.[5] Rifa'a al-Tahtawi can be seen as an intellectual product of an Ottoman administration that experienced conflict and exchange with European powers for centuries, and from the eighteenth century on followed closely Western political and social developments (Altman 1976; Quataert 2005: 75–86; Aydin 2013: 16–18). The history of global Christianity most prominently represented by Catholicism and the entanglement with European history are only two of many examples for my argument that considering the transcendence/immanence dichotomy in different, but very close contexts, proves plausible.

The examples also indicate that we cannot conceive of a similarity between traditions only by referring to comparable theological presumptions. Moreover, exchange between different traditions is also anchored in Arab history itself. This exchange became most visible in a discourse that was shared by Muslim intellectuals like Tahtawi and Christian thinkers like Marrash during the nineteenth century. With scholarship usually considering the period of Marrash and Tahtawi as having "Arabic visions of modernity" (Freitag 2008), Arabs "con-

---

[4] For an extensive account on catholic missions to the Near East and their impact cf. Heyberger (1994).
[5] Revisionism in historiography of the early Ottoman period accentuates continuities, thus relativizing the rupture of 1800 (1798). Cf. Sajdi (2007).

frontation with modernity" (El-Ariss 2013: 51), "Modern Arab identity" (Sheehi 2004), or simply 'Arab modernity,' it seems appropriate to resume the discussion at this point.

3 Contours of a new mode of narration

Nineteenth century Arab thinkers such as Tahtawi and Marrash are often considered part of a movement generally called the *nahḍa*. *Nahḍa*, usually translated as "Arab awakening" or "Arab renaissance" (Tomiche 1993; Patel 2013: 13), denotes a movement that aimed to reform Arab societies beginning in the early nineteenth century. It is often applied to the intellectual discourse that began somewhere between Napoléon Bonaparte's Egyptian campaign (1798–1801) and the process of Ottoman State Reform, or the *tanzimat* (1839–1876) (Brugman 1984: 8–13; Cachia and Badawi 1992; Charif 2000: 35–86).[6]

Scholarship often links the *nahḍa* to its so-called "pioneers" (Sheehi 2004: 13, 196), who were the leading figures of reform in the flourishing cities of the old Ottoman world such as Aleppo, Beirut, Cairo, and Tunis, among others. One of the most famous of these pioneers, Rifaʿa Rafiʿ al-Tahtawi, was a protagonist in the Egyptian educational reform beginning in the early nineteenth century. Egypt's modernization was fostered intensively by the new Khedive's dynasty, which goverened independently from Istanbul and which aimed mainly at reforming education, as well as the economy, the military, and medical institutions in Egypt. Part of this process was the dispatch of missions of promising students to European countries such as Italy and France. Tahtawi was one of these and was sent to Paris in 1826 to acquire new knowledge in natural and technological sciences. After his return to Cairo, he published a travelogue on his experiences in 1834, *The Extraction of Pure Gold in the Abridgment of Paris (Takhlis,* Newman 2004: 85). *Takhlis* quickly gained popularity and was translated into Ottoman Turkish as early as 1839.[7] Nowadays, it is renowned as a milestone in the

---

[6] The origins of the *nahḍa* can be traced to the production and the exchange of texts in the eighteenth century/early nineteenth century (Patel 2013; Hill 2015). The term *nahḍa*, however, was probably not used before the 1870s (Gonzalez-Quijano 2007: 75). For a discussion of the term and its ideological implications also cf. Johnston (2013: 59–60, 123–124).
[7] For renditions on Tahtawi's life in the context of ninenteenth century Egyptian reform, cf. Newman (2004: 15–82), Hourani (1983, 67–83), Delanoue (1982: Tome 2, Première Partie), and Altman (1976).

Arabic literary tradition and often regarded as a forerunner of modern Arabic literature (Brugman 1984: 18).[8]

Takhlis, known as a travelogue (*rihla*; Tahtawi 1958: 56), is not a day-to-day travel report. It bears clear-cut features of an ethno-geographic treatise.[9] Thus, the content of the treatise is hardly centered on the travel adventure of an individual; rather, it is organized as a systematic description of the geography, climate, and city planning of Paris, as well as of Parisians, their manners, and their customs. Furthermore, it evaluates scientific study in France and the revolution of July 1830, with an extensive commentary on the articles of the new constitution. *Takhlis* borrows many European terms (Sawaie 2000; Jalal 2006; 2008) and introduces new concepts to an Arab audience (Salama-Carr 2007: 222–224), but it also alludes to the richness and diversity of the Arabic literary heritage (Wagner 2000). Important for my purpose is the way in which Tahtawi presents Europe as part of a common world, revealing a certain mode of narration.

Ostensibly, Tahtawi had to justify his mission. After *Takhlis's* preface, an introduction precedes the actual travel account with the title "First Chapter. Regarding what seemed to me to be the reason behind our departure to this Land of Infidelity and Obstinacy, which lies far away from us and where there are great expenses because of the high cost of living"[10] (Tahtawi 2004: 101). Tahtawi (2004: 101) then expounds on the purpose of the voyage:

> Originally, man was simple and devoid of adornments; he existed in a purely natural state, and knew only instincts. Then, some people acquired some knowledge that they had not previously had. This was uncovered to them by chance, accident, inspiration, or revelation. The divine law or the intellect judged that this knowledge was useful, and thus it was applied and preserved. For instance, in earliest times some people were completely ignorant of how to cook food by means of fire, since the latter was completely unknown among them. As a result, their diet was restricted to fruit, things ripened in the sun, or raw foodstuffs, as is still the case in some countries today. Then one of them by chance saw a spark coming from a flint as it was hit with a piece of iron or something like that. When he did the same thing, he managed to extract the fire and learned about its properties.

---

8 It is also often seen as a starting point for the *nahḍa* (Salama-Carr 2007: 216; Johnston 2013: 123–124).
9 In its organization, it clearly resonates with Georges-Bernard Depping's *Aperçu historique sur les mœurs et coutumes des nations* (1826) which Tahtawi read in Paris and published in Arabic just before *takhlis* (Stephan: 2012; Euben 2008: 117; Elger 2003: 27; Najib 1981: 25–26). A reprint of Tahtawi's translation can be found in Jalal's study (2008).
10 This and the following quotations are from Newman's translation of Tahtawi's travelogue (2004).

Tahtawi thus does not explain Europe but a general principle of world history. He imagines human origins and man's progressive change toward more refined forms of life. By this he legitimizes the way he approaches the subject of his book. Telling this story of human life, how it is, and how it once must have been or still is, he implies that progress is the leading universal principle in the history of societies. Progress (*taqaddum*), in Tahtawi's view (1958: 60), is a universal principle that is nonetheless not universally happening in the same way and at the same time, as he makes clear with an apposition phrase when discussing the consumption of raw meat: "as is still the case in some countries today" (see above quotation).

Progress does not occur in the same fashion for all humans and at the same time; instead, it is the outcome of different ultimate causes and depends on the natural surroundings. Yet, from a theoretical point of view, it can happen everywhere and is what societies aim at. In the subsequent section, Tahtawi offers the reader a theory of stages – typical of French Enlightenment thought – probably building on Montesquieu, whom Tahtawi read in France (Tahtawi 2004: 292–293). Mankind, the Egyptian explains, can be categorized, according to its proximity to or distance from the original condition (*al-ḥāla al-aṣliyya*) (Tahtawi 1958: 58), into several categories. "The first category is that of wild savages, the second of the uncivilized barbarians, whereas the third comprises people who are cultured, refined, sedentarized, civilized, and have attained the highest degree of urbanization" (Tahtawi 2004: 102). All human communities or nations of the world, as well as individuals, can be classified in these categories, with France and Egypt in the third. Although Egypt is advanced, it still needs some knowledge to reach greater splendor. This knowledge is represented by some sciences, in which European countries are at least in partial terms more advanced than the "Islamic countries" (*al-bilād al-islāmiyya*; Tahtawi 1958: 61). Tahtawi (2004: 105–110) justifies Egypt's borrowing from Europe by explaining that Europeans once learned from Islamic countries. Therefore, he implicitly systematizes an approach to different geo-cultural and historical entities, the West (here: Europe), and the Orient (here: the Islamic countries), which I will come back to at the end of this chapter.

4 Features of the progress story

Understanding this story as containing progress as a new mode of narration, we first of all need to consider in detail what is new about it. For this purpose it seems worthwhile to make some remarks on premodern conceptualizations of history in the Arabic literary tradition. While a comprehensive view is beyond the scope of this chapter, I shall restrict myself to a few features that are related to our premise of the transcendence/immanence dichotomy. In premodern Arabic historical writings, God is usually introduced as the founder of the cosmos, who directed the history of human communities. Transcendence, thus, appears as "the engine of history" (Robinson 2003: 129). The dispatch of messengers and prophets is also an aspect of God's interference, and it was mainly these mediators, by their laws and prophecies, that gave society new directions (Robinson 2003: 133). The people that made change thus were people with names, specific persons that had a prescribed task to fulfill and that disposed of a closer relation to transcendence. In contrast, Tahtawi's story of progress contains a conceptualization of history that is different in three core features:

First, The contingency of change and its multifaceted causes:
Presuming that God is transcendent in the Islamic tradition and that revelation is a human experience of this transcendence, Tahtawi (1958: 59) provides different causes for changes in human behavior, "coincidence" (*ittifāq*) and "chance" (*ṣudfa*), or "revelation" (*iḥyā'*) and "inspiration" (*ilhām*).[11] "Revelation" and "inspiration" seem to be necessarily related to some sort of transcendence, whereas "chance" and "coincidence" seem to be mechanisms relying on their own immanent logic. Whereas the latter two seem to be solely related to human life, the former two denote divine interference. This becomes evident in another sentence of this first section of the introduction in which he juxtaposes two options for change: "divine inspiration" (*ilhām ilāhī*) and "human coincidence" (*ittifāq basharī*; Tahtawi 1958: 59). In other words, what matters here is change, not its actual cause. The reasons for change can be diverse, but Tahtawi stresses the point that change is a universal principle. In this case, it is an experience that is Egyptian or Arab as well as French or European, but it is foremost a human experience, and it does not need to be generated by transcendence.

Second, the approbation of knowledge:
According to Tahtawi (1958: 59), both the *sharīʿa* as the divinely ordained law and human intellect have the ability to approve things as useful knowledge.[12] Tahtawi continues to give diverse reasons behind sustainably changing human behaviors. Anchored in the Islamic intellectual tradition, he conveys that under certain conditions, human intellect can reach results similar to those of

---

11 Here, I rely on Johnston's translations (2013a: 206).
12 This distinction of knowledge seems to be the foundation for his division of sciences (Johnston 2013b).

the revealed law. By combining this Islamic rationalism[13] with the historical narrative about mankind, Tahtawi is able to delineate a normative view on progress.[14] This rationalist worldview, thus, is embedded in the conception of history.

Third, the universal human:
In Tahtawi's account, human beings are presented as creatures without names or characteristics. Thinking man, in his origin as a primitive species, is probably not compatible with the premodern approach to history, in which the human agent appears often as a specific individual, like the prophets or kings who are leaders of the biblical or Islamic community. Society was founded, instructed, and directed by prophets and messengers who receive no mention in Tahtawi's opening narrative; instead, agency is assigned to man in his most simple definition. Thus this story entails the foundation of universal human history. As part of that history, progress serves as a new mode of narration.

With these features in a story of progress, Tahtawi subscribes to a conception of human life as mostly independent from transcendent guidance. Tahtawi imagines human history, takes empirical knowledge and systematizes it in a chronological and causal manner. Thus, 'imagining' is not a placeholder for terms like 'inventing' or 'fictionalizing'. I understand it as that which is thinkable and therefore possible in the view of this author and his implied reader. Tahtawi's story entails a new story about the world.

As a matter of fact, the way Tahtawi thought of societal change here was reflected in his later historiographical project (Tahtawi 2010/2011). He composed a comprehensive history of Egypt of which the first volume (1868) was published before and the second volume just after his death in 1874.[15] Giving the history of Egypt before the advent of Islam in the first volume of this historiography, Tahtawi begins with the geography of the lands and its dynasties. Then he interestingly frames his second volume as a biography of Muhammad, the prophet of Islam, including accounts of the social organization the prophet established.

Instead of inserting Egypt into the traditional history of the Islamic community, Tahtawi includes patterns of Islamic history in Egypt's national history and

---

13 On Islamic rationalism, cf. Mahdi (2001) and R. Taylor (2009).
14 Although there were Arabic/Islamic notions of scientific progress in premodern times, as Khalidi (1981) has shown, they did not seem to be part of the discourse of renewal modifying the approach to human history, as is the case in the nineteenth century.
15 On his late publications cf. Newman (2004: 67–68).

views the latter as an example for the world. More importantly, Tahtawi imagines history according to new principles that can be derived from the aforementioned narrative, depicting immanently organized human society depending on the land where it dwells (pre-Islamic Egypt)[16] and change understood as human progress that can, but does not have to, be successfully triggered by God's interventions (Islamic Egypt). Ancient Egypt, Tahtawi (2010/2011, 3: 32) explains in his first volume, had already achieved "civilization and progress" (*al-tamaddun wa-l-taqaddum*).[17]

5 The concept of *tamaddun*/civilization

Tahtawi's story focuses on people's capacity for progress. The aim of the Egyptian mission to France was to bring home something new in order to change state institutions. Based on the paradigm of progress, the need for comprehensive reform in the nineteenth century in different regions in the Arab world developed to form a broader project that was most profoundly expressed by the term *tamaddun*. This usually translates as "civilization" (Konrad 2011: 175; Zachs 2012; 2005: 67; Schäbler 2004: 23; Sheehi 2004: 12). Tahtawi (1958: 60) had already used the term in 1834 in *Takhlis* when describing the aforementioned third and most advanced category of human societies. *Tamaddun* originally denoted the process of becoming a city dweller (Marrash 1881: 57; Bustani 1977: 843), and city life in general must be subsumed – according to Tahtawi – under the third category of societies in the world.

Tamaddun became a popular concept in the 1850s, most probably peaking in the decades thereafter, and persisted until the twentieth century.[18] It acquired a strong quality of enthusiasm in Fransis Marrash's novel *Ghabat al-Haqq* (1865),

---

16 After an introduction in which ancient Egyptian society is introduced as containing features of progress, Tahtawi (2010/2011, 3: 41–88) defines the geographical borders of Egypt and depicts its landscape and its nature by focusing on the Nile and its value.

17 This approach to history is outlined by Crabbs (1984: 67–82), drawing mainly on Tahtawi's *Manahij al-albab al-misriyya* (1869). Already Hourani (1983: 79–81) refers to this book by depicting Tahtawi's conceptualization of ancient Egyptian history.

18 A similar categorization in which *tamaddun* denotes the most refined group of people can be found in Butrus al-Bustani's *Discourse on Society* (1999). In trying to understand social life in Beirut in a systematic fashion, Bustani also refers to a stage paradigm similar to that elaborated upon in Tahtawi's *Takhlis* and draws on Ibn Khaldun's (1332–82 AD) dualism of country life/city life (Sheehi 2004: 208fn52). The concept of *tamaddun* in the nineteenth century included in fiction and travel writings is discussed in Wielandt's *Das Bild der Europäer* (1980: 130–136) and El-Ariss (2013: Chapter 3).

in which *tamaddun* is presented as a guiding principle for human well-being. Like Lebanese authors of his time, Marrash probably considered it a means of overcoming sectarian tensions that led to clashes in Aleppo, Damascus, and Mount Lebanon during the 1850s and 1860s (Krimsti 2014; Makdisi 2002; Masters 2001: 156–165). Marrash was a physician and a poet from a Greek-Catholic bourgeois family in Aleppo, and he travelled to Paris in 1867.[19] Only at the end of his short life did he shift, as did some other thinkers of his time, from a belief in the universality of progress to a harsh criticism toward European civilization, which in his view revealed a barbarian character (Barut 1994: 81–82; Hulw 2006: 180–193). Before further considering his view on Europe, what is of interest here is the utopian vision that he formulated around the concept of *tamaddun* in 1865.[20]

Marrash embraces *tamaddun* in his novel in various respects. First of all and most prominently, it appears as a reform program he bases on five pillars: political education, the cultivation of the intellect, the refinement of social customs and individual morals, the improvement of cities, and love (*al-maḥabba*) as a cosmological unifying power serving social cohesion (Marrash 1881: 57–95). *Tamaddun* in Marrash's novel most crucially implies thoughts on how contemporary society is best organized. Apart from true moral refinement and scientific progress, *tamaddun* also covers principles of equality, welfare, and just rulership. The narrator explains all these principles within the dynamics of social organization as a closed and coherent system (Marrash 1881: 58) that clearly has as its background Christian as well as Islamic ideals such as charity and justice of the ruler. However, it is installed only by man's ability to lead a civilized social life.

Similar to progress, *tamaddun* is more than just a program. Marrash's *The Forest of Truth* is primarily an allegorical dream narrative (Wielandt 1992: 125).[21] The narrator directs the reader through a dream world that he himself encounters in a deep sleep. This world consists mainly of a thick forest with a few glades that seem without any geographical attribution. At the center of the narration is a dialogue between the "king of freedom" and the "queen of wisdom" who meet with a wise old "philosopher." After their "kingdom of freedom and civilization" (*mamlakat al-ḥurriyya wa-l-tamaddun*; Marrash 1881: 22) has won the war against the barbarous "kingdom of slavery" (*mamlakat al-ʿubūdiyya*; Marrash 1881: 9), their discussion is mainly of the following. How should the prisoners of war be treated? Should they be punished? How should they be in-

---

19 On Marrash's travelogue cf. Wielandt (1980: 98–104).
20 On Marrash's life in the context of his time cf. Wielandt (1992), Barut (1994), Hulw (2006), Moosa (1997: 186–195), El-Enany (2012: 22–24), and Elshakry (2013: 144–145).
21 As Elshakry (2013: 357fn69) suggests Marrash's novel could be read as a play.

tegrated into the kingdom? The philosopher is the one who has answers to every thorny issue the king and queen need to resolve. He also explains the aforementioned five pillars of *tamaddun*, adding that they are part of the human condition and "a law which guides man towards the perfection of his natural and moral conditions" (Hourani 1983: 248).

Tamaddun, as becomes clear in the philosopher's monologues, also entails law (*sharīʿa*) and governance (*siyāsa*). In order to display the human need for law and governance, the philosopher embarks on a historical digression about their origin and with it the origin of the "kingdom of freedom and civilization" (Marrash 1881: 41–54). His story presents mankind throughout its origins. At first it was a community rudimentarily organized socially and located somewhere on a steppe. Accidentally, the leader of this community discovers a promisingly green place on the horizon that turns out to be a forest. He guides his family to it, and in this more fertile environment, he finally builds up his kingdom, which later becomes 'civilized'.

This story line resembles the opening narrative in Tahtawi's travelogue. Human society is presented in its primitive stage and consists of nonspecific human beings. Change then occurs accidentally through man's interaction with his environment, resulting in improvement and eventually mankind's progress and *tamaddun*. Hence, this "historical inference" (*istintāj tarīkhī*; Marrash 1881: 40), by building similarly on the origin of mankind and its inclination toward improvement from a perspective of "general history" (*tarīkh ʿāmm*; Marrash 1881: 42), indicates a similar mode of narration that is expressed with *tamaddun*/civilization.

There are some differences between Marash's and Tahtawi's versions of progress. In the story of *The Forest of Truth*, God does not interfere in the temporal dynamics of the social order which like all other things seems to be part of his "purposeful design" (Elshakry 2013: 145).[22] *Tamaddun* is the cause for change. Thus, *Tamaddun* is conceived of as an internal stimulus that tautologically leads to its own realization. It is, in other words, the foundational principle of human social organization.[23] Second, Marrash conveys that this internal stimu-

---

[22] Based on her study of Marrash's later treatise *Nature's Testimony* (*Shahadat al-tabiʿa fi wujud Allah wa-al-shariʿa*), Elshakry (2013: 144–147) describes Marrash's concept of God's relation to the universe as deistic. She suggests reading Marrash's work as a contribution to natural theology. It might be possible that Marrash was exposed to neo-Thomist ideas during his stay in Paris (Elshakry 2013: 146).

[23] Hence, *tamaddun* itself obtains a transcendent character. Sheehi's (2004: 143) observations of *nahdha* thought confirms this conclusion.

lus is related to a comprehensive program of reform, similar to Tahtawi's, in which change is an inclination of man that is triggered by natural surroundings.

6 Conceiving of the West

Another similarity between Tahtawi's and Marrash's view of progress is related to the belief in exterior impulses. In order to grasp the nineteenth century's new modes of narration, I suggest looking at images of the West as one main impulse. The West, as I argue, forms part of the story about the world and must be considered indispensable for the new modes of narration exemplified by Tahtawi and Marash.

Like Tahtawi who wrote about his journey to France in order to launch into reflections on progress, it is in the end the West that engenders change in *The Forest of Truth*. Just before the narrator awakens from his dream at the end, he finds himself exiled from the forest and alone on a steppe. Looking westward, he discerns a flood of growing greenery approaching him covering the entire desert and giving him feelings of release and delight. By evoking this image, Marrash (1881: 133–134) clearly alludes to his homeland of Syria and his city of Aleppo and its need to acquire Western innovations.[24]

This finale resonates with the introduction to Marrash's novel (1881: 2). In the introduction, the narrator describes himself falling into a slumber that lets him see the kingdoms of the world rising and falling in front of his eyes, including the old Egyptians, the Assyrians, the Greeks, and the Romans, among others. By referring to a history of societal change and progress, he first asserts that the best movers for successful social systems are *reason* (*'aql*) and *science* (*'ilm*; Marrash 1881: 3–4). Secondly, beginning with older ancient civilizations and ending this introduction with the Roman Empire, of which as it seems according to his view the modern world was a late outcome, he also alludes to the idea of the natural rise and fall of civilizations.[25]

This latter idea, as well as the importance given to reason and scientific progress, also formed part of the intellectual movement later described as "Is-

---

24 Similarily, Marrash (2004: 24–26) describes the backwardness of his hometown of Aleppo in his travelogue *Rihlat Baris* from 1867.
25 Conversely to earlier conceptions of the rise and fall of dynasties/states, as in Ibn Khaldun's theory of history (Khalidi 1981: 283–285), a rise in *nahdha* discourse was seen as the main ambition in this era (Sheehi 2004: 143).

lamic reformism" (Kohn 2009).[26] Adherents to this movement looked to the notions of progress articulated in Islamic scriptures (Ivanyi 2007). Like these reformers, however, Marrash some years after the publication of *The Forest of Truth* (1865) underlines the fact that Europeans built their civilization originally on knowledge that they once adopted from Arabic civilizations (Hulw 2006: 186). Tahtawi also proposed in *Takhlis* the idea that Europeans adopted knowledge from Islamic countries. Hence, he legitimized Egypt's adoption of European knowledge, and with it he pronounced the need for "all nations of Islam" to awake from their "slumber" (Tahtawi 1958: 58).

The idea of adopting knowledge, sciences, and technologies seems to justify the "backwardness" of Arabs, which some thinkers began to express in the middle of the nineteenth century (Sheehi 2004: 61–65; 2005: 438–439). The already important role Arabs or Islam played in world history probably fostered the belief that they could regain the scepter of *tamaddun*. The notions of *progress* and *tamaddun* were thus shaped by an idea of circularity, which included the Western world in a common temporality.[27] The West and the Arab world thus became able to be considered as different historical entities in their own right but functioning according to the same principles.

Circularity may have had a twofold impact on the conception of progress. Progress is not merely thought to be linear; it can decrease, and with this, civilizations can reach their end. Civilizations can thus fall back into "earlier" stages of progress, and in Marrash's understanding, *tamaddun* can even degrade toward barbarism (*tawaḥḥush*; Hulw 2006: 182–183). Thus, progress as a mode of narration did not necessarily lead them to believe in the coming "end of history;" rather, most *nahḍa* writers saw themselves and their society as being in one of many circles that improved or lead to a new *tamaddun*. In the stories of *progress* (Tahtawi) and *tamaddun* (Marrash) aspects of circularity and the West's part in it, Arab modernity becomes a complex set of modes of narrations.

7 Conclusion

The new modes of narration in the Arabic literary tradition are centered on the normativity and historicity of progress. This we can find expressed in the stories of Arab modernity I have exemplified in this chapter. According to this story,

---

26 Al-Azmeh (1996: 121–122) observes a continuation between Marrash's understanding of transcendence and later islamic thought.
27 Roussillon (2001: 161) asserts the idea of a universal human temporality for Tahtawi's worldview.

human society can develop independently from transcendent interference. Arab thinkers both made sense of Western progress and valued advances in the reform process during the *Nahḍa* period. Transcendence, however, did not disappear from the stage of history. Arab intellectuals instead reconsidered its role. Transcendent interference in modern Arab conceptualizations of history turned out to be of a particular nature. In addition to the universal principles of *tamaddun* and progress, transcendent interference, or revelation, becomes a marker for the cultural historical entity Arab thinkers saw themselves belonging to. This was later called the Arab nation or the "Islamic civilization" (*al-tamaddun al-islāmī*). The latter expression, used as the title for a historiographical project in the early twentieth century (Philipp 1979: 90–93; Dupont 1996; Sheehi 2004: 160–162; Johnston 2013: 69–71), reveals two themes: a basic and universal understanding of the world consists of civilizations, and a particular designation of one of these civilizations is "Islamic," which alludes to the role of transcendence in history.

Two remarks remain to be made in relation to this last aspect. The option for a history without God has to be put into context. We have to ask on which convictions Tahtawi, Marrash, and others based their conception of an immanent history moved by accident or natural inclinations. In the later nineteenth century, the interaction between European ideas and thinkers in the Arab world certainly played a role, but this cannot be the entire explanation. Examining different ways societies can change must be anchored in the Arabic literary tradition, so that a universal story of mankind, as Tahtawi conceived of it already in 1834 in *Takhlis*, makes sense to its audience. This requires a deeper look into older Arabic historiographical and philosophical conceptions of time and change and their anchorage in the different traditions of Islam and Christianity. Despite similarities between Western and Arab worldviews in the nineteenth century, one must question whether the intertwinement of transcendence and immanence ever existed in the Arab world to the extent that Taylor assumes it did in Western Europe.

Second, in the historical conceptualization presented here, the West is granted a decisive role in engendering change. The reconsideration of transcendence/immanence within a new story about the world thus seems to already pave the way for Western modernity as a thinkable option for fostering renewal and reform. In a discussion of the secular age from an Arab perspective one must take into consideration this inclusivist standpoint and the conceptualization of different cultural entities related to it. Thinking modernity in the Arabic context thus entails thinking cultural difference.

Bibliography

Abu-Lughod, Ibrahim. 1963. *Arab Rediscovery of Europe: a Study in Cultural Encounters.* Princeton: Princeton University Press.
Al-Azmeh, Aziz. 1996. *Islams and Modernities.* New York, London: Verso.
Altman, Israel. 1976. The Political Thought of Rifa'ah Rafi' al-Tahtawi: a Nineteenth Century Egyptian Reformer. Los Angeles: Univ. of California [Diss.].
Ayalon, Ami. 1987. *Language and Change in the Arab Middle East: The Evolution of Modern Arab Political Discourse.* Oxford: Oxford University Press.
Aydin, Cemil. 2013. *The Politics of Anti-Westernism in Asia: Visions of World Order in Pan-Islamic and Pan-Asian Thought.* New York: Columbia University Press.
Badawi, Muhammad Mustafa, and Pierre Cachia. 1992. "Introduction," in *Modern Arabic Literature*, Cambridge History of Arabic Literature, ed. M.M. Badawi, 1–35. Cambridge: Cambridge University Press.
Barut, Muhammad Jamal. 1994. *Harakat at-Tanwir al-'Arabiyya fi al-Qarn al-Tasi' 'Ashar. Halqat Halab.* Damascus: Manshurat Wizarat al-Thaqafa.
Brugman, Jan. 1984. *An Introduction to the History of Modern Arabic Literature in Egypt.* Leiden: E.J. Brill.
Bustani, Butrus. 1977. *Muhit al-Muhit. Qamus Mutawwal li-l-Lugha al-'Arabiyya.* Beirut: Maktabat Lubnan.
Bustani, Butrus. 1999. *Khitab fi al-Hay'a al-Ijtima'iyya wa-l-Muqabila bayna al-'Awa'id al-'Arabiyya wa-l-Franjiyya.* Kaslik: Jami'at al-Ruh al-Qudus.
Charif, Maher. 2000. *Rihanat al-Nahda fi al-Fikr al-'Arabi.* Damascus: Dar al-Mada.
Crabbs, Jack A. 1984. *The Writing of History in Nineteenth-Century Egypt.* Cairo, Detroit: The American University in Cairo Press.
Delanoue, Gilbert. 1982. *Moralistes et Politiques Musulmans.* Tome I. Le Caire: Institut Français d'Archéologie Orientale du Caire.
Dupont, Anne-Laure. 1996. "L'Histoire de l'Islam au Regard des Autres Histoires. Un Article de Jurji Zaydan Traduit par A. Dupont." *Arabica* 43, no. 3: 486–493.
El-Ariss, Tarek. 2013. *Trials of Arab Modernity: Literary Affects and the New Political.* New York: Fordham University Press.
El-Enany, Rasheed. 2012. *Arab Representations of the Occident: East-West Encounters in Arabic Fiction.* London: Routledge.
Elger, Ralf. 2003. "Arabic Travelogues from the Mashrek 1700–1834. A Preliminary Survey of the Genre's Development," in *Crossing and Passages in Genre and Culture*, eds. Christian Szyska and Friederike Pannewick, 27–40. Wiesbaden: Reichert.
Elshakry, Marwa. 2013. *Reading Darwin in Arabic, 1860–1950.* Chicago, London: University of Chicago Press.
Euben, Roxanne L. 2008. *Journeys to the Other Shore: Muslim and Western Travelers in Search of Knowledge.* Princeton: Princeton University Press.
Freitag, Ulrike. 2008. "Arabische Visionen von Modernität im 19. und frühen 20. Jahrhundert: Die Aneignung von Universalien oder die Übernahme fremder Konzepte?," in *Selbstbilder und Fremdbilder. Repräsentationen sozialer Ordnungen im Wandel*, eds. Jörg Baberowski, Hartmut Kaelbe, and Jürgen Schriewer, 89–117. Frankfurt, New York: Campus.

Gonzalez-Quijano, Yves. 2007. "La Renaissance Arabe au XIXe Siècle: Médiums, Médiations et Médiateurs," in *Histoire de la Littérature Arabe Moderne*. Tome I (1800–1945), eds. Boutros Hallaq and Heidi Toelle, 71–113. Paris: Sindbad.

Gran, Peter. 1979. *Islamic Roots of Capitalism: Egypt, 1760–1840*. Austin: University of Texas Press.

Hauerwas, Stanley, and Romand Coles. 2010. "'Long Live the Weeds and the Wilderness Yet': Reflections on A Secular Age." *Modern Theology* 26, no. 3: 349–362.

Heyberger, Bernard. 1994. *Les Chrétiens du Proche-Orient au Temps de la Réforme Catholique (Syrie, Liban, Palestine, XVIIe–XVIIIe siècles)*. Rome: Ecole Française de Rome.

Hill, Peter. 2015. "The first Arabic Translations of Enlightenment Literature. The Damietta Circle oft he 1800s and 1810s." *Intellectual History Review* 25, no. 2: 209–233.

Hourani, Albert Habib. 1983. *Arabic Thought in the Liberal Age, 1798–1939*. Cambridge: Cambridge University Press.

al-Hulw, Karam. 2006. *Al-Fikr al-Libarali 'inda Fransis al-Marrash*. Beirut: Markaz Dirasat al-Wahda al-'Arabiyya.

Ivanyi, Katharina. 2007. "God's Custom Concerning the Rise and Fall of Nations: the Tafsir al Manar on Q 8:53 and Q 13:11." *The Maghreb Review* 32, no. 1: 91–103.

Jalal, Iman al-Sa'id. 2008. *Alfaz al-Hadara fi Misr bi al-Qarn al-Tasi' 'Ashar*. Cairo: Maktabat al-Adab li-l-Tiba'a wa-l-Nashr wa-l-Tawzi'.

Jalal, Iman al-Sa'id. 2006. *al-Mustalah 'inda Rifa'a al-Tahtawi bayna al-Tarjama wa-l-Ta'rib*. Cairo: Maktabat al-Adab.

Johnston, Elizabeth E. 2013a. Reading Science in Early Writings of Leopold Zunz and Rifa'a Rafi' al-Tahtawi: On Beginnings of the Wissenschaft des Judentums and the Nahdha. New York: Columbia University [Diss.].

Johnston, Elizabeth E. 2013b. "Classification and Critique of Sciences in al-Tahtawi's Takhlis (1834)." *Middle Eastern Literatures* 16, no. 3: 282–299.

Khalidi, Tarif. 1981. "The Idea of Progress in Classical Islam." *Journal of Near Eastern Studies* 40, no. 4: 277–289.

Khoury, Raif G. 1983. *Modern Arab Thought: Channels of the French Revolution to the Arab East*. Princeton: Kingston Press.

Kohn, Margaret. 2009. "Afghani on Empire, Islam, and Civilization." *Political Theory* 37, no. 3: 398–422.

Konrad, Felix. 2011. "'Fickle Fate Has Exhausted My Burning Heart': An Egyptian Engineer of the 19th Century Between Belief in Progress and Existential Anxiety." *Die Welt des Islams* 51:145–187.

Krimsti, Feras. 2014. *Die Unruhen von 1850 in Aleppo. Gewalt im urbanen Raum*. Berlin: Klaus Schwarz.

Mahdi, Muhsin. 2001. "The Rational Tradition in Islam," in *Intellectual Traditions in Islam*, ed. Farhad Daftary, 43–65. London: I.B. Tauris.

Mahmood, Saba. 2010. "Can Secularism be Otherwise?," in *Varieties of Secularism in a Secular Age*, eds. Michael Warner, Jonathan Van Antwerpen, and Craig J. Calhoun, 282–299. Cambridge: Harvard University Press.

Makdisi, Ussama. 2002. "After 1860: Debating Religion, Reform, and Nationalism in the Ottoman Empire." *International Journal of Middle East Studies* 34, no. 4: 601–617.

Marrash, Fransis. 1881. *Ghabat al-Haqq*. Beirut: Matba'at al-Qiddis Jawurjiyus li-l-Rum al-Urtudhuks.

Marrash, Fransis. 2004. *Kitab Rihlat Baris*. Beirut: al-Mu'assasa al-'Arabiyya li-l-Dirasat wa l-Nashr.
Masters, Bruce. 2001. *Christians and Jews in the Ottoman Arab World. The Roots of Sectarianism*. Cambridge Studies in Islamic Civilization. Cambridge: Cambridge University Press.
Moosa, Matti. 1997. *The Origins of Modern Arabic Fiction*. Boulder, London: Lynne Rienner Publishers.
Najib, Naji. 1981. *al-Rihla ila al-Gharb wa-l-Rihla ila al-Sharq. Dirasa Muqarina*. Beirut: Dar al-Kalima.
Newman, Daniel L. 2004. *An Imam in Paris: Account of a Stay in France by an Egyptian Cleric (1826–1831)*. London: Saqi.
Patel, Abdulrazzak. 2013. *The Arab Nahdha. The Making of the Intellectual and Humanist Movement*. Edinburgh: Edinburgh University Press.
Philipp, Thomas. 1979. *Ǧurǧi Zaidān, his Life and Thought*. Beirut: Orient-Institut der Deutschen Morgenländischen Gesellschaft.
Quataert, Donald. 2005. *The Ottoman Empire, 1700–1922*. Cambridge: Cambridge University Press.
Robinson, Chase F. 2003. *Islamic Historiography*. Cambridge: Cambridge University Press.
Roussillon, Alain. 2001. "'Ce qu'ils Nomment 'liberté.': Rifa'a al-Tahtawi, ou l'Invention (Avortée) d'une Modernité Politique Ottomane." *Arabica* 48, no. 2: 143–185.
Sajdi, Dana. 2007. "Decline, its Discontents and Ottoman Cultural History: By Way of Introduction," in *Ottoman Tulips, Ottoman Coffee: Leisure and Lifestyle in the Eighteenth Century*, ed. Dana Sajdi, 1–40. London: IB Tauris & Company.
Salama-Carr, Myriam. 2007. "Negotiating Conflict: Rifa'a Rafi' al-TahTawi and the Translation of the "Other" in Nineteenth-Century Egypt." *Social Semiotics* 17, no. 2: 213–227.
Sawaie, Mohammed. 2000. "Rifa'a Rafi' al-Tahtawi and his Contribution to the Lexical Development of Modern Literary Arabic." *International Journal of Middle East Studies* 32, no. 3: 395–410.
Schäbler, Birgit. 2004. "Civilizing Others. Global Modernity and the Local Boundaries (French/German/Ottoman and Arab) of Savagery," in *Globalization and the Muslim World. Culture, Religion, and Modernity*, ed. Birgit Schäbler and Leif Steinberg, 3–31. New York: Syracuse University Press.
Sheehan, Jonathan. 2010. "When Was Disentchantment? History and the Secular Age," in *Varieties of Secularism in a Secular Age*, ed. Michael Warner, Jonathan Van Antwerpen, and Craig J. Calhoun, 217–242. Cambridge, Mass.: Harvard University Press.
Sheehi, Stephen. 2004. *Foundations of Modern Arab Identity*. Gainesville: University Press of Florida.
Sheehi, Stephen. 2005. "Arabic Literary-Scientific Journals: Precedence for Globalization and the Creation of Modernity." *Comparative Studies of South Asia, Africa, and the Middle East* 25, no. 2: 438–448.
Stephan, Johannes. 2012. "Wie man die anderen verstehen soll und wie man über sie schreiben kann. Der Paris-Bericht Rifa'a Rafi' at-Tahtawis (1801–1873) als vielseitige Vermittlung von 'Kultur'." *zeitenblicke* 11, no. 1. http://www.zeitenblicke.de/2012/1/Stephan/index_html (last accessed October 4, 2013).

al-Tahtawi, Rif'a Badawi Rafi'. 1958. *Takhlis al-Ibriz fi Talkhis Bariz*. Ashrafa 'ala Ikhraj hadha al-Kitab wa-Haqqaqahu wa-'Allaqa 'alayhi wa-Qaddama la-hu: Mahdi 'Allam wa-Ahmad Ahmad Badawi wa-Anwar Luqa. Cairo: Wizarat al-Thaqafa wa-l-Irshad al-Qawmi.

al-Tahtawi, Rif'a Badawi Rafi'. 2004. *An Imam in Paris: Account of a Stay in France by an Egyptian Cleric (1826–1831)*, trans. Daniel L. Newman. London: Saqi.

al-Tahtawi, Rif'a Badawi Rafi'. 2010/2011. *al-'Amal al-Kamila*. Vol. 3&4; Tahqiq Muhammad 'Ammara. Cairo: Dar al-Shuruq.

Taylor, Charles. 2004. *Modern Social Imaginaries*. Durham, London: Duke University Press.

Taylor, Charles. 2010a. "Challenging Issues About the Secular Age." *Modern Theology* 26, no. 3: 404–416.

Taylor, Charles. 2010b. "Afterword. Apologia pro Libro Suo," in *Varieties of Secularism in a Secular Age*, eds. Michael Warner, Jonathan Van Antwerpen, and Craig J. Calhoun, 300–321. Cambridge, Mass.: Harvard University Press.

Taylor, Richard C. 2009. "Ibn Rushd/Averroes and 'Islamic' Rationalism." *Medieval Encounters* 15:225–235.

Tomiche, Nadia. 1993. "Nahḍa." *Encyclopédie de l'Islam*, deuxième édition, tome VII, 901–904.

Wagner, Ewald. 2000. "Die literarische Gestaltung von at-Tahtawis Bericht über seinen Aufenthalt in Paris (1826–1831)," in *Beschreibung der Welt: zur Poetik der Reise- und Länderberichte*, eds. Xenja von Ertzdorff and Rudolph Schulz, 427–445. Amsterdam, Atlanta: Rodopi.

Wielandt, Rotraud. 1980. *Das Bild der Europäer in der modernen arabischen Erzähl- und Theaterliteratur*. Wiesbaden: Franz Steiner.

Wielandt, Rotraud. 1992. "Fransîs Fathallâh Marrâshs Zugang zum Gedankengut der Aufklärung und der Französischen Revolution," in *The Middle East and Europe. Encounters and Exchanges*, eds. Geert Jan van Gelder and
Ed de Moor, 116–146. Amsterdam, Atlanta: Rodopi.

Yared, Nazik Saba. 2002. *Secularism and the Arab World: 1850–1939*. London: Saqi Books.

Zachs, Fruma. 2005. *The Making of the Syrian Identity: Intellectuals and Merchants in Nineteenth Century Beirut*. Leiden: Brill.

Zachs, Fruma. 2012. "Cultural and Conceptual Contributions of Beiruti Merchants to the Nahda." *Journal of the Economic and Social History of the Orient* 55, no. 1: 153–182.

Charles Taylor
Afterword

I am grateful for the opportunity to contribute to the discussion in this volume, which is full of interesting points and arguments, and from which I have learned a great deal. I have always seen *A Secular Age* as a very provisional and unfinished work. It in fact draws on a limited range of phenomena and historical experiences, and it obviously needs to be complemented by other accounts and approaches, and in the process amended and altered. I am very glad that the comments that have been made, here as well as elsewhere, have helped to fill out and modify the picture I was trying to paint.

Which is not to say that I agree with all the criticisms; how could anyone? But there is an important space between agreement and disagreement; between seeing an argument as a pure addition to the picture I was trying to offer; and seeing one as simple negation of some element of this picture. This third space is that of misunderstanding. And I mean here not just where I have been misunderstood, but more importantly, where I didn't fully grasp what I was trying to say (that is, the misunderstanding was mine), and the response forces me to clarify and perhaps alter my thesis.

Important loci of such misunderstanding have been my use of the terms "buffered" and "porous," as well my characterizing of the secular age as the site of a "nova;" and of this age as one in which we are aware of our stances in the religious/spiritual domain as "options."

To take this latter point first: Courtney Bender argues that practices that are described by those who pursue them as "spiritual but not religious" are not "ahistorical or anti-historical" (page 293). Here I fully agree. They are often seen as such by those who remain within long-standing historical traditions of faith (and frequently by others as well). And this is often used as a basis to delegitimize these practices, as the on-the-spot inventions of individuals. But I myself don't see them that way, although I may not have made this totally clear in my book.

1

The situation I'm trying to describe, where faith is one option among many (as well as various forms of non- or anti-faith) has been well characterized by Hans Joas in his recent book, *Faith as an Option* (2014). "Option" here means something different from choice. Issues of faith and non-faith are not settled lightly, like choices on a menu. When one enters into or leaves a faith, one feels 'called.' Those who step out wouldn't put it this way, but they nevertheless feel they have no choice in all honesty but to reject faith. "Option" means that for growing numbers of people in the West, or North Atlantic society, as well as some other parts of the world, there is a background understanding to their life of faith/non-faith: they know other people, equally if not more intelligent, or perceptive, who are living another option. The idea that people living within another faith are either weird, or morally deficient, or catastrophically blind, becomes less and less credible. Some of these people will be my friends, others my close kin. This is what it is to see faith as an option.

There are hold-outs: among some more conservative Christians, and also among 'angry' atheists, who don't/can't see things this way, but for more and more people this is their understanding of the context in which they live whatever they have put their faith in.

2

How did this come about? I'd now like to sum this up in a form slightly different from the account in the book. I will mention two large developments, each with two facets.

Disenchantment 1. The first form of this has been coming about over a very long period, centuries in fact. Back in 1500, our ancestors in Europe lived in an 'enchanted' (*verzaubert*) world; one filled with spirits and moral forces, some dangerous (wood spirits), some benign (relics, white magic). Over the last centuries most of us have ceased to see, or – more importantly – to experience the world this way. We are impervious to this dimension of things. We are "buffered selves." This is one of the changes (the main one) that Weber calls "Entzauberung."

Disenchantment 2. The first form of enchantment affected everyone in our civilization. The second was mainly important for the educated minority. It consisted in a notion of the cosmos as expressing and manifesting higher and lower modes of being: for instance, the stars and planets moving ever in perfect circles, versus what exists below the moon, which is changing and only partially realizes the eternal forms above them. A cosmos with levels of being was the context in which societies were embedded, which also reflected these levels in the different social orders, clergy as against lay people; rulers and nobility as against commoners. This too has faded, though over a rather shorter period.

The immanent frame. These different levels of disenchantment have brought about our present shared understanding of our world. We have different ways of ascribing meaning to this world, and particularly between people of faith or without faith; but our general understanding of the universe we share is the one defined by post-Galilean natural science: a universe governed by impersonal causal laws, which can be understood whether or not we see any human meaning in them.

As to our shared understanding of society, it is no longer a reflection of cosmic order, but rather comes about by human action (revolutions, constituent assemblies, seizure of power, and so on) at dateable moments in history. These political structures all claim to be ethically based, and so are meant to embed certain impersonal moral-ethical principles, which have been formulated in our history.

The immanent frame is thus an order of natural laws, human laws, and ethical principles, which we all share, while differing in the ultimate meaning, transcendent or not, that we see in it. This shared understanding is our social imaginary.

Bundling and unbundling: The second big pair of changes is more recent, coming to fruition only in the last century or so. I want to speak of 'unbundlings,' referring to two ways in which religious life has in the past linked certain facets of our life together (bundling), but which have lately come apart.

The first is this: many European societies in the last two centuries were confessional societies. (This is, of course, not true of the United States, but it did apply in some other parts of the Western hemisphere. It applied in my part, namely francophone Quebec.) The people who belonged to the national church also shared many other forms of belonging: family, parish, and nation. To belong to one was (normally) to belong to all. Belongings were bundled. But in the last decades this interweaving of belongings has come apart. The people I share citizenship with, or my kin, or the neighbours in my village, are not necessarily those who share my faith option.

The second form of unbundling is this: Within churches in our civilization, there was an extraordinary variety of spiritual and other activities. The liturgy, of course, but also the celebration of seasonal feasts, the solemnization of rites de passage, special devotions, novenas, pilgrimages, prayers to the Virgin; various charitable organizations and forms of mutual help; and then more private devotions. Different people engaged differentially in these activities, but they were all seen as part of the life of the church (Lacroix 2002). In contemporary society, these activities often split off into separate, dedicated bodies. I may belong to a church, and then also Médecins Sans Frontières, and then practice some form of meditation, and so on; all in a different context or organization.

What has driven these unbundlings? In part the greater mobility, social, geographic, and international, of modern life; the loosening of earlier ties that this brings with it, the newer forms of individualism that it fosters. But also that particular form which we refer to as the 'ethic of authenticity:' the idea that each human being has his or her form of being human and ought to find her form of life and realize it. We can see in twentieth century Western society a steady loosening of closer ties to bundled communities, and a corresponding desire on the part of younger people to step out into the larger society and find their own path. What offsets this process for a while are immigrant populations, who can only survive by holding to their bundled communities. But their children often seek to make their way in the broader society.

The USA was never a highly bundled society in either way, but there too we can observe the loosening of ties to the Catholic urban communities that were still very tight in the immediate post-War period (Ehrenhalt 1994; Wuthnow 1998). And other societies, like Quebec in one way, and the Netherlands in another, which were highly 'pillared,' in the recent past have seen a veritable flight from these tighter identities. More and more people want to be more fully part of the bigger society. This together with the ethic of authenticity has helped drive unbundling.

Disenchantment and unbundling have together brought about a different spiritual landscape. We can see, for example, one consequence of both these changes working together in the laicization of life rituals. People will always want to have recourse to rites de passage to mark the important stages in human life: birth, marriage, the death of loved ones. But in the twentieth century in many Western societies, people very often came to substitute church sacraments with rituals of their own devising. This is most frequent for marriage, and much less in evidence when it comes to funerals. Death is apparently surrounded by mysteries which a quite secularized world has trouble taming.

Or sometimes continuing church rituals are given a quite immanent interpretation by many people who take part. This is very much in evidence in Scandinavian societies, where national and ecclesial belonging are still rather unbundled. But the meaning of Church membership changes. This is the phenomenon Grace Davie (2000) calls "belonging without believing." Complementing this is the phenomenon she calls "believing without belonging," which she sees, among other places, in England. People drop out of active participation in the national church, but yet are happy to see it there, providing occasional rituals, but also just ensuring the continuing presence of the faith in society. This tenuous but still subsistent relation constitutes a kind of "vicarious religion" (Davie 2000).

This phenomenon means that we sometimes exaggerate the degree of 'secularization,' in the sense of abandonment of religion, in some societies, measuring it simply by the drop in regular attendance at church. In many cases, this distance from the church reflects ambivalence, uncertainty, or even something more positive, rather than abandonment of the faith.

José Casanova points out the degree to which 'secularization' in this sense is in Europe an overlay, a kind of generally recognized official story of what is supposed to be happening, rather than an accurate description of things. An amusing side effect of this is that people in Europe when speaking to pollsters tend to under-report their relation to the church, whereas in America many more claim to go to church than do so. These Americans are trying to conform to their "official story." Courtney Bender also makes this point: "the secular is marked not by disenchantment, but by an *oft-repeated claim* that we have been disenchanted," she writes (page 300).

And of course, the older "official story" of sociology, that modernization ineluctably brings secularization, is clearly belied by the American case. It can be argued that this difference is partly accounted for by the fact that unbundling began earlier in America than it did in societies dominated by one national church, common in Europe (and in Quebec). The difference comes not so much from the fact that there is religious competition in the US, as supply side theorists argue; it is probably due rather to the fact that the impact of the age of authenticity, where seekers try to find their own spiritual path, is different in societies where the religious option is dominated by one official body demanding conformity, than it is in a society where faith has been irremediably plural for two centuries already. In the first context (Europe), religion is tainted by its association with power and unearned authority; in the other (the US), it is quite without this negative connotation.

Another consequence is the decline and eventual dissolution of Christendom (see Mounier 1950). By "Christendom" I mean a society and civilization which has been built with the intention of reflecting the Christian faith in all aspects of its life. We emerge from one of the greatest Christendoms, the Latin one. It had its great moments and features, its 'grandeurs'; and also its 'misères,' if I can invoke Pascal. One thinks immediately of the rich culture of literature, music, painting, architecture, Chartres Cathedral, the *Divine Comedy*; and also the attempts to tame warrior impulses, to make a more humane society. But inevitably, there are also the dangers, the down sides: the Inquisition, the forced conformity, the abuses of power, the growth of a smug, self-satisfied 'Christian' culture. Mounier and Bonhöffer were on to something important in their desire to separate the faith from the culture.

But whatever its past highs and lows, Christendom is dissolving. Those who often invoke it most strongly (but safely, in the past, as 'heritage') are secular politicians who want good grounds to exclude Muslims and other outsiders.[1] Indeed, the Christian faith has often been lived outside of Christendom – and is today, in Africa, Asia, as well as de facto in Europe.

What exists in its place is what in *A Secular Age* I call the "nova," the steadily increasing options which are being crafted and defined, and who have to live together, side by side, in society. Courtney Bender's work, including her contribution in this volume, has contributed greatly to our knowledge and understanding of important aspects of contemporary spirituality.

3

But now we come to the difficult parts, the fuzzy areas, which I'm still having trouble working out. One important area of puzzlement, raised by several contributors, surrounds the concept of 'disenchantment,' which I want to link to the distinction of "porous" and "buffered" selves.

Disenchantment (Weber's "Entzauberung") is a concept which has trouble staying in place. It regularly escapes the corral of exact definition. And this is so even in Weber's use. I wanted to confine it to a narrow corral, which I think Weber also had in mind. The "enchanted" world which disenchantment brought to an end was a world full of spirits, and moral forces embedded in things, like relics or love potions. In this world, it was generally agreed that such spirits and forces existed, but that isn't the only difference from our own time, at least in certain societies (including those of the West). There is also the fact that people in those days encountered (or saw themselves as encountering) such forces (in being cured by a relic, or sensing hostile spirits in the forest), and for them this was a straightforward description of their experience, not an interpretive gloss which they were adding, with whatever warrant.

I wanted to stress that there was a real difference in experience, and not simply in beliefs which people held. These forces 'got to' people, in the same way as electric power 'gets to' me today when I switch on the light. I don't think of the electric grid as part of a 'theory' explaining the light going on.

We (I mean most of us in our North Atlantic societies) have been trained out of this experience. We can't have it, even if we try. That's what I mean by our being "buffered." What remains is some sense of the uncanny, and here I'm fol-

---

[1] See the Quebec Charter of Values, which the recent Parti Québécois government tried to foist on us: http://www.assnat.qc.ca/en/travaux-parlementaires/projets-loi/projet-loi-60-40-1.html (last accessed February 17, 2015).

lowing Colin Jager in his discussion of the Gothic novel. But this experience is accompanied by a sense of ontic indefiniteness, similar to that which emerges with the subtler languages of post-Romantic poetry (and, here I agree with Jager, probably related). Now sensing the uncanny has features in common with earlier encounters of moral forces; in both cases, the experience is out of the ordinary; we are encountering something which is beyond the banal, and is in some sense mysterious. But this is no longer a defined force recognized in our world.

So I hope to have chained down 'enchantment' (and thus 'disenchantment'). But it won't stay put. And for a good reason. It is widely felt that the modern training and discipline which has made us "buffered" has excluded too much. That a sense of contact, kinship, attunement to the universe has been made much harder and highly problematic. The art and thought of the Romantic period gave voice to this kind of unease and dissatisfaction with modern identity. It is not surprising that since that period, people have been tempted to view disenchantment as a loss, rather than an achievement, and even to call for a 're-enchantment' of the world.

So when the distinction "porous"/"buffered" is taken up in debate, we often see a different reading than the one I was proposing. Buffered selves are not only those incapable of recapturing the original experience of enchantment, but also and mostly those who have turned their back on any kinship with the extra-human.

Now I think there is an important distinction between the two senses. Because re-enchantment today, as an attainable goal, doesn't mean – I would say, can't mean – returning to the way of experiencing the world of our ancestors of 500 years ago (or less, indeed, considerably less for certain populations). What it must mean is that there can be a way forward in which we can recover new ways of living in attunement with the world and universe we exist within (Taylor 2011).

So I want to retain my narrow, 'corralled' concept of disenchantment, but I understand why the horse keeps jumping the fence; and am even partly reconciled to it. The issues of 're-enchantment' that many people want to debate today are intertwined causally and conceptually with 'disenchantment' in the narrow sense, and clearly defining the difference between what was at stake in earlier 'disenchantment,' and what is at issue in 're-enchantment' today, is so difficult, that keeping the horse in the corral will be next to impossible.[2]

---

[2] I am somewhat consoled by the reflection that Weber's horse also seems to have escaped the corral. He seems to have started with a narrow concept: Entzauberung involved purging the

Moreover, if like me one is on the 'Romantic' side in this question of re-enchantment, one can discern a continuity here. One of the convictions powering post-Romantic poetry, as well as a good part of contemporary ecological concerns, is that the kinship with the universe exists, and that living in attunement with the world is a profound human need/aspiration. But if you take this stance, then it is not possible simply to condemn earlier religious or spiritual notions of kinship with nature as wrong-headed projections of human concerns on the non-human, a kind of 'pathetic fallacy.' We need to go on trying to explain what underlay these earlier forms of spiritual belief and practice, because understanding these may help us to recover new forms of attunement which are possible for us; and vice versa: each will cast light on the other.

So that Hölderlin, for example, invokes "gods" (in some sense; his "das Herz des fühlenden Menschen" ["the heart of the feeling human"] is worth pondering); with all their ontic indefiniteness. It is worth asking why he chose this term.

4

All this brings me to the major question in Jager's paper: what does this whole story of disenchantment and hoped-for re-enchantment mean for our political goals? It is clear that the writers of the 1790s saw these issues in political terms, even after they were dismayed and perplexed by the negative turn in the French Revolution. They wanted to repair not just the break with nature, within us and without, but also the isolation between human beings.

Now a lot of interesting thinking is going on today which stands in some clear relation of succession to that of Schiller and his generation. In our time (at least if you're my age), there was Marcuse, as Jager mentions. But more recently, we have attempts by the sociologist Hartmut Rosa (2010; 2013) to rethink the issue of our attunement with the world in terms of the concept of "resonance," and to work out the notion of the good life which should underpin our efforts to reform our failing democracies. A large-scale collaborative effort is under way, inspired by Rosa and this theory, in a "Research Group on post-Growth societies." The underlying intuition is that our present society not only generates alienation through being exclusively focused on instrumental reason,

---

world of "magic," and he was aware that this was first of all the concern with certain religious traditions, those descended from Judaism, although different variants of Christianity and Islam pursued the agenda with differential zeal and scope. But later Weber begins to use the term in a much broader sense, englobing the denial and sidelining of religion itself. This in spite of his intimate knowledge of Protestantism.

but also because it suffers structurally from a drive to ever-greater acceleration. The problems here are difficult, one might say intractable. But serious work is being done to understand them in greater depth. At any rate, this is one important avenue through which the political entailments of the Romantic critique can be worked out.

I have a sense that I have not so much resolved the fuzziness that surrounds my notion of disenchantment, but offered some (more or less convincing) mitigating circumstances which explains without necessarily excusing it. But I am grateful for the probing criticisms which have forced me to go at least this far.

5

Several papers of this volume raise interesting questions relating the possible relevance of *A Secular Age* to other parts of the world. I'll try to deal with some of these, I'm sure not adequately, but at least by clarifying some issues.

The first question arises out of my self-limitation to what was originally known as Latin Christendom, and then later came to be called 'Europe' (including some of the settler societies European powers planted elsewhere), and still later is often referred to as 'the West.'

Florian Zemmin has identified the reason for this (even though he sometimes seems uncertain of his reading of my intentions). I have long been a subscriber to the family of views that have gone under such names as 'Alternative Modernities' or 'Multiple Modernities.' The underlying idea is that there is no single definition of 'modernity' valid across all differences of civilization and culture. Modernization theories have often assumed this, and have seen human history as passing through a number of stages, basically identical, but which occur in different societies at different times. Naturally, the pioneers were identified here as 'Western' societies, and the others were destined (if lucky) to follow the same stages somewhat later. Obviously, these theories reflected a certain self-congratulation of Western societies.

The underlying idea of speaking of 'multiple modernities' was something like the following. Our contemporary world contains a number of societies which resemble each other in respect of certain institutions: states claiming the monopoly of violence, and also dedicated to bringing about 'development' of some kind in their societies, bureaucracies at the disposal of state power, industrial economies (at least in aspiration), science and its application to technology. These societies also are the site of certain changes: social-geographical mobility, urbanization, expansion of markets. This is an incomplete list. It leaves out the changes of culture and social imaginary that enable the above list of institutions to come into being; for instance the kinds of changes that can make a state of the kind just described minimally legitimate, and therefore effective; the kind of changes in outlook and self-understanding which can allow for the new mobility without dissolving social bonds, and so on.

The intuition of 'multiplicity' here is that, while the first list includes more or less common features, the second doesn't and can't. I say "can't," because developing the culture and imaginary that can sustain the items in the first list amounts to a very different task in societies whose historical cultures are very different. This is already evident within 'Europe:' from the common features of European political culture there have emerged rather different itineraries in the UK, than in France, than in Germany, etc. And the uniformization is far from complete in, say, the present EU: think of Hungary, for instance.

Now 'secularization' is definitely a term from my second list. There are similar processes that are invoked by this term, but the self-understandings involved are clearly very different, to the point where people often question whether the term properly applies to certain societies, rather than distorting our understanding of what goes on. So the idea of a universal process of secularization, valid across all boundaries, is a non-starter. It is one of the constituents of the original, falsely universal, modernization theories. How can we proceed, then, if we want to understand the processes that people often group under 'secularization'?

My answer would be: by the methods of comparative politics, sociology, and history. I don't mean what often goes by the name, for instance, of 'comparative politics' as taught in many political science departments, which defines itself as the search for general, cross-cultural laws. I mean the development of contrastive comparisons, in which the differences point up crucial features of each of the terms. (The godfather of these comparisons in the West is probably Montesquieu.)

But to have contrastive comparisons, you need to have good case studies of the terms to be compared. Hence the idea of doing a study on how what is called secularity, secularization, secularism, in the West emerged in the West. How would this help our general understanding? Well, a study of this kind might produce the following reaction from people familiar with other societies (and this is what I was hoping for from the outset): that's an interesting account of what happened in Europe, but it didn't happen at all like that here.

Great! There have been responses like this, and the comparison can be very fruitful for both sides. We try to define what 'didn't happen here,' or 'what happened instead here,' and this clarifies the story in both places. It can help a study of the society contrasted to the 'West,' and it can help to point up certain things in the West which will change and refine the first story. If I understand him rightly, I think this is part of what Zemmin has in mind.

Of course, drawing the boundaries of a case study is very tricky and controversial. One could argue that I drew mine too broadly. Within the 'West,' or the societies emerging out of Latin Christendom, there are great differences: between Catholic and Protestant societies, between Lutheran and Calvinist, and so on. Very good work has been done in delineating different itineraries of the secular between these different types, notably by David Martin (2005). And I tried to take account of these in my generalizations. But even so, there have been legitimate complaints, for instance from people familiar with Scandinavian Lutheran societies, that I didn't give their histories the weight they deserve. My only plea is the one I made at the beginning of this essay, that *A Secular Age* is incomplete, that it is only a first draft of what the ideal such case study might be; and that I expect it to be further modified by such more focussed studies – just as it needs to be by taking account of the confrontations between Western societies and their (often colonial) others.

But this kind of comparative-corrective road is the only one to follow, and I thought it might be furthered by publishing a work like *A Secular Age*. I still think this, but I recognize more and more how badly I communicated this intent in the book, particularly when reading Reinhard Schulze's contribution to this volume. I have trouble recognizing myself in the goal he imputes to me: "ascertaining the normative *Eigensinn* of the West," "a desire to secure the hallmark of Western excellence" (page 185). It is hard to know where to begin. The whole process of Reform, morphing into the inculcation of disciplines in the *Polizeistaat*, and the construction of the modern sovereign homogenizing state, is such a morally ambiguous process, to say the least; it has involved and still does such a degree of sacrifice of humanity, even if one sets aside certain twentieth century extremes like Naziism and Bolshevism, that I can't see any unvarnished description as a "hallmark of excellence."

Now, of course I deal with all that in the first chapters of the book, and they may fade from memory by the time one gets to the end. I can't complain, the book is too long, and as Jager says, different parts have different purposes.

But once that's off my chest, I return to the self-criticism I offered above, my inability to communicate the intent of my self-limitation. This accounts for some bizarre objections: citing atheists in the Islamic world as counter-examples to my thesis, Schulze asks a rhetorical question: "Does one have to become a Christian first before becoming a legitimate heir of secularism?" (page 188). I have no idea what the phrase "a legitimate heir of secularism" could mean. I certainly never discussed such an odd concept in the book. But it seems that an expression I used twice in the book, "modern secular world," misled Schulze, in spite of many indications to the contrary, into believing that I was offering a universal theory.

This aside, Schulze raises some very interesting issues. One is the troubled one I mentioned above: what are the boundaries of my case study? I already discussed objections to the effect that they are drawn too broadly. But we can also question whether they are drawn too narrowly. And where do they fall exactly? What is often called Latin America, for example, is a region of the world that in one sense emerges partly from Latin Christendom. I say "partly," because although there are many Iberian-originating Creoles in these societies, there is also a substantial indigenous and mestizo population. And then there are globalized milieus in today's world which group people of all origins. The story I'm telling doesn't fully apply to these places and milieus.

Another important issue is the role of narrative. I think this is essential to an enterprise like mine. I also think that one cannot just set aside words like 'correct' or 'true' when assessing narratives (Schulze, page 182). Narrative accounts are hermeneutic exercises. They attempt to make sense of a certain passage of biography or history. It would be hazardous, would almost demonstrate blindness, to claim that one's narrative was 'correct' in the sense of being 'incorrigible,' not admitting of any counter-argument or even improvement. But there is still a claim to truth or correctness involved, which means that the account is vulnerable to certain kinds of objection: in your attempt to make sense of this history, you left out or inadequately described some important phenomena which have to be accounted for. Think of François Furet's objections to some of the marxist historians of the French revolution, that they couldn't account for the high-octane discourse of purity and corruption which accompanied the Terror, trying to explain this purely by the pressure of external threats (the Coalition, the Vendée). It's just that explanatory stories don't rely simply on straightforward facts that can be punctually and uncontrovertibly established, but also on a certain construal of what is to be explained.

Another important issue, this one raised by Johannes Stephan, is the distinction transcendent/immanent. I used this with some hesitation in the book, and many objections have shown me why. The terms admit of too many meanings. What is it to 'transcend'? Transcending what? There are too many unanswered questions. One can speak of any act of heroism or unselfishness as a self-transcendence, as well as speaking of heaven and earth in these terms. But in an important sense something like these terms are centrally involved in the story. Very important is the invention of a watertight distinction between two realms, the natural versus the supernatural. This intervened rather late in mediaeval history, and it probably has few analogues in other civilizations.

The important word here is "watertight." All the older views of cosmic order had higher and lower beings: gods versus mortals, gods versus lowly spirits; in Platonic terms, the Ideas versus the things and events in the flux of time-space. But these levels interacted: you couldn't understand what happens on the lower level without reference to the higher one. For Plato the way things operate in the flux is explained by the Ideas which are beyond it.

The development of the natural/supernatural split opens the way to conceiving a lower order which is explainable on its own terms. This may be radically imperfect, and needs intervention from the supernatural, but it has its own internal principle. Later the post-Galilean science of a universe under unvarying natural law comes to fill in this notion of an explanatorily self-sufficient immanent order.

This both suggests the possibility of doing away with reference to the transcendent altogether; and also ensures that some of the debate about this will take a form in which the watertight distinction is taken for granted, and the big questions revolve around whether one of the two terms should just be denied.

This is analogous with and related to another famous dualism, that of Descartes, separating an immaterial soul from a mechanistically explainable body. This provided and still provides the framework for continuing debates about whether human and animal behavior can be exhaustively explained mechanistically or not. It is accepted (and too easily accepted, I would argue) on both sides that the bodily must be mechanistic; the only issue remains: is there something else immaterial which plays a role here?

The analogy, and mutual reinforcement, of the two dualisms stands out. The Galilean-Newtonian universe, explained in non-teleological (for short, mechanistic) terms is undeniable, as is the existence of bodies. Once we see these as explicable in their own terms (an accepted fact for the universe, but widely presumed for animate bodies, too), then the suggestion cannot but follow (though it cannot thereby be proved) that the other term in each case is superfluous. We can see why in the West so many debates about religion and its foundation or lack thereof flow in the channels laid down by this distinction.

6

Günter Thomas's paper offers an interpretation of *A Secular Age* which is equal and opposite to that of Reinhard Schulze. Where Schulze seems to think that I am uncritically upbeat about Western modernity, Thomas sees me as a Catholic apologist, sighing in nostalgia for the good old days. It's not quite clear what constitute for me these good old days. Sometimes it seems to be the European Middle Ages (surely that's what all good Catholic apologists want to return to). But at other moments, more alarmingly, I want to go back before the Axial turn. This is supposed to be for me "the measure, the gold standard" of religion.

So perhaps I should restate the main conclusions of the book. I took for granted, perhaps too much for granted, that an examination of history cannot produce an unalloyed judgment about what has come to pass, either positive or negative. Western modernity has produced some fine achievements: democracy, individual freedom, various forms of scientific and moral enlightenment, a society which at its best presses less heavily on its inhabitants than many previous forms. But there are also negatives: these achievements are often undercut, and in part reversed. And we have lost modes of relation to nature which were superior to our present dominant instrumental-rational stance, which among other things threaten to destroy our planet. These lists are, of course, incomplete. Suffice it to say that you have to have missed something big if you are either unqualifiedly upbeat or downbeat.

A second enframing assumption is that there are passages of history that are contingent; they didn't have to happen. But at the same time, they can't be reversed; the changes they include produce a ratchet effect. I think this is true of the development of the secular age in the West.

The first feature – the mixing of good and bad in large-scale change – makes nostalgia inappropriate. The second feature – irreversibility – makes it inoperative.

So where have we got to? As I said at the outset, we're in a situation in which faith is more and more seen as an option. This sometimes goes along with a weakening of community ties (in the old Quebec parish, there were forms of mutual aid – e.g., la corvée – which have since disappeared). But there also is a liberation of all kinds of suppressed and marginalized spiritualities or modes of search for meaning, both faith-inspired and anti-faith-inspired; and this is a great boon. It is important to recognize the positive here, in order to give it full scope; but *not* because we have a choice to go back which we should refuse. We don't have that choice.

The book also argues strongly against those who think that either faith-inspired or anti-faith-inspired options enjoy some obvious epistemological or moral superiority which should orient us a priori one way or another. (Hence my arguments against various "Closed World Structures" which foreclose whole categories of options; and also the back-and-forth discussions in the last part of *A Secular Age* on our contemporary "conditions of belief.")

On top of this, and still in relation to Thomas's paper especially, I don't accept the charge of anti-Protestant bias. Reform doesn't mean exclusively the Reformation. What I call the drive to Reform started well before; and continued outside of Reform churches after. Among the cases of top-down remaking of society, I cite Charles Borromeo's administration in Milan, and the Catholic Reformation in seventeenth century France. What the book does have is a lop-sided range of examples; there is too much about Catholic societies, and not enough about Protestant ones. This is one of the things that need to be added, and it would modify the analysis. But not overturn it totally.

A last example of the cross-purposes between Thomas and me: on page 60, he informs us that before the Reformation, "the two-speed model" (sc., of the mediaeval Church) was already in great crisis. But that is precisely my thesis! There are potential strains in all post-Axial religions, between the highest Axial aspirations, on the one hand, and the age-old, ongoing rituals aimed to sustain human flourishing, on the other. But these didn't always result in crisis. It was the Reform thrust in Latin Christendom that brought the tension to the fore, by trying to close the gap between high aspiration and ordinary flourishing. This thrust always came partly from below, as well as from ecclesial and political authority; but the complete make-over of societies as Reformed (either Protestant or Catholic) required state power; and they became inevitably imbricated in the disciplines of civility, and the establishment of the sovereign power of the modern state. This had fateful consequences, quite unintended by the original inspiring figures of Reform. Among these is our modern secular age in the West.

There are a number of interesting and important papers in this volume, and many sections of the papers beyond those I have reacted to, which I haven't got space to comment on. I have learned much from these and am grateful for the opportunity to read these and reply.

Bibliography

Davie, Grace. 2000. *Religion in Modern Europe*. Oxford: OUP.
Ehrenhalt, Alan. 1994. *The Lost City*. New York: Basic Books.
Joas, Hans. 2014. *Faith as an Option: Possible Futures for Christianity*. Stanford, CA: Stanford University Press.
Lacroix, Benoît. 2002. *La foi de ma mère*. Montreal: Bellarmin.
Martin, David. 2005. *On Secularization: Towards a Revised General Theory*. Aldenshot: Ashgate.
Mounier, Emmanuel. 1950. *Feu la Chrétienté*. Paris : Éditions du Seuil.
Rosa, Hartmut. 2010. *Alienation and Acceleration: Towards a Critical Theory of Late-Modern Temporality*. Malmö/Arhus: NSU Press
Rosa, Hartmut. 2013. *Social Acceleration: A New Theory of Modernity*; trans Jonathan Trejo-Mathys. New York: Columbia University Press.

Taylor, Charles. 2011. "Disenchantment – Re-Enchantment." In *The Joy of Secularism: 11 Essays for How We Live Now*, ed. George Levine. 57–73. Princeton: Princeton University Press.

Wuthnow, Robert. 1998. *Loose Connections: Joining Together in America's Fragmented Communities*. Cambridge, Mass: Harvard University Press.

Florian Zemmin
An Annotated Bibliography of Responses to *A Secular Age*

1 Aim and scope of this bibliography

This volume has not been the first word on *A Secular Age*, and it certainly won't be the last; nor, as the great variety of contributions in this volume testify, could any one response do justice to this immensely rich work. In concluding this volume, I do not want to add another particular perspective on *A Secular Age* but, by providing an annotated bibliography, I instead aim at structuring the responses that Taylor's work has already received. This seems a worthwhile enterprise[1] for two reasons: First, it shows which aspects of *A Secular Age* have garnered the most attention and to what extent Taylor's work has been received in individual disciplines. Second, it serves as a tool for future contributions on *A Secular Age*, helping to sharpen those contributions' perspective and enhancing their potential complementarity with other contributions. This bibliography is therefore both looking back and ahead. By providing an overview of previous responses to *A Secular Age* it facilitates future discussions as well.

The bibliography is compiled according to the following criteria: It includes only contributions in English, directly responding to *A Secular Age*, and published in either a journal (printed or electronically) or in an anthology. Excluded therefore are contributions in other languages,[2] unpublished theses,[3] references

---

[1] For a list of reviews of all major works by Taylor, see: http://www3.nd.edu/~rabbey1/reviews.htm (last accessed August 28, 2013). This greatly helpful website hosts the most comprehensive bibliography of Taylor, however, at least in the case of responses to *ASA*, it is not exhaustive. See also: http://oncharlestaylor.wordpress.com/2ary-bibliography/ (February 5, 2015).

[2] The exclusion of other languages does not only serve to keep the task at hand manageable. Most contributions to *A Secular Age* have indeed been written in English. What is more, an extension to other languages would have been of relevance to only a small fractions of the readers of this volume and would have been arbitrary in any case since it would have depended on this author's language skills. Nevertheless, let me refer the reader to the following non-English contributions: In German: From a symposium with papers by Vittorio Hösle, Hans Joas, Ludwig Nagl, and Hent de Vries, published in *Deutsche Zeitschrift für Philosophie* 57, no. 2 (2009): 288–327. In French: Taussig, Sylvie, ed., 2014. *Charles Taylor. Religion et sécularisation*. Paris: CNRS Éditions. In Spanish: Grueso, Delfin Ignacio. 2008. "Tres modos de involucrar el reconocimiento en la justicia." *Praxis Filosofica* 27: 49–71, and Vanney, María Alejandra. 2008. "[Review of] *A Secular Age*." *Anuario Filosofico* 41, no. 1: 207–210. In Italian: Oviedo,

to *A Secular Age* as part of a broader article or book, articles in newspapers and magazines,[4] interviews,[5] and blogs.[6] One blog that deserves more than a mere mentioning in the footnotes is *The Immanent Frame*.[7] It is there that the first academic discussion of *A Secular Age* took place, with Taylor himself among the distinguished group of contributors.

Even with these restrictions, the following bibliography still includes 123 entries, which are numbered and structured primarily chronologically. For each year I then first list anthologies, special issues of journals or other *collections of responses*, with the individual contributions appearing in the order as they appear in the volume. After these collections, individual responses are arranged alphabetically. For each entry I state the author's discipline and, after the colon, the aspects of *A Secular Age* focused upon. For the latter I have formed eight categories. Following the bibliography the reader will find a list of these categories as well as the different disciplines, stating which entries belong to the individual categories or disciplines. The categorization of focal points is intended as a first broad orientation for the reader, rather than a detailed engagement with the author's arguments. The broadest categories are specified in the annotations of the

---

Lluís. 2008. "I cristiani in un mondo secolarizzato: la proposta di Charles Taylor." *Antonianum* 83, no. 3: 511–523; four other contributions in Italian appeared in *Gregorianum* (2013) 94, no. 1: 141–167, 173–179.

3 For example, Chau, Carolyn Anne Sze-Ming. 2012. *A Theological Interpretation of Catholic Witness and Mission in a Secular Age: Charles Taylor and Hans Urs von Balthasar on Faith, Church, and Modernity*, PhD thesis, University of St. Michael's College.

4 It was in newspapers that some of the first responses to *ASA* appeared. Worth mentioning are: Jeffries, Stuart. 2007. "Is that all there is?." *The Guardian*, http://www.theguardian.com/books/2007/dec/08/society1 (last accessed August 28, 2013); Mahoney, Daniel J. 2007. "The Re-Enchantment of the World [Review of Secular Age]." *Wall Street Journal*, http://online.wsj.com/public/article/SB119034571151235021.html (last accessed August 28, 2013); Larmore, Charles. 2008. "How Much Can We Stand?." *The New Republic*, http://www.newrepublic.com/article/books/how-much-can-we-stand (last accessed August 28, 2013); Brooks, David. 2013. "The Secular Society." *The New York Times*, http://www.nytimes.com/2013/07/09/opinion/brooks-the-secular-society.html?ref=opinion&_r=0 (last accessed August 28, 2013).

5 For example, Taylor, Charles, and Ronold A. Kuipers. 2008. "Religious Belonging in an 'Age of Authenticity:' A Conversation with Charles Taylor (Part Two of Three)." http://theotherjournal.com/2008/06/23/religious-belonging-in-an-age-of-authenticity-a-conversation-with-charles-taylor-part-two-of-three/ (last accessed August 28, 2013).

6 Here worth mentioning of the generally excluded blogs are the following: http://onlyagame.typepad.com/only_a_game/2008/10/charles-taylors-a-secular-age.html (last accessed August 28, 2013); Huq, Aziz. 2007. "Keeping God Out of It [Review of Charles Taylor: *A Secular Age* and Mark Lilla: *The Stillborn God*]." *The American Prospect*, http://prospect.org/article/keeping-god-out-it (last accessed August 28, 2013).

7 http://blogs.ssrc.org/tif/ (last accessed August 28, 2013).

individual entries, e.g. adding which of "Taylor's concepts" are dealt with. In light of this bibliography's limited space and its purpose as a first orientation, I hope the contributions' authors will forgive me for not presenting their arguments in as detailed a fashion as they deserve. When suitable, I will quote the summary or abstract of the contribution itself. The most substantial contributions are marked with an asterisk in front of their entry number.

2 Responses to *A Secular Age*: An annotated bibliography

2008

1. *Fides et historia* (2008) 42 no. 2

1a. 27–30. Katerberg, William. "What Would You Choose? Belief in a Cross-Pressured Age."
Mainly a summary, introducing the subsequent responses by Larsen and Walhof.
History: summary

*1b. 31–38. Larsen, Timothy. "We Live in a Cross-Pressured Age."
Fundamental reflections on the usefulness of *ASA* for historians. Larsen also includes remarks on the style of *ASA* and regards as most enlightening Taylor's diagnosis of our present.
History: summary, style, history, story

*1c. 39–48. Walhof, Darren. "Politics, Religion, and the Spaces of Secularity."
Walhof criticizes blind spots in Taylor's conception of the subject matter and lack of engagement with scholarly literature.
Political Science: Taylor's concepts (secularity, religion), present empirical

2. Allen, Brooke. 2008. "The Value of Doubt. [A Review of] *A Secular Age* by Charles Taylor; *Empires of Belief: Why We Need More Skepticism and Doubt in the Twenty-First Century* by Stuart Sim; *Hypatia of Alexandria* by Michael A. B. Deakin; *Modes of Faith: Secular Surrogates for Lost Religious Belief* by Theodore Ziolkowski." *The Hudson Review* 61 no. 1: 199–210.

Allen very much doubts that our age is a secular one – on all three levels of secularity that Taylor distinguishes. He points to Taylor's Christian bias against non-believers and rationalists and bemoans the inaccessibility of *ASA* due to its style.

Philosophy: present empirical, Taylor's intentions (Christian bias), style

3. Benson, John. 2008. "Some Thoughts on Charles Taylor's *A Secular Age*." *Dialog: A Journal of Theology* 47 no. 2: 88–90.

Benson thanks *ASA* for bringing to life the enchanted world of pre-modernity and for illustrating that our modern, disenchanted state is less terrifying and preferable.

Theology: present normative

*4. Calhoun, Craig. 2008. "[Review of] Charles Taylor, *A Secular Age*." *European Journal of Sociology* 49 no. 3: 455–461.

Calhoun values *ASA* for depicting secularism as a worldview of its own, rather than just as a result of the "subtraction" of former religious layers. He points to the limitations of *ASA* as being too narrowly focused on Latin Christendom and on intellectual elites rather than social practice. Calhoun finds two aspects of *ASA* especially noteworthy: First and foremost, Taylor's focus on belief and his linking of individual experience with broader cultural conditions and changes; second, Taylor's genealogy of secular culture as arising out of reorientations within Christian thinking.

Sociology: Taylor's concepts (secularism, belief, fullness), history

5. Gallagher, Michael Paul. 2008. "Charles Taylor's Critique of 'Secularization'." *Studies: An Irish Quarterly Review* 97 no. 388: 433–444.

Gallagher (see also entries 39h, 62) offers an affirmative summary of those aspects in Taylor's story that "cas[t] light on our history and on our current cultural context of faith" (433).

Theology: summary, Taylor's intentions (Catholic stance)

6. Gilman, James E. 2008. "Faith and Fragility in a Secular Age [Review of *A Secular Age* by Charles Taylor; *The Stillborn God* by Mark Lilla; *Modes of Faith* by Theodore Ziolkowski]." *Religious Studies Review* 34 no. 4: 247–253.

Gilman reviews *ASA* together with two other books, reading them as answers to questions about the future role of religion in secular societies and the respective potentials of a religious and a secular worldview. For *ASA*, Gilman mainly summarizes – very affirmatively – some of its key points. He stresses as remarkable that Taylor in his description focuses not only on the "intellectual elite" but also on the "common, ordinary people" (247).

Philosophy: summary, history, present empirical

*7. Gordon, Peter E. 2008. "The Place of the Sacred in the Absence of God: Charles Taylor's 'A Secular Age'." *Journal of the History of Ideas* 69 no. 4: 647–673.

This extensive review contextualizes *ASA* and some of its open and hidden premises in other sociological and philosophical views. Gordon also reads *ASA* against Taylor's own previous œuvre. As a difference from the latter, Gordon stresses the "unabashedly confessional character" of *ASA*, in which Taylor speaks as "a truly Catholic philosopher for modernity" (651). Gordon especially reveals Taylor's hidden premise of an ahistorical transcendent reality.

History, Philosophy: Taylor's concepts (transcendence), Taylor's intentions (Catholic)

8. Gray, John. 2008. "Faith in Reason: Secular fantasies of a godless age." *Harper's Magazine* 316 no. 1892: 85–89.

Gray, who reviews *ASA* together with *Secularism Confronts Islam* by Olivier Roy and *The Stillborn God* by Mark Lilla, appreciates Taylor's argument against the decreasing relevance of religion in secular societies but maintains that the Christian origins of modernity are more comprehensive and fundamental than Taylor suggests.

Philosophy: story

9. Griffiths, Paul J. 2008. "[Review of *A Secular Age*]." *The Thomist: A Speculative Quarterly Review* 72 no. 4: 665–669.

n.a.

Theology

*10. Hurd, Elizabeth Shakman. 2008. "[Review of] *A Secular Age* by Charles Taylor." *Political Theory* 36 no. 3: 486–491.

Hurd appreciates the complexity and forcefulness of Taylor's story. She criticizes his dualism of Christian belief and exclusive humanism as excluding other possible stances and points to the role of the other in the evolvement of Western self-understandings.

Political Science: Taylor's concepts (neo-Durkheimian, fullness, transcendent/immanent), story (parochialism)

11. Lyon, David. 2008. "Possibilities for post-secular sociology." *Canadian Journal of Sociology* 33 no. 3: 693–696.

Lyon (see also entry 43c) points to the general value of *ASA* for theories on contemporary secular societies.

Sociology: summary (appreciative)

12. Marty, Martin E. 2008. "[Review of] *A Secular Age* by Charles Taylor." *Church History* 77 no. 3: 773–775.

Marty comments on the peculiarities of Taylor's (hi)story and what historians may draw from it.

History: history

*13. Miller, James. 2008. "What Secular Age?" *International Journal of Politics Culture and Society* 21 no. 1: 5–10.

Miller questions whether our age is as secular as Taylor suggests and argues that the main difference today is not between believers and unbelievers as Taylor claims but rather between monists and pluralists, be they religious or not.

Philosophy: Taylor's intentions, Taylor's concepts (belief, unbelief), present empirical

14. Morgan, Michael L. 2008. "[Review of] Charles Taylor: *A Secular Age*." *Notre Dame Philosophical Reviews*, http://ndpr.nd.edu/news/23696-a-secular-age/ (last accessed August 18, 2013).

This very appreciative summary highlights Taylor's ability to use language broad enough so as to include a variety of stances whilst still being sufficiently specific.

Philosophy: summary, Taylor's concepts (transcendence/immanence, belief/unbelief), Taylor's intentions (nuanced Christian commitment), story (possible other stories)

15. Rossi, Philip J., S.J. 2008. "[Review of] *A Secular Age*." *Theological Studies* 69 no. 4: 953–954.

Rossi offers an appreciative summary of *ASA*.

Theology: summary, Taylor's intentions (theological agenda)

16. Urbinati, Nadia. 2008. "[Review of] *A Secular Age*." *European Journal of Sociology* 49 no. 3: 462–466.

Urbinati sees Taylor's Christian agenda at work in not denying but rather subsuming all other possible standpoints.

Sociology: Taylor's intentions (Christian bias), story (parochialism)

17. Ward, Ian. 2008. "[Review of] Charles Taylor, *A Secular Age.*" *The Journal of Religion* 88 no. 3: 420–422.

Next to a brief summary, Ward hints at possible lines of criticism awaiting *ASA* and wonders about the place to which *ASA* will be assigned in broader scholarly debates.

Philosophy: summary, Taylor's concepts (religious experience), style

2009

18. "Academic Roundtable on Charles Taylor, *A Secular Age.*" *expositions. Interdisciplinary Studies in the Humanities* (2009) 3 no. 1.

18a. 97–105. Watson, Micah. "Secularism's Fragile Buffered Selves."
Watson questions whether our present is as emptied of religion as Taylor allegedly suggests. Moreover, Watson argues against (his reading of) Taylor that a society would be unsustainable without religious bases.
Political Science: present normative

18b. 106–114. Ledewitz, Bruce. "Charles Taylor and the Future of Secularism."
Ledewitz criticizes Taylor for portraying "traditional belief in God or empty secularism" as the only alternatives available, ruling out any intermediary position (107). To Ledewitz the latter not only exists but is clearly preferable, even more so as traditional belief no longer is an option when taking scientific claims seriously, which Taylor allegedly does not.
Law: present normative, Taylor's intentions (traditional Christian belief)

19. Ballard, Bruce. 2009. "[Review of] *A Secular Age.*" *Philosophia Christi* 11 no. 2: 485–488.

Ballard sees two kinds of apologetics at work in *ASA:* a negative one defending faith and a positive one providing support for belief. He "examine[s] the pertinent arguments for Taylor's negative and positive apologetics, particularly against the test case of hell" (161).

Philosophy: Taylor's intentions (apologetics)

20. Chakrabarty, Dipesh. 2009. "The Modern and the Secular in the West: An Outsider's View." *Journal of the American Academy of Religion* 77 no. 2: 393–403.

In this appreciative summary, Chakrabarty focuses on the buffered self as central to Taylor's story and offers preliminary thoughts on the applicability of *ASA* to modern India.

History: summary, Taylor's concepts (buffered self)

21. Cooke, Bill. 2009. "Charles Taylor and the Return of Theology-As-History." *Intellectual History Review* 19 no. 1: 133–139.
n.a.
Religious Studies

*22. Crittenden, Paul James. 2009. "A Secular Age: Reflections on Charles Taylor's Recent Book." *Sophia* 48 no. 4: 469–478.

Crittenden is very critical of Taylor's alleged advancement of a Christian standpoint as the only viable one. According to him, Taylor not only fails to convince that belief in transcendence is the only solution to present dilemmas, he also argues against straw men to dismiss other standpoints.

Philosophy: Taylor's intentions (Christian bias)

23. Elshtain, Jean Bethke. 2009. "[Review of *A Secular Age* by Charles Taylor and *The Law of God* by Remi Brague]." *Politics and Religion* 2 no. 2: 312–319.
n.a.
Philosophy

*24. Jay, Martin. 2009. "Faith-based History." *History and Theory* 48: 76–84.

According to Jay, *ASA* stands "in the tradition of Catholic apologetics" and has hardly anything to offer to historians. Taylor idealizes a religious past, which in fact was as much cross-pressured as our present.

History: history, Taylor's intentions (Christian apologetic), style

25. Knight, Christopher J. 2009. "Charles Taylor's *A Secular Age:* The Apophatic Impulse," in *Charles Taylor's Vision of Modernity: Reconstructions and Interpretations*, ed. Christopher Garbowski, Jan Hudzik, and Jan Klos, 64–86. Newcastle upon Tyne: Cambridge Scholars Publishing.

Knight analyzes Taylor's Christian convictions and their importance for his work both in previous publications and in *ASA*.

Literature: Taylor's intentions (Christian standpoint)

*26. Kozinski, Thaddeus J. 2009. "Becoming Children of Modernity [A Review of *A Secular Age*]." *Modern Age* 51 no. 2: 161–169.

Kozinski reminds us that, as we all live in modernity, the latter appears as a quasi-ontological reality and as such is immensely difficult to grasp or even define. To him, Taylor offers the best attempt at this so far, describing modern selves as living in an immanent frame, always only realizing one possible spin and grasping only parts of the whole.

Philosophy, Theology: Taylor's concepts (modernity, immanent frame), present normative

27. Laitinen, Arto. 2009. "[Review of] Charles Taylor, *A Secular Age.*" *Ethical Theory and Moral Practice* 13: 353–355.

Laitinen summarizes Taylor's historical narrative, which he finds "quite suggestive, although rich with ideal types and speculation about the motivations of the people involved" (355). On the normative side, he mentions Taylor arguing for the "need for a theistic moral source" (355).

Philosophy: summary, Taylor's intentions (Christian standpoint), style

*28. Long, D. S. 2009. "How to read Charles Taylor. The Theological Significance of *A Secular Age.*" *Pro Ecclesia* 18: 93–107.

Long builds upon two lessons he draws from *ASA* for theologians: "how Christianity became corrupted" and "how communion and agape run askew of the modern moral order, taking up what is good in it and raising it to a higher level" (99). He shows how the Church and theologians adapted to the new prevalence of the immanent and how the latter might be overcome.

Theology: Taylor's intentions (theological premises), Taylor's concepts (agape), present normative

29. Lundberg, Anders. 2009. "[Review of] Charles Taylor[:] A Secular Age." *Acta Sociologica* 52 no. 3: 291–292.

Sociology: summary, Taylor's intentions (Christian standpoint), style

30. May, Collin. 2009. "[Review of] Charles Taylor, *A Secular Age.*" *Society* 46: 199–203.

Whilst mainly appreciative of *ASA*, May criticizes Taylor for putting forth a story that shares with subtraction stories too many false assumptions about pre-modernity.

History: history, story

31. McCurry, Jeffrey. 2009. "[Review of] A Secular Age, by Charles Taylor." *New Blackfriars* 90 no. 1029: 623–626.

Stressing the value of *ASA* for various disciplines, McCurry himself deals with the way *ASA* engages philosophical arguments, not least to argue for embracing Christian belief.

Philosophy: Taylor's intentions (Christian standpoint)

32. Oliverio, William L., Jr. 2009. "[Review of] Charles Taylor, *A Secular Age*." *Pneuma* 31: 137–138.

The Pentecostal Christian Oliverio finds that Taylor portrays his form of experiential belief as suitable for the secular age.

Theology: Taylor's intentions (Christian standpoint), present normative

33. Oviedo, Lluís. 2009. "Christians in a Secularized World: Charles Taylor's Last Endeavor." *Reviews in Religion and Theology* 16 no. 1: 79–85.

Oviedo (see also entry 64) is doubtful whether historical developments are not too complex to allow for a genealogy. More importantly, Oviedo criticizes Taylor for allegedly voicing as many doubts against a Christian standpoint as against its "secular antithesis."

Theology: Taylor's intentions (overly critical of Christianity, too), present normative

34. Roberts, Vaughan S. 2009. "[Review of] *A Secular Age* by Charles Taylor." *Implicit Religion* 12 no. 1: 121–123.

Roberts reads Taylor as making "an appeal for the middle ground, which involves both dwelling and seeking" (122).

Theology: summary, Taylor's intentions (middle ground)

35. Ross, Daniel. 2009. "[Review of] Charles Taylor, *A Secular Age*." *Thesis Eleven* 99: 112–121.

Ross contextualizes *ASA* in Taylor's overall philosophy of meaning and strong evaluations, reading it mainly as a continuation of *Sources of the Self*.

Philosophy: summary, Taylor's intentions (theism)

*36. Schweiker, William. 2009. "Our Religious Situation: Charles Taylor's *A Secular Age*." *American Journal of Theology & Philosophy* 30 no. 3: 323–329.

Schweiker (see also entry 41a) sees *ASA* as interweaving three major themes of Taylor's previous work, the "centrality of questions of meaning," "the historical and social nature of human thought and life," and the relevance of normative outlooks for social relations and history, into a fourth theme, religion and transcendence. Schweiker criticizes Taylor's bias in his conception of fullness and his portrayal of exclusive humanism.

Theology: Taylor's intentions (Christian standpoint), Taylor's concepts (fullness), story

37. Storey, David. 2009. "Charles Taylor's *A Secular Age:* Breaking the Spell of the Immanent Frame," in *Rethinking Secularization: Philosophy and the Prophecy of a*

Secular Age, ed. Herbert de Vriese and Gary Gabor, 177–208. Newcastle upon Tyne, UK: Cambridge Scholars Publishing.

Storey points out the phenomenological and genealogical aspects that make Taylor's account of secularization unique (only mentioning the analytical dimension as a third level of Taylor's account). He then summarizes landmarks of Taylor's story and Taylor's critique of other secularization theories and closes with critical remarks on Taylor's descriptive scope, its relation to history, and Taylor's Christian bias in the notion of fullness.

Philosophy: story, Taylor's concepts (fullness), history

38. Wallulis, Jerry. 2009. "[Review of] *A Secular Age* by Charles Taylor." *Philosophy and Rhetoric* 42 no. 3: 302–312.

This extensive summary includes some tentatively critical remarks on Taylor's conception of fullness.

Philosophy: summary, Taylor's concepts (fullness)

2010

39. Leask, Ian, Eoin Cassidy, Alan Kearns, Fainche Ryan, and Mary Shanahan, eds., 2010. *The Taylor Effect: Responding to a [sic] Secular Age*. Newcastle upon Tyne, UK: Cambridge Scholars Publishing.

These papers are from a conference on *ASA*, held at the *Mater Dei Institute* in Dublin in June 2009. Most of the contributors come from that institution, and almost all display a distinct Catholic perspective.

*39a. 8–25. Abbey, Ruth. "*A Secular Age:* The Missing Question Mark."

According to Abbey, Taylor greatly exaggerates the dominance of exclusive humanism in the West today, and no empirical data supports his claim that religion has become marginalized. This may partly be explained by the fact that Taylor in the end upholds a very narrow understanding of religion, namely as a belief in the Christian God.

Political Science: present empirical, Taylor's concepts (religion)

39b. 26–38. Cassidy, Eoin G. "'Transcending Human Flourishing': Is There a Need for Subtler Language?."

Cassidy criticizes Taylor's conception of the immanent/transcendent divide, which according to him goes along with purely human flourishing being deficient. He reads Taylor as viewing Enlightenment thought and modernity overly critically.

Philosophy: Taylor's concepts (immanent/transcendent), present empirical

39c. 39–52. Costello, Stephen J. "Beyond Flourishing: 'Fullness' and 'Conversion' in Taylor and Lonergan."

Costello explores Taylor's notion of "fullness," which he understands as necessarily referring to the transcendent, and refers to the Jesuit philosopher and theologian Bernard Lonergan for complementing Taylor's conception.

Philosophy: Taylor's concepts (fullness)

39d. 53–68. Dunne, Joseph. "Our 'Ethical Predicament': Getting to the Heart of *A Secular Age*."

According to Dunne, Taylor wants to show the tensions and pressures within both humanism and Christianity, tensions which supposedly are due to our common ethical predicament.

Philosophy: Taylor's concepts (fullness)

39e. 69–83. Leask, Ian. "Deism, Spinozism, Anti-Humanism."

Leask questions the central role Taylor assigns to Deism for the coming about of exclusive humanism. According to Leask, key figures of Deism instead represent a certain anti-humanism, inspired by Spinoza.

Philosophy: history (role of Deism)

39f. 84–94. Shanahan, Mary. "Establishing an Ethical Community: Taylor and the Christian Self."

Taking into account previous works by Taylor, Shanahan "consider[s] Taylor's analysis of the fragmentation of society and its lack of shared projects in the light of Plato's philosophy of friendship," aiming to show how thereby "we can come to view ethics as the fundamental shared project of humanity" (84).

Philosophy: Taylor's intentions (Christian belief, call for shared projects), present normative

39 g. 96–112. Conway, Michael. "The Chaste Morning of the Infinite: Secularization between the Social Sciences and Theology."

Conway reflects rather generally on sociological and historical theories of secularization from a theological standpoint, with *ASA* mainly providing arguments for criticizing the shortcomings of many accounts of secularization.

Theology: story

39 h. 113–123. Gallagher, Michael Paul. "Translating Taylor: Pastoral and Theological Horizons."

Gallagher (see also entries 5, 62) "provides an introduction to Taylor for those engaged in religious education" (114), focusing on Taylor's "positions on modernity, secularisation, religion in general, Christianity in particular, and forms of faith for today" (115).

Theology: present normative

39i. 124–133. Hannon, Patrick. "Ireland: A Secular Age?."

Hannon asks how present-day Ireland fits into Taylor's depiction of secularity. He urges Christian churches to take into account the reality of pluralism and to promote dialog in pursuit of the common good.

Theology: present normative

39j. 134–145. Hogan, Pádraig. "Religious Inheritances of Learning and the 'Unquiet Frontiers of Modernity'."

Hogan contemplates the difficulties of religious education in an age where faith is no longer axiomatic (which it allegedly had been prior to the Reformation).

Philosophy: present normative

39k. 146–159. Kearns, Alan. "Codes of Ethics in a Secular Age: Loss or Empowerment of Moral Agency?."

Kearns reads *ASA* as rightfully cautioning against the fixation on ethical codes, which tends to neglect moral agents. Kearns then argues that some codes manage to avoid this shortcoming.

Theology: present normative

39 l. 160–174. O'Shea, Andrew. "Sources of the Sacred: Strong Pedagogy and the Making of a Secular Age."

To O'Shea, *ASA* helps to explore the meaning of Christianity today, as Taylor "earnestly confronts the historical reality of violence [...] while also attempting a retrieval of the good" (161).

Theology: present normative

39 m. 175–190. Ryan, Fainche. "'Code Fixation', Dilemmas and the Missing Virtue: Practical Wisdom in a Secular Age."

To Ryan, in our age "after virtue," nothing less changed than our "conception of what it is to be human" (175). In the end, true human being can only be realized in the community of the Church.

Theology: present normative

*40. Warner, Michael, Jonathan VanAntwerpen, and Craig Calhoun, eds. 2010. *Varieties of Secularism in a Secular Age.* Cambridge, Mass: Harvard University Press.

Most chapters in this volume, which assembles an impressive range of scholars, evolved from papers originally presented at a conference in Yale in 2008. Whilst the individual chapters engage with *ASA* to varying extents, this collection remains most useful for circumscribing the role of *ASA* in broader debates about religion and secularity.

*40a. 1–31. Warner, Michael, Jonathan VanAntwerpen, and Craig Calhoun. "Editors' Introduction."

The editors orient the reader to the structure and style of *ASA*, refute previous misreading of it, summarize main points of Taylor's story, and engage with its key concepts. Before briefly summarizing the volume's individual chapters, they remark on the colonial encounter, which is absent from Taylor's account, as crucial to the self-understanding of Western Christendom.

Philosophy, Sociology: summary, style, story (parochialism), Taylor's concepts (fullness, belief, immanence, Reform, modern social imaginaries, post-secular)

*40b. 32–53. Bellah, Robert N. "Confronting Modernity: Maruyama Masao, Jürgen Habemas, and Charles Taylor."

Bellah shows that Masao, Habermas, and Taylor are all influenced by Weber's understanding of modernity. "But while Maruyama had little hope that we can learn from premodernity, and Habermas views it with respect and a degree of regret for its loss, Taylor is the only one of my three figures who clearly feels that abandoning the premodern, letting modernity obliterate our spiritual past, would be an irreparable disaster" (51).

Sociology: Taylor's concepts (modernity), Taylor's intentions (Catholic stance, intention to recover pre-modern spirituality)

*40c. 54–82. Milbank, John. "A Closer Walk on the Wild Side."

Milbank – the protagonist of Radical Orthodoxy, mentioned by Taylor in the Epilogue to *ASA* as proponents of the "Intellectual Deviation Story" complementing his own Reform Master Narrative – assesses Taylor's own theological radicalism. He applauds Taylor for showing that secularization was not inevitable but maintains that the recovery of a pre-modern Christian universalism is more feasible than Taylor's conceding to the status quo suggests.

Theology: story, Taylor's intentions (Christian stance), present normative

*40d. 83–104. Brown, Wendy. "The Sacred, the Secular, and the Profane: Charles Taylor and Karl Marx."
Brown mainly engages with chapter five of *ASA*, "The Spectre of Idealism." She maintains that Taylor dismisses materialism too quickly and shows how Marx's materialist arguments continue to hold insights for the history of secularization.
Political Science: Taylor's concepts (Idealism, materialism), story, history

*40e. 105–125. During, Simon. "Completing Secularism: The Mundane in the Neoliberal Era."
During maintains that crucial gaps in *ASA*'s story are due to Taylor neglecting material factors in secularization. He attributes a religious nostalgia to Taylor and, against Taylor's emphasis of spiritual longing, points to people living happily in the mundane. During names as a desideratum the writing of a history of the mundane as neither religious nor secular.
Literature: story, present empirical, Taylor's concepts (secular, religious), Taylor's intentions (religious nostalgia)

*40 f. 126–144. Connolly, William E. "Belief, Spirituality, and Time."
Connolly maintains that immanence can be opened-up without reference to transcendence. After all, the alternative to transcendence is not only an exclusive humanism, as Taylor suggests, but also an "immanent naturalism" or "mundane transcendence" that avoids the reductions of a closed understanding of immanence without attributing its openings to transcendence.
Philosophy: concepts (immanence, transcendence)

*40 g. 145–165. Bilgrami, Akeel. "What is Enchantment?."
Bilgrami identifies certain normative implications following from Taylor's refutation of subtraction stories and his identification of our secular age as constructed. The modern West then did not achieve an advance in rationality (as the subtraction stories have it) but rather developed its own "ideological conceptual system" (146). This system's reductionist understanding of nature and agency fostered both disenchantment and colonialism, and it continues to obscure our view of enchantment in the present – an enchantment which for Bilgrami is not dependent on a transcendental source.
Philosophy: Taylor's concepts (enchantment), present normative

*40 h. 166–192. Jager, Colin. "This Detail, This History: Charles Taylor's Romanticism."

Pointing to the wider circulation of romanticism in present debates about secularism, Jager shows Taylor to be "a Romantic thinker" (167). Taylor's romanticism becomes visible both in his depiction of secularity as well as in his way of telling the story of secularization. Whilst the genealogical mode of *ASA*, ironically, is indebted to Nietzsche, "Taylor looks to romanticism and the expressivist turn in order to find language for what we have lost [in modernity]" (191), aiming to make the reader experience this loss.

Literature: story, style, Taylor's intentions (Romanticism)

*40i. 193–216. Butler, Jon. "Disquieted History in *A Secular Age*."

Butler argues that *ASA* "is not history for historians, meaning history meant to uncover the past for its own sake […]. Rather, it is history for argument about modernity, the cause of the modern condition, and its possible cure. It is a history of lament and failure intended to propel readers toward a history of meaning and fulfillment" (194). Butler then shows the ways in which Taylor's account is not supported by present empirical evidence or historiographical data, as, for example, belief was not all that axiomatic and unquestioned in pre-modern times.

History: history, present empirical, story, style

*40j. 217–242. Sheehan, Jonathan. "When Was Disenchantment? History and the Secular Age."

Similarly to Butler in the preceding chapter, Sheehan maintains that "the story of the 'secular age' is not a history" (225). Rather, as a "conjectural history" it contrasts a *then* with a *now*, not caring for empirical evidence. Whilst such evidence is difficult to access for pre-modern times, the embeddedness of society in a religious framework clearly was not as axiomatic as Taylor claims. His story stands in the tradition of Christian apologetics, with his bias apparent in concepts like "fullness." Sheehan names a history of the religious indifferent as a desideratum for future research.

History: history, story, Taylor's intentions (Christian bias), Taylor's concepts (fullness, immanence, transcendence, religion, secular)

*40k. 243–264. Göle, Nilüfer. "The Civilizational, Spatial, and Sexual Powers of the Secular."

Göle points to the relation of Western secularism to colonialism. "Western secularity cannot be separated from its claim for a higher form of civilization, its impact in shaping and stigmatizing a certain understanding of religion (as backward), its role in spreading models of secular governance to different parts of the world, and, last but not least, its permeation of material cultures in norms of sexuality and private-public distinctions. I will try to illuminate such blind spots in an inwardly West-looking narrative of the secular [as told by Taylor]" (244). Göle shows that Islam is central to current debates about secularity, which are taking place in an "inter-civilizational conversation," as illustrated by headscarf debates in France and Turkey. Moreover, especially in a migrant context, Islam is no longer axiomatic but rather a resource for individual self-fashioning, and as such is "shaped by the secular age," too (264).

Sociology: story (parochialism), present empirical

*40 l. 265–281. Casanova, José. "A Secular Age: Dawn or Twilight?."

Casanova identifies four genealogical accounts of modernity: "(1) the triumphant secularist and anthropocentric progressive stories of enlightenment [...;] (2) the inverse negative philosophies of history, counter-Enlightenment narratives [...;] (3) the positive, mainly Protestant postmillennial identifications of Western modernity and Christian civilization [;] and (4) their opposite, Nietzschean-derived critical genealogies of modernity." To him, "Taylor's account is superior precisely insofar as it is able to integrate successfully the valid insights of most of the competing genealogical accounts" (267). Casanova characterizes Taylor's intention as wanting to open up the immanent frame for transcendence. As such, "Taylor is likely to be recognized as the last philosopher of secular modernity and as the visionary prophet of the dawn of a postsecular age" (281).

Sociology: story, Taylor's intentions (opening up the immanent frame), present empirical (comparison USA, Europe), Taylor's concepts (immanent, transcendent)

*40 m. 282–299. Mahmood, Saba. "Can Secularism Be Other-wise?."

To Mahmood "one of the greatest virtues of the book [i.e. *ASA*] lies in its authoritative dismantling of the idea that religion and secularism are antithetical worldviews" (282). She is very critical, however, of Taylor's identification of secularity with Christianity, maintaining that the Christian self and the very notion of religion were only fashioned by encountering others, especially in colonial times. Moreover, the process of secularization to a large extent is due to the powers of the nation-state, not to transformations within Christianity, as Taylor has it. Mahmood thinks that Taylor's call to dialog will not be fruitful as long as his own position, which he rightfully names as a starting point for dialog, is ignorant of the other positions within itself.

Anthropology: story (parochialism), history (colonialism), Taylor's intentions (Christian stance)

*40n. 300–321. Taylor, Charles. "Afterword: Apologia pro Libro suo."

Taylor summarizes the main threads of his narrative, elaborates on the concepts of "social imaginary" and "fullness," states his intention in writing *ASA*, and encourages further dialog as inevitable in pluralist societies. He accepts the major criticism to "have neglected the way in which Western understandings of religion were informed through the precolonial and then the colonial encounter with other parts of the world" (301). Taylor defends his approach against another major point of criticism, namely historians' questioning of pre-modern enchantment and axiomacy of belief.

Response: summary, Taylor's concepts (fullness, social imaginary), story (parochialism), Taylor's intentions (Catholic stance, dialog)

*41. Schweiker, William et al. 2010. "Grappling with Charles Taylor's *A Secular Age*." *The Journal of Religion* 90 no. 3: 367–400.

This article consists of eight revised texts presented to Taylor by faculty of the University of Chicago Divinity School in 2008. The summaries of these short but fundamental reflections, mainly by theologians working historically, are taken from the introduction (367–368).

41a. 369–373. Schweiker, William. "Theological Ethics."

After summarizing Taylor's depiction of our present human condition and his vision of fullness, Schweiker (see also entry 36) "argues for seeking a third way between Taylor's account of human fullness, grounded in a sense of transcendence, and exclusively humanistic positions" (368).

Theology: Taylor's concepts (fullness), present normative

41b. 373–377. Hector, Kevin. "Theology and Philosophy of Religion."

"Hector argues that secularity, far from being a merely unintended and unwanted consequence of early modern Reform, in fact enables one of Reform's essential goals – that one's Christianity be authentically one's own" (368).

Theology: history (Reform)

41c. 377–381. Betz, Hans Dieter. "New Testament and Graeco-Roman Religions."

"Betz looks at the de facto 'secular age' left in the wake of Augustus's transformation of Roman religion into a ruler cult" (368).

Theology: history (Romans)

41d. 381–385. Otten, Willemien. "Theology and History of Christianity (Medieval)."

"Otten offers some reconsiderations of Taylor's account of the medieval period [as an ideal religious counter-foil to modernity] and suggests that an awareness of medieval humanism enriches our sense of the Christian tradition, even if it deepens our sense of the problems involved in doing theology in a secular age" (368).
Theology: history (medieval), story (confessionalism)

41e. 386–389. Gilpin, W. Clark. "History of Christianity and Theology (Modern)."
"Gilpin reviews Taylor's account of the 'age of mobilization' (1800–1950), concluding that the 'disembedding' of faith from communal religious culture has enabled personal religiosity to be directly negotiated with consumer culture and national identity, without necessary connection to explicitly religious institutions" (368).
Theology: history, Taylor's concepts (belief)

41f. 389–394. Mendes-Flohr, Paul. "Modern Jewish Thought."
Mendes-Flohr offers "a secularization narrative for modern Central and West European Jewry" (368), understood as "a subspecies of [Taylor's] Western narrative" (390).
Theology (Jewish): story

41 g. 395–398. Rosengarten, Richard. "Religion and Literature."
Rosengarten "analyzes George Eliot's *Middle-march* to complicate Taylor's view of the Victorian era as marking a decisive shift in aesthetics from mimesis to creation, which produced in turn a poetics devoted to private sensibility rather than the reflection of public meaning" (368).
Literature: story (disenchantment), Taylor's concepts (porous self)

41 h. 398–400. Riesebrodt, Martin. "Sociology of Religion."
"Riesebrodt analyzes Taylor's conceptualization of secularization and of religion itself, as well as the comparisons that Taylor draws between Europe and the United States" (368).
Sociology: Taylor's concepts (secularity, religion)

*42. "Symposium: Charles Taylor, *A Secular Age*." *Modern Theology* (2010) 26 no. 3.
This issue brings together five responses to *ASA*, rounded up with a response by Charles Taylor.

*42a. 321–336. Kerr, Fergus. "How Much can a Philosopher do?."

Kerr (see also entry 43a) names it as one task of philosophers to "work out philosophical presuppositions that characterize a society's moral and political practices and customs" (324). In doing so, they hardly can remain neutral. Drawing on *ASA* as well as on previous works by Taylor, Kerr maintains that Taylor, as opposed to what some critics have claimed, has never hidden his Christian allegiance, which becomes especially apparent in his critique of British empiricism.

Theology, Philosophy: Taylor's intentions (Christian standpoint), present normative

*42b. 337–348. Ward, Graham. "History, Belief and Imagination in Charles Taylor's *A Secular Age*."

Ward is a foremost representative of Radical Orthodoxy, to which Taylor refers in the epilog of *ASA* as complementing his own story. Ward asks which of the various disciplines addressed by *ASA* might find Taylor's account useful. He argues that social scientists must be disappointed by Taylor's a priori theological stance. Theologians, on the other hand, would require a clearer theological reading of secularization, yet they can well integrate Taylor's story into their own theological reasoning.

Theology: Taylor's intentions (theological premises), story, present normative

*42c. 349–362. Hauerwas, Stanley, and Romand Coles. "'Long Live the Weeds and the Wilderness Yet': Reflections on *A Secular Age*."

Worrying that "Taylor's use of the immanent/transcendent duality may reproduce the habits of a Christianity that still longs to be a civilizational order" (350), the authors plead for abandoning the distinction between immanent and transcendent and to focus instead on liturgical practices. Taylor in his response acknowledges that he should have spent more time on complicating the distinction between immanent and transcendent.

Theology, Political Science: Taylor's concepts (immanence/transcendence), present normative

*42d. 363–381. Baum, Gregory. "The Response of a Theologian to Charles Taylor's *A Secular Age*."

Baum overall agrees with Taylor, enforcing the latter's avocation of dialog between believers and non-believers as not only desirable but as inevitable. Regarding Taylor's story, Baum points to several blind spots and complementary aspects. For example, he maintains that not only exclusive humanism – which might contain a transcendental level, too – evolved out of Christianity and

then led the way, but that also the later immanent frame was very much welcomed and endorsed by some theologians.
Theology: story, present normative

*42e. 382–403. de Vries, Hent. "The Deep Conditions of Secularity."
De Vries focuses on three aspects: "First, I wish to examine whether there is in fact a possible reversibility or revisability to the so-called 'optional' nature of belief that Taylor thinks is characteristic of the secular age; second, I wish to scrutinize Taylor's notion of 'immediacy' of belief in the same milieu; third, I wish to interrogate his use of the term 'fullness' in delineating the temper of the secular age" (382).
Philosophy: Taylor's concepts (belief, fullness), present empirical

42f. 404–416. Taylor, Charles. "Challenging Issues about the Secular Age."
Taylor spends two to three pages on each of the foregoing contributions, clarifying his views but also accepting some critical points made.
Response

43. "Symposium on Charles Taylor with his Responses." *New Blackfriars* (2010) 91 no. 1036.
This issue brings together a very brief comment and five articles critiquing or expanding on *ASA*. Charles Taylor responds to each contribution individually; his responses are summarized at the end of the individual contributions.

43a. 625–626. Kerr, Fergus. "Comment: Christians in a secular age."
Kerr (see also entry 42a) briefly recalls that Western Christians today are living in a secular environment.
Theology: present empirical

43b. 627–645. McLennan, Gregor. "Uplifting Unbelief."
"This article analyses three of Taylor's principal theoretical moves: his basic account of secularity and related rejection of secularist 'subtraction stories'; his comprehension of historico-empirical realities in the light of a sort of philosophy of history; and his presentation of the transcendental quality of the experience of 'fullness'. Motivated to contest Taylor's framing of the 'unbeliever' as spiritual[l]y deprived and intellectually complacent, the coherence, content and rhetorical overkill of his argumentation in each of these areas is questioned" (Abstract). Charles Taylor in his response (645–647) tries to clarify some of the points he sees fundamentally ignored or misunderstood by McLennan.
Sociology, Response: story, history, Taylor's concepts (fullness)

43c. Lyon, David. 648–662. "Being Post-secular in the Social Sciences: Taylor's Social Imaginaries."

"Following the fall of mainstream secularization paradigms, this article suggests opportunities arise for considering social and political life as 'religious' phenomena and, specifically, for using Taylor's pregnant notion of 'social imaginaries' as a bridge between 'secular' and 'post-secular' social science. Thus, themes implicit in *A Secular Age* are made explicit and used to challenge how social science is done in 'post-secular' times" (Abstract). Taylor in his response (662–664) shows quite some sympathy for the post-secular social sciences envisioned by Lyon, which he takes to be necessarily pluralist, avoiding an a priori marginalization of religion.

Sociology, Response: Taylor's concepts (religion, secular, social imaginary)

*43d. 665–676. Tester, Keith. "Multiculturalism, Catholicism and Us."

"[T]he paper argues that the commitment to multiculturalism forces *A Secular Age* to downplay the importance of Catholicism as an institution. It is contended that the book is a great work of catholicity (small 'c') but in need of more Catholicism (capital 'C')" (Abstract). Otherwise, Tester argues, the 'us' Taylor is constantly addressing remains a bit of a mystery.

Taylor in his response (677–679) addresses his understandings of Catholicism, multiculturalism, and multiple modernities.

Sociology, Response: story, style, Taylor's intentions (Catholic and multiculturalist)

43e. Cervantes, Fernando. 680–694. "Phronêsis vs. Scepticism: An Early Modernist Perspective."

"[T]his article attempts a reassessment of some aspects of early modern thought which have been prominent in recent studies. In particular, it focuses on the thin boundary between illusion and reality, on the lure of scepticism, and on the changing role of the Aristotelian notion of *phronêsis* in human action" (Abstract). Taylor in his response (694–698) thanks Cervantes for his insights regarding the emergence of modern Western epistemology, which he, too, wants to think through further, providing first examples here, mainly from Descartes.

History, Response: history (early modernity)

43f. Flanagan, Kieran. 699–721. "*A Secular Age:* an exercise in breach-mending."

"This article considers three aspects of Taylor's *A Secular Age*: the issue of the status and authority of theological insights derived from sociological analyses; the irresolvable ambiguities of secularity, where it marks the disappearance of religion but inadvertently affirms its persistence; and the properties of nostalgia and memory that unexpectedly shape post-secularity and the forms of enchantment it seeks" (Abstract). Taylor in his response (721–724) clarifies that by "Reform" he was not just referring to the Protestant Reformation, and he maintains that his own belief is not "nostalgic," saying he "believe[s] again," not still.

Sociology, Response: story, Taylor's concepts (secularity, belief)

44. "[Reviews of] Charles Taylor, *A Secular Age*." *Philosophical Investigations* (2010) 33 no. 1.

44a. 67–74. Amesbury, Richard. "[Review of] Charles Taylor, *A Secular Age*."
Amesbury's is mainly an appreciative summary of *ASA*, with a short comparison of Taylor's story and the "Intellectual Deviation Story" (Taylor's term) of Radical Orthodoxy.
Philosophy: summary

44b. 75–81. Kinsey, John. "[Review of] Charles Taylor, *A Secular Age*."
Kinsey summarizes *ASA*, briefly pointing out various blind spots, misconceptions, and implicit premises in Taylor's account, chief among them Taylor's Romantic legacy and his progressive Catholic stance.
Philosophy: summary

45. Andrews, Alex, Floyd Dunphy, and Sarah Azaransky. 2010. "A Roundtable Discussion on Charles Taylor's Book *A Secular Age*." *Political Theology* 11 no. 2: 287–298.
These short contributions contain some interesting but rather scattered observations and remarks. Taylor in his response (299–300) picks up three points: the link between civilization and imperialism, the concepts of the porous and the buffered self, and a possible recovery of forms of society based on networks.
Theology, Philosophy, Response: Taylor's concepts (agape, buffered self), Taylor's intentions (dialog, network society)

46. Colorado, Carlos. 2010. "[Review of] *A Secular Age*." *Touchstone* 28 no. 2: 56–68.
Colorado summarizes *ASA*, pointing to Taylor's Catholic background, which, he argues, had remained implicit in previous works and is now explicated, especially in the last sections of *ASA*. Regarding Taylor's notion of *agape* and his cri-

tique of moral codes, Colorado upholds the necessity of politics and law not sufficiently addressed by Taylor.

Religious Studies: summary, Taylor's intentions (Catholic stance), Taylor's concepts (agape, ethics)

47. Mullender, Richard. 2010. "[Review of] *A Secular Age.*" *Ecclesiastical Law Journal* 12 no. 1: 113–117.
n.a.

48. Root, Andrew. 2010. "[Review of] *A Secular Age.*" *Word & World* 30 no. 1: 111–113.

Root's is a very appreciative summary.
Theology: summary

*49. Rundell, John. 2010. "Charles Taylor and the Secularization Thesis." *Critical Horizons* 11 no. 1: 119–132.

Rundell helpfully summarizes Taylor's understanding of modernity, a term synonymous with a secular age, and of modern social imaginaries.

Philosophy, Sociology: summary, Taylor's concepts (modernity, modern social imaginary, buffered self, immanence)

50. Sampson, Mark. "Faith in Modernity: Reflections from Charles Taylor's *A Secular Age.*" *Crux* 46 no. 1: 28–39.
n.a.

2011

51. *The Australian Journal of Anthropology* (2011) 22.

This special issue is the outcome of a working group "of Melbourne-based ethnographers and social theorists." Their common focus is on Taylor's secularity 3, characterized as "the level of religious experience." The papers are problematizing what they perceive as too strict a division between religion and science and between religious and secular stances. Most contributors are critical of an alleged secularist bias underlying these divisions. The summaries of the individual contributions are taken from the introduction or the contributions' abstracts.

51a. 1–13. Baldacchino, Jean-Paul, and Joel S. Kahn. "Believing in a Secular Age: Anthropology, Sociology, and Religious Experience."

This introduction presents the working group from which this special issue originates, the initial questions asked there, and the evolvement of discussions. Whereas the previous reception of *ASA* allegedly mainly dealt with Taylor's depiction of secularity 1 and 2, this group focuses on secularity 3, the level of religious experience. This focus is common to all subsequent chapters, which are summarized here.

Anthropology, Philosophy: Taylor's concepts (secularity, religion)

51b. 14–39. Eipper, Chris. "The spectre of Godlessness: Making sense of secularity."

"'What does it mean to say that we live in a secular age?' asks the philosopher Charles Taylor from a Christian (Catholic) perspective. This paper critiques key aspects of the way he seeks to answer the question, doing so from a methodologically agnostic anthropological stand-point. It focuses on three key elements of his argument: his construal of the problem of immanence, his account of secularisation, and his treatment of science as an (inadequate) antidote to religion. The critique contains within it the ingredients for an alternative, anthropologically grounded approach to secularity, secularism and secularisation. In this spirit, it moves towards examining actually existing secularity as a syncretic phenomenon that is, in significant respects, definitive of modernity" (Abstract).

Anthropology: Taylor's intentions (Christian bias), Taylor's concepts (immanence, transcendence, secularity), present empirical

51c. 40–55. Smith, Karl. "'Deep Engagement' and Disengaged Reason."

"Taylor continues a long-running critique of disengaged reason and its contributions to the malaise of modernity, focusing especially on its conflictual relationship with religious belief and its central role in the disenchantment of the world. My objective here is to relativise and contextualise the relationship between disengaged and engaged modes of being, in part by exploring some of the ways in which we may be deeply engaged in the world and with one another while also employing the critical faculties that enable us to analyse dispassionately, amongst other things, theistic and other interpretations of being-in-the-world" (Abstract). Whilst Smith largely shares Taylor's critique of disengaged reason as it appears in an exclusivist scientism, he "cannot share his faith that a stronger and deeper engagement in any particular religious orientation leads to either greater individual or collective flourishing, or to a better society" (53).

Sociology, Anthropology: present normative, Taylor's concepts (reason), Taylor's intentions

51d. 56–75. Ireland, Rowan. "Religion on Dover Beach."

"How does transcendental religion flourish when a secular frame sets conditions of belief? This question is put in a case study of the Catholic Newman Society at the University of Melbourne (1955–65). The Society [of which Ireland himself was a member] flourished in a secular University where Charles Taylor's 'immanent frame' was supposedly in place. Explanations are found in the particular spirituality nurtured in the Society and in the contingencies of Australian Catholicism in the mid-twentieth century, but also in the conventions of secular discourse in the University. Conclusions drawn from the case are: (i) that there are elective affinities between some forms of transcendental religion and a secular context; (ii) that social science dichotomies that separate the religious and secular obviate appreciation of elective affinities and hybridisation; (iii) that there are parallels between ethnographic inquiry and inner-worldly spirituality that may help us develop a conversational ethnography" (Abstract).

Sociology: Taylor's concepts (buffered self, porous self, immanence, transcendence, religion), present empirical, present normative

51e. 76–88. Kahn, Joel S. "Understanding: Between Belief and Unbelief."
"This paper addresses issues raised in Taylor's work concerning how communities may come to work in normatively secular ways. For Taylor, it seems to be sufficient for believers (and nonbelievers) to acknowledge that their own 'construals' are not shared by everyone. However, this leaves open the question of how the acknowledgement of difference may be turned into respect. A common strategy is to require that faith-based truth claims are 'bracketed out', treating secular and religious discourse as 'non-overlapping magisteria'. This secularising strategy is, however, problematic on a number of counts. The article makes a case for a less confrontational, more cosmopolitan conversation between secular and religious reason in a post-secular age, examining in particular the possibilities for conversation between science and mysticism. It concludes that it is possible to retain a commitment to naturalism and yet also accept some of the most mystical of propositions, thereby establishing a bridge between 'secular' and 'religious' forms of reasoning" (Abstract).

Philosophy: Taylor's intentions (dialog), present normative

51f. 89–103. Branford, Anna. "Gould and the Fairies."
Branford "examines modern Spiritualism from the mid-eighteenth century through to the early nineteenth century, with a focus on the 1917 case of the Cottingley fairies, in which two children claimed to have produced photographs of fairies. On the basis of her case study, she argues that Gould's magisteria are neither separate nor simply overlapping. Rather, their relationship is one of a more complex intertwinement" (8f.). Branford mentions Taylor only in passing and

then hardly depicts his views adequately, as also becomes visible from Taylor's critical response.
Sociology

51 g. 104–124. Baldacchino, Jean-Paul. "Miracles in the Waiting Room of Modernity: The Canonisation of Dun Ġorġ of Malta."
Baldacchino "examines the understandings of the miraculous in a modern Catholic context, focusing on the process of canonisation and the miracles attributed to the recently canonised first Maltese saint, St. George Preca (1880– 1962). [...] Like the other contributors to this volume, he argues that, rather than diminishing religious experience in modernity, the disengaged discourse of modern science provides the religious with new possibilities and a discourse that shapes, and is shaped by, their understandings of the transcendental. [...] One should not dismiss miracles and sanctity out of hand as somehow 'pre-modern', for his paper demonstrates that the grounds of sanctity and the miraculous are much more complex than secularists typically allow" (9–10).
Anthropology: present empirical, present normative, Taylor's concepts (porous self, buffered self)

51 h. 125–133. Taylor, Charles. "Response."
Taylor responds to each contribution individually. Of the various points addressed, he most extensively elaborates his view and vision of dialogue between different positions.
Response: Taylor's intentions (dialog)

52. Froese, Vic. 2011. "[Review of] Charles Taylor's *A Secular Age.*" *Direction. A Mennonite Brethren Forum* 40 no. 1: 90–100.
Froese gives a very appreciative summary that also briefly reflects on the consequences of *ASA* for the church.
Theology: summary, present normative

53. Horton, John. 2011. "Review article: Peggy Lee's question: Charles Taylor, secularism and the meaning of life." *European Journal of Political Theory* 10 no. 1: 113–121.
N.a.
Political Science

*54. Hunter, Ian. 2011. "Charles Taylor's *A Secular Age* and Secularization in Early Modern Germany." *Modern Intellectual History* 8 no. 3: 621–646.

"In this essay I discuss the historical adequacy of Charles Taylor's philosophical history of secularization, as presented in his *A Secular Age*. I do so by situating it in relation to the contextual historiography of secularization in early modern Europe, with a particular focus on developments in the German Empire" (Abstract).

History: history

55. Kollar, Rene. 2011. "[Review of] *A Secular Age*." *The Heythrop Journal* 52 no. 3: 535–536.

This is a very appreciative, short summary.

Theology: summary

56. Lincoln, A. T. 2011. "Spirituality in a Secular Age: From Charles Taylor to the Study of the Bible and Spirituality." *Acta Theologica* Suppl. 15: 61–80.

"The essay indicates the significance of Taylor's work for understanding the present context of the experience of spirituality. It then suggests some possible implications for how biblical perspectives on spirituality might be studied, highlighting Taylor's category of the social imaginary. Finally, it reflects on the potential of Taylor's work for those who are interested in dialogue between a spirituality rooted in biblical perspectives and contemporary forms of spirituality, focusing on his notion of 'fullness'" (Abstract).

Theology: summary, Taylor's concepts (social imaginary, fullness), Taylor's intentions (dialog), present normative

57. Sedgwick, Timothy F. 2011. "[Review of] *A Secular Age*." *Anglican Theological Review* 93 no. 3: 511–516.

Sedgwick's appreciative summary focuses on Taylor's narration of Christianity's history, present, and future.

Theology: summary

2012

58. "Book Discussion: Charles Taylor's *A Secular Age*." *Journal of Religious Ethics* (2012) 40 no. 1.

58a. 123–137. Kavka, Martin. "What is Immanent in Judaism? Transcending *A Secular Age*."

Taking up Taylor's alleged claim that "the desire for a meaningful life can never be satisfied in this life," Kavka proposes that the Jewish model "of a

God who is immanent in social life [through] religious law [...] can mend the relations between varying kinds of believers and unbelievers in a way that Taylor thinks is impossible" (Abstract).

Theology (Jewish): Taylor's concepts (transcendence, immanence), Taylor's intentions (Christian bias), present normative

58b. 138–148. Barre, Elizabeth A. "Muslim Imaginaries and Imaginary Muslims. Placing Islam in Conversation with *A Secular Age*."

Barre takes the "Ancien Régime," the "Age of Mobilization," and the "Age of Authenticity," as depicted in *ASA* as ideal types of social imaginaries, and asks which type the Muslim imaginary represents.

Religious Studies: Taylor's concepts (social imaginary), story (potential universalism)

*58c. 149–170. Hart, William David. "Naturalizing Christian Ethics. A Critique of Charles Taylor's *A Secular Age*."

"I explore [Taylor's] definition of transcendence, its role in holding a modernity-inspired nihilism at bay, and how it is crucial to the Christian anti-humanist argument that he makes. In the process, I show how the critical power of this analysis depends heavily and paradoxically on the Nietzschean antihumanism that he otherwise rejects. Through an account of what I describe as naturalistic Christianity, I argue that transcendence need not be construed as supernatural, that all of the resources necessary for a meaningful life are immanent in the natural process, which includes the semiotic capacities of Homo sapiens" (Abstract).

Religious Studies: Taylor's concepts (transcendence, immanence), Taylor's intentions (Christian bias), present normative

58d. 171–192. Woodford, Peter. "Specters of the Nineteenth Century. Charles Taylor and the Problem of Historicism."

Pointing to parallels between Taylor's historical thinking and that of Wilhelm Dilthey (1833–1911), Woodford maintains that an understanding of the self and the world as historically contingent makes it difficult to argue for the supremacy of any normative stance: "The contrast between the historicist, empirical-genetic side of Taylor's view of historical experience and the philosophical anthropology that identifies 'fullness' satisfied through transcendence as an abiding and necessary goal of human spiritual life creates a vexing and, so far as I can see, irresolvable *aporia* in Taylor's work" (189).

Philosophy: Taylor's concepts (transcendence, fullness, historical self)

59. Bubandt, Nils and Martijn van Beek, eds., 2012. *Varieties of Secularism in Asia: Anthropological Explorations of Religion, Politics and the Spiritual*. London: Routledge.

The introduction presents this volume, whose title seems to be inspired by nr. 40 in this bibliography, as explorations of secularity different from the one described by Taylor for the North Atlantic world (p. 2). In the remainder, however, Taylor figures less prominently as a point of reference than Talal Asad.

Anthropology: story (parochialism)

*60. Dallmayr, Fred. 2012. "A Secular Age? Reflections on Taylor and Panikkar." *International Journal for Philosophy of Religion* 71: 189–204.

Dallmayr compares *ASA*'s assessment of our modern condition with the one advanced in Raimon Panikkar's *The Rhythm of Being* (2010). "Both thinkers complain about the glaring blemishes of the modern, especially the contemporary age; both deplore above all a certain deficit of religiosity. The two authors differ, however, both in the details of their diagnosis and in their proposed remedies. [...] Although sharing [Taylor's] concern about 'loss of meaning', Panikkar does not find its source in the abandonment of (mono)theistic transcendence; on the contrary, both radical transcendence and agnostic immanence are responsible for the deficit of genuine faith" (Abstract).

Political Science: Taylor's concepts (transcendence, immanence), present normative, Taylor's intentions (Christian bias)

2013

*61. Asiedu, F. B. A. 2013. "Theology in a Subjunctive Mood: Reflections on Charles Taylor's *A Secular Age*." *Scottish Journal of Theology* 66 no. 2: 230–240.

After reviewing non-theistic critics of Taylor, namely Quentin Skinner and William Connolly, Asiedu suggests reading *ASA* as representing a "theological discourse in a subjunctive mood," as it "speak[s] about what might be the case and not of what must be, or is the case" (239 f.). Asiedu suggests such an understanding and articulation of theology as more appropriate for our times.

Theology: present normative, Taylor's intentions (contemporary theology)

62. Gallagher, Michael Paul. 2013. "The 'use' of literature in 'A Secular Age': A Note on Romanticism." *Gregorianum* 94 no. 1: 167–173.

Gallagher (see also entries 5, 39 h) points first to the *historical* importance Taylor assigns to Romanticism, suggesting that this importance could be brought out even more strongly, and secondly to the contemporary potential of artistic expressions "as mediations of spiritual openness" (167). He finally connects the stress of literature in *ASA* with Taylor's earlier stress on the importance of imagination, which is often neglected in favor of ideas.

Theology: history (Romanticism), Taylor's concepts (social imaginary)

63. Kirk, J. Andrew. 2013. "'A Secular Age' in a Mission Perspective: A Review Article." *Transformation: An International Journal of Holistic Mission Studies* 28 no. 3: 172–181.

"This review attempts to summarise the author's discussion of secularism under a few key headings and then offers a brief discussion of the material in each case. In the final section it offers some personal reflections on the missiological implications of his main themes" (Abstract).

Theology: summary, present normative

64. Oviedo, Lluis. "The Ongoing Discussion of Taylor's *A Secular Age*." *Antonianum* 88 no. 1: 169–179.

Oviedo (see also entry 33) reviews what he considers the most important contributions in the debate on *ASA*, namely nr. 39 and nr. 40 in this bibliography, together with Taylor's subsequent collection of essays, entitled *Dilemmas and Connections*.

Theology: summary

2014

*65. Horan, Daniel P. 2014. "A Rahnerian Theological Response to Charles Taylor's *A Secular Age*." *New Blackfriars* 95 no. 1055: 21–42.

Horan presents "Karl Rahner's notion of the supernatural existential as a theological response to Taylor's [too rigid] immanent and transcendent divide" (22). Rahner can theologically complement Taylor by explicating the transcendental ground that motivates our search for fullness. He thereby explains why this search is an anthropological constancy as Taylor tacitly presumes.

Theology: Taylor's concepts (immanence, transcendence, fullness)

66. Smith, James K. A. 2014. *How (Not) to be Secular: Reading Charles Taylor*. Grand Rapids, MI: Wm. B. Eerdmans.

This book is intended both as an introductory guide to *ASA* and as a manual of how to live in our secular age.

Philosophy, Theology: summary

Forthcoming

Mirjam Künkler, John Madeley, and Shylashri Shankar, eds. forthcoming. A Secular Age *beyond the West*. Cambridge: Cambridge University Press.

3 Summary

A Secular Age is a classic that is very much alive, and so the discussion it has generated is unlikely to come to an end any time soon. It therefore hardly needs mentioning that the foregoing overview can only be of a temporary nature. And even for the present, the compiled bibliography does not claim to be exhaustive. It should be comprehensive enough, however, to make for a representative overview of the main trends in the reception of *A Secular Age*. The following summary provides such an overview by categorizing the individual entries according to disciplinary backgrounds and aspects of *A Secular Age* dealt with. It also enables the reader to locate those contributions most relevant to their own future contribution within the ongoing debate around *A Secular Age*.

Contributions per year (123 in total)

2008	19
2009	22
2010	56
2011	14
2012	6
2013	4
2014	2

Categorization by disciplines

Occasionally an entry might be situated in more than one discipline. Recommended contributions are marked with an asterisk (*).

Philosophy (35 entries in total)
Entries per year: 2008: 7, 2009: 9; 2010: 15; 2011: 2; 2012: 1; 2014: 1.
Entries nr. 2, 6, *7, 8, 13, 14, 17, 19, *22, 23, *26, 27, 31, 35, 37, 38, 39b, 39c, 39d, 39e, 39f, 39j, *40a, *40f, *40g, *42a, *42e, 44a, 44b, 45, *49, 51a, 51e, 58d, 66.

Theology (41)
2008: 4; 2009: 6; 2010: 20; 2011: 4; 2012: 1; 2013: 4: 2014: 2.
3, 5, 9, 15, 18b, *26, *28, 32, 33, 34, *36, 39g, 39h, 39i, 39k, 39l, 39m, *40c, 41a, 41b, 41c, 41d, 41e, 41f, *42a, *42b, *42c, *42d, 43a, 45, 48, 52, 55, 56, 57, 58a, *61, 62, 63, 64, *65, 66.

Sociology (17)
2008: 3; 2009: 1; 2010: 10; 2011: 3.
*4, 11, 16, 29, *40a, *40b, *40k, *40l, 41h, 43b, 43c, *43d, 43f, *49, 51c, 51d, 51f.

History (11)
2008: 4; 2009: 3; 2010: 3; 2011: 1.
1a, *1b, *7, 12, 20, *24, 30, *40i, *40j, 43e, *54.

Religious Studies (4)
2009: 1; 2010: 1; 2012: 2.
21, 46, 58b, *58c.

Literature (4)
2009: 1; 2010: 3.
25, *40e, *40h, 41g.

Political Science, Law (10)
2008: 2; 2009: 2; 2010: 4; 2011: 1; 2012: 1.
*1c, *10, 18a, 18b, *39a, 39i, *40d, *42c, 53, *60.

Anthropology (6)
2010: 1; 2011: 4; 2012: 1.
*40m, 51a, 51b, 51c, 51g, 59.

Taylor's Response (9)
2010: 9; 2011: 1.
*40n, *42f, 43b, 43c, *43d, 43e, 43f, 45, 51h.

Categorization by focus

Entries may have several foci.

Summary (28)
2008: 8; 2009: 6; 2010: 7; 2011: 4; 2013: 2; 2014: 1.
1a, *1b, 5, 6, 11, 14, 15, 17, 20, 27, 29, 34, 35, 38, *40a, *40n, 44a, 44b, 46, 48, *49, 52, 55, 56, 57, 63, 64, 66.

History: empirical findings of Taylor, criticized or elaborated on (20)
2008: 4; 2009: 3; 2010: 11; 2011: 1; 2013: 1.
*1b, *4, 6, 12, *24, 30, 37, 39e, *40d, *40i, *40j, *40m, 41b, 41c, 41d, 41e, 43b, 43e, *54, 62.

Story: Taylor's narrative, convincing or reductionist/missing parts (30)
2008: 5; 2009: 3; 2010: 20; 2012: 2.
*1b, 8, *10, 14, 16, 30, *36, 37, 39g, *40a, *40c, *40d, *40e, *40h, *40i, *40j, *40k, *40l, *40m, *40n, 41d, 41f, 41g, *42b, *42d, 43b, *43d, 43f, 58b, 59.

Present empirical: "what is" (15)
2008: 4; 2010: 8; 2011: 3.
*1c, 2, 6, *13, *39a, 39b, *40e, *40i, *40k, *40l, *42e, 43a, 51b, 51d, 51g.

Present normative: "what ought to be" (32)
2008: 1; 2009: 6; 2010: 15; 2011: 6; 2012: 3; 2013: 2.
3, *26, *28, 32, 33, 18a, 18b, 39f, 39h, 39i, 39j, 39k, 39l, 39m, *40c, *40g, 41a, *42a, *42b, *42c, *42d, 51c, 51d, 51e, 51g, 52, 56, 58a, *58c, *60, *61, 63.

Taylor's concepts: central terms, concepts and premises in *ASA* (51)
2008: 7; 2009: 6; 2010: 25; 2011: 6; 2012: 5; 2013: 1; 2014: 1.
1c, *4, *7, *10, *13, 14, 17, 20, *26, *28, *36, 37, 38, *39a, 39b, 39c, 39d, *40a, *40b, *40d, *40e, *40f, *40g, *40j, *40l, *40n, 41a, 41e, 41g, 41h, *42c, *42e, 43b, 43c, 43f, 45, 46, *49, 51a, 51b, 51c, 51d, 51g, 56, 58a, 58b, *58c, 58d, *60, 62, *65.

Taylor's intentions: normative standpoint in general, intentions when writing *ASA* (44)
2008: 7; 2009: 14; 2010: 14; 2011: 5; 2012: 3; 2013: 1.
2, 5, *7, *13, 14, 15, 16, 18b, 19, *22, *24, 25, 27, *28, 29, 31, 32, 33, 34, 35, *36, 39f, *40b, *40c, *40e, *40h, *40j, *40l, *40m, *40n, *42a, *42b, *43d, 45, 46, 51b, 51c, 51e, 51h, 56, 58a, *58c, *60, *61.

Style: rhetoric, structure, disciplinarity (10)
2008: 3; 2009: 3; 2010: 4.
*1b, 2, 17, *24, 27, 29, *40a, *40h, *40l, *43d.

Index

9/11: 98, 184, 185

Abbey, Ruth: 314n11, 395
'Abd al-Raziq, 'Ali: 344–345, 344n24
'Abduh, Muhammad: 318, 324, 339, 339n18
aesthetic, aesthetics: 10, 12, 207–209, 211, 218–221, 225, 230, 232, 233n12, 236, 269, 403
affirmation
– crisis of: 271, 271n17, 272–273
– divine: 263, 264, 272–273, 280
– of (ordinary) life: 61n28, 186n17, 268, 269
– of modernity: 65
Afghani, Jamal al-Din al- : 339–340, 339n19
agape: 33, 63, 179, 263, 273, 275, 277, 393, 407, 408
Age of Authenticity: 35, 37, 139, 190, 288, 293, 372, 373, 386n5, 413
Age of Mobilization: 34, 139, 190, 403, 413
agency: 52n9, 160n2, 167, 169, 169n12, 171, 175, 357, 399
aggression: 268, 272, 274–275, see also: violence
Altizer, Thomas: 265, 266
America, American: 13, 35–36, 41–42, 79, 82, 183, 191, 285, 289–292, 293n9, 294, 300, 373, see also: USA
Ancien Régime: 34, 139, 189–190, 413
Anderson, Benedict: 315, 316, 317
anthropology: 26–27, 37, 106, 183, 268, 413
– as an academic discipline: 1, 77, 81, 170, 401, 408–409, 411, 414, 417
anti-humanist, anti-humanism: 12, 60, 65, 240, 269–271, 270n15, 275–276, 278, 396, 413, see also: humanism
apologetic, apologetics 180n6, 188, 324
– in *A Secular Age*: 6, 50n6, 57–59, 59n24–25, 61, 65n36, 179, 264, 272, 276, 280, 351n3, 391, 392, 400
Appleby, Scott: 307n1, 309
Arabic
– literature: 16, 313, 349n1, 350–355, 362–363
– public: 193, 195

– terms: 188, 308, 313, 318, 320, 321, 322, 324
Asad, Talal: 24, 25, 36, 71n1, 138, 148, 169, 169n12–13, 170, 182n10, 209, 211, 318, 321, 321n20, 333, 333n4, 342, 414
Asiedu, F. B. A.: 414
'Attar, Hasan al-: 338
Atheism: 18, 147, 187, 313, see also: Theism
Augustine: 3, 13, 51, 247–258
authenticity: 11, 35n8, 114, 288, 292, 372, see also: *Age of Authenticity*
Automatic writing: 285, 294–298
Axial age (incl. axial religion, axial turn, pre-axial/post-axial religion or religiosity): 39–40, 40n11, 53–55, 54n14–16, 59, 60, 98, 147, 183, 382, 383, 390, 410
Azande: 77–78
Azmeh, Aziz al- : 325, 362n26

Baker, Peter: 191
Bakhit al-Muti'i, Muhammad: 333–335, 333n5, 338, 340–345, 341n22
Bakhtin, Mikhail: 299
Ballard, Bruce: 391
Balthasar, Hans Urs von: 265, 386n3
Banna, Hasan al- : 321
barbarism (Arabic: *tawaḥḥush*): 355, 362
Barre, Elizabeth: 189–190, 315, 413
Barth, Karl: 59n25, 65, 65n39, 266, 266n5
Baum, Gregory: 150, 404–405
Beethoven, Ludwig van: 229n1, 231n4, 232, 238
belief
– and unbelief: 27, 33, 97, 99, 123–124, 129, 182n10, 187, 284, 285–286, 293
– as employed in *A Secular Age*: 2, 5, 16–17, 27–33, 35–36, 39, 51, 52, 52n9, 62, 72, 73–74, 84–84, 97, 99, 105, 123–124, 374, 376, 382, 388, 389, 390, 391, 392, 393, 394, 395, 396, 398, 400, 402, 403, 405, 407, 409, 410
Bellah, Robert: 8, 35, 39, 54n14, 99, 398
Bender, Courtney: 315n13, 369, 373, 374
Benjamin, Walter: 213, 214

Benson, John: 388
Benton, Lauren: 162
Berger, Peter: 23, 28–29, 41, 140, 144
Bergson, Henri: 164n5, 192, 238, 248
Betz, Hans Dieter: 402
Bible: 64, 74, 101, 266
Bilgrami, Akeel: 187, 212n4, 399
Bloch, Maurice: 86
Blumenberg, Hans: 36, 50, 50n3, 100n3
Bonhoeffer, Dietrich: 53n12, 62, 63, 193n21, 265, 265n3, 266
Bouchard-Taylor Commission: 145, 151–153, 177–178
Brooke, Allen: 387–388
Brown, Wendy: 155, 296, 399
Buddhism: 39, 52n9, 55, 187, 270n14, 311
buffered self: 11, 28, 160, 169, 169n12, 170, 212, 213, 217, 220, 229, 230–231, 233–234, 234n13, 370, 391, 407, 408, 410, 411, see also: *porous self*
Butler, Jon: 37, 287n6, 400

Cairo: 308, 316, 333, 353
Calhoun, Craig: 118, 388, 398
Cambridge, Massachusetts: 13, 283, 292–294
Cameron, Julia: 294–296, 298
Campbell, Alexander: 191–192
Casanova, José: 23–24, 37, 39, 41, 138, 143, 144, 146, 147, 331n1, 332–333, 333n3, 341–342, 373, 401
Cassidy, Eoin: 395
Castoriadis, Cornelius: 3, 84
Catholic, Catholicism: 32, 35, 42, 58–60, 132–133, 150–154, 192, 192n18, 210, 237, 242, 274, 280, 352, 352n4, 359, 372, 379, 383
– Taylor's Catholic convictions/bias: 6, 49–51, 58–60, 62–64, 139, 278n22, 381–382, 388, 389, 392, 395, 398, 402, 406, 407–408, 409, see also: Christian bias/conviction
Cavell, Stanley: 260, 266
Cervantes, Fernando: 406
Chakrabarty, Dipesh: 50n4, 188, 391
Christ: see Jesus Christ

Christendom: 14, 181, 323–324, 373–374
– Latin, Western: 30, 50, 187, 210, 230, 276, 311, 313, 351, 377, 379, 380, 383, 388, 398
Christian
– bias/conviction: 6, 12, 14, 31n5, 51, 54, 58, 63, 179, 195, 209, 309, 323, 351, 351n3, 379, 388, 390, 391, 392, 393, 394, 395, 396, 398–399, 400, 401, 403, 409, 413, 414, see also: Catholic – Taylor's Catholic convictions/bias
– culture: 142, 181, 373
– faith: 265n3, 271, 276–277, 323, 325, 373, 374
– theology: 49–70, 245, 257n16, 263–282
Christianity
– as origin of modernity/secularism: 2, 10, 32–36, 38–39, 50, 55, 61, 118, 144, 180, 184, 188, 191, 192, 208–209, 211, 224, 230, 311, 315, 323–325, 379, 383, 389, 404–405, see also: Western Christianity
citizen(s), citizenship: 80, 95, 98–99, 101, 102, 123n1, 132, 134, 135n14, 142, 161, 163, 168, 169, 171, 172, 235, 371
Civil religion: 35, 118
Civilization: 16, 39–40, 160, 179, 208, 216–218, 284, 350, 358–363
– in *A Secular Age*: 14, 17, 39–40, 63n33, 160, 248, 311, 315, 332, 370–371, 373, 377, 380, 401, 407
Cognitive Science/Psychology: 5, 7, 72, 74–75, 78, 85–86
– and rationality: 75–77
– and secularization: 80–83
– and social imaginaries: 84–86
Cognitive Science of Religion (CSR): 5, 7, 71–73, 80, 83, 85–87
Coles, Romand: 314n11, 351n2, 404
colonial, colonialism: 15, 40, 50, 149, 153, 153n6, 154, 163, 179, 188, 289, 308, 310, 311, 313, 323, 325, 331–333, 338, 345, 379, 398, 399, 400, 401, 402
Colorado, Carlos: 407–408
concert: 233n12, 236
– culture: 229, 229n1, 232, 233

– hall: 12, 229, 232, 233, 233n11, 234 – 235, 235n16, 238, 239, 240, 242
Confessional age: 34, 36
Confirmation bias: 75 – 76
Conjunction fallacy: 75 – 76
Connolly, William E.: 58n22, 272, 309, 399, 414
Conway, Michael: 396
Costello, Stephen J.: 396
Credibility Enhancing Displays (CREDs): 81 – 83, 87
Crittenden, Paul James: 392
Cromer (Evelyn Baring, Earl of Cromer): 338, 338n14, 341n22
culture: 17, 49, 119, 127, 130, 176, 193, 208, 208n1, 264
– modern, pre-modern: 26, 66, 98, 100, 114, 181, 229, 245, 249
– popular: 12, 210, 215, 220
– Taylor's culturalist account, cultural imaginary: 6, 14, 25, 26 – 29, 36 – 43, 50, 176, 179, 184, 197, 313n9
– Western, non-Western, Axial: 17, 38, 40, 40n11, 113, 118, 142, 160, 180, 187, 212, 270, 287, 351, 377 – 378

Dallmayr, Fred: 414
Davie, Grace: 37, 41, 213n5, 372
Dawson, Christopher: 179 – 180
de Vries, Hent: 57, 405
democracy: 35, 63, 185, 268, 325, 382
democratic, undemocratic, anti-democratic: 9, 31, 35, 63n33, 99, 103, 118, 141, 148, 160n2, 161, 163, 234, 235, 239, 290, 315
Demolins, Edmond: 322
Denzin, Norman Kent: 186
Derrida, Jacques: 13, 271n17, 260 – 261
desire: 12, 29, 72, 116, 229, 246 – 247, 249, 256, 258, 260n17 – 18, 261, 267, 268, 269n11, 270n13, 271, 274, 372, 412
dilemma of mutilation: 111, 271, 274 – 276
dīn (Arabic term for 'religion'): 313, 334, 335 – 336, 340, 342, see also: *umūr dīniyya*
Direct access society: 28
disenchantment: 16, 17, 26, 28, 29n3, 32, 34, 56, 56n19, 59, 207 – 211, 212n4, 216 – 217, 221, 234 – 235, 237, 246, 284 – 292, 298 – 300, 299n14, 370 – 377, 399, 400, 403, 409
Douglas, Mary : 299n14
Dressler, Markus: 332
Dunne, Joseph: 396
During, Simon: 399
Durkheim, Emile; Durkheimian: 34, 34n7, 35, 40, 41, 79, 83, 84, 293, 320

Egypt, Egyptian: 16, 188, 317, 320, 323, 333, 333n5, 338 – 339, 341n22, 343 – 344, 350, 353, 353n7, 355 – 358, 358n16 – 17, 361, 362
Eisenstadt, Shmuel: 30, 32, 37 – 40, 54n14, 148
Eliade, Mircea: 54n14, 239
enchantment: see disenchantment
enemies: 10, 116, 160, 165
Enlightenment: 13, 96, 98 – 99, 109, 113 – 114, 118, 150 – 152, 184, 187, 230, 270n13, 355, 395, 401
Epistemology, epistemological: 8, 9, 15, 18, 29, 97, 100, 102, 108 – 109, 109n7, 114, 123, 134 – 135, 144, 147, 166, 178, 185, 218, 251n6, 269n12, 318, 321, 323, 343, 382, 406
– epistemological pluralism: 9, 123 – 132, 135
– epistemological skepticism: 124, 132 – 133, 132n10
Esquiros, Alphonse: 320
Europe, European: 14, 24, 36 – 37, 40, 43, 74, 80 – 81, 84, 95, 98 – 99, 109, 114, 137, 141, 143, 150, 162, 165, 176, 180, 184, 187, 210 – 212, 218 – 219, 230, 231n4, 284, 286, 288 – 290, 292, 308, 313, 313n9, 317 – 318, 320 – 321, 323 – 325, 331 – 332, 338 – 339, 338n15, 351 – 356, 359, 362 – 363, 370 – 371, 373 – 374, 377 – 378, 382, 401, 403, 412
Evans-Pritchard, E.E.: 71, 77
existential security: 79 – 81, 83

faith: 59 – 60, 59n25, 115, 128 – 129, 132 – 133, 142, 196, see also: Christian faith
– Taylor's conception of: 52, 56, 58, 62, 123n1, 124, 178, 182n10, 271, 276 – 277,

278n22, 279n24, 285n3, 286, 325, 369–374, 382, 388, 391, 397, 403, 410, 414
Flanagan, Kieran: 406–407
Foucault, Michel: 10, 53, 164, 167, 171, 188–189, 194, 271n17
Fraser, Giles: 264, 265n2–3, 266–267, 278–280
French Revolution: 41, 84, 140, 219, 222–223, 376, 380
Froese, Vic: 411
Fukuyama, Francis: 184
Fullness: 7, 13, 27–30, 37, 39, 44, 51, 61, 65–66, 169n11, 185, 187–188, 189, 213, 219–220, 221, 223–225, 257, 259, 284, 300, 309, 331, 337n13, 388, 389, 394, 395, 396, 398, 400, 402, 405, 412, 413, 415
functional differentiation: 24, 37, 341, see also: social differentiation
Fundamentalism: 141, 183, 309, 323–325

Gallagher, Michael Paul: 388, 397, 414–415
gender: 14, 223
genealogy, genealogical account: 3, 8, 10, 12, 18, 24, 25, 36, 39, 99, 100, 100n3, 182, 184–185, 186, 188–191, 194–195, 215, 269–271, 270n13, 277, 280, 311, 323, 332, 388, 394, 395, 400, 401
Gilman, James E.: 388
Gilpin, W. Clark: 403
God: 28, 33–35, 51–54, 59n25, 63–66, 72, 84, 99, 102, 103, 110, 110n9, 131–133, 162, 166, 167, 187, 190, 192, 194, 230–231, 234–236, 254, 257, 260, 260n17, 264–267, 274–276, 288–289, 296, 297, 312, 315, 324, 336, 341–343, 356, 358, 360, 360n22, 363, 391, 395, 413
– belief in: 2, 8, 74, 78, 82, 124, 125n2, 138, 160, 188, 207, 309, 312, 323
– love of: 27, 28, 273, 280, 286
Göle, Nilüfer: 143, 144, 313, 400–401
Gordon, Peter: 52n10, 58, 63n34, 260n18, 309, 312n7, 389
Gothic
– as melancholy: 213, 214, 216, 225

– as precursor to modern spirituality: 207, 211–213, 220, 375
Gray, John: 389

Habermas, Jürgen: 8, 23, 29n3, 95–109, 114, 117, 146, 155, 180, 185–186, 310, 398
Haidt, Jonathan: 86
Hamilton, Kenneth: 232–233, 233n9, 233n12, 235n16
Hammond, Charles: 295–296, 298
Ḥanafi school of Islamic law: 15, 334–337, 340
Hannon, Patrick: 397
Hart, William D.: 279n24, 413
Hauerwas, Stanley: 65n39, 314n11, 351n2, 404
Hebron: 165
Hector, Kevin: 402
Hegel, Gottfried W.F.; Hegelianism: 3, 13, 26, 50, 53, 96, 102, 104, 107, 114, 178, 257n16, 258–259, 267n8, 280, 341n22
hegemony
– of Europe or the West: 170–172, 187, 194, 195, 210, 323
– of secularism: 6, 7, 9, 42, 43, 97, 99, 160, 197, 274, 314
Heidegger, Martin: 4, 13, 26, 209, 247–260
Henrich, Joseph: 71, 81, 82, 85
hermeneutics, hermeneutical approach: 16, 49n2, 103, 104, 105, 185
– in *A Secular Age:* 25, 26, 30–31, 38–41, 44, 178, 274–275, 351, 380
higher times: 34, 56n19, 138, 238–243, 246–248, 257, 287
history
– conceptual: 25, 29n3, 36, 71n1, 147, 315–316, 318, 333
– historical self-understanding: 4, 15, 299, 323–325, 350, 357
– use of in *A Secular Age:* 1–3, 6, 26, 29, 31–32, 36–37, 44, 50, 53, 57–59, 181, 189–190, 194–195, 209, 211, 219, 221, 257n16, 286, 299n14, 310n6, 312n7, 314, 351n3, 382, 387, 389, 392, 400, 402, 405, 413
Hogan, Pádraig: 397
Holy Spirit: 7, 27, 63–64

Holyoake, George Jacob: 191, 192
Horan, Daniel P.: 415
human flourishing: 27–28, 33–34, 51, 52, 54n16, 55, 138, 139, 215, 270, 270n13, 285n3, 383, 395
humanism: 12, 13, 65n38, 66, 66n41, 66n44, 114, 240, 264, 270–272, 274n19, 275–276, 396, 403
– anti-humanism: 12, 60, 240, 270–271, 275–276, 396, 413
– exclusive humanism: 18, 27, 30n4, 32–34, 53, 60, 62–63, 66, 125, 138, 139, 186n17, 188, 208, 229, 264, 270, 270n13, 272, 280, 286, 389, 394, 395, 399, 404
Hunter, Ian: 411–412
Huntington, Samuel: 184
Hurd, Elizabeth Shakman: 14, 188, 389

Ibn al-Humam: 336–337
Idealism: 96, 178, 399
identity: 14, 26, 28, 35, 85, 117, 141, 163, 169–170, 175–176, 180, 214–215, 229–233, 237–238, 235n1, 353, 375
Illich, Ivan: 62
immanence, immanent: 7, 11, 16, 52, 62, 64, 125, 208, 213, 230, 298, 315, 340, 342, 380, 408
– in distinction from transcendence: 5, 15, 17, 27, 51–53, 61, 63, 74, 217, 229–231, 234–237, 300, 314, 314n11, 333–334, 336, 337, 337n13, 340, 349–352, 356, 363, 380–381, 389, 390, 393, 395, 396, 398, 399, 400, 404, 409, 410, 413, 414, 415
Immanent frame: 4, 5–6, 9, 11, 16, 25–26, 28–43, 62, 123n1, 124–126, 129, 133, 135, 138–139, 178, 188, 189, 211, 212, 215, 217, 241, 245n1, 284, 309–310, 322, 331, 370–371, 393, 394, 401, 405, 410
individual(s), individualism: 35–36, 37, 56, 60, 73–74, 85, 150, 154, 162, 169, 169n12, 170, 176, 230, 231, 288, 292, 313, 315, 316, 321, 342, 372, see also: *Age of Authenticity*

Intellectual Deviation Story: 14, 179, 325, 398, 407
Interdisciplinary, interdisciplinarity: v-vi, 1, 5, 18, 87, 308–309
Islam, Islamic: 5, 119, 141, 142, 165, 171, 176, 187, 189–190, 196, 223, 307–325, 358–359, 362–363, 376n2, 379, 401, 413, see also: Muslim
– Islamic civilization: 16, 315, 363
– Islam in distinction from the West/Christianity: 3, 14, 50, 307, 323–325
– Islamic law: 333–337, 340–345
– Islamic secularity/modernity: 6, 14, 15, 175, 195, 311–313, 317–319, 322–325
– Islamic Studies: 15, 307–310
Israel, Israeli: 9, 10, 159–173, 163, 165,
– Israeli settlers/settlements: 165, 166, 168
– Israel/Palestine: 9, 10, 159–173

Jager, Colin: 270n13, 375, 376, 379, 400
James, William: 34n7, 146, 192, 283–284, 283n1, 286, 296, 296n11, 297–298, 297n12, 300
Jamesian Open Space (incl. open space): 225, 284, 299, 313
Jameson, Frederic: 182–183, 219, 221n10
Jay, Martin: 58–59, 287n6, 392
Jesus Christ: 7, 63–65, 65n39, 110n9, 266–267, 275, 278, 297–298
Jews, Jewish: 50, 114, 116, 165–166, 168, 185, 194, 195, 196, 403, 412–413
– Judaeo-Christian theism: 263
– Judaism: 187, 341n22
Joas, Hans: 23n1, 26n2, 30n5, 34n7, 54n14, 58, 188, 277, 369, 385n2
Jung, Dietrich: 324
Jüngel, Eberhard: 265–266

Kant, Emmanuel; Kantian: 3–4, 27, 34, 96, 101–106, 113, 146, 161, 216, 218, 219, 267n8
Kavka, Martin: 194, 412–413
Kearns, Alan: 397
Kerr, Fergus: 403–404, 405
Khan, Sir Sayyid Ahmad: 339–340
Kierkegaard, Søren: 273
Kinsey, John: 407

Kirk, J. Andrew: 415
kitsch: 266–267, 267n6, 278
Knight, Christopher J.: 392
Kozinski, Thaddeus J.: 392–393

Laitinen, Arto: 176, 393
Larmore, Charles: 130, 131, 131n7, 386n4
Larsen, Timothy: 387
Latin Christendom: See Christendom
Leask, Ian: 396
Le Bon, Gustave: 320
Ledewitz, Bruce: 391
Legare, Cristine: 78
liberal, liberalism: 9, 123–135, 142, 144, 160–164, 160n1, 169n12, 177, 272, 280
Lincoln, A. T.: 412
literature: Taylor's use of: 33, 50, 207–225, 236n17, 414–415
Long, D. S.: 393
love: 7, 13, 60, 64, 115, 118, 184, 185, 213–214, 223, 225, 246–261, 269, 273, 275–277
– divine: 80, 272–273, 275, 277
– of God: 27, 28, 273
– of neighbor: 265, 276
Luckmann, Thomas: 23, 24, 26, 27
Luhmann, Niklas: 27, 37, 40n11, 49n2, 52n11, 147, 197
Lundberg, Anders: 393
Luther, Martin; Lutheran: 49n1, 57, 60, 61, 64, 278, 379
Lyon, David: 390, 406
Lyotard, Jean-François: 180, 183–184

MacIntyre, Alasdair: 175, 180, 264
Mahmood, Saba: 140, 144, 178, 188, 209–210, 311, 331–332, 350, 352, 401
al-Manar: 15, 308, 316–322
Mandair, Arvind-Pal S.: 332
Marcuse, Herbert: 220n9, 222, 223–224, 376
market (economy): 31, 35, 162, 183, 293, 315, 377
Marrash, Fransis: 16, 350, 352, 353, 358–363
Martin, David: 23, 38, 146, 230n2, 379
Marty, Martin E.: 390
May, Collin: 393
McCurry, Jeffrey: 393

McLennan, Gregor: 405
Mendes-Flohr, Paul: 403
Miller, James: 314n11, 390
Morgan, Michael L.: 390
Marx, Karl: 73, 101, 167, 207, 212, 212n4, 219, 265n3, 399
materiality: 341, 342–344
maximal demand: 229, 230, 240, 241, 274, 276, 279n24
Messiaen, Olivier: 237, 241n23
metaphor, metaphorical: 5, 10, 11, 86, 108, 143, 178, 185, 186, 189, 278, 289
metaphysics, metaphysical: 8, 9, 29, 96–97, 102–111, 124, 126, 130–134, 183, 212, 220, 232n5, 250n3, 255, 266, 290, 292–293, 295, 343, see also: post-metaphysical
Middle East, Middle Eastern: 312, 335
Milbank, John: 14, 25, 29n3, 53n13, 64n35, 182, 264, 266, 310n5, 398–399
Mitchell, Timothy: 343
Montesquieu: 355, 378
modern, modernity, see also: multiple modernities; pre-modern
– Arab modernity: 16, 349, 350, 352–353, 362–363
– early modern(ity): 2, 34, 53, 179, 196, 210, 211, 217, 402, 406, 412
– European modernity: 24, 114, 317
– genealogy/story of modernity: 3, 8, 14, 15, 23, 36, 50, 58, 100n3, 139, 181, 183–185, 187–188, 190, 194, 195, 220, 258, 287n6, 299, 307, 308, 323–325, 332, 349, 401, 403
– interpretation of modernity: 64–66, 96, 219
– Islamic modernity: 307–308, 322, 323–325
– modern literature/poetics/music: 10–11, 12, 16, 208, 229, 232, 234, 235n15, 236, 237, 240–241, 354
– modern (moral) order: 10, 164, 188, 195, 236, 269, 285, 393
– modern rationality/science: 29, 73, 249, 339, 252, 261, 277n21, 307, 308, 411

- modern religion/spirituality: 13, 15, 24, 29, 37, 43, 50, 63, 182n10, 209, 213, 283–300, 332, 344, 410–411
- modern self-understanding/identity: 6, 10, 12, 14, 15, 18, 25, 31, 139, 147, 160n2, 169, 169n12, 179, 185–186, 188, 194, 214–215, 220, 222, 232, 237, 239, 245, 258, 271, 288, 308–309, 323, 332, 339, 375, 392–393
- modern social imaginary: 3, 4, 5, 10, 35, 37, 39, 41, 78, 79, 83, 146, 161, 164, 194, 286, 308, 314–316, 322, 398, 408
- modern society: 25, 31–32, 37–38, 57, 62, 100, 110, 124, 127, 230, 315–316, 320
- modern (nation-)state: 10, 34, 162, 164, 169n13, 213, 317, 383
- modernism, modernist: 15, 140, 183, 308, 317, 322–323, 324, 339, 340
- modernization: v, 18, 23, 30, 98, 148, 150, 191, 299n14, 343, 353, 373, 377, 378
- theory of modernity: 6, 25, 26–27, 33, 35, 40, 41, 42, 50, 139, 378, 398
- Western modernity: 12, 14, 29, 38–39, 43, 95, 160, 194, 324, 349–350, 361–363, 381, 382, 401
- morality: 85, 125, 126, 128, 130–131, 134, 176, 196, 216, 265, 268, 272, 276, 277
- moral order 9–10, 32–33, 34–35, 84, 160, 161, 164, 169n12, 170, 171, 175, 176, 182, 186n17, 190–191, 195, 236, 269, 275, 359, 393
- moral orientation/source/power/value: 26, 54, 73, 103, 118, 187, 188, 191, 194, 235, 263, 264, 271–272, 274, 284, 370–371, 374–375, 393
- moral pluralism: 9, 112, 123–135
- moral theory: 42, 85–86, 106, 123–135, 397
Muhaysin, Hamid Mahmud: 319
mujtama' (Arabic for: 'society'): 193, 308, 318–323
Multiple modernities: 17, 37, 39, 148, 311, 314, 377, 406
Music: 4, 5, 12, 208, 229–244
Muslim: 15, 16. 102, 119, 165, 166, 188, 189–190, 195, 308, 310, 312, 313, 313n9, 315, 316, 318, 323–325, 332, 334, 338, 340, 341n22, 344, 345, 352, 374, 413, see also: Islam
mystics, mysticism: 6, 62–63, 292, 410

nahḍa (Arabic Renaissance of the nineteenth century): 16, 350, 353–354, 353n6, 354n8, 360n23, 361n25, 362–363
narrative, narration, narrativity
- modes of narration: 163, 175–176, 179–187, 350, 359, 361–362, 380
- narrative character of *A Secular Age:* 2–3, 17, 26–27, 31–32, 36, 41, 176, 181, 189–191, 194–195, 197, 211, 210, 270, 285, 325
- normative implications of Taylor's narrative and of narrativity in general: 7–8, 57, 175–176, 181–182, 185–187, 188–189, 191, 194, 197, 219, 264, 284, 299n14, 300, 324–325, 349
- reasons for resorting to narrativity: 7–8, 10, 17, 86, 163, 175–176, 179–187, 219, 284, 323, 380, 439
Nassar, Nasif: 193
nation: 16, 172n16, 316, 318, 322, 349, 351
- cross-national comparison: 24, 25, 73, 80, 355
- national belonging: 28, 115, 138, 315, 371, 372
- national expansion: 289
- national identities: 37, 38, 79, 150, 151, 163, 362, 363, 403
- nationalism: 137, 145, 154, 165–166, 313, 317, 321
- nation-state: 10, 161, 162–164, 193, 401
nature: 33, 37, 62, 64, 103, 143, 196, 216–217, 219, 290, 315, 339, 340, 376, 382, 399
natural: 77, 133, 161, 162, 245, 296, 354–355, 360, 363
- natural law: 33
- natural religion: 33, 140
- natural sciences: 72, 277n21, 353, 371
- natural world: 26, 28, 289
- naturalism: 26, 27, 66, 77, 98, 178, 214 339–340, 399, 410
- natural/supernatural: 5, 54, 75, 77–78, 80, 85, 212, 313, 339–340, 380–381, 413

Nietzsche, Friedrich: 3–4, 12–13, 27, 34, 62, 247, 260, 264–267, 269–280, 400, 413
Non-theism: see Theism
Non-West, non-Western: 15, 38, 176, 188, 191, 287, 307–314, 323, 332, 352
normative order: 2, 59, 84, 143, 175, 191–196, 212, 214, 285, 315

Oliverio, William: 394
Onfray, Michel: 188
Open Secularism: 10, 177–178
Ophir, Adi: 315
Orientalism: 179, 187
O'Shea, Andrew: 397
Otten, Willemien: 402–403
Ottoman Empire: 352, 353
Oviedo, Lluís: 385n2, 394, 415

Palestine, Palestinian: 163, 171
– Palestinian Authority: 166, 168
– Palestine/Israel: 9, 10, 159–173
Pärt, Arvo: 230, 237, 241–243
peace: 163, 165, 168, 172, 223, 289
– peacemaking: 10, 160–165, 170
– Perpetual Peace (Kant): 161
Phenomenology: 10, 211
Philosophy: 33, 50, 98, 109, 112, 113, 285
– of religion: 58, 61, 65n36
play, politics of: 219–221, see also: Schiller, Friedrich
plural, pluralism: 6, 9, 29, 42, 60, 62, 64–66, 106–108, 123–135, 153, 213, 293, 390, 397, 402
Popper, Karl: 177
post-metaphysical: 8, 95–120, 265, see also: metaphysics
post-modern, Post-modernism: 180, 182–183, 186, 187, 260, 266
post-secular: 8, 23, 43, 95–120, 390, 401, 406, 407, 410
Post-structuralism: 182–184, 187
Poovey, Mary: 316
porous self: 28, 54, 212, 231, 234n13, 286, 291, 298, 374, 375, 403, 410, 411, see also: *buffered self*

power: 3, 14, 15, 41–42, 54, 79, 140, 148, 176, 209–211, 224, 255, 307, 308, 323, 333n4, 373, 374, 400
– of religion: 142, 154
– of the secular: 144, 171, 246
– of the state: 141, 144, 161, 162, 169, 187, 342, 383
– will to power: 265, 271n17, 279
pre-modern: 15, 34, 50, 62, 73, 84, 98, 207, 230–231, 234, 238, 316, 340, 388, 393, 400, 402
– pre-modern jurists: 334–337, 342
progress: 16, 33, 137, 143, 150, 154, 183, 246, 324
– Arabic: *taqaddum:* 350, 355, 358, 359–362
Protestantism: 6, 7, 14, 57, 59, 59n1, 60, 64–66, 190

Qarafi al- : 334
Quebec: 9, 137, 138, 144–155, 177, 371, 372, 373, 382
Qur'an: 166, 190, 317n14, 324

Radical Orthodoxy: 14, 64n35, 398, 404
Ramadan (month of): 15, 333, 335, 336, 337n12, 342
Ramadan, Tariq: 324, 325
rational, rationality: 61, 72–74, 76, 77–78, 100, 102–103, 109–110, 150, 161, 182, 221, 245, 272, 288, 341, 342, 357, 399
– and the Azande: 77–78
– cognitive science and rationality: 75–76
– and subtraction stories: 87, 98
– procedural: 9, 99, 104, 108, 113, 114, 116–117
– instrumental: 13, 229, 249, 250, 252, 255, 382
Rawls, John: 40, 126, 127, 128, 130, 132–134, 155, 169, 170
Reform: 2, 6, 11, 12, 34, 39, 53–56, 59–61, 138, 139, 190, 207, 218, 225, 229–230, 276, 379, 402, 407
– and rage for order: 56, 59
– in Islam: 318, 319, 320, 322, 324, 338, 350, 353, 358, 359, 361–363
– politics of: 210, 211–215, 220, 383
Reform Master Narrative: 2, 8, 325

Reformation (Protestant): 32, 49n1, 50n5, 56–60, 62, 64, 234, 383
religion: 7–8, 17–18, 36–40, 50–55, 58, 61, 64–65, 102, 108, 128, 129, 133, 140–147, 177–179, 182–187, 192, 193, 208–209, 216, 246, 248, 285, 286, 322–325, 339, 372, 373, 382, 383, 387–389, 391, 394, 395, 401, 402, 408, 410
– art as: 208, 236
– civil: 35, 118
– cognitive science of: 7, 71–87
– comfort theory of: 80, 83, 87
– concept of: 313, 331–333, 339–342, 344, 345, see also: *dīn*
– decline of: 2, 6, 17, 25
– definition of: 15, 27, 57, 71, 138, 331, 340, 343, 344, 381
– invention of: 210, 211
– and public sphere: 96–100, 148, 155, 344
– and society: 196–197, 313, 317
– sociology of: 23–25, 30, 43
– and spirituality: 290, 292–293
– and threat: 79, 81, 151
religious experience: 138, 284, 292–294, 298, 408, 411
revolution: 349, 351, see also: French Revolution
– Quiet Revolution: 150–154
Rida, Rashid: 308, 319, 321, 322–325
Riesebrodt, Martin: 403
Rihani, Amin: 318
Roberts, Vaughan: 394
Romantic, Romanticism: 10–13, 16, 27, 35n8, 96, 113, 114, 218, 220, 229, 288, 300, 400, 407, 414
– art and aesthetics: 10, 33, 209, 217, 225, 249, 270n13, 272, 375, 376
– as disenchantment with modernity: 375
– as free space: 207, 208, 209, 216, 225
– as phenomenology of the secular age: 218
– politics of: 207, 211, 376–377
– post-romantic: 5, 207, 220, 236n17
– Taylor as Romanticist: 16, 63, 179, 218, 219, 224, 376, 400
Rosa, Hartmut: 376
Rosengarten, Richard: 403
Ross, Daniel: 394

Rossi, Philip J.: 390
Rundell, John: 408
Ryan, Fainche: 397

Salafiyya: 324
Sattelzeit: 196
Scandinavia: 79–80, 379
Scheler, Max: 277
Schielke, Samuli: 313
Schiller, Friedrich: 4, 12, 63n32, 207, 212, 216, 217, 218–222, 224, 376
Schopenhauer, Arthur: 268, 271, 273
Schulze, Reinhard: 379–380, 381
Schweiker, William: 57n21, 61, 309, 394, 402
secular, secularism, see also: *Open Secularism*
– definitions of: 2, 7, 16, 17, 25, 30, 31, 38, 40, 43, 73, 81, 137, 148, 149–150, 312, 341
– in Islam: 3, 5, 14–16, 142, 187, 189, 194, 307–325, 331, 333, 338, 341–345, 379, 389, 401, 413
– as normative: 2, 5–9, 31, 57, 58, 75, 83, 87, 100, 123–124, 126–127, 129, 140, 155, 182, 185, 192–196, 316, 325, 363
– phenomenology of: 10, 211
– and social imaginaries: 3, 4, 11, 31, 32, 34–44, 73, 79, 83–87, 146, 191, 308, 314
secularization: 6, 7, 9, 12, 23–44, 53, 63n32, 98, 100, 138, 143, 145, 208, 234, 243, 257n16, 299n14, 300, 309, 311, 324–325, 351, 372–373, 378, 388, 395, 396, 399, 400, 401, 403, 404, 406, 408, 412
– and cognitive science: 79–83
– critique of: 140, 142, 179, 213n5, 373
– as founding myth: 150–154
– and possibilities for cross-cultural comparison: 378–379
– as subtraction story: 2, 14, 29, 36, 63n32, 72–79, 83, 87, 159, 208, 215, 234, 323, 325, 388, 399, 405
Sedgwick, Timothy: 412
Seel, Martin: 194
self: 29, 42, 54, 106, 113, 114–115, 117, 169, 170, 176, 194, 207, 216, 223, 293, 331, 413, see also: *buffered self, porous self*
Shanahan, Mary: 396

shariʻa: 190, 333, 338, 356, 360
Sheehan, Jonathan: 59n24, 66n41, 188, 209, 287n6, 309, 312n7, 351n3, 400
Shelley, Percy: 11–12, 111, 216, 217, 218, 220–224
skepticism: 62, 113, 124, 128–129, 130n6, 131–133, 184
Slingerland, Edward: 72, 86
Social Imaginary: 3–5, 7, 10, 11, 31–32, 34–36, 37, 39, 41–42, 44, 55, 71–74, 78–79, 82–86, 87, 146, 160n1, 161, 164, 164n7, 170, 171, 176, 189–191, 194, 195, 285, 286, 289, 308, 314–316, 319, 322, 351, 371, 377, 398, 402, 406, 408, 412, 413, 415, see also: modern social imaginary
Smith, James K. A.: 415
social space: 81, 138, 229, 234–238, 245n1
Sociology, sociological: 3, 6, 7, 14, 23, 25–34, 36–41, 43–44, 52, 52n11, 58, 79–80, 137–143, 146–148, 197, 212–213, 213n5, 286n4, 292–293, 320, 322, 373, 378, 388, 389, 396, 406
sound: 232, 232n6, 236, 237, 240, 241, 242, 243, 257
Sources of the Self: 26, 32, 35n8, 54, 61n28, 111, 114, 178, 263, 268–273, 394, 397
sovereign, sovereignty, sovereignties: 9–10, 38, 138, 141, 144, 159, 160, 162–164, 166, 168, 171, 172, 379, 383
– popular sovereignty: 10, 160, 162, 164, 166, 169, 172n16
– human sovereignty: 161, 162, 166, 167
supernatural: see natural/supernatural
superstition, superstitious: 81, 110, 245
social (concept of): 316
social differentiation: 2, 7, 16, 62, 312, see also: functional differentiation
society (concept of): 316
spirit, spiritual, spirituality: 13, 17, 36, 54, 56n19, 60, 62–64, 71n1, 83, 111, 186, 192, 212–213, 213n5, 216, 220, 225, 236–238, 241, 273, 283–300, 324, 369, 370–374, 376, 382, 398, 399, 405, 410, 412, 413
Starbuck, Edwin: 283–284, 283n1, 300

state: 34, 34n7, 38, 41, 42, 61, 98, 101, 111, 112, 127–129, 134, 135n14, 138, 140, 141–145, 147, 148, 149, 152–153, 154–155, 161–164, 167–169, 171–172, 177, 193, 213, 321, 338, 342, 344, 353, 377–378, 379, 383, 401, see also: modern (nation-)state
Stein, Gertrude: 296, 296n11
Stephan, Johannes: 380
Storey, David: 394–395
sublime: 288, 290
– urban: 288, 290–291
Subtler languages: 6, 9, 10–13, 111, 112, 114, 209, 216, 217, 220, 222–223, 225, 236–237, 236n17, 243, 249, 280, 287, 375
Subtraction Story: 2, 14, 29, 63n23, 72, 73–75, 77–79, 83, 87, 159, 208, 215, 234, 323–325, 393, 399, 405
Syria: 171, 187, 352, 359, 361

Tahtawi, Rifaʻa al- : 16, 338–339, 350, 352, 353, 354–363
Tayob, Abdulkader: 324, 339
Tester, Keith: 312n8, 406
Theism: 53, 61, 66, 71, 263, 266, see also: Atheism
– causes of: 72, 79–83
– international distribution of: 73, 79
– Non-theism: 7, 72, 73, 79, 80, 82, 87
– Taylor's: 61, see also: Christian bias/convictions; Taylor's Catholic convictions
Theology, connection to *A Secular Age*: 51, 64, 66, 153, 176, 197, 263–268, 392, 394, 396, 402, 414
Thomas, Günter: 381, 383
Thoreau, Henry David: 289
Thorp, Robert: 181
tolerance: 97, 114, 115, 117, 119, 150, 193
Torah: 166
transcendence: 62, 178, 196, 235n14, 270, 274, 288, 291, 292, 298, 312n7, 331–334, 336, 337, 339–340, 342, 343, 345, 392, 394, 399, 401, 413, 414
– as religious fullness: 29, 39, 65, 66
– Reform as loss of: 56
– transcendental schemes: 3, 4
transfiguration: 272–273

Trine, Ralph Waldo: 296–7, 298
Trinitarian (theology): 7, 61–62, 66
Troeltsch, Ernst: 50

umma: 308, 322–323
umūr dīniyya ('religious matters'): 333–336, 340–341, 342, 344
unbelief: 56, 72, 74, 309, 405, 410, see also: belief
– ambiguous space of: 207, 237, 284
– as option: 28, 32, 33, 285, 309, 313
unbundling: 16, 17, 371–373
Urbinati, Nadia: 390
USA: 41, 372

VanAntwerpen, Jonathan: 101, 102, 398
Van der Veer, Peter: 14, 35, 332–333
violence: 161, 171, 268, 269n10, 272, 377
– hermeneutic of: 274–275, 280
– religious: 272, 275, 276–277

Walhof, Darren: 387
Wallulis, Jerry: 395
Walpole, Horace: 213–215
Ward, Graham: 58
Ward, Ian: 391
Warner, Michael: 398
Wasserman, Earl: 216, 217, 218, 222, 223
Watson, Micah: 391

Watts, John: 192
Weber, Max: 16, 29n3, 50, 54n15, 55, 81, 100n3, 139, 142, 189, 246, 300, 370, 374, 375n2
Wenar, Leif: 128
West, Western: 2, 5, 8, 10, 14, 15, 16, 29, 38, 43, 82, 86, 95, 124, 137, 140, 144, 160, 164n7, 169, 171, 172, 176, 185, 187, 188–190, 209, 215, 220, 229, 238, 246, 249, 270, 284, 285, 289, 292, 307–314, 318, 323, 331, 332, 349, 361–363, 370, 371, 372, 377–379, 391, 399, 400
– Western Christianity: 39, 50, 55, 61, 118, 341n22, 351–352, see also: Christendom
– Western secularity: 79, 224
West Bank: 165
Westphal, Merold: 264–265, 276, 278
White, Christopher: 283
White, Hayden: 180
Whitehouse, Harvey: 71, 85
Whitman, Walt: 290–291, 291n7
wilderness: 288–290
witchcraft: 77–78
Withington, Phil: 316
Wood, James: 208
Woodford, Peter: 413

Zemmin, Florian: 178n4, 189, 377, 379